Portuguese Africa

A HANDBOOK

HANDBOOKS TO THE MODERN WORLD

Portuguese Africa

A HANDBOOK

Edited by
DAVID M. ABSHIRE
and
MICHAEL A. SAMUELS

Published in Cooperation with
THE CENTER FOR STRATEGIC
AND INTERNATIONAL STUDIES
Georgetown University
by
PRAEGER PUBLISHERS
New York · Washington · London

Praeger Publishers
111 Fourth Avenue, New York, N.Y. 10003, U.S.A.
5 Cromwell Place, London S.W.7, England

Published in the United States of America in 1969
by Praeger Publishers, Inc.

Library of Congress Catalog Card Number: 69-15740

916.7
P83
71767
Nov., 1970

Printed in Great Britain

CONTENTS

PART IV
Political and International Issues

LIST OF MAPS

NOTE ON THE SPELLING OF NAMES IN PORTUGUESE AFRICA

In the presentation of any publication intended for English-speaking readers which involves the use of foreign place-names, especially those in languages that require transliteration, the question of spelling arises. In the case of Portuguese Africa this is further complicated by the variations of spelling used in epochs before the modernization of orthography, both Portuguese and English.

In the present study, place-names and names of natural features, such as rivers and lakes, are in general spelled in the accepted modern Portuguese orthography. Exception has been made in certain instances, however—for example names that are in such general use as to be familiar to English-speaking readers in a form other than the Portuguese or that refer to geographical features not wholly within Portuguese Africa. Thus, the Province of Mozambique is so spelled because it is familiar to English-speaking readers in that form. But the district, island, and city of Moçambique retain the correct Portuguese spelling. Thus, also, the Zambezi River is spelled as usually encountered in English, and likewise Lake Nyasa, since these are not entirely Portuguese. The District of Niassa, however, is given in the Portuguese form.

With the notable exception of King John II and Prince Henry the Navigator, whose names are well-known in their English forms, names of historical personages are spelled as is customary in Portuguese.

ACKNOWLEDGMENTS

This book, the work of many hands over several years, could not have been completed without the cooperation of various groups and individuals. The Center for Strategic and International Studies gave support—both financial and staff—for this basic research enterprise to fill a gap in area studies. Field research was requisite to an undertaking of this nature, where published material is difficult to obtain. The Gulbenkian Foundation responded to our proposal for a grant to Georgetown University to support extensive field research in Africa and elsewhere.

The authors are especially grateful to Dr. Pedro Theotónio Pereira who had the foresight to appreciate the scope of the project and the unfailing patience to continue his deep interest over a period of years. Of essential help at the beginning of the project was the then United States Ambassador to Portugal, George W. Anderson, Jr. Both lent their efforts through introductions in the Overseas Ministry and with Portuguese outside of government, thus making available all facilities requested by the researchers. Arleigh Burke, Chairman of the Center, enthusiastically encouraged the staff, and James B. Horigan, formerly Dean of the Graduate School, Georgetown University, and member of the Center's Executive Committee, helped make the project possible.

In Lisbon and in Africa, the authors benefited from countless conversations and meetings. Special acknowledgment is made to Dr. José de Almada, Dr. Alexandre Pinto Basto, Viscount Botelho, Dr. Alexandre Ribeiro da Cunha, Dr. J. M. da Silva Cunha, Dr. Vasco Cunha d'Eca, Mr. Albano Homem de Mello, Mr. Antonio Homem de Mello, Mr. José Manuel de Mello, Dr. Adriano Moreira, Dr. Franco Nogueira, Dr. Manuel de Castro Pereira, Mr. Manoel Queiroz Pereira, Dr. V. Xavier Pintado, Ambassador José de Menezes Rosa, Dr. Joaquim P. Quintela de Saldanha, and Dr. Jesus Nunes dos Santos. Valuable assistance was given in Angola by Mr. António de Almeida Abrantes, Mr. José Maria de Lima e Lemos, Dr. Afonso Mendes, Dr. Jayme Monteiro, and Mr. António Rodrigues da Silva; and in Mozambique by Mr. António Rita Ferreira and Dr. António Trigo de Morais. The late Dr. Eduardo Mondlane was particularly hospitable and helpful during a visit to Tanzania by one of the authors.

The authors conferred broadly with State Department officials in Lisbon, Africa, and Washington. Particular appreciation is expressed to W. Tapley Bennett, Jr., U.S. Ambassador in Lisbon from 1966 to 1969, Henry Clinton Reed, formerly in Luanda and Lourenço Marques, G. Harvey Summ in Luanda, Carlos Vieira at the American Consulate in Salisbury, and Wade Mathews, formerly in Lourenço Marques.

Miss Anyda Marchant was of invaluable assistance in analyzing Portuguese sources and in contributing to the historical section. Professors Peter Bauer and Richard Pattee gave wise advice in the early stages of the project. Mr. Robert Moncure guided us to much additional material for the economic sections of the book. Professors Richard J. Hammond, John Marcum, and Douglas L. Wheeler read drafts of some of the chapters at various stages and made helpful suggestions. Mr. Ralph Kostolnik worked under constant stress to produce the maps for the book.

Special appreciation is expressed to many people at the Center who in one way or another aided the project. In particular, Dr. Sevinc Carlson, Mr. Loren S. Patterson, Miss Maureen Heaney, and Mrs. Joyce Hill contributed with research assistance. Much of the great burden of the detailed data collection and the preparation of the manuscript fell on the able shoulders of Miss Maria Clara da Silva, who worked with patience, persistence, and precision.

INTRODUCTION

There has long been a need for a comprehensive interdisciplinary study of Portuguese Africa. Angola and Mozambique together cover an area greater than that of Western Europe, and they comprise the largest area in sub-Saharan Africa under one government.

This survey is aimed at a diversified audience with different interests. For the student of colonial history, Portuguese Africa is unique because Portugal was the first modern European nation to explore the shores of Africa, was the first to penetrate the interior of Central Africa, and is now the last to relinquish political control. This history bears on today's Portuguese mentality and is relevant to current policies.

For the sociologist and the student of race relations, the four centuries of Portuguese influence in Africa constitute a study in contrasts. Along with slavery and forced labor practices there has existed an unusual degree of assimilation and fraternization. Whatever may be the political future of these areas, hopeful questions are raised as to whether this Portuguese-African experience in a world of race tensions may offer a better future rooted in multiracialism than other parts of Africa seem to offer. Of greater international implication is the observation that the success of multiracialism, if it can be made to work in Angola and Mozambique, and if it can actually accelerate and contribute to economic development, might lead to a softening of the more rigid racial attitudes in Rhodesia and South Africa.

For the political scientist, there is significance in the development of local interest groups, in the assembly debates where freedom is greater than in the metropole, and in the educational revolution producing a new generation of African and *mestiço* leaders. For the development economist, backwardness of the subsistence area is matched with expansive hydroelectric projects—one to be the largest in Africa—as well as offshore oil finds and iron ore deposit discoveries. These complement a steadily expanding agrarian sector from which Angolan coffee vies for first place in African production.

For the student of international affairs, Portuguese Africa also has special significance. Heated discussion of Portugal continues in the United Nations, at a time when ethnic nationalism, insurgency, and guerrilla conflict are increasingly important. The Portuguese territories offer an unusual study in that the conflicts in each differ from the others in both tactics and politics. For the strategist, the economic geographer, and the student of African politics, the strategic location of these territories has remarkable significance. Portuguese Guinea is a possible door to the Cape Verde Islands, which could become a major maritime base for a great power, and Mozambique is located on the increasingly important Indian

Ocean. Angola and Mozambique are geopolitically the strategic flanks to transport between white- and black-ruled Africa. This fact is underscored by Communist China's move toward underwriting the Tan-Zam Railway. All this again illustrates how manifold are the international implications of trends in Portuguese Africa, especially in view of the emerging economic interlock of Mozambique, Rhodesia, and South Africa. Portuguese Africa thus becomes an unusually significant strategic study, if by strategic we mean the interplay of geographical, historical, political, economic, and international forces and interests.

This book has been divided and arranged so that the geographer, historian, political scientist, economist, and international affairs specialist can go to the sections that interest them for appropriate reference material. No other single volume brings together such a compilation of data on Portuguese Africa for students of several disciplines. By the same token, however, this collection is important for the writer on current affairs, the intelligence analyst, and the public–policy-maker, to grasp the variety, the scope, and the depth of dependence of one subject on another.

No one can predict the future of these areas, and within a decade much change will take place. The one certain factor is that each aspect discussed here will play an influencing role. This work therefore has tried to produce the basic facts, avoid the polemics, and describe the realities of the situations, whether pleasant or otherwise. It has not tried to fit itself into any ideology, Portuguese or anti-Portuguese, but strives to describe dispassionately the many human attitudes, ideologies, and predilections that come into play.

An interdisciplinary approach has been used to accomplish this. Each of the contributors has a different background from the others and represents, generally, a different institution. The contributors were chosen purposely to provide a mixture of people who are known as scholars of Portuguese Africa and those who are experienced in political and economic analysis in other less developed areas of the world. The Center for Strategic and International Studies, aware that Portuguese Africa is a potential pivotal area in Africa and that, compared with other areas of Africa, there exists a relative research gap, has served as coordinator for the undertaking. Field research extended from 1965 through 1967.

In dealing with French, British, or Belgian Africa, either at the fall of colonialism or today, one encounters a wide variety of studies. In dealing with recent Portuguese Africa, no such variety exists. There is, however, government propaganda and apologia, on the one hand, and extremely anti-Portuguese material on the other. The clash of the Portuguese mystique and the emotional disdain for all things Portuguese-African has made it difficult to extract realities.

Some readers may feel that the book spends too much time on Lisbon's policies and their background, but since Portuguese Africa is still under the control of Lisbon, this approach is necessary if the study is to relate to actual rather than theoretical policy questions. Moreover, even a black-ruled or otherwise independent nation, in either Guinea or Angola or Mozambique, would be dealing with a Portuguese–African heritage—social, economic, political, and racial.

For the convenience of the reader, all currency figures have been converted from escudos to dollars, at a rate of $35 per 1,000 escudos. This conversion has introduced minor discrepancies in the last decimal place of some figures. We have retained the conversion of the totals rather than totaling the dollar figures.

THE EDITORS

PART I

Background

I

Physical, Human, and Economic Setting

IRENE S. van DONGEN

PORTUGUESE AFRICA, the largest remnant of the historical Portuguese empire, today encompasses close to 7 per cent of the total land area of Africa. It comprises two major areas on the mainland, Angola and Mozambique, both located south of the equator, one on the Atlantic coast and the other along the Indian Ocean; Portuguese Guinea, a smaller land wedge north of the equator in the western African bulge; the Cape Verde Islands, which lie in the Atlantic, some 300 miles off Dakar; and two equatorial Atlantic islands, São Tomé and Príncipe, 275 and 125 miles, respectively, from the African mainland.

Each of these five territorial units has the administrative status of an overseas province of Portugal. Together they contain a population of slightly over 13 million, somewhat less than 5 per cent of all the people who call Africa their home. Although a large majority is African, this population includes immigrants from the Indian subcontinent and from China, mostly in Mozambique; and about 400,000 Europeans, who are descendants of early Portuguese colonizers, products of recent immigration, civil servants, or non-Portuguese nationals, are to be found chiefly in Angola and Mozambique. Moreover, quite a significant segment of the population throughout Portuguese Africa is of mixed European and African descent (*mestiços*). In the island provinces, *mestiços* are the true native population, because the islands were uninhabited when they were first discovered.

Because Portuguese-controlled territories in Africa are far-flung, they are diverse in both physical and human landscapes. Portuguese cultural influence is manifest everywhere, however, in language, architecture, institutional structure, and family patterns, but the intensity of this influence varies.[1] A brief general survey of each province should assist in understanding the present Portuguese domain in Africa.

ANGOLA

With a total land area of 481,351 square miles, Angola is Portugal's largest overseas province, about fourteen times as large as metropolitan Portugal, and roughly equal in size to the states of Texas, Arizona, and Colorado combined. Among the African political units lying entirely south of the Sahara, Angola is second in size only to its neighbor, the Republic of Congo (Kinshasa). The long frontier between them forms the northern and the northeastern borders of the province. Angola adjoins Zambia in the southeast and South-West Africa in the south.

Massive and squarish, Angola includes much of the great interior plateau that has led Africa to be called the "plateau continent"; in fact, that plateau surface covers two-thirds of the province. Yet the thousand-mile Atlantic coast creates another Angola open to oceanic influences. It is the latter, maritime Angola, that has shown the strongest imprint of the metropolitan discoverers ever since the founding of Luanda, the present capital of the province, on the northern seaboard, in 1575, and Benguela, on the central coast, in 1617.

The interior plateau consists essentially of an ancient basement, the foundation of the African land mass, upon which later geological formations accumulated. The structure was warped, uplifted, planed down, and somewhat tilted toward east, north, and south. The present slightly rolling main plateau (*planalto*) surface of Angola ranges in elevation from 3,500 to 4,500 feet above sea level, with some higher tablelands and mountain massifs rising above 6,500 feet along the seaward plateau edge, principally in the middle reaches.[2] It is believed that these represent the remnants of an earlier, more extensive plateau surface. Such remnants include the highest points of the province, such as Mount Moco, at 8,597 feet, and the plateau of Humpata, at 7,430 feet.

Through the west-central section of the main plateau runs a west to east broad swell that effectively separates the headwaters of Angolan streams flowing north from those flowing south. In the west, crystalline rocks are prominent either as bedrock or as isolated towering masses (*inselberge*) standing conspicuously on the main plateau; mineralization there is close to the surface. In contrast, except for the northern depression (*baixa*) of Cassange filled with older sediments, the eastern plateau half is largely buried under a thick mantle of relatively recent sand formations, a circumstance that has handicapped geological surveys.

The interior upland drops down to the coastal plain in a series of impressive escarpments linked by level areas and known collectively as the subplateau zone; some scarp faces, like at the Serra da Chela in the south, display sheer falls of several thousand feet. Descent toward the sea is commonly in two steps; in the north, where the elevations of the interior plateau are much lower, the passage is in one step or is fairly gradual. The coastal lowland, as delimited by the thousand-foot contour, is also wider in the north, reaching a maximum extent of some 100 miles just southeast of Luanda. Farther south it narrows behind Benguela to 10 to 12 miles, becomes barely traceable until it practically reaches the third important Angolan seaboard city, Moçâmedes, and then expands again to a 25- to 35-mile breadth before the South-West Africa border is reached.

The coastal plain consists chiefly of deposits of marine or coastal origin banked against or overlying the foothills of the interior crystalline core. In these deposits are found petroliferous structures, which are the basis for northern Angola's petroleum exploitation. The seashores are marked in some locations by cliffs and terraces cut in the limestones and sandstones of the lowland. In other places, the longshore currents have built stretches of beaches, sandbars at the river mouths, and the sandspits that shelter Angola's best harbors. In the extreme south, the shore is underlined by alignments of desert dunes as the Namib Desert of South-West Africa continues into Angola.[3]

The most important national stream, the Cuanza River, drains with its tributaries a great interior area through its 600-mile course, first flowing northward from the central plateau swell and then, in a wide curve, northwest and west into the Atlantic. The Cuanza is also important historically because its lower section, navigable for 120 miles from the sea, supplied a measure of access into the interior, and economically, because of its own and its tributaries' hydropower potential as they cut deeply into the plateau "fall-line." Today the foremost hydropower-producing station in the province, Cambambe, stands on the Cuanza rapids upstream of Dondo. Other streams flowing independently to the Atlantic and entirely within Angola are considerably shorter. In the northern coastal strip, they can be ascended usually only for a short distance in small boats; in the south, they suffer from water deficiencies due to the protracted dry season. Nevertheless, some, like the Dande, Bengo, Cuvo (Cueve), Catumbela, and Bero, have been, or are in the process of being, harnessed for power, irrigation, or ground water supply.

The central Angolan watershed also gives birth to several international rivers. The mighty Zambezi, which flows to the east coast of Africa, rises in the east of Angola, gathering strength after it enters Zambia from several Angolan tributaries across the border. The Cubango, in the southeast (known farther downstream as the Okavango), sustains the vast swamps and marshes in the northern Kalahari reaches of Botswana. The Cunene (Kunene) River, in the southwest, after a 450-mile, almost straight southerly course through Angola, bends sharply to the Atlantic to form, for about 180 miles, the common boundary with South-West Africa; a site at its Ruacaná Falls is now being surveyed jointly by Portugal and the Republic of South Africa for development into a precious source of energy and irrigation for those arid lands. All the northeastern sector of Angola is drained by the headwaters and tributaries of the powerful Cassai (Kasai) River of the Congo Basin, among which the Chicapa (Tshikapa), Cuílo (Kwilu), and Cuango (Kwango) are the most important. In their course north several of these streams have cut deep valleys into the thick cover of the plateau, exposing rich diamantiferous gravels. At its northwestern corner, the province shares with Congo (Kinshasa) the wide and navigable estuary of the Congo (Zaire) River.

Angola lies in the tropical belt where a rainy and a dry season alternate. The altitudes of the interior upland, however, create there an almost temperate zone, while the cool Benguela current along the coast causes atmospheric conditions that are not conducive to precipitation, so that much of the coastal strip is arid. Broadly viewed, average annual temperatures decrease latitudinally and altitudinally and increase with proximity to the sea. At Santo António do Zaire, at the mouth of the Congo, average annual temperature approximates 79° F., whereas Nova Lisboa, in the central uplands, at an elevation of 5,580 feet, has an annual average temperature of 60.5° F. Seasonal temperature ranges are small, as elsewhere in the tropics; for the localities just mentioned, they are 2.5° F. and 5° F., respectively. North and south of the Lower Cuanza, at elevations not exceeding 3,000 feet, the hottest month is March or April, preceding or coinciding

3

with the rainiest month of the year. On the plateau and the eastern fringes of the province, the hottest month is September or October, and in the extreme south it is October or November; increased heat there presages the rainy season. During the dry and cooler season, the *cacimbo*, masses of moist maritime air move at night on to the coastal belt, causing heavy morning dews and mists. Throughout the day, skies may remain clouded then, while on the plateau cloudiness is rare and the relative humidity is very low. Frosts may occur at night at higher elevations. The coolest month is normally July.

Precipitation totals generally decrease, like the temperatures, with the distance from the equator, but they increase with the distance from the ocean and at higher altitudes. The length of the rainy season is from seven to four months with one or two peak periods. The largest amounts of yearly rain, over 60 to 70 inches, fall in the Maiombe forest region of the Cabinda Enclave, the northern plateau around Carmona, in the eastern Lunda District, and in the middle sector of the highlands along the edge of the plateau. Smallest rainfall totals are along the coast, dwindling from the vicinity of Luanda, with about 16 inches per year, to 8 to 9 inches in the Lobito-Benguela stretch, then to less than 2 inches at Moçâmedes. The arid littoral of the south, where as much as two years may elapse between rains, is also noted for its frequent fogs and relative coolness as cold water from the ocean bottom swells up close to the shore. Although this southern coast has virtually no potentialities for agriculture, marine life is abundant in the adjoining seas.

The scant-to-moderate rainfall and the nature of the soils has resulted in a natural vegetation that consists of tall-to-medium grass savanna and relatively dry woodland; the two are characteristic of vast spaces on the plateau. Closed, multistoried tropical rain forest, with woody-stemmed climbers, parasitic plants, and buttress roots, is practically confined to the Maiombe area of the Cabinda Enclave, although, in many valleys and sheltered slopes of the northern sub-plateau zone, a rain-and-cloud forest thrives because of the condensation of moisture brought in by the westerly sea breezes. Here coffee, the leading crop of Angola, finds its natural habitat. This forest passes eastward into a forest-savanna mosaic along the plateau rim. Patches and stream galleries of moist forest can also be encountered through several northern parts.

Throughout the coastal strip increasing dryness from north to south is translated into a cover of sparse low steppe, scrub and thorn bush, abundant succulents like euphorbs and aloe, or fugacious grasses that last only one or two months on the margins of the Moçâmedes Desert. In much of the coastal and subcoastal belts and in some of the drier southern interior, the baobab (popularly *imbondeiro*) is probably the most representative tree as it stands forlornly in the dusty landscape at the height of the dry season, with its misformed trunk and pendulous fruit. Mangrove growth and wild oil palm are common on the alluvial muds of the Congo and other northern river estuaries.

Administratively, Angola consists of fourteen districts within the main body of the province and a fifteenth, the Cabinda Enclave, farther north on the Atlantic, wedged between the seaboards of the Republic of the Congo (Kinshasa) and the Congo Republic (Brazzaville). The names of the districts and their respective seats of administration are given below. Second-order subdivisions are *concelhos* and *circunscrições*, the latter term being reserved for less developed or outlying areas.

District	District Capital
Benguela	Benguela
Bié	Silva Porto
Cabinda	Cabinda
Cuando Cubango	Serpa Pinto
Cuanza Norte	Salazar
Cuanza Sul	Novo Redondo
Huambo	Nova Lisboa
Huíla	Sá da Bandeira
Luanda	Luanda
Lunda	Henrique de Carvalho
Malange	Malange
Moçâmedes	Moçâmedes
Moxico	Luso
Uíge	Carmona
Zaire	São Salvador do Congo

The latest census, taken in 1960, estimated the total population of Angola at 4,830,449, of whom 172,529 were whites and 53,392 *mestiços*.[4] Non-Portuguese nationals numbered only 1,200, one-third of them being of German origin. About 11 per cent of the total population lived in twenty-nine urban centers of at least 2,000 residents; the highest degree of urbanization was to be found in the coastal districts of Luanda, Benguela, and Moçâmedes. Rural population was, in contrast, concentrated in the interior districts of Huíla, Huambo, Malange, and Bié, which contained together roughly 45 per cent of Angola's people. Since then, urbanization has made further progress, and Angola's total population is estimated to have risen to over 5 million. The white population may now have reached 250,000, owing to the intensification of government-sponsored white agricultural settlement, the attractions of economic prosperity, and the presence of metropolitan troops, since 1961, for counterinsurgency operations. Even so, Angola should be considered thinly settled, since its average density of ten persons per square mile is less than one-half of the average population density of the African continent.

Angola Population (Census 1960)

District	Population	Per Cent of Total
Benguela	487,873	10.1
Bié	452,697	9.4
Cabinda	58,547	1.2
Cuando Cubango	113,034	2.3
Cuanza Norte	263,051	5.4
Cuanza Sul	404,650	8.4
Huambo	597,332	12.4
Huíla	594,609	12.3
Luanda	346,763	7.2

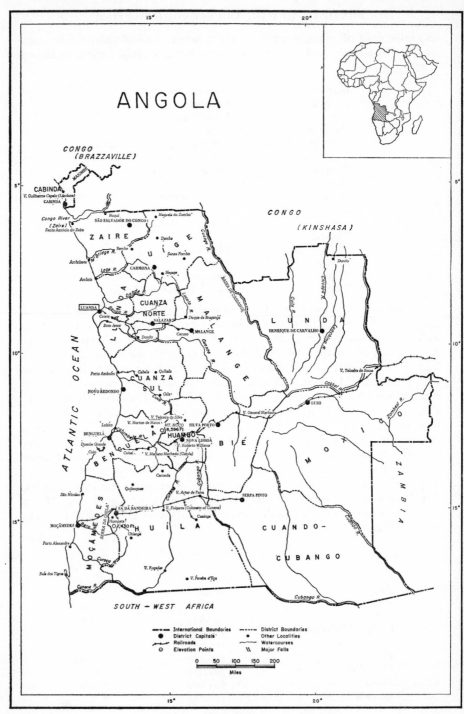

Administrative Subdivisions of Angola

District	Population	Per Cent of Total
Lunda	247,273	5.1
Malange	451,849	9.3
Moçâmedes	43,004	1.0
Moxico	266,449	5.5
Uíge	399,412	8.3
Zaire	103,906	2.1
Total	4,830,449	100.0

Source: Portugal, Província de Angola, Repartição de Estatística Geral, 3° *Recenseamento geral da população, 1960,* I (Luanda: Imprensa Nacional, 1964), 10.

The capital city of Luanda, which almost doubled its population between 1950 and 1960, has long fulfilled the functions of the chief economic and social center of Angola. Luanda, with over 250,000 residents in 1960 and more than one-third of all Angola's white and *mestiço* population, is easily the third largest city in the whole Portuguese community after Lisbon and Oporto. It acts as a focus for more than one-fourth of the province through many commercial links and multiple transport connections and as a consumer of agricultural output. Most of Angola's industry is concentrated in and at the periphery of the capital. Luanda's deep-water port handles the largest share of provincial overseas trade, and its international airport can receive the largest jet aircraft.[5]

Several other Angolan urban centers also play significant roles. Practically all of them are located on the main routes of communications. In the forefront is the urban complex on the central seaboard comprising the modern port community of Lobito, the terminal of the Benguela Railway into Katanga Province of the Congo and into Zambia, and the historic city of Benguela with administrative, trading, and fishing activities. Between the two cities are several satellite townships. The combined population of the area is probably close to 100,000.

Nova Lisboa, with over 40,000 inhabitants, is the collection center for the produce of the central plateau and the headquarters of agronomic investigation. Sá da Bandeira is similarly an agricultural market in the southwest of the interior plateau, in the oldest white farming region of Angola, and is also an educational center. It has a higher number of white and *mestiço* residents than Africans, as has Moçâmedes on the southern seaboard. The latter, a terminal of the southern trunk railroad, is a hub of the fishing industry and on the way of becoming an important iron-ore port. Carmona, in the northern Uíge District, is known as the coffee capital. Malange, the inland terminal of the Luanda rail line, is another fairly prosperous agricultural market city. Cabinda town in the Enclave, a bustling small community, shows signs of impending prosperity and growth as a result of the regional timber trade and petroleum drillings by the Cabinda-Gulf Company.

Most of the northern half of Angola is inhabited by Central Bantu agricultural peoples belonging to three main ethnic clusters: the Bakongo (Bacongo), the Kimbundu, and the Chokwe (Lunda), sometimes known as Kioko. Each cluster

7

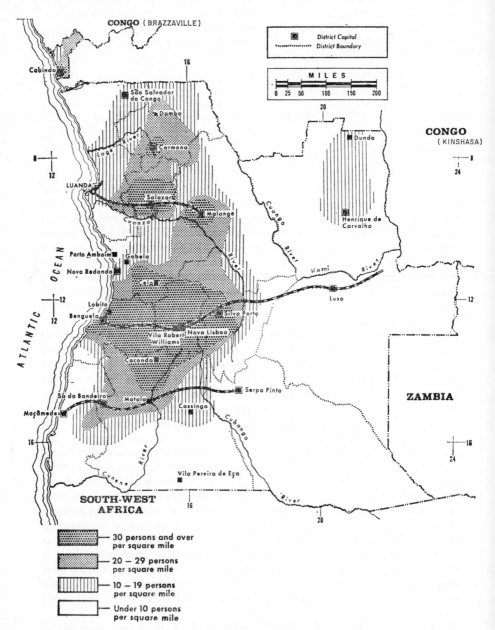

Population Density of Angola

encompasses a number of distinct tribes. Throughout the central and south-central parts of the province, the Ovimbundu and the Ngangela (Ganguela) dominate. The Ovimbundu are the largest ethnolinguistic group in Angola, with over 1.5 million people who are renowned for their fairly advanced crop- and livestock-farming and trading skills. The Nyaneka-Humbe and the Cuanhama (Kwanyama), who live in the southwestern section of the plateau, are also mixed-farmers but are at a disadvantage as cultivators because of limited water supply. Sharing the area with them are the seminomadic Herero pastoralists, who own the vast native cattle herds of southern Angola. In the coastal Moçâmedes Desert and the extreme southeast of the province, population is very sparse. Some Bushman hunters and collectors and some Hottentots live in these inhospitable regions.

Agriculture, inclusive of animal husbandry, represents the chief occupation of most Angolans, engaging about 90 per cent of the active population. Mining and manufacturing have, however, been steadily expanding. In addition to the long-established diamond industry, petroleum came into the picture after 1955 and, more recently, iron ore. Manganese and copper ores have also been mined. For the year 1967, the gross value of mining output was $59.3 million, that of manu-facturing output was $133.9 million, and energy production reached over 390 million kilowatt-hours.

As can be expected, Angola, like all Portuguese African territories, has been drawn into a tight economic partnership with Portugal. Yet other nations too are prominent in the provincial economy as buyers of Angolan products and suppliers of its needs. Through the mid-1960's only some 35 per cent of all Angolan exports went to Portugal, while 23 to 27 per cent was sent to the United States and 12 to 14 per cent to the Netherlands. In import trade 47 to 48 per cent was received from Portugal, 10 to 12 per cent from the United Kingdom, and about 8 per cent each from West Germany and the United States. Since the 1930's, Angola has also handled international transit trade from and to Katanga Province in the Congo (Kinshasa) and the Copperbelt of Zambia over the privately owned central Benguela Railway, which connects with the Congo transport network. In 1966, total transit trade of the port of Lobito was 780,000 tons,[6] although it has become subject to disruption by nationalist guerrilla activity in eastern Angola.

The total rail net in the province now amounts to 2,200 miles of track in three major lines (two of them state-owned) and two shorter lines. Over it moved, in the mid-1960's, some 2.5 million tons of freight and 1.6 million passengers annually. The three main sea terminals of Luanda, Lobito, and Moçâmedes received jointly each year some 1,500 deep-sea ships and handled 3 million tons of international maritime cargo, as well as some 400,000 tons of provincial coastal trade. Among the score or so of secondary ports, Cabinda, Porto Amboím, and Porto Alexandre were the most active. Substantial sums are currently being spent on the improvement of the provincial road network, which now comprises 15,100 miles of major roads and includes 2,200 miles of paved highways. A local air transport organization flies almost 2 million miles yearly within Angola and to South-West Africa.

9

Serious challenges to development are presented by the sheer size of the province, restrictive physical factors in certain regions, and the low density of population resulting in many manpower shortages. Under the Portuguese National Development Program for economic and social growth, which began in 1953 with the First Development Plan and is currently entering its fourth stretch, $528.4 million were officially allocated to Angola up to the end of 1967.[7] Following the 1961 nationalist outbreak on the northern coffee plantations, a short slump occurred in the flow of private investment, but the continued presence of metropolitan troops and government firmness in handling the situation, despite financial burdens, has led to the resumption of economic expansion. In consequence, Angola is traversing at present a period of fairly steady economic build-up.

MOZAMBIQUE

Mozambique, with a total area of 297,846 square miles, is the second largest Portuguese province in Africa, some eight and a half times the size of metropolitan Portugal and slightly larger than Alabama, Florida, Georgia, North and South Carolina, and Virginia combined. It differs from Angola in being an elongated and mostly low-lying segment of the African continent, a sort of eastern coastal fringe to the landlocked interior countries of Rhodesia, Zambia, and Malawi. In its southernmost parts it lies between the sea and the Transvaal region of the Republic of South Africa and the small state of Swaziland. Tanzania adjoins it in the north across the Rovuma River; in the northwest, the province shares with Malawi the southern waters of Lake Nyasa.

The interior African plateau appears only in the west-central and northwestern parts of the province, where generally land areas above 3,500 feet of altitude pass gradually seaward into the transitional zone of low plateaus and hills that covers about one-fourth of the province. Elevations of more than 5,000 feet are uncommon. One example, however, is Mount Binga, the highest point of Mozambique, which rises to 7,992 feet on the Rhodesian border escarpment west of Beira. Also notable are the Angoni Plateau, at 6,500 feet, astride the Malawi border and several mountain massifs such as the Namuli, Tacuane, and Guruè, which are the continuation of the Shire Highlands of Malawi into northern Mozambique.[8]

The coastal lowland, as delimited by 1,650-foot elevations, embraces close to 45 per cent of the territory. It is widest through the southern third of the province where the transitional hilly zone is found only close to the common border with South Africa. In the north it contracts to an average width of some 50 miles between the coastline and higher terrain. The shoreline on the Indian Ocean, 1,750 miles long, is generally low and sandy, backed by numerous marshes and lagoons, and with shallow offshore waters. The several spacious bays forming excellent natural harbors include Delagoa Bay in the south where the busy port and capital city of Lourenço Marques is located. Elsewhere along the coast, navigation demands much caution because of shoals and the swift, southward Mozambique current.

All the rivers of Mozambique flow to the Indian Ocean. The major ones are of international significance, some of them rising hundreds of miles away on the central African plateau. The most prominent is the great Zambezi that rises in eastern Angola and marks the border between Zambia and Rhodesia in the manmade Kariba Lake; it enters the western lobe of Mozambique for a course of 480 miles before expanding into a multiarmed delta. Along the Zambezi valley can be found the farthermost penetration of the coastal lowland into the interior. The Limpopo and the Incomáti (Komati) rivers, which rise on the Witwatersrand plateau in South Africa, the Save (Sabi) from Rhodesia, the Buzi-Punguè fan converging on Beira, and the Rovuma in the north also contribute, with their tributaries, to the extensive river network of the province. Among strictly national watercourses the northern Lugenda, Lúrio, Ligonha, and Licungo are the most significant.

Unfortunately, the water flow of many of these streams is quite irregular because of the regional pattern of rainfall. In the early part of the year disastrous floods frequently sweep the broad valleys of the southern and central streams, whereas during the other months the beds are almost dry and full of sandbanks. The Zambezi has been navigated by boats of low draft from some of its mouths up to Tete. Its navigability spurred the historical Portuguese advance into the interior and the early attempts to cross the width of southern Africa to link the Portuguese-occupied eastern and western seaboards. Recently the build-up of river sediment has led to curtailment of regular navigation schedules, but the giant plan now being elaborated for a plurinational development of the Lower Zambezi Basin should restore sufficient depths to the main channel. Some sections of the Limpopo and the Incomáti are navigable at high waters. Thus far, hydropower has been developed only on the Revuè, a headwater of the Buzi. The Cabora Bassa rapids upstream of Tete are now being harnessed as part of the Zambezi development plan.

The largest part of Mozambique is, like Angola, within the tropical belt and characterized by a succession of wet and dry seasons. The first generally lasts from November to March, coinciding with the warm months of the southern hemisphere; the rainiest periods vary with location and exposure to the northeast monsoon, the bearer of moisture from the ocean. The hottest months in the central and northern coastal strip are January and February with monthly averages between 80° to 85° F. and relative humidities around 80 per cent; in the interior uplands, average temperatures drop to 68° to 70° F. for the same months.

The dry and cooler season lasts five to six months, synchronizing with the period of southwesterly dry winds and southern winters. Southernmost Mozambique extends into the belt of subtropical climates; however, the average temperatures along the coast are boosted by the warm offshore waters of the Mozambique current. As a result, the mild winters of Lourenço Marques with June and July averages of 65° to 68° F. attract to its beaches many tourists from neighboring South Africa who seek to escape the harsh, cold winters of the Rand.

Yearly precipitation totals and relative humidity generally decrease through the coastal plain from the seaboard inland but rise again on the interior plateau. The highest amounts of rain, sometimes over 70 inches, fall in the mountain massifs of northern Mozambique, permitting successful tea cultivation there, and along the Rhodesian border inland from Beira. The northern and central coasts may have 40 to 60 inches, the southern coast between 30 to 40 inches of rain annually. Two large sections in the interior are conspicuous for their dryness: one is the western Gaza District; the other is the enclosed Zambezi valley around Tete. Within the latter area, intense heat combined with drought has earned it the nickname of the hell of the Zambezi. The amount of rainfall received in any one location varies greatly from year to year, with the reliability coefficient approximating only 30 per cent, thus causing wide fluctuations in crop harvests.

Along the coast, particularly in the river estuaries and the delta of the Zambezi, mangrove or marsh-type vegetation is common. Moist montane forest, sometimes with needle-leaf trees, is encountered in patches in the western and northern highlands. The various savanna associations and more or less drier and open woodlands dominate the landscape of Mozambique. Together with occasional tracts of short-grass steppe, they extend over three-fourths of the territory.

Administratively, Mozambique comprises nine districts; four are located north of the Zambezi, two are in the central zone, and three are in the south. Second-order subdivisions are the customary Portuguese *concelho* and *circunscriçao*.

District	District Capital
Cabo Delgado	Porto Amélia
Gaza	João Belo
Inhambane	Inhambane
Lourenço Marques	Lourenço Marques
Manica e Sofala	Beira
Moçambique	Nampula
Niassa	Vila Cabral
Tete	Tete
Zambézia	Quelimane

Though it has a smaller area than Angola, Mozambique has a larger population. According to the 1960 census, total population was 6,578,600 persons, representing an average density of 22 persons per square mile. Some 97,300 of the total were Europeans, 31,500 *mestiços*, and 19,300 Asians, most of them from Pakistan and India. Non-Portuguese Europeans who claimed the province as their legal residence were 2,545, one-third of them being British and 15 per cent of South African origin. More than one-third of the Europeans and Asians and one-fourth of the *mestiços* lived in the capital city of Lourenço Marques, which had a population of 178,000. The cities of Beira, Nampula, and Quelimane each had European communities several thousand strong. Population projections, which assume a growth rate of 1.8 per cent, suggest that the total population of Mozambique should have amounted to more than 7 million people at the end of 1966. There was a further increase of 54,200 by immigration in the non-African community during the period 1961–66.

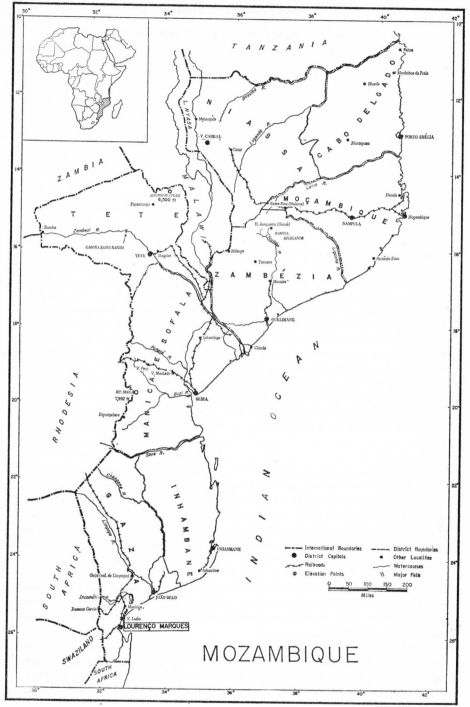

Administrative Subdivisions of Mozambique

Mozambique Population (Census 1960)

District	Population	Per Cent of Total
Cabo Delgado	542,165	8.2
Gaza	675,150	10.3
Inhambane	583,772	8.8
Lourenço Marques	441,363	6.7
Manica e Sofala	783,070	11.9
Moçambique	1,444,555	21.9
Niassa	276,810	4.3
Tete	470,100	7.0
Zambézia	1,363,619	20.7
Total	6,578,604	100.0

Source: Portugal, Província de Moçambique, Direcção Provincial dos Serviços de Estatística Geral, *Anuário estatístico, 1964* (Lourenço Marques: Imprensa Nacional, 1966), p. 30.

The Zambézia and Moçambique districts, north of the Zambezi, are the most populous of the province: almost 3 million people live there. As a rule, the highest densities in Mozambique are found along the coast. Of special significance is the dense coastal settlement in the three southern districts, which, since the turn of the century, have been a reservoir of African labor for the mines of the Witwatersrand, according to the terms of the Mozambique Convention. The least populated area, Niassa District in the north, has a heritage of past devastation by Arab slave traders, endemic sleeping sickness at lower elevations, and few economic opportunities. The highlands of that district, around Cabral, however, have often been suggested as a very propitious region for extensive European agricultural settlement because of their salubrious, almost temperate, climate; few Mozambique areas are so favored.

The great majority of Mozambique Africans belong, as in Angola, to the broad cultural subdivision of Central Bantu. North of and through the Zambezi valley are two main groupings. One is the Maravi-Yao cluster of peoples in the west, related to some extent to those living in Malawi and comprising such tribes as the Nyanja, Nyasa, Zimba, and the Islamized Yao (Ajaua). The other is the Makua-Makonde (Macua-Maconde) cluster in the east, encompassing the large subgroup of Makua, the Lomwe (Lómue), the Podzo in the Zambezi delta, and the somewhat distinct Makonde on the forested northern plateau, separated by the Rovuma River from their kin in southern Tanzania. Scattered among these essentially crop-raising peoples are the Ngoni (Angoni), mixed descendants of an invasion by southern African Zulu, who combine soil-tilling with livestock-raising. There is in addition a sprinkling of East African Swahili along the northernmost seaboard.

South of the Zambezi valley are peoples related to those in Rhodesia, again primarily soil-tillers, subdivided into two numerically quite important groupings. The first is the Shona or Mashona cluster with the Teve, Bargwe, Ndau (Vandau), and Manyika. The second is the Thonga (Tonga) cluster with the Ronga, Tswa,

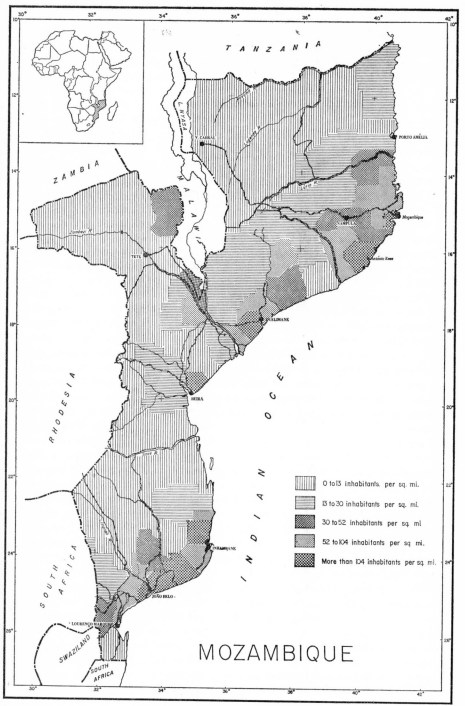

	0 to 13 inhabitants. per sq. mi.
	13 to 30 inhabitants per sq. mi.
	30 to 52 inhabitants per sq. mi
	52 to 104 inhabitants per sq. mi.
	More than 104 inhabitants per sq. mi.

MOZAMBIQUE

Population Density of Mozambique

Hlengwe, and local Ngoni elements known as the Shangana (Changane). Some of the latter own extensive cattle herds in the interior of Gaza District. In contrast to the heavily Islamized north, the tribes south of the Zambezi are either animist or Christian.

The economy of Mozambique is characterized, as in most African countries south of the Sahara, by the importance of agriculture, in which almost 90 per cent of the population is engaged. Industrial development was handicapped in the pre- and post-World War II years by the lack of power, the proximity of more technologically advanced South Africa and Rhodesia, and the distance that the northern agricultural products had to travel for eventual processing in Lourenço Marques, long the only center of industrial enterprise. Mining thus far has been much less important than in Angola. Only second-grade coal has been regularly extracted in some quantity for a number of years, although substantial finds of iron and other ores have recently been reported. The U.S.-affiliated Mozambique Gulf Oil Company finally struck commercially exploitable natural gas deposits in 1966 and 1967, after more than a decade of drilling in the coastal lowland, and other international oil concerns have since shown increased interest.

An outstanding asset to the provincial economy has been its strategic location on the ocean thoroughfare and its capability in serving an extensive extranational hinterland of high productivity. The central rail route connecting the port of Beira with Rhodesia and Malawi has, since the beginning of this century, made that deep-water terminal the foremost gateway to these two countries, to Zambia, and in a minor fashion to the former Belgian Congo. The port of Lourenço Marques and the southern rail system have likewise been a major and early outlet for the great mining and industrial complex of the Witwatersrand and for eastern and northwestern Swaziland; in 1955, the completion of the Pafúri rail link opened to Rhodesia and Zambia an alternate route through the southern Mozambique terminal. Within the next few years, when the northern rail trunk from Nacala toward Lake Nyasa will be linked with the Malawi system, a third international gateway will function in the province.[9] Since Mozambique normally has a balance-of-trade deficit, the income from transit traffic constitutes an invaluable source of revenue. The moderate distances by rail and highway from Salisbury and Johannesburg have also permitted the emergence of a blossoming tourist industry on the seaboard at Beira and Lourenço Marques and in the Gorongosa National Park, noted for its game. Some 250,000 visitors per year spend from $10.9 million to $12.5 million. Furthermore, the province profits from family remittances and the earnings of migrant labor in South Africa and Rhodesia: as many as 250,000 Africans are employed annually across the border.

In Mozambique trade, as in Angolan, metropolitan Portugal is the leading partner, receiving in recent years 35 to 37 per cent of provincial exports and supplying 34 to 35 per cent of its needs. Other members of the Portuguese community account additionally for 4 to 5 per cent of exports and imports. Except for rather special cashew nut exchanges with India, the Republic of South Africa is the second-ranking trade partner, receiving 11 to 12 per cent of exports and supplying 10 to 12 per cent of imports. The United Kingdom competes at times for the second place as importer. The share of the United States usually does not surpass some 5 to 7 per cent of imports or exports.

Mozambique now has some 2,300 miles of essentially state-owned and state-operated rail track of various gauges. Over this network a total of 10.7 million tons of freight and 3.2 million passengers moved during 1967. In 1966 the two international ocean terminals, Lourenço Marques and Beira, were visited by a total of 2,700 deep-sea ships and handled 10.4 million tons of international cargo. About a dozen smaller ports functioned mainly as domestic shipping points, the most significant being Porto Amélia, Nacala, Moçambique, Quelimane, and Inhambane. Some fifteen provincial airports and airfields were served by the local air transport organization which also had flights to Blantyre, Salisbury, Johannesburg, and Durban. The still inadequate road network comprises 7,370 miles of main connections, of which 800 miles are paved, and 9,210 miles of secondary roads. An accelerated road-building program is in progress to meet the defense demands in the north and commercial transport requirements in other sections. Throughout the period 1953–67, Mozambique received $396.3 million under the various stages of the Portuguese National Development Program.

The proximity of and continual contact with countries of Anglo-Saxon cultural heritage, the Moslem imprint on the northern tribes, the presence of a sizable Asian community from the Indian peninsula, and the distance from Portugal have combined to modify the force of Portuguese traditions in Mozambique. This can be observed among both Africans and middle- and upper-class Europeans. Social attitudes are more cosmopolitan and some knowledge of English is current.

PORTUGUESE GUINEA (GUINÉ)

Portuguese Guinea (Guiné), on the western seaboard of Africa, is a 150-mile-deep enclave between the southern reaches of the Republic of Senegal and the north-western sector of the Republic of Guinea. Its total area, inclusive of some sea margins submerged at high tides, is 13,948 square miles or about one-half the size of metropolitan Portugal. Relatively recent marine and coastal sedimentary formations form the largest part of the territory as a low-lying coastal plain and a somewhat higher interior plain with only minor relief features. In the northeast a low plateau surface adjoins the first outliers of the Guinean massif of Futa-Jallon. Nowhere do elevations exceed 950 feet above sea level.[10]

The coastal belt, delimited by the inland reach of the ocean tides, presents a complex pattern of river estuaries, salt and freshwater swamps and marshes, mangrove mud flats, and sandy offshore islands that spill seaward in the central section into the group of the Bijagós, seated on a submarine bank. The territory is drained by two main streams, the Cacheu and the Geba, and an important tributary of the latter, the Corubal. Although meandering sluggishly, flooding in the rainy season, and frequently failing to display precise shorelines because of the fringing mangrove, these watercourses represent the economic and social lifelines of the territory. Their fairly deep channels allow navigation as far as

17

70 to 80 miles upstream for ocean-going vessels of small draft, and practically all the urbanized centers of population, including Bissau, the capital, are located on their banks. Within the coastal zone are found the largest share of the provincial population of about 555,000, most of the non-African population, the most advanced indigenous agriculture, and the densest overland communications network.

Portuguese Guinea lies about midway between the equator and the Tropic of Cancer. Open to the warm waters of that part of the Atlantic, it reaches in the interior toward the margins of the Sahara. Two seasons, one wet and the other dry, mark the rhythm of the year. The onset of the rainy season is preceded by increasing heat that subsides slightly as the rain-bearing masses of marine air move overland around mid-May. Tropical downpours with violent thunderstorms and squalls continue until mid-November, with July and August being the rainiest months and the heat starting to build up again in October and November. Then begins the dry and somewhat more comfortable season (because of lesser air humidity), due to Saharan influences and the winter in the northern hemisphere. Previous average daytime temperatures of 80° to 85° F. in the shade drop to maximum temperatures of 75° F. during December and January. On the seaboard, moist maritime breezes still maintain a fairly high relative air humidity, but the interior is subject to incursions of the harmattan, a dry, dusty, and haze-laden wind from the Sahara that scorches vegetation, contributes to the formation of lateritic hardpan soils, and causes numerous respiratory and eye infections.

Total yearly rainfall of 70 to 120 inches in the coastal zone decreases to 50 to 60 inches in the interior, where at times temperatures higher than along the coast are recorded. However, because of greater seasonal and daily temperature variations, the climate of the interior is considered more salubrious than that of the coast. The interior area is largely covered with scrub savanna or light savanna woodland and is the domain of sparse shifting agriculture and some seminomadic pastoralism. Between the interior and the watery landscape of coastal lands, with their mangroves, swamp forest, rice polders, and an abundant growth of wild oil palm, stretches a transitional vegetational zone. It contains several expanses of fairly dense rain forest where cultivation and logging have made some inroads. The southernmost part of the province also displays a notable stretch of tall, tangled forest around the Cacine estuary on the border with Guinea.

Portuguese Guinea became a separate administrative unit of the Portuguese empire only late in the nineteenth century, having historically been a part of a province of Cape Verde. The relatively restricted size of the territory has precluded partitioning into districts; instead, it is directly subdivided into nine *concelhos*, Bafatá, Bissau, Bissorã, Bolama, Cacheu, Catió, Farim, Gabu, Mansõa, and three *circunscrições*, Bijagós, Fulacunda, and São Domingos.

Present average population density in the province is forty persons per square mile, nearly twice the average density in Africa as a whole. The *concelhos* of Bafatá, Cacheu, and Gabu are the most densely settled, but everywhere population is basically rural. Outside the city of Bissau with close to 25,000 residents,

18

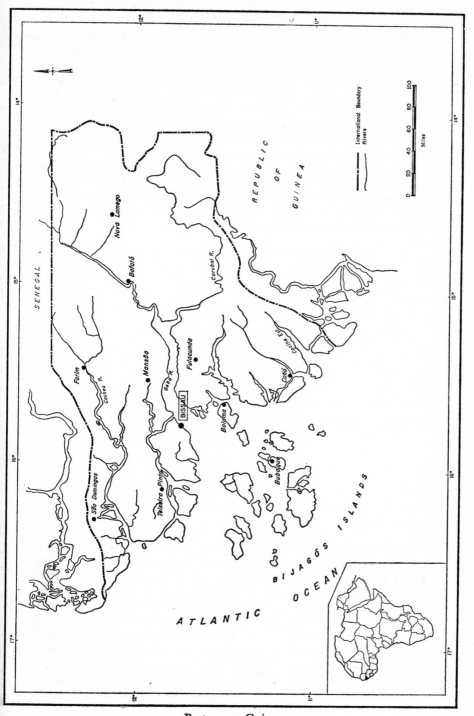

Portuguese Guinea

only Bafatá and Bolama trading centers have a population even slightly more than 3,000. Bolama, the former capital, now moribund, still preserves a municipal status and occasionally functions as a port. But Bissau is incontestably the political, commercial, and transportation heart of the province as it focuses maritime and river traffic to receive imports and to export the products of a basically agricultural economy (most of this trade is with metropolitan Portugal and Cape Verde). Bissau also has an airport at Bissalanca for connections with Cape Verde and Portugal, the major medical and educational facilities, and a few small industrial establishments including an oil refinery at Bandim.

Thus far no minerals have been exploited in the province, though some bauxite deposits reportedly exist. There are no railroads. Total mileage of roads is slightly over 2,000 miles of which only a few sections are asphalt. Under the provisions of various Portuguese development plans from 1953 to 1967, the territory has been allocated $16.2 million for internal improvements.

Portuguese Guinea Population (Census 1960)

Concelhos	Population	Per Cent of Total
Bafatá	70,820	13.6
Bissau	55,625	10.8
Bissorã	44,841	8.7
Bolama	4,642	0.9
Cacheu	70,233	13.6
Catió	37,318	7.1
Farim	56,843	10.8
Gabu	70,292	13.6
Mansõa	40,702	7.9
Circunscrições		
Bijagós	9,332	1.8
Fulacunda	34,703	6.7
São Domingos	23,878	4.6
Total	519,229	100.0

Source: Anuário estatístico, II, *Ultramar* (Lisbon: Instituto Nacional de Estatística, 1964), 10.

Ethnic diversity has long characterized the social structure of Portuguese Guinea. Anthropologists recognize close to twenty local tribes, the most numerous being the Balanta and Manjaco in the coastal zone, the Malinke (Mandingo) in most of the central portion, and the Fula (Fulani) through the northeast and east. Some twenty tribal dialects and a sort of lingua franca, the *crioulo*, a Cape Verdian brand of Portuguese, are spoken. Islam reigns in the north and animism in the south, imported Christianity having had little impact. The reputedly harmful climate of the seaboard, noted for malaria, yellow fever, and other disabling tropical sicknesses before the era of modern medicine, discouraged substantial white settlement. Until the late 1920's, Portuguese Guinea had less than a thousand non-African residents. Traditionally, the majority of its non-African population has originated in the Cape Verde Islands, many of these immigrants being *mestiços*. In the early 1960's, the non-African community was estimated at 8,000, including several hundred Lebanese traders. Today the presence of metropolitan troops greatly inflates those numbers.

São Tomé and Príncipe

The two islands São Tomé and Príncipe, located in the equatorial Atlantic about 275 and 125 miles, respectively, off the northern coast of Gabon, combine to make the smallest Portuguese overseas province in Africa: their total area is only 372 square miles. Both are part of a southwest-northeast alignment of now extinct volcanoes that mark a major fracture of the earth's crust in that part of the Gulf of Guinea. The other members of the volcanic chaplet are the formerly Spanish-held islands of Annóbon and Fernando Po and the mainland mass of Mount Cameroun, rising to over 13,000 feet close to the regional seaboard.

Oval-shaped São Tomé is the larger of the two islands, 30 miles long and 20 miles across, and the most mountainous. Its highest point, Pico de São Tomé, reaches 6,640 feet high; in the west-central and southern sections there are at least ten impressive peaks above 3,500 feet. Numerous streams radiating from the center cut vigorously into the mountain flanks. The western section of the island drops rather abruptly to the sea; the eastern descent is more gentle and fanlike.

Príncipe is roughly rectangular, about 10 miles long and 5 miles across. Its rugged southern half culminates in Pico do Príncipe at 3,610 feet, while in the north a relatively level, lower platform descends gradually to the sea. About 90 miles of sea separates the two islands. Each has a sinuous coastline, a handful of scattered offshore islets, and a few fairly deep embayments sheltering small population clusters.[11]

The over-all insular climate is warm and moist. At low elevations the atmosphere reminds one of a greenhouse: average yearly temperatures are around 80° F. with little daily variation during the eight-month rainy season that lasts from October into May. A somewhat fresher and drier period (the *gravana*) occurs from July to August. At 2,000 feet of altitude, however, the yearly average temperatures decrease to 68° F., and nights are generally cool. March is the hottest month in the islands, and July is the least warm, sometimes without any precipitation. The rain-bearing winds that strike the southwestern slopes of the mountain massifs result in rainfall totals as high as 150 to 200 inches annually for São Tomé and 160 to 175 inches for Príncipe. A luxuriant mantle of virgin rain forest clothes the precipitous terrain, changing above 4,500 feet, where mists abound, into a cloud-mountain forest. Rainfall totals decrease slightly on the eastern and northern flanks of the massifs; the abundant forest growth is still present, but there are now many types of trees introduced by the colonizers as they cleared ground at one time or another for plantations. Only the northern and northeastern lowlands are appreciably drier, with yearly rainfalls of from 40 to 60 inches, some grassy areas, and a light woodland.

Administratively each island is a *concelho*, with three further political

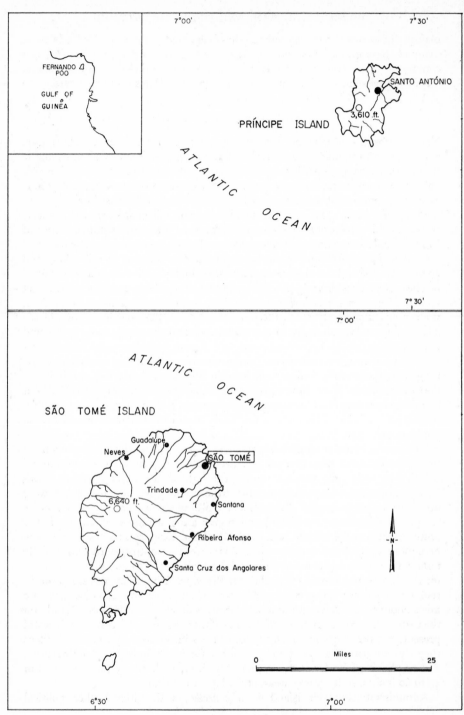

São Tomé and Príncipe

sub-divisions in the case of São Tomé, which has a total population of some 60,000. The city of São Tomé on the northeast coast is the provincial capital and the administrative center of the *concelho* of São Tomé. It has 6,000 residents, some medical and educational facilities, various commercial establishments, and a few rudimentary industrial plants producing soap, soft drinks, and tiles. A new hydroelectric plant on the Contador River may soon permit further industrialization. Its small but active harbor is an obligatory port of call for Portuguese ships operating on the metropole-Angola-Mozambique sea route, and its airport provides connections with the metropole, Angola, and Fernando Po. Some six or seven other settlements located inland from the capital and along the coast comprise several hundred people each. The rest of São Tomé's population is basically dispersed among the cacao estates, which sustain the economy of the islands. Many of the plantations operate as self-sufficient units connected with the city of São Tomé by road or narrow-gauge sections of private rail track; the more isolated depend entirely on schooners. Thus far the difficult terrain has prevented construction of a main road circling the island.

Príncipe, at one time more populous than São Tomé, now has only 5,000 inhabitants, largely concentrated in the more accessible northern part. It has only 30 miles of roads compared with 200 miles in São Tomé, fewer cacao estates, and only one urbanized center, Santo António, with 900 inhabitants. Connections with São Tomé are by plane and schooner.

Portugal generally supplies about 47 per cent of the provincial import trade and other members of the Portuguese community supply an additional 25 per cent. Provincial exports, however, are mostly directed to other countries, as Portugal buys only 35 to 37 per cent of all São Tomé and Príncipe exports, the rest of the Portuguese lands merely 1 per cent. Within the framework of the Portuguese National Development Program, the two islands have received $21 million in aid during 1953–67.

Settlement of these originally uninhabited islands began late in the fifteenth century soon after their discovery by the Portuguese. The racially mixed descendants of successive Portuguese, Spanish, French, and Jewish immigrants and of plantation slaves originating on the western African coast today represent the indigenous Creole society, some 4,500–5,000 strong, most of whom eke out an indifferent livelihood in and around the city of São Tomé. Another group that can be considered "native" is the angolares in the southeast, also numbering a few thousand, who are descendants of runaway slaves from a shipwreck. Formerly roaming in small bands in the mountainous interior, they are now settled and specialize in fishing trades. European residents of the islands, in the capital and on the estates, have seldom numbered more than 1,000–1,200, owing to a climate that discourages permanent European settlement. Thus, the majority of the provincial population has traditionally consisted of African laborers imported under contract from other parts of Portuguese Africa to assist in the plantation work.

The imported laborers have seldom identified themselves with local Creoles or with the soil of the islands. On the other hand, the Creole group has, by and large, either so succumbed to tropical languor or become so impregnated with

23

European Portuguese influences as to mesh entirely with the politics of metropolitan Portugal. As a result, there has been little tendency toward the nationalism
fermenting in the mainland Portuguese territories. The economic difficulties
attendant on production and marketing of the cacao bean do not make São Tomé
and Príncipe precious acquisitions for any African revolutionary party intent on
securing portions of the mainland.

CAPE VERDE ISLANDS

Ten islands and a few islets, located in the Atlantic Ocean some 300 miles east
of Dakar in Senegal, form the Portuguese-African province of Cape Verde, with
a total area of 1,552 square miles, one-fourth larger than the state of Rhode Island.
All of volcanic marine origin, they rise from depths of more than 1,500 fathoms
and are scattered in two subgroups: the northern *ilhas de Barlavento* (windward
islands) and the southern *ilhas de Sotavento* (leeward islands). The northern
subgroup consists of a northwesterly cluster, the islands of Santo Antão, São
Vicente, Santa Luzia, and São Nicolau, and an easterly pair of islands, Sal and
Boa Vista. The *ilhas de Sotavento* comprise the islands of Maio, Santiago, Brava,
and Fogo, the latter being an active volcano 8,770 feet in height whose violent
eruption made news early in the 1950's.[12]

The majority of the Cape Verde Islands display a vigorous and high relief
with peaks culminating at 6,350 feet within Santo Antão and 4,300 feet within
Santiago; only the islands of Sal, Boa Vista, and Maio are low-lying. Because of
the archipelago's location in the semi-arid climatic belt extending across Africa
from the Atlantic to the Red Sea, much of the local landscape is strikingly barren.
Gray and brown crags are interspersed with broad ravines containing intermittent streams (*ribeiras*); bold cliffs surround beaches of rubble; soil cover is
thin and stony on the slopes.

The climate of the islands is characterized by high temperatures throughout
the year and an over-all shortage and unreliability of rainfall. A dry and windy
season lasting from December to June normally changes during July to a three-
month warmer and rainy season that tapers off through November; some years,
however, the rains fail, and a scorching drought desolates the land, causing
famine. The hottest month is September with a monthly average of 80° F.; the
coolest is February when the monthly average temperature falls to about 70° F.
No great temperature variations can be observed between days and nights
because of the stabilizing effect of the surrounding seas. Smallest rainfall totals
are experienced at low elevations in the northern group: São Vicente may receive
4 to 5 inches during only thirteen days of rain a year; on Sal total yearly rainfall
may consist of only one day's torrential downpour. On the seaboard of Santiago
in the southern group, 11 to 12 inches of rain is more or less the yearly norm.
Higher elevations are rainier: at 2,000 feet in Santiago, the yearly volume of rain
may reach 20 inches, and larger amounts fall toward the summits. Insolation is
most intense along the island coasts but the interior mountain masses are often
shrouded through the mornings in fog. Moisture condensation in higher valleys
permits a moderately dense tropical and temperate tree growth, particularly on

Cape Verde Islands

the northeastern slopes exposed to the trade winds, whereas the plant life at lower elevations or on the southwestern slopes is often reduced to succulents and dry scrub.

From an administrative standpoint, the province consists of twelve *concelhos*, six of which correspond to the individual island areas of São Nicolau, Sal, Boa Vista, Maio, Brava, and Fogo. Within Santiago, the largest and most populous of all the islands, are three *concelhos*: Praia, Tarrafal, and Santa Catarina. Santo Antão, the leading island of the northern subgroup, comprises two *concelhos*: Ribeira Grande and Paúl. Santa Luzia Island is included in the *concelho* of São Vicente. The city of Praia on the south coast of Santiago is the official capital of the province and has a population of 13,200. Mindelo, in São Vicente, with some 20,000 residents, is larger and economically more important, ranking as the foremost Cape Verdian port because of its excellent harbor, Porto Grande. Located at the crossroads of several transoceanic routes, Porto Grande is a noted refueling point for Portuguese and some international steamship lines. Similarly, on the island of Sal there is an international airport. There are no railroads in the islands; total road network approximates 800 miles.

When discovered in the middle of the fifteenth century, the islands were uninhabited. Occupation began with a few Portuguese families and Africans imported from Portuguese Guinea, some 550 miles to the southeast. Out of the two stocks there has developed a racially mixed society with cultural patterns similar to those prevailing in rural Portugal. A stumbling block to even a modicum of prosperity in the last decades has been the rapid growth of population as contrasted with the paltry resources of the islands. Salt works and fisheries so far are the only alternatives to tilling the meager soil and to some government and shopkeeper jobs. There is usually a deficit in the provincial trade balance.

Cape Verde Population (Census 1960)

Islands	Population	Per Cent of Total
Boa Vista	3,309	1.5
Brava	8,646	4.5
Fogo	25,457	12.4
Maio	2,718	1.4
Sal	2,626	1.4
Santiago	88,940	44.0
Santo Antão	34,598	17.3
São Nicolau	13,894	5.1
São Vicente and Santa Luzia	21,361	10.3
Total	201,549	100.0

Source: Adapted from *Anuário estatístico*, II, *Ultramar* (Lisbon: Instituto Nacional de Estatística, 1964), 10.

Total population now approximates 225,000, which gives an average density of 145 persons per square mile; ten years ago, when the population was only

148,000, many Cape Verdians were already forced to emigrate for survival. Emigration continues at the rate of up to 4,000 people a year, and many are being encouraged by the Portuguese Government to resettle in other overseas provinces, notably Angola or São Tomé and Príncipe. By comparison to their land area, the Cape Verde Islands have received the highest general development allocations of all overseas provinces, a total of $30 million for the period 1953–67.

NOTES

1. Richard J. Hammond, *Portugal's African Problem: Some Economic Facets* (New York, 1962), p. 35, describes succinctly the Portuguese-African society as follows: "the Portuguese, to an extent unmatched by other Europeans in tropical Africa, have established there not merely a governing and managerial class but a whole urban civilization. More especially there exists a class of skilled European artisans ranging from plasterers to fishermen, from tailors to engine-drivers, which is to be found in the urban settlements up-country as well as in the coast towns. This urban civilization may often have an almost medieval aspect, proportion, and squalor, as it does in the provinces of Portugal itself. . . . But it is unquestionably authentic, and perhaps unique."

2. Different parts of the main and secondary plateaus have received in the geographical literature and on maps such names as the Benguela plateau, Bié plateau, Malange plateau, Huíla plateau, Uíge plateau. The physiographic confines of these entities, however, are imprecise and the names seem to have been borrowed from those used for administrative subdivisions rather than designating distinct morphological units.

3. Significant source materials on the physical landscape of Angola are: F. Mouta, *Notícia explicativa do esboço geológico de Angola* (Lisbon, 1954); Mário de Matos Silveira, *Climas de Angola* (Luanda, 1967), Serviço Meteorológico de Angola, *O clima de Angola* (Luanda, 1955), and *Distribuição da precipitação na província de Angola—Esboço da carta udométrica* (Luanda, 1952), mostly in tables and maps; R. W. J. Keay, *Vegetation Map of Africa South of the Tropic of Cancer* (London, 1959); and an older exhaustive work by J. Gossweiler and F. M. Mendonça, *Carta fitogeográfica de Angola* (Lisbon, 1939), summarized by H. K. Airy Shaw in "The Vegetation of Angola," *Journal of Ecology*, XXXV (1947), 23–48.

4. October 22, 1968, Associated Press dispatch in the *New York Times* claimed that the Angolan population was 6.5 million compared to 5.1 million in 1965.

5. The urban population of Angola is well covered by Ilídio do Amaral, *Aspecto do povoamento branco de Angola* (Lisbon, 1960), and *Ensaio de um estudo geográfico da rede urbana de Angola* (Lisbon, 1962); Irene S. van Dongen, "The Port of Luanda in the Economy of Angola," *Boletim da Sociedade de Geografia de Lisboa*, January–March, 1960, pp. 3–43. A valuable work on African populations is Alvin W. Urquhart, *Patterns of Settlement and Subsistence in Southwestern Angola* (Washington, D.C., 1963). Population figures are all from Portugal, Província de Angola, Repartição de Estatística, Geral, *3° Recenseamento geral da população, 1960*, I (Luanda, 1964), 10, 15, 16, 24, and 25; trade figures are from various releases of Banco de Angola.

6. For 1967 the volume of that transit trade rose to 847,900 tons, about three-fourths originating in or destined to Congo-Kinshasa and the remainder being Zambian traffic. (Personal communication, Benguela Railway Company, 1968.)

7. See Portugal, Ministério da Economia e do Ultramar, *Plano de fomento* (*para 1953–58*), I (Lisbon, 1953), 143; Portugal, Assembleia Nacional, *II Plano de fomento* (*1959–64*), II (Lisbon, 1959), 32–33; and Portugal, Presidência do Conselho, *Plano intercalar de fomento para 1965–67*, I (Lisbon, 1964), 21. These volumes are also the source of developmental funds data for other Portuguese-African provinces.

8. Basic source materials on Mozambique are: Oliveira Boléo, *Moçambique: pequena monografia* (Lisbon, 1961), and his earlier *Moçambique* (Lisbon, 1951); Mozambique, Direcção dos Serviços de Agrimensura, *Atlas de Moçambique* (Lourenço Marques, 1960); C. F. Spence, *Moçambique* (Cape Town, 1963;) Raquel Soeiro de Brito, "Aspectos geográficos de Moçambique," in *Moçambique: curso de extensão universitária*, 1964–65 (Lisbon, 1965), pp. 13–34; M. Pimentel dos Santos, "Situação económica de Angola e Moçambique," *Fomento*, V, No. 2 (Lisbon, 1967), 73–103. Statistical data and other figures cited in this section are largely from Portugal, Província de Moçambique, Direcção Provincial de Estatística Geral, *Anuário estatístico*, 1964 (Lourenço Marques, 1966), pp. 16–26 and 30–43, and their *Boletim mensal* (December, 1966), p. 24, for population increases by migration, and *Boletim mensal* (April, 1967), pp. 62–66 for transport figures.

9. See studies by William A. Hance and Irene S. van Dongen, "Lourenço Marques in Delagoa Bay," *Economic Geography*, XXXIII, No. 3 (July, 1957), 238–56, and "Beira, Mozambique Gateway to Central Africa," *Annals of the Association of American Geographers*, XLVII, No. 4 (December, 1957), 307–35; and Irene S. van Dongen, "Nacala, Newest Mozambique Gateway to Interior Africa," *Tijdschrift voor Economische en Sociale Geografie*, XLVIII, No. 3 (March, 1957), 65–73.

10. This section has drawn on the extensive two-volume monograph by A. Teixeira da Mota, *Guiné portuguesa* (Lisbon, 1954); R. J. Harrison Church, *West Africa* (London and New York, 1957), pp. 272–78; and Agência Geral do Ultramar, *Províncias ultramarinas portuguesas: dados informativos* (Lisbon, 1962–66).

11. The physical and cultural background of the islands has been the object of excellent studies by Francisco Tenreiro, *A ilha de São Tomé* (Lisbon, 1961), and Raquel Soeiro de Brito, "A ilha do Príncipe," *Geographica*, III, No. 10 (April, 1967), 2–19. Other data in this section are from Agência Geral do Ultramar, *São Tomé e Príncipe: pequena monografia* (Lisbon, 1964).

12. Main source materials on Cape Verde are *Cabo Verde* (Lisbon, 1961); an earlier monograph by António Mendes Corrêa, *Ultramar portugués*, Vol. II, *Ilhas de Cabo Verde* (Lisbon, 1954); Orlando Ribeiro, *A ilha do Fogo e as suas erupções* (Lisbon, 1960); and the exhaustive work by Ilídio do Amaral, *Santiago de Cabo Verde: a terra e os homens* (Lisbon, 1964).

II

Early History, European Discovery, and Colonization

DAVID M. ABSHIRE

THE PRECOLONIAL history of sub-Saharan Africa is known only vaguely. In the relative absence of written documents, scholars have had to rely heavily on word of mouth—oral history and traditions—and archaeological discoveries and excavations. Such sources have yielded some information, however, as anthropologists like George P. Murdock, Paul Bohannan, and J. Desmond Clark and historians like Jan M. Vansina, Roland Oliver, and J. D. Fage have demonstrated.

Paradoxically, this continent, so long separated from the mainstream of history and progress, is close to man's beginnings, as is evidenced by skulls and bone fragments found in East Africa. The 25-million year old fossilized remains of Louis Leakey's famed Proconsul, man's earliest known ancestor, were discovered on an island in Lake Victoria. In Tanzania Leakey later discovered what he called the first known human being, by virtue of his capability as a toolmaker, and named him Zinjanthropus—or man from Zinj, the old Arab name for East Africa.[1]

Africa has a longer history than most continents, in terms of human beginnings and geological formation. The continent is principally a great block of rock formed over 200 million years ago, and geologically it has maintained a remarkable stability since Precambrian times, the days of very earliest geological history. The geological materials present in the Congo and South Africa support the concept of Gondwanaland, a once vast southern land mass including South America, Africa, Arabia, India, Australia, and the Antarctic.

Ethnologically, the Bushmen and the Hottentots, the wandering huntsmen and aboriginal inhabitants of the southern part of Africa, are far closer to early man than today's Europeans or the Bantu, who now predominate in Africa. African fauna and flora more closely resemble primeval specimens than flora and fauna elsewhere in the world. Nowhere is this point more graphically illustrated than in the great game preserve of Gorongosa in Mozambique, with its hordes of wildebeests, elephants, buffaloes, lions, zebras, impalas, marabou storks, waterbuck and its lagoons and palm trees and extravagant dawns and sunsets.

Africa may have been not only the cradle of human life but also the home of the very first advances that differentiated humanity from other animals. Not

29

until the later Stone Age did sub-Saharan Africa fall behind the Fertile Crescent and parts of China. Even so, Africa's progress was no slower than Australia's, where European discovery found the aborigines so backward that they could only be compared to the hunters and food gatherers of the Mesolithic Age.[2]

In about the fifth millennium B.C., a great climatic change turned the veritable garden of the northern region of Africa into a desert, driving many humans to the fertile valley of the Nile and the Mediterranean littoral, where civilization then began to flourish. But the change also had the effect of isolating sub-Saharan Africa and pushing some former inhabitants of the Sahara area southward into the lands of the Bushmen and Pygmies.

The ancestors of the Pygmies inhabited Central Africa west of the great lakes from the middle Paleolithic period to about the beginning of the Christian era. The Hottentots and Bushmen, until shortly before the arrival of Vasco da Gama, when their lands were overrun by Bantus, inhabited the region now occupied by South-West Africa, South Africa, Botswana, Lesotho, Swaziland, Rhodesia, and parts of Angola and Zambia.[3] Throughout sub-Saharan Africa's period of isolation, the East African coast remained an exception, as it shared life and trade with Arabia and India.

There are three basic ways in which the peoples of Africa have been distinguished: by race, by culture, and by language. The earliest racial categories, devised by Charles Seligman in 1930, divided Africans into five groupings: Hamites, Semites, Negroes, Bushmen and Hottentots, and Pygmy Negrillos. Seligman's work had a great effect on thinking about Africa for many years and remains current in some circles even today. Nevertheless, it is generally accepted that, as Bohannan has written, Seligman's racial approach forms "a pseudo-scientific rationalization for a common sense, naked-eye view."[4]

Increased European contact with Africa led to a number of detailed ethnographical studies. Under the leadership of Melville Herskovits and Hermann Baumann, racial description gave way to the division of Africa into culture areas. Faced with a desire to organize and classify the peoples of the continent, the advocates of culture categories sought kinship systems, political organization, and religions to justify their divisions. In time, it became clear that there was such a recurrence of each major type that the entire system had only limited usefulness.

The next step of classification was reached through the use of linguistic evidence. The pioneering work was done by Joseph Greenberg, who has so organized the more than 1,000 languages in Africa as to allow historical analysis of human interrelationships. Through careful linguistic study, tribal migrations and cultural innovations become increasingly clear. In this way, Greenberg has postulated that the Bantu originated in the areas between the Cross River and the middle Benue in contemporary Nigeria.[5] Angola and Mozambique, the two largest entities in Portuguese Africa, are largely populated by the Bantu.

The name Bantu refers to numerous Central African peoples who speak languages that have common roots. Seligman noted, "The Bantu might be defined as all those Africans who use some form of the root *ntu* for human being; with the plural prefix this becomes *ba-ntu* (Bantu), i.e., 'the men of the tribe,'

whence the term under which the whole great group has passed into anthropological literature."[6] The Bantus today occupy about one-third of the area of
the African continent. During the past 2,000 years they have displayed "a
capacity for explosive expansion paralleled only by the Arabs after Mohammed,
the Chinese, and the European nations since the Discoveries Period."[7]

Sometime in the latter part of the first century A.D., the Bantu emerged from
the forests of West Africa in waves. Their population increase was apparently
reinforced by their cultivation of food plants adapted from the Cushites of Sudan
and Ethiopia. Their migrations can be traced by the sudden appearance of iron-
working, since it was introduced by the Bantu wherever they went. Utilizing
shifting agriculture, they pushed south into the areas of the Bushmen until
finally they displaced the weaker hunting culture, not only of the Bushmen but
also of their relatives, the Hottentots and Bergdoma.

In the central and southern areas of Africa they had several centers of strength.
The first was the Luba-Lunda complex of kingdoms around the Katanga lakes.
Their predecessors were the Songye Kingdom and, before that, an earlier eighth-
century kingdom since revealed in excavations on the shores of Lake Kisale. The
Luba Kingdom reached its peak in the fifteenth or sixteenth century, its
prosperity based upon the comparatively advanced metallurgy and agriculture
of the highlands of Katanga. It plays only an indirect role in this history,
however.

Closely related to the Luba Kingdom are the Lunda kingdoms, from which the
northeast district of modern Angola takes its name. The Lunda reached their
peak in the eighteenth century. The military strength of the Lunda was never
great, yet they achieved a remarkable expansion, in contrast to the Luba, for
several reasons. Whereas the Luba did not follow positional succession or per-
petual kinship, the Lunda did. They divorced their political structure from their
real descent structure, effectively utilized indirect rule, and peacefully assimilated
local chieftains—all in a very adaptable form of government. With the geography
of the open savanna, their westward expansion was inevitable.[8]

Another strong center of the Bantu in Central Africa was the Kongo Kingdom.
In the fourteenth century, Wene, the son of the chief of a Bantu kingdom
located near present-day Boma on the Congo River, moved southward to
conquer the Congo plateau. Wene took the title of Manikongo (title-holder of
the Kongo) and then extended his conquests farther to include the areas of
Mpemba, Nsundi, Mpamba, Soyo, Mpangu, and Mbata. By the time of the
Portuguese arrival, this had become the largest kingdom in the western part of
Central Africa.

The Bantu kingdoms were interior-located or interior-directed societies. The
stimulus for activity was in the heart of Africa. The coast did yield salt deposits
and shells, which were used as currency, but the sea was regarded as a barrier to
trade and commerce.[9] The earlier population centers, from which expansionist
waves emanated in search of new lands and more profitable hunting, probably
were located toward the continent's center, in the Congo-Lualaba basin, for
example. This pattern of orientation toward the heartlands was to change with
the arrival of the Europeans when the sea became a highway of commerce. Only

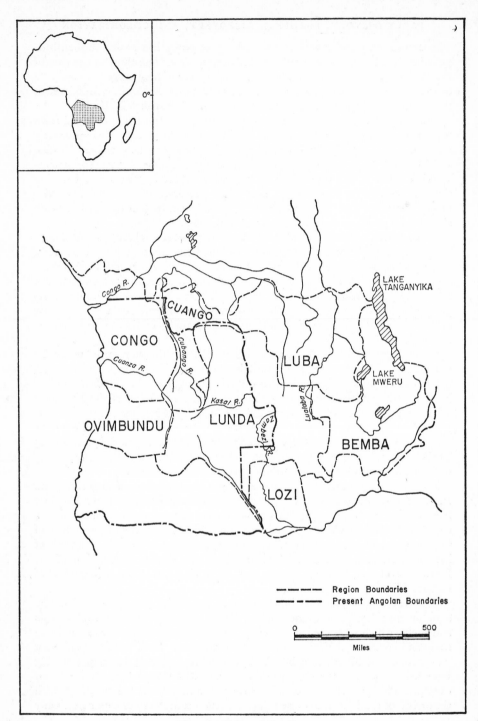

Historic Cultural Regions

then did the weak coastal areas become strong and prosperous. This shifting trade pattern, quite as much as Portuguese military presence, was to produce a constant alternation of the balance of power of African kingdoms during the ensuing three centuries.

EAST AFRICA

In contrast with Angola, which has only a few stone ruins, there are notable stone ruins in southeast Africa that serve as a starting point for establishing the prehistory of that area, in addition to oral tradition and early Portuguese accounts. About 17 miles southeast of Fort Victoria in Rhodesia lie stone platforms, terraces, monoliths, and enormous structures of dry-stone masonry, including a temple almost 90 yards long with walls 10 yards high and up to 5 yards thick. These Great Zimbabwe ruins may have been the seat of a local culture that later moved north of modern Salisbury. Parts of the foundation date from at least as early as the eleventh century. The first Bantu group there probably were the Sothos, followed by ancestors of the Karanga and Shona peoples.[10]

In the first half of the fifteenth century, a Karanga chief, Mutoto, conquered the lands from south of the Umfuli River to the Zambezi. The conquered Thonga began to call him "the master of the ravaged lands," or Mwene-Mutapa (Monomotapa). His Zimbabwe was built at Chitako hill about 100 miles north of the modern Salisbury. By the sixteenth century, the seeds of disintegration of the empire had set in. The ruler had been murdered, and power was seized by another, who in turn was killed by the son of the murdered chief. Such instability brought civil war to the countryside, but the kingdom, even though somewhat diminished, managed to hold together for another three centuries.

Unlike the kingdoms in west-central Africa, this kingdom had long been oriented toward the sea, because of trade with the Arabs for centuries before the coming of the Portuguese. Sofala, south of modern Beira, was a very early trading post for the Arabs, where they acquired gold, ivory, wax, horns, shells, and palm oil. Their goods of exchange, pottery and glass, found their way inland, and discoveries of such items in archaeological excavations have given clear indications of the early history of this part of Africa, in comparison with the vague history of west-central Africa.[11]

About the time of the Portuguese arrival, the Monomotapa was headquartered near the Fura Mountains in the southeast. The Great Zimbabwe was probably unoccupied for a half century, and then occupied by the Rozwe, who were not under the authority of the Monomotapa. Moreover, the areas of modern Umtali and Chipinga were beyond his control. The Monomotapa assumed a vastly exaggerated importance in the minds of the early Portuguese explorers who did not realize that his reputation and glory were mostly remnants of the past.

PORTUGUESE ORIGINS AND MOTIVES

As vital as it is to know about precolonial Africa, it is also important to know about the heritage of the nation that was in the vanguard of European expansion and first placed settlers in tropical Africa. Portugal's peculiar internal history

33

and geographic situation have great bearing on its motives for and methods of conquering its African possessions. An early alliance with England, as this and the next chapter will stress, played an important but erratic role in maintaining Portugal's African presence and has tended to affect Portuguese attitudes and suspicions toward both Great Britain and the United States in recent years.

Portugal's life as a nation is usually dated from 1140, when Afonso Henriques declared himself king of the Portuguese, after pushing the Muslims southward and also freeing himself of the rule of León, the Spanish region to the east and north.[12] Under Afonso's son, Sancho I, the new nation was organized into *concelhos*, or municipalities, with *forais*, or chapters. The *concelho*, however, was not simply or necessarily an urban unit: "among its attributes is the untilled land which may be distributed by *sesmeiro* to those who are willing to cultivate it."[13] Its importance to us is that the *concelho* was to become the basic organizational unit in the subsequent Portuguese overseas colonization.

In the succeeding 100 years, Portugal was fully formed as a nation-state. Sancho's son, Afonso II, summoned a *côrte* at Coimbra, composed of nobles (*fidalgos e homens ricos*) and prelates. Under Afonso III, the son of Afonso II, the kingdom of Portugal, freed from the remnants of both Moorish and Spanish domination, reached its present limits with Lisbon recognized as the capital. Diniz, the son of Afonso III, consolidated the monarchy, negotiated a commercial treaty with England, and formed a royal navy with the help of a Genoese, Emmanuele di Pezagna (Manoel Peçanha). But national existence again became precarious during and after the reign of Ferdinand I, who died with no male heir but an only daughter married to the king of Castile.

The Portuguese people feared Spanish domination. It was not surprising that John of Avis, an illegitimate half brother of Ferdinand, successfully led farmers and merchants alike in a national uprising in the years 1383 to 1385 against the queen regent Leonora, who was about to yield Portuguese sovereignty to the rulers of Castile. The first Anglo-Portuguese treaty had been signed in 1373, and John of Gaunt, Duke of Lancaster, also had his eye on the Castilian throne. Thus it was in part with the help of a small force of English archers that Portugal in 1385 won a monumental victory north of Lisbon at Aljubarrota and then invaded Castile. Politically, this consecrated Portugal's independent national existence and character, and diplomatically it led to a stronger alliance with the English, the 1386 Treaty of Westminster.[14] Underscored at the time by the marriage of John of Avis to Philippa of Lancaster, John of Gaunt's daughter, this is now the oldest existing alliance in the world but one that has caused tensions from time to time, arising from the Portuguese expectation of more than they received.

Aljubarrota and the rise of the House of Avis were followed by the opening of the Portuguese maritime era instigated by the third son of John and Philippa, known as Prince Henry the Navigator.[15] Several elements coming to fruition at the same time brought about the golden age of Portuguese exploration. The Muslims had been driven from the peninsula, and the Portuguese, increasingly aggressive, took the offensive to Morocco, where in 1415 they won a victory at Ceuta. Henry was knighted for his service in that battle on African soil, and he became the spark that ignited the zeal of Portuguese mariners. In his retreat at Sagres, close to Cape St. Vincent, he gathered map-makers, shipbuilders, navigators, mathematicians, astronomers, and practical seamen.[16] There, many of the great navigators of Genoa and Portugal were trained, including Magellan, who later reached the Pacific while sailing under the flag of Spain.[17]

Geographically, Portugal borders the Atlantic, with no direct access to the Mediterranean. The open ocean provided a natural magnet for Portuguese energies, and the development of naval technology made ocean voyages possible.

How did Prince Henry and his contemporaries see the impulse for this movement, which marks the beginning of modern colonization? Prince Henry's chronicler Gomes Eannes de Azurara listed their motives under five headings. The first was to explore the African coast beyond the Canary Islands and a "cape called Bojador," because at that time "neither by writings, nor by the memory of man, was the nature of the land beyond that cape known with any certainty." The second was to find out whether there were Christian peoples in Africa with whom it might be possible to trade; the third, to discover how far the territories of the Moors extended, since "every wise man is obliged by natural prudence to wish for a knowledge of the power of his enemy." The fourth motive was to see if it were possible to find a Christian king who, "for the love of our Lord Jesus Christ" would aid in fighting the Muslims; and the fifth, to extend "the faith of our Lord Jesus Christ and to bring to him all the souls that wish to be saved."[18]

The Christians had lost Constantinople in 1453. The turning of the Muslim flank thus had become a most serious strategic concern. As a part of this endeavor, Prince Henry had dreamed of finding and forming an alliance with Prester John, the legendary head of a Christian kingdom in the horn of Africa.[19] On a strictly commercial level, the Portuguese desired to capture the Venetian monopoly of the spice trade, which had continued even after the fall of Constantinople. For too long the Portuguese had watched without sharing in the wealth gained through the flow of commerce from Italy to Flanders. Lastly, Europe in general, and Portugal in particular, had a balance-of-payments problem: much of the gold in the coffers of Europe had gone to the Italian and Egyptian merchants to pay for the luxury imports from the East. Trans-Saharan caravans arriving in the cities of northern Africa with some salt and slaves sustained the idea that there was more gold to be found somewhere in Africa.[20] Thus, the African continent was of first importance in Prince Henry's eyes.

THE FIRST DISCOVERIES IN AFRICA

Quite early in his career, Prince Henry began to gather information about Africa, and in spite of repeated early failures that were ridiculed at home, several of his expeditions explored portions of the African coast. The Canary Islands were already well known to Portuguese, French, and Spanish mariners. The Arabs had called the Atlantic the "green Sea of Darkness," and the Portuguese navigators, like the Arabs before them, feared the great ocean, whose winds were often disastrous for their small ships. Sailing southward close to the African

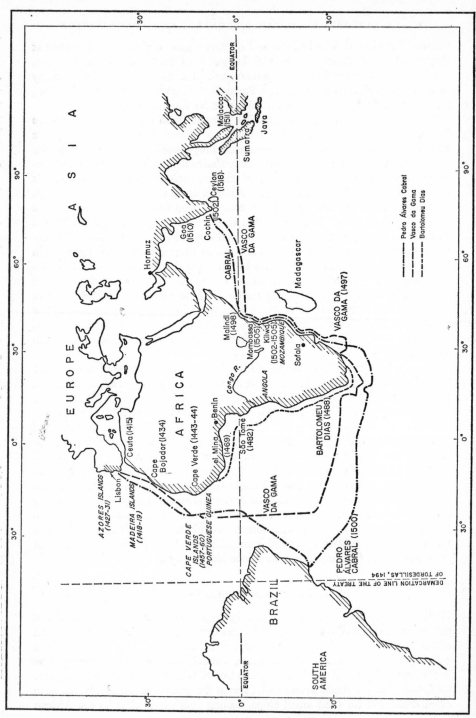

Major Portuguese Sea Explorations

shoreline they found a harborless coast without fresh water for nearly 1,000 miles below Morocco. Cape Bojador, the "bulging" cape, was generally supposed to be the end of the earth. Not until the Portuguese passed it and discovered Cape Blanco and Cape Verde did they find a shoreline of profuse vegetation. In 1442, Antão Gonçalves brought home the first slaves and gold dust from the West African coast. The Senegal seaboard was reached in 1445, followed by what is now Portuguese Guinea the next year when the explorer Nuno Tristão sailed to within sight of the estuaries of the Cacheu and Geba rivers. He dropped anchor off an island of the Bijagós archipelago, but he and his companions were killed by the inhabitants while trying to land. Until the end of the sixteenth century, Guinea was regarded simply as a source of trade, and no attempt was made to bring it under Portuguese rule.

The Cape Verde Islands were uninhabited when discovered in 1457. The earliest to be settled was Santiago Island, and it was from here that the first Portuguese traders moved to Guinea. The equatorial islands of São Tomé and Príncipe were discovered around 1470. São Tomé later became a flourishing colony, the center of the slave trade that rapidly developed between the Kongo and the Guinea seaboards and the Americas, and also an important producer of sugar.

Colonies were founded not only on the equatorial islands of São Tomé and Príncipe and Fernando Póo but also at São Jorge da Mina, on the coast of present-day Ghana. Later, Portuguese fortresses were built at intervals along the African shore where many still stand, the most notable being Elmina Castle.[21] On the north of the Gulf of Guinea, the early Portuguese discoverers established contact, in 1486, with Benin, one of the most highly organized Negro states in West Africa, now part of Nigeria. From there an ambassador was sent to Lisbon, and for more than a century diplomatic contact and friendship were maintained between the two countries.[22]

Although the first trading posts set up in Africa did indeed send gold back home as well as slaves in exchange for Portuguese maize, cloth, and horses, actual profits did not pay for the heavy cost of the expeditions. In 1460, Prince Henry died, heavily in debt.

THE KONGO KINGDOM AND ANGOLA

In late 1482 or early 1483 the discovery of the mouth of the Congo River (called Zaire by the Portuguese) by the great seaman Diogo Cão opened a new chapter in the story. After erecting the customary stone pillars (*padrões*) on the south bank of the river, Diogo Cão contacted the Manikongo, Nzinga Nkuwu. Later he returned to Portugal, taking four Africans with him as hostages for the safety of the messengers who had not reappeared after he sent them with gifts to the Manikongo. In Lisbon the impressed hostages were treated as envoys and exposed to the advances of European civilization. Two years later Diogo Cão returned the hostages and brought rich presents from John II to the Manikongo and a message expressing the hope that he would embrace the Christian faith. The Manikongo was influenced by the hostages' glowing stories, dispatched a small

37

party to Lisbon to learn European ways, and requested John II to send out more missionaries, carpenters, and masons to instruct his people. In 1490, three Portuguese ships arrived in the Kongo, bringing priests and men skilled in various trades.

The experiment of alliance and Christianization started promisingly with the conversion of the Manikongo and his family. However, the cordiality was soon under a strain that involved pro- and anti-Portuguese factions within the royal family. Even the Manikongo had become disillusioned by some of the Portuguese within his kingdom. Upon the death of Nzinga Nkuwu in 1506, a civil war ensued with the victory of the pro-Portuguese side of the family. Nzinga Mvemba, eldest son of Nzinga Nkuwu, became the Manikongo and took the title of Afonso I.[23]

The schism within the Kongo Kingdom involved the Portuguese Fernão de Melo, who in 1499 succeeded Álvaro Caminha as donatário (holder of political and economic rights) of the island of São Tomé and built a slave-trade center there. De Melo was zealous in promoting the economic progress of the island at the expense of the Kongo and he connived with the ship captains, who developed the slave trade with a ferocious disregard for humanity, for the wishes of the Manikongo himself, and for the activities of the various religious groups entrusted, by the Portuguese king Manuel, with extending the sphere of the Catholic faith.[24]

The Kongo port of Mpinda soon developed into a center exporting slaves in return for European cloth and metalware. Not only did the Manikongo begin to sell some of his own people, but either by trade or raids he managed to sell people from the Teke, Hum, and Mbundu. The development of the slave trade had a corrupting influence both on the high ideals of the Portuguese pioneers in the Kongo and on the Manikongo himself.

By and large, however, Portuguese-Kongolese relations flowed smoothly in the period that followed. The capital of the kingdom was renamed São Salvador, after a church built there by the Jesuits. Afonso's son, Henrique, became the first African bishop. Afonso died in about 1543, but his dynasty continued to rule with apparent success for nearly thirty years. Meanwhile, the resident Portuguese had married local women, but their mestiço children were less interested in the advancement of the country than in asserting their own position.

In about 1568, hordes of a warrior tribe, the Jaga, invaded the Kongo Kingdom from the southeast. The origins of the Jaga have not been clearly established, and the best accounts of their activities come from an English sailor, Andrew Battell, who lived with them somewhat later. "It is clear that the Jaga were not pastoralists because they killed and ate the cattle they raided; also, they drank palm wine and preferred to direct their campaigns in areas where wine was available," writes Jan Vansina. He continues: "In a more positive vein, it can be said that they may have had cultural connections with the Lunda-Luba peoples because every single trait of the culture described by Battell, if not already in existence in the lower Kongo area, can be found in the Lunda-Luba culture."[25]

The Jagas were excellent military tacticians and operated with stratagem and surprise. They drove the Manikongo and the Portuguese from the Kongo capital. The Manikongo of the time, Álvaro, requested protection of the king of Portugal and agreed to pay him tribute. Subsequently, a combined army of about 600 Portuguese and Kongolese mounted a counteroffensive and drove the Jaga from the Kongo Kingdom.

Despite this success, the realities of the first major Portuguese campaign in Africa alarmed Lisbon over the future stability of the Kongo area and caused the Portuguese to seek a more stable base in modern-day Angola. Contacts had occurred there in 1519, but were not as propitious as those with the Manikongo. At times this area had belonged to the kingdom of the Kongo, but now, taking advantage of the disturbances caused by the invasion of the Jagas, the king of this Mbundu Kingdom of Ndongo sought to become independent. The title of the king was Ngola, from which the Portuguese later took the name Angola. Relations between the Kongo and the Ngola were not improved when the slave dealers from São Tomé pushed farther south into Angola in search of slaves.

The Manikongo attempted to put an end to this traffic by sending an account of the involved ships to John III, the Portuguese king, who prohibited slaving. However, the Ngola continued to seek direct alliance with Portugal and, as a result of an ambassador sent to Lisbon, the queen mother Catarina (John III having died) sent a mission to the Ngola under Paulo Dias de Novais, a grandson of Bartholomeu Dias. Thus, the foundation of the Portuguese colony really dates from 1575 when Paulo Dias de Novais, the newly appointed governor, who had been given 140 miles of coastline by the Portuguese crown, landed at Luanda with 400 settlers.[26]

Meanwhile, the Ngola had grown increasingly strong. As David Birmingham notes, the Ndongo had gained its power principally through the slave trade. One irony of the Angolan situation of 1575 was that the Portuguese sought to conquer a kingdom whose power they themselves had unwittingly fostered by their commercial activity. The slave trade tended to undermine the states with which Europeans had direct contact while bringing prosperity to those who indirectly supplied slaves.[27]

In addition to this, relations between Dias de Novais and the Ngola deteriorated, and the latter at one point had thirty-odd Portuguese at his court killed. Soon thereafter, Dias de Novais launched a major military campaign to subdue the Mbundu and to take their silver mines. There has been more recent historical speculation that control of valuable salt mines on the south bank of the Cuanza might have been a more realistic aim and that the so-called silver mines were used as a more glamorous lure for support from Lisbon. There may even have been a larger strategic hope that Portuguese penetration up the Cuanza, an obvious African trading route, would one day open up Portuguese trade to the copper supplies of distant Katanga.[28]

The Portuguese met a tough, well-organized enemy. Kongolese troups tried to reinforce Dias de Novais' effort, but they were successfully turned back by the Mbundu. Finally, Dias de Novais reached the junction of the Lucala and Cuanza rivers, and there he built the *presídio* of Massangano, a short distance from Cambambe. It was an incomplete victory. The resistance to the Portuguese had been increased by the strength of the allied Imbangala tribes led by Kasanje. The Ngola held the plateau area; the Portuguese were restricted to the unhealthy lowlands, but they persisted.

This was only the initial phase of the Angolan wars, the first attempt of a European power to make a sizable military effort in tropical Africa. One estimate is that of the 2,000 European troops sent to Angola in the first twenty years of the Angolan wars, over 1,200 either died or had to return because of the fever.[29] If the major advantage of the Portuguese lay in their firearms, that of their enemies lay in the fever and disease that decimated the European ranks.

For the Portuguese mariners there was another lure beyond Africa: the distant goals of India and China. The Portuguese were growing constantly more technically proficient in ocean voyages, and the thought of circumventing their Muslim enemies in this lucrative trade particularly appealed. The way to the Indies, they had come to realize, could be sought around Africa.

Vasco da Gama, rounding the Cape of Good Hope in 1497 and sailing northward into the Indian Ocean, encountered, on the east coast of Africa, the trading settlements that the Arabs had established during the preceding 300 years. Among these were Mozambique, Mombasa, and Malindi, all wealthy from the trade the Arabs carried on between East Africa and southwest Asia. The Portuguese found houses built of coral rock with cement of coral lime, furnished with many articles of luxury, such as Chinese porcelain.

In 1509–10, a Portuguese military expedition, led by Afonso d'Albuquerque, took possession of many of the Arab settlements in East Africa, thus gaining control of the shipping trade that flowed across the Indian Ocean. Mozambique, Hormuz in Iran, Goa on the Indian subcontinent, and Malacca on the Malay Straits became the strong points of empire.[30] Gold, slaves, and ivory went east across the Indian Ocean and the cloth, metal products, and glasswork of Asia traveled west in Portuguese ships.

The discoverers and traders were followed by captains and administrators, such as Almeida, Albuquerque, and Soares, who established their supremacy in seapower by defeating the Arab fleets sent against them and, with a few thousand soldiers, defeated the Indian rulers or frightened them by threat of bombardment into becoming allies. The basis of the Portuguese sea victories lay in a better technology and shrewd tactics. The Muslims continued to fight with manpower-propelled galleys, in hopes of ramming and boarding, but on the high seas they were outmaneuvered and outgunned by sailing vessels equipped with firepower that was new to the area.[31] Within thirteen years of their arrival the Portuguese gained mastery over the western sector of the Indian Ocean.

The capture of the spice trade and of vast overseas dominions brought riches to the Portuguese court, but the newly-found prosperity did not last long. A glut of pepper, the principal import, was followed by a slump in the price. The cost of outfitting national fleets and maintaining so many far-flung garrison outposts ate into the profits of the crown. It was found that the expenses of the overseas empire outweighed the revenues it brought in, so private enterprise was enlisted to provide ships and men in return for a share in the profits.[32]

While making themselves masters of the east, the Portuguese were simultaneously laying the foundation of another empire in the west. Portugal's rights under the Treaty of Tordesillas, signed in 1494 as a result of Columbus's voyages across the Atlantic, included everything that lay within a line drawn 370 leagues west of the Cape Verde Islands. When Pedro Álvares Cabral sighted the coast of Brazil in 1500, he therefore added to the Portuguese empire another territory. By 1530, settlements were founded at São Vicente, near the present port of Santos, and at Piratininga, where modern São Paulo now stands. In 1549, a seat of government was established at Bahía.

COLONIAL ADMINISTRATION

The beginnings of Portuguese colonial administration in Africa are traceable in the Atlantic Ocean islands, which, it will be recalled, were uninhabited when first discovered. With settlement came the need for some sort of government administration. In the beginning, the Azores, Madeira, the Cape Verde Islands, and São Tomé were governed by *donatários* or *capitães donatários*, nobles or soldiers who exercised full authority subject to appeal to Lisbon and royal inspection.

The larger Portuguese empire that later developed in Asia and Africa can be described as a commercial and maritime empire cast in a military and ecclesiastical mold.[33] The earliest system of administration in the forts established along the African coast called for a military commander, or *capitão*, who directly represented the king; a *feitor*, who was in charge of commercial relations with the inhabitants and who sometimes served also as the *capitão*; a *missionário* or priest (the posts were also the seats of religious missions); and sometimes an *ouvidor*, or royal judge. These outposts were gradually known by the name of *feitorias*, after the fiscal officer. Relations with the interior were carried on through trading expeditions and missionary activity and through the conversion of native chiefs and kings to Christianity, which meant acceptance of the king of Portugal as feudal lord. There were three such protectorates in the territory of present-day Angola, the most important being the kingdom of the Kongo, ruled by the Manikongo. In the general area of present Mozambique, there were several protectorates established over Zambezi kingdoms, the most important being that of the chief known as the Monomotapa.

SPANISH DOMINATION AND STAGNATION

After the first outburst of vigor in early discoveries and colonization, events in Portugal took a downward turn that had profound effects on the new empire. Spain and Portugal stood together on the doctrine of the closed sea to protect their dominions against interlopers and intruders, whether they were Portugal's old allies, the English, or Spain's old vassals, the Dutch. The architects of this policy, such as King Manuel, never meant it to result in placing Portugal under the Spanish crown. Yet, precisely such a development occurred as a consequence of the fanaticism of the Portuguese king, Sebastian, a young religious fanatic whose militancy outran his means. With the news of the Kongo disaster at the hands of the Jagas, he had issued to Dias de Novais the charter for the conquest

41

of Angola and ordered Gouveia, a former captain of São Tomé, to retake the Kongo. He also instructed Barreto to conquer the Monomotapa.

As to his more immediate actions, he led the flower of Portuguese youth to a terrible disaster that resulted in his own death at the hands of the Muslims, at Alcacer-el-Kebir in North Africa. While the traumatic shock of this defeat reverberated through Portugal, the dead king's closest relative, a feeble and childless great uncle, Cardinal Henriques, assumed the crown while a watchful relative, Philip II of Spain, made ready to lay claim to it. In 1580, the Portuguese crown came under Spanish dominion.

The first Spanish king of the Portuguese, Philip II, did well by his foreign subjects, but the same cannot be said of Philip's successors. Yet, this first Portuguese stagnation and decline was not due simply to the fact that the Spanish kings who followed Philip II were less zealous in their duties toward the Portuguese, embroiling them in their European intrigues and wars and taxing them for part of the cost. Portugal had exported much of the best of its diminishing population and suffered heavy losses in voyages and battles waged to secure *presídios* and settlements that stretched half-way around the globe. The incoming gold quickly passed to financiers in Holland and Germany, and during the period of Spanish domination the Portuguese lost the maritime supremacy that was basic to their commercial empire in the East.[34]

During the earlier period of Spanish overlordship, Portugal's African colonies had developed falteringly. Francisco d'Almeida became governor-general of Angola in 1592 and founded a system of colonial administration, despite the opposition of the Jesuit missionaries, local Portuguese landholders, and recalcitrant tribes. Almeida, acting on orders from Lisbon, ended a system whereby conquered chiefs became subject to the *donatário* or his designate and directed that all chiefs would be subjects only of the crown.

Frustrated in his policies by the Jesuits and other slaveholders, Almeida was succeeded in his post by his brother Jerônimo, who was more lenient in enforcing the new laws. His ambition was to take the town of Cambambe, but this was to be achieved by another governor, Manuel Cerveira Pereira in 1605. Yet, the hoped-for silver mines were not there; neither had the Portuguese taken the salt mines south of the Cuanza. The disillusionment brought to a close the first stage of the Angolan wars.

The next period of the Angolan wars, from 1605 to 1641, took place in the shadow of this disillusionment and with the realization that only commerce in human beings offered prosperity for the Portuguese in Angola. Other Europeans, such as the English and Dutch, acquired their slaves by barter, whereas the Portuguese acquired theirs as prisoners of war, and this necessitated successful military campaigns. Birmingham notes that slave "campaigns were never permitted by official policy, and had to be justified by excuses such as punishing chiefs who had given refuge to runaway slaves or had failed to pay tribute."[35] The underpaid governors thus developed a sizable supplement to their small income.

The decisive blow against the Mbundu was struck by Governor Luís Mendes de Vasconcelos. He, like other governors, arrived in Luanda with great idealism and he entertained notions of re-establishing friendly relations with the Ndongo and ending the Portuguese alliance with the Imbangala tribes whom Vasconcelos had heard would eat their captured Mbundu. Angola was too unprofitable and the tribes too uncooperative for such idealism, and soon he successfully headed campaigns, with many Imbangala, that reached and destroyed the Ndongo capital near Mbaka on the Lucala River. Subsequent governors, however, restored relations with the Mbundu, and their remarkable queen, Nzinga, even got the Portuguese to help drive the Imbangala from their lands.

Portuguese policy fluctuated almost with each governor, and another one, Fernão de Souza, foolishly launched a new war against Nzinga. The weakening of the Mbundu, and the migration of many of them inland to avoid the Portuguese, resulted in increased power going to two new states, Kasanje, founded by an Imbangala chief by that name, and Matamba, which was conquered by Queen Nzinga and made her headquarters. Both of these states, on the upper side of the Cuango River, became involved in vigorous slave-trading, some of it with the Dutch.

Meanwhile, in 1617, Manuel Cerveira Pereira, who held a royal commission to subjugate the more southerly regions of Angola, founded the city of São Felipe de Benguela, on a site between the Maubambo and Coringe rivers.[36] He began at once to war upon the local tribes and to contend with other Portuguese officials, all of whom were driven by a consuming desire to discover the copper and silver mines that were to make their fortunes.

The formation of the Dutch West India Company, in 1621, was the signal that the Dutch had designs on the Portuguese empire, and the Dutch assault subsequently was to take place in many areas of the world. In search of slaves, they attacked Portuguese Africa in 1641 and captured and occupied Luanda and Benguela. Many Portuguese traders and refugees fled inland to such *presídios* as Massangano, Cambambe, and Mbaka, where some settled permanently. The weakened Kongo Kingdom and the queen of Matamba favored the Dutch with the new opportunity for slave trade, whereas some tribes from Ndongo, Imbangala, and Kasanje fought with the Portuguese. In 1648, the Dutch were expelled by an expedition commanded by Salvador Correia de Sá, mounted and financed in Brazil, but the Dutch continued for some decades to be a threat.

In the aftermath of their success, the Portuguese launched offensives against the monarchies that had sided with the Dutch. Luís Lopes de Sequeira led a Portuguese army of 3,000 African bowmen, 200 European troops, 150 settlers, and 100 African riflemen to a decisive victory over the Kongolese at Mbwila in 1665.[37] The Kongo never regained its strength. As slave-trading partners, the Portuguese were again allied with Queen Nzinga in Matamba, and this in turn brought on war with their earlier ally, Ngola Ari, ruler of Ndongo. In 1671, Portuguese military successes ended the Ndongo as an effective state.

As these African kingdoms degenerated, those at a greater distance grew in strength and prosperity. They were too far inland to fear the Portuguese military, yet close enough to become rich partners in the slave trade. Alliances shifted, and in the middle states such as Kasanje, the Portuguese would back their African candidate in succession quarrels. Wars were intermittent, with a state such as

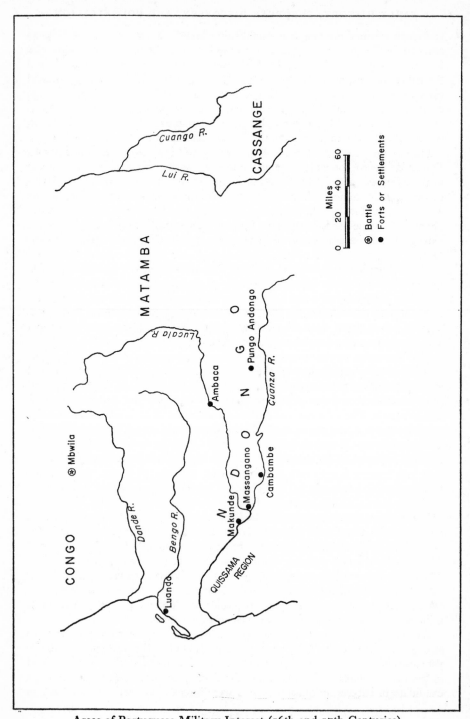

Areas of Portuguese Military Interest (16th and 17th Centuries)
Adapted from David Birmingham, *The Portuguese Conquest of Angola* (London, 1965), p. 52.

Matamba suddenly becoming friendly in hopes of better opportunity for trade in slaves, acting as a middle man between the Portuguese and inland states such as the growing kingdoms which the Portuguese had never seen.

The peace with the Matamba, in 1683, marked the end of the most militant expansionist phase of Portuguese activity radiating from Luanda, despite another outbreak with the Matamba in 1744. The concern of the Portuguese, however, was with the increasing slave trade of the English, Dutch, and French, originating from inland areas such as Lunda, but exiting through the Loango Kingdom in the north, bypassing Angola.

Upon arrival in Angola, the Europeans usually did not establish themselves in settlements, but tended to scatter and penetrate the inland areas either for adventure or in hopes of finding riches. The Portuguese government envisaged a threat in these private explorations and, to assure control over the most remote areas and encourage trade, they established several inland forts. To the south, radiating from Benguela, the Portuguese had penetrated the plateau zones, transforming the treacherous, tranquil swamp area of the Bongo River into a significant locale for population concentration and the exportation of slaves. In about 1682, the Caconda fort was built at the headwaters of the Lutira River, under the command of Sergeant Pedro da Silva.[38] This became the future base of military operations, first for protection, later for conquest, and flourished as a gateway for trade. As for the Luanda hinterland farther to the north, Portuguese settlements up the Lucala River (an affluent of the Cuanza) had reached Ambaca, founded in 1614. Up the Cuanza itself Portuguese settlements extended almost 200 miles inland to the small *presídio* of Pungo Andongo, founded in 1671, and beyond that Portuguese traders operated farther east to trade fairs. The most notable was that of Cassange, beyond the Cuango River, about 380 miles from Luanda just within the modern-day northeastern district of Angola called Lunda. In view of the frequent hostility of both nature and native, this seventeenth-century commercial penetration of Angola by tiny settlements and trade fairs was extraordinary in the annals of European survival deep in tropical Africa.

Mozambique, the Monomotapa, and Interior Expeditions

When Vasco da Gama rounded the Cape of Good Hope, he stopped at the mouths of two rivers, the Limpopo and the Quelimane, and then dropped anchor at Mozambique Island before proceeding toward India. This island was one of the Arab city-states that at the time were found all along the eastern seaboard of Africa and that were the entrepôts for the trade that flowered between Africa, Arabia, and India. The inhabitants of these cities were predominantly African, but they were ruled over by Arab sheiks, who competed for trade and power.[39]

At the turn of the century, Pedro Álvares Cabral, on his way to India, first sighted Sofala, just south of the modern city of Beira. Upon his return from India, his curiosity over Sofala as the Arab export port for the legendary gold trade led him to send a squadron there. Portuguese first visited Delagoa Bay in 1502, took over and settled Sofala in 1505, but shifted their principal efforts to Mozambique Island three years later, as a better and more secure way station for

India. Francisco d'Almeida (not to be confused with the later governor of Angola) was headquartered in Goa as Viceroy of India, and in 1505 his authority was defined so as to include Mozambique.

The first European to penetrate into the interior of southern Africa was a Portuguese, António Fernandes. He was a *degredado*, a criminal who had been offered a pardon in return for his enlisting in the Indian service. This was a usual practice by which the Portuguese crown obtained some of the manpower it needed for the exploration of Africa and the way to India. Little is known about António Fernandes. He is assumed to be the ship's carpenter spoken of by the chroniclers Góis and Barros as having sailed in the fleet of Vasco da Gama or that of Pedro Álvares Cabral. In any case, he was in Sofala in 1505 and presumably aided in the construction of the fort there that year, the first European building in southern Africa. Fernandes was probably illiterate, but a narrative of his journeys into the interior was written by Gaspar Veloso, one of the officers in Sofala.[40] The exact date of Fernandes' departure on his first trip is assumed to have been at the beginning of the dry season, about April, 1514. He went with a train of African bearers carrying the presents—muskets, cloth, and glass beads —for the local chiefs he expected to encounter. Because of the hostility of some unfriendly tribes, he did not travel directly from Sofala to the mines at Manica, but skirted the Inyanga highlands, then stayed to the south of the Chimanimani Mountains, entered the Sabi (Save) valley, and from thence reached the Mazoe River. Near the Pungué River he first saw natives mining gold ore, and several days later he arrived at the Machona gold fields. He went thereafter northeastward until he reached the present district of Lomagundi in Rhodesia. There he became the first white man to encounter the great chief, the Monomotapa, whose kingdom covered the whole territory from Lomagundi to Beira. (The name "Monomotapa" is applied to both the territory and the chief who controlled it.) Fernandes stayed in the domains of the Monomotapa long enough to make two expeditions to other gold fields, arriving back in Sofala five days short of four months after he had left.

His second journey probably took place during the rainy season of 1514–15 and lasted more than four months because of delays caused by tropical storms and tribal wars. This trip took him to the gold fields of Que Que, and then Batonga and the area around the present Fort Victoria in Rhodesia. Since he did not mention the Great Zimbabwe ruins, it has been estimated that he passed some 30 or 40 miles to the south.[41]

Between 1530 and 1570, the Portuguese founded tiny settlements on the Zambezi, one at Sena, 160 miles from its mouth, and another at Tete, about 300 miles from its mouth, and just below the Cabora Bassa rapids. On the coast, meanwhile, settlements were started at Quelimane in 1544 and a station was begun near Catembe.

As dreams of gold faded, some churchmen sought a higher mission. A Shona leader was baptized while visiting Mozambique and he asked for missionaries to come to his village near Inhambane. Dom Gonçalo da Silveira, a Jesuit, responded in 1560 and thus headed the first Christian mission to southeastern Africa. All the village was converted, although the Africans ultimately rejected

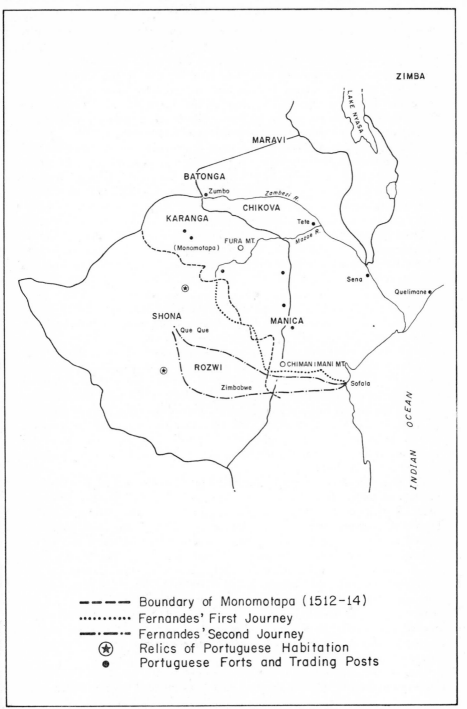

ZIMBA

LAKE NYASA

MARAVI

BATONGA
Zumbo
Zambezi R.

CHIKOVA

KARANGA
Tete
Mazoe R.
(Monomotapa) FURA MT.

Sena

Quelimane

SHONA

MANICA

Que Que

ROZWI
CHIMANIMANI MT.
Zimbabwe
Sofala

INDIAN OCEAN

– – – – Boundary of Monomotapa (1512–14)
•••••••••• Fernandes' First Journey
– • – • – Fernandes' Second Journey
⊛ Relics of Portuguese Habitation
● Portuguese Forts and Trading Posts

African Habitation, Portuguese Forts, and the Voyages of
António Fernandes, 1512–15

these missionaries who criticized polygamy and rain-making ceremonies. Meanwhile, Silveira traveled with a Portuguese trader as a guide up the Zambezi to Sena and Tete, and on beyond to Fura Mountain, headquarters of the Monomotapa. After a friendly reception, resulting even in the Monomotapa's baptism, Silveira encountered Arab traders who spread suspicion as to Silveira's being the source of witchcraft. This, coupled with his marital teachings, induced the Monomotapa to order him to leave. Silveira nevertheless baptized fifty converts, and the next day the Monomotapa had him strangled.

Following the news of this murder, King Sebastian determined to seize the gold of the Monomotapa while also taking North Africa and Angola. In 1569, Francisco Barreto, the first man to be appointed governor solely of Mozambique, received troops from Lisbon only to have fever kill a sizable portion of them at Sena. Barreto, weakened further by two battles, retreated and himself became a fatality.

In 1571, another expedition to reach the mines was mounted under Fernandes Homem. Instead of following the Zambezi route, he went from Sofala to Manica and successfully negotiated with a chief near Umtali, but he was disappointed by the limited amount of gold being mined there. The information from his expedition in 1609 was incorporated in a remarkable journal by João dos Santos.

Failure to find minerals dampened Portuguese ambitions to mount more aggressive expeditions into the highlands. It should be remembered too that the insatiable King Sebastian had died, and Portugal had passed under control of Spain in 1580. Nevertheless, Portuguese traders increasingly infiltrated Mashonaland. As the home government became less interested and less willing to back them with military assistance, the art of playing tribal politics became more important to local Portuguese. This was truly put to a test when the Zambezi valley faced the onslaught of the savage cannibalistic tribe known as the Zimba, based in the area of modern-day Tanzania. Part of the tribe erupted eastward to strike at Kilwa and Mombasa, and the other part scourged the Zambezi area to the south. Portuguese and Africans retreated in their wake, and Sena was overrun for a time, as Portuguese power in the Zambezi fell to a new low by the turn of the century.

The next Monomotapa, Kapararidze, changed loyalties and tried to drive all Portuguese traders from the country. In a major counteroffensive, Diogo de Menezes with 300 European troops and supposedly 12,000 African spearmen burned the villages that were the headquarters of the Shona chief, Chikanga, moved to Fura Mountain, won a battle, and killed Kapararidze in 1632. A Portuguese puppet was put in his place—and thus was accomplished a long-sought objective of bringing this ancient ruling structure within their orbit.

Beginning in 1612, the Portuguese had taken up the search for silver with an offensive up the Zambezi River against another tribe, the Chikova. About the same time, Gaspar Bocarro led an expedition to Lake Nyasa, first in a vain search of silver mines and then of copper. After crossing the lake he moved eastward to Kilwa, on the Indian Ocean, adding another spectacular trek to Portuguese explorations.

Late in the sixteenth and early in the seventeenth centuries, Portuguese soldiers and merchants in the Zambezi valley had founded large estates through conquest. These estates were in a sense land grants from the Monomotapa, whom they would back in various tribal wars. The Portuguese took African wives, learned the language, and participated in the local culture. By the middle of the seventeenth century, the Portuguese Government had itself begun to support this system of Zambezi estates and started to grant what became known as *prazos da coroa*, since the titles were in theory granted for three generations by the crown. They were given as reward for distinguished service and on condition that the female descendants would become the holders and marry white Portuguese. Some of the *prazeros* were to acquire great power; with their private armies, hundreds of slaves, and feudal way of life, most paid no attention to the Portuguese governor or to any high principles offered by Lisbon. Attempts to curb their independence met with little success.[42]

As the seventeenth century advanced, Portuguese traders increasingly permeated the Monomotapa lands. Their strength was due more to their facility at playing tribal politics and to possession of the flintlock than to any support from Lisbon or Goa, which at best was uncertain and subject to long delays. Even in their own settlements, the Portuguese were enormously outnumbered: in Tete perhaps forty Portuguese lived with some 600 baptized Africans or *mestiços*. After 1680, some local Portuguese began to recognize their risky position and to observe that their success was based primarily on their political cunning and ability to solicit African support. Yet, many other Portuguese soon violated these earlier principles of success with the Africans and became overconfident landlords who antagonized the friendly Africans. The antipathy of the Monomotapa grew until he allied himself with the Rozwi, and together they mounted a fierce offensive. The Portuguese were destroyed in small groups and driven off the Mashonaland plateau altogether.[43]

They were also suffering even more serious reverses along the coast, as the Arab cities north of Mozambique were in revolt. In 1698, after a long siege in their great Fort of Jesus at Mombasa, the Portuguese were driven out by the Omani Arabs. The defense and the attempted rescue had been under incompetent commanders.[44] Pemba Island and Kilwa fell shortly thereafter. By the early part of the eighteenth century, the Portuguese had withdrawn south of Cape Delgado, which thereafter remained as the northern limit of their expansion. In sum, both along the coast and in the interior, the beginning of the eighteenth century saw the Portuguese fortunes in Mozambique at a new low.

Despite these political reverses, Portuguese traders relentlessly held on and continued to permeate the area. In fact, by 1714, a new fair or post was established farther up the Zambezi than ever, at Zumbo, where the Luangwa River joins the Zambezi.

ADMINISTRATION

It is evident that throughout the first 300 years of the Portuguese presence in Africa, contact with Africans occurred chiefly at military posts, religious missions, and trading posts, all of which represented a sort of far frontier of the Portuguese empire sparsely populated with Portuguese settlers. It is not surprising that during these centuries the colonial administration remained the same.

49

From about 1500 to 1822, administration in Portuguese Africa was, at least on paper, divided between areas of direct military-civil control under governors, concessions awarded to individuals and companies, and native protectorates. But there was a difference between east and west. Until the middle of the eighteenth century, Portuguese East Africa with its *prazos* was governed under the authority of the viceroys of Portuguese India. Angola was controlled economically from Brazil, as it amounted to its dependency.

The Metropolitan Overseas Council was founded in July, 1643. By 1650, a typical African territory had an administration consisting of a governor or captain-general, a chief of police and treasury head, a council consisting of officials and local citizens, and an *ouvidor*, or chief justice, who was the second-ranking man in the colony. In 1670, the first administrative code was promulgated, setting forth the duties of the captains and other officials of fortresses and settlements.

The economic and political development of Portugal's overseas empire in the eighteenth century must be seen against the course of events in Lisbon. During the Spanish occupation, the Anglo-Portuguese treaty of 1386 had been suspended, but with independence and the Bragança dynasty, a new treaty was negotiated in 1642. In 1661 the alliance was further reconsecrated with the marriage of Charles II to Catarina of Bragança, in which as a dowry England received Tangier and the island and territory of Bombay, plus trading concessions with Brazil and India. England in return agreed in a secret clause to defend not only Portugal but the colonies as well.

In the latter part of the seventeenth century, Portugal was rapidly losing ground financially, and its exports of sugar, tobacco, wine, fruit, and salt were inadequate to pay for needed imports of cereals and manufactured goods. The balance-of-payments crisis, however, was averted by the discovery of gold in Brazil and by hostilities between France and England, leading to English consumption of Portuguese rather than French wine. This new trade was formalized in the Methuen Commercial Treaty of 1703, which in turn was born during the war of the Spanish succession in which Portugal joined the English, Dutch, and Austrians against Louis XIV, who wanted his grandson Prince Philip on the throne of Spain, which would thus have made that country his satellite. The treaty, aimed at weakening France and Spain economically as a part of the war strategy, had lasting impact on Anglo-Portuguese economic relations. It assured Portuguese wines preferential duties in exchange for admittance of British woolens to Portugal. The Spanish and French bitterly denounced the treaty as placing Portugal in a subservient economic position to England. Many Portuguese later argued that it stifled Portuguese industry, although it gave a valuable boost to the wine industry, even if it did lead to English control.[45]

From 1755 to 1777 Portugal was in effect ruled by a dictator, the Marquis of Pombal, the remarkable minister of state of Joseph I. In the king's name, he made all the decisions, great and small, in a way typical of authoritarian government. The Portuguese crown, in the paternalistic tradition, concerned itself with petitions from individuals seeking redress of wrongs suffered in the colonies, the supervision of the gold and diamond mines of Brazil, and the settlement of disputes with foreign and ecclesiastical officials.[46] Pombal began his career as ambassador to London, where he observed the importance of the English East India Company. Upon coming to power, he founded a number of trading companies that were given monopolies and government subsidies.

Because of the extreme stagnation into which the nation had sunk, Pombal had few native resources. To create an army and build forts, he was forced to bring in German, French, English, and Spanish mercenaries. To create industries, he sent to France for weavers, watchmakers, and iron-founders and to Italy for china-manufacturers. He even had to import his merchants and his university professors. His great efforts were ephemeral and Portugal lived off the wealth of Brazil.[47] In the latter part of his rule, the country encountered an acute economic crisis, mostly brought about by a decline in the production of Brazilian gold, diamonds, and sugar but also the result of a basic principle in the Portuguese monarchical structure. Like the Spanish, the Portuguese crown claimed the residual ownership of all private wealth. The resources of its colonies were crown property, which individuals might exploit only with the consent and close supervision of the king and his officials and to the enrichment of the royal treasury. This principle discouraged the initiative of those who might otherwise have undertaken new enterprises, and it hampered the development of such enterprises as were attempted because of the long delays involved in the necessary submission of so many matters to Lisbon.

A number of Pombal's actions had an effect on the future development of Portuguese Africa. His famous decree suppressing the Society of Jesus in the Portuguese territories (which preceded similar action in Spain and France) had far-reaching results. Although the Jesuits were the best teachers and missionaries in Portuguese Africa and Asia, in Angola, by the 1640's, the Italian Capuchins had come to be the most successful missionaries.

Underlying all these developments was the inescapable economic predominance of the slave-traders. In the latter part of the eighteenth century, Francisco de Sousa Coutinho, a protégé of Pombal came to Angola as governor. In this capacity, from 1764 to 1772, he made valiant efforts to diversify its economic life by establishing an iron foundry, promoting the growing of food supplies, and investigating the possibilities of exploiting sulfur and asphalt deposits. He built a new coastal *presídio* at Novo Redondo to prevent foreign traders from smuggling south of Luanda and also to improve overland communications between Luanda and Benguela. He encouraged expansion into the Benguela highlands, to include building up Caconda and establishing trade fairs farther east. He tried to overhaul the administration, to cut down on corruption and to bring more effective control over some of the wealthy settlers in virtually autonomous domains in the backlands.

His example was not followed by his successors. The abandonment of his work must have been complete because Miguel António de Melo, who later (1795–1800) was governor of Angola, wrote to Rodrigo de Sousa Coutinho, his son and then minister of state: "But as nothing that my predecessor advocated was done and as the good things that he initiated were destroyed, what shall I be able to do, without any means and after twenty-eight years of neglect?"

Angola reverted to the stagnation and easy-going ways Sousa Coutinho had tried to eliminate.[48]

The trade in human beings thwarted the local economic development of Mozambique. In earlier years, near Tete, for example, there had been some commerce in wheat, millet, maize, coffee, sugar, oil, gold dust, and ivory. The crops were cultivated, however, by slaves. In the heyday of the slave trade, the slave masters succumbed to the use of quicker returns from selling these slaves off, until they had in effect exported the labor supply upon which their earlier prosperity was based. As decadence set in, many of the Portuguese themselves left for Brazil.[49] At the end of the eighteenth century, the plight of Mozambique was far worse than that of Angola. Meanwhile, in 1752, Mozambique had been separated from Goa and given its own governor.

North of the Zambezi, patterns of trade began to shift as Arab traders attempted to circumvent Portuguese control by skirting to the north and using Zanzibar as a base. The tribe stretching from the Zambezi delta toward Cape Delgado was the Makua and inland from it were the Yao peoples—important traders of slaves and ivory. Indeed, by offering better terms than the Portuguese, traders from Zanzibar acted as a magnet in pulling trade northward from the Makua and Yao tribal areas. Mozambique Island had diminished in importance since the seventeenth century, as ships used the so-called inner passage of the Mozambique Channel less frequently and instead stayed eastward of Madagascar where Port Louis on Île de France (named Mauritius in 1810 when taken over by the British) had become an important way station for traffic to Bombay and Calcutta.[50] Thus, the loss of much of the ivory trade dealt a second great blow and forced a further concentration on the slave trade.

On the extreme southwest coast of Mozambique, the Portuguese had a small trading post (factory) on magnificent Delagoa Bay, but little thought was given to the area until foreigners, beginning with the Austrians, made attempts to set up similar posts near by. A British captain, William Owen, visited Delagoa Bay in conjunction with a coastal survey in 1822 and later entered into a compact with native chiefs and began to argue that the Portuguese could not justify their claims to all the bay area. Though only a minor incident at the time, this event assumed importance when reviewed in retrospect, as discussed in the following chapter.

Of major significance was the push of Zulu warrior tribes into the Mozambique area. One clan of the Nguni-speaking Bantu, or Zulu, the Shangana, had fled Shaka, the Zulu king, and moved into Mozambique between the Save (Sabi) and Limpopo rivers in about 1825, and within a decade many had also dispersed in the Lourenço Marques area. Some of them plundered areas near Sofala. Other Nguni groups crossed the Zambezi near Zumbo and dispersed in the Yao areas, and some moved north of the Rovuma River, and some even reached Cape Delgado.[51]

TRANSFORMATIONS

Oliveira Martins states that, as far as Angola was concerned, the plans formulated by Pombal and Sousa Coutinho were chimerical, since every attempt at developing the resources of the colony was undermined by the fact that the greatest profits were those made in the slave trade.[52] Charles Boxer says that the slave trade, even more than disease, "formed the greatest handicap" in the economic development of both Portuguese Africa and Brazil. It is difficult to believe, however, that even without the slave trade Portugal, limited by both its resources and Iberian attitudes, could have fostered major economic development in Africa before modern transportation and medicine. Geography, demography, and climate—and all the realities of the tropics—made this a white man's grave and furnished obstacles to real development. Africa, with its swampy and malarial coastal areas, presented health barriers that made European settlement difficult and discouraged settler occupations. Without question, though, the economic dominance of Brazil and its demand for slaves paradoxically made it doubly difficult for Angola to become a second Brazil. This was true especially because the vast majority of emigrants from Portugal preferred Brazil to Angola.

Meanwhile, the slave trade had worked a profound change in the Africans themselves. The whole social and political structure of the kingdoms and chiefdoms with which the Portuguese were involved was altered by the trade and the attendant disruption of traditional life caused by the forced migrations of people, reduction of population, new diseases introduced by the white man, and famines resulting from frequent wars. The political power of native kingdoms waxed—like that of the Ovimbundu who were so successful as middlemen in the slave trade—or waned in direct relationship to their position in that trade. The stage was set for the even more profound transformation that the nineteenth century was to bring.

In large part, though, this nineteenth-century transformation was a product of events determined outside of Portuguese Africa. The independence of Brazil came about 1822. The following year Benguela voted to join Brazil in a confederation, although Portuguese troops smashed the effort. If the special relation between Angola and Brazil was thus ended, so also was the priority position that Brazil had held in the Portuguese empire.

Other events were almost as momentous. A constitutional monarchy was established in Portugal after 1826, and with it came a greater influence of liberal thought. An 1836 decree called for the abolition of the slave trade. Furthermore, England was pursuing policies to abolish the slave trade in Africa and install a system of free trade; this was in direct conflict with the Portuguese mercantile system. Thus the centuries-old Portuguese policies in Africa were threatened with erosion at a time when they had long been an anachronism. The loosening of the foundations of the Portuguese-African system was concomitant with the serious effects of the Napoleonic wars on the metropole, its subsequent economic ruin, and, lastly, in the second and third decades of the nineteenth century, a civil war over the monarchy. Portugal often verged on anarchy.

Indeed, it is surprising that a politically and economically bankrupt Portugal remained in Africa at all. It not only did, however, but the severance of Brazil created a new colonial movement in Portugal among part of the intellectual, military, and political leadership. To this group, not simply empire in Africa but extension of the metropole to include Africa became a redeeming way out of the vicious economic, political, and international impasse in which Portugal was caught. Reform in the metropole could perhaps be the product of reform in Africa. Any danger of a Spanish take-over of the narrow Portuguese Kingdom could be offset by the vast holdings in Africa. Economic stagnation in the metropole could be cured by extracting a profit from overseas. Portuguese stature in Europe could be recouped by making Angola a new Brazil. As one Portuguese writer expressed it later in the century, "only the colonies can give us in Europe the influence and position which otherwise would be denied us so justifiably because of the narrow boundaries of the Metropolis, and its situation in the peninsula."[53]

The personification of the new movement, its progenitor and leader, was the able Sá da Bandeira, who became minister for naval and overseas affairs in 1835, later led the campaign for the decree to abolish slavery, dreamed of a new economy based on free trade, and once again placed Portugal's role in Africa on an ideological basis of the traditional "civilizing mission." As we shall see, his influence in Portugal spanned four decades until his death.

Throughout this period, following it, and until this day, there were anti-imperialist, anti-Africanist voices in Portugal. Perhaps these could be personified by the gifted literary historian Oliveira Martins. To them, Portugal could never find the answers to its home problems or its future in far-off Africa. This group, however, was in the minority, and the scramble for Africa by the great powers was to find destitute Portugal a real contender.

NOTES

1. As Sir Mortimer Wheeler has aptly said, "Asia leads the way in human progress, but it is by no means certain that the Garden of Eden, or its more scientific equivalent, should not be located in Africa." Roland Oliver (ed.), *The Dawn of African History* (London, 1961), p. 1.
2. Roland Oliver and J. D. Fage, *A Short History of Africa* (New York, 1964), p. 13.
3. George Peter Murdock, *Africa: Its Peoples and Their Culture History* (New York, 1959), pp. 48 and 52.
4. Paul Bohannan, *Africa and Africans* (Garden City, N.Y., 1964), p. 67.
5. Joseph H. Greenberg, *The Languages of Africa* (Bloomington, 1966), p. 38. Guthrie sees the origin of the Bantu as being in the upper part of the Congo. For a discussion of the compatibility of the two theories, see Roland Oliver and Gervase Mathew (eds.), *History of East Africa*, I (Oxford, 1963), 81.
6. C. G. Seligman, *Races of Africa* (London, 1966), p. 118.
7. Murdock, *op. cit.*, p. 271.
8. Jan M. Vansina, *Kingdoms of the Savanna* (Madison, 1966), p. 82. Seligman, *op. cit.*, p. 132, treats the Lunda Kingdom as flourishing in the eighteenth and early in the nineteenth centuries.
9. David Birmingham, *The Portuguese Conquest of Angola* (Oxford, 1965), p. 3.
10. Until recently it was supposed that the Great Zimbabwe ruins were the remnants of works created by Bantu tribes under Arab inspiration—especially the Shona (in their language the word *dzimbabwe* means "stone houses" or "chiefs' graves"). Now, however, through the analysis of carbon samples, it is

believed that they dated from about the ninth or tenth centuries. Much of Zimbabwe has suggested "a specific connection with the Megalithic Cushites, an interpretation bolstered by the wealth of stone phallic representations reminiscent of those on the Azanian Coast and in southern Ethiopia." Murdock, *op. cit.*, pp. 210–11. Roland Oliver speculates further that the Zimbabwe-Monomotapa culture and the Ankole-Ruanda culture may have a common ancestry. As for the latter culture, it will be recalled that the governing class were pastoral, while the subjected class were cultivators. Oliver, *op. cit.*, pp. 57–58. On Zimbabwe see also Rowland J. Fothergill, *The Monuments of Southern Rhodesia* (Bulawayo, Published by the Commission for the Preservation of Natural and Historical Monuments and Relics, 1953), pp. 71–74, and Roger Summers, *Zimbabwe: A Rhodesian Mystery* (Johannesburg, 1963).

11. From his examination of the geological characteristics of human debris found in the coastal areas of Mozambique, Professor C. van Riet Lowe concludes that the colony's contribution to the story of prehistoric human development is destined to be an appreciable and important one, but very little detailed investigation has been made as yet: "During the centuries of Arab, Chinese, and possibly other foreign exploitation and infiltration before the appearance of the earliest Portuguese navigators, Mozambique was the gateway to South Africa, and in it, I am convinced, must lie the most important secrets of the Zimbabwe Culture." He refers to the interrelationship of the various ruins in Mozambique and the interior, especially Rhodesia, and notes the presence of medieval and other glass beads and glazed wares found in Sofala that can be matched by material from Ceylon, Cairo, Zanzibar, Zimbabwe, and Transvaal. C. van Riet Lowe, *A Contribution to the Prehistory of Moçambique* (Lourenço Marques, 1944), p. 3.

12. On July 25, 1139, Afonso had been victorious over the Moors in the battle fought supposedly at Ourique, and this year is sometimes cited as marking the beginning of nationhood. Eight years later Afonso I took Lisbon with the help of passing Crusaders, some of them English knights on their way to the Second Crusade. They were amazed at the mingling of races in Lisbon, already a meeting-place for the trade between north and south, a middle point between the Gothic ports in Galicia and Oporto and the Muslim sea-towns of the Algarve. H. V. Livermore (ed.), *Portugal and Brazil: An Introduction* (Oxford, 1953), p. 54.

13. *Ibid.*

14. The treaty of May 1386 contains a clause according to which it was renewed or modified each time one of the signatories died. During the Spanish occupation, this treaty was suspended and in the treaty of 1661 it was declared that only the treaties from 1642 onward would be considered valid.

15. Prince Henry was both a creator and a product of the age. Portuguese interest in exploration and commerce preceded the House of Avis and Aljubarrota. H. V. Livermore, *A New History of Portugal* (Cambridge, 1966), pp. 106–7.

16. Not only the technical preparation of the mariners but shipbuilding was also decisively advanced. Oliveira Martins, speaking of the vessels that antedated the explorations says: "What were these ships like? The reader has certainly at some time seen, in the evening at sundown, the arrival of vessels returning from the sea on the beaches of Ovar or Povoa-de-Varim. He has seen their construction and the types of these primitive ships and the picturesque appearance of their crews: there is a thirteenth-century squadron." Oliveira Martins,

História de Portugal, I (Lisbon, 1908), 173. The single-masted square-sail *barca* was replaced by the three-masted light and long caravel, without oars, which could sail with side winds as well as before the wind. The new and swifter ship had the maneuverability to avoid the shoals of the African coast. Since the caravel was dangerously low in the water in stormy seas, Vasco da Gama was to round the Cape of Good Hope in a truly ocean-going vessel, the round ship called *nau*, somewhat similar to the later galleon. See Edgar Prestage, *The Portuguese Pioneers* (New York, 1967), pp. 331–33.

17. "Columbus was a Genoese in the service of Spain; Magellan, a Portuguese, was also in the service of Spain; but the voyages of both, no less than those of Bartholomeu Dias and Vasco da Gama, were technically prepared by Portugal," Hugh Trevor-Roper, *The Rise of Christian Europe* (New York, 1965), pp. 191–92. Also see Charles McKew Parr, *Ferdinand Magellan, Circumnavigator* (New York, 1964).

18. Gomes Eannes de Azurara, *The Chronicle of the Discovery and Conquest of Guinea*, I (London, 1896, printed for the Hakluyt Society), 27–29.

19. Speaking of Prince Henry's own ambitions, the Portuguese historian Oliveira Martins distinguishes among these motives. Did the Prince expect to reach the kingdom of Prester John by sea? "It seems to us that this was not so. To explore the terrible sea in search of the islands of whose existence there was some vague knowledge, to explore and gradually occupy the western coast of Africa, these would appear to be enterprises not linked at that time with that of the voyage to the kingdom of Prester John. Not that that voyage did not preoccupy the Prince's attention, but he believed it was to be achieved by a different route, by land . . . . In the Prince's ambitious scheme two enterprises were joined: to conquer the Moroccan empire, or at least its sea-coast, in order to guarantee a Portuguese monopoly in the trade with the Sudan; and at the same time to conquer the islands of that unknown sea, while visiting and exploring the whole length of the western coasts of Africa." Oliveira Martins, *op. cit.*, pp. 165–66.

20. By far the best account of the religious background of the Portuguese age of discovery is found in Francis M. Rogers, *The Quest for Eastern Christians* (Minneapolis, 1962). Rogers' writings emphasize this period of Portuguese history in the light of modern ecumenism. Of related interest is Francis M. Rogers, *The Travels of the Infante Dom Pedro of Portugal* (Cambridge, 1961). An older classic work is Prestage, *op. cit.* For the general economic background see the standard texts: Carlton J. H. Hayes, "Economic Expansion," *A Political and Cultural History of Modern Europe*, Vol. 1, Ch. 2; Shepherd B. Clough and Charles W. Cole, "The Expansion of Europe," *Economic History of Europe* (Boston, 1952), Ch. 5.

21. See A. W. Lawrence, *Trade Castles and Forts of West Africa* (London, 1963), Part Two, "Elmina Castle," pp. 103–30; also Prestage, *op. cit.*, pp. 191 and 204–6.

22. Basil Davidson, *African Kingdoms* (New York, 1966), p. 102. Chapter 5 gives an illustrated account of the metropolis of Benin. See also J. W. Blake, *Europeans in West Africa* (2 vols., London, 1941–42).

23. "In truth, Dom Afonso was not a vulgar, arrogant and ignorant native chief; he dressed like a European, he could read and write, he knew the history of Portugal and the Gospels, he spoke our language correctly, and was intelligent, generous and reflective," Ralph Delgado, *História da Angola*, 2nd ed. (Lobito,

1961), I, 83. For some of the controversy over dates and routes of Diogo Cão's voyages, see Prestage, *op. cit.*, pp. 208–11.

24. *Monumenta Missionária Africana*, I, 183, cited in Delgado, *op. cit.*, p. 90. Delgado states that the inhabitants of São Tomé were given the privilege of obtaining slaves in Kongo by a royal grant of March 26, 1500. The ship captains were authorized to deal in slaves on their own account.

25. Vansina, *op. cit.*, p. 67.

26. Paul Dias de Novais received his *carta de doação* from Dom Sebastião on September 6, 1571. Gastão de Sousa Dias, *Os portugueses em Angola* (Lisbon, 1959), pp. 62–65.

27. Birmingham, *op. cit.*, p. 14.

28. Birmingham, "The African Response to Early Portuguese Activities in Angola" (unpublished paper presented to the University of California Project "Brazil-Portuguese Africa," February 6, 1968), pp. 4–7.

29. Pero Rodrigues, *História* (1954), referred to in *ibid.*, pp. 11–12.

30. Donald L. Wiedner, *A History of Africa South of the Sahara* (New York, 1962), pp. 103–4.

31. Carlo M. Cipolla, *Guns, Sails, and Empires: Technological Innovation and the Early Phases of European Expansion, 1400–1700* (New York, 1965), pp. 102–3.

32. For the Portuguese expansion in the East, see Boxer, "The Portuguese in the East, 1500–1800," in Livermore, *Portugal and Brazil*.

33. Charles R. Boxer, *Four Centuries of Portuguese Expansion, 1415–1825* (Johannesburg, 1961).

34. For additional reasons for the Portuguese decline, see H. Morse Stephens, *Portugal* (New York, 1891), pp. 177–83, Oliveira Martins, *op. cit.*, and Charles E. Nowell, *A History of Portugal* (Princeton, 1952), pp. 105–7. For an account laying stress upon Portuguese maritime disasters, see James Duffy, *Shipwreck and Empire* (Cambridge, 1955). Boxer (*Four Centuries*, pp. 89–90) contests the view that Portugal's overseas expansion brought about the decay of agriculture and industry in the metropole, and a population decrease. For Livermore's views noting the depopulation of the countryside, see *A New History of Portugal*, pp. 150–51.

35. Birmingham, *The Portuguese Conquest of Angola*, p. 25.

36. Delgado, *op cit.*, II, 47–48, says that on May 17, 1617, Cerveira Pereira, enchanted by the fine harbor of the Baía de Santo António, and influenced by the apparent abundance of water, fresh fruits, and vegetables, wood, the fertility of the soil and labor supply, and deluded by what appeared to be a fine climate, since he was there during the *cacimbo*, actually chose the worst spot from the health point of view, to place his settlement. Delgado also gives a forceful picture of the desperate rivalries among the Portuguese for control of the newly discovered lands and the mineral wealth that was supposed to exist in them.

37. Delgado (*op. cit.*, III, 304) says that the Portuguese were faced by an African army of some 20,000 men, and that the Portuguese triumph was aided by the overconfidence of the king of the Kongo on seeing what small numbers opposed him and by the usual Portuguese tactic of killing off the leaders of their enemies at the beginning of the battle.

38. *Ibid.*, IV, 60–61. Also see Alvin W. Urquhart, *Patterns of Settlement and Subsistence in Southwestern Angola*, Foreign Field Research Program sponsored

by the Office of Naval Research, Report No. 18 (Publication 1096: National Academy of Sciences, National Research Council, 1963), pp. 129–30.

39. The coast of Kenya, Somalia and Tanganyika, from Kisimayu in the north to Kilwa in the south and including the off-lying islands of Pemba and Zanzibar, was known to Mediterranean antiquity as Azania. Murdock, *op. cit.*, p. 204. The great trade route from Azania to India via southern Arabia has been termed the Sabaean Lane, since it was probably the Sabaeans of southern Arabia who first made the long passage around the eastern horn of Africa and reached the Azanian coast. It has been assumed that the Azanians were Negroes but the suggestion has been made that they were Megalithic Cushites. Yemenite Arabs, Persians, Chinese, and Indonesians all had a part in the trade through this region before the arrival of the Portuguese. Murdock, *op. cit.*, pp. 212 ff.

40. This information is drawn from a study by Hugh Tracey, "António Fernandes, Southern Rhodesia's First Pioneer, A.D. 1514–1515," given in manuscript form to Caetano Montez, at the time Chief of the Statistical Services of Mozambique, who translated it into Portuguese. It was published in Portuguese with the title, *António Fernandes, Descobridor do Monomotapa, 1514–15* (Lourenço Marques, 1940). Tracey assumed that Fernandes made two trips into the interior and that Veloso's letter contains information obtained in both. Caetano Montez, the translator and editor of Tracey's study, disagrees with this, though he does not deny that Fernandes made more than one trip. But he believes that the information in Veloso's letter was obtained in the first trip. Montez takes exception to a number of Tracey's interpretations of the distances covered by Fernandes and other details.

41. Portuguese chroniclers of the sixteenth and seventeenth centuries mention various places they called Zimbaoe, some of which could not have been the Great Zimbabwe. Diogo de Alcaçova, the factor at Sofala, in a letter to King Manuel of Portugal dated November 20, 1506, states that the principal settlement of the Monomotapa was a twenty-four-day journey from Sofala, near the ruins of "Zimboae." The chronicler Barros stated that this "capital" lay at 170 leagues from Sofala. See Manuel Nunes Dias, "Os campos de ouro do Monomotapa no Século XVI," in *Actas*, Vol. II of III Colóquio Internacional de Estudos Luso-Brasileiros (Lisbon, 1960), especially note 58 on p. 134.

42. James Duffy, *Portuguese Africa* (Cambridge, Mass., 1959), pp. 43, 82–85.

43. A. J. Wills, *The History of Central Africa*, 2nd ed., (London, 1967), pp. 40–43; Eric Axelson, *Portuguese in South East Africa, 1600–1700* (Johannesburg, 1960), pp. 182–95.

44. Charles R. Boxer and Carlos de Azevedo, *Fort Jesus and the Portuguese in Mombasa, 1593–1729* (London, 1960), pp. 82–85. Also Axelson, *op. cit.*, pp. 155–75.

45. See opinions on the treaty in Nowell, *op. cit.*, pp. 159–60; William C. Atkinson, *A History of Spain and Portugal* (Baltimore, 1960), pp. 230–32; Boxer, *Four Centuries of Portuguese Expansion*, pp. 73–74; Livermore, *Portugal and Brazil*, pp. 67–68. For extensive background, see A. D. Francis, *The Methuens and Portugal* (Cambridge, 1966).

46. Boxer, *Four Centuries of Portuguese Expansion*, pp. 80–81. The best life of Pombal is Marcus Cheke, *Dictator of Portugal* (London, 1938). See also Livermore, *A New History of Portugal*, pp. 212–42.

47. Oliveira Martins, *op. cit.*, II, 207ff.

48. Gastão Sousa Dias, *Os portugueses em Angola* (Lisbon, 1959), p. 231, citing *Arquivos de Angola*, Vol. I, Doc. II, and Silva Correia, *op. cit.*, II, 45.
49. David Livingstone, *Missionary Travels and Research in South Africa* (New York, 1858), pp. 675–76.
50. Mabel V. Jackson Haight, *European Powers and South East Africa* (New York, 1967), pp. 22–27, 31–35, 37–40, and 83–103. Axelson, *op. cit.*, p. 118.
51. Haight, *op. cit.*, pp. 44–45.
52. Oliveira Martins, *O Brasil e as colónias portuguêsas* (Lisbon, 1893), p. 99.
53. Manuel Ferreira Ribeiro, *As conferências e o itinerário viajante Serpa Pinto* (Lisbon, 1879), p. 754, quoted in Douglas L. Wheeler, "The Portuguese in Angola, 1836–91: A Study in Expansion and Administration" (Ph.D. dissertation, History Department, Boston University, 1963), p. 10.

III

From the Scramble for Africa to the "New State"

DAVID M. ABSHIRE

MUCH EARLIER than Livingstone's famed exploration of Africa in the 1850's, several Portuguese made documented journeys through parts of the continent that had been previously unknown to the outside world. Francisco de Lacerda was the most memorable of these figures. A Brazilian mathematician and advocate of the abolition of the slave trade, Lacerda became governor of the Rivers of Sena, a district of Mozambique. He foresaw that the British occupancy of the Cape of Good Hope, in 1795, portended far-reaching British ambitions that could extend into Central Africa. As revealed by his proposals to the Portuguese authorities, this determined explorer was in the tradition of Prince Henry, except that his vision was landward.

Lacerda planned an overland crossing of Africa, from coast to coast. The aims of his expedition, he argued, would be to create a commercial advantage for the crown and the people, for extending the conquests "over lands and tribes hitherto unknown," and, by opening a line of communication between the eastern and western coasts of Africa, to make them mutually supporting economically and militarily. This line of communication would allow ships from Asia to discharge cargo at Mozambique for the overland journey to Benguela, thereby avoiding "the danger and the delay of doubling the Cape of Storms. Thus the custom-house duty would increase, and the industry of the whites, as well as the blacks, would be fostered."[1]

Lacerda successfully appealed to the tradition, enterprise, and hopes of former governor of Angola Francisco de Sousa Coutinho in gaining official support for his project. In 1798, he led a group of twenty Portuguese and fifty native soldiers from Tete, on the Zambezi River, to Lake Mweru in the kingdom of Cazembe in the Luapula valley. There the great explorer died of fever, leaving behind him a map and a diary. The British editor of that diary, Richard Burton, was to write: "This journey of Dr. Lacerda shows that the Portuguese never abandoned the idea of a 'viagem a contracosta,' and we can hardly characterize their claims to having crossed Africa as 'hanging on a slender fibre.' "[2]

A few years later two *pombeiros* (agents for slave-traders), Pedro João Baptista and Amaro José, were dispatched by their employer, a Portuguese trader, on an expedition to find a way from Angola to Mozambique. Leaving in November,

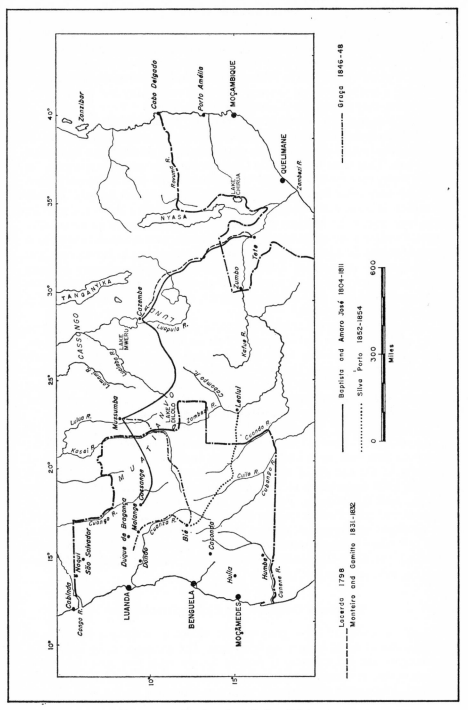

Portuguese Explorations Before Livingstone

1804, they reached Cazembe after two years, but they were detained there, although well treated, for four years owing to trouble in the kingdom and the refusal of the tribes beyond to let them pass. When at last they were allowed to depart, they arrived at Tete in February, 1811, thus becoming the first travelers to record a transcontinental journey. Leaving Tete in May and following the same route, they returned to Cassange three years later.[3]

About a quarter of a century later, in 1831–32, Majors José Correia Monteiro and António Pedroso Gamitto, of the Portuguese Army, were sent to explore the Zambezi headwaters and inquire into the possibility of establishing a trade route to Angola. They went from Tete to Cazembe but were unable to continue. No useful trade, they concluded, could be established with such barbarous people.

There were other Portuguese explorers in the nineteenth century. António Francisco da Silva, better known as Silva Porto, was both a settler and a trader who lived among the Africans of Bié in the interior of Angola for almost fifty years, founding a village which he called Belmonte, near the modern town now named for him. In 1853, he journeyed across the continent to Barotseland, and while in route encountered David Livingstone. His contemporary Joaquim Rodrigues Graça, in 1846–48, traveled to the headwaters of the Zambezi and the territory of Lunda on the borders of Cazembe, concluding treaties of friendship with several local chieftains.[4]

Thus, long before world attention was focused on Africa, Portuguese explorers like Lacerda and Silva Porto had made their daring and ambitious expeditions. But, possibly because they wrote in Portuguese, the accounts of their travels were little known outside Portugal. The widely circulated accounts published by the Scottish missionary David Livingstone and the renowned newspaper reporter H. M. Stanley, sent by the proprietor of the *New York Herald* to find Livingstone, first excited world interest in Central Africa.

Livingstone began his celebrated journey at Cape Town, proceeded to Linyante near the present frontier between Zambia and Botswana, ascended the Zambezi, then went on to Lake Dilolo, and, finally, on May 31, 1854, reached Luanda. In the autumn of 1855, his party returned to Linyante, discovered Victoria Falls, and went on to Tete in Mozambique, going thence to the eastern African coast at Quelimane. From some Africans he had heard vague stories of Lacerda and other Portuguese who had gone before him. In 1857, in London, he published his famous *Missionary Travels and Researches in South Africa.* His two other journeys were undertaken to explore the headwaters of the Zambezi, the Shire Highlands, the area between Lake Nyasa and Lake Tanganyika, and the upper reaches of the Congo River.

Economic Changes and Local Discontent

During the period of these journeys, the economic landscape, especially of Angola, was involved in new configurations. The abolition of the slave trade undermined the old economy of Angola, for the trade had been the biggest source of state revenues. Consequently, in the second quarter of the nineteenth century, Portuguese policy was in large part motivated by the need for new

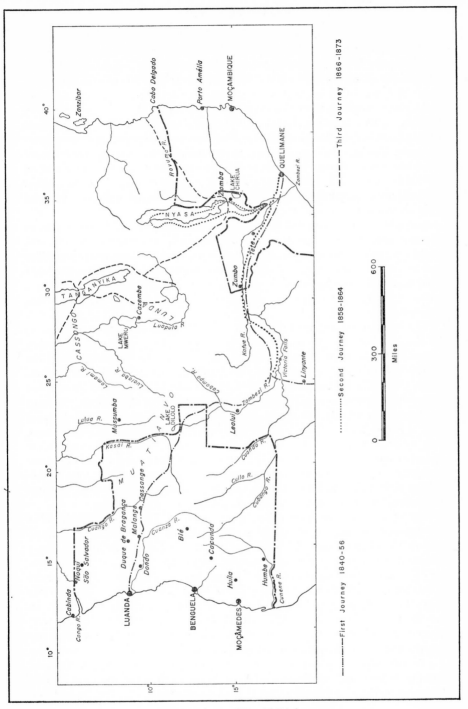

Explorations of David Livingstone

revenue and new sources of production. There was further need to establish firmer control of the interior of Angola and the Atlantic coast north of Luanda, because many foreigners who traded with the interior were bypassing Portuguese customs by taking northern routes and shipping from points outside the Portuguese domain. In order to prevent contraband shipments from the northern coast, the Portuguese, in 1792, had built a coastal fort at Ambriz, but the English later forced its evacuation. In 1783, the Portuguese occupied Cabinda but were soon driven out by the French. In 1825, however, the governor of Angola proposed that the Portuguese reoccupy Ambriz, noting that the move would eliminate foreign slaving from there. Nothing was done, though, and it was Sá da Bandeira, in 1838, who actually ordered the reoccupation of both Ambriz and Cabinda, although Ambriz was actually reoccupied only in 1855 and Cabinda not officially until the 1880's.

Although the main thrust of the Portuguese efforts was along the coast, a series of major annexations in the interior took place with a spurt of energy. The area called Duque de Bragança was annexed as a result of the vassalage of the tribes well to the south. In 1840, a small settlement was established at Moçâmedes, a place that soon became known for its healthful climate. In the next decade, a series of small settlements on the Huíla plateau beyond Moçâmedes was established.[5]

Meanwhile, the interior of the Luanda and Benguela districts was the scene of several minor revolts against Portuguese rule. The very rugged Dembos region is northeast of Luanda at the headwaters of the Dande River. Dom Aleixo de Água Rosada e Sardónia, a Congo prince, roused the Dembos to refuse to pay taxes. The Portuguese crushed this revolt and imprisoned the prince, but intermittent opposition to Portuguese rule continued to occur there. Another conflict broke out near Benguela, when the African brothers of the Ferreira Gomes family led an effort to move on Benguela and drive out the Europeans, only to be crushed by a few whites and unfriendly Africans. Actually, these incidents were spotty considering the vastness of the wild areas the Portuguese attempted to rule. Worse stirrings of discontent occurred in the Luanda hinterland as news of the abolition of the slave trade became known. Many African chiefs were too deeply involved in the slave trade to wish its passing.[6]

Further revolts were triggered in 1860, again by attempted taxation. The Portuguese commander at the Cassange trade fair tried to impose on the independent-minded Jaga peoples the *dízimo* tax, or tithe, in place of the normal yearly tribute of ten porters. The Portuguese had previously maintained their "sovereignty" and had been able to regulate the trade fair by moral suasion and friendly influence, having recognized that they could not rule by force. The new tax policy for such areas of tenuous Portuguese rule was clearly a blunder. In fact the governor-general in 1863 concluded just that. Greedy merchants were blamed for fomenting the war, and it is probable that the tax at Cassange was actually imposed with no authority from Luanda.

The war followed a customary pattern, involving tribal factions, with the Portuguese backing a usurper leader. At first the Portuguese and their African auxiliaries suffered reversals and fell back to Malange, but they rallied and

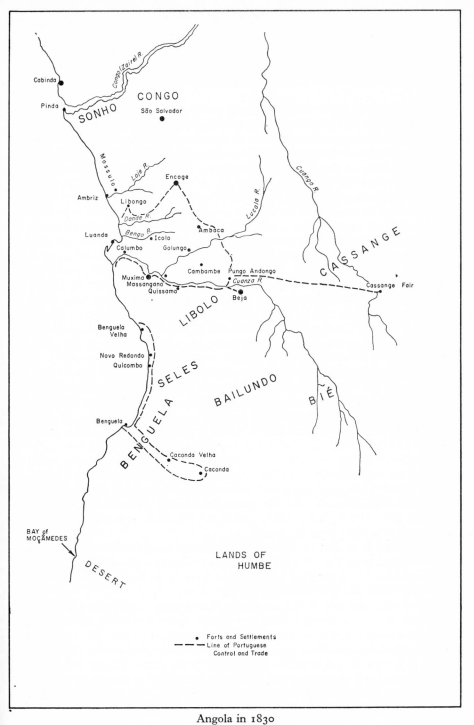

Angola in 1830

Adapted from Douglas L. Wheeler, "The Portuguese in Angola, 1836–91: A Study in Expansion and Administration" (Ph.D. dissertation, Department of History, Boston University, 1963), p. 417.

effected a compromise peace in 1863 that, on paper, recognized Portuguese authority. The Jaga leader was anxious to keep friendly relations with the Portuguese, but without the tax. The Portuguese did not reoccupy Cassange for some time, although Portuguese traders continued to penetrate the area.[7]

This pattern of expansion and retraction of Portuguese military control was also followed in the Huíla areas to the south, as well as in the Kongo area in the north. After the occupation of Ambriz on the coast, Quibala and Bembe, inland, were occupied partly for the purpose of working the malachite mines found there and partly to assist the Portuguese in pressing their claims against the British to the mouth of the Congo River. The British in fact landed in a small naval force at Quissembo, just north of Ambriz.

To further its position in the Kongo, the Portuguese Government interfered in the succession dispute over the Kongo throne. The Portuguese Government supported the legitimate African, the Marquis of Catendi, who was crowned Dom Pedro V (after the king of Portugal). Anti-Portuguese revolts occurred in Ambriz and Bembe. In 1859, Dom Nicholas, another African of the royal line but ineligible for the throne under the rules of succession, wrote to Lisbon journals that he deserved the throne. He claimed that he was better educated and that the Portuguese had no right to rule the Kongo or place troops at São Salvador. Dom Nicholas, although educated in Lisbon, had later worked as a clerk in Luanda and Ambriz and had developed sufficient British and Brazilian connections to be suspected of involvement in independence movements.

In 1860, about 700 new troops arrived in Africa to move as a unit into Ambriz, Bembe, and São Salvador. But the white man's army fresh from Europe did not fare well. By late 1861, it had been devastated by malaria and yellow fever, and those still living returned to Portugal.

Douglas Wheeler notes that 1861 ended the expansionist phase that had begun with the 1836 decree to abolish slavery.[8] During this period the area of Portuguese control doubled, and most often this expansion had been achieved by relying on African auxiliaries. At the end of the phase, as we have seen, independent tribes, some former Portuguese allies and trading partners, began to revolt at their attempted "vassalization." The Portuguese, increasingly overextended, too often tried to substitute force for politics and failed miserably, especially when new troops were brought from Lisbon.

The period from 1861 to 1877 saw a Portuguese retreat from frontier posts in the interior, but in the late 1870's there was a military expansion, and mission expansion too, on to the plateaus of Angola. Reasons for this expansion were in part international and involved Mozambique as well.

The Portuguese role in the interior of Mozambique late in the eighteenth and early in the nineteenth century was mostly confined to the Zambezi valley, with its settlements at Sena, Tete, and, intermittently, at Zomba. The economic and political configurations of Portuguese involvement continued to be in the form of the vast *prazos*, which had grown into feudal states. Though these huge estates were the first serious attempts to settle Portuguese, there was no progress and, indeed, no real attempt to develop there a plantation or agrarian economy.

66

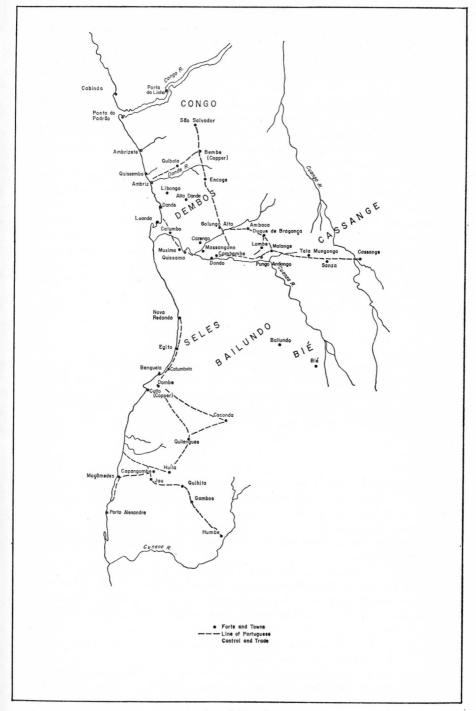

Angola in 1861

Adapted from Douglas L. Wheeler, "The Portuguese in Angola, 1836–91: A Study in Expansion and Administration" (Ph.D. dissertation, Department of History, Boston University, 1963), p. 418.

Their principal function was to serve as a superstructure for control, conduct, and protection of trade, mostly in slaves and ivory.

The *prazeros* were Portuguese, more often *mestiços* and Indians, mostly Goans. In other cases, there was absentee ownership, the opulent owners living in Brazil, India, or Portugal. Two major exceptions were the most famous *prazero* families, da Cruz and Pereira. Pereira had been a trusted guide with Lacerda and had been rewarded with even more lands than he had already held. The da Cruz family had a large estate, Massangano, near Tete. About the middle of the nineteenth century, the two families began to fight one another, beginning the wars of the Zambezi that lasted almost until the end of the century.

To the south of this area there lived, in the latter half of the century, a Goan, Manuel António de Sousa, called Gouveia, who continuously expanded his domain. His headquarters was in the Gorongosa hills, near the modern-day game preserve. The Portuguese gave him military rank, and the Africans between the Zambezi and the Pungué came under his influence, the Manica king in the 1870's and the Barué king in the 1880's. He blocked the advances of the Nguni or Landin tribes from Gaza. For his help in suppressing the *prazeros*, he was invited to Lisbon and honored.[9] Once again, we see that wherever the rule of influence of the Portuguese Government in Mozambique existed, it did more by proxy than by direct action.

ALLIANCE STRAINS

When Livingstone and Stanley had whetted the appetites of the British, French, Germans, and Belgians, the Portuguese and their oldest ally, Great Britain, found themselves increasingly at cross-purposes over some of the Portuguese Africa border areas. In Angola, there had been tension over Ambriz and coastal zones to the north. As for Mozambique, in 1861 a British naval force seized Inhaca Island, which dominated the bay of Lourenço Marques. The Portuguese were alarmed, needless to say, and they hoped to gain allies by concluding a treaty with the Transvaal (although six years later) that recognized the Portuguese claim to the entire bay, including the disputed territory on the southern part of the bay, the so-called English river. Britain refused to recognize the treaty, and the Portuguese successfully proposed arbitration. In 1875, the arbitrator, President MacMahon of France, ruled in favor of Portugal. The judgment was based upon priority of discovery and claims dating from the sixteenth century.

Portuguese treaties with the Transvaal had lasting ramifications. Under a treaty of December, 1875, Portugal undertook to build a railroad from Lourenço Marques toward Pretoria. This treaty contained a significant clause guaranteeing Portuguese neutrality in case of war and free passage for arms and ammunition. Under a second treaty, that of May, 1876, Portugal was authorized to build the railway from Lourenço Marques to Orange Free State. The economic development of Mozambique was truly commencing.

A number of Portuguese, including Silva Porto, Sá da Bandeira, and João de Andrade Corvo, sometime navy and overseas minister and sometime foreign minister, realized fully that Livingstone's much publicized journeys had shattered the protective isolation that the Portuguese had enjoyed in Africa. Counter-measures were urgently needed. In 1867, Sá da Bandeira published a map show-ing the Sanyati and Umniati rivers as the limit of Portuguese territory, thus including much of Mashonaland and part of modern-day Rhodesia. Andrade Corvo and Luciano Cordeiro founded the Lisbon Geographical Society (Sociedade de Geografia) in 1875, and used it to revive Portugal's ancient terri-torial claims. Sensing the coming struggle, Andrade Corvo prodded the king to stand up for Portuguese rights in Africa. He recognized the danger that the Portuguese might lose credit for the discoveries of Lacerda, Baptista, and Amaro José and weaken their claims and spoil chances of annexing the great central plateau between Angola and Mozambique. It is little wonder that this group reacted so quickly in 1876. They heard that Leopold II of Belgium had called an international conference in Brussels on the exploration of Central Africa and had not invited the Portuguese. This conference heralded the birth of the Congo Free State, the personal fief of King Leopold. Other European activities, including the growth of steamship lines to West and East Africa, the com-petition for legitimate coastal trade, and the discovery of diamonds at Kimberley, were ending the comfortable isolation of Angola and Mozambique.

Andrade Corvo immediately sent explorers Brito Capelo, Roberto Ivens, and Serpa Pinto to Angola to survey the region between the two Portuguese colonies. The Geographical Society financed the expedition, which sailed from Lisbon to Luanda in July, 1877. Circumstances altered their plans on arrival in Angola, however, and Serpa Pinto set out on an expedition of his own to cross the continent, following the trade route into Lealui in Barotseland and then turning south to reach the Indian Ocean at Durban. On his return he met with the same sort of sensational public success that Livingstone had enjoyed. His erstwhile companions, Capelo and Ivens, did not achieve such widespread notice, but their expedition to Cassange and Malange and northward along the upper reaches of the Cuango produced the first thorough survey of that part of the province. In 1884, the government sent them on another expedition to open up a coast-to-coast route. From Moçâmedes they traveled to Lealui, then north to Katanga, and from there south to Zomba and down the Zambezi to Quelimane.

In the same year, Serpa Pinto, accompanied by Augusto Cardoso, led an expedition from the east coast to Lake Nyasa for the purposes of strengthening Portugal's claims to prior discovery and settlement and establishing the territorial link between Angola and Mozambique.

With the increasing interests of other nations in Central Africa, this link was now becoming a matter of urgency. In 1879, Stanley began acquiring areas of the Congo in the name of the International Association of the Congo, founded by Leopold II as a cover for his colonizing plans. In 1880, the French explorer Savorgnan de Brazza arrived at the right bank of the Congo River and planted his flag on the north shore of Stanley Pool, where the city of Brazzaville stands today. The scramble for Africa had begun.[10]

This scramble re-energized Portuguese expansionism beyond the goal of exploration and toward the achievement of tribal alliances, pacification, and occupation. The Portuguese pull-back of the 1860's was due partly to increased tribal opposition in certain areas and partly to the financial costs of maintaining extended positions. Nevertheless, Portuguese policy in the 1880's and 1890's again called for expansion into the interior of northeastern Angola, because both Germany and Belgium were hungry for the Cassange and Lunda areas. Almost as many Germans as Portuguese began to appear in Lunda. The pundits and strategists of the Geographical Society in Lisbon agitated that the lands not be lost and that political considerations be placed first.

Therefore, in 1883, a Portuguese garrison reoccupied Cassange, and a treaty with the Jaga incorporated Cassange into a newly created *concelho*. The Portuguese had never really claimed the territory east of the Cuanza River where their ancient trading partners, the Lunda, were located. They next not only took this area but also laid plans to annex the lands beyond the Kasai River. Beginning in 1884, an intrepid army officer, Henrique Dias de Carvalho, led a scientific and political expedition into the Lunda area, planting thirteen stations between Malange and Mussumba, the capital of the Lunda area now in modern-day Katanga. In order to avoid hostilities, the expedition was made up almost entirely of Africans.

Time passed before any attempt was made to incorporate the area into the Angolan administration. The Lunda and Mussumba itself came under fierce attack by the Chokwes from the southwest, and the Lunda desperately needed arms and aid; Dias de Carvalho successfully negotiated a treaty with them in 1887. However, negotiations in 1891 between the Portuguese and the more powerful Leopold drew the boundary line of eastern Angola at the Kasai River. Though Portugal lost the part of the Lunda Kingdom that is now a part of Katanga, it gained the lands that it had not even claimed two decades earlier, thanks to the daring and skill of Dias de Carvalho.[11] The Angolan district of Lunda includes the valuable diamond areas that were for a period the economic mainstay of the entire province.

Expansion into central Angola followed the trade routes. The great plateau area could be approached by routes from Moçâmedes by way of Caconda, from Benguela by way of Caconda, or more directly by way of Bailundo. From Bié, trade routes led to the upper Zambezi and Barotseland. Silva Porto had long ago established himself on the plateau and persistently urged the Portuguese Government to pacify and control the area and to move into Barotseland as well. Paradoxically, not until a military expedition under Paiva Couceiro arrived in Bié did Chindunduma, the rather friendly chief of the Bié Ovimbundu, become provoked into fighting the Portuguese. He reacted unexpectedly and even slapped Silva Porto, by now an old man. The following day the despondent Silva Porto blew himself up with gunpowder kegs. A Portuguese counterattack under Artur de Paiva led to the capture of Chindunduma, with the help of American missionaries in the area.[12]

THE PARTITION OF AFRICA

Charles E. Nowell, speaking of Portugal's role during this period, comments that "Portugal played an active and important role in the partition of Africa.

The common assumption that the little kingdom rested supinely on ancient exploring laurels while the others did the work is both unfair and untrue." Through the rules established by the great powers for the division of Africa, Portugal "fully earned the substantial territory it holds today." That it did not gain more resulted from lack of manpower, lack of financial resources, and a heavy public debt: "These prevented Portugal from wielding influence in the Councils of Europe, where, in the last analysis, the African questions were decided."[13]

Portugal's claim to dominion over both sides of the lower Congo River produced the impulse that resulted in the Conference of Berlin. In 1884, Great Britain had recognized the Portuguese claim to both banks of the Congo River, and Portugal agreed to preserve freedom of navigation. The Anglo-Portuguese treaty led to countermoves by Leopold, in concert with France and Germany. The Kaiser had already staked out Germany's claim to the territory of South-West Africa. As a result, the British weakened on their 1884 recognition, and the Portuguese recognized that, with British recognition less assured, Portugal would lose. Lisbon proposed an international conference, in the hope that the antagonism among the great powers would create divisions in its favor.

Portuguese aspirations were not realized at the conference, convened by Bismarck in Berlin on November 15, 1884. There followed the division between France and Leopold of the vast Congo Basin, with the recognition of Leopold's private colony as the "Independent State of the Congo," or Congo Free State. After much haggling, Portugal was conceded the present northern frontiers of Angola, including parts of the ancient kingdom of the Manikongo, the south bank of the Congo River, from its mouth nearly to Matadi, and, northward, the Cabinda Enclave. Nevertheless, the Portuguese felt bitterly that the great powers had been allowed to annex vast areas without historical claim or effective occupation and that these same two criteria were applied adversely to Portugal as a weaker power. Significantly, only the U.S. delegate talked about the right of Africans to decide their own destinies and suggested that the validity of occupation should also rest upon "the voluntary consent of the inhabitants."[14]

The portrayal of the outcome of the conference as a Portuguese defeat produced a change of government in Lisbon. The subsequent foreign minister Barros Gomes, did not, however, follow a diplomacy very different from that of his predecessor, Barbosa du Bocage. He too sought French and German recognition of Portuguese territorial claims and ambitions. He signed boundary treaties with Germany establishing the Angolan–South-West African borders, and the Mozambique and German East African boundary, in each case making some territorial concessions in hopes of future German support. Treaties were also signed with the French relative to Portuguese Guinea and Cabinda. In another clause in the same convention, the French recognized Portuguese influence in the territories between Angola and Mozambique, subject to the rights previously acquired by other powers. At French insistence, however, such territories were not truly defined on the grounds of irrelevancy. As Hammond says, "in effect, therefore, the clause was no more than a friendly gesture."[15] Nevertheless, Portugal had published, along with the protocol to the convention, the so-called rose-colored map, tinted pink to show that the vast territory lying between Angola and Mozambique was already a part of the Portuguese empire. It was this map that Barros Gomes displayed before the *côrtes* in 1886, as if the dreams of Lacerda were now a geographical reality and Portugal's title indisputable.

In June, 1887, Lord Salisbury disputed such title and stated British unwillingness to recognize claims of Portuguese sovereignty in areas not under "effective occupation." To his government it did not matter how many ruined forts, churches, and other relics the Portuguese could show. It mattered only whether the Portuguese could keep law and order in the areas and control them. The Anglo–Portuguese alliance was stretching thin.

The doctrine of effective occupation had actually been accepted at the Berlin conference for coastal areas but not for the interior. The Portuguese therefore redoubled their efforts to bar such acceptance.[16] Barros Gomes argued with the British that the principle had never been applied to South-West Africa and the Congo Free State.

The ensuing developments bore out Lacerda's warnings about the British. Late in the summer of 1888, *The Times* of London carried an unsigned article, by Harry Johnston, the aggressive British consul in Mozambique, that described a British "Cape-to-Cairo" route. This vast scheme cut the Portuguese rose-colored map in two. The British dreams turned to action. J. S. Moffat, acting on behalf of the young diamond magnate Cecil Rhodes, signed an agreement with Lobengula, chief of the Matabele in what is now Rhodesia. Whatever the Portuguese may have suspected of Lord Salisbury, he was far more moderate than was Rhodes, who personally detested the Portuguese. Rhodes aimed to control Mashonaland, to eliminate the influence of the Boers' Transvaal, and to confine Portugal to a narrow eastern coastal strip.

In 1889, Rhodes's British South Africa Company was granted a royal charter under which it obtained the British Government's permission to occupy and administer all the territory lying to the north of Bechuanaland and west of Mozambique. Farther east, Rhodes's company and the Mozambique Company of Paiva de Andrada were vying for position, and Andrada did not retreat. When Serpa Pinto boldly led an expedition up the Shire River, Britain immediately took this as a threat to its influence in Nyasaland and to the Scottish missionary station at Blantyre. Harry Johnston delivered a warning not to advance any farther, and Serpa Pinto halted for a time. But soon some of his force twice crossed the Ruo River, whereupon the acting consul for Nyasa, David Buchanan, declared the region a British protectorate.

On January 11, 1890, there followed what has generally been interpreted as Salisbury's ultimatum. In Lisbon the British minister told Barros Gomes that, if the Portuguese troops continued to occupy the land in dispute, he had instructions to leave their capital and hand over the archives to the British consul. Barros Gomes asked the minister to put this information in writing, and he complied. The opposition Portuguese newspapers dramatically announced that an ultimatum from Portugal's so-called ally had been delivered. The recall of the minister, they said, could only be interpreted as a threat of war. Gomes urgently requested arbitration over the disputed territory. When Salisbury

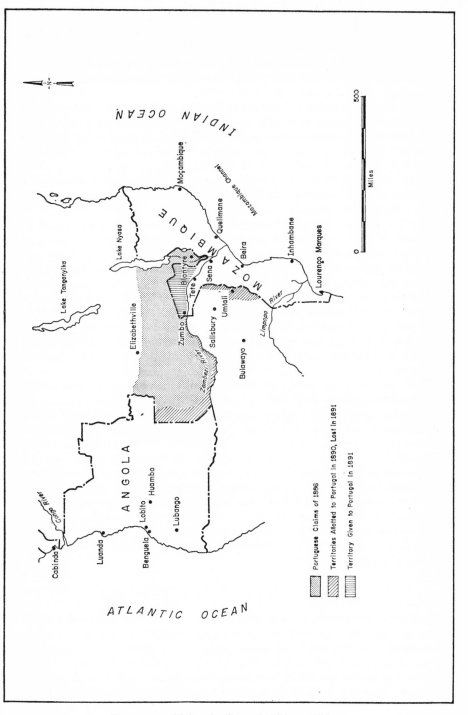

Portuguese Claims in Central Africa, 1886–91

Adapted from R. J. Hammond, *Portugal and Africa, 1815–1910*, with the permission of the publishers, Stanford University Press, p. 104. © 1966 by the Board of Trustees of the Leland Stanford Junior University.

refused, the humiliated and angered Portuguese Government backed down. The public was irate; the government of Barros Gomes fell. In August, the new government negotiated a treaty, but the *côrtes* rejected it, and Salisbury's attitude appeared to be hardening even more. However, in November a *modus vivendi* was worked out between London and Lisbon.

Such an understanding did not soften Rhodes, and in southern Africa a series of incidents continued to inflame emotions. Rhodes attempted a treaty with Gungunyane, supposedly a Portuguese vassal, who was chief of the Shangana (formerly Vátua) of Gazaland. Rhodes wanted to gain control not only of Gazaland but of Gungunyane's claim to the Mozambique coast. Even Salisbury became concerned lest Rhodes's ambitions produce a further Portuguese humiliation that would disturb the stability of the Portuguese monarchy and play into the hands of more radical Portuguese political forces.

In May, 1891, another new Portuguese Government—in the wake of a financial situation at home so desperate that Portugal later went off the gold standard (in 1892)—negotiated a new treaty with the Salisbury government. This time the *côrtes* approved. The treaty was signed the following June, thus roughly setting the present boundary between Mozambique, Malawi, Zambia, and Rhodesia and ending Lacerda's dream of Portuguese transcontinental dominion.[17] But so also were ended Rhodes's dreams of territorial control from Rhodesia to the sea. In compensation for some losses farther south, including parts of Manicaland, Portugal received that large wedge of territory between modern-day Zambia and Rhodesia that the Cabora Bassa hydroelectric project has made so important today.

But, for the Portuguese, the psychological consequences of the famous ultimatum burrowed deep into the political life of the nation. "Since the Napoleonic invasion the Anglo–Portuguese Alliance had guaranteed the throne of the Braganças [dynasty in Portugal]," maintains Livermore, "and Salisbury's ultimatum had struck at the roots of the monarchy."[18] Popular support of the monarchy rested in part upon the assumption that the Portuguese crown was a magic link to British protective power, and the common view of the ultimatum demolished this concept. Republicanism began to increase rapidly, and an uprising in Oporto even tried to proclaim a republic, imitating events in Brazil in 1889. The outbreak was easily suppressed and the republican party outlawed, but political strife continued with the increased curtailment of civil liberties. The crown itself, rather than the rapidly changing government, became the object of disdain.

BRITISH ATTITUDES AND PORTUGUESE REACTIONS

The Victorian concepts of imperialism became the ostensible justification of the English viewpoint that Portugal was not able to fulfil her international duties and mission and that the "white man's burden" there should be passed to those more capable. Livingstone in his *Missionary Travels* had emphasized the many kind and generous acts of the Portuguese, "because somehow or other we have come to hold the Portuguese character in rather a low estimation," partly because of "the pertinacity with which some of them have pursued the slave-trade" and partly because of the "contrast which they now offer to their illustrious ancestors, the foremost navigators of the world."[19] Lord Salisbury privately gave his opinion on the differences between British and Portuguese national characteristics: "the quiet taciturn energy and resources of our race, and the boastful fecklessness of the other."[20] It often was assumed that the break-up of Portuguese Africa was simply a matter of time and that, if the empire disintegrated, the English should be primary heirs to it.[21]

Such British attitudes and assumptions served as justification for a series of secret agreements to divide Portuguese possessions if the empire were to crumble. When Portugal sought a loan in 1898, with talk of the colonies as collateral, Britain and Germany secretly agreed to claim their own spheres of influence if Lisbon were to default. Despite such scheming, however, Britain's attitude was ambivalent. In the final analysis, "the British did not want to partition the Portuguese colonies with any other power," as William Langer says, "they wanted no other partner in south Africa and liked to think of the Portuguese colonies as a British preserve."[22] In fact, London did all it could to keep partition from materializing. As for the loan, the Portuguese Government raised the necessary funds in Paris on its tobacco and match monopolies without having to pledge the colonies as collateral.

It was in the face of such changing foreign attitudes and intrigues that a new and tougher generation of Portuguese colonial leaders reviewed their country's determination to remain in Africa. They began to take the concept of effective occupation seriously, although they realized that the rules applied to the great powers would be different from those applied to Portugal. When Lourenco Marques was threatened by a revolt in the interior, António Enes was sent out as high commissioner and undertook a military campaign that, eventually on November 6, 1895, destroyed Gungunyane's main army at Coolela. Following this, Mousinho de Albuquerque led a small patrol into Gungunyane's headquarters to make a spectacular capture. Both Enes and Albuquerque were gifted writers, and their descriptions of great African victories added to their reputation as national heroes in Portugal at a time when there was resurging popular commitment to the overseas areas.[23]

At the close of the century another turn of events affected the Anglo–Portuguese Alliance. Britain verged on war with the Boers. The Portuguese thought they saw a chance to obtain British indebtedness, to nullify the Anglo–German treaty of 1898, and to cause the British to reaffirm the historic Anglo–Portuguese treaties. Thus, the Portuguese quickly responded to a British request to forbid arms to pass through Lourenço Marques to the Transvaal and to permit British bases in Mozambique. In addition, the two parties reaffirmed the treaties of 1642 and 1661, which had even committed England to defend the Portuguese colonies.[24] The alliance was dramatized outwardly by the visit of the British Channel Fleet to Lisbon in December, 1900.

Portuguese policy in Mozambique toward the close of the century, unlike that in Angola, moved toward employing the concessionary company with foreign capital for the development of the territory. We have already noted that the

Mozambique Company, whose concession covered most of the present district of Manica e Sofala, included European and South African capital. The Niassa Company in the north of the territory, the wild and primitive area of the Yao and Makua, was backed with English capital but accomplished little. The Zambézia Company, in Tete District and Quelimane, comprised many *prazos* and also included diverse European and South African capital, and unlike the two other companies it did not have to administer the area. Subconcessions were to contribute to the first really substantial agricultural advances in the valley area.

The complete pacification of Mozambique took until the second decade of the twentieth century. By the turn of the century, southern Mozambique had been largely dominated. In the Manica and Sofala areas, however, a period of violence followed the death of Gouveia in his once secure domain, despite the attempts of the Mozambique Company to usher in a new order. Pacifying Gorongosa was especially difficult, but in 1902 several hundred Portuguese troops accomplished the task, and from then on the area was under military administration. In 1897, Mousinho de Albuquerque had established forts along the coast near Mozambique Island, and in 1906 the inland tribes were dominated. In 1910, the Arabs on Angoche Island were defeated. In Niassa District, forts were established along the Rovuma River to interdict arms supply to the Yao and Makua chiefs from the Germans in Tanganyika, and, in 1912, the Portuguese took the Kraal (near Vila Cabral) of Mataka, the Yao chief who then fled to German territory.[25] The Mozambique pacification campaigns, of great diplomatic and psychological importance for Lisbon, were executed with little loss of life and often resembled police actions made logistically difficult due to the extreme distances.

In Angola, meanwhile, the period from 1891 through 1918 marked the final phase of conquest. In extreme southern Angola, the Portuguese had an isolated garrison at Humbe, near the Cunene River. When disease infected the cattle of the Cuanhama tribe, part of the garrison tried to persuade the Africans to allow their cattle to be vaccinated, which led instead to a massacre of the soldiers and a general uprising. In 1904, 300 Portuguese and loyal Africans were attacked and killed at Cuamato in a disaster of such proportions that, within two years, 2,000 troops were dispatched to the area to destroy Cuanhama power. The Cuanhama held out until 1915, however, because of their prowess in war, the isolation of Cuanhamaland, and the supply of arms and, in 1914, some troops from Germany.

As for west-central Angola, rebellion became more prevalent among the Bailundo (Ovimbundu), who were stirred by the rum trade, conscription for contract labor, and a contraction in the wild rubber trade. Portuguese control was established within two or three years. Eastward, the Portuguese pushed their outposts into Moxico District along their route to the upper Zambezi, signing treaties with chiefs and establishing a penal colony on the site of Luso. The final campaign to control the vast areas was not completed until 1917, and afterward most of the outposts were garrisoned by African troops instead of Europeans.[26]

Most difficult was that region of chronic trouble, the Dembos, northeast of Luanda around the Dande River, with rugged, difficult terrain. Africans, *mestiços*, and Portuguese *degredados* (exiled criminals), kept up a center of insurrection.

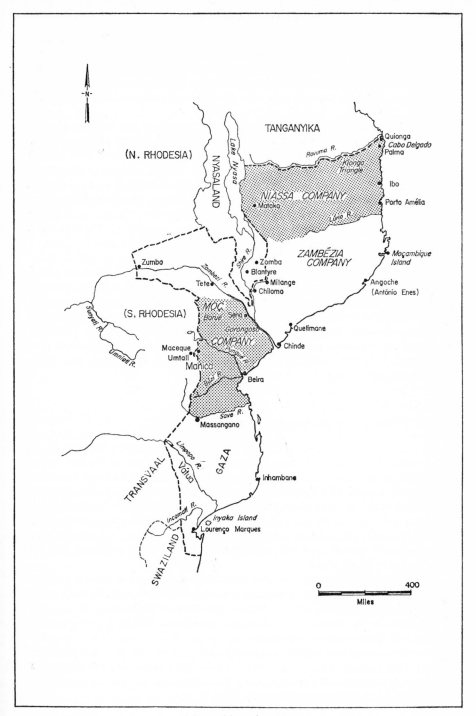

Mozambique in 1914

There were no battles for the Portuguese to win, only an almost invisible enemy to fight. Nevertheless, Captain João de Almeida and the intrepid Artur de Paiva carefully reconnoitered the area in 1907. The new intelligence became the basis for a series of successful small actions; but some fighting continued until 1910. Farther to the north, campaigns against the Bakongo continued from 1913 until 1918.[27]

In Portuguese Guinea, the problems of conquest of the interior seemed insoluble. The very title of this land remained in doubt between 1838 and 1870, when the dispute with the British over Bolama was referred to the United States, with President Grant ruling in favor of Portugal. Though assured to the title of the land, the Portuguese still had to deal with tribal hostility in the interior. Campaigns of 1884 and 1886, against the Papéis, during which the Portuguese gained the Fulas as allies, were failures. The Portuguese were primarily restricted to the towns and under constant pressure from one tribe or another. During the period of 1891 to 1910, rebellions of the Papéis, Balanta, and Malinke were frequent.

Success awaited the arrival of Captain Teixeira Pinto from Portugal in 1912. He disguised himself as a French trader and, wandering through the lands of the rebellious Malinke in the vicinity of the Oio River, spied out the enemy's positions. After his return to Bissau, he began a successful three-year campaign with the assistance of his Malinke lieutenant, Abdul Indjai. Teixeira Pinto's force included only about six Europeans with over 400 African allies. The final defeat of the Papéis in 1915 meant that Portuguese Guinea was more or less conquered, with the exception of three tax disputes in 1917, 1925, and 1936, and the current conflict.[28]

THE COMING OF FOREIGN MISSIONS

Late in the nineteenth century foreign interests of another type began to focus on Portuguese Africa. Protestant missions, so active in much of the rest of the continent, chose to enter into lands where the much earlier Catholic activities had already ended. The Protestants, as well as the new Catholic missions that responded to the challenge, had a considerable effect on the development of the Africans with whom they came in touch. They became agents of many types of social, economic, and political change. Individually and collectively, missionaries exercised a strong influence, both directly and indirectly, first over small villages and later over whole tribes.

The English Baptists were the first Protestant missionaries in Angola, settling in 1878 at São Salvador, seat of the ancient kingdom of the Kongo. In their wake, the Portuguese re-established the Catholic mission in order to compete with the Protestants and to reassert their historical precedence. Within a few years the Kongo had again lost its independence and passed to Portuguese control, under circumstances that one Baptist missionary described as follows: "the poor old King [of the Kongo] had in 1884 affixed his mark and seal to a document acknowledging the suzerainty of Portugal, under the impression that he was thanking a brother monarch for some presents sent him."[29]

The Baptists were soon followed by American and Canadian Congregational-ists and Plymouth Brethren who settled in central Angola, the latter near the border of the Belgian Congo and Northern Rhodesia. American Methodists settled in Angola in 1884 and in Mozambique in 1889. An important Swiss Protestant mission was founded in the Lourenço Marques District in 1881, and the Anglicans conducted limited operations in the northwest corner of Mozambique, including a large station on Likoma Island in Lake Nyasa. In Angola, the most pervasive Catholic effort was conducted by the Holy Ghost Fathers, of French or Alsatian nationality. The foreign complexion of Catholic missions was less pronounced in Mozambique, although, after the establishment of a republic in 1910 in Portugal, the Jesuits were replaced by foreign orders.

Besides strictly religious activity, the early years of missionary endeavors emphasized literacy, educational, and medical tasks. African languages were put into print, and a religious literature began to develop. An example of the rate of development of these activities is provided by the Baptists, who published the first Kikongo edition of the New Testament in 1893 and whose first medical missionary arrived in São Salvador in 1907, preceding by six years the estab-lishment of a permanent hospital.

One important irritant confronting Protestant missions was the Portuguese idea of "civilizing." To be "civilized"—that is, assimilated to Portuguese norms —one had to be Catholic: "The concept of Portugueseness explains and justifies the special position accorded in all Portuguese dominions to the Roman Catholic Church and missions. Protestantism hardly exists at all in Portugal, whereas the Roman Catholic Church has been intimately connected with Portuguese history. . . . Naturally, therefore, to become Portuguese should also mean to become Roman Catholic."[30] While it was never impossible for one who professed another faith to become assimilated, "that he should do so must seem to the Portuguese paradoxical and inconvenient—he is denying in one breath what he has affirmed in another."[31]

Plainly, the criterion for becoming civilized in Portuguese Africa meant to become culturally Portuguese and religiously Catholic. Although at first both Protestant and Catholic missions found it convenient to stress African languages in their educational efforts, the Catholics showed more willingness to use Portuguese than the Protestants did. In 1921, the government, in the now famous Decree 77, forbade the use of African languages in mission schools.[32] Unwilling to accept the national intent of this decree, the Protestant missions did not adapt their rudimentary school system to fulfill language requirements. So widespread was the Protestant linguistic intransigence that over 200 schools in northern Angola alone were immediately closed, thus, according to one missionary, "cutting the sinews of this very important branch of our work, and condemning thousands of native children to illiteracy and ignorance."[33]

The effect of Decree 77 on Catholic missions was less disastrous. In the early days, the Holy Ghost Fathers had founded a seminary in Portugal, displaying a far-sighted realization that the use of Portuguese nationals as missionaries would be a definite asset. In the years following the 1921 decree, the Catholics showed more interest in emphasizing the Portuguese nature of their activities than the

Protestants did, while the Protestant school system suffered. Also important was the willingness of Catholic missionaries of whatever nationality to speak Portuguese, whereas the Protestants, mostly English-speaking, had more difficulty with that language and were less interested in learning and using it.

While the decree did not prohibit speaking an African language in teaching the Gospel, it stirred up much bitterness, although its enforcement was not uniform. Whereas in northern Angola the letter of the law was forcefully applied, one broader-minded, practical governor-general of Mozambique had Portuguese taught in the schools, without forbidding the local language.[34]

Though the way was sometimes smooth, Protestant mission activity, especially in northern Angola, generally ran a rocky course, and there was greater involvement in political affairs there than elsewhere in Portuguese Africa. Late in 1913, the recruitment of contract workers in northern Angola for São Tomé resulted in an uprising led by a local Bakongo chief, Álvaro Tulante Buta. Though Buta had himself been educated by Catholics, Baptist missionaries were falsely accused of being instigators of the rebellion. A combination of wise action by the Portuguese colonial minister, the English Government, and Carson Graham, a missionary, kept local administrators from prolonged retaliation. Some of those falsely accused led the later mediation, but among others the bitterness was not soon to die.[35] The Portuguese Government nevertheless respected its commitment to the General Act of the 1884 Berlin Conference, which guaranteed religious toleration and did not expel the missions. Despite this forebearance, the clash of Protestant and Catholic attitudes was enough to plant the seeds of eventual conflict.[36]

The success with which this essential disagreement was resolved varied in different parts of Portuguese Africa, depending upon the mutual attitudes of various missionaries and the Portuguese, the degree of active competition in proselytizing, and factors within the indigenous societies.

In northwest Angola, the Protestant mission sentiment against the Portuguese has deep historical roots of which the Bakongo uprising of 1913 described above is an example. In both the Belgian and the Portuguese Congo, the situation was further complicated in 1921 not only by Decree 77 but by the beginning of a messianic movement under the guidance of "Prophet" Simon Kimbangu. The Lord was supposed to have appeared to Kimbangu in a town in the Belgian Congo. Soon there were reports of marvelous cures, and many adherents of the Protestant missions in northern Angola sought out the "savior" in the Belgian Congo. Prophets began to multiply and appear in northern Angola as well. The adventist teachings of the prophets resulted in a refusal of Africans to work or accept missionary medical help: "As the movement grew it became more and more imbued with magic, and practices akin to the witch-doctor's sorceries, especially in the Kivimba district north-east of São Salvador. . . ."[37] In the Belgian Congo, around Thysville, where the Bakongo tribes related to those in northern Angola lived, many Africans left the Protestant mission to join the prophet movement, until the Belgian, and later the Portuguese, government tried to repress it, with the result that many innocent people suffered from indiscriminate police repression.[38]

The Congo area was certainly not typical of all Portuguese Africa. On the whole, the Portuguese Government, in spite of the underlying causes for opposing Protestant missions, maintained a consistent theoretical position, but the application of policy varied with officials and with areas. Two writers on missions have testified in more recent times that the government was cordial and appreciative toward evangelical missions and that, in fact, "The Protestant missionaries had more liberty in Angola than in Portugal."[39]

ADMINISTRATIVE ADVANCES AND HOME CRISIS

Because of an increased awareness of local requirements, it became recognized even in Lisbon that the policies followed in the preceding decades were both unrealistic and unworkable. Such men as Paiva Couceiro, Eduardo da Costa, António Enes, Mousinho de Albuquerque, and, later, Norton de Matos, agitated for and obtained a new policy of decentralization and administrative autonomy for the overseas provinces. Enes defended such a policy: "I wish to see each province administered and governed from within the province, following rigid norms established and financed by the metropolis."[40] At the Congresso Colonial Nacional, of 1901, decentralization was defended by Costa, who put forth an eight-point program: decentralization; more autonomy; the metropolis to regulate and inspect, approve or disapprove only; more power to the governors and their staffs; no local councils; separate codes for Africans and Europeans; division of the provinces into districts and *circunscrições*; and, lastly, administrators to be appointed by the governors.[41]

In his report to the government, *Moçambique*, first published in 1893, António Enes stated: "We have, then, good land and labour to work it; we lack only capital and initiative."[42] Administrators in Angola and Mozambique, such as Enes, Mousinho de Albuquerque, and Paiva Couceiro set to work to provide what was lacking. Before 1895, Portuguese Africa had been a hodgepodge of concessions, missions, and captaincies and military commands. Administrative reforms began in the field, with the local administrative areas, or *circunscrições*, founded in Mozambique in 1895. A more substantial program was inaugurated, at least on paper, in Mozambique by 1907 and in Angola in 1911. In 1906, the Escola Superior Colonial was founded by the Lisbon Geographical Society for the training of colonial administrators and then in 1926 was integrated with the colonial administration. The landmark Colonial Reform Act of 1907 sanctioned the reforms that had taken place in the field and was followed by decrees in 1908, 1910, 1911, and 1912 that tended to increase local autonomy in the colonies.

After 1907, the Portuguese-African administrative system was based upon three local units: the *concelho*, the more rural *circunscrição*, and the *capitania-mor*. The latter, destined to disappear, was a military command in areas still to be pacified. *Postos*, the most rural administrative unit, also began to be formed. However, there were still areas governed by private concessionaries in Mozambique (the *prazeros*), and the large areas of the same province remained administered by the Niassa and Mozambique companies.[43]

At this time, Portugal was witnessing a demise of the monarchy and the rise of

81

republicanism. By 1906, political and financial turmoil had driven the weak ruler, Carlos, to invest in João Franco unusual powers. Franco soon became a dictator, ignoring the *côrtes* and all parties, suppressing newspapers, and reactivating an earlier decree authorizing deportation of political enemies to Timor without trial. The day after signing the latter decree, February 1, 1908, Carlos and his eldest son were assassinated. The second son, Manuel II, reigned for two years, with six changes of government, restoration of civil liberties, and increasing republican activity through the secret society, the Carbonária. This society infiltrated the armed forces, and on October 5, 1910, obviously incapable of governing, Manuel fled Lisbon after a cruiser on the Tagus had turned its guns on the royal palace.[44]

The proclamation of the First Republic in 1910 accelerated the trend toward decentralization and provincial autonomy for the Portuguese-African possessions again termed "colonies." These principles, embodied in the constitution of 1911 and codified in 1914 and 1916, allowed each colony to adopt its own organic charter. Highly influential in this administrative reform was Norton de Matos and his very progressive 1913 directive for Angola, which brushed aside proponents of military rule and established the circumscriptions as the civilizing vehicle for political development of the Africans.

The sixteen-year history of the republican regime (1910–26) was rocky and made all the more precarious by World War I. With the republic came a reaffirmation of the alliance with England. However, the very eve of World War I found Britain and Germany again involved in a secret draft treaty that enlarged Germany's share of the Portuguese colonies in the event of Portugal's default on a loan. The German ambassador in London wrote at the time that conditions justifying intervention were so vaguely phrased that almost any pretext would serve.[45]

When the war broke out, the Portuguese ambassador in London requested and received British assurances of protection against German attack on Portuguese Africa from South-West Africa and Tanganyika. German attacks took place nevertheless. Toward the end of 1915, Britain was hard-pressed by a shipping shortage, and Lisbon responded to London's request to seize seventy-two German vessels interned in Portuguese ports. Germany's official declaration of war against Portugal came only in March, 1916, after Germany had been defeated, in May, 1915, in South-West Africa and had already been badly shaken in Tanganyika.

For the western front, Portugal volunteered its best division, but it was poorly trained and ill prepared. The Portuguese troops were not psychologically motivated for the war, as became evident when they broke before a furious German offensive in April, 1918. On the home front, strikes and disorders grew, but English loans propped up the government and the war effort continued. In East Africa, after the successful campaign of the British in Tanganyika, the able German general Paul von Lettow-Vorbeck escaped into Mozambique with 2,000 followers to fight a guerrilla war, sustained by trading captured booty to Africans for their support.[46]

The great political confusion in Portugal was reflected in administrative confusion overseas. In World War I, most administrative functions had been taken over by the military. All prior decrees dealing with the colonies were revoked in 1918, restored in 1919, and then revised by decrees in the following three years. The principal element remaining from all these changes was Norton de Matos' 1913 directive, made law in 1914. Six years later, the high commissioners in each territory were given wide powers, assisted and advised by an elected legislative council and an appointed executive council. It was at this time that Angola reached the verge of bankruptcy due to political events at home and abroad.[47]

The aftermath of war and debt had brought into being one government crisis after another in Lisbon, as well as a gigantic financial scandal involving the newly formed Angola Metropole Bank. "The most revolution-ridden Latin American state had never been more unstable than the Lusitanian republic between 1910 and 1925," writes Professor Nowell. "Furthermore, during these years the situation showed no sign of mending but only grew worse as time passed; after sixteen years of republicanism the country was ready to try something else."[48]

During this turbulent period, Lisbon's desperation tended to produce a continuing decentralization and financial autonomy in Africa, which would have been most fortunate had there been a better base for economic development. In Angola, the discovery of diamond deposits had led to the establishment of Diamang (Companhia de Diamantes de Angola), largely with British and Belgian capital allied with the Union Minière in Katanga. The company became a large employer of Africans and, in fact, a state within a state. This one note of prosperity, albeit a big one, was inadequate to rectify the deficits of the colony. The monumental Benguela Railway was begun by an associate of Rhodes, Robert Williams, in 1903, and made slow progress up to and across Angola's central plateau, owing to shortage of capital. In 1929 it reached the Congo border. Meanwhile, it produced settlements and maize trade along the way as it eased the penetration of the interior and, particularly, changed the life of the Ovimbundu.

The first rail line in Angola, from Luanda inland, started by a private company in 1886, reached Malange and promoted the economic development of the hinterland to a limited extent only. As elsewhere in Africa, there was a lag in the import of capital for development of large plantations.[49] Farther south, the isolation of the town of Sá da Bandeira was not ended until 1923, with the opening of the railway from Moçâmedes. In the 1920's, as high commissioner of Angola, Norton de Matos was given wide authority, and he pressed forward with rare aggressiveness, especially in the field of transportation. But his development ideas vastly outran his financial means, and indebtedness skyrocketed.

In a somewhat more prosperous Mozambique, the Niassa and Mozambique charter companies continued their speculation with little success and little capital. The Zambézia Company, unlike the other two companies, did not have to divert its resources to expensive public administration, and it achieved better results in the Tete and Quelimane districts with sugar, sisal, and copra.[50]

At the heart of the greater prosperity of Mozambique were the railways. During the Boer War of 1899, the siege of Mafeking disrupted the previously established overseas trade routes to British Central Africa via the Cape, and Beira (the Rhodesian–Beira rail line was completed in 1896) benefited as the new gateway to developing Southern Rhodesia.[51] The rail line from Lourenço Marques to Transvaal, completed in 1894, carried increasing amounts of traffic, although this shortest route to the rich Witwatersrand region of the Transvaal suffered from restrictive commercial measures, which gave the advantage to Durban, Cape Town, and Port Elizabeth harbors. The signing of the Mozambican convention in 1909, however, assured the port of Lourenço, Marques the traffic of at least 47.5 per cent of South African imports in exchange for Mozambique African labor.[52]

Although there was talk of gold and copper in the colonies, investors in Portugal seldom put their limited capital there. Some of the Portuguese who did, however, reaped handsome profits and did so, occasionally, by benefiting from forced labor practices. Nevertheless, despite earlier government policies against foreign investment, it was mostly British, French, and Belgian money that created the capital for the Mozambique Company, and yet there was not enough money to build the Beira–Rhodesia Railroad, a job that by default went to Rhodes's company. The Benguela Railway, despite foreign financing, had a capital shortage that delayed completion until twenty-five years later. The railroad from Lourenço Marques to the rich Transvaal, although provided for in the 1877 treaty, was six years in finding an entrepreneur, the American Colonel Edward McMurdo, who then had trouble in raising the funds and died, apparently insolvent, amid charges of watered stock. In all these enterprises, "what stands out is the difficulty they had in attracting investment capital— second only to their chronic shortage of labor in impending economic development."[53] Indian coolie labor had to be imported to complete the first part of the Benguela Railway.

Richard Hammond suggests that the Portuguese did not "hold on to their African dominions merely for what could be got out of them. . . . Though the bankruptcy of the Portuguese state could largely be put down to expenditure on the colonies, a proposal that Mozambique be sold to finance the development of the remainder found few takers. The Portuguese felt—and feel—that their overseas possessions have been a symbol of their place in the world, even a warranty of their independence as a nation."[54] The Portuguese increasingly embraced the view that their very survival as a nation depended upon the successful defense of their African empire against not only other European powers but their oldest ally as well. Salisbury himself once indicated that he thought it logical for the Portuguese to argue that loss of their whole colonial empire would probably result in their absorption by Spain.[55]

BANKRUPTCY AND THE "NEW STATE"

The military government first came to power in Portugal on May 28, 1926. By then, public debt charges in Angola were absorbing as much as 25 per cent of the total revenues and the situation elsewhere overseas was not much better. Military expenses continued to increase. The deepening financial crises were followed by serious questions as to the ability of Portuguese Africa, and indeed of Portugal itself, to survive. The increasingly desperate Portuguese Government investigated the possibility of a League of Nations loan, but that body made international financial controls a prerequisite. Under these circumstances, it seemed possible that Portuguese Africa might pass to international political control.

Popular protest against League of Nations control of finances then forced the hand of the military government to give power to a civilian professor of economics at Coimbra, António de Oliveira Salazar, who avoided a loan but at the same time reduced military expenditures. Salazar hoped eventually to develop the overseas areas with Portuguese rather than massive foreign capital, with less local autonomy and closer supervision by Lisbon. For the present, he was determined to balance the budget at home and in the overseas provinces and to bring a prompet nd to all talk of giving up any part of Portuguese Africa. His policies were adopted amid renewed international suggestions that Portugal should be relieved of her colonies. Not surprisingly, the new government eyed all foreign activities and loan offers with distrust and was determined to follow economic policies quite the opposite of the "new economics" of the mid-1930's. Indeed, the acceptance of Salazar rather than the loan and its controls was more than an economic and political turning point. It was a precursor of the Portuguese mentality of the next forty years.

In 1930, Salazar (as interim colonial minister) and, later, Armindo Monteiro (as colonial minister), promulgated a new Colonial Act, restricting local autonomy, although not entirely eliminating it, and giving Catholic missions a privileged position as "an instrument of civilization and national influence."

The new administrative system in Portuguese Africa was established by the Colonial Act of 1933, later incorporated into the constitution of the same year. The first principle of the act involved the affirmation of the unity and solidarity of a Portugal consisting of peoples ethnically, economically, and administratively varied but united in goals and interests. Other principles included the special character of colonial legislation, normally pertaining to the colonial minister; extensive grants of power to the colonial governors, including tutelary intervention of the colonial minister; financial autonomy; economic organization subordinate to the principle of national unity; establishment of a special judicial system for the Africans; and, finally, gradation of decentralization according to the degree of development of the various colonies and division into colonies of "general government" and colonies of "simple government."[56]

The subsequent policies of the Salazar and Caetano regimes for Portuguese Africa are treated in later chapters, as is the resurgence of the question of Portuguese Africa in international debate. These developments are best understood by considering the historical experiences, outlined in this chapter, that helped build the Portuguese mentality: the sensitiveness toward their oldest ally, which at times saved them, at other times bullied them; the suspicions of plotting by the great powers to divide Portuguese Africa among themselves; a deep Portuguese Catholicism identified with a civilizing mission in a way that antagonized Protestants; a fierce determination to stay in Africa despite the opposition of great powers and the fact that it was the white man's grave. The colonies were an economic burden that drained the metropole and yet the Portuguese never lost the idea that developing colonies and profiting from them could "save" Portugal at home. The Portuguese phenomenon and dilemma were well summed up by Sir Harry Johnston, who knew both Africa first hand and the European power politics of his day:

> Of all European powers that rule in tropical Africa none have pushed their influence so far into the interior as Portugal. And the Portuguese rule more by influence over the natives than by actual force. The garrisons at Dondo, Malange, and other places in the interior range perhaps from fifty to two hundred men, and these are nearly entirely native soldiers. The country is so thickly populated that the inhabitants could in a moment sweep away the Portuguese if they disliked their rule. What Portugal wants for the development of her magnificent colonies is money and men. She is too poor and too thinly populated to be able to supply these essentials herself and she is too much afraid of foreign aggression to invite them from other nations.[57]

Though the Portuguese heritage was slow in providing men and money, it did leave another legacy. Despite the earlier slave trade and forced labor, there developed a coexistence between blacks and whites that merits separate treatment.

NOTES

1. See R. F. Burton, *The Lands of Cazembe: Lacerda's Journeys to Cazembe and also Journey of the Pombeiros J. P. Baptista and Amaro José Across Africa from Angola to Tete on the Zembeze and a Résumé of the Journey of M. M. Monteiro and Gamitto* (London, 1873), pp. 19–20.

2. *Ibid.*, p. 12.

3. The date of departure from Cassange (1804) is confirmed. *Ibid.*, pp. 201–2, in a reference letter dated November 11, 1804. There has been a dispute whether Pedro João Baptista and Amaro José were *mestiços* rather than Africans. This is clarified in the diary of these two *pombeiros*. The entry for October 20, 1806, notes that upon their arrival at Cazembe's sister's farm, she referred to them as "white people." *Ibid.*, p. 186. On their arrival at the court of Cazembe, the African guide, introducing them to the king, said "I bring you some white men here from the king they call Muenuputo, king of Portugal." *Ibid.*, p. 187.

4. In 1852, the Portuguese Government commissioned the Austrian Friedrich Welwitsch to make a botanical survey of Angola, where he spent the next nine years. In the last years of the century, a Portuguese naturalist, José Alberto de Oliveira Anchieta, traveled sometimes with the support of the Portuguese Government, in all parts of Angola collecting specimens for museums in Lisbon.

5. An excellent account of this period is found in Douglas L. Wheeler, "The Portuguese in Angola 1836–91: A Study in Expansion and Administration" (Ph.D. dissertation, History Department, Boston University, 1963), pp. 71–102.

6. For accounts of African resistance movements see Hélio Felgas, *As populações nativas do Congo Português* (Luanda, 1960), and Wheeler, *op. cit.*

7. Wheeler, *op. cit.*, pp. 157–63.
8. *Ibid.*, pp. 180, 189, and 191.
9. James Duffy, *Portuguese Africa* (Cambridge, Mass, 1959), pp. 230–32.
10. For further background, see A. J. Wills, *The History of Central Africa*, 2nd ed. (London, 1967); George Martelli, *From Leopold to Lumumba: A History of the Belgian Congo, 1877–1960* (London, 1962); and Eric Walker (ed.), *The Cambridge History of the British Empire*, Vol. VIII, *South Africa, Rhodesia, and the High Commission Territories* (Cambridge, 1963).
11. Wheeler, *op. cit.*, pp. 324–29.
12. *Ibid.*, pp. 329–38; Duffy, *op. cit.*, pp. 199–200.
13. Charles E. Nowell, "Portugal and the Partition of Africa," *The Journal of Modern History*, XIX, No. 1 (March, 1947), 1.
14. Actually, at the time of the Berlin Conference, Bismarck was far more concerned over Heligoland and the settlement of other problems with Great Britain, and he took little interest in colonial expansion. For the general diplomacy of the period, see William Langer, *European Alliances and Alignments, 1871–90*, 2nd ed. (New York, 1950); *The Cambridge History of the British Empire*, Vol. III (Cambridge, 1959). For a modern Portuguese attitude including the comment on the U.S. position, see the speech by Franco Nogueira in *Portugal Information Bulletin*, V, No. 8 (London, 1966), 6. See also S. E. Crowe, *The Berlin West African Conference, 1884–85* (London, 1942). General background of the period is found in A. J. Wills, *The History of Central Africa*, 2nd ed. (London, 1967). Also see Ronald Robinson and John Gallagher, *Africa and the Victorians* (New York, 1961).
15. R. J. Hammond, *Portugal and Africa, 1815–1910* (Stanford, 1966), pp. 103–5.
16. Philip R. Warhurst, *Anglo-Portuguese Relations in South-Central Africa, 1890–1900* (London, 1962), pp. 3–4.
17. *Ibid.*, pp. 78–103; Hammond, *op. cit.*, pp. 133–47; Roland Oliver, *Sir Harry Johnston and the Scramble for Africa* (London, 1957), pp. 173–80; H. V. Livermore, *A New History of Portugal* (Oxford, 1966), pp. 306–10. For an example of British anti-Portuguese attitudes at the time, see J. Scott Keltie, *The Partition of Africa* (London, 1895).
18. Livermore, *op. cit.*, p. 309.
19. David Livingstone, *Missionary Travels and Research in South Africa* (New York, 1858), p. 698.
20. Letter from Salisbury to Sir Robert Morier, February 11, 1891 (Salisbury Papers), quoted in Warhurst, *op. cit.*, p. 37.
21. Reasons for the differences in attitude of Salisbury and Rhodes are well summed up by Warhurst (*ibid.*, pp. 5–7 and 45–46). Whereas both concurred in the generally held opinion that Portugal was in decay and that the break-up of empire might be near, Salisbury "had no intentions of allowing unfair measures against her." Whereas Rhodes's focus was on southern Africa, Salisbury was concerned with the difficulties of the traditional British policy of splendid isolation and was not unaware of the coming need for allies. Thus he saw no reason needlessly to antagonize the Portuguese—and certainly not merely to satisfy Rhodes's commercial acquisitions. With Germany in South-West Africa, neither was Salisbury unaware of the possibility of a link-up between the Germans and the Boers of the Transvaal. Rhodes, had he his way, may well have pushed through Mozambique to the sea, regardless of the cost to relations with Lisbon and previous agreements with the Portuguese.

He feared having the English in Rhodesia and his own interests there, being shut up, without outlet to the sea, like "rats in a trap." (Quoted in *ibid.*, p. 77.)

22. William L. Langer, *The Diplomacy of Imperialism, 1890–1902*, 2nd ed. (New York, 1951), p. 529.

23. António Enes, *A guerra de África em 1895*, 2nd ed. (Lisbon, 1945), and *Moçambique*, 3rd ed. (Lisbon, 1946); Joaquim Mousinho de Albuquerque, *Moçambique* (Lisbon, 1899); Douglas Wheeler, "Gungunhana," in Norman R. Bennett (ed.), *Leadership in Eastern Africa* (Boston, 1968), pp. 167–220; and Douglas Wheeler, "Gungunyane the Negotiator," *Journal of African History*, IX, No. 4 (1968), 585–602; Charles Nowell, *op. cit.*

24. Hammond, *op. cit.*, pp. 256–58. Livermore interprets these events as Salisbury demanding that Portugal declare war on the Boers or face a British blockade of Lourenço Marques (*op. cit.*). However, see José de Almada, *Aliança Inglêsa*, Vol. II (Lisbon, 1947).

25. Duffy, *op. cit.*, pp. 233–34.

26. Wheeler, *op. cit.*, pp. 320–46; Duffy, *op. cit.*, pp. 326–28.

27. See David Magno, *Guerras Angolanas* (Porto, 1934).

28. Archibald Lyall, *Black and White Make Brown* (London, 1938), pp. 187–91; A. Teixeira da Mota, *Guiné Portuguesa*, II (Lisbon, 1954), pp. 33–34.

29. R. H. Carson Graham, *Under Seven Congo Kings* (London, 1931), p. 1.

30. Stephen Neill, *Colonialism and Christian Missions* (New York, 1966), p. 293.

31. *Ibid.*

32. This action was noticeably later than similar measures in other African areas—for example, in French Equatorial Africa, where French became the mandatory language in 1906.

33. Graham, *op. cit.*, pp. 194–95.

34. *Ibid.*, pp. 194–98.

35. *Ibid.*, pp. 132–72.

36. Clifford Parsons, an English Baptist missionary who lived nearly twenty years among the Bakongo, points out that both Catholic and Protestant clergy have made efforts to ameliorate the authoritarianism of the Portuguese colonial administration, the former being hampered by their "special relationship" with the Portuguese government and the latter by their "foreignness." "What has really been under attack," he states, "has been the Protestant practice of giving the laity [in this case the Africans] a significant part in church government, for any training of Africans for responsibility has been viewed with suspicion." "The Makings of a Revolt," in *Angola, A Symposium: Views of a Revolt* (London, 1962), p. 70. Hugh Kay, presenting "A Catholic View" in the same symposium (p. 85), outlines the strictly controlled position of the Catholic hierarchy in Angola and Mozambique under the Missionary Agreement with the Portuguese Government, and states that "God and Empire are so closely linked in this colonial theory that African languages tend to be stifled, indigenous cultures ignored, and the African somewhat depersonalised."

37. Carson Graham, *op. cit.*, p. 186.

38. For a good summary of this and other subsequent movements, see Eduardo dos Santos, *Maza* (Lisbon, 1965), pp. 259–315. The Protestant activity among the Ovimbundu farther south did not so antagonize the Portuguese. See Adrian C. Edwards, *The Ovimbundu Under Two Sovereignties* (London, 1962), pp. 76–89. See Mary Floyd Cushman, *Missionary Doctor* (New York, 1944).

However, the climb was always uphill. Two of the greatest problems were Protestant resentment of the subsidies and special privileges granted to Catholic missions and the tendency of converted Africans, whenever faced with insecurity, to revert to witchcraft and superstition in ways that set back not only religion but economic and medical advances. G. M. Childs, *Umbundu Kinship and Character* (London, 1949), pp. 222–23.

39. R. H. Glover and J. H. Kane, *The Progress of World Missions* (New York, 1960), p. 284.

40. António Enes, as quoted in Adriano Moreira, *Política ultramarina* (Lisbon, 1956), p. 272.

41. Duffy, *op. cit.*, p. 243.

42. António Enes, *Moçambique*, p. 26.

43. Some valuable sources on the pre-1910 period include António Eduardo Villaça, *Relatório, propostas de lei e documentos relativos às possessões ultramarinas*, Vol. I (Lisbon, 1899); Bahia dos Santos, *op. cit.*, esp. Chs. 6 and 7; Gerardo A. Pery, *Geografia e estatística geral de Portugal e colonias* (Lisbon, 1875), esp. pp. 323ff.; Paiva Couceiro, *Angola, estudo administrativo* (Lisbon, 1898); Joaquim Mousinho de Albuquerque, *op. cit.*; José Gomes dos Santos, *As nossas colónias* (Lisbon, 1875); "Estudos sôbre a administração civil das nossas possessões africanas, 1901" in Eduardo da Costa, *Colectânea de suas principais obras militares e coloniais*, (ed.) Bello de Almeida, 4 vols. (Lisbon, 1939); Aires de Ornelas, *A nossa administração colonial—o que é, o que deve ser* (Lisbon, 1903).

44. William C. Atkinson, *A History of Spain and Portugal* (Baltimore, 1960).

45. Herbert Feis, *Europe: The World's Banker, 1870–1914* (New Haven, 1930), p. 257, writes: "Great Britain by this agreement abandoned—at least seemed prepared to abandon—a small and defenseless ally. Sir Edward Grey probably conceived it as a means of promoting conciliation with Germany without sacrificing any essential British interest; in fact, the expected end would bring valuable territorial accessions to Great Britain. It might have appeared like weak and muddled sentiment to continue to support a colonial administration as inhumane and withering as the Portuguese. The recent conduct of that administration had aroused the indignation of the world. The treaty was never ratified. Sir Edward Grey insisted upon publication as a condition of ratification. Germany was afraid that publication would make its plans more difficult. Perhaps Sir Edward Grey had counted upon that fact. The outbreak of the war ended the discussions . . . . But still, financial failures, which might have cost a state of more primitive civilization its independence, were permitted Portugal because of its historic place in the European world."

46. See Paul von Lettow-Vorbeck, *East African Campaigns* (New York, 1957), pp. 223–63. Lettow-Vorbeck had an unusual ability to get along with the Africans. Of his original force in Tanganyika of 5,000, only 5 per cent were Europeans. Holland Thompson (ed.), *The World War* (New York, 1921), pp. 972–73; *Encyclopaedia Britannica*, 14th ed. (London, 1929), p. 769.

47. For special sources on the period 1910–32, see J. M. R. Norton de Matos, *A nação una* (Lisbon, 1953), and *Regulamento das circunscrições administrativas da província de Angola* (Lisbon, 1913), a codification of the system of civil administration; Rocha Saraiva, *Curso de administração colonial* (Lisbon, 1914); Jayme Pereira de Sampaio Forjaz de Serpa Pimentel, *O problema colonial português* (Lisbon, 1910), esp. pp. 25–44; Paiva Couceiro, *Angola: dois anos de*

governo (Lisbon, 1910); João Lopes de Moura, *Administração nas colónias portuguesas* (Lisbon, 1910), Francisco Pinto da Cunha Leal, *Calígula em Angola* (Lisbon, 1924), an attack on Norton de Matos; and Américo Chaves de Almeida, *O problema da África oriental portuguesa* (Lisbon, 1932), an attack on the administration of José Cabral in Mozambique.

48. Charles E. Nowell, *A History of Portugal* (Princeton, 1952), pp. 231–32.
49. See Irene S. van Dongen, "The Port of Luanda in the Economy of Angola," *Boletim da Sociedade de Geografia de Lisboa,* January–March, 1960, pp. 12–13.
50. James Duffy, *Portugal in Africa* (Baltimore, 1963), pp. 141–42. Historical rail construction and developments in Luanda's interior are examined by Irene S. van Dongen, *op. cit.,* pp. 9–12. For a history of the Benguela Railway, see "The Benguela Railway," in *Standard Bank Review,* September, 1966, monthly publication of the Standard Bank of West Africa, London. The Niassa Company, a British-French–chartered company, almost passed under control of German bankers in 1914, possibly a first step by the Germans toward the intent of the Secret Draft Treaty of 1914. Feis, *op. cit.,* p. 254.
51. See William A. Hance and Irene S. van Dongen, "Beira, Mozambique Gateway to Central Africa," *Annals of the Association of American Geographers,* XLVII (1957), 308–9.
52. Irene S. van Dongen, "Transportes Africanos Internacionais," *Jornal Português de Economia e Finanças,* VI, No. 63 (October 15, 1958), 12. William A. Hance and Irene S. van Dongen, *op. cit.,* pp. 307–35. For the continuing competition between Durban, Port Elizabeth, East London, and Lourenço Marques, see Manfred Shaffer, *The Competitive Position of the Port of Durban* (Evanston, 1965).
53. R. J. Hammond, "Economic Imperialism: Sidelights on a Stereotype," *The Journal of Economic History,* XXI (published for the Economic History Association by the Graduate School of Business Administration, New York University, 1961), 589.
54. *Ibid.,* p. 596.
55. Letter from Salisbury to Sir G. Petre, quoted in Warhurst, *op. cit.,* p. 68.
56. Marcelo Caetano, *Tradições, princípios e métodos da colonização portuguêsa* (Lisbon, 1951), pp. 275–76.
57. Quoted in Roland Oliver, *op. cit.,* p. 30.

IV

The Portuguese Racial Legacy

DAVID M. ABSHIRE

LIKE ALL other Europeans and the Muslims in Africa, the Portuguese generally held themselves to be a superior people uplifting inferior ones. Such ideas of superiority were used at times as moral justification for the slave trade and for the later system of contract labor in Portuguese Africa. Official government attitudes about race fluctuated often through the decades and centuries; in general, the Portuguese did not accept the African as they did the East Indian. After the abolition of slavery in the nineteenth century, many fortunes in Lisbon were built upon forced labor in Africa, with consciences put to rest by the idea that only in this way could Africans be turned into productive, civilized beings.

Despite their obvious record of discrimination, the Portuguese, as conquerors and settlers of overseas empires, were to a degree different from the British, Dutch, Belgians, and even the French and Spanish, in many of the attitudes and practices they adopted toward the lands and peoples they discovered and colonized. After citing numerous cases of color prejudice in different times and places in the Portuguese overseas possessions, Charles R. Boxer admits that such instances do not alter the fact that by and large the

> Portuguese did mix more with coloured races than did other Europeans, and they had, as a rule, less colour prejudice. . . . Though much of the history of Portuguese expansion is one of constant friction and fighting, yet the Portuguese often secured for themselves a friendly feeling which their European rivals regarded with puzzlement or with envy.[1]

While the Portuguese tendency toward nonracist attitudes is generally acknowledged, the degree of tolerance, the reasons for it, and the many vacillations in Portuguese race attitudes have been matters of some debate. Scholars have sought reasons for such tolerance in the history of the Portuguese people themselves. This chapter will examine that background and its possible influence on the fraternization of the Portuguese with other races. A later chapter will consider current racial conditions in Portuguese Africa, conflicting trends in discrimination and multiracialism, and, finally, the degree of participation of Africans in government and the modern sector of society.

These concerns are important for an understanding of colonial history in Africa, an understanding of present-day Portuguese policies, a comprehension of the legacy that might be left in Portuguese Africa if the present Portuguese rule were to be altered or ended, and a more complete knowledge of various racial experiences at a time when racial strife may well be the major issue facing the entire world.

Portuguese Beginnings

"Africa begins at the Pyrenees," goes an old saying. Dan Stanislawski adds that Europe ends at the Sierra Morena, and that on the great central tableland of the Iberian peninsula exists a blend of European and African cultures.[2] The Iberian peninsula was certainly the historical buffer zone and battleground between Europe and Africa. The inhabitants of Portugal included both European and African elements at the time of the Roman conquest, and the subsequent Moorish rule greatly increased the African contribution to the Iberian mixture.[3]

For more than seven centuries, the Portuguese who lived south of the Douro River were a subject people, less civilized than their later conquerors, the Moors. What memories there were of Roman imperial splendor had long since faded. The period of Moorish domination coincided with the age in which the genius of Islam flowered, with its philosophers, poets, mathematicians, and men of other arts and learning. Most of the Portuguese submitted to Moorish rule and adopted many cultural practices of the Moorish rulers, not only with regard to sanitation and habits of personal hygiene but also in their political, legal, and religious institutions. The Portuguese intermarried with the Moors and demonstrated an ability to coexist with Moorish cultural norms despite their own continued adherence to Catholicism.

The two great proselytizing religions, Islam and Christianity, both contain the unifying principle that religion is the exclusive, universal, and permanent distinction between one man and another. Whereas Islam urges tolerance, physical separation, and good relations among Christians, Muslims, and Jews, all of whom are considered people of the Book, Christianity does not. In practice, the Islamic Arabs converted societies that were often already highly developed and multiracial, using a variety of methods—threats, force, bribes, and persuasion. The Christians, on the other hand, converted a much less civilized society that was not so multiracial, using similar tactics. Islam, furthermore, does not admit of separation between church and state, whereas Christianity does. Islam does not exclude war, conquest, and the sensual life; Christianity does. Both religions recognize slavery.

The peculiar history of the Iberian peninsula, the development of its political and religious institutions, and its interior racial policy show a mixture of ideas taken from both religions. The ferocity of the Spanish Inquisition, the way to salvation through faith, not acts, quietism, Iberian mysticism, the extravagant religious justifications of cruelty, greed, injustice, vice, and sensuality and the high value put on bravery and physical courage perhaps find their effective origin in Islam. We must not forget that the Inquisition, the expulsion of the Moors, and the age of discovery all coincided. A religious fervor that combined the sword, torture, and the cross at home was the experience from which Portuguese traders and adventurers derived.

Under the Muslims, both Spanish and Portuguese Christians (the Mozarabs), had their own Christian liturgy. As individuals they frequently rose to high places in government while absorbing Eastern cultural and even religious influences. This period produced some liberality in Portuguese Catholicism that carried over long after the Moorish captivity and may well have contributed to their subsequent adaptations of Catholicism in tropical climates and to different peoples after the age of discovery.[4] The mild treatment subsequently accorded the Brazilian natives by the Portuguese, Nicolas Debbané maintains, was probably a carry-over of the treatment accorded the Portuguese by the Moors, who had treated the Portuguese as members of the household rather than as beasts of burden.[5]

The Moorish practice of polygamy influenced Portuguese marriage customs by increasing extramarital relationships and contributed to miscegenation during the later periods of Portuguese colonization in the tropics. Gilberto Freyre concludes that exposure to the Moors led to the idealization of the Moorish woman, the enchanting, seductive Mooress, "a charming type, brown-skinned, black-eyed, enveloped in sexual mysticism, roseate in hue, and always engaged in combing out her hair or bathing in rivers or in the waters of haunted fountains."[6]

This cultural exposure, again according to Freyre, later led Portuguese men to become attracted to Indians of the New World, to Africans, and, even more particularly, to mestiças. He cites the old but revealing Brazilian saying, "White woman for marriage, mulatto woman for loving, Negro woman for work."[7] Although Freyre's theories on the development of Portuguese racial attitudes are possibly more descriptive than scientific, they nevertheless have been aptly termed Luso-Tropicology.

Visiting Bahía in 1718, L. G. de la Bardenais noted that the Brazilian Portuguese preferred an African or mestiça girl to the loveliest white girl: "Frequently, I asked them how they had come by a taste so bizarre, that induced them to ignore their kind. I believe that as they are cared for and nurtured by slaves, they received these inclinations with the milk from their breasts."[8]

Another influence on Portuguese culture and history in the fifteenth and sixteenth centuries was that of the Jews, many of whose daughters were married by Portuguese nobles for their dowries.[9] Jews mingled with Portuguese Christian and Muslim society as stock-jobbers, court doctors, and tax collectors. This situation changed as a result of the crisis over the proposed marriage of Manuel I to the daughter of Isabella of Spain, which was conditioned upon Manuel's agreeing to expel from Portugal any Jews who refused baptism, as had been done in Spain. Manuel agreed and later achieved at least the technical although forced conversion of most Jews into "new Christians,"[10] thus accelerating Jewish assimilation. "It may be seen that, in the case of the Jews as in that of the Moors, there was great vertical mobility that ended in a mingling of strains in the marriages between those of diverse ethnic stocks."[11]

Before the Muslim conquest, Africans were brought by Arab slave-traders across the Sahara to the Iberian peninsula. By the middle of the thirteenth century, African slaves were being sold at fairs even in northern Portugal, but it was particularly in the south, the Algarve, that racial mixing was greatest.[12] It is

93

difficult to determine how extensively the Portuguese assimilated Africans at that time or in later periods, but, considering the earlier influx under the Arab slave-traders, the later influx after the Portuguese discoveries, and the absence of many pure-blooded Africans in Portugal today, much absorption must have taken place. In the mid-sixteenth century, slaves, mostly African, made up a tenth of the population of Lisbon and a majority in the Algarve.[13]

THE EARLY AFRICAN EXPERIENCE

Until the voyages along the west coast of Africa and to Brazil, the Portuguese, despite their acquaintance with Africans, had viewed the world as Christian with a Muslim fringe. The Portuguese, however, and Europeans in general, did not place the Moors and non-Muslim Africans on the same spiritual plane. They felt that the latter, from the religious point of view, should not be treated as infidels but as neutrals.[14] Prince Henry's chronicler, Gomes Eannes de Azurara, wrote with pity in 1488: "I hear the prayers of the innocent souls of those barbarous nations, whose forefathers from the beginning of the world have never seen the divine light."[15]

Portugal's initial political experience in Africa was with the Kongo Kingdom during the era of Manuel I. This unequal partnership with an African state constituted an approach to a backward society that was unparalleled in its seeking conversions to Christianity rather than conquest and domination. From the viewpoint of race relations, the dramatic climax of the experiment occurred when Manuel persuaded a reluctant pope to make Dom Henriques (the son of the Kongolese ruler Afonso I) the first black Catholic bishop.[16] Manuel's *regimento* of 1512, called "a blueprint for acculturation," attempted to codify the partnership of Portugal and the Kongo. The author of the edict noted prophetically, "Our plans can be carried out only with the best people."[17] It was one thing for Lisbon to decree, quite another for local Portuguese to execute.

The disparity between policy and execution was to become a recurring problem for the next five centuries. The emigrant Portuguese, technicians, missionaries, or traders, divided into two camps: those who supported the racially liberal Manuelian tradition and doctrine and those who supported the Portuguese traders of São Tomé, whose racist policies were based on economic motives and fear of social and sexual competition. The latter opposed the *regimento*, as well as Afonso's special trade privileges with Lisbon. They determined to prey on such trade, even if they had to commit robbery on the high seas. In large part, the inevitable greed and prejudice of some men on the spot, not only at São Tomé but in the Kongo Kingdom, led to the breakdown of Portuguese relations with the Manikongo and the death of the Manuelian dream of "collaboration and equality."[18]

In the ensuing centuries, however, the dream never fully died for some Portuguese. During the early colonization of São Tomé, miscegenation was a matter of official internal policy, and bachelors were provided with African women by the crown. A royal edict of 1515 declared slave mothers and *mestiço* children of such unions to be free. Another royal decree in 1528 reprimanded the governor for opposing the election of *mestiços* to the town council.[19] Yet the São Tomé racism had external, economic roots. As such, the antagonism between the São Tomé planters and traders and the supporters of the Manuelian tradition presaged the dualism reflected in the subsequent racial history of the Portuguese-speaking world.

The Portuguese were not alone in their greed for the wealth that came from the slave trade. Even before the collapse of the Kongo Kingdom, King Afonso himself became increasingly involved in the slave trade, which was an accepted institution among many African tribes: "The first slave caravan which belonged jointly to a priest of the capital and to a white trader is mentioned during the war of Afonso with Munza. Afonso brought 400 prisoners of war back from Ambundu, 320 of whom were shipped to Portugal."[20] A slave market was situated at Stanley Pool, near what is now Brazzaville. Afonso's worry about the kidnaping and sale of his own people in no way deterred him from dealing freely in slaves from neighboring tribes.

The next phase of Portuguese activity in West Africa took place south of the Bengo River in Angola. It has been appropriately noted that the Portuguese attitudes toward peoples south of the Bengo River formed a curious contrast with the efforts to convert and Europeanize the Kongolese by peaceful means.[21] The southern tribes were politically, although not necessarily economically, less advanced. Then, too, the Portuguese were disillusioned by the failure of their policies in the Kongo Kingdom after a promising start. The new, hardened attitude resulted from the experiences of a pioneer Jesuit missionary in Angola, Father Gouveia, who, in 1563, advocated "what one of his colleagues in Brazil termed 'preaching with the sword and the rod of iron.' "[22] Gouveia was influenced by his harsh years of captivity by the king of Ndongo and the Ngola's outright rejection of Christianity. Whereas Portuguese commercial interests rejected the idea of conquering and holding tribes in subjection, Gouveia "advocated conquest and political domination, not for commercial reasons, but in order to impose Christian teachings."[23]

The death of Viceroy Francisco de Almeida in 1510, the sacking of Sepulveda in 1554 by the Hottentots, and other such events left deep impressions of savagery, brutality, and bestiality. Randles asserts that as early as the sixteenth century these attitudes and reactions led to the formation of the African stereotype. Perhaps as an example of this, the famous poet Camões later dubbed Africans "the vicious and avaricious savages." Although the Portuguese were greatly concerned about the spiritual welfare of the Africans, they were generally not even classified as "noble savages," the phrase sometimes used to refer to Indians in the Americas.[24]

The Portuguese attitudes related primarily, however, to the unconquered Bantu and Hottentot tribesmen, who were often at war with the Portuguese, and their allied tribes. Portuguese attitudes toward Africans who were integrated into their settlements were not quite the same, and in this respect the Portuguese differed from the later Dutch and British colonizers. A *mestiço*, Luís Lopes de Sequeira, led the Portuguese troops in the victory at Mbwila in 1665. And, in 1684, Lisbon decreed that color should not be a bar to military promotions and appointments in the colony's garrisons and militia. By 1713, the Luanda municipal council noted that the town's militia regiment had racial equality.[25]

In studying racial attitudes in settlements like Luanda, one must avoid lumping together the rulers in Lisbon, the ruling class in the settlement, and the ordinary Portuguese. In its stated policy on race relations, the government in Lisbon generally differed from local practices. In the mid-seventeenth century, John IV intervened in the harsh actions of the governor of Angola and warned him to treat Africans more leniently.[26] The writings of a Portuguese conquistador, António de Oliveira Cadornega, give some clues to policy on the spot. Fear and obedience were necessary to keep the heathen Bantu in their place, Cadornega maintained. He warned against Portuguese who failed to conduct themselves in a lordly manner around the Africans and who did not treat them as servants and slaves. There were, of course, many Portuguese who did not do so and who "went native" as well; otherwise Cadornega would not have so warned. Not only in the earlier period of the Kongo Kingdom but also later in the colonies of Angola and Mozambique, many lower-class Portuguese married Africans and adopted tribal ways.

This retrogression and intermingling, this abandonment of the concept of European superiority, was disapproved of by many members of the ruling class in the colonies, just as Cadornega himself condemned it. But even he, a noted separatist on race, describes a situation markedly unlike the British, Belgian, French, and Dutch colonizing environments:

> The soldiers in the garrison and other European individuals father many black children of the black ladies for want of white ladies with the result that there are many mulattoes and coloureds (*pardos*). The sons of these unions make great soldiers, chiefly in the wars in the backlands against the heathen inhabitants. They can endure severe hardships and very short commons, and go without shoes. Many of them become great men. When this conquest began, all the most important conquerors, with the exception of a few who brought their families, accommodated themselves with mulattas, daughters of respectable settlers and conquerors by their female slaves or free concubines.[27]

Unlike the Manuelian period of attempted partnership, the seventeenth century was a period in which the governing class in Angola was involved in wars and conquests, as described in an earlier chapter. Assimilation and miscegenation continued in the settlement areas, and African and Portuguese troops fought together against alien tribes.

Because of the limited number of Portuguese in Angola, assimilation took place only on a small scale. Since the Portuguese were settled along the coastal areas of Angola, "a powerful merchant class, possessor of a large number of slaves and free African customers" emerged, and "the formation of a detribalized class of Africans linked to the Portuguese, and the appearance of a numerous class of *mestiços*" took place.[28] Significantly, these Africans and *mestiços*, unlike most of the tribes, supported the Portuguese against the Dutch when the latter attacked Angola and seized Luanda in 1641. The Angolan situation, however, differed markedly from the situations in Mozambique, Portuguese India, and Brazil.

MOZAMBIQUE AND INDIA

King Manuel's East African policy had struck the same high note as had his dealing with the Kongo Kingdom. He instructed his viceroy, Francisco de Almeida, to do no harm to the Africans in the offensive against the infidels.

As noted elsewhere, Portuguese East African settlements, especially in the Zambezi valley, were characterized by *prazos*, or large estates. Over the centuries, however, the basic trend of Zambezi valley society, in contrast to the Portuguese municipalities such as Luanda and Mozambique Island, was regressive. Whether European or *mestiço*, the original *prazo* holders became like tribal chiefs and controlled vast areas. By the late seventeenth century, the crown insisted that land titles pass to the eldest daughter and be retained only upon marriage to a white man born in Portugal. But state attempts to produce a European society were of little avail, and interracial mixing occurred. As a consequence of the almost total absence of white women, the number of *mestiços* increased, but "their descendants reverted to barbarism, and became submerged in the indigenous population. Miscegenation made it impossible to maintain the standards of colonization."[29]

Mozambique, administratively under the viceroy of India, was isolated further from Lisbon's rule and influence than was West Africa. In Asia, the Portuguese Government encouraged interracial marriage, whereas in Angola and Mozambique, miscegenation was not originally promoted as state policy. In India, the mixed-marriage policy initiated by Afonso de Albuquerque showed his personal preference for selected Indian women as compared with the "black women" of Malabar.[30] The over-all policy was, nevertheless, "that religion and not colour should be the criterion for Portuguese citizenship, and that all Asian converts to Christianity would be treated as the equals of their Portuguese co-religionists." But laws passed to this effect in 1562 and 1572 were not fully implemented for two centuries. By a decree of April 2, 1761, Portugal's dictator, Pombal, informed the viceroy of India and the governor-general of Mozambique that converted Asian subjects must have the same legal and social standing as whites born in Portugal: "His Majesty does not distinguish between his vassals by their color but by their merits."[31]

The Amerindians of Brazil were given equally favourable treatment, but the Africans in Portuguese Africa were not accorded the same status, although persons of African descent might become clergymen and be admitted to the University of Coimbra. During the sixteenth and seventeenth centuries in São Tomé, the Cape Verde Islands, and Angola, seminaries for African clergy were established, institutions that were lacking in Mozambique.[32]

THE SLAVE TRADE

Slavery is said by some to have its origins in war. Originally, conquered people were eaten or killed, and, later, when cannibalism was rejected, taken as slaves or killed. The doctrines of natural inferiority, rights of the conqueror, spiritual freedom of slaves, and so on were justifications of existing institutions and conditions. There were some highly developed societies of the ancient world that were not based on slavery, but most were. Some anthropologists believe that slavery was a step forward in civilization in that it was "better" than killing and cannibalism and created a labor base for development. In any case, slavery in Africa was a characteristic of inter-African tribal relations for centuries before the age of discovery.

Early Christianity stressed that free men could be slaves to sin and slaves could be spiritually free. The physical condition of servitude became secondary to the condition of the spirit. Such attitudes continued throughout medieval Europe and into the Renaissance: "To many deeply religious Portuguese, Spaniards or Britishers, the slave trade—with its more hideous side shrouded by lack of knowledge of real conditions—was a way to take the prisoners of African tribes, transport them to the New World, bring them up under fatherly discipline which needs to be stern, but far more importantly, offers them the light of eternal salvation." Even the humanists, philosophers, and jurists of the Renaissance did not challenge this institution, and "it was as if the learned volumes on law and statecraft had been produced in a different world from that which contained Negro captives awaiting shipment at Elmina Castle, the disease and sickening stench of the slave ships, and the regimented labor of colonial plantations."[33]

Professor Frank Tannenbaum, on the other hand, stresses that slaves were always baptized by the Portuguese before the dreaded sea journey to Brazil, and once there they were instructed in Christian doctrine: "As a Catholic, the slave was married in the church, and the bans were regularly published."[34]

Though there might be some objections of conscience voiced, the slave trade, as Basil Davidson writes,

> carried all before it. As elsewhere in the world, those who dealt in slaves could make their fortunes. . . . If 'everyone in Liverpool' was investing in the trade, so was 'everyone in the Congo.' There grew up along the coast a tightly organized and self-defending system of monopoly. It was interested in importing European firearms, strong drink, textiles, and metal goods, and in buying from the peoples of the interior as many captives as were required in payment.[35]

The captors of the slaves were not permitted to sell them directly to the European slave-traders but were required to deal with brokers appointed by the colonial government. The brokers were in turn required to observe the implementation of the government regulations, the most important of which were those requiring the sale to European markets of captives only taken in war or purchased from outside the Congo. Davidson points out, this pattern of trade and contact

> left the coastal peoples inextricably enmeshed in a system of spoliation which could not possibly make way to new techniques from Europe. Moreover, it had an additional disadvantage from the standpoint of African development. It isolated the peoples of the interior from any contact with Europe except

through the sale of captives. The chiefs of the coastal peoples throve and defended their power by purchasing European firearms; those in their rear, deprived of any direct link with Europeans, were reduced to impotence or involvement in the trade themselves. Increasingly, they chose or were driven to involvement.[36]

The Portuguese themselves followed the same system; small trading expeditions were dispatched into the interior, consisting of servants—sometimes free men and sometimes slaves—and *mestiço* or African *pombeiros* who might be gone for weeks, months, or years, often bringing or sending back 400, 500, or 600 slaves.

As in the Kongo Kingdom and elsewhere in Africa, the slave trade in Angola was based upon the sale of prisoners of war. There was extensive cooperation between the Portuguese and the Kongolese chiefs in the sale of slaves, and the African rulers failed to resist the tempting trade.[37] From the sixteenth century almost to the twentieth, the slave trade grew in volume and intensity and was indeed "the one great continuing event in Central African history." The trade bred wars—Europeans against Africans, and Africans against Africans—since the slave market was fed largely by new prisoners of war. "Although raids and wars cannot always be attributed to the desire to capture slaves," Vansina maintains, "the perennial raids of the Lunda on the Sala Mpasu, of the Yaka and the Imbangala on the populations of the Kwango" were to be explained "mainly as wars for slaves."[38]

Domingos de Abreu e Brito late in the sixteenth century estimated, as a result of his general investigations of Angola on behalf of the crown, that within two decades alone, over 50,000 slaves were sent to Brazil.[39] Perhaps as many as 1 million slaves were exported from Angola between 1580 and 1680. In the middle of the sixteenth century, the Spanish priest Las Casas challenged the institution of slavery.[40] Although slavery was gradually abolished in Europe as Pombal abolished it in Portugal, the African trade continued.

Abolition in Europe was a gradual process. The British were among the first to abolish colonial slavery. Their doing so in the West Indies in 1833 caused economic difficulty, as cheaper production of sugar by the slave economies of Brazil and Cuba undercut the British sugar market. The British Government thus developed an economic interest in ending slavery in other countries. They had a further strategic and economic motive for severing the close trade link between Angola and Brazil. When Brazil declared its independence from Portugal in 1822 and sought British recognition, British Foreign Minister George Canning made such recognition conditional upon a Brazilian agreement, eventually ratified in 1827, to make it illegal for Brazilians to engage in the slave trade. Such illegality, if it did anything, stimulated demand, and as Tavares Bastos, the Brazilian abolitionist propagandist, estimated, the trade increased from a low of 14,000 slaves in 1842 to a high of 58,000 by 1847.[41] The human cargo was carried by ships of many countries, including Brazil, Portugal, Spain, and the United States. As British efforts at interception increased, U.S. vessels derived special advantages through their immunity from British attacks and gained an increasing share of the trade.

Until Brazil itself moved toward abolition of slavery, the traffic never ended. In the early part of the nineteenth century, Brazilians were convinced that, in an agrarian economy, sudden abolition of slavery would have catastrophic consequences. As moral justification, they pointed to miscegenation and to the fact that elite Africans voluntarily came to Brazil to be educated and that few Africans—even slaves—desired to return to Africa. Then, too, the Portuguese argued, something was being done for the spiritual destiny of the Africans. On the most practical level, Brazilians noted that the British antislave crusade was a recent development. In the first years of the century, Liverpool had been crowded with more than 1,000 slave-trading ships, and even British priests and diplomats used slaves, as Cunha Matos fondly pointed out in 1827.[42] He could have added that none of the great fortunes of Lisbon came from the slave trade (something not true in the later days of forced labor) but that the profit from the trade had helped build the fortunes of Liverpool. It also built the smaller fortunes of Bahía and Recife and supplemented the salary of the governor-general of Angola.

There were actually three slave systems in the Western Hemisphere, argues Tannenbaum. On one extreme were the British, Americans, Dutch, and Danish, and on the other were the Spanish and Portuguese, with the French somewhere in the middle. The characteristics of the first extreme involve no effective slave tradition, no slave law, and virtually no concern about Africans in relation to religious institutions. The middle group, the French, lacked a slave tradition and law, although it possessed the same religious principles as the Iberians. As for the Spanish and the Portuguese, "the spiritual personality of the slave transcended his slave status." Tannenbaum concludes: "If one were forced to arrange these systems of slavery in order of severity, the Dutch would seem to stand as the hardest, the Portuguese as the mildest, and the French in between, as having elements of both."[43]

The views of Debbané, Freyre, Tannenbaum, and Pierson have been challenged most recently by David Brion Davis, following Boxer's lead, as exaggerating national and cultural differences and overemphasizing mild servitude and racial harmony.[44] Wherever slavery existed, there were masters who were stern with their servants and free in the use of the *palmatória*, the dreaded wooden hand-paddle. In describing Portuguese mildness, Freyre drew exclusively on evidence from northeastern Brazil in his *Casa Grande e Senzala*. Because he perhaps overstressed the slavery in the domestic household rather than that in the fields, he may have put too much emphasis on the favorable aspects of slavery in Brazil as compared to slavery in North America.

Nevertheless, consequences weigh heavily in the debate. The Portuguese and Spanish system favored manumission, or freeing of slaves, while the British West Indian and U.S. system generally opposed it. The former system promoted Christianization while the British West Indies system (although not that of the United States) opposed it. Abolition came in Brazil comparatively peacefully, in the United States violently; the Latins were far quicker to accept former slaves into their society.

The great Portuguese eighteenth-century colonial governor-general, Sousa Coutinho, foresaw the economic and other dangers of a society based upon the slave trade. But he recognized that the obstacles to his constant efforts to attract industry and European colonization were too great to overcome. Nevertheless, in 1764, he prohibited slavery in Angola. It was reinstated by his successors only to be attacked again by another governor in 1791. In 1807, still another governor, António de Saldanha, proposed total abolition to the home government. The next initiative was therefore Lisbon's. But when Sá da Bandeira, as prime minister, issued a decree in 1836 abolishing the slave traffic throughout the Portuguese possessions, it was found impossible to enforce the decree initially. In fact, the governor of Mozambique immediately flouted it.

ATTITUDES IN PORTUGUESE AFRICA AND BRAZIL COMPARED

Although Sá da Bandeira abolished slavery in Portuguese Africa long before similar steps were taken in Brazil, in the former (excluding the islands), there was never as much miscegenation as in Brazil. In modern-day Angola, the Europeans make up about 4 per cent of the population, mestiços somewhat over 1 per cent, and Africans 95 per cent. In contrast, over one-fourth of Brazil's population is mestiço.[45] The explanations are several. Fewer whites settled in Angola. There were fewer plantations where race-mixing presumably is more common. The Portuguese penetration of the interior of Angola was slower than penetration in Brazil. Brazil was an empty land, sparsely populated by Indians, in which both the Portuguese masters and the African slaves were interlopers. Economic and cultural assimilation of many races in Brazil, and in the Portuguese islands where tribal ties were broken, was not hindered as it was in Angola, where the African tribal structures dominated society. In fact, the influence of traditional society was so great that, at times, the Portuguese were assimilated into African culture. This occurred also in Mozambique.[46]

In the areas where larger numbers of Europeans settled, however, the story is entirely different. The seventeenth, eighteenth, and nineteenth centuries were periods of an increasingly multiracial society in the Portuguese-African islands, in the European coastal settlements, and in a few inland-settlement areas of Angola and Mozambique. Here the tribal society was not strong. Multiracialism and miscegenation were common, as attested by George Tams's description of the grand ball of the governor of Luanda, where a beautiful, wealthy, former slave, turned slave-dealer, was the belle of the ball,[47] and Captain Owen's account, in 1825, of the mixed ball at Government House on Mozambique Island.[48] The golden era in race relations, after the time of King Manuel, was reflected in the Constitutional Charter of 1826, which stressed racial equality. As Sá da Bandeira wrote in 1873: "The Portuguese inhabitants of the provinces of Africa, of Asia, and of Oceania, without distinction of race, colour, or religion, have rights equal to those enjoyed by the Portuguese of Europe."[49]

As to Portuguese behavior on the nineteenth-century frontiers of the Angolan colony, the account of Livingstone is of considerable interest. In the spring of 1854, while en route to Luanda, he arrived at Cassange, "the farthest inland station of the Portuguese in western Africa."[50] Cassange was a village of thirty or forty traders' houses surrounded by manioc and maize plantations, under the command of a Captain António Rodrigues Neves. A comparatively high standard of civilization had been maintained. All the traders were officers in the militia. In addition, there were some slaves and some free Negroes, both of which, on Easter Sunday, mixed without social restrictions with the merchants. Livingstone found no Portuguese women, and most of the traders would stay at the outpost for only a few years: "It is common for them to have families by native women," recorded the missionary doctor. "It was particularly gratifying to me, who had been familiar with the stupid prejudice against color, entertained only by those who are themselves becoming tawny, to view the liberality with which people of color were treated by the Portuguese." To Livingstone, this was in sharp contrast to South Africa. "Instances, so common in the South, in which half-caste children are abandoned, are here extremely rare. They are acknowledged at table, and provided for by their fathers as if European." Colored clerks mixed socially with European employers. "The civil manners of superiors to inferiors is probably the result of the position they occupy—a few whites among thousands of blacks; but nowhere else in Africa is there so much good-will between European and natives as here."[51]

Although frontier practices, such as "going native," were hardly affected, there was a strong reaction against tolerance toward the end of the nineteenth century. According to Richard J. Hammond, the imperialist revival then taking place in Portugal "was marked by a rejection, at least on paper, of what had come to be regarded as dangerous sentimentality tending to race-suicide."[52] There developed in this reactionary period of the 1890's the seed of the *indigenato*, or policy of dual citizenship. That policy has been described by some writers as smacking of both racial and economic discrimination against the backward masses of Portuguese Africa—although such discrimination was practiced by a multiracial, not an all-white, elite. The Portuguese colonial leaders of the 1890's may have been efficient administrators, but they were not liberal in race relations. Most of the leaders who sought greater autonomy for the colonies from Lisbon—António Enes, Mousinho de Albuquerque, Henrique de Paiva Couceiro, and Eduardo da Costa—were opposed to miscegenation.

In the years following the 1890's, racist tendencies dominated government actions and leaders. A typical racial purist was General Norton de Matos, a prominent colonialist, administrator, and cabinet minister in the period after World War I and a candidate for the presidency against the Carmona-Salazar ticket in 1948 (he later withdrew under pressure). Separatist tendencies, so strong in Norton de Matos earlier in this century, have appeared in recent years, as illustrated by the exclusion of Africans, even as laborers, in the Cela colonization scheme in Angola.

Portuguese racial purists like Norton de Matos and Vicente Ferreira strongly objected to the sociological writings of Gilberto Freyre that stressed details of Portuguese miscegenation. Such influences lasted until they were attacked by the Salazar government through laws and propaganda that exaggeratedly claimed that all Portuguese had always been racially tolerant, free of ambiguities, fluctuations, and blemishes.[53]

Freyre points out that miscegenation does not rule out an attitude of superiority.

Moreover, though miscegenation may have demonstrated a lack of skin-color prejudice, it did not always promote race harmony. It has been argued that, in Mozambique, not until the arrival of European wives after the turn of the century did the African men begin to lose some of their hostility toward Portuguese who were involved in miscegenation.[54] As for Angola, Francisco Tenreiro has observed that "Cities, like Luanda and Benguela, centers that attracted the peoples of the interior . . . from the beginning allowed human relationships between Blacks and Whites, unprecedented in African history." These relationships, he argued, "allowed, through miscegenation, the upward movement of the more capable people without regard to the color of their skins." It is true that *mestiços* predominated in these cities. Luanda was, in fact, as a Brazilian visitor called it more than fifty years ago, a *"mestiço* city."[55]

Much of the miscegenation in Portuguese Africa has been the product of necessity, of the situation of the male European living without women of his own kind in the tropics, with its climate and diseases that white women would not endure. In the Dutch Cape Colony, as a result of early settlements, a colored or racially mixed population of Europeans, slaves, and Hottentots was also produced even though the Cape Colony was certainly not in the tropics. But, almost immediately, there came an attempt to sharpen the color line and develop a caste system, a reaction quite untypical of Portuguese race attitudes in general.[56] The French racial attitude was perhaps the most like the Portuguese. On the other hand, the *mestiços* in Portuguese Africa are not viewed by European settlers and by Africans with the same contempt that exists in much of French West Africa.[57] Furthermore, French assimilation policy was implemented in only one of France's African colonies, Senegal, and even there it was implemented only in the four communes.[58]

In sum, the Portuguese racial legacy in Africa is an anomaly. The Portuguese slave trade and, following it, policies of forced labor have justified African resentment. So long as the Portuguese continue their African rule, such resentment will not disappear by simply noting that other Europeans, Arabs, and Africans themselves were accomplices in the trade. At the same time, the Portuguese have shown a tolerance, an ability to coexist with Africans, and a willingness to accept them as other Europeans seldom did. "The strong point of the Portuguese," wrote Archibald Lyall after his 1936 trip to Guinea, "is their remarkable capacity for getting on with the natives." The gentle nature of the Portuguese, he added, "seems subtly attuned to [that] of the Negroes." He noted that, otherwise, the Portuguese would not have been able to hold Portuguese Guinea with only 264 local African volunteers commanded by six white officers and eleven NCO's.[59]

Tendencies toward coexistence may reflect their own very old racial mixtures, not wholly European. They also reflect Portuguese characteristics in Africa: a willingness to accept and compromise, sometimes to the point of laxity, characteristics fought by Enes and Norton de Matos in their desire for greater economic development and in their push toward a racial policy in the form of *indigenato*.

An analysis of what this racial legacy—a strange mixture of slave-trading and nonracism—means for Portuguese Africa today and in the future is contained in Chapter X.

NOTES

1. Charles R. Boxer, "The Colour Question in the Portuguese Empire, 1415–1825," *Proceedings of the British Academy 1961* (London, 1962), p. 137.
2. Dan Stanislawski, *The Individuality of Portugal* (Austin, 1959), p. 9.
3. It is likely, however, that the brown-skinned, curly-haired type was more characteristic, and cultural forms were more Mediterranean than Nordic, more African than European. Gilberto Freyre, *The Masters and the Slaves: A Study in the Development of Brazilian Civilization*, (trans.) Samuel Putnam (New York, 1964), p. 179.
4. *Ibid.*, p. 226.
5. Nicolas J. Debbané, "L'Influence Arabe dans la Formation Historique, la Littérature et la Civilisation du Peuple Brésilien," Cairo, 1911, cited in *Ibid.*, p. 202.
6. Freyre, *Masters and Slaves*, p. 19.
7. *Ibid.*, p. 20.
8. José Honório Rodrigues, *Brazil and Africa*, (trans.) R. A. Mazzara and Sam Hileman (Berkeley, 1965), pp. 55–56.
9. In fact, Freyre goes so far as to say that "Portuguese imperialism and imperialistic expansion were based on Jewish prosperity," *op. cit.*, p. 211.
10. H. V. Livermore, *A New History of Portugal* (Cambridge, 1966), pp. 125–27.
11. Freyre, *op. cit.*, p. 210.
12. For an excellent discussion of the Portuguese contact with slave-trading before 1500, see Anthony Luttrell, "Slavery and Slaving in the Portuguese Atlantic," in *The Transatlantic Slave Trade from West Africa* (Edinburgh, 1965), pp. 61–80.
13. J. Lúcio de Azevedo, *Épocas de Portugal económico* (Lisbon, 1929), pp. 75–76. By the middle of the sixteenth century, Lisbon had more slaves than free men and the Algarve was almost entirely populated by African slaves. H. Morse Stephens, *Portugal* (New York, 1891), p. 182.
14. W. G. L. Randles, *L'Image du Sud-Est Africain dans les littérature européenne au XVIe siecle* (Lisbon, 1959), pp. 115–16.
15. Gomes Eannes de Azurara, *Crónica do descobrimento e conquista da Guiné* (Paris, 1841), p. 9; pp. 4–5.
16. Charles R. Boxer, *Race Relations in the Portuguese Colonial Empire, 1415–1825* (Oxford, 1963), p. 19.
17. Jan M. Vansina, *Kingdoms of the Savanna* (Madison, 1966), pp. 48–57.
18. *Ibid.*, pp. 50–52; A. da Silva Rego, *Portuguese Colonization in the Sixteenth Century: A Study of the Royal Ordinances (Regimentos)* (Johannesburg, 1959), pp. 42–50.
19. Boxer, "The Colour Question in the Portuguese Empire, 1415–1825," pp. 116–17.
20 Vansina, *op. cit.*, p. 52.
21. Boxer, *Race Relations in the Portuguese Colonial Empire*, p. 22.
22. *Ibid.*, p. 22. Comments Silva Rego on the *regimento* of 1520 (*op. cit.*, pp. 52–53): "The real importance of such a document lies, however, in the fact that during King Emmanuel's reign, Portuguese native policy was entirely based on friendly and commercial relations with everybody. . . . Further

experience convinced them that the happy events of the Congo could not be repeated elsewhere. This change, however, in Portuguese native policy took place in John III's time."

23. David Birmingham, *The Portuguese Conquest of Angola* (Oxford, 1965), pp. 10–11.

24. Rodrigues, *op. cit.*, pp. 5–6.

25. António de Oliveira Cadornega (ed.), *História geral das guerras angolanas*, 3 vols. (Lisbon, 1940–42), III, 30, cited in Boxer, *Race Relations in the Portuguese Colonial Empire*, pp. 31–33.

26. *Ibid.*, p. 26.

27. *Ibid.*, pp. 30–31.

28. Jofre A. Nogueira, "Aspectos fundamentais da miscigenação étnica na província de Angola" in *III Colóquio Internacional de Estudos Luso-Brasileiros* (Lisbon, 1959), p. 188.

29. Eric Axelson, *Portuguese in South-East Africa 1600–1700* (Johannesburg, 1964), p. 193.

30. Boxer, *Race Relations in the Portuguese Colonial Empire*, pp. 64–65.

31. *Ibid.*, pp. 69–74. Pombal also abolished slavery in Portugal.

32. Boxer, "The Colour Question in the Portuguese Empire," p. 122.

33. David Brion Davis, *The Problem of Slavery in Western Culture* (Ithaca, 1966). This statement can be misleading. A Spanish priest, Bartolomé de las Casas (1474–1566), later known as the "apostle of the Indians," made the famous attack on colonial abuses against the Amerindians. He first proposed to relieve these abuses through Negro slavery but later repented the concept. In his debate with Ginés de Sepúlveda, he attacked the enslavement of all aboriginal people. See L. Hanke, *Bartolomé de las Casas* (Philadelphia, 1952).

34. Frank Tannenbaum, *Slave and Citizen: The Negro in the Americas* (New York, 1947), p. 64.

35. Basil Davidson, *The African Slave Trade: Precolonial History, 1450–1850* (Boston, 1961), p. 153.

36. *Ibid.*, p. 154.

37. *Ibid.*, p. 156.

38. Vansina, *op. cit.*, pp. 247–48.

39. Quoted in A. Albuquerque Felner, *Um inquérito na vida administrativa e económica de Angola e do Brasil em fins do século XVI (1591)* (Coimbra, 1931).

40. See Hanke, *op. cit.*; Davis, *op. cit.*, pp. 169–73.

41. A. C. Tavares Bastos, *Cartas do solitário*, 3rd ed. (São Paulo, 1938), p. 161.

42. Rodrigues, *op. cit.*, pp. 126–28.

43. Tannenbaum, *op. cit.*, p. 65. In support of Tannenbaum, see Stanley M. Elkins, *Slavery: A Problem in American Institutional and Intellectual Life* (Chicago, 1959), pp. 27–80.

44. Davis, *op. cit.*, pp. 223–61.

45. Oscar Soares Barata, "Aspectos das condições demográficas de Angola" in *Angola* (Curso de Extensão Universitária, Lisbon, 1964), p. 153.

46. I. R. Sinai, *The Challenge of Modernization* (New York, 1964), p. 101, is perhaps a bit too harsh on tribal society, which had its virtues, but makes a point that, "the tribal society was probably the most unsuccessful, the most stagnant form of society that mankind has ever known. African traditional history records migrations, battles, and conquests, but it never tells of any mental transformations or changes in social structure."

47. George Tams, *Visita às possessões portuguesas na costa occidental d'Africa* (Oporto, 1850), I, 225–26, cited in Richard J. Hammond, "Race Attitudes and Policies in Portuguese Africa in the Nineteenth and Twentieth Centuries," *Race*, IX, No. 2 (October, 1967), 206–7.

48. Boxer, *Race Relations in the Portuguese Colonial Empire*, pp. 126–27.

49. Sá da Bandeira, *O trabalho rural africano e a administração colonial* (Lisbon, 1873), pp. 13–14; cited in Hammond, *op. cit.*, p. 207.

50. David Livingstone, *Missionary Travels and Researches in South Africa* (New York, 1858), p. 396.

51. *Ibid.*, pp. 399–400. In Livingstone's later travels in Mozambique, he became increasingly concerned about the slave trade. In exploring the Rovuma River, he found great evidence of the trade and involvement of Portuguese officials. Of significance also is Livingstone's comment about his visit to Luanda: "The Portuguese home government has not generally received the credit for sincerity in suppressing the slave trade which I conceive to be its due" (pp. 429–30).

52. Hammond, *op. cit.*, p. 207.

53. It is significant that one of Norton de Matos' Portuguese critics attacked him as follows: "he detested such liaisons between whites and blacks or *mestiço* women, forgetting that men who come to these parts do not make vows of chastity. Let [him] not forget our ethnic origins and the influence of some centuries of Arab rule in the Peninsula, and seek to change the characteristics of our race in its most fundamental aspect, making us like unto the Anglo-Saxons." Júlio Ferreira Pinto, *Angola: notas e comentários dum colono* (Lisbon, 1926), pp. 368–69, quoted in *ibid.*

54. Conversations with José de Almada, Lisbon and Sintra, April, 1967.

55. Francisco Tenreiro, "Angola: problemas de geografia humana," *Angola* (Curso de Extensão Universitária, Lisbon, 1964), p. 53.

56. John A. Barnes, "Race Relations in the Development of Southern Africa," in Andrew W. Lind, *Race Relations in World Perspective* (Honolulu, 1955), pp. 167–85. Also see John H. Wellington, *Southern Africa*, II, Ch. 16, "The Asian and Coloured Populations" (Cambridge, 1955), 232–36. One famous mixed marriage was that of the Dutch surgeon Van Meerhoff to a Hottentot interpretess. Marriages between colonists and Christianized slaves were not permitted after 1685, and the so-called Bastards (European-Hottentot) were accepted neither into Dutch society nor into the European part of the Dutch church.

57. For the attitude in French West Africa, see Georges Balandier, in Lind, *op. cit.*, p. 156.

58. Michael Crowder, *Senegal: A Study of French Assimilation Policy* (London, 1967), pp. 1–9.

59. Archibald Lyall, *Black and White Make Brown* (London, 1938), p. 190.

V

African Peoples

MICHAEL A. SAMUELS and NORMAN A. BAILEY

MUCH IN THE way that Portugal's contact with non-Europeans provided the historical background for her relations with Africa, so both strife and accommodation have been prominent among the various African peoples who presently inhabit Portuguese Africa. Recent historical investigation has revealed a continental history of migrations and consolidation and wars and alliances as a result of the inhospitality of nature and the interaction of human ambitions. The present chapter will sketch this heritage as it relates to the inhabitants of Portuguese Africa. With few exceptions, these peoples are among the least well studied in Africa.

Any discussion of African peoples must dwell on the tribal groupings into which they are divided. Chapter II provided a brief discussion of the three major ways of classifying African peoples—racially, culturally, and linguistically. All these means are part of the process that has been applied to discover exactly what people mean when they refer to "tribe." Unfortunately, no foolproof system has been devised to simplify tribal classification. As Bohannan has observed, "some African tribes are what have been described as village states; others are empires of several million people spread over hundreds of thousands of square miles. Some African tribes form language groups; still others are congeries of indefinite or indiscriminate groups that have been classified together under a term, usually pejorative, by their neighbors."[1]

In many areas of Africa, common interest and identification extend for only a short distance, frequently encompassing only a few villages. As communications have improved, the range of contacts has expanded. With this expansion has come an identification with a larger community. More often than not, the most noticeable characteristic of such a community has been the linguistic similarity of its members. Thus, for descriptive purposes in this chapter, ethnic distinctions have been based on language and, occasionally, on similarities in customs or other factors.[2] But language may mislead. It should be noted that the most serious disputes and deeply rooted antagonisms frequently occur within a language group.

THE CAPE VERDE ISLANDS

The first people arrived on the island of Santiago after it was divided in 1462 into two captaincies under the jurisdiction of António de Noli and Diogo Afonso. Fogo, Boa Vista, and Maio were the next islands to be inhabited. The growth of the population by the sixteenth century encouraged some people to move to São Nicolau and Santo Antão. The first people to go to Brava did so because of volcanic eruptions on Fogo in the seventeenth century. Other islands were populated later.[3]

The first Europeans came from the Algarve and Minho districts of Portugal or were Jews who left Europe because they found themselves a target of growing persecution there. Later came immigrants from the island of Madeira. African slaves, from many of the tribes of what is presently Portuguese Guinea and nearby lands, were brought in to work the land.[4]

At the present time, persons of mixed Portuguese and African origin account for at least 60 per cent of the population on all islands except Santiago, where they are outnumbered by Africans. Europeans are only a small minority on all the islands and represent at most only 2 per cent of the population.[5]

The miscegenation and cultural assimilation processes were less complete on Santiago than on the rest of the islands. As a result, vestiges of African culture are more noticeable there than elsewhere.[6] However, social democratization took place after the abolition of primogeniture in 1863 allowed the fragmentation of large estates. The estates were subsequently sold to people of other classes who had established themselves in commerce and were able to raise their social position to that of the latifundia owners.

On the other islands, small landowners had no way of acquiring large numbers of slaves nor was there a way to resupply slaves. As a consequence, far from their tribes of origin, the Africans lost their cohesion as social and cultural groups and many of their customs, including habits of food and dress.[7] The African cultural elements in the islands as a whole have lost many of their original characteristics under the influence of Catholicism and Western civilization. There remain, however, some clear reflections of African origins; other customs exist in which the two cultures are so completely intermixed that it is very difficult, if not impossible, to tell whether the African or the European influence is greater.[8]

For example, the mortar and pestle, introduced by Africans from the Guinea coast, is still commonly used. The basis of the Cape Verdian's diet is not bread but corn, a result of the African cultural heritage. The African game of *ouri* is played quite frequently. The women's habit of carrying children on their backs and their use of headscarves are other African elements found throughout Cape Verde. There is also a tendency toward polygamy among the lower classes. Weddings are rare and large numbers of children are a guarantee of "social security" for the parents when they are no longer able to work.

Besides these widespread traces of African culture, there persist on Santiago some practices that are today unknown on the other islands. One important remnant in Santiago is the *batuque*, a dance of African origin. Another interesting remnant of African tribal life there is the *tabanca*. *Tabanca* originally meant a small population center, and it still has this meaning among some peoples in Africa. The Africans of Santiago, being far from their own tribes, felt the need for some type of union with others of the same culture, customs, and language, and so they formed the *tabanca*, a mutual assistance society similar to tribal associations presently found in many urban areas throughout Africa.[9]

The *tabanca* headquarters function as a "chapel" for religious rites, a place for dances, an infirmary, and a prison. The head of the *tabanca* is a king or chief and his assistant is the religious leader. There is also a queen who governs the women and the young girls. The members of the *tabanca* help each other in building homes, give moral and material assistance to each other in cases of sickness and death, and pay monthly membership dues.

Nevertheless, whatever remnants there are today of African culture, they do not represent a cultural bloc. Consequently, it is difficult to describe social classes in Cape Verde, since individuals are grouped together more as a matter of convenience than because of their cultural or ethnic ties. Integration has long been a fact of life in the Cape Verde Islands.

The language is a creole dialect comprised of archaic Portuguese that has been modified and simplified through contact with African languages. It varies slightly from island to island: the language spoken on Nicolau, for example, is almost modern Portuguese, while that spoken on the other islands is more archaic. The creole dialect on Cape Verde is much more Portuguese than that of São Tomé or Príncipe. Nevertheless, the islands as a whole have their own characteristic creole literature and songs (*mornas*).[10]

Three factors differentiate the creole dialects from contemporary Portuguese: phonetics, morphological simplification, and the remnants of archaic patterns. The phonetic patterns undoubtedly reflect African influence. The morphological system, however, contains no words that do not have their roots in Portuguese, and the African influence is insignificant.[11]

São Tomé and Príncipe

São Tomé became populated after 1485 when it was given as a *donatária* to João de Paiva. Thereafter, it played a prominent role in the slave trade, especially as an intermediary between the Kongo and Portugal. The location of the islands on major sea routes, both to India and between Africa and South America, facilitated diverse racial and cultural contacts. The immigrants included Portuguese and people from Madeira, Genoa, and France, who brought technical skills of sugar-cane farming.

In 1493, about 2,000 Jewish children of about eight years of age were separated from their parents and taken to São Tomé in hopes of converting them to Christianity. According to Valentim Fernandes, only 600 of them had survived by 1499, and in 1532 there probably were not more than 50 or 60. Thus, this group disappeared because of the high mortality rate and because those who lived to maturity mixed and blended with the African population.[12]

From Africa, slaves from many tribes were brought in to work the land. They came from the Gulf of Guinea (Mina, Benin, and Gabon, especially), from the Kongo, and, later, from Angola. In recent years, contract laborers have come from Angola, Mozambique, and Cape Verde.[13]

There are now six distinct groups on the islands: (1) *filhos da terra* or *mestiço* descendants of the early African slaves; (2) *angolares*, or descendants of some Angolan slaves who survived a 1540 shipwreck and now are fishermen; (3) *fôrros*, or descendants of slaves freed when slavery was abolished; (4) *serviçais*, or contract laborers living temporarily on the islands; (5) *tongas*, or children of *serviçais* born on the islands; and (6) Europeans.[14] Although these groups show distinct social stratification, four centuries of contact has largely destroyed cultural differences. Vestiges of African culture can be found, but they are well integrated into a Luso-African culture. For example, rural homes are similar to those in northern Portugal, fishing methods and habits of dress are Portuguese, and bread, rather than corn, is in the diet.[15]

As in Cape Verde, the common language is a creole dialect formed through contact between archaic Portuguese and African languages. The resulting creole reflects more African attributes, especially in its verbal structure, than the creole of Cape Verde.[16]

PORTUGUESE GUINEA

The Portuguese presence has changed Guinea least of all. Educational facilities are few, and Catholic missions engage in only minimal activity. In 1960, only 4 per cent of the population was Christian, while 38 per cent was Muslim and 58 per cent was animist.[17] The largest foreign element in Guinea is not the Portuguese but Syrians and Lebanese, who are established throughout the province as traders.[18]

Although there are seventeen separate African tribes and languages in Portuguese Guinea, they are divided into three principal ethnolinguistic groups.[19] There are the nomadic and Muslim Fula (Peul or Fulani), who inhabit the north and northeast sectors of the province; the Malinke (Mandinga), a settled Muslim people who live in the north-central areas of the province; and a heterogeneous group of Sudanese Negroes whom Murdock has classified among the Senegambians, who live in the central areas of the province and along the coast. This last group is largely made up of animists practicing a mixed economy.[20]

Guinea presents an excellent example of a recurring feature in Portuguese Africa, the separation of tribal groups that were divided by international boundaries established by European agreements of the past century. Since these boundaries are not well patrolled, possibilities for migration and, especially in present-day Africa, for contact and influence across national frontiers have increased. All major African peoples in Portuguese Guinea have large numbers of their fellow tribesmen in neighboring Senegal or Guinea. Because of the international border situation, it is quite easy for any of them to wander into a neighboring country. Zartman has estimated that about 10 per cent of the slightly more than 500,000 people of Portuguese Guinea have gone to Senegal in recent years to avoid the troubles resulting from a growing insurgency against the Portuguese.[21]

According to the 1950 census, the following were the major ethnolinguistic groups:[22]

Tribe	Number	Per Cent
Balanta	146,300	29.1
Fula (Fulani)	108,400	21.5
Manjaco	71,700	14.2

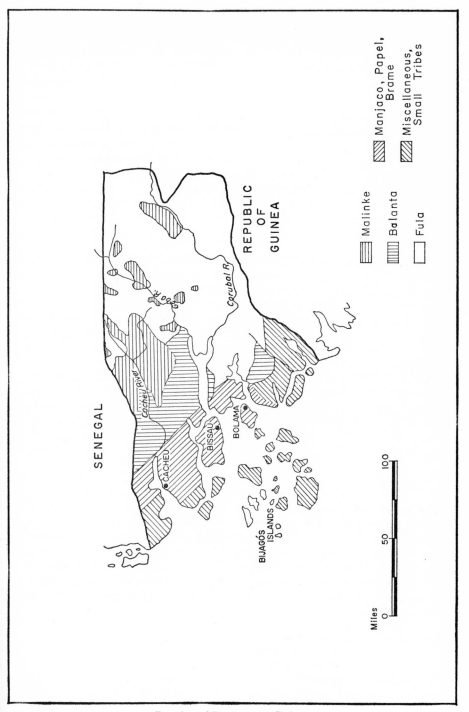

Peoples of Portuguese Guinea

Tribe	Number	Per Cent
Malinke (Mandinga)	63,800	12.6
Papel	36,300	7.2
Brame	16,300	3.2
Others	47,100	9.3

The Senegambian peoples, who encompass the Balanta, Manjaco, Papel, Brame, and some others, occupy unhealthful coastal land into which they were pushed by Malinke invasions. As a result, these coastal peoples fought among one another, isolated themselves, and established their own strategic villages, a pattern that mitigated cultural mixing. In the nineteenth century, with the expansion of the Fula from the Futa-Jallon, these peoples were once again raided and their new area depopulated as captured prisoners were sent to central Sudan. It was among these Senegambian peoples that the Portuguese experienced the greatest difficulty in pacification. Into the 1930's, tribal uprisings, especially among the Papel, continued.

The Balanta were also resistant to the Portuguese. This dynamic people has also had occasional small wars with the neighboring Malinke. The latter, descendants of the peoples of the empire of Mali and well-known as traders, have played a very important role in the diffusion of Islam. Their resistance to the Portuguese, however, was noticeably weaker than that of the coastal peoples, among whom European presence was more consistent. The Malinke are actively engaged in agriculture, as well as trade, and frequently feud with the pastoral Fula among whom they live—the eternal feud between farmer and herder.

The Fula of Guinea, at the western end of a culture group that extends across the Sudan, have a strong hierarchy of chiefs, which contrasts sharply with the relatively chiefless Balanta. The Fula have mingled racially and culturally on the same scale as the town Fulani, their settled kin of Nigeria, thousands of miles away. The Fula chiefs still rely on the Portuguese to maintain their authority among their own people, and they seem to be strong allies of the Portuguese.

ANGOLA

The overwhelming majority of the 5 million Africans of Angola is Bantu-speaking. Before the Portuguese discoveries in the fifteenth century, the Bantus had won the area by conquest. The original inhabitants, Bushmen and Hottentots, now live in the extreme southern portion of the province. There are about 100 tribes in Angola sufficiently different from their neighbors to be considered separate peoples. However, almost 70 per cent of Angola's African population speaks one of the four main languages—Umbundu, Kimbundu, Kikongo, or Chokwe-Lunda.[23]

Language Group	1960 Population
Umbundu (language of the Ovimbundu people)[24]	1,450,000
Kimbundu	1,100,000

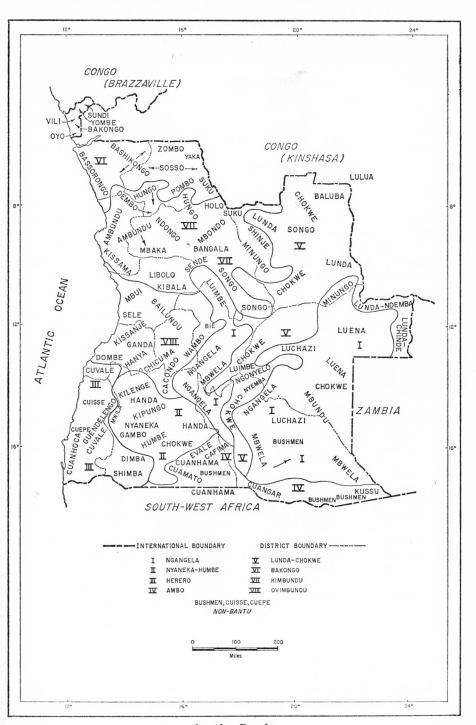

Angolan Peoples

Language Group	1960 Population
Kikongo (language of the Bakongo people)	500,000
Chokwe-Lunda	360,000
Ngangela	330,000
Nyaneka-Humbe	200,000
Ambo	60,000
Herero	25,000
Hottentot, Bushman	7,000
Vátua	6,000
Shindonga	4,500

In general, these language groups are not mutually intelligible. Within a given language group a number of tribes share enough words and grammatical features to allow understanding. That the above list may present a false picture of uniformity, however, is shown by the following table indicating some of the tribes within the major groups.[25]

Ovimbundu	Kimbundu	Bakongo	Ngangela
Bailundu	Ambundu	Bashikongo	Luchazi
Bié	Mbaka	Sosso	Luena (Luvale)
Wambo	Ndongo (Ngola)	Pombo	Luimbe
Kiyaka	Mbondo	Zombo	Ngangela
Ngalangi	Dembos	Bassorongo	Nyembe
Kibula	Hungo	Congo	Mbwela
Ndulu	Bangala	Yaka	Mbane
Kingolo	Holo	Suku	Mbunda
Kalukembe	Shinje	Guenze	Nkangala
Sambu	Munungo	Coje	Ngonyelo
Ekekete	Songo	Vili	Avico
Kakonda	Kissama	Yombe	Ngongeiro
Kitata	Libolo	Kakongo	Yahuma
Sele	Kibala	Oyo	Gengista
Mbui	Sende	Sundi	Nkoya
Kissanje	Luango		Camochi
Hanya	Ntema		
Ganda	Puna	*Chokwe-Lunda*	*Nyaneka-Humbe*
Chicuma	Cari	Chokwe (Kioko)	Mwila
Dombe	Bambeiro	Lunda	Gambo
Lumbo	Haco	Mataba	Humbe
Sumbe	Esela	Kakongo	Handa
		Mai	Kipungu
			Kilengi
			Donguena
			Hinga
			Kwan Kua

The largest group in Angola is the Ovimbundu, who live on the central highlands at an average altitude of 4,000 feet. The largest city in that region is Nova

Lisboa. The Benguela Railway passes directly through Ovimbundu territory, and there is a fairly extensive network of all-weather roads. European settlement of the region has been encouraged by favorable climate, and the European settlement, or *colonato*, of Cela is in the area.

The present Ovimbundu developed after conquests by the Jaga, who invaded this area during the sixteenth and seventeenth centuries. The Jaga, who came from the northeast, were not a culture group or a tribe as such but rather a warrior people who added to their numbers captured children from other peoples, whereas their own children were put to death.[26] This conquering horde settled in the highland region and mingled with the original inhabitants, the remnants of whom still exist on the southern and eastern fringe of the Ovimbundu. As late as the nineteenth century, the word *jaga* still meant ruler in the language of the Ovimbundu.

Through the slave trade, the Ovimbundu had many contacts with the Portuguese during the seventeenth and eighteenth centuries, and the first permanent Portuguese settlement was a fort at Caconda, built in 1682. Late in the eighteenth century and well into the nineteenth, other forts were built that enabled the Portuguese to extend their trade with the Ovimbundu, who acted as middlemen between the interior and the coast. Trading caravans traveled as far as the Congo River in the north, the Kalahari Desert in the south, and the great lakes of eastern Africa, seeking slaves, ivory, beeswax, corn, and palm oil to exchange at the ports of Benguela and Catumbela for cloth, guns, and rum of European manufacture. Between 1874 and 1911, the Ovimbundu reached the apogee of their commercial prosperity, based upon the newly important rubber trade that replaced the international slave trade. Many caravan leaders became immensely wealthy by local standards.

The Portuguese attempted to establish direct control over the Ovimbundu in 1890. This effort culminated in the so-called Bailundu War of 1902–3 against the most powerful of the Ovimbundu kingdoms. Other groups supported the Portuguese, who emerged victorious, and by 1910 the whole region was under effective Portuguese control. Meanwhile, construction began on the Benguela Railway, and Catholic and Protestant missionaries increased their religious activities.

The establishment of Portuguese rule coincided with the collapse of the rubber trade, and with it ended the great Ovimbundu caravans. Although Ovimbundu traders are still active locally, most of the people are now farmers who raise mostly corn and also beans, manioc, potatoes, and tobacco for local consumption and trade. Cattle, sheep, goats, pigs, and fowl are raised on a small scale, but the Ovimbundu are less pastorally inclined than most southern Angolans. Unlike many other Bantu culture groups, Ovimbundu men work in the fields along with the women, especially at the clearing stage, and often the women have their own fields to cultivate and the men theirs. Large iron-ore deposits are found in the Ovimbundu region, so traditionally the Ovimbundu have been skilled as ironworkers and also in pottery, basketry, leather-working, and wood-carving. The Ovimbundu have been considered among the best traders in Africa after the Zanzibar Arabs and the Ibos, partly because the Lebanese,

Greeks, and other peoples so important in African trade are almost unknown in Angola.

For centuries, travelers, officials, and missionaries have noted the readiness on the part of the Ovimbundu to accept European values.[27] European dress and merchandise such as radios and bicycles are universally admired and acquired whenever possible. Material benefits are sought after, and "making money and being rich are regarded with unambiguous approval."[28] Another example of the greater adaptability and desire for change of the Ovimbundu as compared with other tribes in Angola has been their readiness to accept Christianity, in either its Catholic or its Protestant varieties. Where there are large numbers of converts, the church school has replaced the hut of the headman as the center of village life. Indeed, the village itself, formerly known by the name of the first headman, may now be known by the name of the catechist. Protestants seem to have had more success among the Ovimbundu than elsewhere in Angola. Though the Catholics have also had good results, some observers feel that Protestant catechists have stronger ties to their people and more influence than Catholic catechists. But among the Ovimbundu, more so than elsewhere, the democratic nature of a locally controlled Protestant church has given large numbers the ability and desire to control their own institutions. Recently, official pressures have attempted to reduce the opportunities for such control.

Theoretically, the Ovimbundu are still divided into thirteen paramount chiefdoms and nine tributary chiefdoms, each with its remnant of a royal court and a shadowy substructure of subordinate chiefs and village headmen. In actual practice, detribalization has gone far among the Ovimbundu, and the old customs are dying out. Recent observers have noted that even the kinship structure is sometimes unknown. The traditional chiefs and headmen are looked upon as links to a dying past.

The Ovimbundu are a highly homogeneous ethnic group who lack major intertribal tensions. Though signs of such tension did exist prior to definitive Portuguese occupation, it is no longer present. Ovimbundu influence is spreading to neighboring peoples, and small tribes that are not historically Ovimbundu, such as the Sende, Kissanje, and Sele in the north and the Ganda, Hanya, and Dombe in the south, can be considered within the Ovimbundu orbit.

The Ovimbundu display little hostility toward the northern peoples, the Bakongo and Kimbundu, with whom they have had little contact, and toward the Nyaneka-Humbe peoples to the south. Perhaps because traditional communication routes have gone from the coast, a more bellicose relationship exists with the Ngangela and the Chokwe. The former, as well as the Kimbundu-speaking Songo, were the sources for domestic and exportable slaves. In recent years, the Ovimbundu have absorbed large numbers of Ngangela, and the latter show a certain fear and distrust of the Ovimbundu.

Though the Chokwe were not a source for the slaving activities of the Ovimbundu, there is no love lost between the two. Occasionally, however, a Chokwe village may prefer an Ovimbundu catechist to one of its own people. The Chokwe are a rapidly expanding people. Their not infrequent encroachment on Ovimbundu land has led to numerous cases of conflict. As the Chokwe expand, and as both groups settle in urban areas, this conflict might take on increasing significance.

The Kimbundu peoples, the next largest group in Angola, are located to the north of the Ovimbundu, around Luanda and throughout its interior. Since late in the sixteenth century, when Portuguese interest switched away from the Kongo Kingdom, the Kimbundu have been in closer touch with Europeans than have any other Angolan peoples. While the Portuguese had mostly concentrated their efforts along the Angolan coast by the time of the scramble for Africa, early colonial administration and Portuguese civilization had already begun to have a strong effect among the Kimbundu.

The Kimbundu-speaking people whom the Portuguese first reached had no central authority, although political links did exist among the various tribes. Because of the threat in the north from the Bakongo, who had earlier pushed the northern frontier of the Kimbundu south of the Dande, a temporary central authority developed in the Ngola of Ndongo, who variously allied himself with or fought against the Portuguese. After the Portuguese destroyed this short-lived unity, no other centralizing force again arose.

Though there have been no important ethnological studies of the Kimbundu, it is clear that they are related linguistically to the Ovimbundu and culturally to the Bakongo. A large number of detribalized people who live in the center of the Kimbundu area speak Portuguese, sometimes as their first language, and are Christians, a large majority being Catholics, and they show little allegiance to the vestiges of traditional Kimbundu tribal authority. Luanda has provided a strong urban influence, as have Malange and, lately, Salazar. More noticeable than any similarities, however, is their diversity. A discussion of the Kimbundu therefore requires a mention of some of the major tribes who comprise the larger ethnolinguistic group.

About 60 per cent of the Kimbundu population is made up of four main tribes, Ambundu, Mbaka, Ndongo, and Mbondo. The Ambundu have been most fully assimilated into modern Angolan life, probably owing to their proximity to metropolitan Luanda. Their hard work and success in taking advantage of educational and other urban opportunities have produced bitterness and jealousy among such Kimbundu groups of the interior as the Mbaka. Many Kimbundu consider the Mbaka arrogant because they claim to be "pure Kimbundu" and never to have submitted to the Portuguese. Furthermore, there remains, no doubt, some recollection of the active slave-procurement by the Mbaka, who, contrary to Ovimbundu slave-traders, did not hesitate to raid and enslave people from neighboring Kimbundu tribes. The general separation among these tribes has been shown by the traditional restraint on intertribal marriages, a restraint that is only now beginning gradually to break down.

The northernmost Kimbundu people are the Dembos, who have been greatly affected by the Bakongo. They strongly resisted the Portuguese and, in 1919, were the last people in the north to lose their independence. In spite of being industrious, the Dembos have continued to keep aloof from modern influences; they remain poorly educated and cling to traditional institutions. Their heritage of resistance has not died; in spite of its proximity to Luanda, the Dembos area remains a hotbed of nationalist insurgency, their guerrilla tactics of today being more modern versions of their activities fifty years ago.

Some of the Kimbundu peoples, such as the northern Hungo and Holo, have remained even farther away from Portuguese influence. The same might have been said of the Kissama, who inhabit the area south of the mouth of the Cuanza, until recently, when oil-prospecting in the region began to attract many Kissama into salaried jobs.

Some vestiges of the Jaga invasions remain among the Kimbundu, although considerably fewer than among the Ovimbundu. Thus, the Kibala ruling class is descended from the Jaga invaders. In fact, the Kibala and their neighbors, the Esela, provide a peaceful transition between the Kimbundu and the Ovimbundu although they are already affected by the expansion of Ovimbundu culture and language. Other signs of the earlier Jagas exist just beyond the eastern Kimbundu fringe, most noticeably among the Imbangala, who may still quite accurately reflect their Jaga ancestors.[29] Until Portuguese domination, the Imbangala were a hostile, active, trading people; their relations with all their neighbors have never been overly friendly.

Farther to the east, the Munongo, Shinje, and Songo present a linguistic and cultural transition from Ovimbundu and Kimbundu to the Chokwe. These tribes have experienced constant intermixing with their stronger neighbors on all sides.

Whereas the Kimbundu and Ovimbundu are fully contained within Angola's boundaries, the third largest ethnolinguistic unit, the Bakongo, belongs to a tribal group whose home stretches across the Angola-Congo border. The Bakongo offer a good example of how such a division has shaped contemporary events.

If one were to rely strictly on the current demographic picture, the Bakongo would be of much less importance than the 1960 census figure of 500,000 would indicate. Reports have given estimates, sometimes inflated, that from 200,000 to 600,000 people, mostly Bakongo, have, in the wake of the 1961 rebellion against the Portuguese, fled from northern Angola to the Congo (Kinshasa).[30] Regardless of what the actual numbers are, it is clear that since 1961, through migrations, war, and government resettlement programs, important changes as yet neither fully investigated nor completely final have taken place.

The Bakongo include a number of disparate tribes. Besides language, the only item they have in common is a heritage of having been a part of the once great Kongo Kingdom and of having descended from the Manikongo. There is some evidence that much of the power of the Manikongo was created in the minds of the Portuguese. Even that power had begun to disappear within a century after the Portuguese arrived on the scene, especially as a result of the slave trade and the internal mercantile rivalries it created. According to Vansina, "it is clear that by 1720, Kongo had broken up into a set of chiefdoms, which themselves kept dividing and subdividing until, by 1780 or before, a chiefdom consisted only of a capital town, the *mbanza*, of 200 huts or more, and a few villages or *libata* of fifty huts each—or less. No chiefdoms were bigger in size than 12 miles or so across."[31] In spite of the passage of more than two centuries during which the Bakongo have lacked even a semblance of effective centralized

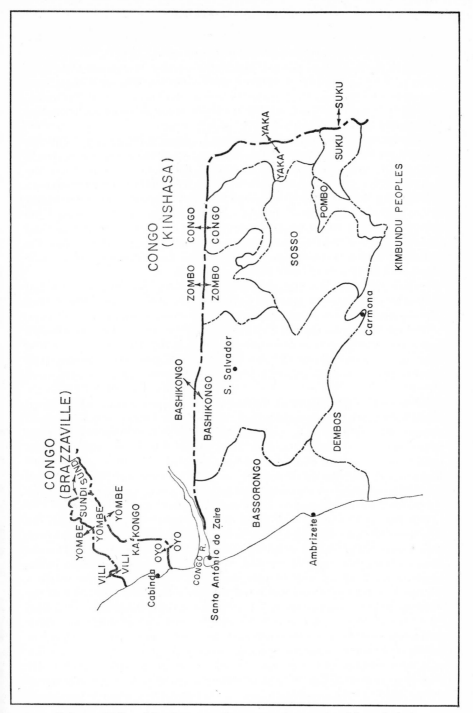

Bakongo Tribes (showing extensions across international boundaries)

power, twentieth-century Bakongo have given the old kingdom a luster it probably never had in reality, and the memory of the kingdom remains a very important unifying force. An important contemporary form of that force has been the Abako political party in the Congo (Kinshasa), which has derived much of its support through visions of the political unification of the Bakongo.

Such visions, however, in no way cloud the reality of a group historically divided and highly differentiated. The largest Bakongo tribe in Angola is the Bashikongo, whose lands include the former (and now almost mystical) political and spiritual capital of São Salvador. Together they and their eastern neighbors, the Sosso, account for about half of all Angolan Bakongo.

Two smaller yet significant tribes, the Bassorongo and the Zombo, are industrious peoples who have adapted to modern economic and social changes more easily than the Bashikongo and the neighboring Sosso. The Zombo, especially, held a position not dissimilar to that of the Ovimbundu as important middlemen in the slave trade between Luanda and Stanley Pool. After some early hostility, they have largely cooperated with the Portuguese. On the eastern fringe of northern Angola live the Yaka and the Suku, neither of which is culturally tied to the Bakongo; the former, like the Imbangala, are descendants of the Jaga[32] and are the traditional enemies of the Bakongo. The main body of these tribes lives in the Congo (Kinshasa).

Of importance to all these northern Angolan peoples is the fact that since late in the nineteenth century, and especially since World War I, the source for modern ideas and opportunities has been not in Luanda but in Léopoldville (Kinshasa). Young men have gone there for economic, educational, and social reasons. Encouraging such migrations were the Baptist missionaries in the Belgian Congo, who frequently engaged better-educated Angolan Bakongo in church and school positions in many areas under their jurisdiction. Easy migration across the border has put the Bakongo in touch with messianic movements taking place or centered in the Congo, such as the Kimbangu movement mentioned on p. 80. Since the 1920's, messianic movements have arisen frequently among the Bakongo. The following sects have large numbers of adherents in Angola:

1. *A religião salvadora* (The Religion of Salvation) of Zacarias Bonzo, who lives in the Congo (Kinshasa). Besides more religious sentiments, this cult is a strong advocate of "Africa for the Africans."

2. *Estrêla Vermelha* (Red Star) of Simão Toko. Once a Baptist teacher, Toko gained a large following in the former Belgian Congo. Because of his conviction that he was Christianity's last prophet and that Christ's second coming would be expedited through the removal of Europeans, the Belgian Government returned Toko to Angola, where, in spite of attempts by government authorities to limit his influence, his views spread both within and beyond the Bakongo. Now exiled to the Azores, Toko has been engaged, through radio appeals in recent years, in urging his followers to coexist with the Portuguese.

3. The *Maiangi* sect in Cabinda, "for Negroes only," celebrates its own form of mass, advocates the destruction of all fetishes, and forbids its believers to enter other churches.[33]

In the Cabinda Enclave, the general Bakongo international connection is repeated. The five different tribes that comprise the 55,000 people in the Enclave all extend into neighboring countries. The northern Vili, Yombe, and Sundi are smaller fragments of more numerous tribal groups outside Cabinda. Between the Yombe and Sundi, two who inhabit the eastern extension of the Enclave, there have been frequent village clashes. Many of the southern Kakongo and Oyo peoples have migrated to the town of Cabinda, where they have actively sought assimilation into European culture. Fine craftsmen and fishermen, these Cabindans have a higher standard of living than most Africans in Angola. There is every indication that they will adapt to and take advantage of the economic boom caused by the discovery of oil in Cabinda.

As the Bakongo are descendants of the great Kongo Kingdom, so is the next largest group, the Chokwe-Lunda, descended from the Lunda empire of the Mwato-Yamvo. In the seventeenth century, ancestors of the Chokwe started their migration across the Kasai River into what is presently Angola's Lunda District, where they soon merged with the inhabitants, probably Ngangela and Mbwela. After a consolidation, at the end of the nineteenth century, the Chokwe successfully attacked the Lunda Kingdom in Katanga. When the Lunda dynasty was restored in 1897, many Chokwe remained in Katanga, and hostilities between the two groups have continued until this day. Their merger for the purpose of the present discussion can be justified only on historical and cultural bases.

During the period of slave-trading, the Chokwe sought captives among their neighbors and became important slave suppliers to the Ovimbundu and others. This heritage, together with the rapid Chokwe expansion in all directions within the past half-century and their antagonism toward most nearby tribes, has led to a continually strained atmosphere in areas where their presence has been felt. Famed as artists, the Chokwe are a highly mobile people who have remained basically rural. Their geographic distance from centers of Portuguese interest and their early hostility to missionaries have kept them isolated from many of the modernizing influences that lead to urbanization and a weakening of tradition.

Not all the peoples in this grouping, however, are Chokwe. Groups of more than 10,000 Lunda live among the Chokwe in Lunda District and in the eastern corner of the "Dilolo Boot" on the Zambia border. These Lunda remain very isolated from any but traditional influences.

Because of the strength of the Ovimbundu to the west, the Chokwe to the north, and the Lunda to the east in Katanga, the intervening peoples have customarily bent in the direction of prevailing external pressures or have run away from it. These people, generally grouped together as Ngangela,[34] form a group of tribes many of which have ethnolinguistic links. There is, however, practically no sense of tribal solidarity among them. Furthermore, there have been few studies of them, and our information remains inadequate.

It seems likely that these people were early settlers on interior lands that now form part of Ovimbundu and Chokwe territory. Many Ngangela have, in fact, been fully acculturated into the life of those newcomers. They were a source of slaves for the Ovimbundu and the Chokwe, although they seem currently more able to accommodate to the former than to the latter. The lack of historical personality for these people is symbolized by the very name, Ngangela, under which they were classed; it is a slightly derogatory Ovimbundu word for "other peoples."

Three large tribes of the Ngangela peoples, the Mbunda, the Luchazi, and the Luena (Luvale) spill over into Zambia as a result of continuing migrations in search of improved conditions. The Luena language has extended its influence, because the Plymouth Brethren missionaries in the area have concentrated on it in their work. The Brethren have not, however, introduced modern advantages to a degree comparable with other areas of active missionary work. Only in very recent years have they begun to stress the literary and educational side of their activities.

Other Ngangela tribes have remained practically isolated from European influence. The Ngangela, the Mbwela, Ngonyelo, and Nyembe live scattered in the sparsely populated Cuando-Cubango District and to the south of Silva Porto. Some of these latter tribes, through their language and their pastoral activities, show signs of contact with the Nyaneka-Humbe people to the west.

The Nyaneka-Humbe are the only other large ethnolinguistic group. Though largely farmers, these peoples have a high regard for cattle, some of which are considered sacred. In past centuries, their cattle attracted Ovimbundu raiding parties, but a more peaceful mingling between the groups at their borders has led to occasional friendly and sometimes even close relationships.

The Nyaneka-Humbe are among Angola's most conservative peoples. Lacking any meaningful central authority and organized only at village level, the tribes have had little contact among themselves. Nor has any contact with new ideas changed them very much. This is surprising in light of the fact that the oldest continual Catholic missionary activities, those of the Holy Ghost Fathers, have been centered in their midst since 1881; similarly, the nearby European settlement at Sá da Bandeira has existed since 1884. Though contract labor in South Africa has attracted the Humbe and though its youth occasionally wander to urban areas for temporary employment, when they return to their villages they bring with them little impetus for change.

Half of the people in the remaining ethnolinguistic groups, which account for only 100,000 people, are members of the Cuanhama tribe. The main entity of the Ambo peoples whose largest numbers are in South-West Africa, the Cuanhama have had a historic importance far out of proportion to their numbers. Tall, strong, and vigorous people whose culture shows signs of the Nilotic culture of East Africa, the Cuanhama were organized as warriors long before the Portuguese thought of conquering them. Yearly raids against the Nyaneka-Humbe, Ngangela, Herero, and even the Ovimbundu produced them both cattle and slaves. During Portuguese attempts at conquest, the Cuanhama inflicted several smashing defeats on the Europeans. Only after the Cuanhama had allied themselves to a losing German cause in World War I did the Portuguese succeed in defeating them. Among both Africans and Portuguese alike there still remains a great deal of respect for, if not also some fear of, the Cuanhama.

The other peoples in the south include the cattle-oriented Herero, the still primitive Shindongo, and vestiges of the pre-Bantu Bushmen and Hottentots. Though the latter have historical and anthropological importance, their population does not exceed 10,000.

MOZAMBIQUE

The current tribal pattern in Mozambique is largely the result of the Bantu migrations from the north and west and the nineteenth-century migratory reversal in the wake of the Zulu uprisings in South Africa. The most obvious characteristic of the resulting demographic pattern is a strict differentiation among tribal groups in the manner in which they trace descent. The tribes north of the Zambezi are mostly matrilinear and are heavily Islamized. Those south of the Zambezi are patrilinear and either animists or Christians. An intermediate group around the Zambezi shows traits from both north and south.

According to the 1950 census, the major ethnolinguistic groups in Mozambique are as follows:[35]

Makua-Lomwe	2,293,000
Thonga	1,460,000
Shona	1,155,000
Chopi (Tonga)	240,400
Nyanja and Chewa	166,000
Makonde	136,200
Yao (Ajaua)	119,900
Barore	44,400
Ngoni (Nguru)	14,300

In the north is found the largest ethnolinguistic group in the province, the Makua-Lomwe peoples, estimated in the 1950 census at 40 per cent of the total African population of Mozambique. Of these, the Makua outnumber the Lomwe more than three to one. Though little is known of their past, the Makua are thought to have been the first Bantus to reach the Indian Ocean coast.[36] Mostly agriculturalists, the Makua have no central political structure but are organized in small tribal units. They are one of the few groups found only within Mozambique, not spreading into neighboring countries. Their generally friendly relationship with the neighboring Yao is favored by the common religion of Islam. In contrast with this friendship is their traditional enmity toward the Makonde, which has led the Makua to build stone and clay lookout towers near their villages. The less numerous Lomwe have not been as influenced by Islam as have the Makua. In recent years, many Lomwe have migrated into Malawi, where they now represent the second largest ethnic group.

The next largest northern tribe, the Makonde, inhabits a plateau in Cabo Delgado District bordering on Tanzania, where 300,000 of their fellow tribesmen live across the Rovuma River, which forms the Tanzanian border. More than 10,000 Makonde have fled to Tanzania in the last few years. A fierce people, noted for their artistic wood-carvings, the Makonde have succeeded in keeping most of their tribal customs and not becoming Islamized, in spite of long contact with Arabs.

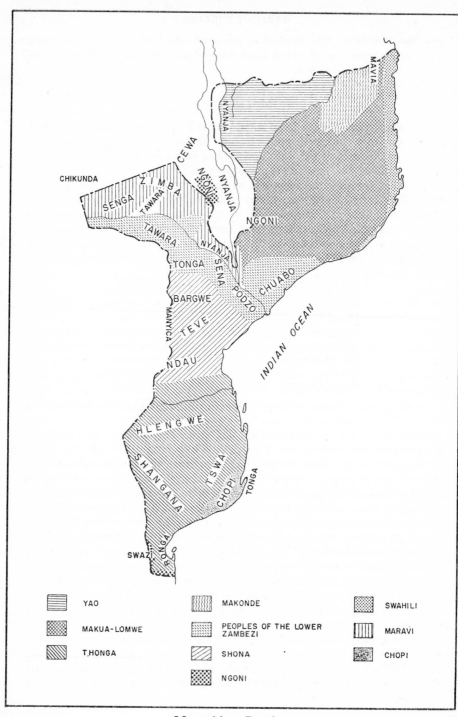

Mozambique Peoples

Livingstone, who met some Makonde and was attacked by them when exploring the Rovuma River in 1862, attributed their aggressiveness to the fact that they lived in the direct line of the Arab slave route between Kilwa and Lake Nyasa, had been preyed on by the slavers, and were, therefore, suspicious of all strangers.[37] The Makonde were the only tribe hostile to the Livingstone Expedition during the six years it spent exploring between the coast and Lake Nyasa. Not being Muslims, they were considered in recent years potentially more receptive to Christian proselytizing than the Makua, and a number of Catholic missionaries were working among them until they were evacuated in 1964.

The Yao, neighbors of the Makonde, also had centuries of exposure to the Arabs. They eventually became almost completely Islamized, and they still wear long Arab robes. For hundreds of years, the Yao functioned as middlemen for Arab slave-traders in eastern Africa, much like the Ovimbundu in Angola, and they were serious competitors with the Portuguese for trade in the interior. Late in the nineteenth century, numbers of Yao moved away from Portuguese pressure into Nyasaland.

Around Lake Nyasa, the Yao are heavily intermixed with the Ngoni, and Nyanja. Many villages often contain all these tribes, and the number of inter-marriages is increasing.[38] Though the Nyanja were a constant source of slaves, and the Ngoni are descendants of the marauding bands that crossed the Zambezi in 1835, current relations among these peoples seem quite peaceful. An important twentieth-century mitigating influence has been that of the two Anglican missions at Massumba and on Licoma Island in Lake Nyasa. Given the paucity of Christian missionary activity in the entire northern part of Mozambique, these two missions have greatly affected the region. Significantly, those who have had contact with the Anglicans, mostly Nyanjas, are now literate, not in Portuguese but in English.

Related to these people culturally are the Chewa and others in Tete District. Bordering on Malawi, these people frequently cross the international boundary, looking for wage labor and educational opportunities.

The other major group of peoples in the north are Swahili-speaking coastal inhabitants, many of whom are of Makuan descent. Active traders themselves, they have had centuries of contact with Arab traders and are strongly Islamic. As a result, both Islam and Kiswahili continue to spread southward along the coast and into the interior.

Little is known about the intermediate tribal groups in the valley of the lower Zambezi. Throughout history the Zambezi has been a major route to the interior for Africans as well as foreign peoples. Consequently, the tribes, chief among whom are the Chuabo, Podzo, Sena, Tonga, Tawara, and Chikunda, have mixed considerably among themselves.

More is known about the peoples south of the Zambezi. This partially reflects the greater Portuguese interest there than in the north, but much of the information exists only because these peoples extend into South Africa and Rhodesia, where African customs and traditions have been studied more thoroughly.

The largest southern group is the Thonga. Mostly located south of the Save

River, the Thonga peoples comprise four major tribes, the Ronga, Shangana, Tswa, and Hlengwe. By the sixteenth century, the Thonga had arrived at about their present position. As a result of the uprising of Shaka in Zululand, several Nguni tribes headed northward away from Shaka before 1821.[39] After a struggle, Soshangane became sole leader of some of the wandering Nguni and began to consolidate an empire, Gaza, among the Thonga. The Portuguese were not forced to abandon their forts, but they could remain only by paying tribute. On Soshangane's death, a succession dispute developed between two of his sons. When one of them, Mzila, won, the Portuguese claimed tribute from him. Though they did not succeed in subjugating Mzila, the Portuguese renewed their efforts in East Africa during his reign. His successor, Gungunyane, by then chief only of the Shangana, and partially financed by Cecil Rhodes, was defeated by the Portuguese and deported to the Azores.[40]

The Thonga proudly recall the grandeur of the past century, but no political and few cultural ties remain among the major tribes. There is little Thonga consciousness. Male Thonga, however, attain some feeling of belonging to a larger group when they work, as about 40 per cent of them do, in South African or Rhodesian mines.[41] In the mines, the workers find social compatibility among those who speak their language, which is frequently used by local authorities for education and communication. Migratory labor has now become a pattern among the Thonga and is discouraged by neither Portuguese and tribal authorities nor by family groups. A byproduct of work in the mines has frequently been some education, including literacy in Shangana (which cannot be taught in schools in Mozambique) and in English. Another result has been the entry into Mozambique of some of the many "Ethiopian sects," similar to the prophetic movements of Angola.[42]

Men of two smaller tribes, the Chopi and the Tonga, from the coastal areas in Gaza and Inhambane districts, also actively participate in the stream of migrant labor. Not connected with the Thonga, these tribes have had a greater opportunity than all other tribes in Mozambique except the Ronga to acquire modern education because of an active Methodist mission and some Catholic activities in their midst. The Chopi, especially, are responsive to the temptations of urban life and are numerous in Lourenço Marques.

North of the Thonga live the more than 1 million Shona. An even larger number of Shona live in Rhodesia. There are five major Shona tribes in Mozambique, the Manyika, Bargwe, Teve, Zezuru, and Ndau. The Shona live well with the Thonga; their numbers, in fact, have been increased through migrations from South Africa, Rhodesia, and southern Mozambique.

Two Ngoni remnants exist in the south of the province. Important among these, along the Swaziland border, are the Swazi, who have not lost their identity since their entry into Mozambique earlier this century.

Much as in Guinea, non-Africans control most of the trade of Mozambique. In eastern Africa, the foreign groups are Indians, Goans, Pakistanis, and Chinese, all of whom have retained many of their own ethnic characteristics.

It is evident that, even among the most numerous ethnolinguistic groups in Mozambique, no tribe is clearly dominant in number, language, or culture.

Christian proselytizing has been inadequately financed and organized, and modernization has set in very slowly. As recently as 1964, less than 15 per cent of the population was Catholic and only 4 per cent was Protestant. As modernization begins to loom on Mozambique's horizon, it may be that their experience in South Africa and Rhodesia, combined with their numbers, will allow the Thongas to take advantage of new opportunities sooner than other groups.

NOTES

1. Paul Bohannan, *Africa and Africans* (Garden City, 1964), pp. 124–25.
2. To say that the history of precolonial Africa is tribal history is misleading. The fallacy of regarding the "tribe" as the basic unit of African society is argued by Vansina: "What the historians mean by the term is that the tribal history covers the history of the community or the society in question, and even here no distinction is usually made between the politically sovereign community— a political unit—and the cultural community—a cultural unit. Furthermore, many historians imagine that the cultural community, the 'tribe,' is perennial. It does not disappear; it does not alter throughout the ages, although it does migrate; and its migration routes can conveniently be charted. This notion of the perennial tribe is meaningless." Jan M. Vansina, *Kingdoms of the Savanna* (Madison, 1966), p. 14.
3. Oscar Soares Barata, "O povoamento de Cabo Verde, Guiné e São Tomé," *Cabo Verde, Guiné, São Tomé e Príncipe* (Lisbon, 1966), pp. 928–29.
4. António de Almeida, "Das etnonímias da Guiné Portuguesa do arquipélago de Cabo Verde e das ilhas de São Tomé e Príncipe," *ibid.*, p. 141.
5. Moshe Y. Sachs (ed.) *Worldmark Encyclopedia of the Nations: Africa* (New York, 1967), p. 218.
6. Nuno de Miranda, *Compreensão de Cabo Verde* (Lisbon, 1963), p. 41.
7. *Ibid.*
8. *Ibid.*
9. *Ibid.*, p. 49.
10. Sachs, *op. cit.*, p. 218.
11. Miranda, *op. cit.*, p. 62.
12. Francisco Tenreiro, *A ilha de São Tomé* (Lisbon, 1961), p. 68.
13. Almeida, *op. cit.*, p. 144.
14. *Ibid.*
15. Tenreiro, *op. cit.*, pp. 182–84, 212.
16. Jorge Morais Barbosa, "Cabo Verde, Guiné, São Tomé e Príncipe: situação linguística," *Cabo Verde, Guiné, São Tomé e Príncipe* (Lisbon, 1966), p. 158.
17. A. Teixeira da Mota, *Guiné Portuguesa*, I (Lisbon, 1954), 239 and Agência-Geral do Ultramar, *Guiné* (Lisbon, 1967), pp. 48–49.
18. Richard Pattee, *Portugal na África*, contempornâea (Coimbra, 1959), p. 252.
19. Valuable sources on the peoples of Portuguese Guinea include José Mendes Moreira, *Fulas do Gabu* (Bissau, 1948); Jorge Vellez Caroço, *Monjur: O Gabu e a sua história* (Bissau, 1948); António Carreira, *Vida social dos manjacos* (Bissau, 1947), and *Mandingas da Guiné Portuguesa* (Bissau, 1947); Luís António de Carvalho Viegas, *Guiné Portuguesa*, 3 vols. (n.p., 1936–40); Conde de Castillo Fiel, "Geografia humana de la Guinea Portuguesa," *Archivos del Instituto de Estudios Africanos*, II, No. 4 (June, 1948); M. M. Sarmento

Rodrigues, *No governo da Guiné*, 2nd ed. (Lisbon, 1954). See also bibliographical note 4 on pp. 249–50 in Richard Pattee, *Portugal na África contemporânea* (Coimbra, 1959). There is no general agreement on spelling of tribal names.

20. George Peter Murdock, *Africa: Its Peoples and Their Culture History* (New York, 1959), pp. 265–69.

21. I. William Zartman, "West African Refugees from Portuguese Guinea in Senegal" (unpublished paper presented at the Center for African Studies, St. John's University, New York, November, 1967), p. 11.

22. António Carreira, "Apreciação dos primeiros números discriminados do censo da população não civilizada de 1950 da Guiné Portuguêsa," *Boletim Cultural da Guiné Portuguêsa*, XVI, No. 21 (January, 1951).

23. José Redinha, *Distribuição étnica da província de Angola*, 2nd ed. (Luanda, 1965), p. 9.

24. The word "Ovimbundu" is the name of the people, "Umbundu" is their language and the adjectival form, and "Ochimbundu" is a single individual. For purposes of clarity here, Ovimbundu is used throughout.

25. The following lists are adapted from *ibid.*, pp. 11–20, with spellings changed. Other major works consulted included, on the Bakongo, Hélio Felgas, *As populações nativas do Congo Português* (Luanda, 1960); Mário Milheiros, "Registro etnográfico e social sôbre a tribo [dos Sossos] [dos Congos] [dos Sólongos]," *Mensário Administrativo* (November, 1953–October, 1954); Marcel Soret, *Les Kongo Nord-Occidentaux* (Paris, 1959), and Manuel Alfredo de Morais Martins, *Contacto de culturas no Congo Português*, Estudos de Ciências Políticas e Sociais, No. 11 (1958). On tribes of other regions, see Gladwyn Murray Childs, *Umbundu Kinship and Character* (London, 1949); Adrian C. Edwards, *The Ovimbundu Under Two Sovereignties* (New York and Oxford, 1962); D. A. Hastings, "Ovimbundu Customs and Practices as Centered Around the Principles of Kinship and Psychic Power," (unpublished doctoral dissertation, Hartford Seminary, 1933); W. D. Hambly, *The Ovimbundu of Angola* (Chicago, 1934); Merran McCulloch, *The Ovimbundu of Angola* (London, 1952), and *The Southern Lunda and Related Peoples* (London, 1951).

26. This strange custom, observed by Andrew Battell and others, is reported in G. M. Childs, *op. cit.*, p. 185.

27. Edwards, *op. cit.*, pp. 31–32.

28. *Ibid.*, pp. 73–74.

29. The Imbangala present a good example of the difficulty in drawing major tribal and linguistic boundaries in Africa. Their inclusion among the Kimbundu must be justified by geographical convenience rather than by linguistic or cultural similarity.

30. United Nations, *General Assembly Report of the Special Committee on the Situation with Regard to the Implementation of the Granting of Independence to Colonial Countries and Peoples*, A/6700/Add. 3 (October 11, 1967), p. 213. Though some refugee estimates are clearly inflated, the Bakongo population of Angola is much smaller than in 1960.

31. Vansina, *op. cit.*, p. 190.

32. Murdock includes both the Yaka and the Imbangala among the Cuango cluster, which follows the drainage basin of the Cuango River. Most Cuango peoples are in the Congo (Kinshasa).

33. Summaries of these groups are found in Eduardo dos Santos, *Maza* (Lisbon,

1965), pp. 259–316. Other relevant studies include: M. Milheiros, "Qual é a religião das tribos gentílicas angolanas?", *Revista do Gabinete de Estudos Ultramarinos*, No. 1 (January–March, 1951); Serra Frazão, *Associações secretas entre os indígenas de Angola* (Lisbon, 1946); J. M. da Silva Cunha, *Movimentos associativos na África negra*, Estudos, Ensaios e Documentos No. 27, Junta de Investigações do Ultramar (Lisbon, 1956), and *Aspectos dos movimentos associativos na África negra*, Estudos de Ciências Políticas e Sociais No. 23 (Lisbon, 1959); A. Dias da Silva, "Cabinda e seus povos," *Mensário Administrativo* (Luanda), No. 31/32 (March–April, 1950); Pattee, *op. cit.*, pp. 524–25; A. A. Mendes Corrêa, "Sociedades secretas africanas e a ciência social," *Boletim da Sociedade de Geografia de Lisboa*, No. 4/6 (April–June, 1954).

34. Murdock, however, does not see them as a distinct group but divides their various parts among the central Bantu and the southwestern Bantu.

35. Repartição Técnica de Estatística. *Recenseamento geral da população em 1950*, III (Lourenço Marques, 1955), 72–73. Though providing some indication of African distribution, the census statistics do not provide the degree of accuracy necessary to distinguish the population along the more satisfactory ethnolinguistic lines presented in A. Rita Ferreira, "Caracterização e agrupamento étnico dos indígenas de Moçambique," *Boletim da sociedade de estudos de Moçambique*, XXVII, No. 3 (July–August, 1958). Furthermore, the publication of detailed census figures from 1960 has been inexplicably delayed.

36. Abel dos Santos Baptista, *Monografia etnográfica sôbre os Macuas* (Lisbon, 1951), p. 15.

37. David and Charles Livingstone, *Narrative of an Expedition to the Zambezi* (Lisbon, 1865), p. 435.

38. J. C. Mitchell, *The Yao Village* (Manchester, 1956), pp. 16, 30, and 59–60.

39. The Shaka uprisings and the effects caused by the subsequent migrations are discussed in J. D. Omer-Cooper, *The Zulu Aftermath* (Evanston, 1966). For sections especially relevant to Mozambique, see pp. 57–78.

40. Douglas L. Wheeler, "The Portuguese and Mozambique," in John A. Davis and James Baker (eds.), *Southern Africa in Transition* (New York, 1966), pp. 186–87.

41. Keith Irvine, foreword to Henry A. Junod, *The Life of a South African Tribe* (New Hyde Park, N.Y., 1962), pp. x–xi.

42. A. Rita Ferreira, *O movimento migratório de trabalhadores entre Moçambique e a África do sul* (Lisbon, 1963).

PART II

Government and Society

VI

Government and Administration

NORMAN A. BAILEY

A RECURRING feature of Portugal's contact with Africa has been a tendency to govern her African territories as integral elements of the Portuguese state. In recent years the organs of local and provincial government have been strengthened and, at least in theory, given greater autonomy. Nevertheless, Portugal's African territories are still part of a highly centralized state.

In the sixteenth and seventeenth centuries, Portugal's African possessions were generally termed "conquests" or "overseas dominions," although the term "provinces" was also used at times, first about 1576 and with greater frequency after 1633. During the eighteenth century, "colony" was the term most often employed. Article 132 of the Constitution of 1820 referred to "provinces," and this term was retained in the Constitution of 1842. After 1910 the term "colony" was used again. In 1911, the Overseas Ministry became the Colonial Ministry. Since 1951, Portuguese Africa has officially been organized into five "overseas provinces."[1] The overseas provinces have no legal counterpart in metropolitan Portugal, which is administratively divided into districts, each with a civil governor named by the minister of the interior and each containing several levels of subdivision.[2]

CENTRAL GOVERNMENT

Since all top-level policy decisions emanate from Lisbon, and since the actions of provincial and local governmental bodies in Portuguese Africa are subject to Lisbon's ultimate veto, a brief review of the political structure of metropolitan Portugal is necessary.

At least in part because of a particularly turbulent popular presidential election in 1958, the president of Portugal is now elected for a seven-year term by an electoral college consisting of the members of the National Assembly and the Corporate Chamber, as well as representatives of each district and all overseas legislative bodies.[3] The president, who since the *coup d'état* that instituted the Second Republic in 1926 has always been a high-ranking military or naval officer, appoints the prime minister and the rest of the cabinet. According to the Portuguese Constitution, the prime minister is responsible only to the president, not to the National Assembly. In fact, according to the terms of the Constitution, the president should be the most powerful member of the government. There is speculation that General de Gaulle modeled the Constitution of the French Fifth

Republic, at least in part, on the Constitution of Portugal. Nevertheless, in practice, for four decades, political power was centered with Prime Minister António de Oliveira Salazar.

Under Salazar, Portugal's political base was a shifting coalition of the armed forces, rural interests, and the church. It is often forgotten that Salazar was brought in by an already established (since 1926) military dictatorship that enjoyed popular acquiescence if not widespread support. Popular revulsion at the extreme political and economic instability of the First Republic, established in 1910 after the overthrow of the Bragança dynasty, was instrumental in maintaining Salazar in office. Salazar's rule was always manipulative and highly personal.

In 1968, Salazar, after a serious illness, was replaced as prime minister by a close associate, Professor Marcello Caetano, one of the authors of the Portuguese corporate constitution. Caetano promised a continuation of the Salazar government's policies with reference to the African provinces, but domestically various steps were taken to liberalize press regulation and step up industrial development. Caetano also visited Angola, Mozambique, and Guinea, something that his predecessor had never done.

The cabinet in Lisbon may legislate by decree on matters of concern to all of Portugal, metropolitan and overseas. In matters concerning more than one overseas province, but not metropolitan Portugal, the overseas minister may legislate by decree, after consulting the Overseas Council. The Overseas Ministry, principal executive organ for the overseas provinces, includes many departments overlapping certain metropolitan ministries, including Justice, Education, Health, Public Works, and Customs Administration. Thus, it is in a way a little government of its own, responsible only to the prime minister and eventually to the president. The Overseas Council (Conselho Ultramarino) functions as an advisory agency on legislation, as the organ of adjudication of disputes over administrative jurisdiction, and as the agency that decides on the constitutionality of metropolitan decrees affecting the overseas provinces. The overseas minister is additionally advised by a Conference of Overseas Governors held every three years.[4]

The legislative branch of the Portuguese central government consists of the National Assembly and the Corporate Chamber. The National Assembly may legislate for the overseas provinces only with reference to the modification of their charters, the conclusion of agreements with foreign powers concerning them, the authorization of the contracting of loans, and the delimitation of the powers of the organs of the central and provincial government with regard to the granting of concessions.

Thus, the National Assembly is ordinarily quiescent with respect to the overseas provinces, save when examining provisions of development plans (*planos de fomento*) for metropolitan and overseas Portugal. Nevertheless, when situations of crisis occur, as in 1961, debate within the Assembly may be prolonged, bitter, and meaningful. Both the Corporate Chamber and the Assembly substantially modified Overseas Minister Adriano Moreira's liberal proposals for changes in the overseas statute. The overseas deputies took an active part in the floor debate and in the committees.

The members of the National Assembly are elected to four-year terms by direct but limited suffrage. Total representation of the overseas provinces is twenty-three of a total of 130 deputies. The deputies representing the overseas provinces need not be residents of those provinces, although now they usually are. Normally an effort is made to name authorities on the overseas territories to the Overseas Committee of the National Assembly, but much more could be done to bring the native-born of all races from Portuguese Africa into legislative and executive positions in the central government.[5] Some Lisbon authorities claim that there has been a practical problem in increasing the number of representatives from Africa. Good candidates for representatives often do not want to leave their businesses in Africa to go to Lisbon. Furthermore, the failure of the legislature to be politically meaningful on many issues discourages prospective candidates.

The Corporate Chamber is made up of representatives of local governmental units and administrative, moral, cultural, and economic organizations, in accordance with the corporative theory of the Estado Novo. All laws submitted to the National Assembly must first be reviewed by the Corporate Chamber. Although purely consultative, the inherent power of the organizations represented and the personal stature of many members makes it a rather effective body, as was demonstrated by the debate and changes in the draft of the new Overseas Organic Act of 1963. The Chamber, more conservative than either the Assembly or the overseas minister at the time, reduced the degree of provincial autonomy envisioned in the original draft, by retaining the overseas minister's power to veto legislation of the provincial assemblies. The overseas provinces are represented in the Corporate Chamber in accordance with the provisions of the statute of each province.

PROVINCIAL AND LOCAL GOVERNMENT

The present structure of provincial government in Portuguese Africa is outlined in the Overseas Organic Act of 1963. After extensive study and consultation with officials and private citizens from the overseas provinces, new statutes were promulgated, in consecutive decrees of November 22, 1963.[6]

The principal executive officer in the overseas provinces is the governor-general, in the case of Angola and Mozambique, and the governor, in the case of Cape Verde, São Tomé e Príncipe, and Guinea. These officials are appointed by the cabinet in Lisbon upon the nomination of the overseas minister: "The Ministry of Overseas Affairs is, in effect, the executive branch of overseas government, while the provincial administrations are its agencies which implement and adapt to local conditions the directives received from Lisbon."[7]

The governors have wide powers to legislate by decree on native affairs and on other matters outside the authority or competence of the National Assembly in Lisbon, the Overseas Ministry, or the legislative councils of the provinces. They may also legislate by decree when a legislative council has for any reason been prorogued. Before issuing a decree they must, however, in all cases, consult the provincial government council. The governors administer public finances and, subject to formal approval of the overseas minister, levy taxes and incur expenditures as they see fit, with the advice of the economic and social councils and the approval of the legislative councils.

The provincial cabinet, headed by a secretary-general, consists of a number of provincial secretaries appointed by the governor, with administrative rank equal to that of inspector. In Mozambique, for example, there are six secretariats, consisting of political and civil administration; health, labor, and welfare; education; economy; colonization; and public works and communications. Also directly under the authority of the governor are the administrative departments, which in Mozambique consist of agriculture and forestry; survey; customs; economy and statistics; geology and mines; education; public works; health and hygiene; veterinary services; and African affairs. The governors are also assisted by a Government Council (Conselho de Governo), consisting of the governor, the secretary-general and the provincial secretaries, armed forces commanders, the attorney-general, the director of the treasury, and members of the Legislative Council.[8] The most important function of the Government Council is the assistance it renders to the governor in the preparation of the yearly budget.

Legislative councils were established in Angola and Mozambique by the Organic Act of 1953 and in the other African provinces by the Organic Act of 1963. There are thirty-six members of the Legislative Council of Angola, in addition to the governor-general, who is presiding officer. The attorney-general and the director of the treasury are ex-officio members. The rest are elected— fifteen by direct suffrage, three by taxpayers paying over $510 per year, three by economic organizations, three by workers' organizations, three by cultural-moral organizations, three by African authorities, and three by administrative officials. The Legislative Council of Mozambique has the same ex-officio members and twenty-seven elected delegates, nine by direct suffrage and the rest distributed in the same fashion as Angola. Guinea, Cape Verde, and São Tomé e Príncipe have similar but smaller legislative councils, and a lower percentage of members are elected by direct suffrage.

To be a member of the legislative council of an overseas province, the candidate must be a native-born Portuguese citizen, over twenty-one years of age, literate, a resident of the province for at least three years, and, except for the representatives of African authorities and Portuguese administration, not a civil servant. The suffrage is limited to literate males over twenty-one, females who have completed the first cycle of the academic high school, heads of families, whether literate or not, and taxpayers paying over $3.40 per year exclusive of the head tax (paid by most adult males).[9] Late in 1968, the Portuguese Government introduced a bill into the National Assembly liberalizing the suffrage requirements. There will no longer be any property or tax-paying requirements nor any special restrictions on women. Any literate citizen will have the right to vote.

The provincial legislatures have sole legislative authority while in session over all matters exclusively concerning their respective provinces. Specific authority exists over the general lines of the budget, authorization to the governor to contract loans, sanctioning the annual report of the Technical Commission for

Planning and Economic Integration and implementation of the report, and election of representatives to the Overseas Council in Lisbon and the Government Council of the province. The draft of the yearly budget is presented to the Government Council for advice and then to the Legislative Council for approval and is finally promulgated by gubernatorial decree.[10]

In 1963, under the terms of the new Organic Law, economic and social councils were established in Angola and Mozambique. These consist of fifteen members, seven appointed or ex-officio, and eight elected, two each by administrative bodies, moral and cultural institutions, and employers and employee organizations. The economic and social councils elect the delegates to the Corporate Chamber in Lisbon from Angola and Mozambique, advise the governor-general on economic and social matters, and submit proposals to the legislative councils.[11]

REGIONAL AND LOCAL GOVERNMENT

Angola and Mozambique are administratively divided into districts with a governor appointed by the overseas minister and assisted by partly appointed and partly elected district boards.[12] These are further subdivided into *concelhos*, in relatively advanced areas with some degree of local autonomy and representative institutions, and *circunscrições* in more rural areas. The chief executive officer in both subdivisions is the *administrador*. The most rural administrative subdivisions are the *postos*, governed by *administradores de posto*.[13] Cape Verde, São Tomé e Príncipe, and Guinea form a single district each. Guinea is divided into nine *concelhos* and three *circunscrições*, Cape Verde into thirteen *concelhos*, and São Tomé e Príncipe into two *concelhos*.

After adoption of the Organic Law of 1963, many former *circunscrições* were elevated to *concelhos*, and the eventual aim is to replace all *circunscrições* with *concelhos*. At present there are *câmaras municipais* (municipal councils) in all provincial and district capitals and in all *concelhos* with 500 or more registered voters.[14] The presidents of the *câmaras* are appointed by the governor-general, but the aldermen are all elected by direct or corporate suffrage. *Concelhos* with fewer than 500 electors and *circunscrições* with more than 300 have *comissões municipais* (municipal commissions); *freguesias* (wards of cities) and *postos* with at least twenty electors have a *junta local* (local council).[15] These lesser local government bodies are also made up of appointed presidents and elected aldermen. All local government bodies below the district level are subject to the overall supervision of the provincial Department of Civil Administration. The *juntas distritais* also perform supervisory duties with respect to the local councils within their jurisdiction.

PUBLIC ADMINISTRATION

The principles upon which present-day Portuguese administration is based in Africa remain those enunciated by Marcello Caetano in 1951:

European and overseas Portugal forms a political unity, differentiated administratively in its various parts, because each one must have the organization and

137

the laws that best fit its position, its economy, its population, and its social development.

These differentiated laws and administration correspond to a common spirit of nationality, a political and spiritual community reflected in certain uniform juridical rules, applied in territorieswith a moral personality and financial autonomy.[16]

The events of 1961 in Angola, however, resulted in considerable intellectual ferment in Portugal and in the overseas territories.[17] This led to the decision to re-examine administration in the overseas provinces as well as their political structure and relations with the metropole. As a consequence, the Overseas Council was called into session in October, 1962, with representatives of the legislative councils and government councils of the overseas provinces joining the regular members of the Council. As a result of its deliberations, which lasted the rest of the year, the new Organic Law of the Overseas Provinces was passed on June 24, 1963. This Organic Law currently regulates African administration and political institutions.[18]

The overseas minister, at the pinnacle of overseas administration, is assisted by a number of related bodies that are the outgrowth of a development going back at least to the foundation of the Junta das Missões Geográficas e de Investigações do Ultramar in 1936.[19] Since then, many other bodies, formed to study various aspects of the overseas provinces, have published an impressive number of scholarly and popular works. The most important of these organizations is the Instituto Superior de Ciências Sociais e Política Ultramarina, which has developed from the Escola Superior Colonial established in 1906 for the purpose of training overseas administrators. It offers three general courses of study at the undergraduate and graduate levels.[20]

In 1961, two important bodies were created in each province. The *juntas de povoamento* supervise and make studies of immigration and land concessions. The make-up of the *juntas* is fixed by each legislative council, but the presidents are appointed by the overseas minister. The *institutos do trabalho, previdência e acção social* supervise and enforce labor and social legislation, as well as making studies of labor and social conditions. The labor inspectors under these institutes have the powers of arrest and of fixing sanitary regulations on the spot.

Financial autonomy of the overseas provinces is guaranteed by Article 148 of the Constitution, modified by special provisions in times of emergency, as set forth in Article 175. The basic monetary institutions affecting the overseas provinces are the Bank of Portugal, the Ministry of Finance, the National Overseas Bank, the Bank of Angola, and the Exchange Funds (Fundos Cambiais) of Angola and Mozambique.[21]

By means of various economic boards, metropolitan Portugal assures prices and markets for some goods from its overseas provinces.[22] Usually these prices are above, sometimes below, world market prices. In 1957, intra-overseas trade was freed, with exceptions in the cases of Cape Verde, São Tomé, and Príncipe. Despite reiteration of the ideal of absolute internal free trade in the Constitution (Article 158) and in Article LXXI of the Overseas Organic Law of 1953, the various overseas provinces maintained separate customs regimes imposed by the overseas ministry until 1962. On January 1, 1962, internal tariffs began to be reduced successively until, by 1972, Portugal and the overseas provinces were to constitute a single market. According to Article LXXII of the new Overseas Organic Law of 1963, all issue banks were to be headquartered in Lisbon, the escudo was to become the unit of currency everywhere, and free convertibility was foreshadowed.

Somewhat before the Angolan insurrection of 1961, the Portuguese secret police, the Polícia Internacional e de Defesa do Estado (PIDE), was introduced into the overseas provinces for the first time. Since 1961, both PIDE and the armed forces have taken a more direct, though sometimes conflicting, role in overseas administration. Provincial governors and about half the district governors are ordinarily military officers. A provincial Polícia de Segurança Pública (Public Security Police) was created in 1961, a Corps of Local Militia in 1962.

The Catholic Church plays an integral role in the administration of health, education, and welfare. Article 60 of the Missionary Statute placed rudimentary education almost entirely in the hands of the church, although more recently the state has begun to build and administer rudimentary schools. In 1926, the year of the national revolution, the Estatuto Orgânico das Missões Católicas Portuguesas was promulgated. Missionary activity is still regulated in part by this Organic Statute, now amended.[23] An agreement of 1940 with the Vatican is the most important document of the modern period with reference to the position of the church in the overseas Portuguese provinces. At the same time, a Missionary Accord was signed with the Vatican.[24]

NATIVE ADMINISTRATION

Native policy is discussed in a later chapter. Here it is well to note, however, that since 1926 Portugal has followed a policy toward Africans still living under tribal conditions that is halfway between the indirect rule of the British and the assimilation policy of the French. Chiefs and other traditional officials have been viewed as part of a transitional phase of the development toward African assimilation into Portuguese society.

In urban areas and in rural areas where tribal ties have been loosened, authority rests in a *regedor*, either a recognized traditional chief or an appointed local authority of no traditional standing. *Regedores* are appointed by district governors after consultation with local inhabitants, and they receive a salary plus an annual gratuity. Village headmen, who serve under the *regedores*, are appointed by the administration and, instead of a salary, receive an annual gratuity based on the amount of taxes collected in their villages during the year. From time to time, a *banja*, or meeting, is held by the people of a region with their administrator, *regedores*, and headmen. At this meeting, problems are discussed, minor disputes are settled, and complaints are heard. The *regedores* may appoint local councils if they wish, and they are represented in the legislative and government councils. The duties of the *regedores* are to maintain order in their districts, assist in tax collection, and keep the authorities informed of developments. Neither *regedores* nor headmen have any authority over the expenditure of revenue. An infrequently applied law provides for a good *regedor* to pass into the regular administrative cadres.[25]

The position of an African chief during a transitional period is a difficult one. It often involves divided loyalties and an attempt to maintain traditional ways in a changing society. Tribal organization is disappearing rapidly in Angola, as noted in an earlier chapter, but it is still strong in Mozambique, where 90 per cent of the *regedores* were traditional chiefs in 1965.[26]

LEGAL STRUCTURE

The first Political, Penal, and Civil Statute especially for the Africans of Angola and Mozambique, taking into account their customs and traditions, was enacted in 1926. In 1929 the act was amended to provide for the establishment of African tribunals. The Portuguese Criminal Code applies intact in all the African provinces, and the Civil Code applies in Cape Verde and São Tomé and Príncipe, where the policy of dual citizenship (the *indigenato*) never existed. The Portuguese Civil Code is applied in Guinea, Angola, and Mozambique to all citizens choosing to be governed by it rather than indigenous law. In case of conflict of laws, written law prevails. Principles applied in the application of modified customary law include the tolerance of some local cults, the prohibition of magic and sorcery, the prohibition of tattooing and body mutilation, the strengthening of the family through the abolition of some customary practices, and a distinction for purposes of punishment between crimes committed under the influence of animistic beliefs and those committed without such excuse.

Portuguese civil and criminal law is applied in the African provinces by ordinary and special courts, municipal courts, and labor courts. The ordinary courts consist of courts of first instance, appeal courts, and provincial supreme courts of justice. The special courts are administrative tribunals that sometimes hear cases *ab initio* and sometimes take appeals from the ordinary courts. Final appeal is to the Metropolitan High Court in Lisbon.

A very subjective application of African customary law is made by courts presided over by Portuguese administrative officials. Each official is assisted by two African advisers on tribal law in civil cases, and procedure generally follows custom, consisting of the complaint or petition, discussion, evidence, allegations, decision, and execution. At present, local jurisdiction is limited to minor offenses such as insults, minor damages, adultery, and small debts. Appeal to the regular courts is always possible. In certain areas, rather complex African judicial systems still exist in accordance with custom, enabled to impose rather heavy penalties in the form of fines (imprisonment is a prerogative of ordinary or special courts).[27] In the Bakongo area of northern Angola, for example, certain cases can be appealed to the Manikongo. Due to the reforms of 1961 that granted citizenship to all inhabitants willing to assume its responsibilities, administrative and ordinary court adjudication has become more important at the expense of customary courts and procedures.

In Portuguese Africa, local government and public administration are inextricably intertwined, because the executive officer at every level of local government is an administrative official. There is a remarkably high degree of both political and administrative hierarchic centralization in the Overseas Ministry. The full ministerial cabinet in Lisbon deals with Portuguese Africa only in times of crisis. The legislative organs are generally bypassed, again except for times of crisis. Thus, both official provincial and local bodies and private African interest groups are tied in fact, as well as in theory, directly to the prime minister through the overseas minister. In the next chapter we shall trace the political process in Portuguese Africa as conditioned by the formal structures that have been outlined.

NOTES

1. Title VII of the Constitution of 1933 as amended, "Do ultramar português." See Marcello Caetano, *Do conselho ultramarino ao conselho do império* (Lisbon, 1943), pp. 29–30, and Franco Nogueira, *The United Nations and Portugal: A Study in Anti-Colonialism* (London, 1963), pp. 176–77. There are slight discrepancies between the two accounts. See also Francisco Leite Duarte, *A posição dos dominios ultramarinos no estado Português* (Lisbon, 1945), and *Constituição política da República Portuguesa* (Lisbon, 1963), especially pp. 39–48.
2. See A. Martins Afonso, *Princípios fundamentais de organização política e administrativa da nação*, 12th ed. (Lisbon, 1963).
3. In the presidential elections of July, 1965, 151 of the 600 electors were from the overseas provinces.
4. Any treaty, convention, or agreement signed by an overseas province with any other province or territory, national or foreign, must be approved by the overseas minister. See J. M. da Silva Cunha, *Administração e direito colonial* (Lisbon, 1956), and Caetano, *op. cit.*
5. Only five of the deputies at the 1953–54 session were native-born representatives of the overseas provinces. República Portuguesa, *Anais da assembléia nacional e da câmara corporativa*, VI Legislatura, Sessão Legislativa 1953–54 (Lisbon, 1955).
6. *Estatuto político-administrativo da província de Angola* (Lisbon, 1963); *idem*, same date, all other provinces. These statutes are to some measure the equivalent of state constitutions in the United States.
7. Roberto de Saboia de Medeiros Fernandes, *Portugal and Its Overseas Territories: Economic Structures and Policies, 1950–57* (unpublished doctoral dissertation, Harvard University, 1959), p. 4. The powers of the governor-general include protection of nationals and foreigners; expulsion or refusal of entry; appointment, promotion, and dismissal of officials below a certain rank; day-to-day operation of government departments; a general police power; reception of petitions; initial outlining of budgets; the granting of concessions and contracts with the approval of the overseas minister; and the protection and improvement of the conditions of the native population. The chief executive officer of an overseas province may not leave the territory of the province without the authorization of the overseas minister and must inform the minister whenever he leaves the provincial capital.
8. The Government Council, together with the governor, may legislate in times of emergency, and in Cape Verde, São Tomé and Príncipe, and Guinea, the

Government Council elects the representatives of the province to the Corporate Chamber in Lisbon.

9. See Oliveira Lírio, *Legislação eleitoral* (Coimbra, 1964?). Requirements for electors to the National Assembly, pp. 49–50; overseas representation in the Corporate Chamber, pp. 146–47. In 1964 there were 175,241 registered voters in Angola and 96,569 in Mozambique. The latter figure represented an increase of 46,560 over 1963. The members of the legislative councils enjoy immunity from arrest and prosecution during their terms of office. Upon the request of the governor, the overseas minister may dissolve the Legislative Council and order new elections.

10. A Technical Commission for Planning and Economic Integration was established in each province under the terms of Article LXIX, paragraph IV, of the Lei Orgânica of 1963. Private members of the legislative councils may introduce any bill except bills calling for expenditures above the approved budget or for reductions in income below those foreseen in the budget. The governor may veto a bill that he himself has introduced if he finds it no longer opportune, in which case his veto is final. If he disagrees with a bill introduced by a private member, he may present it to the overseas minister for final judgment, or he may send it back to the Legislative Council, which by a two-thirds vote may override his veto. If the governor believes that a bill violates either the provincial statute or the Portuguese Constitution, he may present the matter to the Overseas Council in Lisbon, the decision of which is binding.

11. Expenditures may not exceed those established in the budget submitted by the governor; tariffs and other trade taxes are imposed by Lisbon; annual ordinary or current budgets must be balanced; borrowing abroad requires approval of the government in Lisbon.

12. *Quatro anos no governo do distrito do Uíge* (Carmona, 1965) has an excellent account of the powers of the *juntas distritais*.

13. For a review of administrative subdivisions of Angola and Mozambique see Chap. I.

14. The area of jurisdiction of a Câmara Municipal and of the *concelho* are not necessarily the same.

15. The administrative head of a *freguesia* is called a *regedor*.

16. Marcello Caetano, *Tradições, princípios e métodos da colonização portuguesa* (Lisbon, 1951), pp. 35–36.

17. See Franscisco Pinto da Cunha Leal, *A pátria em perigo* (Lisbon, 1962), and Manuel José Homem de Mello, *Portugal, o ultramar e o futuro* (Lisbon, 1962). Homem de Mello's recommendations for reform are found in summary form on page 119. Francisco de Paula Dutra Faria's *Debate inoportuno* (Lisbon, 1962) is a reply to Homem de Mello; Fernando Pacheco de Amorim's *Três caminhos da política ultramarina* (Coimbra, 1962) is a reply to Cunha Leal. See also Cunha Leal's more recent indictment, *Ilusões macabras* (Lisbon, 1964).

18. *Organic Law of the Portuguese Overseas Provinces* (Lisbon, 1963). See Adriano Moreira, *Continuity* (Lisbon, 1962), pp. 7–8, for the questions the Overseas Council dealt with. See also Gonçalo Mesquitela, *O ultramar português na organização política da nação* (Lisbon, 1962). Mesquitela was an elected member of the Legislative Council of Mozambique and a representative to the Overseas Council in 1962. For cogent and sometimes biting criticisms of the new organic law, many paralleling the present author's (see Chap. VII), see the debates in the National Assembly, April 2–23, 1963, especially pp. 263, 273,

290, 305, 326–27, 399–400, and 426 and pp. 551–54 of Vol. II. A compilation of all overseas legislation originating in metropolitan Portugal can be found in *Nova legislação ultramarina.* See especially, for the contemporary period, Vols. VII, VIII, IX, Xa, Xb, and XI (Lisbon, 1962–63). The most useful short summary of overseas administration is Honório José Barbosa, *Informações jurídicas para conhecimento da orgânica administrativa do ultramar português* (Lisbon, 1964); see pp. 54–55 for the organization of the Overseas Ministry, p. 55 for the autonomous organs, and pp. 55–56 for the consultative bodies.

The line officials of the Portuguese overseas administrative service are: *governador-geral* (provincial), *governador* (district), *intendente, administrador* (three grades), *administrador* or *chefe de posto,* and *aspirante* (an *intendente* acts as vice-governor in some districts). Administrative cadres are divided between line and staff services. Officials above the rank of *administrador* are appointed by the overseas minister and may be sent anywhere. *Administradores* and below are appointed by the provincial governors and may be used only in a single province if they so desire. A regular administrative official is appointed initially for a five-year term, subject to a satisfactory report after two years. Reappointment after five years is permanent. Any industrial, commercial, or professional activity by the administrative cadres is prohibited. Graduates of the Instituto Superior enter the service as *administradores de posto.* All others enter as *aspirantes* by means of competitive examination. There are various grades in the Portuguese overseas administrative service, characterized as A through Z: (A) governors-general; (B) provincial governors; (C) general secretaries, provincial secretaries, *inspectores superiores*; (D) district governors, administrative inspectors, sixteen other categories; (E) fifty-two categories, no line; (F) district *intendentes*, 111 other categories; (G) thirteen categories, no line; (H) first-class *administradores*, fifty-five other categories; (I) twenty categories, no line; (J) second-class *administradores*, forty-nine other categories; (K) twenty-four categories, no line; (L) third-class *administradores*, 120 other categories; (M) forty categories, no line; (N) 114 categories, no line; (O) forty-two categories, *administradores de posto*; (P–Z) only staff categories.

Salaries in the administrative service range from 25,000 escudos per month to fifty. Category C is the highest that can be attained by an administrator through regular promotion. By law, 50 per cent of all district governors must be career officials. The provincial secretaries are named by the overseas minister upon the nomination of the provincial governor. The district governors are also named by the overseas minister but are responsible to the governor-general Lower-ranking officials are appointed and removed by the governors, with the approval of the minister. The *administradores*, chief executive officers in the *circunscrições* and *concelhos*, have a staff consisting of two *aspirantes*, or lowest-ranking officials, and a secretary. João Ferreira Semedo and António Manuel da Costa Moreira (eds.), *Estatuto do funcionalismo ultramarino*, 2nd ed. (Coimbra, 1960), pp. 465–502.

The autonomous services have their own regulations. These include the Serviços de Portos; Caminhos de Ferro e Transportes de Angola e Moçambique; Correios, Telégrafos e Telefones; Administração do Porto de Bissau; Fundo do Fomento de Moçambique; Imprensa Nacional de Angola e Moçambique; and Luz e Agua de Luanda. The judicial system, meteorological service, armed forces, PIDE, civil aeronautics, civil identification, and others come under separate statutes as well (p. 8). As of December, 1968, the value of the escudo equalled 3.4 U.S. cents.

19. The Overseas Ministry consists of the minister's personal cabinet (a chief of cabinet and two secretaries); a general secretariat; the directorates-general of political and civil administration, development, treasury, and education; the inspectorates of administration, indigenous affairs, health, development, treasury, and customs; the consultative and technical bodies, and the related organs. The consultative and technical bodies are regulated by Section IV of the Organic Law and consist of the Overseas Council, the Conference of Overseas Governors, and the Overseas Economic Conferences. Silva Cunha, *op. cit.*, pp. 354–64, and Manuel Gonçalves Monteiro, *Elementos de direito aduaneiro e de técnica pautal*, Estudos de Ciências Políticas e Sociais, 2 vols., Nos. 73–74 (Lisbon, 1964). The ministry alone employs 40,000 people. Overseas services not centralized in the Overseas Ministry include higher education, civil aeronautics, meteorological services, police, military, merchant marine, and engineering research centers. Placement of the administration of justice under the Justice Ministry is now under study.

20. Other agencies involved with African studies include the Agência Geral do Ultramar (which concentrates on the publication and distribution of popular works), the Centro de Estudos Geográficos at the University of Lisbon, the Arquivo Histórico Ultramarino, and the Instituto de Medicina Tropical. Other recently formed institutes include the Centro de Estudos de Antropologia Cultural, the Centro de Estudos de Antropobiologia, the Centro de Estudos de Desenvolvimento Comunitário, and the Instituto de Investigação Científica. All are attached to the Junta de Investigações do Ultramar. In addition, each province now has a *conselho de protecção da natureza* chaired by the governor, for the protection of soils, flora, and fauna.

21. The National Overseas Bank (Banco Nacional Ultramarino) is the bank of issue in Cape Verde, São Tomé and Príncipe, and Mozambique. It is a private bank, in form at any rate. The precise link between the bank and the government is hard to establish. The Bank of Angola, also private, is the bank of issue in Angola. Both overseas banks can extend long-term credit for economic development. The Exchange Funds in Angola and Mozambique are administered by the banks of issue, subject to the regulations of Exchange Councils (*Conselhos de Câmbios*), made up of government officials, a director of the bank of issue, and a representative of local business organizations. Caetano, *Colonização Portuguesa*, esp. pp. 36–37, and Vicente Loff, *Ordenamento e coordenação dos serviços e organismos executivos da política económica nacional de âmbito ultramarino* (Lisbon, 1960).

22. The services of economic development of the Overseas Ministry comprise the departments of economy and of public works. There are, in addition, three special interministerial committees dealing with economic matters: the Economic Council, the Council of Ministers for Foreign Commerce, and the Corporate Council. The former metropolitan commodity boards were replaced as of 1961 by provincial boards of foreign commerce, cotton, cereals, coffee, and rice. The officially recognized corporative bodies in metropolitan Portugal and overseas can control the entry of new firms into their industrial sectors. Fernandes, *op. cit.*, p. 229, Fernandes calls the corporate bodies "oligopolistic cartels."

23. See A. da Silva Rego, *Curso de missionologia* (Lisbon, 1956); António Lourenço

Farinha, *A expansão da fé na África e no Brasil* (Lisbon, 1942); and J. Alves Correia, *A dilatação da fé no império português* (Lisbon, 1936).
24. *The British Survey*, Main Series (November, 1965), pp. 8–9.
25. Richard Hammond, *Portugal's African Problem: Some Economic Facets*, Occasional Paper No. 2, Carnegie Endowment for International Peace (New York, 1962), 9.
26. See A. Richards (ed.), *East African Chiefs* (London, 1960); L. A. Fallers, *Bantu Bureaucracy* (Cambridge, 1965); A. Rita Ferreira, "Nota sôbre o conceito de 'tribo' em Moçambique," *Boletim da Sociedade de Estudos de Moçambique*, XXVII, 108 (January–February, 1958); Max Gluckman, *Custom and Conflict in Africa* (New York, 1955), and *Order and Rebellion in Tribal Africa* (New York, 1963).
27. See James Duffy, *Portuguese Africa* (Cambridge, Mass., 1961), p. 301; F. F. Olesa Munido, "La Orientación etnológica en el proyecto definitivo de Código Penal para los indígenas de Moçambique," *Cuadernos de Estudos Africanos*, Vol. VI (1949); Augusto Castro Júnior, "Aspectos do direito e da justiça entre os povos incivilizados em geral e em especial em relação aos indígenas de Angola," *Mensário Administrativo*, Vols. XXXV and XXXVI (July and August, 1950); António dos Santos Carvalho, *Legislação da metrópole em vigor na provincia de Moçambique* (Coimbra, 1955); Artur Augusto da Silva, *Usos e costumes jurídicos dos fulas da Guiné Portuguesa* (Bissau, 1958); Adriano Moreira, "Administração da justiça aos indígenas," *Revista do Gabinete de Estudos Ultramarinos*, Nos. 5 and 6 (January and June, 1952); Narana Coissoró, *As instituições de direito costumeiro negro-africano* (Lisbon, 1964); José Gonçalves Cotta, *Projecto definitivo do código penal dos indígenas da colonia de Moçambique acompanhado de um relatório e de um estudo sôbre direito criminal indígena* (Lourenço Marques, 1946); and Adriano Moreira, *Estudos Jurídicos*, Estudos de Ciências Políticas e Sociais, No. 40 (Lisbon, 1960).

VII

The Political Process and Interest Groups

NORMAN A. BAILEY

It is something to be assessed in terms of political science, which has viewpoints of its own.   Adriano Moreira

ADMINISTRATIVE POWER

THE STUDY of the process of decision-making is the study of the strategies of the use of power. In any of the societies usually called "underdeveloped," there are two well-defined sectors, that which operates within the traditional societal modes, whether tribal or feudal, and that which operates in accordance with the evolved techniques and complexities of the technical society developed in Europe and North America in the nineteenth and twentieth centuries. A rough measure of the degree of "development" of a society is the degree of its complexity—or, in other words, the relative size of the two sectors mentioned above.

In many of the most advanced societies, of course, there still remain traditional elements, as with the Lapps in Norway, Sweden, and Finland and the Indians and Eskimos in the United States and Canada, but these elements are tiny in relation to the total population of the countries involved. At the other end of the scale there are countries such as Bhutan, where the modern sector is entirely or almost entirely lacking, but these are now rare. Most common are what Fred W. Riggs has called "prismatic" societies—those between the fused or traditional society, with its lack of specialization, and the highly complex, modern, or diffracted society with its extreme specialization.[1] In such societies, the ordinary interaction of official and private groups in the process of decision-making are further complicated because there are, in fact, two societies living side by side within the boundaries of the state. We have already seen, in earlier chapters, some of the problems that this has caused for Portuguese Africa.

In such a transitional society, the administrative service acts as a powerful pressure group, behaving in relation to other pressure groups more as one of them than as a regulating agency or corps of civil "servants." Although this is also true elsewhere, it is particularly marked in a transitional society. In Portuguese Africa, this fact is further complicated by the existence of four overlapping administrative services dependent respectively on the Overseas Ministry, other metropolitan ministries, and provincial and municipal authorities.

Mozambique and Angola make an interesting administrative contrast.

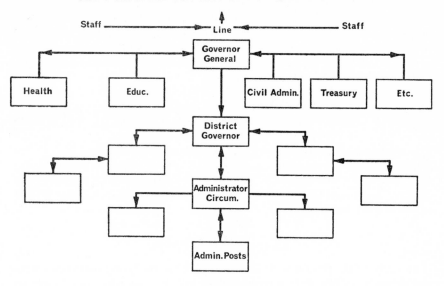

Chart 1
Mozambique. Administrative Process. Flow of Information and Orders

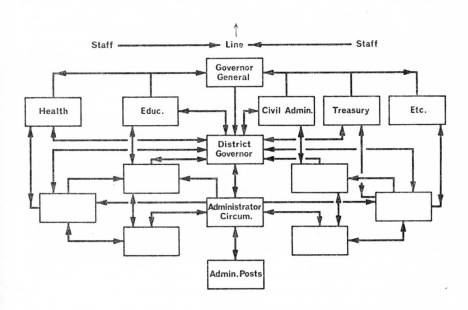

Chart 2
Angola. Administrative Process. Flow of Information and Orders

Formally, both have the same administrative structure, on paper, decentralized horizontally but centralized vertically (despite a recent tendency toward vertical decentralization as well, which will apparently be continued in the new administrative code). In practice, however, Angola operates in a horizontally decentralized fashion, while the Mozambique administrative services are highly centralized in every way, in a manner common to transitional societies, with the flow of information and requests moving to the central line officers and thence up to the governor-general, and orders flowing from the governor-general's office to the line and staff subordinates.

In Mozambique, the status of the administrative structure leads to the constantly reiterated complaint of a stifling bureaucracy, doing little, consuming much, and subjecting private groups and individuals to inordinate delays and indignities—the daily and usually quite justified complaint found in almost all prismatic societies.[2]

In Angola, on the other hand, there is a much greater degree of administrative decentralization, with staff offices acting as executive departments, as they sometimes do in diffracted societies, and with secretaries and directors accepting a considerable degree of responsibility for executive decisions within the field of their competence and authority. The flow of information and requests moves not only or even primarily to the line officers but rather directly to hierarchical staff superiors. Orders also move down the line within the staff departments. This system, more rapid and effective than the centralized one, makes decision-making more efficient. As a result, although political criticisms are heard in Angola, *administrative* criticisms are very rare, and, when they are heard, they are usually directed against a particular individual or office rather than the bureaucracy as such. There is no significant difference in the actual number of public officials in the two provinces.

Administrative problems in Portuguese Africa are manifold, as they are in all societies except, perhaps, traditional ones. Of the problems common to all administrative systems, only two need be mentioned as being particularly relevant to Portuguese Africa. Finding sufficient administrators of high quality is a grave problem for a country as small and poor as Portugal, leading to frequent situations where efficient administrators and technicians are frustrated by a lack of depth in their department or, conversely, by incompetent superiors. The other problem, extensively discussed by Adriano Moreira, is the same as that analyzed by Victor Thompson in his classic work on administration[3]—namely, the clash between technicians and traditional bureaucrats, with the technician usually hierarchically inferior to the bureaucrat, and, even if not inferior, subject to the necessity of implementing whatever judgments are handed to him by the political authorities.[4] This latter problem is obviated to a substantial extent in Angola by the authority exercised by the staff (executive) departments; in other words, the technicians often make the decisions and carry them out, subject, of course, to the general lines of political policy from Lisbon.

Various specific criticisms have been directed at the administrative services of Portuguese Africa. It is sometimes alleged, particularly in Mozambique, that the bureaucracy is excessively large. In terms of numbers purely, this can hardly be sustained. In Angola, for example, there were in 1965 a total of 786 line administrators from governor-general to *ajudante de administrador de posto*, to administer a territory of 481,351 square kilometers and 5 million inhabitants. What is undoubtedly true is that an inefficient and parasitic administrative structure is always too large, whatever the actual number of functionaries. Coordination of the four administrative services mentioned above is a serious problem for Portuguese Africa, leading often to three or four agencies all dealing with the same problem, laying claim to the same scarce resources, and generally being less effective jointly than any one of them could be alone. The solution to this problem, however, lies not in the administrative but in the political field, with the inevitable eventual decision either to continue the present trend toward federalism to its logical conclusions or to reverse the trend and make Portugal again in fact a "unitary state."

Recruitment and promotion policies have been a constant preoccupation of those responsible for overseas administration. Recent policy has tended toward liberalization, with various decrees of 1961 authorizing the provinces to fix the size, recruitment, salaries, and the like of their own provincial civil services, providing for interdepartmental and interservice transfer, transfer from provinces with *governo simples* to provinces of *governo geral*, promotion out of turn of two hierarchical steps for "exceptional merit," creation of the new post of *inspector superior* accessible to career administrators, direct promotion from *administrador de posto* to *administrador de circunscrição*, and reservation of 50 per cent of governorships of districts for intendents and inspectors with academic degrees. The new legislative code published in 1966, superseding that of 1962, attempted to encourage vertical decentralization in the administrative structure by providing governors and administrators with greater power of local decision.[5]

Some of the reforms themselves have created problems, however. No administrator without a higher academic degree can be promoted permanently above a certain level, "H." In practice, most such higher degrees are issued by the Instituto Superior in Lisbon (see Chapter VI). This fact, and the fact that, before recent improvements, the degrees of the Instituto were not really the equivalent of university degrees, have led to the pejorative name of *coliseu* (coliseum) for the Institute among career administrators, and to such bitter remarks as "We are legal illiterates—they are functional illiterates." The value of experience over formal training, and vice versa, is a problem that has no solution, except to say that every effort to find and utilize talent and initiative should be made, no matter what the formal background of the individual, and the hands of the provincial governments should not be tied by rigid regulations admitting of no flexibility.

Another complaint, that native-born inhabitants of the African provinces are not sufficiently represented in the administrative cadres, has recently been reduced by expanded recruiting. In Angola, for example, in 1965, out of 1,753 employees of the metropolitan government in line and auxiliary positions, 715 were born in overseas provinces. Out of 182 high administrative officers, 34 were native-born, and out of 52 political figures (deputies to the National Assembly, members of the economic and social councils, legislative councils, and so on),

25 were native-born.[6] It is interesting that recent rapid development in Angola and Mozambique and the consequent attractiveness of private employment to the Europeans have led to increased Africanization of the administrative cadres.

LOCAL POWER: DECISION-MAKING

In Portuguese Africa the administrative services act as powerful pressure groups in competition with private organizations. This is particularly true because of the official corporate structure of the Portuguese Government (although rudimentary in the overseas provinces, as we shall see) and because government power is centralized and the metropolitan economic structure is oligarchic. Thus, competition between the administration and local economic groups can be, and often is, strong. In addition, there is the added circumstance that all executive officials in the overseas provinces, all the way down to the presidents of municipal councils, are appointed, not elected. It is unquestionable, however, that the various provincial and local bodies of self-government exert a substantial influence on decision-making. We shall try to trace through the decision-making process, first by an enumeration and evaluation of local government, local private bodies, and continental Portuguese groups with influence in the overseas provinces, and then by a description of their interaction in the making of decisions.[7]

In the elections of 1964 for the legislative councils of all the overseas provinces (including Macau and Timor), of the common list of voters registered, the number that actually voted ranged from 77.1 per cent in Cape Verde to 95.15 per cent in São Tomé and Príncipe. Voting is not obligatory in Portugal. Of the total number of 111 delegates elected to the legislative councils, 70 were native-born.[8] Both the economic and social councils and the legislative councils, although not by any means rubber stamps, are sounding boards for public or, more precisely, private group opinion, more than they are legislative bodies proper. In the case of the official representatives of economic, administrative, religious, and local bodies, this function is obvious, but, even in the case of members elected by direct suffrage, their function appears to be, and they understand it to be, defense of the interests of the district they represent in the council. The representational system is arranged to prevent the development of factions or *de facto* political parties in the councils, and, in practice, such factions do not appear to exist. Legislative functions are also important, of course. If the Legislative Council refuses to pass a bill presented by the provincial government, as we have seen (Chapter VI), the governor-general may send the bill to the overseas minister for his decision. This has never, in fact, occurred but, should it occur, the minister would obviously either have to dismiss the governor, if he decided against him, or dissolve the council and order new elections.[9] As a consequence, the process used by the Legislative Council when faced with a bill it does not like is not to reject it but to amend it out of existence.

In Portuguese legislative practice, a bill is first voted on "in generality" and then article by article. If a bill is passed by the council "in generality," no matter what happens afterward the governor cannot veto it and has no choice other than to withdraw the bill when it has been reduced to little more than the preamble. The budgetary powers of the Legislative Council are also more than nominal. In the session of December 4, 1964, the Legislative Council of Angola excised from the budget presented by the governor a provision for the re-establishment of a tax abolished in 1956. This change had been suggested by the committee charged with considering the budget.

The functions of the *juntas distritais* are to advise the governor of the district, to supervise the local government bodies in the district, and to adapt laws of superior bodies to local conditions. In addition to these functions, the *juntas distritais* also appear on occasion to perform another—that of protection of local government bodies from interference by higher bodies and superior administrative officials. In the district of Benguela in Angola in 1965, for example, the *junta distrital* supported the *câmara municipal* of the city of Benguela in the issuance of a contract for street-lighting in the face of adverse decisions by the Department of Public Works in Luanda.

The *câmaras municipais*, *commissões municipais*, and *juntas locais* in Portuguese Africa suffer from the same disabilities as local government bodies almost everywhere—a lack of funds from their own resources. The effects of district and provincial subsidies on the independence of these bodies is obvious, as is the fact that their presidents are appointed at the provincial level. All this is particularly marked in Mozambique. The percentage of total receipts from their own sources is much lower than in Angola, and the appointive presidents are likely to be career administrators or military officers rather than local businessmen, as is often the case in Angola. In addition, the municipal councilors in Mozambique are likely to be employees of metropolitan companies rather than independent merchants or industrialists, as in Angola. The percentage of total expenditures of local government bodies on administrative costs is also higher in Mozambique than in Angola.

A reading of the debates in the legislative councils of Angola and Mozambique, as well as interview data, reveals a preoccupation with the role of pressure groups that is amply justified by the reality of the decision-making process and amplified by the fact that the principal local pressure groups are officially represented on all provincial and local councils.

PRESSURE GROUPS

The pressure groups most often mentioned as locally powerful are the economic (invariably first), the church, the administration, ethnic and local organizations, the armed forces and the police, as well as the large metropolitan companies and banks. Among the economic groups, power relationships seem to be skewed in an odd fashion for a transitional society, with the commercial and industrial associations exerting more and more effective influence than the agricultural associations or the associations of landlords.

In discussing economic pressure groups in Portuguese Africa, a clear distinction must be made between organizations that are part of the official corporate structure of the Portuguese state and organizations that are independent of that structure. The formal corporate structure is weak in the overseas provinces, so weak as to lead one extremely well informed observer to claim in a publication of 1963 that, despite decree-law 27.552 of 1937 extending the corporate system (which did not exist even in the metropolis until some twenty years later) to the overseas provinces, the corporate system was, in fact, practically nonexistent.[10] None of the *grémios*[11] or *sindicatos* existing in Portuguese Africa are yet part of any over-all union or federation, much less any of the metropolitan corporations.[12] There were, in 1965, three *sindicatos* with twenty-four sections and eight *grémios* with three sections existing, at least on paper, in Angola, and twelve *sindicatos* and six *grémios* in Mozambique.

The corporate system is much better organized in Mozambique than in Angola, where at times official initiatives for the formation of *grémios* have been sabotaged by the prospective members themselves. There also exist a number of officially run, largely African cooperatives in both provinces, cooperatives in name only, because they are tightly controlled by the administrative authorities.[13] A distinction must, of course, be made between independence and power—the fact that an organization has official connections does not necessarily mean that it will lack power in comparison with a more independent organization. In actual practice, however, the *grémios* and *sindicatos* are considerably less powerful in the overseas provinces than the independent economic associations, in Angola to the point where the official corporate structure is of negligible significance. In Mozambique, the relationship is somewhat more favorable to the *grémios* and *sindicatos*, both because they are inherently stronger and because the independent associations are weaker than in Angola. The labor unions (*sindicatos*) in Mozambique have developed substantial power and, if led by vigorous leaders, can and do make life quite miserable for employers inclined to ignore minimum wage levels and regulations on working conditions. This influence will be strengthened in the future as more *sindicatos* are authorized to sign collective contracts with employers (in 1965 only the bank and railway employees could do so in Mozambique, and none could in Angola). All *sindicatos* provide their members with medical assistance and employment services.

There are six types of independent economic associations in Portuguese Africa: industrial, commercial, retailers, agricultural, landlords, and cooperatives.

Overseas, as in the metropole, these associations . . . continue to assume a certain economic preponderance in the direction of their representative activities, and despite their purely private character, their functions are considered in the public interest, the government using them as "connecting links" between its own services and organs and individual activities.[14]

These economic associations, and particularly the industrial associations of Angola and Mozambique and certain of the commercial associations (which are not federated provincially but cover a particular city or region), are the single most powerful pressure groups in Portuguese Africa, receiving no government subsidy as a rule, often led by men at odds with the provincial or even national government, and ordinarily well financed. Their influence will presumably increase in the future, with economic growth and recent initiatives toward joint action and toward the formation of their own staffs of economists and technicians to make studies at the request of members. Whether their power will increase *relatively*, however, is another question, having to do principally with the actions of certain metropolitan groups to be mentioned later. The agricultural associations do not have the influence that one would expect, principally because so much of large-scale agriculture is in the hands of companies based in the metropolis. For the same reason, the total relative power exerted by the economic associations in Mozambique is less than in Angola. Some private cooperatives, such as that of the cattle-ranchers in Mozambique, also have appreciable influence.[15]

Strictly local pressure groups other than the economic are of less importance. Daily newspapers in Mozambique are entirely in the hands of either the church or the Banco Nacional Ultramarino. The weekly press in Mozambique and the dailies and weeklies of Angola exert some influence, but all are subject to political censorship. There are a number of organizations such as the Associação dos Naturais de Angola (ANANGOLA), the Liga Africana (in Angola), the Associação Africana (in Mozambique), and the Associação dos Naturais de Moçambique. With the exception of the last mentioned, however, most of these organizations have been intervened by the government since 1961 and their officers in many cases imprisoned, or at any rate deprived of office. *A Voz de Angola, A Voz de Moçambique*, and *O Brado Africano* are published by various of these organizations, which also engage in social and sports activities, social welfare projects, granting of scholarships, and the like. The only one that can be said to have retained any substantial independent influence is the Associação dos Naturais de Moçambique. The portion of the population still living under tribal conditions influences decisions directly through the *regedores*, represented in the Legislative Council and in the *juntas distritais*, and indirectly because of their economic and, more recently, international importance.

The leadership of some of the economic organizations and of some of the *associações dos naturais* is politically opposed to the present regime in Lisbon, but overt political opposition groups are, of course, absent. There is substantial dissatisfaction with some of the economic policies of the present government, as is indicated by the fact that the official candidate for the presidency, Admiral Tomas, took 67 per cent of the vote in Angola in 1958, compared with 75 per cent in continental Portugal, while the opposition candidate, General Delgado, whose campaign was managed in Angola by the then president of the industrial association of the province, took the district of Benguela, commercial-industrial heart of southern Angola. It is also significant that the organization of the União Nacional (the official party) overseas is practically nonexistent. The nationalist opposition is based abroad and is properly the subject of another chapter. It should be mentioned here, however, that the several nationalist groups exert a direct military influence on decision-making in Guinea, Angola, and Mozambique, as well as an obvious indirect influence.[16]

The organizations centered in metropolitan Portugal that strongly influence decision-making in Portuguese Africa include the church, the central government, metropolitan trusts and banks, and the armed forces and the police. The

153

first three have always been present, of course. The church exerts power principally in two ways—through its enormous influence with the Christianized rural population and through the activities of individual prelates, such as the now deceased cardinal-archbishop of Lourenço Marques and the bishop of Beira. Both dioceses own daily papers. It cannot be said, however, that the influence of the church is directed in any particular direction, but rather it depends on personalities. The central government, of course, sets the political guidelines outside or beyond which organs of provincial and local government may not go. Industrial and agricultural trusts, the Banco de Angola in Angola, and the Banco Nacional Ultramarino, in the remainder of Portuguese Africa, have enormous power. The Banco de Angola has until recently exercised a monopoly of commercial banking in Angola, and the Banco Nacional Ultramarino has done so in São Tomé and Príncipe, besides being the bank of issue. A measure of its influence in Mozambique is that, until 1965, it was able to prevent the entry of any other metropolitan banks into the province and prevent completely the formation of a bank with local capital. Standard Bank of South Africa and Barclays (DCO) traditionally operated in Mozambique but have limited themselves to financing export-import trade with the United Kingdom, Rhodesia, and South Africa.

The armed forces have been an increasingly important influence in Guinea, Angola, and Mozambique since 1961. In the zones of military activity, their control is naturally almost complete, but this, except in Guinea, is minor. More important is the influence exerted by officers holding civil positions, particularly as governors of districts and presidents of municipal councils. By law, half the district governors must be career administrators, but almost all the others are military officers. Because provincial governors and governors-general are usually military officers as well, these officer-governors can often bypass official channels and obtain rapid action on their requests. As with the church, however, this power is not exerted in any particular direction, but rather it depends on the personality and interests of the individuals involved. The military presence in Portuguese Africa has naturally created some problems of relationship with local pressure groups, if for no other reason than that it complicates the picture and increases the quantum of local power. Resentment of military prerogatives and interference is also common among the civil administrative cadres. The Polícia Internacional e de Defesa do Estado (PIDE, International Police and for Defense of the State) entered the African provinces of Portugal also on a wholesale basis in 1961. The scope of its actions has included interventions, not always successful, in local organizations, sometimes indirectly through the electoral process and sometimes directly by removing and, at times, imprisoning officers. Given the intense local patriotism and pride of the local population of all races, such activity may well prove to be counterproductive in the long run.

INTERACTION OF METROPOLITAN AND LOCAL GROUPS

Interaction of various groups with the administration takes place both formally and informally. Because of the link with metropolitan Portugal, the formal organs are more important than one would normally expect in a transitional society, since most private organizations of influence are represented in administrative and legislative bodies. The Associação Industrial de Angola (AIA), for example, is represented on nineteen different boards and councils.[17] The commercial associations participate in the deliberations of the Legislative Council, the Economic and Social Council, *juntas distritais, câmaras municipais,* the Junta de Comércio Externo, the Customs Board, the Instituto do Café, the Serviço de Transportes, and many others. This official representation is an effective method of applying pressure, *if* the boards and councils themselves have the power of decision, either directly or through provincial secretaries and directors of services. This is the case in Angola, less so in Mozambique.

The economic associations of Angola in 1962 formed a Gabinete de Estudos Económicos in order to make their influence felt in a more effective way. In Mozambique, a Gabinete Regional das Associações Económicas was founded in the same year and for the same purpose, presided over on a rotating basis by the president of one of the member organizations. In 1964, in Lourenço Marques, five metropolitan, sixteen Angolan, and twelve Mozambican economic associations met for the first time and founded a Conselho de Coordenação das Associações Económicas Portuguêsas. It is interesting that none of the official economic organizations of the Portuguese state corporate system were invited or attended the meeting. If these organs of unity continue and are successful in coordinating the activities of their members, they should in the future attain great influence within Portuguese society, given the accelerated rhythm of economic development in both metropolitan and overseas Portugal.

In a society such as Angola, with a complicated system of social stratification based on rank, wealth, and color rather than on a single factor,[18] and where there is no longer any connection between the traditional tribal elite and the educated African elite in a largely detribalized territory, it is natural that "associations of class" should assume an overriding importance. This fact is reinforced because of the substantial destruction of the effectiveness of the Liga Africana and ANANGOLA, only now beginning to regroup into some sort of coherent force after the events of 1961. As a result, the economic associations are represented, not only by their official delegates, but, in the overwhelming majority of cases, members of the Legislative Council, *juntas distritais,* and *câmaras municipais,* elected by direct or restricted suffrage, are also, in fact, important members of the economic associations. In this way, the effectiveness of the associations is doubled. Their aggressiveness and the fact that substantial portions of the Angolan economic system are locally owned, not only in commerce but in industry and agriculture as well, gives them a position of prominence in the province rivaled only by the administration and metropolitan organizations such as the armed forces.[19] Elections for *vogais* (members) of *juntas distritais* and *câmaras municipais* are often contested in Angola, because they are positions of real importance and influence, and the *vogais* are ordinarily independent businessmen with financial and personal stakes in the areas they help to administer. The government shows its recognition of these facts by inviting local powerfuls to join higher bodies (but less controllable by the associations), such as the

Legislative Council. Such government offers are sometimes met with refusal or with later intransigence if the post is accepted. Because of the decentralization of public administration in Angola, the local pressure groups can operate more effectively by approaching the official most directly concerned with the matter at hand and can generally obtain a rapid decision. Approaches are often made directly to Lisbon, as well, to the overseas minister or the prime minister, depending upon the subject. Because of the power of the economic associations, administrative officials such as district governors sometimes use them to pressure higher government organs, as in petitioning for a larger share of the highway budget.

In Mozambique, although the formal system of representation is practically the same, the actual interaction of groups, and of these with the administration, is very different. For the reasons already expressed, the economic associations are much less powerful than in Angola, and the Catholic Church, the *sindicatos*, and the metropolitan trusts and banks much more so. This makes for a more inflexible decision-making process, compounded by the overcentralized administrative system. In addition to this, rural Mozambique is much more primitive than rural Angola; the vast bulk of the Africans still live according to tribal rules and organization and under traditional chiefs, and a much smaller percentage of them speak Portuguese than in Angola. This fact increases the power of the administration and the church, the two organizations with greatest influence over the traditional sector of this transitional society. In the modern sector, control by metropolitan economic organizations is very great.

An example of this power is instructive. Early in 1965, the president of the Associação dos Naturais de Moçambique, a large and important organization, who was also a member of the Mozambique Legislative Council, published in its organ, the *Voz de Moçambique*, a photo of the Banco Nacional Ultramarino (BNU) in Lourenço Marques with a caption quoting Winston Churchill: "Never did so many owe so much to so few." He was immediately thereafter fired from his job in a company dependent on the BNU for financing, and the newspaper *Notícias*, owned by the BNU, refused to continue printing the *Voz de Moçambique* on its presses. Several months later, he was still unemployed. No single private agency or combination of agencies in Angola has this kind of power. Local and district elections are very seldom contested in Mozambique, and a large percentage of officeholders are private and public employees rather than independent businessmen, as in Angola. These councils, then, in Mozambique, are principally useful as sounding boards for the governor-general and the provincial secretaries rather than as reflections of an effective local power network. Nevertheless, as we shall see later, they are by no means entirely without influence, nor are the economic associations completely powerless. The Industrial Association and the Commercial Association of Beira may be pointed to as having substantial influence, and the power of the economic associations is growing, not receding.

The process of decision-making through official bodies, then, is one of prior consultation with important local groups through both formal and informal channels. The groups then suggest changes in a proposal, or they make one themselves in administrative units in which they are represented. The matter is next taken to the Government Council and the Economic and Social Council. The latter provides the first opportunity for other groups interested in the matter to take a hand in its formulation. The Economic and Social Council gives an opinion on the bill and may submit an entirely new proposal. The bill then goes to an *ad hoc* committee of the Legislative Council, which may also suggest changes in its report to the plenum. Finally, the bill is voted in its generality and by articles, as described earlier, providing the opportunity for the virtual destruction of the measure if the Legislative Council so determines. The process of initiation of a proposal may also start in local bodies, such as municipal councils and district councils. More commonly, however, the initiative is administrative.

THE ELECTORAL PROCESS

This brief outline of the process of decision-making leads to the question of the choice of candidates for the legislative councils. The administration is formally represented, not only by permanent *vogais* (the attorney-general and the director of the treasury) but by elected representatives and traditional authorities, who must be assumed to be hand-picked.

The process of nomination to the legislative councils in Angola and Mozambique differs. In Angola, ordinarily, a group of local businessmen meet and decide to approach one of their number and ask him to stand for the Council. This usually requires a good deal of persuasion, because the position entails considerable personal sacrifice in time and money. If the chosen candidate accepts, he is then suggested to the administration, which declares him acceptable or not. If acceptable, he is officially presented. Since he represents local economic forces and is acceptable to the administration, he is likely to be unopposed in the election. Ordinarily, only if he is declared unacceptable and decides to run anyway will the administration put up a candidate against him. In the elections of 1964, one district was contested in Angola (Cabinda), by three candidates, and one district in Mozambique (Moçambique), by two candidates. In Cabinda the official candidate won by 50·3 per cent of the total vote, in Moçambique by 93 per cent. This system, at least in Angola, assures that the Legislative Council will be controlled by men acceptable to both the economic associations and the administration, which makes the outcome on controversial proposals rather unpredictable. In Mozambique, a larger percentage of the *vogais* elected by direct suffrage are invited by the provincial government to join the Council, and only then are local pressure groups asked to decide if the candidate is acceptable—in other words, the nominating process is usually reversed.

Since the abolition of the *indigenato*, the electoral rolls in Portuguese Africa have increased tremendously (see Chapter VI), and the time is not far off when a majority of the electorate will be "nonwhite." It is difficult to see that this will have any immediate effect as long as the economic associations in Angola and the administration in Mozambique retain their present share of power. In any case, the economic and social councils, although purely advisory bodies, have more real power than the legislative councils, because they must be consulted on every issue, including urgent ones. They are made up only of representatives of locally powerful groups, and they meet throughout the year.

The interrelationship of official and unofficial bodies can be illustrated by mentioning a trip made to Mozambique by the president of the Commercial Association of Luanda in 1964. While there, he discovered that the system of import-licensing in Mozambique was much simpler than in Angola. Upon his return, the Commercial Association of Luanda asked for and received the support of the other commercial associations in the province and made official overtures to the administration through its representation on the Customs Board. Nothing was done. Then, because the president was also a member of the Legislative Council (representing taxpayers who pay more than 15,000 escudos per year), he presented a bill incorporating the changes desired. The regulations were then changed through administrative action, without the bill actually going through the legislative process.

Powerful overseas groups, then, are effectively represented in bodies of provincial and local governments. The same is not true of the metropolis. There, decrees and laws of general application are passed without sufficient consultation with the inhabitants of the overseas provinces (a notable exception was the new Organic Law of 1963). As a consequence, the process of metropolitan decision-making consists of a law being passed in Lisbon, promulgated in the province, and then eventually (often years afterward) modified or repealed, because of official and unofficial local reaction. An example of this was a recent action of the Legislative Council of Mozambique in excising a provision in a local enabling act that simply repeated the provisions of a metropolitan law. Although it was an *ultra vires* act of the Legislative Council, this was perhaps the only formal method available of demonstrating disagreement with the general law. From the standpoint of governmental and administrative effectiveness and efficiency, it would be preferable to provide for adequate prior consultation, rather than to wait for the drawn-out and diffuse process of local reaction.

CASE STUDIES

While in Angola, the author had the opportunity to trace through two case studies of local and community power processes. The two issues involved were one of "commercial dispersion" versus "commercial concentration," an issue of province-wide scope, and that of "clandestine" quarters, an issue in Luanda, Nova Lisboa, and other cities of the territory.[20]

By a law of November 30, 1935, Angola began the process of commercial regulation. Commercial concentration was first made mandatory in 1937 and strengthened by laws of 1948 and 1954. According to these laws and the administrative regulations designed to implement them, retail outlets could be established only in designated areas, and competition in the sale of the same merchandise by various outlets, even in the legal areas, was severely restricted. The rationale for this regulation was that it made inspection and taxation easier for the administration and was, for obvious reasons, supported by the local retailers, who were thus protected from competition. It also resulted in a sort of de facto segregation, was very inconvenient for the native population, and prevented the development of a class of native merchants.[21] In a law of November 29, 1961, a timid start was made in altering the regulations by providing for local markets, but these functioned only at harvest time, since a permanent commercial structure still had to fulfill various requisites that made it impossible for merchants to establish themselves without substantial capital.[22]

In 1964, the provincial administration introduced a bill providing for what was called "commercial dispersion." The pressures for this liberalization came from various sources. In the first place, illegal mercantile establishments had become a problem, especially in Luanda, Lobito, and Benguela. Secondly, the commercial associations, made up largely of large importers, wholesalers, and distributors, were interested in increasing the number of retail outlets; and, finally, the church was interested in providing more convenient facilities for the native population and the possibility of opening businesses of their own.[23] In deference to strong pressures by the local retail associations, however, the government bill provided merely that the district governors could determine whether to allow commercial dispersion in their districts. Before making their decision, they were required to hear the opinion of existing local economic associations. It would obviously be much easier for the retailers to exert pressure at the district than at the provincial level. In addition, anyone petitioning for permission to open a commercial establishment, even if dispersion were allowed, had to have completed the second year of primary schooling, in addition to certain other prerequisites.

On October 15 and 16, the Economic and Social Council, dominated by the representatives of large-scale commerce and industry, as well as by the administration, met to consider the bill. The deliberations of the Council resulted in an entirely new text, requiring that district governors subordinate their decisions to the general directives of the governor-general. Both texts were then sent to a committee of the Legislative Council, made up of three elected representatives and the attorney-general. The committee accepted the changes made by the Economic and Social Council and reported both texts to the plenum of the Council, which debated the issue in the sessions of November 6, 17, and 18. By a vote of 24 to 4, it was determined to use the text presented by the government, and that text was then approved "in generality" by a vote of 27 to 1. As it passed into the voting by articles, it was amended to bring it more into line with the version of the Economic and Social Council. In the course of the debate of November 17, which became particularly Byzantine with reference to various licenses and forms to be required of merchants, the president of the Commercial Association of Luanda (a member of the Legislative Council elected by substantial taxpayers) expressed clearly the political climate that had led to the introduction of the bill:

I only wish to manifest, once again, the anxiety of commerce to live with a bit more freedom, and not be suffocated always by the straitjacket of licences and forms which are not and cannot be followed in practice.

It seems to me that we are wasting time, discussing constantly matters that are of no practical interest.[24]

Following the passage of the bill, the governor-general in any case allowed the district governors great discretion in allowing and forbidding commercial dispersion. The general pattern of decisions by the summer of 1965 seemed to indicate that military governors were less responsive to pressure by the local retailer associations and thus more likely to permit dispersion.[25]

It will be noted that the original bill, although passed "in generality" by a vote of 27 to 1, was extensively amended by the Economic and Social Council, the committee of the Legislative Council, and the Legislative Council itself, by votes as close as 15 to 10.

The issue of "clandestine" quarters (*bairros clandestinos*) in the principal cities of Angola was chosen for study because, unlike the issue of commercial dispersion, there were no powerful, organized interest groups to offset the administration. Rather, it is an example of the power that can be exerted by individuals acting informally together to achieve a common end and, how, in an authoritarian society, it may be done.

As in practically all developing countries, Angola faces the phenomenon of such rapid urbanization that all efforts to keep up with it in terms of housing have failed. Considerable progress is being made in the construction of *bairros populares*, built with provincial and municipal funds, and *bairros económicos*, built by private firms for their workers. Nevertheless, each sizable Angolan city has a shanty-belt of jerry-built huts, called *muceques*, similar to the *casuchas* and *favelas* of Latin America. In most cities, the *muceques*, since they are formed on state land or someone's private land, are included in the term "clandestine quarters." In Luanda, however, that term is limited to a somewhat different phenomenon. As economic and industrial development takes place and the total urban population continues to grow, the middle class grows as well. Land is purchased by some members of the new middle class and the Municipal Council is petitioned for permission to construct houses and tie in with the municipal electric, water, and sewage services. The stage is set for conflict.

In 1960, the municipality of Luanda established a department of urbanization, charged with carrying out long-range urban planning and dealing with the problems of increasing immigration from rural areas. The department was given authority to grant all residential building permits. Partly because of insufficient personnel, partly because of the disruption caused in the city by destructive floods and landslides, and partly because of inevitable bureaucratic delays, requests for building permits were allowed to pile up without action. By the end of 1961, individuals owning land, but without building permits, began to build houses on the land clandestinely, with work proceeding mostly at night. As time passed and the municipal government failed to move against the transgressors, others began to build, some on their own land and some on state land. The houses built in this way are not huts or miserable shanties but substantial buildings, some of two or three stories. The municipal government refused to provide these illegal quarters with water or sewage or electricity but was overridden by the governor-general, who stated that, if the houses were allowed to stand, they must be provided with at least water and sewage for health reasons. The Municipal Council then decided to send the police to destroy the houses. The inhabitants of the clandestine quarters, now numbering in the thousands, hearing of the plans for police action, took immediate action themselves. They proceeded to name their quarters and streets after President Américo Tomás, Prime Minister António de Oliveira Salazar, Foreign Minister Alberto Franco Nogueira, Portuguese heroes of the guerrilla warfare of 1961, and various saints. They saw to it that a number of journalists and press photographers would be on hand when the police arrived. They staged sit-ins at Luanda's city hall. On the Sunday of the police "invasion," they stood in front of their developments, waving small Portuguese flags and singing the Portuguese national anthem. When the police charged, they threw sticks and stones at them, flung themselves on the ground, continued to sing, and began shouting, "They're attacking the street of Doctor Oliveira Salazar," "They're destroying the Avenue of Admiral Américo Tomás," and so forth. After about ten minutes of this the police withdrew, utterly defeated.

Since that time, the municipality has provided water and sewage, in accordance with the orders of the governor-general. The inhabitants have, themselves, linked up their houses with the electric system. Since the construction is illegal they do not pay for any of these services. The Council confines itself to passing resolutions and levying fines, which the inhabitants gladly pay in lieu of taxes or rent or electric, water, or sewage bills. By 1965, truckloads of sand were being moved in at night from the cliffs near Luanda to the sea and dumped, to create more land to build more illegal houses.[26]

Other Angolan cities have resolved the problem of "clandestine quarters" by legalizing them wholesale, so as to be able to regulate them and apply rental charges. This was done by Nova Lisboa, for example, the second-largest city of the province. The city created *bairros de transição*, with nominal charges leading to ownership, but applying heavy fines for construction outside these regulated *bairros*. In emitting an opinion in support of the Municipal Council's initiatives, the district attorney of Huambo District explained the reasons for and the pressures behind the moves in the following terms:

Let us examine the problem in its crudest reality. Urbanization in a city such as Nova Lisboa, as in Luanda and most, if not all, the cities of Angola, cannot be carried out with the esthetic planning of quarters, gardens, and social centers. Here, urbanization must confront an immediate and determining circumstance: the people of the city cannot protect themselves from the rain with the plans and dreams of the city planners. That is to say, the city must be immediately present. We cannot wait for tomorrow, because if we do, families which do not have houses will have to construct them anywhere and by any means, without thought to the future of the city. And we cannot condemn them, either on paper, or in the courts, or even in our consciences, because essential necessities have no future, but only a present. And according to all ethics, all morals, all right, and our whole manner of being Portuguese, no òne can condemn a person for wishing to give a house, a home, a shelter to his family.[27]

The same problem exists in Mozambique, but to a lesser extent, because of the lower level of urbanization.[28]

GENERAL TRENDS

There is no doubt that the general trend of at least the last decade or more (since the Organic Act of 1954) has been toward greater provincial and local autonomy in the overseas provinces. Despite the statement in the Portuguese Constitution that Portugal is a unitary state, the fact is that the present situation is one of nascent federalism, with the overseas provinces coming into greater administrative equality with continental Portugal. There is every indication that the new administrative code currently being drafted will accelerate this trend, providing for more effective organs of local government.

If the tendency toward greater provincial autonomy continues, the next step would be elected district governors and, eventually, elected provincial governors. Should this happen, it would perhaps be wise, considering the overwhelming predominance of Angola and Mozambique among the overseas provinces, to constitute the others as districts, equal in rank to the metropolitan districts, with elected or appointed governors (to conform with the situation at that time in Portugal), and with continental Portugal, along with the adjacent islands, one province; Cape Verde and Guinea another; São Tomé, Príncipe, and Angola a third; and Mozambique a fourth.[29]

There are forces, notably from continental Portugal, working in the opposite direction of greater centralization rather than federalization. The eventual outcome is, of course, unknown. At the moment, however, metropolitan and overseas pressures for local autonomy appear to have the upper hand.

NOTES

1. Fred W. Riggs, *Administration in Developing Countries: The Theory of Prismatic Society* (Boston, 1964).
2. See, for instance, Manuel Simões Vaz, *Problemas de Moçambique* (Lourenço Marques, 1951), and Associação Comercial de Beira, *Relatório do conselho director e parecer do conselho fiscal, exercício de 1964* (Lourenço Marques, 1965).
3. Victor Thompson, *Modern Organization* (New York, 1961).
4. See Adriano Moreira, "Relações entre a técnica e a administração," *Ensaios, estudos de Ciências Políticas e Sociais*, No. 34, 3rd ed. (Lisbon, 1963).
5. At present the *administrador de posto*, whatever the regulations may say, must make many decisions on his own in areas where he may have no competence, simply due to the lack of supporting personnel. Francisco Alfredo Fernandes, *O posto administrativo na vida do indígena* (Lisbon, 1955?).
6. Typewritten document of the Department of Civil Administration (Luanda, 1965). Similarly, Lord Hailey reported that out of a civil staff of 81 in Portuguese Guinea in 1950, 50 were from the overseas provinces (p. 378). Felgas reports more than 1,000 African officials in his district (Congo), of all ranks, when he was governor: Hélio A. Esteves Felgas, *As populações nativas do Norte*

de Angola (Lisbon, 1965), p. 65. On the subject of public administration and administration in transitional societies, besides the works already cited, consult Aaron Wildavsky, *The Politics of the Budgetary Process* (Boston, 1964); Harold F. Alderfer. *Local Government in Developing Countries* (New York, 1964); A. L. Adu, *The Civil Service in New African States* (New York, 1965); J. G. March and H. A. Simon, *Organizations* (New York, 1958); H. A. Simon, *Administrative Behavior*, 2nd ed. (New York, 1957); Robert K. Merton *et al.*, *Reader in Bureaucracy* (Glencoe, 1952); K. G. Younger, *The Public Service in New States* (New York, 1960); Peter Blau, *The Dynamics of Bureaucracy* (Chicago, 1955); R. Apthorpe, "The Introduction of Bureaucracy into African Politics," *The Journal of African Administration*, July, 1960; and F. A. Nigro, *Modern Public Administration* (New York, 1965).

7. On the general problem of the measurement of power, see, *inter alia*, Nelson W. Polsby, *Community Power and Political Theory* (New Haven, 1964); Robert A. Dahl, "The Concept of Power," *Behavioral Science*, Vol. II (1957); James G. March, "Measurement Concepts in the Theory of Influence," *Journal of Politics*, Vol. XIX (1957); Herbert A. Simon, "Notes on the Observation and Measurement of Political Power," *Journal of Politics*, Vol. XV (1953); and James G. March, "An Introduction to the Theory and Measurement of Influence," *American Political Science Review*, Vol. XLIX (1955). On local government in Africa, see L. Gray Cowan, *Local Government in West Africa* (New York, 1958); Ronald Wraith, *Local Government in West Africa* (New York, 1965); Fred Burke, *Local Government in Uganda* (Syracuse, 1964); and J. K. Nsarkoh, *Local Government in Ghana* (Accra, 1964). On Portuguese Africa, see Adriano Moreira, "The 'Elites' of the Portuguese 'Tribal' Provinces," *International Social Sciences Bulletin*, Vol. VIII, No. 3 (1956); and José Júlio Gonçalves, "Ensaio sobre as 'Elites,' " *Técnicas de propaganda, élites, quadros e outros estudos* (Lisbon, 1961). This is an area where the Portuguese have neglected research and where much useful and interesting work could be done.

8. *Novidades* (Lisbon), April 8, 1964.

9. A case of this kind almost arose in Angola in 1962, but before the matter could be submitted to the overseas minister for resolution, the governor general resigned.

10. Adriano Moreira, *op. cit.*, p. 11.

11. *Grémio* is a cooperative organization of enterprises in the same line of business; it enforces a standard of principles and ethics within the group.

12. Consult Adriano Moreira, *Direito corporativo* (Lisbon, 1950).

13. A. Rita Ferreira, *O movimento migratório de trabalhadores entre Moçambique e África do Sul* (Lisbon, 1963), p. 170.

14. Vicente Loff, *Ordenamento e coordenação*, p. 71.

15. Some of the information in this section and the following is from Associação Comercial da Beira, *op. cit.*; *Boletim da Associação Industrial de Angola*, XVI, No. 62 (December, 1964–January, 1965); Associação de Fomento do Distrito de Quelimane, *Relatório e contas do exercício de 1963* (Quelimane, n.d.); Câmara Municipal de Lourenço Marques, *Orçamento para o ano 1964*; Sindicato Nacional dos Empregados de Escritório da Província de Moçambique, *Relatórios do conselho geral e da direcção; balanço e contas do exercício de 1964* (mimeo); and Associaçao Comercial de Luanda, *Relatório e contas da gerência de 1964*. It is worth noting that a sense of social responsibility is developing,

at least in Angola. In Carmona, for instance, many public buildings and facilities were built by local agriculturists, and the new airport of Benguela was financed in part by public subscription in a campaign directed by the local newspaper.

16. See, among other references listed in Section IV of this book, *Africana Newsletter*, I, No. 3 (Summer, 1963); Alejandro Botzáris, *Africa e o comunismo*, II, Estudos de Ciências Políticas e Sociais, No. 46 (1961); Mário de Andrade, "Le nationalisme angolais," *Présence Africaine*, No. 42 (1962); and Hélio Esteves Felgas, *Guerra em Angola* (Lisbon, 1962).

17. It is well to point out that frequently there is considerable overlap on such boards, and power lies in fewer hands than is at first discernible.

18. See A. Lima de Carvalho, "Angola: Diferenciação, estratificação e mobilidade social—alguns problemas introdutórios fundamentais," *Angola* (Lisbon, 1964).

19. The church also exerts less influence in Angola than in Mozambique, due to a tradition of noninterference and the personalities involved.

20. The research techniques used in these decision-making studies were extensive interviewing of government officials, legislative representatives, and private individuals who took some part in the process; attendance at meetings of deliberative bodies; and a content analysis of official documents, legislative records, and newspapers. The results obtained were checked by a rudimentary reputational analysis in Angola, by a study of the nominating process for the legislative councils of Angola and Mozambique, and by the tracing through of a single but similar decision in Mozambique. See Norman A. Bailey, "Local and Community Power in Angola," *Western Political Quarterly*, XXI, No. 3 (September, 1968).

21. *Quatro anos no governo do Distrito do Uíge* (Carmona, 1965), pp. 40–42.

22. *A Província de Angola*, August 15, 1964.

23. See *Boletim Oficial de Angola*, Anexo, Conselho Legislativo, Acta da Sessão No. 131 (November 6, 1964), p. 2651.

24. *Ibid.*, Acta da Sessão No. 132 (November 17, 1964), p. 2671.

25. Documentary sources used in studying the process of decision-making in the case of commercial dispersion included legislative records, reports and memoranda of the economic associations, and newspapers.

26. There are now two clandestine districts in Luanda, the Bairro Dr. Alberto Franco Nogueira, wealthier and built in part on land owned by the inhabitants, and the Bairro Santa Barbara, lower middle class and built entirely on state land or land reclaimed from the sea. As of mid-1965, there were cases pending in the courts over the question of whether land reclaimed from the sea was state land or "belonged to God" (that is, to those who reclaimed it).

27. Junta Distrital do Huambo, *Parecer do delegado do procurador da república junto da vara* (Justino Miguel da Costa, April 19, 1965), typewritten—translation by author.

28. An amusing item in the July 19, 1965, issue of the *Diário de Moçambique* announced a decision of the municipality of Nampula to destroy the houses of three of its citizens who had "demanded the provision of light and water to their properties of clandestine construction."

29. Macau and Timor are outside the scope of this study, but it would appear that, because of their geographic distance, they would have to form a fifth province with two districts, or three, if Portuguese India is returned to Portuguese sovereignty. For a similar Portuguese view and prescription, see Manuel Dias Belchior, *A missão de Portugal em África* (Lisbon, 1960).

VIII

Native and Labor Policy

NORMAN A. BAILEY

NATIVE POLICY

THE POLICY of the Portuguese Government toward the indigenous population of its African territories has passed through four phases. Until the liberal revolution of 1820, Portuguese policy was one of recognition of the authority of African kings and chiefs under the overlordship of the king of Portugal. This overlordship was often nonexistent because of inadequate resources for effective supervision. The formal structure was complemented by a trading relationship through which the Portuguese purchased local products and slaves in exchange for manufactured goods, principally cloth, arms, and rum.

The second phase covered most of the nineteenth century, under the liberal monarchy, when the free Africans were officially Portuguese citizens with the same rights and duties as any other citizen. In practice, however, very little changed. Occupation was no more effective than previously, and local potentates continued their undisturbed rule and their trade with the Portuguese on the coast.

The third phase came with the colonial generation of the 1890's, when a series of *ad hoc* measures backed by warfare brought most Africans under effective Portuguese rule and when African labor began to be used for colonial purposes. The racial attitude of this generation has been covered in Chapter V. During this phase, the Portuguese native policy in Africa was one of "tendential assimilation," officially respecting local institutions and customs while gradually attempting to bring the Africans into contemporary life. This phase reached its culmination with the passage of the Native Statute (Estatuto dos Indígenas) in 1954, a restatement of the similar 1928 statute. This statute was similar in text and spirit to the subsequent International Labor Organization Convention No. 107 of 1957 on "The Protection and Integration of Tribal and Semitribal Populations in Independent Countries" and to typical paternalistic practice in many countries toward "noncivilized" populations. It perpetuated a division between Portuguese "citizens" and Portuguese "nationals," the latter consisting of the majority of the African populations.[1] In theory, the system was to be one of transition leading to the eventual integration of the entire population into Portuguese citizenship. For this purpose a category had been developed earlier, that of the *assimilado*, an African who, having fulfilled certain conditions and applied for citizenship, was granted that status with the rights and duties it entailed. In actual practice, by 1960, when the present phase of native policy emerged, few Africans (fewer relatively in Guinea and Mozambique than in Angola) had taken advantage of this provision, because, among other reasons, opportunities were limited and by doing so they lost the right to use reserved land, were subject to more onerous taxation, were deprived of free medical assistance, and were barred from being recognized as traditional chiefs. When the system was in effect, however, to be an *assimilado* was attractive enough that many claimed to be *assimilados* who legally were not. They wanted to reap the benefits of both statuses.[2] Only *assimilados* had the right of unrestricted free movement within a province, *indígenas* requiring permission of the *administrador* to leave their *circunscrição*. Even with the drawbacks involved, seven times as many Africans in Angola became *assimilados* as in Mozambique.

Despite the fact that a special system for the protection of aboriginal peoples is recognized by the International Labor Organization and practiced by many states, the manifest slowness of the official assimilation process led to a change in native policy in 1960, accelerated in 1961.[3] In September, 1960, by provincial *portarias*, a new status was introduced for more advanced Africans who did not wish to become *assimilados*. Such people were provided with a *cartão de identidade* and given free movement within the province. Africans retaining full indigenous status, and thus having a *caderneta* for identification, were granted free movement within their district. The fully assimilated population continued to be identified by a *bilhete de identidade*.

In September, 1961, the Native Statute was repealed and all inhabitants of the Portuguese-African territories were legally placed on an equal footing, with equal access to the rights and duties of citizenship. This was a partial and more realistic reversion to the liberal nineteenth-century position. Movement within the province was made free for everyone, and in September, 1962, the *cartão de identidade* was officially suppressed and issuance of the *bilhete de identidade* authorized for all inscribed on the civil registry. Under the provisions of the reforms of 1960–62, any African may, by simple declaration, choose to be governed by the Portuguese civil code and thus assume full Portuguese citizenship. There is no test or fee for this. If he does so, he is issued a *bilhete de identidade* and may vote if he fulfills the other suffrage requirements. By mid-1965, over 1 million Angolans and about 300,000 Mozambicans were registered on the civil rolls. Registration is permanently open.[4]

Prior to 1961, certain lands were preserved for African subsistence cultivation through a system of land reserves. Legislation was extremely complicated and contradictory, however, and African lands might be expropriated for any one of a number of reasons by many different government bodies. In 1961, previously confused land concession laws were codified. Africans in their reserves hold inalienable property in common. Any African choosing the civil code may hold real property as an individual. The procedure for obtaining land concessions was facilitated, utilization requirements for maintaining concessions were raised, and anyone applying for a concession of more than 100 acres had to submit proof of financial capability.[5]

Thus, a new phase of native policy in Portuguese Africa opened in the 1960's.

According to the new legal structure, an African may remain under the protection of special laws and arrangements if he prefers to continue a traditional existence. Should he prefer to assume the rights and duties of Portuguese citizenship, however, he is free to do so without test or fee, and hundreds of thousands have done so. In fact, in São Tomé and Príncipe, where no tribal organization existed, the entire population, except for temporary migrant labor, was granted citizenship. How long the period of transition will last and how well the new policies will work depends on many factors. External factors are discussed elsewhere in this book. As to internal factors:

> The answers to all these questions will depend upon how the high ideals of the Portuguese government are implemented by the European Portuguese working in harmony with the indigenous peoples in such a way that Africans will feel that their cultural values are appreciated and that nothing stands in the way of the advancement of the African peoples.[6]

LABOR POLICY

Until the nineteenth century, the economic system of much of Portuguese Africa was based upon slave labor. As explained in earlier chapters, the liberal revolution of 1829 gave rise to agitation for abolition, a movement supported by British pressure for an end to the slave trade. In 1836, the slave trade was abolished, in 1869 the children of slaves were declared free, and, in a decree of April 29, 1875 (to take effect one year later), slavery was abolished. Abolition of slavery in the Portuguese territories followed Great Britain (1833), France (1848), and the United States (1863) but preceded Brazil (1888) and Ethiopia (1924).

Issued soon after the official Portuguese abolition of slavery, the Labor Regulations of 1878 were designed to provide for a completely free labor system. But with the official end of slavery came economic stagnation, there being little or no entry into the market economy on the part of the vast bulk of the African population. As a result of this situation, the same generation of colonial reformers who were responsible for the administrative reorganization of the African territories also advocated the introduction of a system of compulsory or forced labor, for limited periods of time, with remuneration. It was claimed that to do so was simply to apply provisions similar to the vagrancy laws in Portugal itself. These ideas were put into practice in 1899. Section 1 of the Native Labor Regulations of that year read:

> All natives of Portuguese overseas provinces are subject to the obligation, moral and legal, of attempting to obtain through work the means that they lack to subsist and to better their social condition. They have full liberty to choose the method of fulfilling this obligation, but if they do not fulfill it, public authority may force a fulfillment.

Similar regulations were re-enacted several times until 1928.

While forced labor was used by all the colonial powers in Africa and, prior to colonization, by the African chiefs themselves, the Portuguese practices gained publicity, as they had done in earlier days, when David Livingstone devoted special attention to incidents in the Portuguese slave trade.[7]

Not long after issuance of the regulations of 1899, there began an international press controversy about contract labor in São Tomé. This involved charges that the five-year contracting of Angolan workers for the cacao plantations of São Tomé was forced, that living and working conditions were unsatisfactory, and that no workers ever returned. Even before the controversy broke into the international arena, the Portuguese themselves had undertaken corrective measures; however, in the passion of international controversy, instead of making much of what the government was doing to correct them, and expanding their corrective activities, they chose to deny that the abuses existed. As to Angola, critical publications such as John Harris's book in 1913, entitled *Portuguese Slavery*, and Edward Ross's report in 1925 continued to appear. The latter elicited a Portuguese response in the Sixth Assembly of the League of Nations. The Portuguese attempted some reforms and a defense of their position. The major Portuguese reform effort came with the Native Labor Code of 1928, which forbade recruiting by administrative officials for private companies and restricted forced labor to works of public utility, such as road-building.[8]

This law had little practical effect. Abuses continued for several reasons: lack of administrators, occasional collusion between administrators and private users of African labor, the extremely sparse population of Angola and Mozambique, and the preference on the part of the Africans for subsistence cultivation of their traditional lands rather than for working in sometimes distant and strange regions for remuneration maintained at an artificially low level by a system of maximum wages. Yet this labor system continued until 1955, when the law was revised, increasing the penalties for administrative recruiting of labor for private firms and further restricting the number of tasks of public utility for which compulsory labor could be used. The legislation of 1955 also provided, for the first time, detailed regulation of the hours and conditions of work. Under the new provisions, working conditions improved, but, with certain kinds of forced labor still permitted, continuing problems were inevitable. Particularly marked was the situation in northern Mozambique, because of the introduction of compulsory cotton cultivation.[9] Compulsory cultivation, however, is a different kind of abuse than forced labor, in that this is work imposed on the African farmer on his own lands, not forced labor on the property of someone else.

The abuses did not go uncriticized. The archbishop of Luanda, in a pastoral letter against the practice in 1956, and the bishop of Beira, in a long pastoral letter in 1954, condemned the continuing labor abuses.[10] As A. Rita Ferreira noted, "It is clear that recourse to compulsory labor and maximum salaries perverted during many decades the free functioning of the labor market and salary levels."[11]

Definitive reform of the native labor system began in 1960, with the revocation of penal sanctions for breach of work contracts, the setting of minimum wages, the establishment of labor inspection, the ratification of the International Labor Organization's Conventions on Child Labor and the Abolition of Forced Labor, and other measures. In 1961, the new Code of Rural Labor was promulgated.

All rural workers and unskilled urban workers come under the provisions of the general Portuguese labor code and union regulations as well as provincial laws.[12]

The general principles upon which the Code of Rural Labor is based are freedom of choice of work, equality of pay for equal work irrespective of extraneous factors such as race and sex, and the prohibition of labor recruitment, for any purpose, by administrative officials. The detailed provisions of the Code are similar to those of the famous Article 123 of the Mexican Constitution of 1917. They provide for an 8-hour day and a 48-hour week; collective bargaining; a 2-week paid vacation every year; no labor under 14 years of age (16 in some occupations); a 6-hour day for all workers under 18; free housing, transportation, and food for rural workers, with an option on the worker's part to take the equivalent in cash; compulsory accident and illness insurance and compensation; and temporary work contracts limited to 12 months if the worker is alone, 36 months if accompanied by his family.[13]

Major defects in the system of labor legislation were the lack of a social security system and the inadequate level of health and accident insurance. The former was remedied by the passage of a social security act in 1965, to be administered by the labor and social welfare institutes.[14] Penalties for violation of provisions of the code vary from $6.80 to $1,700.[15] Also in 1961, a decree revoked all previous laws on cotton cultivation and declared such cultivation free of coercion, setting heavy penalties for violation.

Enforcement of the Code of Rural Labor is in the hands of the labor and social welfare institutes. These institutes, founded in 1962, operate in the labor field through a corps of labor inspectors and assistants. All administrators can also make labor inspections, order changes, and levy fines. Acceptance of and compliance with the code has generally been better in Angola than in Mozambique, where many businesses are owned by metropolitan Portuguese trusts and where local managers generally operate on the principle that profits are made only through low salaries. The Labor Inspection Service is also better organized and more active in Angola than in Mozambique. In 1964, in Angola 11,000 inspections were made, and fines totaling $115,000 were levied for infractions of the Labor Code and of provincial labor legislation. Opposition to fulfilling the terms of the code is found in Angola principally among plantation-owners and in Mozambique in urban retail commerce. Corruption in the Labor Inspectorate is avoided by paying the inspectors well ($275 per month) and by having them make their visits accompanied by local administrators.[16]

A new system of labor courts went into effect on January 1, 1966; this involved the creation of two additional labor courts to handle the increasing volume of labor disputes and minor disputes arising out of the administration of labor laws as authorized in 1965. The court that had existed in Luanda since 1960 was upgraded. These courts provide more expeditious handling of labor disputes and have led to the formation of a small corps of judicial authorities versed in dealing with labor problems.

Except for difficulties during a short initial period, especially in Mozambique, implementation of the Code of Rural Labor has not hampered recruitment of labor. Market habits and the desire for manufactured goods have apparently by now become sufficiently instilled in the African population for the normal economic incentives to operate effectively.

According to the 1965 figures of the Provincial Labor Institute, the number of wage-earners in Angola was just over 400,000. There were 357,851 in private industry and 28,818 employed by the provincial and local governments. A large number of workers, such as house-servants and unskilled farm-laborers, who are wage-earners at least part of each year, are not included in these statistics.

Wage-earners in Angola were employed by activity in 1965 as follows:

Private Industry

Agriculture	144,667
Fishing	16,225
Cattle-ranching	5,721
Mining	30,249
Manufacturing	29,838
Civil construction	40,747
Communications and transportation	31,683
Commerce (banks, wholesale, retail)	25,000
Services	40,000
Not specified	3,221
Total	367,351

Government (Estimate)

Provincial	
Permanent	27,478
Contract and temporary	7,000
Local	
Permanent	1,540
Contract and temporary	5,000
Total	41,018
Grand total	408,369

Of the total number of employed workers in Angola, aside from government employees, 241,351 are considered unskilled laborers, largely employed in agriculture, while approximately 65,500 are listed as semiskilled and 65,000 as skilled.

Minimum-wage levels (there no longer are maximum-wage levels) in force in 1965 varied between $34 and $204 per month for workers not entitled to extensive fringe benefits (almost entirely urban semiskilled and skilled workers) and between $23 and $75 per month for rural and unskilled workers (depending on district) plus housing, food, medical care, insurance, transportation, schools, canteens, and other fringe benefits. The actual level of wages in 1964 was considerably higher in Angola than in Mozambique, because of a greater shortage of labor in the former province and greater employer resistance in the latter. The median monthly rural wage for unskilled labor in Angola was $7.50 in cash and $11.60 in fringe benefits, a total of $19.10. In Mozambique, rural salaries, including fringe benefits, for unskilled daily labor ranged from $8.80 to $17.20 per month, depending on the district, and, for industrial unskilled labor, they ranged from $10.20 to $18.50.[17] The growing shortage of labor in Mozambique is exerting a constant upward pressure on wages, however. A recent investigation in a multiracial public housing development in a Lourenço Marques suburb found 9.7 per cent of the families with cash incomes above $51 per month, 77.4 per cent with between $20.45 and $50, and only 12.9 per cent with under $20.45, but all were higher than $13.60.[18]

In Angola, the concentration of the skilled and semiskilled laborers is in the urban areas of Luanda, Lobito, Benguela, and Nova Lisboa. The average monthly salary, depending upon the nature and level of skill, was from $60 to $120 in 1965.

The government has shown interest in the problem of unemployed laborers and the shortage of skilled workers, and the Angolan Labor Department opened an artisan training school in 1966, offering six-month courses in various trades, particularly those useful in construction. The initial program called for approximately 250 graduates in the first year.

The organization of trade unions (*sindicatos*) in Portuguese Africa has been discussed in Chapters VI and VII.

THE INTERNATIONAL LABOR ORGANIZATION REPORT

At the beginning of 1961 the government of Ghana, through its permanent representative to the International Labor Organization, filed major and far-reaching charges against Portugal. Ghana claimed that the cornerstone of Portuguese native policy, particularly in Angola and Mozambique was, and continued to be, the African's obligation to work, despite Portugal's ratification of the Abolition of Forced Labor Convention in 1960. Furthermore, Ghana maintained that the development of Portuguese Africa was carried out by forcing Africans to work by every available means. Part of Ghana's case was based upon citations of earlier Portuguese native-labor regulations, such as the Native Labor Regulations of 1899 noted earlier in this chapter. Ghana also produced witnesses, newspaper accounts, and other documents.[19] Other charges were that the Benguela Railway was partly maintained by forced labor; that such situations were worse than slavery; that forced labor was generally used in the European-owned sugar, coffee, and sisal plantations; that wages were low and not fixed, the highest paid African on these plantations receiving only about three cents a day; that under the Portuguese–South African labor contract, over 100,000 Mozambicans were shipped to mines in South Africa under recruitment that included bribing the chiefs.

Acting upon the complaint by Ghana, the International Labor Organization established a commission to investigate conditions in Portuguese Africa. The commission was composed of three experts, from Switzerland, Uruguay, and

Senegal. The commission reviewed documentary evidence and traveled nearly 9,000 kilometers in the two major African territories, following an unannounced itinerary and with freedom to consult, interview, and visit anyone and any place of its choosing.

The findings and recommendations of the commission came as a surprise in view of the fact that the charges of Ghana and the documents and publications presented by the UAR had won rather wide public acceptance. Portugal had done so little to open Angola and Mozambique to the press that many people assumed that Portugal had something to hide. Almost any charge therefore created suspicion.

Early in the investigation, the commission notified Ghana that its original complaint was unsupported by evidence, and Ghana was afforded an opportunity to substantiate its claims further, without avail. Subsequent to hearing the only two witnesses produced by Ghana, the commission made its on-the-spot visit to Angola and Mozambique.

The commission recognized the difficulties facing the Portuguese in carrying out in full their own laws and recommendations, with great distances, imperfect communications, mining and agricultural concessions over large areas under company influence, difficulties in knowing how well the African population in obscure and inaccessible areas understand their own rights, language problems, and "the difficulty of having any real understanding of what is happening in the African mind in the absence of a substantial African Administrative cadre in either government or industry."[20] The commission noted that "it was favourably impressed by the degree of freedom exercised by a very large majority of those with whom it came into contact in both Angola and Mozambique (government officials, employers and workers alike, Africans and Europeans) in expressing their views to it without constraint or inhibition."[21] Further, the commission noted that, instead of historical evidence, it could consider only conditions in Portuguese Africa after the Portuguese ratification of the Abolition of Forced Labor Convention of 1957, which went into effect in Portuguese Africa on November 23, 1960. This excluded, for example, the charges made in the "Galvão Report," which dealt with facts prior to 1949. It also recognized that "forced labor was for many years a major factor in the economies of many African countries."[22]

After stressing the "far-reaching changes" that had occurred "in Portuguese policy, legislation, and practice," the commission concluded its observations by declaring itself "fully satisfied with the bona fides of these changes" and "rejects as entirely without foundation the suggestion made in support of the complaint that 'Portugal only ratified the Convention as a cover to continue her ruthless labor policies.' "[23]

It is fortunate that economic incentives appear to be operating effectively in Portuguese Africa, for there has always been some form of at least de facto forced labor at the beginning of every industrialization process, through law or taxation or such devices as the enclosure acts in England. The situation was particularly difficult in Africa, where the traditional social structure in many areas provided that agricultural labor be done by women, while the men fought, hunted, or herded cattle.[24] On the other hand, some of the African tribes in the Portuguese territories have traditionally been oriented toward a market economy. One example is the Ovimbundu of Angola, for whom "making money and becoming rich are regarded with unambiguous approval."[25] The reaction to the Code of Rural Labor in 1961 indicates that other tribes as well have changed their traditional attitudes. There have been dramatic reactions to wage incentives among African workers in both Portuguese and non-Portuguese Africa.

Some African countries since independence have reinstated forms of forced labor to aid in the process of modernization. Guinean President Sékou Touré, for example, announced, as soon as his country had won its independence, "We will be the first African Government to establish compulsory labor."[26] Despite earlier traditions to the contrary, Portugal has rejected the concept and has begun to solve the difficulty.

LABOR MIGRATION

A special problem for Mozambique is the heavy current of labor migration to the mines and factories of South Africa and Rhodesia. Labor emigration to South Africa from the Lourenço Marques area, principally from among the Thonga peoples, began as early as late in the 1860's. The first formal agreement for furnishing workers for the Rand mines was made with the Transvaal Government in 1897. In 1901 the Witwatersrand Native Labour Association (WNLA) began to recruit in southern Mozambique. The WNLA was formed by the larger South African mine-owners in an attempt to deal with their ever increasing problem of labor shortage. Operating initially on a legal basis in Mozambique, the WNLA soon began to engage in questionable and illegal behavior, including the formation of a corps of armed "runners" or "emigration police," uniformed in such a way as to be confused with the regular police in the minds of the Africans, and numbering at one point as many as 6,500, as well as the establishment of labor recruitment and collection camps on Portuguese territory and the suborning of African chiefs for the purpose of having them turn over their subjects for work in the mines. In addition, the WNLA actively encouraged illegal emigration, above the total provided for in the agreement between the South African and Portuguese governments. As the development of wage-consciousness among southern Mozambicans proceeded, however, and with attempts on the part of the Portuguese authorities to curb these abuses, the WNLA gradually gave up these practices and now operates within the law.[27]

The current agreement with the South African Government provides for not more than 100,000 contract workers per year, all to come from the area of Mozambique south of the 22nd parallel. Besides the legal emigrants, there has always been a large number of illegal emigrants, at times reaching a figure three times that of the legal workers. At one time, the financial return to Mozambique from labor emigration was substantial, but currently it does not exceed 2 per cent of annual provincial income.[28] This return in no way compensates for the undesirable effects of the emigration, including family dislocation and the loss of needed labor.

Several reasons have been given for this migration, especially the presumed preference of the Thonga women for men who have been to the mines and brought back the *lobolo*, or bride-price. There is no doubt that the migration originally began, at least in part, because of the loss of cattle through war and drought, requiring that the bride-price be paid in cash; presently, the primary reason for the emigration is that wages in South Africa and Rhodesia are considerably higher than in Mozambique.

There has also been a largely unrecorded emigration from Mozambique to the southern part of Malawi because of the development of tea plantations there. These emigrants have often preferred to remain in Malawi. As a result, areas in Malawi that were sparsely populated at the turn of the century had 380,000 Lomwe-speaking people permanently settled there in 1945, as compared to none in 1896, 120,000 in 1921, and 136,000 in 1931.[29]

Thus, any cure for labor emigration must begin with continuing the economic growth of Mozambique, resulting in better local conditions and higher wage levels. Improved conditions have already resulted in a lower level of emigration, averaging in the 1960's about 250,000 per year to South Africa and Rhodesia, with perhaps 100,000 of that number illegal.[30] Mozambique law now levies heavy fines on activities designed to promote illegal labor emigration, including a $170 fine per person recruited, and dismissal from office of public officials aiding such efforts. There is also a minor current of emigration from Angola to the mines of South-West Africa, averaging perhaps 10,000 workers per year.[31] Instability of the labor force due to internal migration and repeated changing of jobs has proved to be a problem in both Angola and Mozambique.[32]

Labor migration is a phenomenon by no means limited to Portuguese Africa, of course: "In many areas the migration of labor has become a commonplace of modern African life."[33] Almost all underdeveloped countries, including Portugal itself, have experienced this phenomenon, as rural underemployed attempt to find remunerative employment in urban and mining areas. Labor mobility is, of course, a good thing, if in fact those moving are able to fit into a healthy, growing economy. As Marcello Caetano has noted, "When working conditions offered to the African are such that he feels himself better off in the plantation, in the fisheries, in the factories or mines than in his village, the problem of manpower will be to a great extent solved."[34]

South Africa has been the most attractive magnet for migrant labor from other parts of Africa. Before it declared independence, Rhodesia also had some 200,000 African workers from Zambia, Malawi, and other nearby states. This movement of individuals in quest of employment and better working conditions creates innumerable complications from the point of view of social legislation, labor standards, and the protection of local Africans against people from outside.

NOTES

1. Note the position of the Indians in the United States (a system of apartheid) and Brazil, the Ainu in Japan, the bushmen in Australia, the Eskimos in Canada, the Lapps in Sweden, and others. Examples of discrimination against groups that could hardly be called "aboriginal" are legion, such as the Tamil in Ceylon, the Arabs in Israel, etc.

2. Amparo Baptista, "Indígenas e assimilados, inexactidões estatísticas," *Jornal Português de Economia e Financas*, IV, No. 44 (March 15, 1957). See also José Carlos Ney Ferreira and Vasco Soares da Veiga, *Estatuto dos indígenas portugueses das províncias da Guiné, Angola e Moçambique*, 2nd ed. (Lisbon, 1957); J. M. da Silva Cunha, *Questões ultramarinas e internacionais* (Lisbon, 1961); Terence O. Ranger, "Revolt in Portuguese East Africa: The Mokombe Rising of 1917," in Kenneth Kirkwood (ed.), *African Affairs*, No. 2 (London, 1963). For the indigenous political systems to which the Portuguese have had to adapt, see Orlando Ribeiro, *Aspectos e problemas da expansão portuguesa*, Estudos de Ciências Politicas e Sociais, No. 59 (Lisbon, 1962); M. Fortes and E. E. Evans-Pritchard, *African Political Systems* (London, 1940), Isaac Schapera, *Government and Politics in Tribal Society* (London, 1956); Lucy Mair, *Primitive Government* (Baltimore, 1962).

3. Adrian C. Edwards, *The Ovimbundu Under Two Sovereignties* (New York, 1962), pp. 136ff.

4. On this subject, besides works already cited, see J. M. da Silva Cunha, *O sistema português de política indígena* (Lisbon, 1952). For some additional foreign criticisms, see Perry Anderson, *Le Portugal et la fin de l'ultracolonialisme* (Paris, 1963); Len Addicott, *Cry Angola* (London, 1962); James Duffy, "La présence Portugaise en Angola," *Presence Africaine*, No. 41 (1962).

5. Adriano Moreira, "A propriedade no ultramar," in *Ensaios*, 3rd ed., Estudos de Ciências Políticas e Sociais, No. 34 (Lisbon, 1963); A. de Sousa Franklin, "The Portuguese System of Protecting Native Landed Property," *Journal of African Administration*, January, 1957; Lucy Mair, *Native Policies in Africa* (London, 1936); Marcello Caetano, *Os nativos na economia africana* (Coimbra, 1954); Genipro de Eça d'Almeida, *Colonização: um problema nacional* (Lisbon, 1945); Ralph von Gersdorff, "Endeavor and Achievement of Cooperatives in Mozambique," *The Journal of Negro History*, XLV, No. 2 (April, 1960); Augusto Casimiro, *Angola e o futuro* (Lisbon, 1958).

6. Eduardo Mondlane, "Mozambique," in C. W. Stillman (ed.), *Africa in the Modern World* (Chicago, 1955), p. 244.

7. Livingstone's charges were disputed by F. J. de Lacerda, *Exame das viagens do Doutor Livingstone* (Lisbon, 1867). Since the British coveted the Portuguese territories, it was claimed that Livingstone was not objective.

8. See Vasco Dias de Oliveira, *Mão-de-obra indígena* (Luanda, 1924), and J. M. da Silva Cunha, *O trabalho indígena: Estudo de direito colonial* (Lisbon, 1959). A vivid description of forced labor and other labor practices in the 1920's can be found in the novel *Terra morta*, by the white Angolan writer, Castro Soromenho (Lisbon, 1961).

9. The most useful single work on Portuguese-African labor policy is Silva Cunha, *O trabalho indígena*; there is a bibliography of works on the subject on pages 297–305. See also J. P. Paixão Barradas, *Legislação sôbre trabalho indígena* (Lisbon, 1957), and Caetano, *Os nativos na economia africana*.

10. Sebastião Soares de Resende, *Hora decisiva de Moçambique* (Lourenço

Marques, 1954). The Bishop of Beira informed the author in July, 1965, that the free system of cotton production introduced in 1961 is working very well. Another Portuguese criticism will be found in António Carreira, "Problemas do trabalho indígena na colónia da Guiné," *Boletim Geral das Colónias* (December, 1948). For foreign criticisms, see Marvin Harris, *Portugal's African "Wards"* (New York, 1958); Basil Davidson, *The African Awakening* (London, 1955); and James Duffy, *Portugal in Africa* (London, 1962).

11. A. Rita Ferreira, "Estrutura da população activa em Moçambique," *Ultramar*, IV, No. 4 (1964), p. 10 of pre-published MS. For a view that the 1955 labor legislation was among the best in Africa, see André Durieux, "Essai sur le Statut des Indigénes de la Guinée, de l'Angola et du Mozambique," *Mémoires de l'Académie Royale des Sciences Coloniales*, V, Part III, New Series (Brussels, 1955), 68: "fruits d'une longue expérience, et sources d'heureuses conséquences. . . . Eût-il même apporté des realisations marquées de succès durable et fécond."

12. For labor legislation in force in Angola as of 1963, see Instituto do Trabalho, Previdência e Acção Social, *Documentos, legislação do trabalho em Angola*, Vol. I (Luanda, 1963).

13. For English versions of the 1960–62 labor reforms, see "Rural Labour Code for Portuguese Overseas Provinces," *International Labour Review*, Summer, 1962, and Adriano Moreira, *Portugal's Stand in Africa* (New York, 1962), pp. 225–61. For a recent attack on Portuguese native and labor policies, supposedly by a long-term American resident of Angola, see anonymous article; "Kingdom of Silence," *Harper's Magazine*, May, 1961. An authoritative defense of these policies will be found in António de Oliveira Salazar, "Realaties and Trends of Portuguese Politics," *International Affairs*, April, 1963.

14. Afonso Mendes, *A Huíla e Moçâmedes: considerações sôbre o trabalho indígena* (Lisbon, 1958). Mr. Mendes was subsequently president of the Labor Institute in Angola.

15. "Rural Labour Code for Portuguese Overseas Provinces," in *op. cit.*

16. In the month of May, 1965, the labor service in Angola made 457 visits in six cities and levied seventy fines. *Diário de Luanda*, June, 16, 1965, p. 6.

17. Instituto do Trabalho, Previdência e Acção Social de Angola, "Salários mensais em numerário, por percentagem dos trabalhadores rurais e equiparados durante o ano de 1964" (mimeo), and "Evolução dos salários por sector de actividade, por zonas geográficas e por profissões" (typewritten, deals with Mozambique).

18. A. Rita Ferreira, "Estrutura da população activa em Moçambique," p. 25 of MS. In 1968, the UPI reported that Mozambican employers in the building trades were pressing for an increase in minimum wages from $5.25 to $10.20 per day. *New York Times*, November 6, 1968.

19. International Labour Organization, *Report of Ad Hoc Committee on Forced Labour* (Geneva, 1963), and "Report of the Commission Appointed under Article 26 of the Constitution of the ILO to Examine the Complaint Filed by the Government of Ghana Concerning the Observance by the Government of Portugal of the Abolition of Forced Labour Convention, 1957 (No. 105)," *Official Bulletin*, XLV, No. 2, Suppl. II (Geneva, April, 1962), 149. See also George Martelli, *The Future of Angola* (London, 1962), pp. 17–18. As late as December, 1959, the African Consultative Commission of the ILO could mee

in Luanda: *Boletim Geral do Ultramar*, January–February, 1960, pp. 137–43. For an attack on the methods and conclusions of the ILO Commission, see Marvin Harris, "Race, Conflict, and Reform in Mozambique" (typewritten manuscript, 1965), pp. 22ff. An American missionary charged that no one in Angola would think of denying that forced labor existed. Another witness, again a missionary, alleged that an African, working on the land, who could not prove that he had produced a certain amount of coffee or had effective control of a certain amount of land was regarded as lazy and idle and was subject to forced-labor recruitment. The United Arab Republic joined with Ghana in presenting in evidence many documents and books, including *The African Awakening* by Basil Davidson (New York, 1955), *Portugal's African "Wards"* by Marvin Harris (New York, 1958), *Portuguese Africa* by James Duffy (Cambridge, Mass., 1961), *Santa Maria: My Crusade for Portugal*, by Henrique Galvão (Cleveland, 1961), and *Angola: Journey to a War*, a television documentary, produced by an American television company, NBC.

20. International Labor Office, *Official Bulletin*, XLV, No. 2, Suppl. II (April, 1962), 231–32.
21. *Ibid.*, p. 232.
22. *Ibid.*, p. 233.
23. Detailed information on specific labor practices is found in *ibid.*, p. 234.
24. See Hélio Felgas, *Aspectos políticos da Africa actual* (Lisbon, 1962), p. 20, and W. H. Friedland and C. G. Rosberg (eds.), *African Socialism* (Stanford, 1964), esp. pp. 15, 16, and 19. On the position of women in the traditional African economy, see J. A. Barnes, *Politics in a Changing Society: A Political History of the Fort Jameson Ngoni* (London, 1954).
25. Edwards, *op. cit.*, pp. 73–74. For African response to improved conditions and wage incentives, see Augusto António, "Os indígenas africanos e o trabalho," *Revista do Ultramar*, III, 17 (June, 1950), and Augusto Casimiro in Caetano, *Os nativos na economia africana*, pp. 303ff.
26. George Balandier, *Ambiguous Africa* (New York, 1966), p. 266.
27. A. Rita Ferreira, *O movimento migratório de trabalhadores entre Moçambique e a África do Sul* (Lisbon, 1963), pp. 102–4 and 129–34.
28. *Ibid.*, pp. 135ff.; Hélio Felgas, *Emigração indígena de Moçambique para os territórios limítrofes* (Lisbon, 1955), particularly useful for historical summary; M. D. W. Jeffreys, "Lobolo e o preço da criança," *Boletim da Sociedade de Estudos de Moçambique*, XXXI, 132 (July–September, 1962).
29. UNESCO *Bulletin*, E/CN. 14/LU/ECOP/2 (July 20, 1965), p. 3.
30. For criticisms of this labor migration, see Judith Alves Martins, "A destribalização da mulher negra em geral com alguns apontamentos sôbre o problema em Moçambique," *Estudos Ultramarinos*, Vol. II (1961), and Marvin Harris, "Labour Migration among the Mozambique Thonga: Cultural and Political Factors," *Africa*, XXIX, No. 1 (January, 1959), A. Rita Ferreira, "Labour Migration Among the Mozambique Thonga," *Africa*, XXX, No. 2 (April, 1960), is a reply to Harris.
31. Mendes, *op. cit.*, and José Maria Gaspar, *Problemática do trabalho em Africa* (Lisbon, 1965).
32. *Estudo sôbre o absentismo e a instabilidade da mão-de-obra africana*, Vol. III (Lisbon, 1960).
33. Lord Hailey, *An African Survey* (London, 1957), p. 1359.
34. Caetano, *Os nativos na economia africana*, p. 224.

IX

Education, Health, and Social Welfare

MICHAEL A. SAMUELS AND NORMAN A. BAILEY

IN RECENT YEARS, it has become increasingly clear that the level and quality of education and health play a significant role in economic and political development. Before highlighting recent developments and problems, and possible future trends, past traditions will be explored. A later chapter on agriculture will discuss various settlement plans that might, however, be seen as part of social as well as economic development.

EDUCATION

From the earliest contact with Africa, education has been an integral part of Portugal's "civilizing" mission. Though literacy in Portuguese and Catholic doctrine were stressed, European technical skills were occasionally included. Afonso, the sixteenth-century Catholic Manikongo, sought in vain for an increase in the technical side of early Portuguese educational aid. The Portuguese, however, were less interested in, or less capable of, providing secular skills than religious instruction. For almost four centuries, education was mostly a function of the Catholic missionaries, both Portuguese and Italian. Restrictions on Catholic activity by Pombal in 1759 and the liberal government of 1834 proved to be setbacks to Portuguese educational work in Africa.[1] Nevertheless, Catholic missions and their educational work reached farther into the African interior than did any activity other than the slave trade.

The first specific government provision for education in the overseas provinces was authorized by decrees of 1845 and 1869.[2] As a result of them, there slowly developed what might be called a village system of education. Government schools, staffed by parish priests, partially educated Africans, or random soldiers were common in forts and in centers of effective administration. Most of the students in such schools were neighboring Africans, few of whom succeeded in acquiring basic literacy. Meanwhile, in the 1860's and 1870's in Luanda, interested citizens organized private primary schools.

The 1878 arrival of the English Baptists in northern Angola presaged a flow of Christian missionaries from several European countries and America.[3] From their activity flowed in turn a natural educational expansion, which often accompanied the expansion of administrative control toward "effective occupation" of the interior. The educational pattern that soon developed was a dual one: government and private education in populated areas and administrative centers, mission education for Africans in rural areas. Only rarely did these two systems coincide, and then they did so only through the activities of Catholic priests, who were sometimes used both as missionaries and as parish priests.

By the turn of the nineteenth century, several traditions had developed. The modicum of education had stirred many Westernized *mestiços* and Africans, aware of growing opportunities, to use local newspapers to demand, unsuccessfully, more educational opportunities.[4] The government spoke about providing education but gave it a very low priority. The schools that did develop served to encourage an administrative system parallel to that in the metropole and to provide the opportunity for a limited number of children to learn something of Portuguese culture and language.

For the mission, education had a different function. Because growing numbers of Africans desired education, Catholic missions were able to use it as an incentive to attract converts. Financial support for their schools came largely from the government, and classes were sometimes in Portuguese but frequently in the local African language. Though the curriculum of most schools included little more than the catechism, in Angola a seminary and in Mozambique a technical school became the first postprimary schools before World War I. The Protestants had a greater concern for literacy, since reading the Bible and other Christian texts was an important facet of their program. The Protestants, somewhat more than the Catholics, frequently attempted to proselytize through an African clergy, and thus their activities were conducted almost exclusively in African languages, many of which they reduced to writing for the first time. Some of the better Protestant students learned English or, more rarely, Portuguese. The use of African languages limited the level to which the schools could develop and began to alienate the Portuguese, many of whom were already skeptical about the presence of foreign missionaries.

The arrival of the First Republic brought many consequences for education. The decrease in government funds to Catholic missions for almost a decade practically crippled their educational activities. Protestant missions, however, were given increased moral support. At the same time, government educational plans, rather than actions, were numerous. A significant action was the establishment of bureaus of native affairs, which officially separated the education for rural Africans from that for Europeans and assimilated Africans. In later years, the failure of the bureaus to take charge of African education meant that rural Africans would continue to be educated by missions or not at all.[5]

Decree 77 of 1921 stands as an educational milestone. It forbade the use of African languages in schools, except for the purpose of teaching religion and for help in the early stages of teaching the Portuguese language. The government felt that, since the educational goal was the integration of Africans into Portuguese society and culture, use of African languages was senseless and divisive. The majority of Africans were, of course, far removed from centers where there existed a functional need to use Portuguese; thus, there was neither much demand for nor potential practice in what was for many a foreign language. A basic result of this decree was to give a natural advantage to Catholic missions. This advantage was compounded by Protestant intransigence or linguistic inadequacy in Portuguese. The purposes of Protestantism were better served by communicating the Christian message in African languages and providing written materials for its continued reinforcement.[6]

The next major educational event for Portuguese Africa was the signing of a Missionary Accord with the Vatican in 1940. The following year a Missionary Statute made Catholic missions the arm of the state in educating Africans.[7] This statute gave specific meaning to the 1930 Colonial Act, which had given Catholic missions a privileged position in education. The previous dual system now assumed a more formal shape. For European and assimilated African children, there was a system that duplicated the system of metropolitan Portugal. For the vast majority of Africans under mission tutelage, there was "education for adapting" (*ensino de adaptação*), or "rudimentary education" (*ensino rudimentar*) as it was called after 1956. The purpose of this three-year primary course was to introduce Africans to Portuguese language and culture. Though legal means existed for a transfer to the state school system, artificial age barriers and natural rural hindrances kept such transfers to a bare minimum.

The deficiencies of this system were compounded by two traditional factors: first, the impoverishment of Portugal itself and, second, a prevalent educational laxity in the metropole, where the illiteracy rate was among the highest in Europe. Meanwhile, the outside world was beginning to comment on the sad state of the schools of Portuguese Africa. Although Lord Hailey used statistics of doubtful accuracy, he noted that, in Angola for 1950–51, there were 13,586 pupils in primary schools, 2,277 in secondary schools, 1,548 in technical schools, and 154 in normal schools, "not a very noteworthy achievement for an administration which has in its charge a population of over 4 million people."[8] Official realization of, and concern for, the bad state of educational affairs by late in the 1950's led to an increased government interest in education at all levels. This increased interest was given further impetus by the beginning of Angolan insurgency in 1961. Since that time, there have been significant changes in both quantity and quality of education.

GENERAL SCHEME OF EDUCATION

Though in 1961 the government abolished the legal distinction between citizens and indigenous inhabitants, large cultural and social differences have remained. A major aim of the educational system is to reduce the differences and to assimilate the Africans, the basic tool still being the teaching of the Portuguese language. The desire to spread their language provides the impetus for the Portuguese in their policy of educational expansion.

A major feature of the school system reflects the Portuguese view of their country as multiracial. In contrast to the pattern in the rest of southern Africa, there is no racial division either within the school system or within the schools themselves. Although rural elementary schools may be completely African, and the universities are heavily European, urban schools reflect a complete racial and social mixture. One interesting effect of such a situation is that it places great difficulties in the path of someone attempting to make observations about racial balance in the schools. Such an attempt must be done subjectively.

As was pointed out in Chapter VI, top-level policy decisions emanate from Lisbon. Within the Overseas Ministry, there is the General Directorate for Education (*Direcção Geral do Ensino*), which establishes a general scheme of development and coordinates the activities of each province. For problems at the secondary and university levels, relevant sections of the Ministry of National Education have ultimate jurisdiction. Each province has an education department within the administration (*direcção dos serviços de educação*), which reports to the governor-general. In Angola and Mozambique, an appointed provincial education secretary works with the governor in coordinating educational activities, being, in effect, a minister of education. The education department is divided into two parts, one charged with normal administrative duties and one with inspection. The latter is responsible for the quality of education, through supervision of course content, teacher performance, and teacher training.[9] One function that could be assumed to be included in an educational department is noticeably lacking. Educational statistics are collected and published not by the educational department but by a central, provincial-wide statistical department (*serviços de estatística*). A lack of coordination between these two departments leads to the collection and dissemination of many facts that lack educational relevance, the omission of other more relevant ones, and a lack of information about and interest in current statistics by those most directly concerned with education.[10]

Officially, children begin school at age six, attending a preprimary year in which they are introduced to the Portuguese language. Through mostly oral, activity-centered methods, the preprimary grade was conceived as a kind of head-start program for children lacking skills in Portuguese. Those for whom such a year is unnecessary are promoted three months after the school year has begun. The remainder of the primary course continues for four years.

In most rural school posts, however, inadequate facilities and teachers with low educational qualifications preclude the offering of the full course. Thus, although the former dual system has now become a unified one, and all students study the same subjects from the same textbooks, rural posts do not function very differently from their predecessors, the rudimentary schools. The full four-year course is available in primary schools (*escolas primárias*) usually centrally located in areas of major population concentration.

For the two types of schools, there are three levels of teacher. The lowest-qualified teacher is the *regente* or *monitor*, seen as a temporary expedient to fill the classrooms in a period of rapid expansion. The majority of the rural school posts are filled with such teachers who have completed only the four-year primary course. Many have also attended an additional special training course, which provides preservice and in-service three-month courses designed to perfect their skills in using the textbooks from which they will teach.

A four-year postprimary course, including both the first two years of secondary school and two of teacher training, prepares rural teachers (*professores de posto*). Though these teachers are not supposed to teach beyond the third primary class, many of them prepare students for the primary school promotion exams. A shortage of teachers and personal inclination have led many *professores de posto* to seek positions in primary schools in nonrural areas. Teachers of the above two levels are usually Africans. The most highly qualified primary teachers and the only ones who, by law, can teach in *escolas primárias* attend a two-year teacher training course after five years of secondary school or five years of experience as *professor de posto*. This training course has become available outside Portugal only in this decade. Practically all teachers trained at this level are Europeans or *mestiços*.

Although the certificate of the fourth class is an important minimal qualification for employment, it does not provide entrance to secondary school. There is a special examination, composed in the Ministry of National Education in Lisbon, for entrance to each of the secondary streams, technical and academic (*liceu*). Although many urban children are able to pass the admission examination immediately after the four-year primary course, rural children frequently spend an extra year in an "admission" class, preparing for the entrance exam, restudying the lessons of the previous year. Some missionaries consider this extra year an integral part of the course they offer. Since the official school program no longer includes such a year, to consider it integral must reveal deficiencies in the regular four-year course.

The first cycle (two years) of secondary education would be considered primary or presecondary in many countries. Portugal has now recognized this and is engaged in trying to unify the program for these years in a kind of middle school. After the second cycle in the *liceu* (three years) or in the technical school (three or four years), administrative and technical jobs and specialized courses attract many youths. The shortage of educated manpower in both private industry and government has led to the availability of employment at this level. Further pre-university education, however, is available in the last cycle of the *liceus* and in advanced technical institutes. Many students in the latter are sent parttime by their employers.

Since 1963, two universities have been opened, one in Angola and the other in Mozambique. Each of these universities is integrated into the Portuguese university system, and professors are often sent from similar positions in metropolitan Portugal. Both were authorized to award final degrees in 1968 for the first time. The universities are attuned to the technical needs of a developing society. There are courses in engineering, medicine, veterinary science, agronomy, forestry, and training for secondary teachers. Private industry has failed in attempts to encourage the establishment of an economics faculty. Noticeably lacking are courses in law, the humanities, and the social sciences, which can be studied only in Portugal. It would seem that the lack of qualified staff and the potential social and political effects of such courses will discourage their introduction.

Other than in the above-mentioned schools, postprimary training is available in agricultural schools, craft schools (*escolas de artes e ofícios*), nursing schools, and social service schools. Private firms and government agencies, such as the post and telegraph services and the Labor Institute also provide in-service technical courses.

An Appraisal of Recent Developments

In the past decade, much time and attention have gone into the development of education in Portuguese Africa. The awareness of educational deficiencies, the revealing light of international attention, an increased familiarity with what is happening elsewhere in Africa, a growing social awareness, the desire for better-trained manpower to meet needs of economic development, a need to provide a competitive alternative to the growing appeal of nationalist movements—these have been some of the factors explaining the increased activity in education. As a result, school opportunities have widened, and some old patterns have changed, but many problems have remained and new ones have arisen.

To even the most casual visitor to Portuguese Africa, the most obvious change has been a vast increase in primary school enrollment. Most urban areas are approaching the fulfillment of the legal requirement of free and compulsory education for all children between the ages of seven and twelve who live within 3 kilometers of a school. A low population density and centuries of educational neglect have hindered development in rural areas. Nevertheless, the enrollment increase attests to the progress. In Angola, there was an increase of primary attendance of 270 per cent, from 68,759 to 267,768, between 1956 and 1967.[11] In Mozambique, total attendance is higher and the rate of increase, though less dramatic, was still appreciable. In the eleven years between 1957 and 1968, attendance rose 93 per cent from 264,233 to 510,170.[12] Though attendance is higher in Mozambique, observers claim that Angolan students stay in school longer and thereby receive a more complete education. Ninety per cent of the students in Mozambique attended missionary schools as recently as 1965.

Although the government began to reduce the power of the Catholic Church ten years ago, it has been more successful in Angola than in Mozambique. Furthermore, there has been a need for the government to establish primary schools in certain areas for political reasons. In areas in Guinea, Angola, and Mozambique, where strategic hamlets have been set up, the primary school, along with the dispensary and a piped water supply, is one of the main attractions. There are more new government schools in Angola than elsewhere in Portuguese Africa. The vacuum caused by the removal of Methodist and Baptist missions has led the government to begin numerous schools in Angola. Only in northern Mozambique has there been an even partially parallel situation. But the unrest leading to the withdrawal of Catholic missionaries from among the Makonde has not allowed the development of government schools.

A marked feature of the school system of Portuguese Africa is the large number of private schools. There are three types of these—Protestant mission schools, institutions that attract children of parents wealthy enough to pay for special schools, and schools provided by private companies. Plantations and factories above a certain size are required to provide schooling for the children of their workers. In Angola, for example, the Benguela Railway and the Lobito Mining Company operate schools not only for the children of their workers but also for some from nearby villages. Since the official school system does not adequately extend to all areas, such private schools are very important. Diamang enrolled over 2,200 pupils in its schools in 1962, a creditable figure, but surprisingly low when the vast expanse of its operation is considered.[13]

An important difference among the African provinces appears in their textbooks. The latest major education decree of 1964 allowed each province the authority to develop its own system of primary school textbooks, adapted to local conditions, within the confines of a national system that determines the amount of knowledge that must be attained by the end of the fourth grade. Though Guinea and Mozambique have not taken the opportunity to do so, Angola has not only Africanized its textbooks (stressing, of course, multiracial living and friendships), but in so doing has adopted modern, "active" teaching methods, more advanced than in Portugal and much of Africa. Though such textbooks provide more challenge for the teachers, they add life to the frequently drab, painful memorization undergone by most Portuguese schoolchildren.

The history of Portuguese administration and education in Africa shows that there has been a complete failure to adapt Koranic schools for entry into a total system. Nor have Catholic missions made strong attempts to develop schools in the Muslim areas of interior Guinea and northern Mozambique. In the former alone, the seventy-nine Koranic schools were half again as many as within the official system, although official students outnumbered Arabic students by 13,040 to 758 in 1964.[14] Koranic schools were widespread among the Yao and Makua in northern Mozambique.

The existence of Koranic schools complicated the already difficult task of computing the literacy rate in Portuguese Africa. Besides those who can read in Arabic must be placed those in Guinea and northern Angola who have had contact with French-speaking neighbors and those in Mozambique who have become literate in English through contact with former British colonies or English missionaries. Furthermore, large numbers of migrant laborers from southern Mozambique become literate in an African language, usually Shangana, through adult education courses provided in South Africa. In spite of these various paths toward literacy of the adult male population, no more than 5 per cent in Guinea, 10 per cent in Angola, and 15 per cent in Mozambique could be considered literate.

The present decade has seen a new educational force in Portuguese Africa. In response to African desires and the need for creating a more educated base and with a view toward providing necessary services to those whom they consider their constituency, most nationalist movements have established educational programs. (The nationalist movements are discussed in Chapter XVII.) The Portuguese Government has even cooperated with some of the more moderate movements by providing teaching materials and scholarships, eager to spread the Portuguese language and culture even among those who disagree with them politically.

The largest nationalist movements, however, have developed educational programs on their own. In Guinea, the PAIGC (*Partido Africano da Independência da Guiné e Cabo Verde*) claimed to have had 8,000 students in its schools in 1966. It has already published its first textbook, a primary reader in Portuguese containing some words in the local creole and some patriotic, ideological passages. There are also reports the PAIGC runs a secondary school in Conakry.[15]

The two main Angolan nationalist groups displayed different attitudes toward education. The MPLA (*Movimento Popular de Libertação de Angola*) felt that war needs had priority among their expenditures. As a result, by the middle of 1967, it claimed to be educating only ninety students at primary level and vaguely hoped to begin a secondary school.[16] This contrasted with earlier reports that it was actively developing education outside Angola and had already educated 1,000 pupils in "improvized" schools.[17] Though the MPLA claimed that it had developed teaching materials in Portuguese, it was clear that it had been hindered by the requirement of the Office of the United Nations High Commissioner for Refugees that the language of instruction be that of the country hosting the refugees.

In the case of Angola, this requirement meant either French (the two Congos) or English (Zambia). The GRAE (*Governo Revolucionário de Angola no Exílio*) did not see this as a problem. In fact, much of its support came from people who had themselves been educated in French, and among whom, more often than not, normal conversation was conducted in French. Furthermore, GRAE still retained its pocket of resistance in the Dembos area, where, at one time, an estimated 92 schools with almost 7,000 students were giving primary instruction in Portuguese. Many of its schools in and around Kinshasa, however, were teaching in French, and textbooks were Congolese. The same was true of its secondary school in Kinshasa, which enrolled 300 pupils.[18] By early in 1968 however, there were indications that the level of GRAE's educational activity had declined significantly.

Of the Mozambique nationalist movements, only FRELIMO claimed a well-organized educational system. In mid-1966, Eduardo Mondlane stressed that "the most important preoccupation of FRELIMO . . . was the planning, establishment, and directing of schools in the liberated and semiliberated areas." The nature and extent of that system, however, is worthy of question, since FRELIMO claimed to have 10,000 pupils in 100 schools with a student-teacher ratio of 250 to one.[19] Such a ratio would not only limit meaningful learning, but would mean that FRELIMO had teachers in, at most, only 40 per cent of its schools. FRELIMO did, however, maintain an apex institution in Tanzania. Originally financed from private United States sources, the Mozambique Institute provided secondary and limited technical (nursing) education, which functioned partially to provide the educational qualifications necessary for admission at more advanced schools in other countries. Political turbulence, however, led to the closing of the Institute in the spring of 1968.

Most nationalist organizations are aware of the strong desire among young Africans for an access to the education that they perceive as the major key to future doors. Although these groups have reacted to this awareness, they have been hindered by a lack of funds, a shortage of teachers, and a force that they greatly underestimated, a similar awareness by the Portuguese Government. In no way less impressive than the growth of official primary education in Portuguese Africa has been the large expansion of secondary schools, both academic and technical. The secondary school expansion presents an effective answer to the critics of earlier Portuguese educational policy who claimed that post-primary expansion was being denied for political reasons. On the contrary, expansion may have been motivated by a desire to draw increasing numbers of the population of Portuguese Africa into modern life.

The statistics in the accompanying table do show, however, that the Portuguese are aware of the need to stress technical-school expansion over *liceus*. Although precipitated in part, no doubt, by political reasons, the technical emphasis represents an awareness of the complaints elsewhere in Africa about the overly academic nature of the school system, a need to produce technically skilled manpower to satisfy the rapidly growing needs of the economy, and a natural extension of the expansion in technical education in metropolitan Portugal in the 1950's. The government has successfully controlled this expansion by providing for more vacancies in technical schools and a scale of tuition charges that has made technical schools more attractive than *liceus* to students from lower socio-economic classes.

Lower tuition charges have combined with other factors—such as belief in greater employment relevance and lack of confidence in the existence of opportunities in positions for which *liceus* usually provide a preparation—to lead most people in the lower socio-economic classes to favor their children's attendance at technical schools. The racial complexion of school attendance has been affected in recent years by increased immigration from Portugal. Thus, many of the secondary school places have been filled by children of immigrants rather than by Africans.

It must be stressed, however, that increased opportunities in secondary education in Portuguese Africa are a new phenomenon.[21] Only after more school places became available and after Africans gained the belief, now current in urban areas, that they *could* continue their schooling beyond the primary years did the complexion of the educational system begin to change. The first generation of recipients of the benefits of the change are only now in the middle of their secondary school course. As each year passes, percentage of Africans in each secondary school becomes appreciably greater.

Nevertheless, membership in lower socio-economic classes involves many pressures on Africans to leave school early. School-leaving age is also lowered by the lack of a tradition of literary culture in the students' homes. Another pressure is caused by the urban nature of the schools. There are few boarding facilities associated with secondary schools, greatly affecting students from rural areas or from homes in parts of the cities that are not conducive to study requirements.

Although the government does provide some scholarships, their number is clearly inadequate. It is in the provision of scholarships and other support for secondary school students, including parttime employment, that private companies and the government have not yet grasped their responsibilities. Private support and provision for primary education have been an important feature in the expansion of educational facilities, yet contemporary economic and political realities demand a new awareness by the growing industrial base of Portuguese Africa that Africans need to be given support at a higher level and then absorbed into the economy as skilled technicians. A similar awareness among some

Secondary School Attendance[20]

	1955–56 Students	1960–61 Students	Growth Since 1955 (Per Cent)	1966–67 Students	Growth Since 1955 (Per Cent)	Growth Since 1960 (Per Cent)
Angola						
Academic	3,729	7,486	101	16,700	351	122
Technical	2,164	4,501	108	15,559	620	244
				1965–66 Students		
Mozambique						
Academic	n.a.	4,639	—	9,028	—	95
Technical	n.a.	4,621	—	11,483	—	157

187

Lisbon-based private foundations would greatly aid an equitable secondary school development. At present, programs of scholarships to provide secondary school opportunities for the best students in the schools in the fortified villages and other resettlement centers in areas of continuing insurgency are lacking.

The Portuguese, noticeably in Angola, have begun to show a concern for the need to Africanize the curriculum in order to make schooling more relevant for all the inhabitants in the overseas provinces. Such concern has not yet extended into the secondary schools. Not only is the secondary curriculum exactly the same as in the metropole, but its remaining as such is assured by the continuing of effective control of all secondary education in Lisbon. The Portuguese have failed to take advantage of the cultural and historical diversity in Africa to enrich the curriculum not only in Africa but also in Europe. In fact, the school system, through dancing, sewing, and history lessons, makes a point of stressing the differences among the various Europeans in Portugal. It would not be difficult to make some African additions to the cultural pluralism already prized within the Portuguese nation.

The stress given to technical schools has derived from a belief in the need to equip larger numbers of people to make social and cultural advances. Practical steps to implement this belief are less than a decade old. Yet certain contradictions still remain. These can best be seen in administration and agriculture. Though the lower levels of local administration have begun to fill up with local residents (few Africans, though, because the major wave of qualified Africans is still moving through the schools), nowhere in Portuguese Africa has there begun an administration course for either advanced or middle-level administrators. This has led to the use of untrained novices. It has also limited the amount of research into the administrative systems of Portuguese Africa.

In 1961, Mozambique began to organize elementary agricultural education. Agricultural activities are in the curriculum for rural schools as a practical belief in the oft-quoted Deweyan view of making education relevant to life. Furthermore, schools at Tchivinguiro in Angola and Limpopo in Mozambique (but none in Guinea) provide secondary-level apex institutions for training agricultural technicians. Nevertheless, the number of such institutions and programs has remained largely inadequate to provide the manpower to meet the needs of a largely agricultural society. As a result, most people trained as agriculturalists are required to fill bureaucratic staff positions rather than to traverse the interior as extension workers.

Despite recent advances, the educational systems of Portuguese Africa are far from reaching the stage where the overseas provinces are self-sufficient in trained manpower. This has meant a continuing need to attract such people from Portugal. Although the continuing insurgency and a historical reluctance to migrate to Africa has limited the number of skilled immigrants, various occupations are nevertheless dependent upon people educated and trained in Europe. Nowhere is this more obvious than in the supply of teachers. Though several thousand Africans are being trained as *monitores* and *professores de posto*, total enrollment was low in the four complete normal schools (*magistério primário*) begun since 1961. Thus, in 1965, there were only 208 such students in Angola, 88 in Mozambique, and none in Guinea.[22]

The situation is even more pronounced when it comes to secondary school teachers. No special programs have been devised to train teachers for the lower classes of secondary schools, such as has been done in many other African areas. Furthermore, the Portuguese university system has not expanded to meet contemporary needs in education. Nor have the pedagogical sections of the universities of Angola and Mozambique made significant contributions to filling the demand for qualified teachers in the expanding system. Nevertheless, though overburdened, teachers have appeared from Portugal and have frequently done so through a type of technical assistance program unusual in the underdeveloped world of today—many of these immigrant teachers plan to stay and make their careers in Africa. The availability of such people has allowed planners to avoid a more comprehensive educational plan for the various African provinces and to rely on Portugal. As the system continues its rapid development, however, it will have to begin generating its own manpower.

HEALTH

Health problems have been studied in Portugal since the 1902 founding of the postgraduate Institute of Tropical Medicine in Lisbon. Before he became a nationalist leader, Eduardo Mondlane wrote that

> The Portuguese Government has done everything within its power to eliminate disease in Mozambique. The health department . . . is one of the most forward looking and most successful in Africa. These ten years have seen a tremendous expansion of health services to reach most parts of Mozambique.[23]

Furthermore, more than in education, public and private corporations have carried a heavy burden of the responsibility for health programs.

At the opening of the Conference of Health Education in Pointe Noire, Congo (Brazzaville), in June, 1962, Dr. C. M. Norman Williams noted that "all social and economic progress in Africa depends very closely on the health and the nutrition of the population."[24] Although Africa's health problems cannot be compared either in extent or in severity to the problems of Asia, the productive capacity of the continent nevertheless depends to a very high degree on health education and eradication of diseases that sap the vitality of the African peoples.

The problem is particularly acute if we bear in mind the fast-growing population of Africa. Most of the African states will double their population during the next thirty or forty years. Whereas this population explosion has many advantages for the areas of Africa that are still underpopulated,[25] there will still be a problem of feeding a much larger population. By the year 2000, Africa south of the Sahara will have to feed twice the population it has today. Health, therefore, is not only a problem of longevity; it is indispensable to a productive Africa.

African health problems derive from many causes typical of the tropics, such as poverty, widespread endemic disease, poor soil productivity, and climate. A considerable number of Africans die as a result of diseases caused by malnutrition.

189

One of the gravest problems of contemporary Africa is the paucity of protein in the ordinary diet. This stems not only from the lack and unequal distribution of available food products but also from the unwillingness of the African to change his dietary patterns. Inadequate sanitation has continued to be a problem, as affected by inadequate housing, lack of piped water and sewage systems, and ignorance of cleanliness and personal hygiene.

Ignorance of the seriousness of the prevalent diseases and of preventive and curative measures is compounded by the relative lack of scientific knowledge about many tropical diseases.[26] Often, when one disease is eliminated or its incidence is reduced, another takes its place. Epidemics break out from time to time, such as the infectious hepatitis epidemic that occurred in Mozambique in 1964, with 1,916 known cases. Sometimes solutions to other problems cause increase in diseases. For example, with irrigation projects creating new sources of infestation, bilharzia continues to be an important health problem in Mozambique.[27]

Much of Portuguese Africa lies in the tropical and subtropical zones. In some regions, such as Guinea, the danger of disease typical of the tropics is particularly great. Such ailments as malaria, sleeping sickness, yellow fever, yaws, bilharzia, and smallpox are common. Diseases that have been brought in by non-Africans, such as measles, tuberculosis, pneumonia, veneral infections, and poliomyelitis, also create serious health problems.

The health situation in all Portuguese territories in Africa still leaves much to be desired, as is the case with most of Africa. The Portuguese authorities have been making advances in recent years. The leadership in solving the challenge of health problems has come from the overseas ministry, the Institute of Tropical Medicine in Lisbon, and the growing number of doctors serving in the armed forces. To help solve the various problems, a reorganization of the overseas health and welfare services of Portugal was carried out by a decree issued in 1964. It added social welfare services to health services in Guinea and Mozambique. The Angolan health structure was modified, as new administrative divisions were created, with special emphasis on health education, school health, industrial health, preventive medicine, environmental sanitation, assistance to the sick, invalid, and elderly, and mental health. Public health, pharmaceutical services, and specialized services for the control of endemic diseases were emphasized in Mozambique. Maternal and child welfare services were given special attention, especially in Angola and Mozambique.[28]

Efforts have been made to increase the number of doctors and medical auxiliaries, such as midwives, pharmacists, nurses, and others who, as field-workers, are indispensable in the fight against disease in Africa. The three experts who went to Portuguese Africa on a World Health Organization mission n 1962 at the request of the Portuguese Government mentioned, among the facts that impressed them, the devotion of the medical personnel, whatever their professional level and the nature of their functions, and the complete confidence shown by the local population, African and European, in the sanitary services.[29] In 1963, the training of rural health technicians, who educate the rural population in general hygiene and sanitation and provide preventive and minor curative welfare services, was started in Angola. In 1964, new regulations concerning the technical schools of health and welfare services were established, which have paved the way for better training facilities.[30] The Psycho-Social Service, termed "Angola and Mozambique's version of the Peace Corps," also contributes to the fight against disease.[31]

Any discussion on health suffers from inadequate, out of date, and, at times, contradictory statistical information. Health data have been taken from official and unofficial Portuguese sources and from the *Third Report on World Health Situation* of the World Health Organization (WHO). Comparison of these figures is complicated because definitions vary. For example, WHO considers all clinics, dispensaries, and the like as "hospitals," while the Portuguese figures differentiate among types of medical installations. The WHO figures on hospital beds in Angola refer to state hospitals only, whereas there are actually more hospital beds in private than in public hospitals, in accordance with the terms of the Code of Rural Labor. WHO figures on birth and death rates and infant mortality rates are quoted, but it should be noted that the Portuguese themselves have published no official over-all figures of comparable type and that relevant figures for most rural areas are lacking. In fact, statistics give little accurate indication of health conditions throughout Portuguese Africa.

Angola

Medical and hospital care has improved in recent years and compares favorably with what is provided in other African territories. The number of doctors in 1965 was 492, of whom 352 were in government service. In 1963, there were 1,787 auxiliaries, such as midwifery aides, fully qualified nurses, visiting nurses, and rural health sanitarians.

In 1966, there were 338 hospitals and institutions for in-patient care, providing some 5,700 beds in the state hospitals, or 1.1 beds per 1,000 population. Out-patient care was provided at 865 locations. There were 79 specialized medical centers, such as maternity centers, tuberculosis dispensaries, and mobile trypanosomiasis teams.[32] Special programs exist for the control of major communicable diseases, such as trypanosomiasis, tuberculosis, and leprosy, and vaccination against smallpox and poliomyelitis. Between 1960 and 1964, over 2 million people were immunized against smallpox, poliomyelitis, yellow fever, and other communicable diseases.[33] The most frequently diagnosed diseases remain bilharzia, intestinal parisitoses, venereal diseases, and malaria.

In 1964, over 300,000 inhabitants in urban centers and over 1 million inhabitants in rural areas were provided with piped water supplies. Over 250,000 inhabitants in urban centers and over 1 million in rural areas were served with sewage systems.[34] In 1964, the government budget had an estimated expenditure of $138 million, of which $4.5 million (3.2 per cent) was devoted to the provision of health services. This was equivalent to an expenditure of $0.90 per head on these services as compared with $0.75 in 1961.[35] Yet health expenditures are not growing as rapidly as other budgetary expenditures.

Besides the health activities of public authorities, several of the large private and semiprivate enterprises located there have provided medical, educational, and recreational facilities for their employees and their families. In urban areas, labor unions (*sindicatos*) are a vital source of health assistance. The Benguela Railway, Diamang, the Lobito Mining Company, and the Cassequel Agricultural Corporation have programs of a scope and quality that deserve special mention.[36] Protestant missionaries also have traditionally provided excellent health services in rural areas, although, since 1961, their activities have been reduced considerably.

Mozambique

Although the population of Mozambique is larger and health conditions have improved steadily, it still has fewer doctors than Angola; however, it has more hospitals and hospital beds and a better ratio of beds per 1,000 population. The climate, the distribution of the population, and migratory labor have all been factors hampering the fullest health supervision. Lack of knowledge has been a principal obstacle to the campaign against such diseases as leprosy. Of the 10,000 known lepers in Mozambique, only 3,239 were in leprosaria.[37] The main health problems in Mozambique stem mostly from communicable diseases. Diarrhoeal infections are the major causes of infant mortality, the extent of which, although very high in the province, is not known precisely.

Mozambique has special services to combat leprosy, tuberculosis, and sleeping sickness. There is also the Institute for Medical Research, to which is attached a mission to study and combat bilharzia, and a nutrition commission. It also maintains a training program for medical personnel. The army, provincial police corps, labor unions, state railways, and various government and municipal agencies likewise have medical programs and facilities.

In 1964, there were 382 doctors in Mozambique, 223 of whom were in government service, or a ratio of 1 doctor to 17,800 persons. There were also 1,962 auxiliaries.[38] The number of hospitals at the end of 1964 was 395, providing 10,455 beds, with a ratio of 1.5 beds per 1,000 population.[39] There was a total of 1,093 specialized health centers, including school health centers, maternity and child welfare centers, and leprosy clinics.

As bilharzia continues to be an important health problem because of new irrigation projects, over 1 million bilharzia patients were treated in out-patient clinics in 1963. Compared to 1955, the number of syphilis patients decreased with the use of antibiotics, but cases of gonorrhoea increased. It is estimated that about 80 per cent of the population has been immunized against smallpox, as smallpox vaccination has been compulsory since 1920. A malaria pre-eradication project was started in 1961 in a pilot zone of the Save River, in collaboration with WHO. This has already begun to be extended to other areas.

A control campaign was initiated in 1959 in Nampula and the districts of Zambézia and Cabo Delgado for yaws, which occurs frequently in the coastal areas. The percentage of yaws cases diagnosed in health centers dropped from 5 to 8 per cent in 1952 to 0.7 per cent in 1964. In 1963, close to 21,000 people were immunized against tuberculosis. New tuberculosis cases increased to 1,933 in 1964 as compared to 1,379 in 1950. A control service was established in 1950 for leprosy, as the disease is endemic throughout the territory. As sleeping sickness is also found in the territory, tsetse control programs have been undertaken. Over 1 million people were immunized against communicable diseases in 1964.[40]

In 1963, the total health expenditure by public and general government health agencies amounted to $7.3 million, of which $6 million was incurred by the central government departments. This was equivalent to an expenditure of $1.10 per person. A further $820,000 was spent for the expansion and improvement of health facilities.[41]

Portuguese Guinea

The territory of Guinea offers particularly difficult problems of public health. The heavy rainfall, tropical vegetation, inadequate communication facilities, and relative density of the population all pose problems of a special kind. The diseases that create the greatest problems are malaria, tuberculosis, leprosy, trypanosomiasis, and intestinal parasitoses.

In 1963, Portuguese Guinea had 34 doctors, a ratio of 1 doctor to a population of 15,400. There were 202 auxiliaries. There were 31 hospitals providing 839 beds, or 1.6 beds per 1,000 population, and there were 29 specialized health centers.[42]

In 1963, over 612,000 antimalarial tablets were distributed free, as malaria is still quite prevalent in the territory. In the same year, 6,687 cases of ankylostomiasis were treated, although only improved conditions, especially in the rural areas, would eradicate the disease. Close to 160,000 people were immunized against various communicable diseases.[43]

The government budget for 1964 involved an estimated expenditure of $725,000 for the provision of health services. This was equivalent to an expenditure of $1.45 per person on these services. Included in the total given above was a sum of $185,000 for the campaign against trypanosomiasis and a further sum of $52,000, over half of which was donated by the Gulbenkian Foundation for the antituberculosis campaign.[44]

The Cape Verde Islands

The Cape Verde Islands have always been handicapped by erratic rainfall, poor soil, and a low yield of food crops. This territory is, economically, one of the least promising of Portugal's overseas territories. Living is precarious on its ten islands and the monotonous diet of corn has weakened the inhabitants. Influenza and malaria have the highest incidence among communicable diseases.

In 1964, Cape Verde had 25 doctors, 21 of whom worked in government service, a ratio of 1 doctor to 4,580 people.[45] There were 10 hospitals, with 499 beds, making a ratio of 2.2 beds per 1,000 population.[46] Out-patient facilities were available at 39 locations. There also were 4 maternity and other specialized centers.[47]

In 1960, a tuberculosis campaign was started. In addition to the leprosy control program that is in operation, other projects have been initiated to control various other diseases. Over 31,000 people were immunized against tuberculosis, smallpox, and yellow fever in 1964.

In 1964, the total general government current expenditure on health services amounted to $305,000. This was equivalent to an expenditure of $1.40 per person on these services. A further sum of $78,000 was spent on projects included in plans for the development and improvement of health facilities.[48]

São Tomé and Príncipe

The two islands of São Tomé and Príncipe belong to the heavy rainfall area. Malaria presents the greatest problem. In 1964, there were 18 doctors, of whom 14 were in government service, a ratio of 1 doctor to every 3,300 persons.[49] The number of auxiliaries such as midwives, nurses, and pharmacists was 113. There were 41 hospitals and maternity clinics, providing 2,093 beds. There also were 4 maternity and child health centers, 1 dental clinic and 1 tuberculosis dispensary, and a leprosy unit. The ratio of beds to population was 3.5 to 1,000. Out-patient care was available in 63 locations, most of which were private health centers. The number of specialized health units was 18. Over 8,000 people were immunized against smallpox, tuberculosis, and other communicable diseases in 1964.[50]

Príncipe Island had serious epidemics of sleeping sickness from the end of the last century until 1914, when the disease was completely eradicated. When tsetse flies showed up again in 1956, it was decided to eradicate them to prevent the reintroduction of the disease, although none of the flies was found to be infested. The subsequent eradication campaign has been deemed successful.[51]

SOCIAL WELFARE

Until the passage of the Native Statute of 1954, social welfare in Portuguese Africa was largely the responsibility of the Catholic Church, Protestant missions, and private charity. Under the terms of the statute, however, a provincial commission of rural welfare was established in each of the overseas territories to centralize and coordinate welfare activities in the rural area. In 1962, it was merged into the provincial institutes of labor and social welfare, so that now both urban and rural welfare activities are coordinated and directed by a single agency.

Rural Welfare Activities

Government Programs. The Portuguese Government views the idea of "community development" as an integral part of its over-all program for its African territories.[52] This concept underlies the ambitious government program of rural welfare, which is in operation in both Angola and Mozambique, carried on by the so-called Psycho-Social Service. Administratively, each psycho-social team is made up of a leader (*chefe de brigada*), an assistant, a male nurse, a social worker, and African demonstrators, one specializing in agricultural problems. The teams attempt to teach and demonstrate the basic principles of hygiene, home economy, farm management, and so on. The government realizes that the problems of public health, education, and social advancement are closely interrelated and that no real progress in the assimilation of Africans into Portuguese society can be achieved without control of disease and malnutrition and diffusion of literacy. Each team spends two months in a region, six to eight days in each village. The *colonatos* and other centers of rural population are the focus of the activities of these teams. The service also publishes posters and pamphlets and broadcasts radio programs on hygiene, literacy, and so forth.[53]

In Mozambique, as of mid-1965, there were twenty teams in operation, equipped with radio and movie equipment. In 1963 these teams made a total of 1,240 visits through the territory. Although the psycho-social program has had some impact, its activities have been brief and scattered. Attempts have yet to be made to concentrate attention for longer periods of time in a single area and to train local leaders to carry on the program with a stronger long-term impact.[54]

On a broader basis, the effects of the rural *regedorias* might well be extended until *freguesias rurais* develop, each with a production cooperative. A program of this kind has been successful among the Bakongo, since the beginnings of unrest in 1961.

The rural cooperative program of the Cotton Institute of Mozambique is one of the most successful ventures of its kind. Headed by a dedicated and realistic young agronomist, the program emphasizes the training of local leaders to take over when the Institute's teams are no longer in the particular rural area. The Institute works in various phases: in the first, an African employee gains the confidence of the population and leaders in a given village; then, practical instruction in the improvement of agricultural techniques is provided and a communal warehouse established. When this aspect of the program is functioning smoothly, classes are given for the women of the community in sewing, cooking, and hygiene, and a chapel, social center, and club are formed. Finally, a true cooperative for production and consumption is founded, including an "Agricultural Club" for the children, where they grow and sell their own produce. After this, the entire system is turned over to the local leaders the team has been training, and then the team leaves to repeat the process in another village.

Private Enterprise. The social welfare activities of large private enterprises should not be overlooked. Many of these concerns, notably the Benguela Railway, the Lobito Mining Company, Diamang, CADA, and the Cassequel plantations, in Angola, and Lusalite (Lusalite–Sociedade Portuguêsa de Fibro-Cimento SARL), in Mozambique, provide housing, piped water supply, electric current, churches, libraries, and recreational facilities for employees and their families, besides the medical and educational facilities already noted. Often, in areas located away from centers of population, these amenities are sometimes the only examples of the advantages of civilized living available to the rural population.

Diamang, besides maintaining the Dundo Museum of local arts, crafts, and antiquities, has studied insects of their area and supports large local sports festivals and other social activities. Other private enterprises likewise provide such auxiliary services for their employees. The Labor Institute now provides seaside vacation camps in Angola for workers and their families and boarding facilities for migrant workers.

Urban Welfare Activities

A problem more pressing than rural welfare is posed by the substantial influx of individuals and families from the rural areas to slums in the cities and towns, especially in Angola and Mozambique. About 25 per cent of the population of Luanda, for example, lives in shanty slums (muceques). The center of the city and certain suburban areas are largely European, mestiço, and fully acculturated African in composition, with some less acculturated Africans, mestiços, and Europeans concentrated in the muceques, where temporary housing and the lack of electricity, water, and sewage systems present problems of health and hygiene. Although wages are higher than in the rural areas, living costs are higher also.[55] Unemployment has not yet proved a serious problem.

Problems of urbanization due to the influx of rural populations are not, of course, phenomena confined to Portuguese Africa; they are almost ubiquitous among the underdeveloped countries. The rest of the African continent is also plagued with them, and the teeming favelas and casuchas of Latin America bear witness to the attraction of urban living for peoples of its regions. In Africa, however, the situation is complicated by residual tribalism in the urban areas, causing complicated meshing with newly developing interest groups, administrative units, and secret organizations.

Voices have been raised proclaiming that the social problems of urbanization could destroy the Portuguese future in Africa and that measures to deal with it have been inadequate.[56] Although the slum areas of the principal cities suffer from lack of physical facilities, more important are the social and psychological implications of a large group emerging from a traditional society into a transitional one. Daniel Lerner has observed that those in the process of modernization are in some ways more content than those who stay locked in traditional society; otherwise, they would not migrate.[57] The first generation of urban dwellers may not miss amenities that they lacked in their rural villages. At the same time, however, their problems are manifold and, in the slums, they are more concentrated and articulate.

Professor Pattee lists several reasons why Africans leave their tribal areas and join other masses in urban slums. Those attracted to the city are seeking relatively well remunerated work (or believe that such work is available), joining relatives already in the city, striving to better themselves personally, or hoping to free themselves from the obligations of primitive society.[58] Economic motivation would be lessened by improvement of rural conditions and avoidance of over-concentration on industrialization, thus avoiding the situation in which Venezuela, for instance, finds itself, trying (rather unsuccessfully) to persuade urban dwellers, many of them unemployed, to return to the land and become farmers again. In a province as underpopulated as Angola, it would be most unfortunate if such a situation were allowed to develop.

Attempts to deal with the housing situation by decree were made in 1922, 1948, 1954, and 1956, but they have been inadequate. Still, considerable progress is being made in the construction of low-cost housing (bairros populares), built with provincial and municipal funds, and similar bairros económicos, built by private firms for their workers. Plantations of more than a certain size are required by law to provide housing for their workers. One typical state-housing project in Luanda, for example, has 120 units consisting of kitchen, bathroom, and two bedrooms. Rent is $5.50–$6.50 per month, applicable to eventual purchase of the house. The multiracial project has water, light, sewage, a school, and a club. The houses cost $1,500–$1,700 to build.

The government has also given attention to the more traditional services for poverty-stricken and underprivileged inhabitants. In 1962, there were eighteen welfare institutions in Angola, including orphanages and old-peoples' homes. Government subsidies are provided for many such establishments operated by the Catholic church and by Protestant missions. In 1962, there were 187 Catholic missions, staffed by 1,439 persons, and 87 Protestant missions with some 1,109 personnel. Most of these missions maintain schools and institutions for the relief of distressed persons. There also existed in 1962 in Angola 10 mutual aid societies with 27,865 members and 2,646 pensioners, as well as a public employees savings fund (*Cofre de Previdência dos Funcionários Públicos*).

The dimensions of social welfare efforts in Mozambique may be measured by the outlay for general welfare and public assistance programs. In 1964, $930,000 was disbursed in relief payments to unemployed persons, orphans, indigent widows, and aged persons and as subsidies to charitable institutions operated by private or church organizations. Grants-in-aid to poor but deserving students and the repatriation expenses of destitute families to their countries of origin are also provided.[59]

Aside from these relief programs, the government has general public welfare programs, such as public housing projects, town planning, and local improvements. In 1965, $1.2 million was actually disbursed in these programs. In 1964 the Mozambique Government reported 6,746 persons in 173 welfare institutions. There were also 226 Catholic missions with a staff of 1,588 and 14 Protestant missions, with 459 branches, staffed by 572 missionaries and aides, many of which, like those in Angola, maintain establishments for the underprivileged. In 1964, there existed 27 mutual aid societies in Mozambique, with 35,129 members and 2,100 pensioners.

Social welfare services in Portuguese Guinea are provided by several agencies.[60] The Administrative Committee of the Development and Welfare Fund (Commissão Administrativa do Fundo de Fomento e Assistência) is presided over by the governor. It is in charge of welfare agencies such as charity hospitals, old peoples' homes, orphanages, and sports, cultural, and recreational groups, which, even though privately maintained or under the aegis of church authorities, are considered to be of value to the whole community. The Department of Civil Administration (Repartição Provincial dos Serviços de Administração Civil) and the administrative bureaus of the *concelhos* and districts also provide some welfare services. The Provincial Committee for School Welfare maintains school lunch programs in various urban centers. Subsidies from public funds are granted to private charities. There is a system of public pensions for aged and disabled persons and also provision for transportation of sick people to Portugal for necessary medical attention.

Angola and Mozambique each has its own system of prisons. In Angola, there exist both local and provincial prisons. In 1963, 3,118 people spent some time in local jails, while 934 were in the provincial penal colonies of Roçadas, Bié, and Damba. The latter, an agricultural colony, provides the only rehabilitation program for criminals.[61] The penal system in Mozambique is similar to that of Angola.

NOTES

1. Jan M. Vansina, *Kingdoms of the Savanna* (Madison, 1966), pp. 45–58; Eduardo dos Santos, *O estado Português e o problema missionário* (Lisbon, 1964).
2. Ávila de Azevedo, *Política de ensino em África* (Lisbon, 1958), pp. 122–26.
3. C. P. Groves, *The Planting of Christianity in África*, III (London, 1955), 110–28 and 180–82; J. Alves Correia, *Civilizando Angola e Congo* (Braga, 1922).
4. M. António de Oliveira, *A sociedade angolana do fim do século XIX e um seu escritor* (Luanda, 1961). This period is now being studied by Douglas L. Wheeler.
5. Education during the period 1878–1914 in one province, Angola, is described in Michael A. Samuels, *"Educação* or *Instrução?* A History of Education in Angola, 1878–1914"* (doctoral dissertation, Columbia University, 1969).
6. For a sample Protestant reaction, see R. H. Carson Graham, *Under Seven Congo Kings* (London, 1931), pp. 194–97.
7. Azevedo, *op. cit.*, p. 143.
8. Lord W. M. Hailey, *An African Survey* (London, 1956), p. 1216.
9. Ministério do Ultramar, *O ensino no ultramar* (Lisbon, 1966).
10. Thus, in Angola, for example, in contrast with practically all the rest of Africa, no office of a major educational administrator contains statistical or other information charts on the walls.
11. Many of the Angolan statistics and a general review of Angolan education appear in Michael Samuels, "The New Look in Angolan Education," *Africa Report* (November, 1967), pp. 63–67. See also Província de Angola, Direcção dos Serviços de Estatística, *Estatística da educação*, 1966–67 (Luanda, 1968).
12. Direcção Provincial dos Serviços de Educação, *Panorama do ensino na província de Moçambique* (Lourenço Marques, 1965), pp. 15; E. Andrade Pires, *Evolução do ensino em Moçambique* (Lourenço Marques, 1966), p. 12; United Nations, General Assembly, *Territories Under Portuguese Administration*, A/AC. 109/ L. 538/Add. 2 (April 15, 1969), p. 24.
13. Diamang, like many large firms, also provides training and adult education schools for its employees. It provides a traveling cinema for showing educational films and entertainment features. *Companhia de Diamantes de Angola*, pamphlet published by the company (Lisbon, 1963).
14. *Boletim Geral do Ultramar*, XLII, 491 (May, 1966), facing 232; United Nations, General Assembly, *Report of the Special Committee*, A/6700/Add. 3 (October 11, 1967), pp. 136–37.
15. I. William Zartman, "Guinea: The Quiet War Goes on," *Africa Report* (November, 1967), pp. 69–70; J. J. Gonçalves, "A informação na Guiné, em Cabo Verde e em São Tomé e Príncipe," *Cabo Verde, Guiné, São Tomé e Príncipe* (Lisbon, 1966), pp. 255–60.
16. United Nations, *op. cit.*, p. 230.
17. *Ibid.*, p. 308.
18. GRAE, *"La Lutte Armée en Angola"* (mimeographed, n.d.), p. 16.
19. United Nations, *op. cit.*, pp. 287–88.
20. For secondary school statistics, see Secretaria Provincial de Educação, *Síntese das actividades dos serviços, 1964–65* (Luanda, 1966); unpublished figures of the

Repartição de Estatística Geral (Luanda, 1966); Pires, *op. cit.*; Serviços de Educação, *op. cit.*

21. In 1960, Marvin Harris wrote, "the present administration has no intention of hastening its own eventual doom by exposing its impressionable wards to that portion of the western world's intellectual heritage which was acquired after the sixteenth century." Marvin Harris, *Portugal's African "Wards"* (New York, 1958), p. 15.

22. *Boletim Geral do Ultramar*, XLII, 491 (May, 1966), 232.

23. Eduardo Mondlane, "Mozambique," in C. W. Stillman (ed.), *Africa in the Modern World* (Chicago, 1955).

24. Henri Dupin, *Expérience d'education sanitaire et nutritionnelle en Afrique* (Paris, 1965), p. 13.

25. Recent studies have indicated that many areas of Africa are actually over-populated, in spite of a small population, because of limited soil fertility. See William Hance, "The Race Between Population and Resources," *Africa Report* (January, 1968).

26. In 1955, the Medical Institute of Mozambique was established under the auspices of the Institute of Tropical Medicine in Lisbon. Extensive research has been done in malaria, bilharzia, ankylostomiasis, infectious hepatitis, and anemia. World Health Organization, *Third Report on World Health Situation*, Nineteenth World Assembly, A 19B and b/4 (April 7, 1967), Part II, mimeo., review by country and territory, p. 35. A similar institute was founded in Angola in 1965. See Agência Geral do Ultramar, *Dados Informativos*, 4 (1968), and Secretaria de Saúde, Trabalho, Previdência e Assistência, *Síntese da actividade dos Serviços e Organismos, 1963–1966* (Luanda, 1966).

27. *Ibid.*, pp. 33–34.

28. *Ibid.*, pp. 1 and 32.

29. See Ernani Braga *et al.*, *Rapport de la Mission de L'OMS sur la situation sanitaire de la Guinée Portugaise, l'Angola et la Mozambique* (Geneva, 1962), p. 2.

30. World Health Organization, *op. cit.*, p. 2.

31. "Mozambique: Land of Good People," *National Geographic Magazine*, CXXVI, No. 2 (August, 1964), 218–21.

32. World Health Organization, *op. cit.*, pp. 1–3. According to the official figures provided by the Portuguese Government for 1965, Angola had 352 doctors, with 140 in private practice; 3 central, 6 regional, 6 subregional, and 11 specialized hospitals; 12 private clinics; 59 rural hospitals and 78 private hospitals—a total of 175 hospitals providing 13,299 beds, 5,928 of them in state hospitals and 7,371 in private hospitals.

33. *Ibid.*, pp. 2–3.

34. *Ibid.*, p. 3.

35. *Ibid.*

36. *The Benguela Railway*, pamphlet issued by Companhia do Caminho de Ferro de Benguela; *Angola—Companhia Mineira do Lobito*, pamphlet published by the Companhia Mineira do Lobito; Bureau International du Travail, *Bulletin Officiel*, XLV, No. 2 (April, 1962), 208–9.

37. Ralph von Gersdorff, *Moçambique* (Bonn, 1958), p. 100.

38. World Health Organization, *op. cit.*, p. 33. According to the official figures provided by the Portuguese Government for 1965, Mozambique had 315 doctors with 220 in private practice.

39. *Ibid.*, pp. 32–34. According to the official figures provided by the Portuguese Government for 1965, Mozambique had 3 central hospitals, 6 regional hospitals, 6 subregional hospitals, 59 rural hospitals, 11 specialized hospitals, 7 private clinics, and 40 private hospitals, making a total of 132 hospitals providing 7,396 beds in state hospitals.

40. *Ibid.*

41. *Ibid.*, p. 35.

42. *Ibid.*, pp. 38–39.

43. *Ibid.*, p. 39.

44. *Ibid.*, p. 40.

45. *Ibid.*, p. 12. According to the official figures provided by the Portuguese Government for 1965, Cape Verde had 32 doctors.

46. *Ibid.* According to the official figures provided by the Portuguese Government for 1965, Cape Verde had 2 central hospitals, 1 regional hospital, 8 rural hospitals, and 2 leprosaria, making a total of 13 hospitals providing 580 beds in state hospitals.

47. *Ibid.*, pp. 12–13.

48. *Ibid.*, p. 13.

49. *Ibid.*, p. 44. According to the official figures provided by the Portuguese Government for 1965, there were 24 doctors in São Tomé and Príncipe, with 4 in private practice.

50. *Ibid.*, pp. 44–45. According to the official figures provided by the Portuguese Government for 1965, São Tomé and Príncipe each had 1 central hospital, and together they had 51 private hospitals and 1 leprosarium, making a total of 54 hospitals providing 390 beds in state hospitals and 2,556 beds in private hospitals.

51. J. Fraga de Azevedo, M. da Costa Mourão, and J. M. de Castro Salazar, *The Eradication of Glossina Palpalis Palpalis from Príncipe Island (1956–58)* (Lisbon, 1962), pp. 105–75.

52. The idea of "community development" as viewed by the Portuguese is discussed by Alfredo de Sousa in a pamphlet published by the Junta Provincial de Povoamento de Angola, entitled *Organização e programas de desenvolvimento comunitário*. Dr. Sousa refers to the definition of community development formulated by the United Nations, in XX Rapport du C.A.C. au Conseil Economique et Social, Annex III (New York, 1954). Another work by the same author is "Desenvolvimento comunitário em Angola," *Angola* (Lisbon, 1964).

53. The activities of these teams in Angola, especially in the *colonatos* and other communities created or fostered by the government, are set forth in Junta Provincial de Povoamento, *Relatório das actividades, 1964*, No. 3 (Luanda, 1965).

54. See Amadeu de Castilho Soares, *Política de bem-estar rural em Angola* (Lisbon, 1961); Homero Ferrinho, "Cooperativismo e promoção rural," mimeo.; Jacques Denis, *Une colonie agricole européenne en Afrique tropicale* (Brussels, 1956); de Sousa, *op. cit.*; and Junta Provincial de Povoamento, *op. cit.*

55. Illídio do Amaral, "Subsídios para o estudo da evolução da população de Luanda," *Garcia de Orta*, VII, 2 (1959). Also see A. L. Epstein, *Politics in an Urban African Community* (Manchester, 1958), p. 12. The community studied by Epstein was Luanshya, a mining town of the copperbelt in Zambia (then Northern Rhodesia). Epstein has done perhaps the most thorough study of an

urban African community. He points to the unstable aspect of the urban population, many of whom, after the age of about 45, tend to return to rural villages because of the lack of old-age assistance. See H. Flegg and W. Lutz, "Report on an African Demographic Survey," *Journal for Social Research* (Pretoria), No. 10 (December, 1959). To a large extent, the social problems of the large urban centers of Mozambique are the same as those of Angola. For example, the same phenomenon of instability and youth of the population, as well as the lack of women, has been found in Lourenço Marques, and this is undoubtedly true of other urban areas.

56. Soares, *op. cit.*, p. 175. Pages 174–249 of this work provide an overview of the social and political problems of urbanism in Angola. See also Francisco Tenreiro, "Angola: Problemas de geografia humana," in *Angola* (Lisbon, 1964), pp. 37–60.

57. This situation has been analyzed by, among others, Daniel Lerner, *The Passing of Traditional Society* (New York, 1958), pp. 73–74, and James C. Davies, *Human Nature in Politics* (New York, 1963), esp. pp. 98–99.

58. Richard Pattee, *Portugal na África contemporânea* (Coimbra, 1959), p. 661.

59. The revenue for these disbursements is obtained by means of a 5 per cent surcharge on the income tax, grants from municipal and other public authorities, a 5 per cent tax on entrance tickets to all places of amusement and Public Assistance Stamp Taxes levied on a variety of public documents. See Unclassified Report from Lourenço Marques, *Department of State*, Airgram No. A-128, March 7, 1967.

60. *Guiné: anuário turístico* (Bissau, 1964).

61. Information drawn from *Angola: anuário estatístico, 1963* (Luanda, 1964), p. 85.

X

Current Racial Character

DAVID M. ABSHIRE AND NORMAN A. BAILEY

AN EXAMINATION of the racial situation in Portuguese Africa today necessitates a distinction between the concepts of multiracialism and nonracism. Though frequently overextended in meaning, the term "multiracialism" means solely the presence of more than one race. "Nonracism" means a lack of social and other discrimination based on racial differences. In contrast, racism includes a belief in the natural inferiority of some racial groups and in the need for social and legal measures to reflect that inferiority.[1]

Two examples show possible extreme positions of the above concepts of multiracialism and nonracism. Both the Cape Verde Islands and the Republic of South Africa have a high degree of multiracialism. The position of the former as an important Atlantic fueling station led to a mixture of Europeans and Africans. The latter contains Europeans, "cape coloureds," Bantu, East Indians, and others. Few areas in the world have achieved the level of nonracist society that Cape Verde has. Likewise, few have established a more racist social system than South Africa.

MISCEGENATION

The general attitude toward miscegenation is an important factor in the nature of racial tensions in society. A critical difference exists on this issue between most Portuguese and peoples from certain other societies. Even Thomas Okuma, a former Protestant missionary very critical of Portugal, has written:

> In many societies "miscegenation" is a fear-ridden word. White Southerners in the United States say that they are against integration because they fear miscegenation. South Africa's policy of separateness of races (apartheid) is justified on this basis. Products of miscegenation are called half-castes and half-breeds; words connoting scorn and degradation. In the Union of South Africa they are classed as "coloureds." Whatever the term of classification, the products of miscegenation are "outs" in both the white and black communities, in most societies. . . . The Portuguese, on the other hand, deny that miscegenation is an unhealthy practice. They humorously say that "God made white men and God made black men, but mulattoes were made by the Portuguese."[2]

We can go a step beyond Okuma's observation that miscegenation is not frowned upon by most Portuguese; it is actually encouraged and approved, although with limited practical results. Portuguese nationalism has incorporated nonracism and miscengenation into its ideology. The visitor to Portuguese Africa is commonly told that a man is Portuguese regardless of color. The distinguishing factor is being culturally Portuguese. Portuguese officials commonly use this nonracism as one of the justifications of their continued political rule in Africa. Whether or not it is a valid justification, it remains an established fact.

The Portuguese racial contact in Africa has much in common with similar contacts in Brazil. Though realizing that future research into differences between African and Brazilian societies is of great importance, it is useful to review some observations about the latter. Related to the question of miscegenation is a Portuguese attitude that can be described as "the mystique of whiteness." Donald Pierson noted about Brazil: "The general tendency is for the predominantly European portion to absorb the lighter *mestiços*, while the mulattoes absorb the Negroes. This means that the Brazilian population is constantly acquiring a more European and less Negroid appearance."[3]

Many people in Portuguese Africa as well as in Brazil consider miscegenation a process of "improving the race." Guerreiro Ramos, a black Brazilian scholar speaking of his country, feels that this trend "is reassuring, in that it democratically resolves the racial question which covers prejudice that should not be eliminated by inverting the ideological terms, proclaiming, for example, that blackening of the national population would be desirable. This position would be a kind of racism against racism."[4]

For two decades, until the 1961 uprising and the consequent arrival of large bodies of Portuguese troops, miscegenation was declining in Angola, according to Justino Teixeira, partly because of the increased number of Portuguese, especially women, settling there. The remaining miscegenation had assumed a clear pattern:

> In interracial marriages most Portuguese prefer *mestiços* to Africans. At the same time the *mestiços* tend to marry their own kind, thus not increasing the percentage. Among Africans, 95 per cent tend to marry their own kind and only 5 per cent tend to marry *mestiços*.[5]

Though interesting, these conclusions can lead to an error commonly made by both Portuguese and non-Portuguese writers. The incidence of mixed marriages in Portuguese Africa has little to do with the extent of miscegenation; most miscegenation takes place outside wedlock. One reason for this is illustrated by Archibald Lyall's comments on his 1936 visit to Cape Verde. He found that marriage was looked upon as an unnecessary expense among the lower class, that at least two-thirds of the island children were born out of wedlock, and that, in 1912, the estimate of these ran as high as 98 per cent: "This does not matter to them, for the Capeverdians are very fond of children, and no stigma attaches to bastardy."[6] These proportions are, of course, no longer correct today, but they speak for a characteristic tendency in Portuguese Africa, especially in more remote areas. Such an informal situation with reference to marriage is not uncommon in many developing areas, as well as in some pockets of poverty in the developed countries.

Prejudice does of course exist in Portuguese Africa, but the emphasis and character of that prejudice is of interest. It is similar to that found in Brazil. Charles Wagley, distinguishing between race prejudice of appearance and race prejudice of origin, noted the presence of the former but not the latter in Brazil. He compared Brazilian racial attitudes with attitudes in the United States: "In the United States, they are aimed against all people of known Negro ancestry, regardless of physical appearance. Thus, such attitudes, derogatory stereotypes, and forms of prejudice and discrimination are aimed against a large group that varies from Caucasoid to Negro in physical appearance."[7] Prejudice based on appearance is perhaps not even as prevalent in Portuguese Africa as in Brazil, since the percentage of *mestiços* among the top social strata is higher in Angola than in Brazil. Nowhere in Portuguese Africa are the kinds of black and white stereotypes and categories found in the form so common in other parts of the world.

When answering a question about the possibility of Asian migration to Portuguese Africa, a cabinet minister in Lisbon explained that, since miscegenation with Orientals would not result in a gradual emergence of European characteristics, as in the case of Euro-African unions, it would not produce the "whitening" or Europeanization of race. Similar discussions about the relative advantages of miscegenation often appear within the Portuguese-speaking community in a manner without parallel elsewhere.

The success of Portuguese race policy certainly cannot depend only upon the rate of miscegenation. The formation of a completely nonracist society in Portuguese Africa will depend more on economic, cultural, and political factors than on the annual rate of miscegenation, but attitudes toward race mixing can affect those factors decisively.

Cultural Differentiation

A discussion of the degree to which a multiracial and nonracist society exists in Portuguese Africa must differentiate between modernized and traditional segments of society. The morals and manners of tribal groups differ widely from those of nontribal society, even in the early stages of detribalization that prevails in parts of Angola's urban and rural sectors.

In traditional societies in the process of modernization, there is a lack of homogeneity, a wide variance in morals and manners, and a great unevenness in economic development. The young Portuguese sociologist A. Lima de Carvalho has described Angola as "a socio-cultural field" that "does not constitute a cohesive unity" but is differentiated in all its principal dimensions. The population subunits are in fact socially, culturally, ethnically, and linguistically distinct. The formally organized superstructure and the local substructures, whether primarily African or not, are dissimilar: "These cultures have their own historical and developmental dynamics and they reflect, as any other society, the painful struggle between the being and the becoming ... the same 'process' of accumulation and transmission of experience, knowledge and practice."[8]

With few exceptions, people in the modern sector discriminate against those in the traditional sector. It is difficult to describe the nature and character of that discrimination and the degree to which it is racial rather than social, economic, and political. An appropriate criterion of the racial issue, argues Lima de Carvalho, should be defined thus: a person's "rank" in society is determined by his degree of education, financial status, job and family relations, and other factors, whether that person is African, *mestiço*, or white. In a system such as Angola's, there is opportunity for social mobility, and there are varying proportions of *mestiços* at all levels of society.[9]

Two levels of social mobility are important, one involving movement into the modern sector and one involving movement within the modern sector. The government sector has been a greater field for social mobility than has the private. Though lessened discrimination may increase upward mobility, enlarged economic opportunities and more widespread availability of education may be more significant factors. Because most Portuguese Africans are illiterate, and most illiterates are African rather than European, economic discrimination is practiced by the more advanced members of the society—the whites, *mestiços*, and Africans—against the less advanced members, most of whom are Africans. Basically, then, this is a social discrimination similar to that in Brazil rather than racial discrimination as it exists in North America or South Africa. The more advanced parts of Portuguese Africa, however, with their social mobility, could serve as the yeast of change for the several million people who still live in traditional social units, if the Portuguese Government would face the problems of black and white social mobility with a greater sense of urgency.

DEMOGRAPHIC CHARACTER

Many discussions of the possible paths to independence for the Portuguese possessions in Africa differentiate inadequately between the racial composition of various African entities, and they tend to relegate Angola and Mozambique to a category similar to neighboring states. The accompanying table lists the racial population mix of some major African countries as well as areas not independent today or under white minority rule.

Countries Ranked by Total White Population

South Africa	3,100,000
Angola	250,000
Rhodesia	217,000
Mozambique	130,000
Congo (Kinshasa)	113,200
Madagascar	90,000
Zambia	75,000
South-West Africa	69,000
Kenya	49,000
Tanzania (Continental)	22,300
Cameroun	17,000
Ivory Coast	12,000

Countries Ranked by Total White Population

Uganda	11,600
Swaziland	10,000
Congo (Brazzaville)	10,000
Guinea	10,000
Malawi	8,491
Portuguese Guinea	2,000

Countries Ranked by Percentage of African Population

More than 99 Per Cent	*More than 98 Per Cent*	*Other*	*Per Cent*
Ghana	Madagascar	Kenya	97
Cameroun	Uganda	Mozambique	97
Ivory Coast	Guinea	Zambia	96.7
Portuguese Guinea	Tanzania (Continental)	Swaziland	96.2
Malawi	Congo (Brazzaville)	Angola	94.5
Gabon		Rhodesia	94.3
Congo (Kinshasa)		South-West Africa	83.7
Nigeria		South Africa	69.8

Source: Colin Legum (ed.), *Africa: A Handbook to the Continent* (London and New York, 1966), and P. H. Ady (ed.), *Oxford Economic Atlas: Africa* (Oxford, 1965), p. 10.

Thus, we see that Angola has the second largest white population in sub-Saharan Africa and that its percentage rank is about the same as Rhodesia's. Its white population is over four times that of Kenya, which has the largest white population in British Africa. The Angolan white population increased by about 80 per cent from 1940 to 1950 and by about 119 per cent between 1950 and 1960, a trend that has accelerated during the 1960's. Mozambique has the fourth largest white population in Africa, several times that of Kenya and somewhat larger than that of Congo (Kinshasa). Also significant is the fact that, at the time of independence, less than 1 per cent of the population of Britain was in the colonies, whereas today over 5 per cent of the Portuguese live in the overseas provinces. In a sense, even this 5 per cent underestimates the personal relationships involved. Some Portuguese have relatives who have lived, if not continuously, then intermittently in Angola and Mozambique for generations. One author, for example, spent some days in Angola with a descendant of Salvador Correia de Sá, who helped drive the Dutch from Angola over 300 years ago. Portuguese founded Luanda in 1575 and Benguela in 1617, and such urban centers, with Beira and Lourenço Marques, are Portuguese in character and culture. Plainly, there is now a greater Portuguese identity in Angola and Mozambique than existed in the British, French, and Belgian areas.

Civilian settlement schemes are discussed elsewhere, but it is interesting to note that the presence of a large body of troops is accelerating these trends. Inducements are being offered to soldiers to settle in Africa after completing their service. Such inducements have included free transportation for them and their families, free land of from four to fourteen acres, and a small monetary subsidy. Another purpose of soldier settlement has been to increase a readily available defense reserve.[10]

On the other hand, Portuguese Guinea, with only 2,000 Europeans, is entirely different in character from Angola and Mozambique. It cannot be categorized with the white settled areas of Africa and is more typical of the small states in West Africa. Also different are the Cape Verde Islands, São Tomé, and Príncipe, where the overwhelming *mestiço* population makes them almost uniracial. The differing racial composition of the Portuguese territories is another reason why movements toward independence or other political forms may proceed differently for each and why some movements may eventually differ from ones elsewhere in Africa.

VARIATIONS IN ATTITUDE AND SOCIETY

Not all the components of Portuguese Africa exist at the same level of multiracialism and nonracism. Generalizing presents severe dangers of misrepresentation and misunderstanding. Accurate analysis shows that three basic types of societies exist in Portuguese Africa: (1) those that are already multiracial and nonracist, (2) those in which multiracialism and nonracism is in a formative stage, and (3) those which contain impediments to multiracialism and nonracism. Since one territory may display a mixture of categories, each territory deserves separate analysis.

The Islands

By the middle of the twentieth century, the Cape Verde Islands had become largely multiracial in terms of color and nonracist in terms of social attitudes. Uninhabited when discovered by the Portuguese, these islands had a high rate of miscegenation and were never dominated by a tribal social structure as other parts of Portuguese Africa were. The high percentage of *mestiços* in the population, the progress toward social democratization, and pride in the few remnants of African culture make these islands the showplace for the Portuguese emphasis on racial equality.

While also having large percentages of *mestiços*, São Tomé and Príncipe present a scene quite different from that of Cape Verde. Society is heavily structured along lines that frequently parallel racial differences. At the top, however, are both Europeans and *mestiços* (the *filhos da terra*) who own lands that account for over 95 per cent of total production. Many of the workers on the cacao plantations of the islands are contract laborers, both Africans and *mestiços* from Cape Verde. The workers have little social contact with the rest of the population, as they live in the traditional plantation manner.[11] In the highly stratified society, contacts are rare between Europeans and *angolares*, Europeans and *tongas*, and even between *fôrros* and *angolares*.[12] This high degree of social stratification exists in spite of a cultural uniformity that has blended African and Portuguese culture.

Guinea

The racial future of Guinea is far different from elsewhere in Portuguese Africa, because the European population in Guinea is minuscule. In Guinea, an impediment to multiracialism is, quite simply, the fact that the white and *mestiço* populations are so small. Unless the Hamitic admixture found among many

Guineans is taken to indicate multiracialism, Guinea must be considered a uniracial territory, with a climate hostile to European colonialization and with little, if any, agricultural land available for European settlement.

In the last century, Guinea had an African governor,Colonel Honório Barreto. Thereafter, the percentage of nonwhites in important positions declined.[13] Recently, this situation has begun to change but, in 1964, an African, J. Pinto Bull, served in the Legislative Assembly in Lisbon, while being Inspector of Administration and, formerly, secretary-general of Guinea.

Angola

Angola may be categorized as formatively multiracial, partly because the percentages of whites and *mestiços* are still small. In the more modern sector, however, multiracialism permeates all strata of society, as compared with that in Brazil, for example, where the highest stratum is almost totally white.

Especially significant is the fact that the provincial civil service in Angola contains an appreciable number of nonwhites. There are many nonwhites in the lower ranks, while their incidence is not as great in the upper echelons. There is no legal bar against nonwhites reaching the upper echelon, except the lack of educational qualification that time and increased educational opportunities can overcome. The situation already contrasts favorably with the marked discrimination in the civil service in, for example, the Belgian Congo before independence. There, admission to higher grades was restricted to citizens of Belgium and Luxembourg. Africans were regarded not as Belgian nationals but only as subjects. It was not legally possible, therefore, for an African to qualify for a higher administrative position in the Congo, whereas Africans in Portuguese Africa can qualify for all civil service jobs.[14]

A study of miscegenation in Angola by a Portuguese teacher in Sá da Bandeira, Jofre A. Nogueira, noted its momentary decline as European settlements developed and the white population became more stabilized. Writing prior to the mass troop arrivals in Portuguese Africa, Nogueira asserted that the proper conditions for miscegenation were disappearing but that conditions for a more complete social and cultural assimilation were increasing.[15] The spread of the Portuguese language, the primary condition for a more complete social and cultural assimilation, is rapidly increasing. Other conditions not foreseen by Nogueira have already led to a rapid increase in the *mestiço* population and in miscegenation as well. While the *mestiço* population was almost stable from 1940 to 1950, it increased rapidly from 1950 to 1960, as it had from 1930 to 1940. The 1960 census figures reflect the altered trend with respect to the *mestiço* population, as indicated in the accompanying table.

Population of Angola According to Racial Types
(Estimates and Census, 1930–60)[16]

Year	Total	European	Mestiço	African	Other
1930	3,343,500	30,000	13,500	3,300,000	n.a.
1940	3,738,010	44,083	28,035	3,665,829	63
1950	4,145,266	78,826	29,648	4,036,687	105
1960	4,830,449	172,529	53,392	4,604,362	166

The figures for *mestiços* considerably understate the true size of that population, since, in many cases of racially mixed parents, the child was recorded as Portuguese and white. After the first generation, *mestiços* frequently classified themselves as white or black, depending upon the milieu in which they lived. It should be noted, however, that the 10-year increase in total *mestiço* population of 80 per cent may to some degree reflect a change in the tendency to record *mestiços* as whites.

Mestiços are concentrated in west-central Angola, mostly in the urban areas, and along rail lines and river valleys.

Since 1961, Portuguese troop strength has risen to over 50,000, and the government has provided settlement inducements. Many Portuguese officials in Angola argue that this influx of Portuguese will result in a still greater increase in the birth rate of *mestiços*. Typical is the comment of one Portuguese officer, who hoped that each Portuguese soldier would leave at least six *mestiço* children behind him. Another official said, "It is the *mestiços* who will have the future of Angola in their hands."[17] This aspiration is, of course, partly propaganda for the visitor, a phenomenon that in itself is unique, since, historically, racial propaganda has tended to justify either separation, as in South Africa, or genocide, as in Nazi Germany. The aspirations are also indicative of a policy pushed very hard in the last years of the Salazar government, in conscious opposition to racist tendencies of the type that emerged with the generation of the 1890's.

The 1961 insurgency in Angola is revealing on the race issue. At the time, it was widely predicted that, within weeks or months, the Portuguese would be pushed out of Angola. Since the seventeenth century, relations with the Bakongo (and the neighboring Dembos who were under their influence) have been worse than relations with other tribal groups in Angola, because of the particularly harsh treatment meted out to them by some Portuguese settlers and because of the political boundary, splitting the Bakongo between Angola and the more prosperous Congo. Also, it must not be forgotten that the Dembos were about the last tribe to be subdued in Angola and that they have periodically rebelled against the Portuguese. Though not sanctioned by the government, settler abuses and land confiscation in this part of Angola stirred lasting resentment among Africans and Protestant missionaries there.

After the conflict of 1961, the government acted rather decisively to eliminate such abuses. The government's previous denial that abuses existed reflects, in part, its ignorance as to the extent of them, as well as, perhaps, a desire not to know about them. Among reasons why predictions as to the removal of the Portuguese did not come true, the character of race relations is important. Luciano Lôbo may have been guilty of a poor metaphor when he wrote that African troops and civilians fought bravely against the attackers "like a vaccine, which creates antibodies, immunizing the body from attack,"[18] but the paramount question is why only comparatively small numbers of Africans, principally Bakongo, fought the Portuguese. Greater support of the insurgents could easily have swept the Portuguese Government out of Angola, since Portuguese military capability on the spot was minuscule at the time. Historically, as on that occasion, the Portuguese have always been too weak militarily to fight alone in Angola and elsewhere, and, whenever they fought one tribe, they had the support of others. Until 1961, their African troops were generally more numerous than their white troops. This is not to say that Portuguese attitude toward race was solely responsible for the fact that more Africans did not join the conflict in 1961. But other tribal groups apparently saw this conflict as between the unpopular Bakongo and the Portuguese rather than a general conflict of black against white. The orthodox view in America and Europe has been one of whites fighting blacks in Africa, whereas, today and historically, whites and blacks have been allied against other blacks. The Portuguese have made judicious use of the principle of divide and rule.

Claims about widespread Portuguese discrimination and racism in Angola are genuinely believed in the rest of Africa. They have gained credence through the many individually motivated acts of racial-social discrimination. An observer would find it difficult to know whether these were officially sanctioned or even encouraged. Some of the members of nationalist movements have lived as exiles, voluntary and involuntary, much of their lives, and as such have been exposed to such propaganda. One such person was Angelino Alberto, representative of NtoBako,* who lived in Kinshasa and was convinced that the Portuguese were involved in massive discrimination. In 1962, he testified before a U.N. committee to that effect.[19] After visiting Angola, he was surprised to find that many of his ideas on Portuguese discrimination were myths.[20] When Laurence Appalloo, as Ghanaian Secretary of Government for Technical Education, attended the Second Inter-African Education Conference in Luanda in November, 1957, he expressed delight with Angola, its educational system, and its lack of discrimination.[21] The lack of a color bar in Angola was apparent to visitors, for example, in the absence of "whites only" notices, so conspicuous in British, French, and Belgian colonies, and the freedom of beaches and swimming pools to all races.

In his Albert Londres prize-winning book, *Quand le vent souffle en Angola*, the French journalist José Hanu gives vivid illustrations of nonracism in Angola. He mentions, for example, a funeral procession of about 2,000 people—whites, Africans, *mestiços*, cub-scouts, Children of Mary, and choir boys holding candles and censers—following a small, flower-bedecked truck carrying two coffins. The coffins held two teen-age boys, one African, one white, and were now to be buried in the same tomb. Hanu also describes having seen white, African, and *mestiço* soldiers mixed together under the command of white and *mestiço* officers, a situation unlike that in other African countries when under European dominance.[22]

As in Portuguese Guinea, the number of *mestiços* and Africans in more responsible positions has risen in recent years. A list of important Angolan members in the 1964 Legislative Assembly included Burity da Silva, Carlos Alves, president of the Municipal Council of Carmona, Dr. Custódia Alves, and Dr. José Pinheiro da Silva, professor at the university in Angola. The last, educated at Coimbra, the son of a Cabinda merchant, has subsequently been promoted to Provincial Secretary for Education. The Angolan Director of the Treasury in the 1960's and the editor-owner of the province's oldest newspaper are *mestiços*, and

* See Chapter XVII.

there are *mestiço* planters (*fazendeiros*) who own 2,500 hectares or more of coffee, cotton, and cacao, while many white families live in the worst slums of Luanda, Nova Lisboa, and other cities alongside Africans and *mestiços*.

In Benguela, for example, under the influence of locally owned businesses, social mobility in top society is more pronounced, and the elite has more of a *mestiço* and African character than in Luanda. At the Benguela airport, in July, 1967, one of the authors observed an interesting scene in the crowded lobby. Well over half the well-dressed crowd awaiting the plane were *mestiços* and Africans, all obviously in good circumstances. There was much camaraderie. The District Governor, the popular Santos Prado, arrived to escort the Angolan Secretary of Finance, an African, to the plane, and bid him farewell with a typical Portuguese embrace.

The position of Goans in the history of Angolan assimilation deserves more thorough investigation. Late in the nineteenth century, *assimilados* sought to assimilate Goans into the Angolan community, in order to eliminate competition for the few available jobs. At the same time, some lack of acceptance was shown toward many Goans who filled vacancies as parish priests. After 1930, part of the program of the *assimilado* organization, the Liga Nacional Africana, was to get the government to give Angolans equal chance for jobs and to de-emphasize employment of Goans and Cape Verdians in Angola.

The strong desire of many rural Africans to enter into this multiracial society is expressed in the following African dance (*batuque*) song:

Eu queria que o meu menino
Desta terra se partisse
Que saísse
Que fugísse!
Ser um preto di rispeito
Cumós pretos di Luanda
Ser preto civilizado . . .
Ter camisa
Ter carteira com falanga
Ter sapato
Ser igual os brancos, enfim.

I wish that my boy
Would leave this land
He must leave
He must flee!
Become a respectable black
Like the blacks of Luanda
Be a civilized black . . .
Have a shirt
Have a briefcase with a handle
Have shoes
Be equal to the whites, in short.[23]

Mozambique

A few areas of Mozambique provide racial patterns not dissimilar to those in Angola. In smaller towns, such as Nampula and Quelimane in the north and João Belo and Inhambane in the south, there is a friendly mixing and a minimum of class consciousness. The towns in the Zambezi valley, with the exception of historic Tete, have a strong *mestiço* influence. Quelimane, on the coast, has almost the same racial mixture as Benguela in Angola.

Though the racial situation in northern Mozambique is fairly good, certain hostilities have traditionally existed, especially with the Makonde tribe, which is split between Tanzania and Mozambique. Furthermore, there have traditionally been few Portuguese in the north, thus limiting opportunities for contact and the growth of multiracialism. In the northwest, near the Malawi border, hostilities have also existed. Large-scale emigration to Malawi has taken place, and the influence of the Anglican missions is strong. As to race relations in these areas, Dr. Hastings Kamuzu Banda has said that, before 1961, Portuguese Africans were treated harshly by the Portuguese but that they are now treated much better, a fact that he attributes to Malawi's independence and Portuguese interest in maintaining good relations.[24]

Since the South African and Rhodesian societies are admired because of their economic and technological dynamism, their influence is strong in Lourenço Marques, Beira, and elsewhere. The Portuguese Government finds it necessary to broadcast antiracist propaganda on the Lourenço Marques radio station, and some Africans of Mozambique exhibit the defensive reactions of clowning and fawning subservience typical of a group made to feel inferior. These reactions are not common in Angola or in rural Mozambique. Despite the provisions of the Rural Labor Code, differential wage and salary rates still prevail in many establishments: "Numerous cases can be found, for example, of professionals carrying out exactly the same functions, but paid differently according to their racial extraction."[25]

Even miscegenation is less common in Mozambique than in Angola. For example, in the Limpopo colonization scheme, which includes both Europeans and Africans, there were in 1966 some forty marriages of children of European colonizers, and not one was mixed. Authorities there say that miscegenation tends to occur more among Europeans on isolated farms and villages or "in the bush."

In the last decade, since the abolition of the *indigenato*, the social situation in southern Mozambique has improved, and some African and *mestiço* Mozambicans have entered the provincial administration. Moreover, public segregation according to race is forbidden by law, as it is elsewhere in Portuguese Africa, and the law is enforced.[26]

One of the most striking aspects of Mozambique is the sizable Chinese, East Indian (mostly Goan), and Pakistani populations. Beira, for example, has an excellent Chinese primary school and a special Chinese cemetery. Lourenço Marques has many shop-owners and traders of Chinese and Indian origins, and these groups are importantly represented at the top social levels. It may be interesting to note that of 3,975 members of the various economic associations in Mozambique as of 1963, 1,138 were non-European. Most of these, however, were East Indians and Chinese, not Africans.

At the top level of much of Mozambique society, there are no Africans and few *mestiços*. An exception to this is the wealthy African mayor of Nampula, Pedro Baessa. Nampula has special significance, since, with its cement, cashew, and railway developments, it is one of the fastest growing towns in Mozambique and contrasts vividly with the previous backwardness of this northern area. Though other examples could be cited, the number of nonwhite top-level officials is still small, though growing, which has led to charges that such integration is merely token.

There is a general feeling among the Europeans, *mestiços*, Chinese, and East Indians in Portuguese Africa that the average African is less intelligent than the average non-African and innately incapable of taking command or management positions. This is important in hiring, although not yet pervasive, since there is a shortage of skilled and semiskilled labor and little unemployment. It creates a sense of inferiority among Africans, who have very strong ideas of justice and shame. For example, when asked if he would prefer housing projects to be mixed or uniracial, an African worker in Lourenço Marques said: "Mixed but with equal justice. Living together is difficult when there is no money. To speak up and be heard is also difficult when one is poor."[27]

An Overview

Although the various parts of Portuguese Africa currently provide strikingly different racial situations, they contain a common thread. It is significant that Portuguese attitudes do not provide a basis for an official policy of segregation. The colonial administrative generation of 1890, while not moving toward complete segregation, did practice social segregation and moved toward racial discrimination through a hardened native policy. A motive of this move was economic, in terms of accelerating economic development by manipulating an unskilled labor force. Today, segregationist and racist policies would not accelerate but would markedly hinder economic development and would introduce the larger problems of skilled labor that are so conspicuous in South Africa. The recent observers who have argued that Portuguese Africa is now tending in a racist direction misinterpret what could more accurately be called a Europeanization of Portuguese Africa. This process has involved the erosion of African cultural institutions and the glorification of Portuguese or other European cultural values. This change of values has taken place even though European immigration is small relative to the over-all African labor force. Discrimination from an attitude of cultural superiority, however, is not the same as discrimination from an attitude of racial superiority.

In Luanda and Lourenço Marques, there are no settlements comparable to Harare, the solidly African township of 60,000 in Salisbury, Rhodesia. In Portuguese law there is no tendency toward such things as the Land Apportionment Act of Rhodesia or the former Jim Crow laws in parts of the United States.

Any restaurant or hotel in Angola or Mozambique can be immediately closed down for refusing the right of admission solely on the basis of color. It should be noted that many restaurants in Mozambique post signs reserving their right to refuse admission but legally, on the basis of dress or conduct, something open to wide interpretation, needless to say.

Looking toward the future, it would seem that, if Angola and Mozambique were unrestrained by Lisbon's rule, they would nevertheless resist the imposition of a color bar, much as Senegal did under a racist Vichy regime. As in the case of Senegal, some elements of racism would no doubt surface.[28]

Where Africans do not fully participate is among the economic and political elite. In this regard, one is struck by the unfavorable contrast with such African capitals as Accra, Lagos, or Nairobi. Compared to other areas in southern Africa, however, the number of nonwhites in the elite is considerable. In the municipal elections of 1962 in Guinea, Angola, and Mozambique, 25 per cent of the elected village, town, and city aldermen were nonwhite.[29]

The predominant Portuguese conviction that Portuguese are color-blind works against a widening of the elite. Portuguese officials say that there has been no discrimination against Africans and that, as education efforts bear fruit, more Africans will achieve high positions in the military, business, and administration. The Portuguese educational efforts, and the Portuguese lack of a color bar, indicate that there is also much truth in this assertion. Laxity and a late start in higher educational efforts are principal reasons why more skilled Africans with leadership and executive qualities cannot now be found. The Portuguese Government does not discriminate either in favor of or against Africans in education. A policy of providing Africans with special opportunities in education has from time to time been considered, but so far it has been rejected. Such a policy decision, could, of course, be made only in Lisbon, under the present government. The refusal to view race as a problem means that, along with reduced racial prejudice, there is a lack of special measures to advance Africans.

An interesting issue, though, is whether the general Portuguese nonracism toward Africans has produced an African nonracism toward whites. As yet, beyond a reporting of the anti-Portuguese attitudes of the nationalist parties made in a later chapter, no study has presented the African view of racial attitudes in Portuguese Africa.

But the larger question is whether politics will stand still to await African educational development. The process of modernization in Portuguese Africa, as everywhere else in the world, will create new tensions—in the labor force, in the growing cities, and in the younger population, which is becoming an increasing proportion of the total. To lack prejudice based solely on race is a passive trait and alone may be inadequate to meet the problems of the future. The urgent need is for leaders of society to search actively for nonwhites who can be educated as members of needed, stable professions such as medicine and engineering. This urgent requirement is important whatever may be the political future of Angola and Mozambique. The degree to which that future will be under Portuguese influence may well depend upon the degree to which the Portuguese can meet the challenge of equality of economic opportunity, lack of which is now the Achilles' heel of their racial practice. For, despite the relative lack of racial prejudice among the Portuguese, and the introduction of the virtues of miscegenation into the Portuguese ideology, the character of Portuguese Africa is such that an economic gulf exists between the majority of Africans and the economically better-off Europeans, Asians, and *mestiços*.

NOTES

1. The ramifications of prejudice are well discussed in Gordon W. Allport, *The Nature of Prejudice* (New York, 1958).
2. Thomas Okuma, *Angola in Ferment* (Boston, 1962), p. 26. For American attitudes see Gunnar Myrdal, "Race and Ancestry," *An American Dilemma: The Negro Problem and Modern Democracy* (New York, 1944), Chap. 5.
3. Donald Pierson, *Negroes in Brazil: A Study of Race Contact at Bahia* (Chicago, 1942), p. 123.
4. Oliveira Viana Arianizante, *O Jornal* (Rio de Janeiro), December 13, 1953, quoted in José Honório Rodrigues, *Brazil and Africa*, (trans.) R. A. Mazzara and Sam Hileman (Berkeley, 1965), p. 84.
5. Justino Teixeira, article in *Diário de Luanda*, reprinted in *Afrique Nouvelle* (Dakar: December 6, 1955), cited in Richard Pattee, *Portugal and the Portuguese World* (Milwaukee, 1957), pp. 245–46.
6. Archibald Lyall, *Black and White Make Brown* (London, 1938), p. 54.
7. Charles Wagley, *An Introduction to Brazil* (New York, 1963), pp. 140–41.
8. A. Lima de Carvalho, "Angola: diferenciação, estratificação e mobilidade social: alguns problems introdutórios fundamentais," *Angola, Curso de Extensão Universitária, Ano Lectivo de 1963–64* (Lisbon, 1964), pp. 136–37.
9. *Ibid.*, p. 153.
10. A. B. Herrick *et al.*, *Area Handbook for Angola* (Washington, D. C., 1967), p. 72.
11. Francisco Tenreiro, *A ilha de São Tomé* (Lisbon, 1961), pp. 210–11.
12. *Ibid.*, pp. 200–1.
13. It is interesting to note, however, that Lyall, in his extensive 1936 visit to Guinea, found it a colony with excellent relations between Portuguese and Africans, far better than in adjoining French areas. Lyall, *op. cit.*, p. 240.
14. Georges Brausch, *Belgian Administration in the Congo* (London, 1961), p. 29.
15. Jofre A. Nogueira, "Aspectos fundamentais da miscegenação étnica na província de Angola," *III Colóquio Internacional de Estudos Luso-Brasileiros*, Actas, I (Lisbon, 1957), 188.
16. Oscar Soares Barata, "Aspectos das condições demográficas de Angola," *Angola*, p. 124.
17. Drew Middleton, *New York Times*, May 5, 1966.
18. Luciano Lôbo, "Horizontes novos em Angola," *Boletim da Sociedade de Estudos de Moçambique*, XXXI, No. 130 (January–March, 1962), 137. See also Eduardo de Azevedo, *Terra de esperança* (Lisbon, 1954), for excellent descriptions of multiracial slum life; J. L. Ribeiro Tôrres, *Mozambique: A Study in Integration* (London, 1965) (the authors have been unable to consult this work); António Augusto, "Medições da Niassa—Moçambique," *Anais da Junta das Investigações Coloniais*, Estudos de Antropologia, Vol. V, No. 140 (1948); José Redinha, "Conceito indígena da superioridade do branco," *Garcia de Orta*, Vol. IV, No. 3 (1956); Alfredo Athayde, "Contribuição para

o estudo psicológico dos indígenas do ultramar Português," *Anais da Junta de Investigações do Ultramar*, Vol. VIII, No. 3 (1953); A. K. Strangeway, "The Advance of African Women in Angola," *African Women*, Vol. I, No. 4 (June, 1956); Bandeira Duarte, "Conceito Errado?," *Mensário Administrativo*, Vol. XLIX/L (Luanda: September–October, 1951); and José Júlio Gonçalves, *Técnicas de propaganda, elites, quadros e outros estudos* (Lisbon, 1961).

19. United Nations, *Official Records of the General Assembly*, 17th Sess., 4th Committee, Trusteeship, II (November, 1962), 482.

20. *Ibid.*, p. 541.

21. Quoted in Horácio de Sá Viana Rebelo, *Angola na África dêste tempo* (Lisbon, 1961), pp. 37–39.

22. José Hanu, *Quand le vent souffle en Angola, ou le dialogue pathétique du Portugal et de l'Afrique* (Brussels, 1965), pp. 72–73.

23. Azevedo, *op. cit.*, p. 39.

24. *The Rhodesian Herald*, July 8, 1967.

25. A. Rita Ferreira, "Estrutura da população activa em Moçambique," *Ultramar*, IV, No. 4 (1964), 4.

26. Oscar Soares Barata, *A questão racial* (Lisbon, 1964); and José Osório de Oliveira, *Contribuição portuguêsa para o conhecimento da alma negra* (Lisbon, 1952).

27. *Promoção social em Moçambique*, Estudos de Ciências Políticas e Sociais, No. 71 (Lisbon, 1964), p. 100. For an example of white superiority sentiment seldom seen in print but sometimes encountered verbally, see Armindo Monteiro, *The Portuguese in Modern Colonization* (Lisbon, 1936).

28. See Michael Crowder, *Senegal: A Study of French Assimilation Policy*, 2nd ed. (London, 1967), pp. 39–42.

29. João da Costa Freitas, *Policy of Peace and War* (Lisbon, 1962), p. 21.

PART III

Economy

XI

Development, Finance, and Trade

FRANK BRANDENBURG

THE FIRST part of this chapter is essentially a descriptive account of certain basic characteristics of the economies of Angola and Mozambique. Then follow sections on their internal and external financial situations and their foreign trade. The reader will do well to refer to other chapters for an understanding of the historical context in which the economies of Angola and Mozambique have been developing and the natural resources available to them. Agriculture, industry, and transport receive only brief mention here, since they are discussed elsewhere in the book.

COMPARATIVE ANALYSIS: ANGOLA AND MOZAMBIQUE

The capacities for economic advance in Angola and Mozambique are in many ways representative of conditions in much of the less-developed world today. Rates of population growth and illiteracy are high. Per capita income is low. Economic life shows a heavy orientation toward exports, and the economies of the two provinces are dualistic in the sense that one part is largely traditional and outside the money economy while the other is essentially modern and relatively efficient.

In other ways, the two economies are relatively unique in respect to conditions encountered in the less-developed world generally. First, unlike many poor countries, both Angola and Mozambique have large territory, rivers that can be used for irrigation or production of power, fairly extensive areas of under-developed land suitable for cultivation, and certain valuable minerals. The list of minerals known to exist in Angola and Mozambique is long, though some occur in only limited reserves. All in all, even though much capital and technical know-how are required to expand profitable economic occupancy beyond the present productive areas, Angola and Mozambique are certainly endowed with a better physical base than many, perhaps most, low-income countries.

Second, unlike much of Asia and parts of Latin America and Europe, Angola and Mozambique have low population densities, about 10 and 22 persons per square mile, respectively, along with significant expanses of underdeveloped and undeveloped land situated in areas enjoying moderately temperate climate. A combined effect of these two factors should be to make both territories relatively attractive for white immigration. However, across the centuries, Portuguese contemplating emigration from the mother-country have much preferred to go to more developed foreign lands. Notwithstanding much recent encouragement by Lisbon, including financial assistance, emigration to the overseas provinces continues but on a moderate scale, as indicated in Table 1.

Table 1
Portuguese Emigration, 1960–65

	1960	1961	1962	1963	1964	1965
Emigration to foreign countries:						
France*	3,593	5,445	8,242	15,223	32,637	57,315
Rest of Europe	211	579	918	1,876	4,165	14,180
Brazil	11,498	15,209	12,531	10,080	3,764	1,981
Other (mainly North and South America)	15,156	10,507	10,179	10,170	13,320	14,012
	30,458	31,740	31,870	37,349	53,886	87,488
Emigration to overseas provinces	10,415	(−6,919)	17,291	8,405	11,222	14,123
Total	40,873	24,821	49,161	45,754	65,108	101,611

* Permanent work-permits granted in France to Portuguese nationals, according to *Monthly Bulletin of the French Institute of Statistics*, totalled 24,781 in 1963, 43,751 in 1964, 47,330 in 1965. Discrepancies between the French and Portuguese statistics are explained in large part by illegal emigrations from Portugal, which are not reflected in official Portuguese data.

Source: OECD, *Portugal (Economic Surveys)* (Paris, December, 1966), p. 11.

Third, geographical location is of greater importance in the economies of Angola and Mozambique than it is for many low-income countries. Ports on both seaboards offer the shortest routes to ocean transport from neighboring areas in the interior of Africa—for the Katanga region of Congo (Kinshasa), Zambia, Malawi, Rhodesia, the Transvaal of South Africa, and Swaziland. Mozambique has a decided edge in respect to three "invisible" contributions to the balance of international payments: transit-trade revenues, despite the 1966 closing of the oil-pipeline from Beira to Rhodesia; tourism; and earnings of migratory laborers. Angola's income from transit traffic, via the Benguela Railway and Lobito terminal, is considerably smaller. Likewise, Mozambique sends about fifteen migratory workers to adjoining countries for every one sent by Angola, and the flow of tourists into the former is several times larger than tourism into Angola.

Fourth, economic growth in the two territories has not been achieved at the expense of monetary stability or efficiency in public utilities. With so many countries around the world beset by the crippling effects of rampant inflation, Angola and Mozambique offer object-lessons in the capabilities of advancing economic development by sound money policies. Both territories have consistently enjoyed relative monetary stability. More exceptional still is the high degree of efficiency attained by the management of the railroads, port and dock facilities, and municipal utilities. Performance in these sectors of economic activity appears strikingly enviable alongside that of most less-developed countries.

Fifth, the two economies are further unique in respect to economic relations with the rest of the world. Sizable investment and economic aid by wealthy industrial nations have been a basic condition of development in many parts of the world. In the case of Angola and Mozambique—where adverse propaganda against Portuguese rule in Africa and fairly tight government controls on the operation of various private enterprises in Portuguese territories have been the rule until quite recently—there has been little foreign investment or receipt of international economic assistance. Unlike former French territories in Africa, which through association with the European Common Market now enjoy special access to Western European markets, Angola and Mozambique enjoy only the advantages accruing from most-favored treatment by Portugal, while they suffer from the disadvantages of having a metropole that is one of the poorest countries in Europe. Throughout the Salazar era, foreign equity investment was rare as a rule, and outside investment and outside aid have meant essentially Portuguese investment and Portuguese metropolitan aid. Newest developments show a shift toward opening the two territories to large-scale foreign investment and toward soliciting aid funds from countries other than Portugal.

These observations do not imply that similarities of the two economies with other underdeveloped regions of the world may not, on occasion, outweigh the uniqueness of each economy individually. Annual per capita income in Angola is somewhat higher than in Mozambique, roughly some $90 for the former against $80 for the latter. If subsistence output is included, per capita incomes in the two entities would probably amount to twice as much.

Mixed Ownership and Directed Economic System

The Portuguese in Africa adhere to a set of guidelines on economic structure and types of ownership resembling economic policy in much of Western Europe and Latin America, including Portugal and Brazil. The state not only owns a large proportion of the means of production but also plays a critical regulatory and supporting role in the marketplace. Emergency measures adopted by Salazar to rescue the Portuguese national economy in the course of the difficult years of the 1930's and the war years of the 1940's were carried over virtually intact into the 1950's with a variety of new rules and regulations added. As a result, there was a restricted climate for private enterprise in Portugal and in Angola and Mozambique.

In the two provinces, government has been under considerable pressure to complete the basic economic infrastructure required to support further growth and, in the process, narrow the disparity between backward and advanced regions. Most basic transportation and communication facilities—roads and railroads, airports and local airlines, port facilities, telephone and telegraph—along with municipal services and some electric-power generation and distribution facilities are now under state ownership and are expected to remain so. Some notable exceptions include entities with either partially or completely private ownership, such as the Benguela Railway and the Porto Amboím Railway in Angola, the intercontinental air transport company, TAP (Transportes Aéreos Portugueses), all ocean and coastal shipping except for a government-operated route along the seaboard of Mozambique, the consortiums controlling the distribution of electric power from Cambambe in Angola, and the planned dam at Cabora Bassa in Mozambique.

Mineral development in Angola and Mozambique is reserved mainly for private investment, although the government frequently participates as a minority shareholder and names directors to corporate boards. The joint government-private form of ownership will probably continue to be the preferred structure for large promotions in mining. On the other hand, manufacturing, banking, finance, and general commerce are sectors of business activity in which the government rarely seeks or accepts an equity position, although it may play a strong supportive role in the form of incentives and other stimulants, especially in the case of new manufacturing and export industries.

The situation in agriculture is somewhat more complex for two main reasons. First, the kinds of ownership structures are more varied and include many forms of private, cooperative, corporate, and state proprietorship and second, there is some perplexity within Portuguese Government circles as to the direction that agriculture should take in Portuguese Africa. Major issues concern such questions as whether to enlarge present agricultural settlement schemes and promote new ones, whether to divide large, unused private and public lands into smaller holdings, and whether private, cooperative, or communal tenure should have precedence. In both Angola and Mozambique, there is a fair amount of unused or grossly underdeveloped land suitable for cultivation that remains idle because of tribal settlement preferences, the presence of malaria or the tsetse fly, lack of owner initiative or capital, and other factors. Such obstacles seriously prevent Portuguese Africa from achieving higher levels of agricultural productivity. Encouraging immigration from countries other than Portugal, for example Japan, could be decisive in determining the levels of future land-utilization and increasing farm output. Cooperatives, rather than individual private enterprise, may prove especially advantageous in dairy-farming, citrus-fruit–growing, and the cultivation of special crops. Nothing in Portuguese tradition would inhibit a diversification of land use or immigration of non-Portuguese settlers.

ENTREPRENEURSHIP AND MANPOWER

A serious problem of economic development in Portuguese Africa is the shortage of competent people who understand development in the practical terms of production and distribution of more and better goods at lower costs. Heavily influenced by the traditional Portuguese mentality, local entrepreneurs tend to be more responsive to external economic forces like fluctuations in world commodity prices than to business opportunities arising from changing conditions in the domestic economies of Angola and Mozambique. While an autarkic approach to development is rarely preferable to an outward-looking approach sensitive to the economic advantages of foreign trade, the removal of institutional and other inhibitions to the spread of an atmosphere conducive to enterprising activity focusing more effectively on local markets would doubtless accelerate growth, particularly in Mozambique. There is a widespread small-scale entrepreneurship among artisans, but the number of local people willing to innovate and assume new risks appears lower in medium-size agricultural manufacturing ventures than in medium-size commercial and transportation activities. This has been mostly due to (1) lack of capital and sources of loans; (2) restrictive influences of some government taxation and red-tape procedures; (3) too few attempts to draw Africans into the process; (4) a certain tendency among Portuguese in Angola and Mozambique to engage in ventures of the fly-by-night type and an unwillingness to equip themselves with desirable know-how, trusting rather to their lucky star. Except for a handful of corporate ventures in commercial agriculture, mining, industry, and transportation, the experience of organizing large-scale business is lacking. Foreign (non-Portuguese) entrepreneurs have traditionally not been allowed to do much for either agriculture or trade. However, lately they have been invited to participate in mining and manufacturing, where their contributions have been instrumental in bringing about rates of growth in industrial production that have been much higher than those in agriculture and trade.

Outside of the traditional Portuguese preference for trading, enterprising activity in Angola and Mozambique is influenced to a certain extent by differences in the evolution of business structures in each province and the different sets of values held by immigrants. Mozambique initially developed in the British way of Cecil Rhodes, with large foreign-financed companies, such as the Mozambique Company (Companhia de Moçambique). The territorial economy evolved around its ports and railroads serving the rich mining areas of neighboring countries. Because performing services that are associated with transportation require a fair degree of labor specialization, Mozambique developed a business elite oriented toward management rather than hardy, risk-taking individualism. One result was the clustering of its European population and entrepreneurs at Lourenço Marques and Beira. Also, Portuguese immigrants in Mozambique were much attracted by employment in government services. As a result, along with some native Africans, immigrants of Chinese, Indian, and Goan origin have assumed most of the entrepreneurship in small industry and commerce.

Angola, on the other hand, has always attracted many immigrants who looked upon it as a permanent place of settlement where they could become independent farmers or set up small private business firms of their own. These immigrants were and are essentially individualistic, imbued with a private-enterprise ethic.

Another difference between the two provinces is the presence of Islam in Mozambique. Some Portuguese have claimed that it has led to deterioration in the industriousness of the male, who, by virtue of the acceptance of polygamy and related customs, depends on his wives and children to earn a livelihood for him. One suspects that this is an excuse to justify the Portuguese dislike of Arab influence, which is strong in northern Mozambique, and the fear of underground connection with pan-Arab agitators as well as of opposition to the teachings of the Catholic Church. African society, even without Islam, has usually tended to polygamy, hard labor in the fields for women and children, and relative leisure for the adult male. The Portuguese have done little to alter this traditional pattern within tribal life, although contract labor, migratory labor, the example of the Portuguese farmer living alongside the African, Christianity, urbanization, and a variety of other factors have to some extent induced the temporary or permanent departure of Africans from tribal norms.

In the modern sectors of the economy, the family-owned enterprise is quite conspicuous. Too often it has caused an indifferent level of managerial skills and has foreclosed the advancement of potential talent among outsiders. Low volume output and high prices typically win out over large volume and low prices. Productivity gains are seldom shared with employees and customers. Absentee ownership, particularly in large agricultural holdings, is common. Too little concerned about efficiency and reinvestment of earnings, the proprietor-family behind the firm hardly serves as a source of new hope and confidence.

The shortage of entrepreneurs has stimulated the government to assume entrepreneurship responsibilities, especially in Mozambique, where a large part of the territory's income depends on the efficient operation of utilities connecting ports to neighboring countries and where irresponsibility in industrial enterprises supporting these essential utilities would be costly. The administration of public utilities in Angola and Mozambique is among the most efficient anywhere in the low-income regions of the world. Portuguese Africa can doubtless stimulate private entrepreneurship a great deal more by encouraging an atmosphere favorable to greater economic freedom and by lowering barriers that hinder creative activity and the emergence of responsible management.

The labor force outside the subsistence sector as a whole receives low wages, even though organized labor in industry, commerce, and government service has managed to carve out a niche for itself alongside the middle and upper strata of society, and even though there exists a shortage of skilled and semiskilled manpower. Among the main causes are traditionally low levels of wages for lower social classes in metropolitan Portugal and the lack of interest of upper social echelons in a more equitable distribution of national wealth. A study made in 1966 by the U.S. Department of Labor[1] placed the total number of wage- and salary-earners (exclusive of domestic and seasonal labor) in Angola at 408,400 persons, with an average monthly wage of $15–$20 for unskilled workers and $60–$120 for skilled and semiskilled workers in the major urban centers. For Mozambique, 1960 estimates were of 894,000 wage- and salary-earners, including Mozambicans employed in South Africa and Rhodesia. As an increasing number of people become dissatisfied with life in the countryside and head for urban areas, labor-intensive enterprises in nonfarming activities can expect a ready source of cheap labor. In both labor-intensive and capital-intensive industries, provision for higher wage levels, which the government has vowed to implement, carries the danger of increased costs without corresponding increases in productivity.

In the course of development, as the proportion of the labor force employed in nonfarm occupations increases, the absolute number of people that remain in agriculture will still be high and probably will continue to rise for many years. "Talk of an African industrial revolution on the European or North American scale," as George Kimble reminds us, "is an extravagance while the agricultural productivity of the average African remains low and almost stationary. So long as it does, the market for manufactures must remain small, and its rate of expansion slow."[2] The biggest problem of labor productivity is how to increase both the incentives for farm people and the funds earmarked for agriculture.

Increasing productivity has been one of the goals of education in Angola and Mozambique. Importance is now attached to vocational and technical education and, at the university level, to engineering, the agricultural sciences, and medicine. In an effort to increase the economic skills and human capabilities of Portuguese Africa, the encouragement of new immigration has been adopted. Portugal has allowed limited entry of high-level manpower and technicians of non-Portuguese nationality, whereas over-all immigration has been restricted almost wholly to Portuguese nationals.

Statistics on net immigration (the difference between arrivals and departures) suggest that recent advances in protective medicine, hygiene, and sanitation, along with greatly improved transportation and communications, have been making Angola and Mozambique more attractive as areas of Portuguese settlement. Nevertheless, the extent of attractiveness between 1960 and 1965 as shown in Table 1 on page 220 was a net immigration of only 61,456 Portuguese to the overseas provinces, despite a loss of 6,919 in 1961 when insurgent activities in Angola reached a high pitch.[3] A yearly average of 10,000–12,000 immigrants can hardly represent the scope of immigration that Portuguese officials believe necessary if a decided contribution is to be made toward the skilled-labor pool and acceleration of economic development in Portuguese Africa.

Since colonization based on Portuguese immigration has not attracted the amount of enterprising or skilled people desired, a vigorous policy encouraging immigration from other countries might prove effective if it were adopted. Given the nonracial nature of society in Portuguese Africa and the experience of Brazil with immigration policy, Portuguese Africa could profit greatly from inviting Japanese immigrants. The Japanese who went to Brazil made a decisive contribution to its economic development and have fitted admirably well into Brazilian society. By contrast, Chinese and Indian immigrants have not been as adaptable in mixing with other races, either in Africa or Latin America. Above all, however, local Africans should be given more opportunity. The African has often been discouraged from engaging in certain types of employment, in order to maintain the potential opportunity for Portuguese immigrants.

THE PORTUGUESE NATIONAL DEVELOPMENT PROGRAM

Growth on all fronts of economic activity represents a relatively new goal that Portugal has set for itself and its African territories. It is true that development plans for guiding and promoting the growth of the two provincial economies first existed in the 1930's, but concerted effort by the metropolitan Portuguese and provincial governments to increase incomes and improve the living standards of all people in the Portuguese community did not truly get under way until 1953, with the First Six-Year National Development Plan (*Plano de Fomento I*). Areas of developmental concern include agricultural reform, accelerated extraction of mineral resources, build-up of infrastructure, greater savings and investment, availability of credit, and increases in entrepreneurial and manpower skills. They further include provision of hospitals, clinics, schools, and libraries; construction of low-cost housing; making available basic foodstuffs and consumer goods at reasonable prices; allotment of funds from the government budget to grossly underdeveloped communities; and enforcement of labor rights. Unfortunately, economic policy goals have turned out to be paper thin.

Between 1953 and 1959, plan implementation depended almost totally on revenue made available within the provinces themselves, mainly for expenditure on transport, electric power, irrigation, and agricultural settlement. Metropolitan Portuguese assistance consisted almost entirely of long-term loans totaling $600,000 for Angola and $12.5 million for Mozambique.[4] Beginning with the Second Six-Year Plan (*Plano de Fomento II*) of 1959–64, and with the establishment of a National Development Bank in 1959 to make long-term loans for agricultural and industrial development, Portugal committed itself to assist the

Table 2

Investment Allocations (in Millions of Dollars) by Sector Under the Third Six-Year Development Plan, 1968–73

	Metropolitan Portugal	Overseas Provinces*
Agriculture, forestry, and livestock	511.0	177.0
Fishing	63.8	29.3
Mining and manufacturing	1,090.0	741.0
Local improvements	100.7	4.2
Power	617.0	79.5
Distribution network	—	9.9
Transportation and communications	949.0	354.0
Housing and urbanization	282.0	23.0
Tourism	415.0	6.9
Education and research	195.0	93.5
Health	81.7	35.9
Total	4,305.2	1,554.2

* Including Macao and Timor (negligible items).

Source: Dillon Read & Co., Inc., *Republic of Portugal*, circular (November 2, 1966), pp. 11–13.

overseas provinces with development grants and loans from the metropole. Under the Second Six-Year Plan, about half of the funds for development of Angola and Mozambique were earmarked from metropolitan sources, both public and private. Moreover, the Transitional Development Plan (*Plano Intercalar de Fomento*) for 1965–67 directed additional sums from metropolitan tax revenues for financing projected investment in the overseas territories, mostly in Angola and Mozambique, to supplement funds from development bonds and some non-Portuguese sources.

Portugal and its provinces are presently guided by the Third Six-Year Development Plan covering the period 1968–73. The current plan envisages a global investment target of $5.86 billion, of which $4.3 billion would be invested in metropolitan Portugal and adjacent islands and $1.6 billion in the overseas territories. The $5.9 billion breaks down to roughly twice the annual volume of investment under the Transitional Plan and represents an increase of 54 per cent for the overseas territories. Yearly increases in gross domestic product are programmed at from 6.1 to 7 per cent in the case of metropolitan Portugal, from 5 to 7 per cent in the case of Angola, and from 6.5 to 7.1 per cent in the case of Mozambique. Main objectives of the plan include increased production, productivity, and economic integration of the escudo zone created in 1961 and improved income distribution, both among individuals and by regions.

Sources of investment funds under the current plan for development of the overseas territories are set at 36 per cent from the public sector, 30 per cent from credit institutions and private industry, and 34 per cent from foreign sources. Expenditures by the metropolitan Portuguese Government, included in the estimate of public-sector funds, are programmed at $235 million, or 15 per cent of total investment. Compared with allocations under the previous development plan, both Angola and Mozambique are scheduled to receive significantly higher investment. Like previous plans, major outlays are earmarked for mining and manufacturing and transportation and communications.[5]

Economic and social advance for Portuguese Africa, as envisaged in the current development plan, requires high rates of economic growth, simultaneous advance in many sectors of economic activity, and the special build-up of specific development zones. In the period 1953–62, gross domestic product per capita at current prices appears to have increased at an average annual rate of over 7 per cent in Mozambique and over 5 per cent in Angola. Since prices, except import prices, in these provinces were relatively stable, increases in GDP at current prices approximated those at constant prices. While these rates of growth were below those of Japan, Israel, and a handful of other countries, they were much above those for the United States and the averages for both high-income countries and other less-developed countries around the world. The growth rate of GDP per capita slumped somewhat between 1963 and 1965, but it apparently remained above 4 per cent a year in both Angola and Mozambique. New investments are expected to keep the annual rate of GDP per capita above the 4 per cent level, although maintenance of this level of growth clearly depends on restraining inflationary pressures, arising in part from heavy expenditures for defense and on attracting new sources of outside funds.

Table 3

Investment Allocations Under the Third Development Plan, 1968–73, by Province (in Millions of Dollars)

	Cape Verde	Guinea	São Tomé and Príncipe	Angola	Mozambique	Total
Agriculture, forestry, and livestock	3.4	2.7	6.4	69.4	72.6	154.5
Fishing	9.1	0.9	1.2	18.0	—	29.2
Mining and manufacturing	0.6	16.6	4.2	508.6	221.1	751.1
Local improvements	1.2	0.6	0.3	12.6	3.9	18.6
Power	0.8	1.1	—	42.1	34.7	78.7
Distribution network	0.1	0.2	0.1	4.7	3.5	8.6
Transportation and communications	11.2	12.6	6.1	128.6	185.7	344.2
Housing and urbanization	3.5	3.1	0.3	12.7	15.6	35.2
Tourism	0.2	0.4	0.1	3.9	0.3	4.9
Education and research	2.4	2.5	2.4	46.2	34.1	87.6
Health	2.1	2.1	0.6	16.3	14.0	35.1
Total	34.6	42.8	21.7	863.1	585.5	1,547.7

Source: Banco Nacional Ultramarino, Boletim Trimestral, No. 73 (Lisbon, 1968), p. 25.

Table 4

Sources of Financing Under the Third Development Plan, 1968–73, by Province (in Millions of Dollars)

	Cape Verde	Guinea	São Tomé and Príncipe	Angola	Mozambique	Total
National	27.0	29.4	21.7	494.5	413.9	986.5
State	25.8	27.7	12.6	269.0	201.1	536.2
Central administration	25.8	24.5	12.6	68.0	76.2	207.1
Provincial administration	—	—	—	196.9	94.5	291.4
Local administration	—	2.3	—	4.1	9.1	15.5
Autonomous organizations	—	0.9	—	—	—	0.9
Funds and firms	—	—	—	—	10.2	10.2
Beira Railway	—	—	—	—	11.1	11.1
Credit institutions	1.1	—	1.9	18.5	17.0	38.5
Industrial participation	0.1	1.7	7.2	207.0	195.8	411.8
External	7.7	13.4	—	368.4	171.7	561.2
Total	34.7	42.8	21.7	862.9	585.6	1,547.7

Source: Banco Nacional Ultramarino, Boletim Trimestral, No. 73 (Lisbon, 1968), p. 25.

Economic and social advance is further conceived in terms of the concentration of sufficient productive and growth-generating activity in one location to make it economically sound, simultaneous with decentralization of economic activity to provide jobs in widespread locations and prevent population pressures from building up in any one area. A major problem in this respect is the desire to de-emphasize the relative importance of the industrial and commercial complexes centered in Luanda and Lourenço Marques. For Angola, the Luanda–Dondo–Malange belt and the Lobito–Benguela–Upper Catumbela–Nova Lisboa complex have been proposed as two basic zones of development, in addition to several secondary centers. Nine main development zones are proposed for Mozambique, stretching from the Porto Amélia zone in the north to the greater Lourenço Marques zone in the south.[6]

A most difficult and pressing problem for Portuguese Africa is reconciling economic growth with needed social advances. Critics of Portuguese rule in Africa claim gross neglect of the social dimensions of development. They maintain that it is difficult to defend Portugal's policy when, after four centuries of rule, nine of every ten people in Portuguese Africa are illiterate; poverty and communicable diseases are widespread; infant mortality rates are high; and housing, sanitation, and educational opportunities are so obviously inadequate. Of course, tropical possessions of European powers, Portuguese and non-Portuguese, showed little progress until perhaps the turn of the century for Asia, the 1920's for Africa. Only then did medical and educational advances begin. Portugal was slower than other colonial powers in instituting social reforms. Today, this lag, despite other solid achievements since about 1958, may be the weakest link in the Portuguese equation for development of its African provinces.

THE INTERNAL FINANCIAL SITUATION

In recent years, the financial situation in Angola and Mozambique has been characterized by a strong demand for credit, a steady rise in the means of payment, and a flow of public funds from Portugal heavier than normal. Alongside these trends, the two territories have been experiencing the effects of a new exchange system, revised customs duties, new regulations to control the remittance of profits, and higher taxes. The value of exports has doubled in the last fifteen years for both provinces, and invisible income has also grown, though less rapidly.

CURRENCY, BANKING, AND EXCHANGE

Although the basic currency unit of Angola and Mozambique is the escudo, issued by the Banco de Angola and, in Mozambique, by the Banco Nacional Ultramarino (National Overseas Bank) in Portugal, the practical effect of exchange regulations is to create separate provincial currencies. Both the Angolan escudo and the Mozambican escudo are accepted on a par with the Portuguese escudo in official transactions (the equivalent of 28.5 escudos to the dollar), but, owing to greater confidence in the latter, along with delays and difficulties in the transfers of provincial currency to metropolitan destinations, the value of the Portuguese escudo is often considerably more on the free market. The strength of Portugal's currency relative to the territories was reflected in the free-exchange rate of the Angolan escudo in 1964, when it fluctuated from 33 to the dollar early in the year, to 35 in midyear, and 30.5 at year's end. Since August, 1965, the free rate of the Angolan escudo has continued to be higher than that of the Portuguese escudo.

Exchange restrictions prohibiting the direct use of foreign currencies in the two provinces and transfers from one province to another are not always respected outside the regular exchange system. United States, British, Rhodesian, and South African currencies are often accepted by local tradesmen as means of payment. Moreover, it is common knowledge that many Portuguese investors transfer some of their capital gains between the provinces or to Portugal through the free-exchange market. A result is an understatement in official statistics of the amount of Portuguese investment that circulates between the segments of the Portuguese community. While the amount of such investment flowing through free channels remains unknown, stability of the free-exchange rate in Angola since 1965 would seem to indicate that the inflow has been significant enough to offset Angolan remittances abroad made outside official channels.

Though the commercial credit needs of both territories are better served today than they were in the first half of the 1960's, it is generally believed within the two territories that additional banks are desirable.[7] Until late 1965, when the Banco de Crédito Comercial e Industrial de Angola (BCCIA or Commercial and Industrial Credit Bank of Angola) was first established, Angola had only two commercial banks. One, the official Banco de Angola, not only engages in commercial credit but serves as the bank of issue for the province. The other, the Banco Comercial de Angola, controlled by the private Banco Português do Atlántico in continental Portugal, normally has attracted more long-term savings deposits than the Bank of Angola, since the latter paid no interest on savings. Half of the initial capital of the BCCIA was subscribed by the Banco Borges e Irmão of Portugal and the other half was reserved mainly for subscription in Angola and Mozambique. More recently, the Banco Totta-Aliança of Portugal and the Standard Bank of South Africa (in which Chase Manhattan Bank has a minority participation) combined to establish banks in Angola and Mozambique (Banco Standard-Totta); the private Banco Pinto e Sotto Maior of continental Portugal likewise opened agencies in Angola and Mozambique. Furthermore, Barclays Bank has offices in Mozambique.

A broadening of activities by existing banks and easier terms for mortage and personal loans are also needed. Shortage of long-term loan sources greatly handicaps medium- and small-size enterprises. Until 1966, commercial banks were not allowed to accept term deposits of over a year, which prevented them from granting long-term loans and thereby held back economic advance. It is too early to evaluate the effect of a 1966 regulation authorizing commercial banks to set up autonomous "financing departments" to handle long-term deposits and loans. The absence of attractive interest rates has discouraged savings and, thus, has handicapped a build-up of private capital reserves in the overseas provinces as well as within the metropole. Aside from some foreign investment, financing to private enterprises has come almost entirely from the semigovernment-owned Banco do Fomento Nacional (BFN or National Development Bank) in Lisbon, operating through agencies in Angola and Mozambique since 1959. The BFN has concentrated on financing electric-power development and manufacturing and construction industries; more recently, it has extended credits to primary production. In 1964, it sent a study mission to Angola and Mozambique to help define the scope of its future action.

The situation in respect to home mortgages and personal loans is hardly better. Ordinarily, both types of loan must be fully secured and are obtainable by the average resident of Angola or Mozambique only from the Postal Savings Bank, where many local residents keep their meager savings, or from private housing cooperatives. Shortage of mortgage funds and the stiff terms attached to them explain, in part, the declining rate in house construction in both provinces for a short period following 1963.

Table 5

Money Supply in Angola and Mozambique (in Millions of Dollars), 1961–66*

	1961	1962	1963	1964	1965	1966
Angola						
Currency in circulation	39.0	47.6	50.3	55.6	61.8	60.9
Demand deposits	111.3	117.6	129.2	141.0	168.6	186.0
Time deposits	2.5	2.9	3.6	4.6	9.5	14.5
Total	152.8	168.1	183.1	201.2	239.9	261.4
Mozambique						
Currency in circulation	41.8	45.6	47.5	49.3	52.5	
Demand deposits	122.8	124.7	129.2	132.6	144.6	
Time deposits	5.8	8.2	9.3	11.5	12.3	
Total	170.4	178.5	186.0	193.4	209.4	

* Years ending December 31.

Source: Dillon Read & Co., Inc., *Republic of Portugal*, circular (November 2, 1966), p. 43. The 1965 and 1966 figures for Angola are from Banco de Angola, *Relatório e contas—exercício de 1966* (Lisbon, 1967), p. 180.

The means of payment, as Table 5 shows, have increased considerably in recent years, more in Angola than in Mozambique, in respect both to currency in circulation and bank deposits, even if one takes into account creeping inflation or the fall in real value of money, a phenomenon that the two provinces have in common with other countries around the world.

As it can be seen, in Angola, from 1961 to 1966, currency in circulation has increased 56 per cent, bank deposits somewhat more than 75 per cent. The comparable figures for Mozambique from 1961 to 1965 were 25 per cent and 18 per cent, respectively. The rate of increase in the means of payment in Angola probably exceeds that province's rate of real productivity gains as measured by GDP growth, while in Mozambique the increase in the means of payment is probably less than the real productivity gains.

The exchange system in Angola and Mozambique, based on the economic integration policy adopted by Portugal in 1963 for all its territories, operates through four main mechanisms—the Junta Provincial de Câmbio (Provincial Exchange Board), the Fundo Cambial (Exchange Fund), the Fundo de Compensação (Compensation Fund), and the Fundo Monetário da Zona do Escudo (FMZE, Escudo Zone Monetary Fund). The Junta authorizes and coordinates all official exchange transactions, while the Fundo Cambial, comprising all provincial exchange holdings, consists of a Fundo de Reserva (Reserve Fund), deposited by the territories in Portuguese escudos in the Banco Central de Portugal, and working balances of foreign exchange holdings of provincial commercial banks maintained at a maximum level, determined by the Junta, to service day-to-day transactions. The Fundo de Compensação is managed by the Banco de Portugal and is really a monthly clearing house for interterritorial transactions, as it serves to debit or credit deficits against or to a territory's account in a Reserve Fund. Finally, the FMZE facilitates the stabilization of the exchange position of Angola, Mozambique, and other Portuguese provinces, in respect both to each other and to Portugal itself. From the capital of the FMZE, which was obtained jointly from Banco de Portugal, Banco Nacional Ultramarino, and Banco de Angola, provinces in deficit to the Reserve Fund are authorized to make monthly withdrawals to cover their deficits. Thus, the FMZE works for Portugal and its provinces much the same way as the International Monetary Fund operates on behalf of the world community.

It is important to distinguish between foreign exchange and Portuguese exchange. The former is handled through the working balances, the latter through the compensation and reserve funds. In effect, this means, in the case of Angola for example, that there is always a surplus of foreign exchange, since that province enjoys a positive commercial balance with non-Portuguese areas. The surplus is credited to Angola's "working balances" until they reach their maximum level, when the excess is transferred to the Reserve Fund to offset possible Angola deficits in that account. Hence, while non-Portuguese exchange is readily available in the working balances for covering payment orders issued against these balances, payment orders against Portuguese exchange are delayed until funds are available in the Reserve Fund. The system thereby operates to the immediate benefit of foreign corporations remitting profits abroad, since funds are obtainable without delay from the exchange board. On the other hand, Angolans, remitting "invisibles" to Portugal and importers from Portugal usually have to wait two or three months until the exchange board authorizes a transfer of funds.

The exchange system works to the relative advantage of foreign firms in Angola, because the exchange board permits Portuguese firms to remit to Portugal a lower percentage of profits than the foreign firms can return to their parent companies. At the end of 1965, for example, Portuguese firms could remit only 20 per cent of their profits, whereas foreign companies were allowed to remit full profits. Similar regulations now control the transfer of rents and other savings of Angolan businessmen and firms. This modification of the basic exchange legislation of 1963 has reduced the transfer of local savings out of

Angola, which reached serious proportions in 1963 and 1964; it has also encouraged new foreign private investment.

The difficulties in fund transfers and substantially higher rates of interest in other countries have led to considerable illegal exodus of capital from Portuguese territories and metropolitan Portugal. It is estimated by some that the amount of money secreted by Portuguese nationals abroad, mainly in Western Europe and the United States, runs into the tens of millions of dollars. The shortage of medium and long-term capital available from commercial banks makes the recovery of this money important. At the end of 1966 stiff penalties were introduced in Portugal to discourage offenders.

PROVINCIAL BUDGETS

Government budgets in Angola and Mozambique have increasingly been conceived in terms of necessary development rather than public administration, as was traditional. This has meant that the sources and uses of government revenue are heavily influenced by the National Planning Commission in Portugal and provincial planning commissions in the territories. It is to these organs that provincial administrations look for guidance in setting goals and administering economic plans. The intimate ties existing between these planning agencies and direct supervision of planning by the provincial governors facilitate coordination. Nevertheless local officials are aware that both planning and budget-making procedures require improvement.

The Third Development Plan, like the previous plans, is neither all-inclusive nor compulsory; it provides guidelines and calls for annual appropriations from provincial governments. Anticipated revenue and expenditures to implement the development plans in Angola and Mozambique are an important, but not the sole, consideration of the two provinces when they prepare their annual

Table 6

Government Budgets in Angola and Mozambique, Revenue and Expenditures
(in Millions of Dollars), 1962–66

		1962	1963	1964	1965	1966
Angola						
Receipts		118.0	171.2	162.5	183.4	197.8
Expenditures		106.9	163.5	149.6	173.9	187.3
	Surplus	11.1	7.7	12.9	9.5	10.5
Mozambique						
Receipts		171.5	178.5	178.5	196.0	206.5
Expenditures		168.0	171.5	171.5	189.0	205.5
	Surplus	3.5	7.0	7.0	7.0	1.0

Source: Banco de Angola, *Relatório e contas—Exercício de 1966* (Lisbon, 1967), p. 193. Mozambique, Direcção Provincial dos Serviços de Estatística, *Boletim Mensal*, Year 8, No. 3 (March, 1967), p. 99.

Table 7

Revenue and Expenditures (in Millions of Dollars) in Angola, 1966

Ordinary receipts

Direct taxes	23.9	
Indirect taxes	35.5	
Special industrial contributions	10.5	
Diverse taxes	4.3	
Profit from participation in private industry	9.9	
Income on investment	1.7	
Repayments	2.9	
Committed receipts	68.5	
		157.2
Extraordinary receipts		40.6
Total receipts		197.8

Ordinary expenditures

Debt	8.1	
Government expenses and retirement provisions	2.1	
General administration	28.2	
Department of the Treasury	3.2	
Department of Justice	2.1	
Development services	52.6	
Armed forces	22.0	
Miscellaneous	28.2	
		146.5
Extraordinary expenditures		
Development Plan	29.6	
Other	11.2	
		40.8
Total expenditures		187.3

Source: Banco de Angola, *Relatório e contas—exercício de 1966* (Lisbon, 1967), pp. 195–201.

public budgets. Never ignored is the legal right of a province to utilize all taxes collected within its own boundaries to meet expenditures in that province alone. Never overlooked, either, is the constitutional mandate prohibiting budget deficits. Another major stipulation is that the local governor is required to submit annual budgets for approval to the legislative council.

Total budget expenditures on a cash basis, as well as total receipts,[8] have been reaching slightly higher levels in Mozambique than in Angola, as shown in Table 6.

Although the data in the table indicates a gross surplus for every year, the two provinces have actually been operating on a deficit, as a result of the increase in public debt. Revenue obtained from international loans is included in receipts, but the increase in public debt, which amounts to more than the given surpluses, is excluded. At the end of 1966, this total public debt, resulting from loans and advances from Portugal and issue of public bonds, amounted to roughly $189 million for Angola and $207 million for Mozambique and equaled roughly one year's government revenues in each province. Debt-servicing represented 5.5 per cent of ordinary expenditures and drew on 5.15 of ordinary receipts in Angola.[9]

Under existing accounting procedures, double entries are made for certain receipts. When such entries are made net revenue is less than stated.

Table 8

Revenue and Expenditures (in Millions of Dollars) in Mozambique, 1966

Ordinary receipts		
Direct taxes	25.0	
Indirect taxes	29.8	
Special industrial contributions	11.0	
Diverse taxes	8.7	
Profit from participation in private industry	1.9	
Income on investment	0.2	
Repayments	9.4	
Committed receipts	100.2	
	———	186.2
Extraordinary receipts		21.3
		———
Total receipts		207.5
Ordinary expenditures		
Debt	8.6	
Government expenses and retirement provisions	2.1	
General administration	28.0	
Department of the Treasury	3.9	
Department of Justice	2.5	
Development services	82.1	
Armed forces	27.7	
Miscellaneous	24.6	
	———	179.5
Extraordinary expenditures		26.0
		———
Total expenditures		205.5

Source: Mozambique, Direcção Provincial dos Serviços de Estatística, *Boletim Mensal,* Year 8, No. 3 (March, 1967), p. 99.

TAX STRUCTURE

The tax structure in Angola and Mozambique is cumbersome, complicated, and regressive. Indirect taxes, mainly import and export duties and excise taxes, provide considerably more revenue than direct taxes. There is no sales tax as such, although a wide variety of taxes are levied on almost every commercial transaction. Direct taxes, mostly the head tax and taxes on individual and corporate incomes, account for less than 20 per cent of ordinary receipts in the two provinces. The biggest single source of budgetary income in Mozambique, regularly providing almost half the total revenue, actually comes from government-owned enterprises, especially the railroads and ports administration. As direct taxes often involve multiple taxation of the same income, and indirect taxes are obviously too numerous and too frequently earmarked for specific purposes or entities, the entire tax system could benefit from consolidation. The main direct taxes payable in Angola and Mozambique are the following.

1. General minimum tax, payable by every male, and every female in government service, between eighteen and sixty years of age, the amount of the tax varying from $4 to $16 a year, depending on the location of residence. This tax has replaced the former head tax paid by male Africans.

2. Industrial tax, the net effect of which, in specific taxes in this category, is a tax rate of about 19 per cent on the difference between production costs and sales prices. Basic tax is 10 per cent of the difference, to which are added surtaxes of 70 per cent, earmarked for specific government uses, sometimes a tourism tax of 3 per cent, and a stamp tax varying from 11 per cent to 16 per cent of the basic tax. Both individuals and firms engaged in almost every line of industrial activity are required to pay the tax.

3. Personal income tax is charged on the income of government employees, salaried workers, and professional people. The first two groups pay rates of from 1 to 6 per cent of salaried income plus 4 to 6 per cent on any nonsalaried income, while professional people pay according to a complicated schedule usually amounting to from $70 to $150 a year.

4. Urban building tax is a tax on income from rentals, charged at the rate of 10 per cent of taxable income (total rental income minus 20 per cent for maintenance costs). As surtaxes of as much as 6 per cent of the basic tax are added, mainly for funding specific items in municipal budgets, the over-all urban building tax may reach a maximum rate of 16 per cent. Income from buildings less than ten years old is exempt if the cost of the building was at least $100,000 in a major city, $17,000 in a rural settlement.

5. Concession tax is charged on profits from concessions granted by the government for agricultural, livestock, timber, fishing, and mining exploitation; the rate is 1 per cent on the first $700, 4 per cent on further $700 to $3,000, and 6 per cent for income over $3,000. In addition, there is a stamp surtax of from 3 to 8 per cent of the basic tax. Annual profits of less than $2,000 are exempt, as are subsistence cultivation of all types and agricultural and timber concessions less than ten years old.

6. Excess profits tax is actually a second tax on income subject to any of the

taxes in all the foregoing categories but the first. Rates increase with higher levels of income, reaching 40 per cent on individual incomes of $3,000 or more annually and 8 per cent on corporate incomes of $50,000 or over.

7. Real estate transfer tax is rated at 10 per cent of the amount of the sales price, unless the transaction represents the first sale of an apartment building where the seller had paid the industrial tax on its construction. In the latter instance, the rate is 3 per cent.

8. Extraordinary tax for the defense of Angola was imposed in June, 1963; the tax is now payable by all individuals and companies in that province, whether Portuguese or not, whose earnings exceed the equivalent of about $17,000 a year. Depending on the income level, the rate is from 4 to 30 per cent.

While the multiplicity of taxes levied on the population is clearly excessive, the great majority of individuals in Angola and Mozambique pay, in effect, relatively low taxes. In addition to the need for consolidation of the tax structure —direct and indirect taxes alike—some relief is in order for existing businesses. Present taxation of business profits is too high to encourage new investment in certain areas. The granting of some tax holidays avoids this barrier in respect to new investment in Angola.

External Financial and Economic Relations

A significant aspect of the external economic and financial relations of Angola and Mozambique concerns the relationship of each of these provinces to metropolitan Portugal, upon which the provinces have depended long and heavily for markets, investment capital, and economic, technical, and military aid.[10] Portugal, in turn, has found in its provinces not only a captive market for exports and a convenient source of primary products, but also a haven for investment and a favorable balance of international payments to offset Portugal's traditional deficit with foreign countries.

Both development of natural resources and the establishment of agricultural, commercial, and industrial enterprises in the African provinces is controlled by the Portuguese Government through the granting of concessions. In the case of concessions of land, only companies representing at least 50 per cent Portuguese capital participation were eligible, until recently. Otherwise, foreign firms were limited to buying land for which firms or persons already have full title or to taking over government land concessions granted prior to 1937. At present, the climate for over-all foreign investment is more favorable. Two important decrees were issued in 1965, one being the foreign investment law[11] and the other the industrial protection law. Under the first, firms in nonstrategic fields may be established with 100 per cent foreign capital participation, and the totality of profits plus the entire original investment may be remitted abroad. Under the second, greater protection is provided for industries in the overseas territories, from both foreign and Portuguese competition, and restrictions are abrogated on textile-manufacturing, previously imposed to protect the manufacturers in metropolitan Portugal.

The major Portuguese overseas corporations and the major Portuguese banks are now convinced that substantial amounts of foreign capital, including venture capital, are absolutely essential to economic development. Nevertheless, the official Portuguese attitude is not easy to define; policies and practices are often ambiguous. Many potential investors, as well as already successful ones, complain of obstacles such as red tape, delay, and not knowing exactly where they stand. Sometimes one agency of the government will be helpful while another will hinder. When such an attitude is matched by frequent reluctance to invest in underdeveloped areas for fear of political uncertainties and less return than in the developed areas, the result can deter the inflow of foreign capital. At the same time, as the discussion of industry shows,[12] the attitude toward foreign investment in Angola and Mozambique is more favorable than in some other areas in Africa.

In Chapter XV, financial relationships between Portugal and its African provinces are discussed, and the consequences of their association within the political climate created by conditions since 1961 are pointed out. The rest of the present chapter will, therefore, be devoted to a survey of the external trade of Angola and Mozambique.

External Trade and Balance of Payments

Both Angola and Mozambique depend heavily on external trade, although the extent of dependence is not the same: in Mozambique's balance of payments, the "invisibles" play a greater role. Their structures of imports are remarkably alike, but the total value of imports is slightly higher for Angola. Some exported raw materials are competitive, principally in the metropolitan market, and occasional rivalry is displayed by the two provinces.[13] Apart from the metropolitan Portuguese market, directions of trade are somewhat different: the OECD countries are more important in Angola's trade, whereas South Africa and some Asian countries are more involved in Mozambican exchanges.

Nearly all import, export, and re-export trade movements in the two provinces require prior authorization by local officials, except for trade within the escudo zone. Such authorization is granted almost automatically for commodities liberalized in that zone, although fewer have been liberalized for the provinces than for metropolitan Portugal. Portugal normally abstains from imports from countries outside OECD when they might affect provincial industries adversely. Exchanges within the escudo zone are permitted freely and are subject only to customs duties and registration to facilitate payments. For a few commodities imported by the provinces from the metropole, prior authorization may be required on occasions to protect producers within a specific province.

Angola

Table 9 shows the growth of external trade of Angola since 1952, the year immediately preceding the start of the Portuguese National Development Program. During the period 1952–66, the total annual value of provincial trade more than doubled. Despite considerable fluctuations in the world market prices of certain export commodities, the balance of trade has been positive, except for the years 1957–60, when heavy imports of capital goods to implement the early stage of the Second Six-Year Development Plan met with low quotations for coffee, the leading Angolan export since the 1950's.

Table 9

External Trade (in Millions of Dollars) of Angola, 1952–67

Year	Exports	Imports	Total Trade	Balance
1952	96.4	88.5	184.9	+7.9
1953	123.7	85.2	208.9	+38.5
1954	103.5	96.4	199.9	+7.1
1955	98.2	94.0	192.2	+4.1
1956	115.1	110.7	225.8	+4.4
1957	117.7	123.8	241.5	−6.0
1958	129.0	130.7	259.7	−1.7
1959	125.5	131.8	257.3	−6.3
1960	124.8	128.4	253.2	−3.6
1961	135.6	114.3	249.9	+21.3
1962	149.2	136.4	285.6	+12.8
1963	164.0	147.4	311.4	+16.5
1964	205.4	165.0	370.4	+40.4
1965	201.2	196.1	397.3	+5.1
1966	222.8	208.2	431.0	+14.6
1967	237.9	274.6	512.5	−36.7

Sources: For 1952–63, Angola, Direcção de Economia, Repartição de Estatística Geral, Comércio externo (Luanda: Imprensa Nacional). For 1964–66, Banco de Angola, Relatório e contas—exercício de 1966 (Lisbon, 1967). Figures from 1967 come from International Monetary Fund, Direction of Trade (August, 1968).

The main commodities in Angolan trade in 1966 are shown in Table 10. Coffee accounted then for close to one-half of all exports. Diamonds, fish products, sisal, iron ore, timber, maize, and cotton fiber are also important in the export flow, and, in some years, sugar and petroleum products have contributed significantly. The latest investments in the Cassinga iron ore mines should cause iron-ore exports to reach higher levels in 1968. Likewise, when the offshore deposits in the Cabinda Enclave come into full production, crude and refined petroleum should become a major export.

In provincial imports, automotive equipment and parts have occupied first rank throughout the period under consideration, owing to continual expansion of transportation facilities. Iron and steel products for construction and engineering works have been also flowing in at a fast rate. Table wines, textile goods, and various foodstuffs to supplement Angola's own food production are the most commonly imported consumer goods.

Portugal has traditionally ranked first as the country of origin of Angolan imports. During the 1960's, between 43 and 49 per cent of all imports came from the metropole. For 1965–66, the percentage decreased somewhat, because of declining imports of home textiles. Portuguese capacity for absorbing Angolan

Table 10

Main Commodities in Angola Trade (in Millions of Dollars), 1966

	Value	Per Cent of Total
Exports		
Coffee	107.2	48.1
Diamonds	39.4	17.6
Fish products (fish meal, fish oil, and dry, canned, and fresh fish)	14.1	5.8
Sisal	10.5	4.7
Iron ore	4.7	2.0
Timber (round and sawn)	4.3	2.0
Maize (grain and meal)	4.1	2.0
Cotton fiber	3.7	1.7
Other	34.8	16.1
Total	222.8	100.0
Imports		
Motor vehicles and parts	21.3	10.3
Iron and steel	17.7	8.6
Wines and alcoholic beverages	16.8	8.0
Textiles (yard goods and manufactures)	13.6	6.5
Foodstuffs	13.0	6.2
Medicine	5.5	2.6
Other	120.3	57.8
Total	208.2	100.0

Source: Banco de Angola, *Relatório e contas—exercício de 1966* (Lisbon, 1967), pp. 146, 148, and 164.

production, however, has been much less, as indicated by Table 11, and only from 15 to 30 per cent of provincial exports have normally been directed to the metropole. In 1965–66, the figures rose to 35 per cent, because raw diamonds previously exported for cutting to London were being cut in Lisbon. Exports and imports to other Portuguese overseas provinces are usually of the order of 2 to 3 per cent each.

The United States has been the foremost foreign country of destination of Angolan exports, taking at times as much as 25 per cent of all exports and ranking third or fourth as a source of imports. In several post–World War II years, it has even surpassed metropolitan Portugal as the leading Angolan customer (see chart 3 p. 243). The Netherlands, West Germany, the Congo (Kinshasa), and sometimes Spain and Italy are also generally significant as countries of destination of products from Angola, whereas the United Kingdom, West Germany, France, and Belgium–Luxembourg are more important as countries of origin of provincial imports.

241

Table 11

Angola Trade with Metropolitan Portugal and Its Contribution to Escudo Zone
Balance of Trade (in Millions of Dollars), 1952–66

Year	Exports to Portugal		Imports from Portugal		Balance of Trade with Portugal	Balance of Trade with Third Countries	Net Contribution to Escudo Zone
	Value	Per Cent of Total	Value	Per Cent of Total			
1952	28.87	30	44.45	48	−15.57	+19.95	+4.37
1953	19.14	15	41.30	48	−23.20	+60.62	+37.41
1954	21.56	21	45.85	48	−24.29	+31.43	+7.14
1955	22.12	22	43.96	47	−21.84	+25.90	+4.06
1956	19.07	17	50.29	45	−34.72	+35.66	+0.94
1957	21.70	18	56.03	48	−34.33	+28.28	−6.05
1958	23.27	18	60.27	47	−37.00	+35.28	−1.71
1959	22.85	18	61.39	49	−38.53	+32.20	−2.83
1960	30.13	24	59.99	48	−29.85	+26.18	−3.67
1961	26.07	19	50.12	37	−24.04	+45.25	+21.21
1962	29.92	20	56.49	38	−26.56	+39.37	+12.81
1963	36.54	22	63.38	43	−26.84	+44.34	+17.50
1964	61.35	29	80.71	49	−19.35	+59.71	+40.35
1965	70.80	35	93.13	40	−22.33	+27.44	+5.11
1966	77.56	35	87.29	42	−9.73	+23.45	+13.72

Sources: For 1952–63, Angola, Direcção de Economia, Repartição de Estatística Geral, Comércio externo (Luanda, 1964); For 1964–66, Banco de Angola, Relatório e contas—exercício de 1966 (Lisbon, 1967).

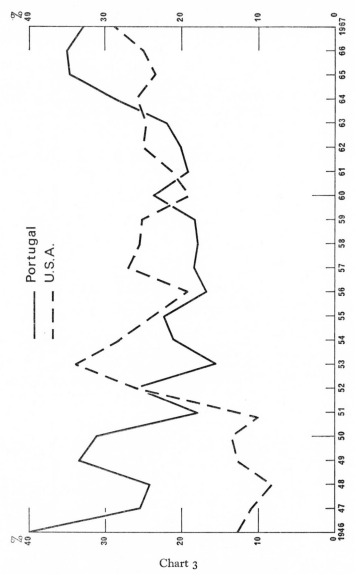

Chart 3

Angola Export Trade with Metropolitan Portugal and the United States, 1946–67
(in Percentages of Total Export Values)

Source: Adapted from Vasco Fortuna, "Estructuras Económicas de Angola,"
Angola (Lisbon, 1964), p. 499, and Banco de Angola, *Relatório e contas-exercício de
1966* (Lisbon, 1968).

Table 12

Balance of Payments (in Millions of Dollars) in Angola, 1964 and 1966

	1964			1966		
	Debit	Credit	Balance	Debit	Credit	Balance
Current transactions (total)	199.71	215.74	+16.03	234.44	258.02	+23.58
Trade	169.12	151.20	−17.92	167.40	188.37	+20.97
Current invisibles (total)	30.59	64.54	+33.95	67.04	69.65	+2.61
Tourism	0.17	8.72	+8.54	1.54	13.09	+11.55
Transport	9.35	1.99	−7.35	15.05	5.95	−9.10
Insurance	0.03	0.52	+0.49	0.22	0.87	+0.65
Return on investments	0.11	24.82	+24.71	2.03	14.07	+12.04
State	19.04	4.51	−14.53	24.85	1.54	−23.31
Other services and profits	1.68	8.96	+7.28	23.03	22.61	−0.42
Private transfers	0.21	15.02	+14.81	0.32	11.52	+11.20
Capital transactions	11.34	4.17	−7.17	3.95	10.64	+6.69
Total	211.05	219.91	−8.86	238.39	268.66	+30.27

Source: Banco de Angola, *Relatório e contas—exercício de 1964* (Lisbon, 1965), and *Ibid., Exercício de 1966* (Lisbon, 1967).

Table 13

Balance of Payments of Portugal with Angola (in Millions of Dollars), 1964–65

	1964			1965		
	Debit	Credit	Balance	Debit	Credit	Balance
Current transactions (total)	124.9	174.5	+49.5	137.7	160.6	+22.9
Merchandise	51.8	79.5	+27.7	51.4	82.2	+30.9
Current invisibles (total)	73.1	95.0	+21.9	86.3	78.4	−8.0
Travel	0.2	7.7	+7.5	0.2	8.4	+8.2
Investment income	0.5	17.9	+17.4	1.1	16.0	+14.9
Government	69.5	29.5	−40.0	82.3	19.8	−62.5
Transport and other services	1.5	9.8	+8.3	1.6	13.6	+12.0
Private transfers	1.4	30.1	+28.7	1.0	20.5	+19.4
Capital movements	20.4	—	−20.4	6.6	—	−6.6
Short term (net)	—	2.1	+2.1	—	1.9	+1.9
Long term (total)	25.3	2.8	−22.5	16.0	7.6	−8.4
Private sector	3.4	0.2	−3.2	5.9	4.0	−1.9
Official sector	21.9	2.6	−19.3	10.0	3.6	−6.4
Unbalanced transactions and errors	1.2	—	−1.1	—	0.2	+0.2
Total	146.5	174.5	+28.0	144.3	160.8	+16.5

Source: Banco de Portugal, as adapted by OECD, Economic Studies—Portugal (Paris, 1966), pp. 53–54.

245

Trade balances between Angola and Portugal have consistently favored the latter. In contrast, the trade with third countries has constantly shown a surplus of varying magnitude, compensating in most years for the adverse trade relationship with Portugal. Thus, between 1952 and 1966, Angola made a total positive contribution of $150.5 million to the trade of the escudo zone. Furthermore, Angolan trade has certainly exerted a substantial stimulation on metropolitan economic activity.

In regard to the provincial balance of payments, the situation in Angola is less favorable than in balance of trade particularly if invisibles are taken into consideration (Table 12). Positive "invisible" items appear in the 1964 and 1966 balance statements only in connection with transport and state transfers. The former may have its explanation in the transit earnings of the Benguela Railway, the latter in the metropolitan payments to support the provincial government and development programs.

Substantial negative items appear for tourism, investment income, and private transfers. The negative balance for tourism might be accounted for by the assignment to this category of the expenses of Portuguese nationals traveling between the province and the metropole. Private transfer deficits are unmistakably due to the remittance to Portugal of business profits and part of the earnings of white Angolans.

Data on the balance of payments between Portugal and Angola are available only for 1964 and 1965 (Table 13). They show the substantial balances in favor of the metropole for trade, private transfers of return on investments, and services. Balances are in favor of Angola, on the other hand, in respect to the current inflow of government and private funds.

Mozambique

The yearly trade values for Mozambique are only about three-fourths of the trade values of Angola (see Table 14). Trade balances ran consistently at a heavy deficit for the period 1952–64. An over-all expansion of provincial trade has occurred, though, at about the same rate as in Angola.

It is the trade with third countries rather than with metropolitan Portugal that is responsible for the consistently negative trade balances of Mozambique (see Table 15). Portugal receives a higher percentage of total Mozambican exports than of total Angolan exports, or between 40 and 47 per cent, mainly because of raw sugar and cotton shipped to metropolitan processing plants. Imports from Portugal are lower, and their proportion in total import flow is somewhat more constant than in Angola; during 1952–64, it was between 26 and 32 per cent. In 1965–66, it rose, however, to 35 per cent. The net contribution of Mozambique to escudo zone trade during the period under consideration was totally negative, to the amount of $595.5 million. The basic economic problem of the province has been obtaining sufficient foreign exchange sources from "invisible" sources to compensate for trade deficits.

The main commodities in Mozambique trade for 1966 are shown in Table 16. The leading export items have been all of agricultural origin, mining production thus far has failed to make any impact, and the trade and fisheries output is also

Table 14

External Trade of Mozambique (in Millions of Dollars), 1952–66

Year	Exports	Imports	Total Trade	Balance of Payments
1952	46.65	76.37	123.02	−29.71
1953	56.66	80.08	136.74	−23.41
1954	55.33	85.75	141.08	−30.41
1955	53.48	90.54	144.02	−37.06
1956	53.02	95.76	148.78	−42.73
1957	65.52	104.86	170.38	−39.34
1958	72.06	115.67	187.74	−44.66
1959	66.64	120.82	187.46	−54.18
1960	73.46	127.61	201.07	−54.14
1961	89.18	130.20	219.38	−41.02
1962	91.56	136.78	228.34	−45.22
1963	101.36	142.66	244.02	−41.30
1964	106.50	157.15	263.65	−50.64
1965	108.74	179.33	283.08	−65.59
1966	112.56	208.98	321.54	−96.42
1967	132.54	200.45	332.99	−67.91

Source: For 1952–62, Mozambique, Serviços de Estatística Geral, Comércio externo (Lourenço Marques, 1963). For 1963–66, Mozambique, Serviços de Estatística Geral, Boletim Mensal (Lourenço Marques, 1967). For 1967, The Economist Intelligence Unit, "Portugal and Overseas Provinces," Quarterly Economic Reviews, No. 1, 1969, p. 14.

much lower than in Angola. If recent information about mineral discoveries in the province is correct, minerals may become a substantial proportion of Mozambican exports during the next decade. The import list is similar to Angola's, except for a substantial inflow of crude oil destined for the new refinery in Lourenço Marques.

Outside of Portugal, Mozambique's principal trade partners are South Africa, India (which has been until recently processing and re-exporting the largest share of the province's cashew-nut crop) the United Kingdom, West Germany, and Rhodesia. The United States takes only about 6 per cent of Mozambique's exports and supplies about 7 per cent of its imports.

The balances of payments for Mozambique for 1964 and 1966 are very favorably influenced by the great contribution in the "invisible" sector of income from transit trade handled by Mozambique transport facilities on behalf of South Africa, Rhodesia, and Malawi and, to a lesser degree, on behalf of Zambia and Swaziland. It is not known whether the heading "private transfers" includes the remittances of African migratory workers employed in the South African and Rhodesian mines or whether the African remittances are accounted for under "miscellaneous," which would explain the negative balance under "private transfers" despite the fact that these remittances rise to substantial sums. The flow of capital for Mozambique appears to be negative unless incoming investment bypasses official channels, which is extremely likely because of the

Table 15

Mozambique Trade with Metropolitan Portugal and Its Contribution to Escudo Zone Balance of Trade (in Millions of Dollars), 1952–66

Year	Exports to Portugal		Imports from Portugal		Balance of Trade with Portugal	Balance of Trade with Third Countries	Net Contribution to Escudo Zone
	Value	Per Cent of Total	Value	Per Cent of Total			
1952	21.3	47	22.8	30	−1.5	−28.2	−29.7
1953	25.8	46	23.6	30	+2.2	−25.6	−23.4
1954	22.9	41	22.6	26	+0.3	−30.6	−30.3
1955	23.3	44	25.6	28	−2.3	−34.8	−37.1
1956	21.3	40	28.6	30	−7.3	−35.2	−42.5
1957	29.3	45	32.3	31	−3.0	−36.3	−39.3
1958	31.8	45	32.6	28	−0.8	−43.8	−44.6
1959	31.5	42	32.3	27	−0.8	−53.4	−54.2
1960	35.2	43	36.4	29	−1.2	−52.9	−54.1
1961	36.7	41	38.7	30	−2.0	−39.0	−41.0
1962	36.3	40	39.7	29	−3.4	−38.0	−41.4
1963	36.1	36	44.7	31	−8.6	−32.7	−41.3
1964	34.5	32	50.0	32	−15.5	−35.2	−50.7
1965	40.2	37	60.4	35	−20.2	−45.6	−65.8

Sources: For 1952–64, Mozambique, Serviços de Estatística Geral, *Comércio externo* (Lourenço Marques, 1965). For 1965, Banco Nacional Ultramarino, *Boletim Trimestral*, No. 73 (Lisbon, 1968).

proximity of South Africa and the intimate relations of many of Mozambique's businessmen in Lourenço Marques with Johannesburg business firms.

The balance of payments statement between Mozambique and metropolitan Portugal (Table 18) shows some special features in their financial relationships. According to it, Lisbon would receive more regular government income from the province than it gives to it in subsidies. However, this is more than offset by the metropolitan contributions to local development, especially in 1964.

Table 16

Main Commodities in Mozambique Trade (in Millions of Dollars), 1966

	Value	Per Cent of Total
Exports		
Cashew nuts (shelled and unshelled)	21.1	19.4
Cotton fiber	19.4	17.9
Sugar and molasses	10.2	9.4
Petroleum products	8.5	7.8
Vegetable-oil products	8.2	7.5
Tea	7.2	6.6
Timber	6.8	6.3
Sisal	6.1	5.6
Copra	5.9	5.4
Other	15.3	14.1
Total	108.7	100.0
Imports		
Textiles and clothing	25.2	14.4
Motor vehicles and parts	20.1	11.5
Iron and steel	12.9	7.4
Wines and alcoholic beverages	9.4	5.4
Petroleum	8.5	4.9
Corn and wheat	5.6	3.2
Medicine	3.5	2.0
Other	89.2	51.2
Total	174.4	100.0

Source: Banco Totta Aliança, *Portugal—Some Facts About Its Economy* (Lisbon, 1968), pp. 76–77.

Table 17

Balance of Payments (in Millions of Dollars) in Mozambique, 1964 and 1966

	1964			1966		
	Debit	Credit	Balance	Debit	Credit	Balance
Current transactions (total)	173.04	169.19	−3.88	226.80	213.85	−12.95
Trade	121.52	90.40	−31.08	166.91	104.72	−62.19
Invisibles (total)	51.57	78.75	+27.23	59.88	109.16	+49.24
Tourism	8.64	8.05	−0.59	7.45	10.08	+2.62
Transport	3.64	39.06	+35.42	4.16	61.11	+56.94
Return on capital	13.47	0.49	−13.02	14.21	0.84	−13.37
Private transfers	11.62	6.72	−4.90	13.16	11.55	−1.61
Miscellaneous	14.17	24.46	+10.29	20.79	25.51	+4.69
Capital transactions (total)	11.79	7.91	−3.88	11.51	10.50	−1.01
Short-term	2.17	0.80	−1.36	2.90	0.45	−2.45
Long-term	9.62	7.14	−2.48	8.52	10.01	+1.47
Total	184.83	177.10	−7.73	238.31	224.35	−13.96

Source: Mozambique, Serviços de Estatística Geral, Boletim Mensal (Lourenço Marques), monthly.

Table 18

Balance of Payments of Portugal with Mozambique (in Millions of Dollars), 1964–65

	1964			1965		
	Debit	Credit	Balance	Debit	Credit	Balance
Current transactions (total)	57.95	117.09	+59.14	48.26	130.05	+81.79
Trade	37.98	48.77	+10.79	35.66	64.05	+28.39
Invisibles (total)	19.97	68.32	+48.35	12.60	66.00	+53.40
Travel	0.03	4.66	+4.63	0.12	6.56	+6.35
Investment income	4.70	10.29	+5.59	0.31	12.20	+11.97
Government	13.56	20.36	+6.80	10.21	20.02	+9.81
Transport and other services	0.49	8.30	+7.81	0.52	9.09	+8.54
Private transfers	1.19	24.71	+23.52	1.32	18.05	+16.78
Capital transactions (total)	22.05	—	−22.05	—	2.91	+2.91
Short-term (net)	—	2.75	+2.75	—	0.95	+0.95
Long-term (total)	28.39	4.05	−24.33	20.58	22.54	+1.96
Private sector	0.91	2.97	+2.06	2.68	5.66	+2.98
Official sector	27.48	1.08	−26.40	17.90	16.88	−1.02
Unbalanced transactions and errors	—	0.24	+0.24	0.49	—	−0.49
Total	80.00	2,117.33	+37.33	48.75	132.96	+84.21

Source: Banco de Portugal, as adapted by OECD, *Economic Studies—Portugal* (December, 1966), pp. 53–54.

NOTES

1. *Labor Digests on Countries in Africa*, Nos. 93 and 121 (Washington, D.C., 1966), pp. 2–3.
2. George H. T. Kimble, *Tropical Africa: Land and Livelihood*, I (Garden City, 1963), 326.
3. *Portugal*, Economic Surveys, OECD, Paris (December, 1966), p. 11.
4. From data in Leonard Rist, "Capital and Capital Supply in Relation to the Development of Africa," in E. A. G. Robinson (ed.), *Economic Development for Africa South of the Sahara* (New York, 1964), pp. 446 and 457.
5. Banque de Paris et des Pays Bas; Dillon Read & Co., Inc.; Banca Commerciale Italiana, *Republic of Portugal $15,000,000 c/o External Loan Bonds due 1977*, Prospectus (September 8, 1967), pp. 11–13.
6. See L. M. Teixeira Pinto and R. Martins dos Santos, "Problems of Economic Development of Angola: Poles and Prospects" in Robinson, *op. cit.*, pp. 198–221, and Vasco Fortuna, "Estruturas económicas de Moçambique," in *Moçambique* (Lisbon, 1965), pp. 204–7.
7. To facilitate development financing, the banking system in the territories was revised in 1965 (Decrees 46,243 and 46,492). This has enabled existing banks in Angola and Mozambique to establish new branches, and a number of other banks have been authorized to establish offices in these two territories.
8. In Portugal, although the statutory interest rate is set at 5 per cent per annum, most of the government's borrowing has been at lower rates. Pending the revision of measures, the government in January, 1967, authorized a new series of 5 per cent treasury bonds totalling $35 million. *Diário de Notícias* (Lisbon), January 27, 1967. The government hopes that the higher interest rate will attract savings and will reduce the exodus of capital. The proceeds from the bonds are to be used exclusively for investments in plans approved by the Council of Ministers for Economic Affairs.
9. *Bank of London and South America Review* (February, 1968), p. 127.
10. The exact amount spent for military expenses in the African provinces is difficult to estimate since the Portuguese budget scatters these expenditures among different ministerial budgets. Announcements made by the Portuguese Government indicate such expenditures run to two-thirds of the extraordinary government expenditures of $157.5 million. (See *Diário de Notícias*, December 29, 1966.)
11. See Banco de Angola, *Investment of Foreign Capital in Portuguese Territories* (Lisbon, 1965).
12. See Chap. XIII.
13. Richard J. Hammond, *Portugal's African Problem: Some Economic Facets* (New York, 1962), p. 10.

XII

Agriculture and Other Primary Production

IRENE S. van DONGEN

PORTUGUESE AFRICA, like most of Africa south of the Sahara, is still basically an agrarian and rural society, notwithstanding recent industrialization and urbanization trends in Angola and Mozambique. The usual problems of rural societies are encountered, and there are further challenges owing to the tropical environment. Because tropical life seems so abundant, and plant growth so rapid compared with temperate climates, misconceptions have long existed among Western peoples as to the inexhaustible fertility of tropical lands. Only recently has this illusion been partly dispelled by the progress of scientific research and a longer acquaintance with the tropics.

BACKGROUND FOR AFRICAN AGRICULTURE

Except for a few favored areas, the soils of tropical Africa range from relatively poor to poor soils leached of needed organic and mineral nutrients, and many are difficult to work as well as maintain in good condition. As long as there is a dense forest cover continuing to contribute to the humus reserves through the addition of dead leaves, branches, and other litter, a measure of natural balance between elements supplied and extracted is maintained. Dense vegetation also protects the soil from erosion by tropical downpours and from the wide seasonal ranges in temperature and humidity noticeable in the grassland zones. Once the tree cover is stripped off, the fertility and structure of tropical soils deteriorate rapidly.

Water supply for crops often may be in excess or fall short of the amounts required. Both the quantity and the periods of recurrence of the annual rainfall are conspicuously unreliable through many parts of Africa. The practice of setting fire to dried bush toward the end of the dry season in the savanna zone inflicts considerable damage to certain plant species. Pests and diseases of animal and plant life proliferate to an extent seldom found in the middle latitudes.

In only a few regions of Africa can the inhabitants be considered effective farmers when measured by modern standards. Traditional habits of land tenure, the implements or techniques in use, the assignment to women of most agricultural tasks, or the social prestige attached to the mere possession of large herds whatever their state of health, all inhibit proper soil-utilization and livestock-raising. Productivity is further impaired by widespread tropical diseases that sap bodily vigor and by the reluctance of many Africans to work for sustained periods.

The European colonizer injected novel elements into African societies long-established in shifting subsistence agriculture, seminomadic herding, and barter exchange, among them being agricultural organization geared to world economy, application of capital and mechanical devices, and an insistence on persevering labor. Frequently, however, the European brought methods of cultivation more suited to his former environment than to tropical lands, and had to pay the price of learning. His striving for quick gains and his impatience with manpower difficulties have, in general, not endeared him to local populations. He has insistently demanded considerable financial outlays from the colonial administrations, to provide an infrastructure capable of supporting a rational and profitable development of agricultural resources. But, as a result of European arrival and pressure, many former subsistence farmers have become producers of cash crops. Such also has been the case in Portuguese African territories.

AGRICULTURE IN ANGOLA

The primary production sector of the Angolan economy (crops, livestock, forestry, and fisheries) regularly contributed from 20 to 25 per cent of the gross national product in the 1960's, compared with 4.7 per cent contributed by the secondary sector and 69 to 72 per cent by the tertiary sector.[1] In spite of agriculture's large share in the economy, for various reasons, only about 2 per cent of Angola's arable land is under active exploitation.

Agricultural activities in Angola display a wide scale of entrepreneurship, ranging from large and modern European corporate plantations to traditional tribal subsistence plots. Between these two extremes lie less important European or *mestiço* plantations and farms, individually or family-owned; fairly well established African farms, concentrating on valuable cash crops like coffee or on market-gardening; government-sponsored agricultural development schemes (*colonatos*) for Europeans and Africans; small European quasi-subsistence farms; and the average African holdings, producing subsistence staples plus a small volume of a cash crop recommended by the local administration. Similarly, livestock-raising activities range from a few European-owned ranches to traditional African herding; they also include several European dairy farms and attempts at mixed crop–livestock farming by Europeans and Africans.

Government supervision of primary production in Angola was originally vested in the Department of Agriculture (Serviços de Agricultura) and Department of Veterinary Services and Livestock Production (Serviços de Veterinária e Produtos Animais). In the last few decades, more government agencies have arisen to provide technological advice to Europeans and Africans alike, and other organizations have assisted with marketing or production improvement of specific crops. Detailed soil surveys have been carried out since 1954 and have already covered an area larger than metropolitan Portugal. An important element in the governmental control of the production and sale of African agricultural products is the system of country markets (*mercados rurais*) originally established in the 1930's and additionally defined through several decrees in 1963–64.

Research on the crops and livestock is being undertaken at the Instituto de

Investigação Agronómica de Angola and the new Instituto de Investigação Veterinária in Nova Lisboa. It is still too early to see the outcome of the creation in 1965 of the Concelho de Coordenação Agrícola, which is supposed to coordinate all production, and of the recent establishment of the long-awaited Credit Bank (Caixa de Crédito Agro-Pecuário). Furthermore, the results of an agricultural census in Angola, taken early in the 1960's by the Missão de Inquéritos Agrícolas, have not been published, except for a small-scale, preliminary endeavor at regionalization.[2]

There is no doubt, however, that the Portuguese authorities firmly intend to consolidate and augment Angola's agricultural potential. Since the beginning of the Portuguese National Development Program inaugurated in 1953 with the *Plano de Fomento I* (1953–58), followed by *Plano de Fomento II* (1959–64) and *Plano Intercalar de Fomento* (1965–67), $157.5 million was allocated for the general improvement of the primary sector and the specific development of agricultural settlement projects. Some of the allocations have not been entirely used, but heavy government investment in upgrading agriculture is continuing under the present *Plano de Fomento III* (1968–73).

Crops grown in Angola fall into three main categories: crops of major export significance, crops of some significance either on the export list or for internal consumption, and crops of minor importance.

Crops of Major Export Significance

The seven leading export crops of Angola for the last decade, by order of their export value for 1967, were coffee, sisal, maize (corn), cotton, cane sugar, oil palm products, and manioc. By order of volume exported, coffee again came first, followed by maize, manioc, sisal, cane sugar, oil palm products, and cotton.[3] Most of the coffee and sisal are exported, but a substantial share of the production in other major crops is consumed locally.

Coffee. Coffee is one of the most important commodities in world trade, after crude petroleum or grains. In the last two decades, tropical Africa has greatly expanded its cultivation of coffee, to compete with the long-standing sources of supply in Central and South America. The largest African producer, the Ivory Coast, accounted for 8.1 per cent of the world's coffee output in 1967, and Angola, the next largest African producer, followed with 6.1 per cent.[4] Angola's coffee has been consistently bought by the United States, the world's largest coffee-consumer, which frequently receives over one-half of the Angolan harvests. Another important buyer is the Netherlands. Portugal is only third on the list.

Since 1965, annual coffee production has exceeded 200,000 metric tons. Coffee exports in 1965 represented nearly 47 per cent of all export values of the province; in 1967, 195,500 tons were exported, valued at $120.6 million, and coffee rose to 53 per cent of the total exports.

Coffee is the chief crop of the northwestern quarter of Angola, as maize is of Angola's central belt. Some 98 per cent of Angolan coffee belongs to the species *Coffea robusta*,[5] used primarily for making "instant" coffee. It is grown essentially under the shade of partly cleared moist forest in the subplateau zone, within two broad regions located north and south of the Cuanza River. A small quantity

255

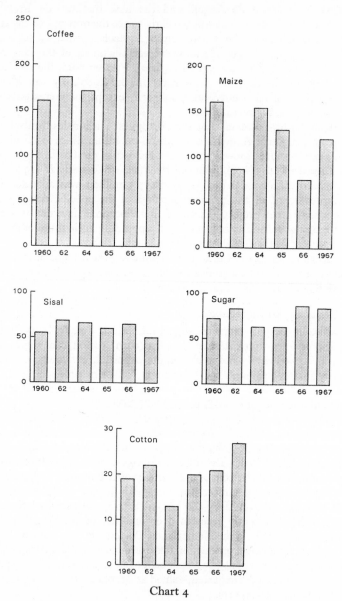

Chart 4

Some Major Export Crops in Angola, 1960–67. (Commercial Production, in Thousands of Tons)

Source: Adapted from Banco de Angola, Department of Economic Studies, *Economic Survey and Financial Survey of Angola, 1965* (Lisbon, 1966), pp. 16 and 34, and *ibid.*, 1967 (Lisbon, 1968).

is also grown in the Cabinda Enclave. The different varieties of Angolan *robusta* are quoted on the world market, according to their area of origin, as Ambriz, Amboím, Cazengo, and Cabinda. The first two are the most highly prized. The small production of *arabica* is chiefly from the central plateau, inland from the cities of Lobito and Benguela.

Since 1950, the region north of the Cuanza River, embracing the Cuanza Norte, Uíge, and Zaire districts, has been the most important coffee-producer. Prior to the uprising of 1961, one-third of the regional harvest came from African farms while most of the remainder came from medium- and small-size European *fazendas* and *roças*. Profits from coffee-growing have stimulated the growth of Carmona, the northern coffee capital. Transactions in coffee have enriched the city of Luanda, whose port handles the lion's share of northern coffee exports. Small coastal settlements like Ambriz and Ambrizete have also benefitted from coffee traffic. The insurrection of March, 1961, which took, in one night, the lives of about 1,000 northern coffee-growers and threatened to set aflame all the north of Angola, caused only moderate damage to coffee plantations. Equipment was destroyed but coffee plants were left untouched, since some of the African rebels hoped to secure the abandoned European coffee-holdings for themselves. After the military operations, some Portuguese soldiers remained in the area as coffee-farmers. This, and the coming into full bearing of sizable acreages put under cultivation just a few years before, resulted in increasing coffee production during the 1960's.

The coffee region south of the Cuanza River, in the *concelhos* of Amboím and Seles of the Cuanza Sul District, is smaller in area and output. Local production is dominated by three or four companies, the largest being Companhia Angolana de Agricultura (CADA). CADA is a model corporate agricultural enterprise in Africa, with an African staff of over 10,000, for whom it provides above-average educational and welfare facilities; yearly coffee production is in excess of 10,000 tons. Its great Fazenda Boa Entrada and many other coffee farms lie in the vicinity of the town of Gabela. However, several factors, including a deficiency of transportation facilities, have prevented Gabela from becoming as prominent as Carmona in the north.

The present total coffee acreage is about 550,000. Some 200,000 people (growers and traders) in Angola make a living from coffee. Technical advice in cultivation and coffee-marketing has been extended to growers since the early 1940's by an autonomous government organization, formerly known as the Coffee Export Board (Junta de Exportação de Café), and, since 1961, as Instituto do Café. Its offices are in Luanda and Lisbon, and it has experimental stations for *robusta* near Carmona and Gabela and in the Dembos area and for *arabica* at Ganda. It operates hulling plants in several locations, insures marketing facilities, and has contributed to the success of African coffee-farmers. Curiously, many coffee-growers in Angola combine petty trade with coffee-farming because of the average would-be-grower's original lack of capital.

Though seemingly prosperous, Angolan coffee-growing has been beset with numerous problems, such as continual labor shortages, lack of development funds, several periods of depressed prices on the world markets, and, lately, the specter of overproduction. Joining with other countries in an effort to control world surpluses, Portugal took part in several meetings of the International Coffee Organization and signed the International Coffee Agreement in 1962, which allocates a yearly coffee-export quota for each producing country, sometimes allowing a special increment. When Angola's 1965–66 harvest overshot its quota of 2,214,127 60-kilogram bags by some 297,500 bags, the government restricted new coffee-plantings and allowed only the replacement of aged and nonbearing trees.

Sisal. In Africa, Angola ranks a poor second to Tanzania in sisal production. Its sisal-growing developed later than in Mozambique, but now it produces over twice as much. Remarkable progress was made in the past decade through mechanization, and now sisal is grown on 280,000 acres. The Banco de Angola estimates that 201 estates produced sisal in 1964, with a total capital investment of about $34 million and employment of 25,000 persons.[6]

The 1967 sisal exports, over 47,000 tons worth $6.6 million, were much lower than in the preceding years.[7] As a rule, sisal may represent from 5 to 12 per cent of total Angolan exports. Profits were twice affected during the last decade by sudden price declines on the world markets. Nevertheless, sisal is still considered a promising crop among European farmers. As elsewhere in Africa, the large amounts of capital required to purchase the machinery to process the fleshy leaf hinders increasing participation in the sisal industry by Africans.

The chief sisal-growing area has traditionally been the western part of the Benguela subplateau and plateau, where the *concelhos* of Cubal, Ganda, and Bocoio account for 60 per cent of total production. All arable land around Cubal is under sisal. The Provincial Sisal Experimental Station is located at Ganda. Other areas of importance are the Cuanza Norte and Malange districts. The central plateau producers have recently formed a cooperative in Benguela to coordinate sales and have put up a factory to manufacture cord and other sisal products. Internal demand has so far accounted for about 12 per cent of the total output.

Maize (Corn). Angola has long been a steady exporter of maize of fair quality to Western European markets. Maize-growing, and the associated trade in maize, helped to attract European settlement on the central plateau, beginning early in the 1920's.

At present, the maize belt of Angola has expanded from the former corridor along the Benguela Railway north to Malange, but Vila Roberto Williams in the *concelho* of Caála still remains a leading maize handling center. A second important region is around Sá da Bandeira. Some maize is raised all over Angola, except in drier areas, where manioc, sorghums, or millets are grown in its stead. As much as 95 per cent of the total production comes from African plots, though some Europeans have attempted mechanized maize-cultivation, and maize is a major crop at the *colonato* of Cela. The Ovimbundu show special skill for growing maize, which they often rotate with beans. Maize is, unfortunately, a soil-depleting crop, and where it is grown the already poor local soils are further impoverished. In the absence of fertilizers and regular manuring, yields are quite low, even by African standards. On the other hand, maize can withstand occasional dry spells, suits African farming habits, and is both a staple food and a cash crop. Further incentive for growing maize was provided through the circumstance that, for a long time, many Angolan laborers received part of their wages in provisions, including a substantial family ration in maize as grain or meal (*fuba*).[8]

Maize production not entering the channels of trade is estimated to vary between 150,000 and 200,000 tons per year. Harvests fluctuate greatly because of weather inconsistencies. In 1967, 100,000 tons of grain, valued at $5.9 million, were exported together with 11,500 tons of maize flour and meal, worth $612,000.[9]

Maize trade has been organized under the Maize Marketing Board (Grémio do Milho) and the Junta de Exportação de Cereais, recently renamed Instituto dos Cereais. The Maize Marketing Board buys the grain at fixed prices from European middlemen along the Benguela Railway and ships the bulk maize to mechanical-loading installations at Lobito, the port for nine-tenths of all Angolan maize exports. Maize traffic sometimes constitutes up to 20 per cent of all national freight traffic on the central rail trunk. The Instituto dos Cereais maintains cleaning, grading, and storage facilities at many points on the Railway. Its work is more appreciated than that of the Grémio, which has often been criticized because it adds to the number of intermediaries between the African farmer and the consumer.

Since late in the 1950's, an additional hardship to Angolan maize-producers has been an unfavorable competitive position in the world market. Also, Portugal, formerly a large importer, is beginning not only to be self-sufficient in maize but even to have exportable surpluses. This condition stems partly from a change in taste for bread in metropolitan Portugal, where the dark-colored maize-flour bread of rural areas has become less popular than the wheat loaf.

Sugar. Over $17 million is invested and 16,000 persons are employed in the growing and milling of sugar cane, one of the oldest industries in Angola. The industry is controlled by three Lisbon-based companies: Companhia de Açúcar de Angola, with a main plantation and mill at Fazenda Tentativa, 90 miles northeast of Luanda and a secondary area inland from the small port of Cuio south of Benguela; Sociedade Agrícola do Cassequel, with extensive cane fields and a modern factory near Catumbela, between Lobito and Benguela; and Sociedade de Comércio e Construções, with a smaller acreage and a mill near Bom Jesús on the lower Cuanza. Plans were abandoned for a fourth operation, Companhia Açucareira de Cuanza, originally scheduled to begin production in 1965 with a capital of $6.8 million and planned output of 75,000 tons. All the plantations are located on the alluvial soils of river valleys in the coastal lowland.

Angola's producers have protested against the introduction of sugar-beet cultivation into metropolitan Portugal. Yet, Portugal has greatly expanded sugar consumption in recent years, and the overseas provinces are seldom able to fill the sugar quota allocated to them by the metropole for the home supply. Portugal now consumes 175,000 to 200,000 tons of sugar a year and is very anxious to avoid currency losses to foreigners. But sugar in Angola must compete with coffee in securing labor. Expansion of output has also been handicapped by the level of fixed prices in metropolitan and overseas Portugal and by the large capital investment needed for the irrigation of cane fields in the rain-deficient coastal strip. This helps to explain the slow increase in land use for sugar cane, to about 22,500 acres in the mid-1960's.[10]

Of the 1967 sugar production, 67,000 tons, or 60 per cent, was used in Angola, and the rest was exported to Portugal and other Portuguese provinces in western Africa. The exported tonnage valued at $3 million equaled only 1.3 per cent of the total Angolan exports,[11] though prior to World War II sugar represented about 15 per cent of exports, the decline being explained by the relatively greater increase in the amount and value of other export products. Some two-thirds of production is in raw white sugar, and most of the rest is raw brown. Refining is customarily done in Portugal. Molasses is also exported, as well as converted locally into industrial alcohol.

Government decrees of 1964–65, allowing a long-needed adjustment in prices, may prove an incentive to increase future acreage under cane.

Cotton. Portugal's desire to have its overseas possessions produce more cotton in order to supply the textile industry at home has been the motivating force behind increased cotton-growing in Angola and Mozambique. Cotton production was long regulated by the Cotton Export Board (Junta de Exportação de Algodão) which, though represented in Angola, was seated in Mozambique. The Board operated on the lines of the former Cocoa Marketing Board in Ghana, collecting a small sum on every kilo sold for the Cotton Farmers' Welfare Fund (Fundo do Algodão). It was assisted by a research center, the Centro de Investigação Científica Algodoeira. Cotton cultivation by small African farmers was further supervised by European concessionaries, who were given a buying monopoly at fixed prices in delimited zones. They ginned raw cotton and distributed selected seeds to Africans for the next planting. Severely criticized, the cotton concessionary regime was abolished in 1961 in favor of free cultivation and sales. The Instituto do Algodão, successor to the Board, was to reorganize the industry and promote the creation of African cotton-growers' cooperatives.

Yet, no spectacular changes occurred in the cotton production through the 1960's. Although yields rose, the total area under cotton was reduced from over 125,000 acres in 1959 to 90,000 acres in 1963.[12] The main varieties grown are the "Triumph Big Ball" and "0–52," both medium-length fibers. The chief cotton-growing region is still in the eastern sector of the Malange District, on the northern plateau and the adjoining depression of Cassange. That area contains over fifty cotton-marketing centers and a dozen gins, and it accounts for about two-thirds of the entire crop. Other areas of significance are in the Cuanza Sul District and around Catete, near Luanda.

Annual harvests had averaged around 20,000 tons of seed-cotton until 1967, when 27,000 tons were produced.[13] Exports of fiber have stagnated at between 4,500 and 6,000 tons. Some 6,000 tons were exported in 1967, with a value of $3.3 million. Some cotton is retained in Angola to be transformed by the Sociedade Algodoeira do Fomento Colonial ("Textang") in Luanda into cotton thread, yard goods, knitwear, and pharmaceutical cotton. Another textile mill is under construction at Dondo, close to the Cambambe hydropower plant, and, in 1967, a major ginning and pressing mill was opened at Novo Redondo. Since 1958, cottonseed oil has been produced near Luanda and at Malange, the seedcake being sold as cattle feed to local European farmers.

Oil Palm. The Angolan output of oil palm (*Elaeis guineensis*) products cannot compare with that of the large African producers, Nigeria and the Congo (Kinshasa). Except in the Cabinda Enclave and some parts of the north, the natural environment is not propitious for *Elaeis* palm cultivation because of the long dry season and relatively low yearly rainfall. Wild palm groves exploited by Africans in the Enclave and in the northern sector bear fruit that is low in oil; the tallness of the trees and their scattered location in the forest make collection of the fruit difficult. The African share of the oil palm harvest probably accounts for about 30 per cent of the total. Planted groves are found principally in the domains of the CADA, the largest palm-oil producer of Angola, and of the Companhia de Açúcar de Angola. The latter company's production at Dombe Grande in the Benguela District is really outside the ecological zone of the *Elaeis* palm. These large plantations are all near the coast. Throughout the coffee areas of the northern interior, many semiwild groves could be improved and utilized by European farmers, but this resource is untapped.

Palm oil, extracted from the softer part of the *Elaeis* fruit, is both exported and used locally as a source of fats in the African diet and in the manufacture of soap. The hard kernels, which require special treatment, have only recently been crushed in Angola; normally, they have been shipped out whole.[14] Exports of oil palm products in 1967 were 15,500 tons of oil, 6,900 tons of kernels, and 1,500 tons of kernel oil, valued at $5.2 million.

Manioc. Manioc (cassava) is Angola's biggest crop in volume. It is a basic African food staple like maize, sorghums, and millets. The root dominates subsistence agriculture throughout the north and much of the east; in the central belt it is a significant supplementary crop. No government agency is involved in its commercialization, and, therefore, information on manioc is extremely scanty, except for the export records that relate to manioc in its cut-and-dried form (*crueira*) or in flour and starches.[15] Total yearly production is believed to vary between 1.0 to 1.4 million tons, practically all grown by Africans. Manioc has a better resistance to long dry seasons, strong winds, and pests than maize, and it yields well, even in quite poor soils. One acre planted with manioc can produce up to 50 tons of fresh root and 12 tons of dried manioc. It does not grow well, however, at the higher, cooler elevations.

Manioc for export now comes chiefly from Moxico District and is shipped through Lobito; production in the Malange area is shared between consumers in the city of Luanda and overseas markets through the Luanda port. In the 1960's, exports of manioc products ranged from 45,000 to 112,000 tons per year, over nine-tenths of this as *crueira*. The leading buyers are Portugal and France, where the product is used in manufacturing tapioca and starches.

Crops of Some Significance for Export and Internal Consumption

Crops in this category are tobacco; beans; such grains as wheat, rice, sorghums (locally *massambala* and *massango*) and millets (*mexoeira*); oil seeds other than *Elaeis* palm fruit; and, lately, various tropical fruits such as bananas.[16]

Tobacco. Commercial tobacco cultivation, long concentrated in the Malange region to supply the processing factories in Luanda, has shown new vigor in the Huíla, Benguela, and Moçâmedes districts, which now raise three-fifths of Angola's tobacco crop. Three cooperatives were formed there in 1965, one in Benguela, one in Quilengues in Huíla, and one at the *colonato* at Matala also in Huíla. In the Malange area, dark tobaccos, raised by African farmers, dominate; in the central and southern regions, European growers, who are in the majority, raise the Virginia type of tobacco. The total tobacco acreage of Angola is now 25,000. In 1967, exports were 2,600 tons, and a further 1,800 tons was used in the provincial tobacco industry. Production of finer grade tobaccos in overseas territories has begun to be looked upon with favor by metropolitan manufacturers; previously, their buying in Portuguese Africa equalled only about a fourth of total home requirements, despite frequent Angolan complaints.

Beans. Previously grown for subsistence by both Europeans and Africans, beans from Angola were in extraordinary demand during World War II in Allied countries, and, in the immediate postwar period, they still represented about 10 per cent of annual exports. Subsequently, production fell drastically, as farmers turned to more profitable crops and the government withdrew technical assistance to bean-growers. Yearly exports in the 1960's have averaged 10,000–15,000 tons.

Traditional bean-growing areas are the Benguela–Bié plateau and, to a lesser extent, Malange District. A great variety of beans from red to white are grown. Most of the bean cultivation is now done by Africans.

Wheat. In many African territories, where cooler uplands beckoned to Europeans, white farmers attempted in the past to raise wheat, the staple of Western civilization, only to be frustrated by rust, mildew, and repeated harvest failures. Portugal also looked toward the plateaus of Angola to supply its necessary wheat. Notwithstanding all efforts and much ink expended in newspaper exhortations, results have always fallen short of goals. Gradually, three-fourths of wheat acreage passed into African hands. Yields are low and the grain is of inferior quality, owing to poor soils and fungoid diseases. Despite yearly harvests of 20,000–35,000 tons, not only are exports nil, but Angola has to import each year about three-fourths of its wheat requirements (slightly above 50,000 tons), either as flour or in grain that is ground in several modern mills originally erected to process Angola-grown wheat.[17] The two largest mills are located near Luanda and Silva Porto. To continue sustaining the growing of wheat on the central plateau, government regulations require the bakeries of Lobito and Benguela to incorporate some of the home product into their daily batches of dough, thus lowering the quality of bread distributed through these two cities.

Rice. Rice is raised by Africans on dry land in the northern, central, and eastern sectors of the province. Irrigation would be expensive, and there is no tradition for it. Yearly production probably reaches 20,000 tons, of which 2,000–3,000 tons are exported. The largest amount comes from Malange District, the Sanza Pombo area, and from Moxico and Bié districts, where the production is supervised by a Grémio dos Descascadores do Arroz. The best quality is from Luanda District. A number of rudimentary decorticating mills are scattered through the producing areas. Varied government decrees through 1964–65, aimed specifically at the improvement of Angolan rice production, have not changed the situation appreciably.

Millets and Sorghums. These African cereals are entirely subsistence crops, raised for food and for making village beer. They are grown throughout the dry southern belt of Angola, sometimes alone, sometimes in association with maize or manioc as secondary crops. Both are noted for drought resistance, and, since their growing season is only 3 to 4 months long, they can germinate and bear fruit during the short rainy period in the south. Furthermore, they tolerate quite poor soils. No estimates of the quantity produced are available, though occasionally 1,000 to 2,000 tons of these grains may be exported.

Oil Seeds. Angola is one of the smaller African exporters of peanuts (locally *ginguba*); practically all the crop is grown by African farmers in the Damba and São Salvador areas of the north and in the Moxico and Bié districts where peanut oil substitutes for palm oil. Production is generally placed at 30,000–40,000 tons, of which 2,000 to 5,000 tons are exported. Some sesame seed is also raised, of which 1,000 to 2,000 tons are exported.

In many African countries, the castor plant is found in a wild state or is cultivated on a small scale. Originally, castor beans were exported as such from Angola but, soon after World War II, a Portuguese company became interested in producing castor oil for industrial use, notably as a lubricant for jet planes, and exporting it to Portugal and the United States. An extracting plant of 22,000-ton capacity was set up at Catumbela, near Lobito, and the company obtained a buying monopoly of the castor-bean production of the central plateau. Notwithstanding other protectionist measures, results have been extremely discouraging, possibly because of the low level of fixed prices for the bean. Normally, the extracting plant was able to obtain but one-fourth of the raw material needed to operate at full capacity. Castor-bean production of some 7,000 tons in the early 1950's dwindled to below 1,000 tons after 1961. After the original monopoly was ended in the mid-1960's, exports again showed a rise, to 3,000 tons of beans for 1966.

Vegetable-oil extraction, with production of feedcake for livestock and, frequently, soap- and paint-manufacturing on the side, is an expanding industry in Angola, the main plants being located in Luanda and Malange. Production of various oils currently approximates 10,000 tons.

Fruit. Both tropical and temperate varieties of fruit are grown in Angola because of the range in altitude. Temperate fruit from the plateau has seldom been of sufficient standards to be exported; it does not compare favorably with similar fruit raised in South Africa and Rhodesia. Tropical fruit such as papayas, bananas, pineapples, and guavas are of fine quality and plentiful for internal consumption. On the other hand, the looks and taste of local citrus fruit (oranges, grapefruit, limes, lemons) generally leave much to be desired. A mission near São Salvador and a German-owned plantation near Luso seem to be the only two sources of superior oranges and lemons in the province, the latter exporting some citrus fruit.

A new development is the increase of banana shipments to Portugal, which consumes at present 32,000–35,000 tons of bananas per year. A South African fruit-handling firm projects an investment of $850,000 in refrigerated storage in Lisbon, Luanda, and Lobito, so as to handle 40,000 tons of bananas yearly from Angola. Exports for the last 4 or 5 years have increased steadily, to 6,600 tons in 1967. Much of the land to be put under bananas in the near future is in the lower valley of the Catumbela, only some 20 miles from the port of Lobito. The Angolan administration has tried its best to secure refrigerated space for banana transport aboard ships calling on the seaboard but has been unsuccessful, and the banana-growers are thinking of acquiring their own ships for fast sea-transport, as stocks of fruit frequently spoil. In 1967, the administration also formed a committee, the Grupo de Trabalho para o Fomento Fruteiro do Ultramar, to study the fruit-supply situation and attempt to correlate the supply of Angolan fruit with the needs of metropolitan Portugal.

Crops of Minor Significance

The remaining significant crops include European-type potatoes and vegetables, cacao, olives, cashew nuts, sweet potatoes and yams, and the formerly important wild rubber.

Market-gardening of fresh vegetables is fairly well developed near larger urban centers on small Portuguese holdings and by African cultivators. Vegetables are further supplied to Luanda over the northern railway by the Grémio de Produtores de Hortaliças of Malange and by road from Cela. Sweet potatoes and various types of yams are raised on a small scale by Africans in all regions favorable to root crops. European potatoes, grown only on the cooler plateaus, are sometimes exported.

Early attempts at cultivating cacao failed in most of Angola because of insufficient rainfall. Only Cabinda Enclave offers suitable ecological conditions for growing cacao trees. The output long stagnated at about 300 tons a year for export; in 1966, production suddenly shot up to double that figure, but in 1967 it was only about 500 tons.

On the southern Angolan seaboard, an area exists where homesick Portuguese farmers introduced the olive tree, the vine, and the pomegranate. Thus, a fragment of the Mediterranean agricultural landscape was created in the lower valleys of the Bero and Giraúl, near Moçâmedes city. By now, the cultivation of the olive tree, bearing olives for local consumption, has become traditional. Its success recently caused the Chamber of Commerce of Moçâmedes to plan to import additional plants in order to expand the area to over 3,000 acres, up to 120,000 trees, with the eventual purpose of extracting olive oil. Other coastal settlements in Moçâmedes District have also been importing nursery olive plants from Portugal.

The cashew nut grows wild in the sandy soils of the coastal strip. In the face of its tremendous success in Mozambique, the Angolan administration plans to encourage its exploitation and make additional plantings near Santo António do Zaire and in other northern seaboard areas.

Though some texts still refer to Angola's rubber, the formerly active collecting of latex from *Funtumia elastica*, a tree in the northern forest zone, or from the root of *Landolphia thollonii* in the savanna regions, is now only a museum curiosity. Planting of *hevea* rubber was attempted and abandoned; a request was recently made by Portugal to the FAO to re-examine the possibility of cultivating that product in Angola. Experts reached the disappointing conclusion, however, that only the Cabinda Enclave enjoyed the climatic conditions necessary for the crop.

Livestock-Raising

In recent years, increased attention has been paid to existing livestock resources and the possibility of their more rational development, with a threefold aim: (1) to insure a reliable supply of meat and dairy products for the fast-growing local urban centers and metropolitan troops stationed in Angola; (2) to reduce related imports; (3) to enlarge the range of exports and, in particular, to remedy the deficiency of meat supplies in metropolitan Portugal, into which considerable quantities of meat are imported every year. The Commission for Livestock Development (Comissão do Fomento Pecuário), created in 1957, was recently reinvigorated, and intensive livestock-raising by the more progressive farmers is being encouraged by many means, including official distribution of prizes for the best breeders and free transport of imported stud animals.

Livestock censuses are seldom reliable in Africa, for African owners cannot or will not supply the necessary information. Few pastoralists are literate, and many are fearful that the administration may have designs upon their animals. Cattle or small livestock are rarely stall- or barn-fed; they live in the open, frequently under seminomadic conditions. It is more appropriate to refer to the African care of cattle as herding rather than raising. European ranchers are still a small minority.

According to the estimated 1967 livestock figures, the province had about 2.1 million head of cattle, 715,000 goats, 315,000 hogs, 137,000 sheep, and a few thousand horses, mules, and donkeys.[18] This represents roughly 1 head of cattle for 2.5 inhabitants, a fairly low ratio; many other sub-Saharan African territories with a substantial area under grass cover fare much better. Kenya, Tanzania, and Rhodesia, for example, have almost 1 head of cattle per head of population.[19] Despite the existence of other sources of protein from small livestock and fish, it is quite desirable that Angola's small number of cattle should be speedily increased—particularly as the view, often expressed by some scholars, that cattle is for an African only a status symbol or a bride-price is not altogether correct. Cow's milk, fresh or sour, is a main food staple in rural southern Angola.[20] And the increasing tempo of urbanization naturally demands further increases in milk and beef supplies for the large cities.

Huíla District contains 65 per cent of all cattle, over one-third of all goats, roughly one-fifth of all hogs, and one-sixth of all sheep. Away from Sá da Bandeira, the European agricultural center of the Huíla plateau, or the *colonato* at Matala, most cattle are of rustic native breeds. They are owned by the Cuanhamas and other Ambo peoples, in an extension of a large African herding-zone centered on the Ovamboland of South-West Africa. The natural pastures of the region are known as "sweet pastures" (*pastos doces*), because they provide palatable forage throughout the year. Obstacles to an expansion of southern herds have been the saturation of better areas, existence of some virulent animal diseases transmitted at times across the border from South-West Africa, and a great regional shortage of water during the protracted dry season; cattle suffer and lose weight, as they must travel long distances from one watering point to another. Some receive water only every 2 to 3 days. As a consequence, since late in the 1950's, the provincial Geological Services has pursued a detailed survey of surface and underground water reserves in the south while, at the same time, teaching the local population to construct shallow wells and rudimentary water-storage reservoirs. Formerly, the search for water was carried out by World Mining Consultants, Inc., of New York, and Aero Service Corporation of Philadelphia. In addition, a range-management program is now being elaborated by the new Huíla Pasture and Water Board (Comissão de Pastos e Águas do Distrito de Huíla). The adjoining Moçâmedes District has a further 6 per cent of the cattle total.

The Benguela, Huambo, and Cuanza Sul districts, through the northwestern half of the central plateau, form another important livestock-raising region in Angola. Here, cattle, and sheep particularly, are often in European hands; the native stock has mostly been improved by the introduction of pure-breed cattle from Europe, South Africa, and North America. In these districts, Africans do not own wandering herds but raise livestock in association with crops; some even use oxen for agricultural work. Nova Lisboa has had a good milking herd for some time and, since 1964, has had a modern dairy plant. On the other hand, throughout this zone, the low quality of natural pastures has been a great handicap to livestock-owners. This applies especially to the local winter season, *cacimbo*, from May to October, when local "sour" or "high veld" (*pastos acres*) lose their palatability and the diet of the animals needs to be supplemented by hay or cultivated forage.[21]

A transitional zone of somewhat better natural pastures, "middle veld" (*pastos mistos*), stretches between the central and southern cattle areas, and there are concentrations of African herds around Quilengues and Caconda in northern Huíla District. Otherwise, cattle-raising has never been important in the rest of Angola because of a lack of pastoral tradition among the northern tribes and the occupation of sizable areas by one of the scourges of the African continent, the tsetse fly. The fly commonly harbors the single-cell parasite that causes trypanosomiasis, or sleeping sickness. Perhaps as much as one-third of the province is infested.[22] Through the northern half of the coastal lowland, as far south as Benguela, the tsetse exists along practically every watercourse. The northwestern and northeastern interior is also affected, and there are unwelcome tsetse concentrations in the upper basin of the Cuanza, on the eastern Angolan border adjoining Zambia, and in the extreme southeast.

With appropriate sanitary precautions, the tsetse fly is perhaps not as forbidding now as in the past. Some Europeans have managed to raise healthy medium-size herds on the northern plateau around Malange. Fine beef has been raised by some enterprising Portuguese near Porto Amboím. The *colonato* of Cela has a very active dairy-produce cooperative with two plants, obligated by contract to buy all milk offered by local settlers. A new road between Luanda and Nova Lisboa passes nearby and has greatly eased problems of distribution. Cela's cattle herd is now estimated at over 6,000. Another dairy cooperative, operated since 1940 by settlers from the Azores, functions at Catofe, near Quibala in Cuanza Sul District, within a tsetse region. One of the largest cattle ranches of the country, belonging to Companhia Agro-Pecuária de Angola,[23] is near the mouth of the Cuanza River. Some of Luanda's households are supplied daily with fresh milk from two small herds in the vicinity of the capital. In the northeast, Diamang maintains a model herd of crossbred European-native cattle for the benefit of its mining staff.

Besides dressed meat for provincial markets, dairy products (fresh milk, cream, butter, and cheese),[24] and 1,000–2,000 tons of overseas exports of dried hides and skins (which come mainly from African herds in the south) there exists a processed-meats and animal-fats industry. The latter now reaches a combined output of some 5,000 tons a year. Only pork meat has been used so far, following the custom in the Iberian Peninsula. Processing is largely located in and around Sá da Bandeira and in Huambo District, in small establishments preparing home-made types of products comparable in quality to the sausages and hams of metropolitan Portugal. Raising sheep for wool on the central plateau has also been attempted for the past 10 years, by a Portuguese consortium, but with no remarkable results.

Probably of greater economic portent for the future are two endeavors aiming at outside markets. The first, though still on an experimental basis, is the raising of Persian lamb (caraculo) in the semi-arid subcoastal strip inland from Moçâmedes. A flock of several thousand bearing ewes exists already, and periodic auctions of black and gray skins are held in Angola and Germany in the hope of ultimately creating in southern Angola prosperous Persian lamb ranches, such as those in neighboring South-West Africa. In 1967, some 3,000 skins were offered for sale in Luanda, a decline from the 5,000 of the previous year.

The second is the export of frozen beef by Sociedade Frigorífica do Sul, "Sofrio." Sofrio has two meat-packing plants, in Moçâmedes and Sá da Bandeira, each with a slaughtering capacity of 50 head per day and cold storage capacity of 400 and 700 tons, respectively. Meat shipments to Portugal began late in 1961, and meat is also supplied to Luanda. Due to periodic shortages of animals for slaughter, exports have, however, seldom risen above 2,700 tons per year. Another meat-packing concern, Sociedade de Carnes de Angola (Socar) has a larger plant under construction near Nova Lisboa on the central plateau. Capital investment for the two plants approximates $1.4 million.[25]

A distinctive type of animal product for which Angola has been traditionally noted on the world market is beeswax. Today bee-keeping and the collection of wild honey and wax is on the decline in several formerly productive areas, like Malange District, because of other cash-earning possibilities. Moxico District and some outlying sectors of Cuando Cubango District continue, however, as important wax-producers. The greatest share of commercialized production passes through purification installations in Benguela, so Angolan wax is largely known in the trade as Benguela wax.[26] In the present decade, 700–900 tons of beeswax have been exported yearly to a wide range of markets.

AGRICULTURE IN MOZAMBIQUE

The contribution of the primary-production sector in Mozambique is generally about 25 per cent of the gross national product, compared with 10 per cent for the secondary sector and 65 per cent for the tertiary sector. Although the progress of industrialization has resulted in some exports of manufactured products, the share of agriculture still comprised over 80 per cent of exports in the mid-1960's.[27] African agriculture has been encouraged by such factors as a greater density of population, the extent of the coastal lowland, and more favorable conditions of rainfall and fertile alluvial soils than in Angola. Furthermore, the traditional African labor movement to the mines in Transvaal frequently introduced the Mozambican African to the better farming practices of the South African Bantu.

On the other hand, prior to the Limpopo scheme, white agricultural settlement was at a disadvantage, because of the small areas of favorable temperate climate, the division of political control over the colony until the 1940's, and the fact that the independent settler had to disburse costs of sea-passage between Lisbon and Mozambique, higher than those between Lisbon and Angola. Most European agriculture in Mozambique was, thus, in the hands of large corporations.

According to the agricultural census in progress from 1960 to 1965, some 2,940 cash farm and plantation units operated in the province, largely in Moçambique, Zambézia, Manica e Sofala, Gaza, and Lourenço Marques districts. They occupied a total area of over 4 million acres, of which 830,750 acres were under effective cultivation. Land-owners were largely Portuguese nationals, with a sprinkling of other Europeans and about 130 Asians. The paid labor force involved totaled 129,500 people, equivalent to 3.8 per cent of all agricultural manpower in the province; total yearly salaries and wages reached $12 million.[28] Almost one-half of the total paid labor force was concentrated on the coconut and tea plantations of Zambézia District. That district also led in the value of non-African agricultural production, with close to 40 per cent of Mozambique's total.

In comparison, Africans worked some 7 million acres of the province, with an average of 2.5 to 9 acres per family; the most extensive African cultivation was in the Inhambane and Moçambique districts. The latter district and Zambézia District accounted together for 52 per cent of total African-marketed output.[29]

The Portuguese administration in Mozambique has long shown a more systematic approach to the assessment of local agricultural resources than in Angola. Data pertaining to agriculture are periodically compiled in a special volume of statistics.[30] Information collected during the recent agricultural census has already been released for the northern and central districts;[31] only the information covering three southern districts remains to be processed. Since 1943, the Cotton Research Institute (Centro de Investigação Científica Algodoeira, or CICA) has contributed much to the ecological and agricultural knowledge of the province. Also in Mozambique, the first African agricultural cooperatives in Portuguese Africa were started by the staff of Serviços de

Agricultura e Florestas, which also supervised the drainage of some swamplands in the south. In 1961, steps were taken to organize elementary agricultural schooling at the level of the African farmer by training future instructors at agricultural experimental stations; since then, these instructors have started apprenticeship classes in several rural areas. As in Angola, the province has its own Instituto de Investigação Agronómica, started in 1965, to carry out basic research in agriculture.

Within the framework of the Portuguese national development program, some $130 million was allocated to Mozambique between 1953 and 1967 to promote agriculture and other primary production. The latest development plan (*Plano de Fomento III*, 1968–73) foresees an additional investment of some $80 million in that sector.

As in Angola, the crops grown in Mozambique may be classified as crops of major export significance, crops of some significance in export or internal exchanges, and crops of minor significance.

Crops of Major Export Significance

The six leading export crops of Mozambique have been cotton, cashew nuts, cane sugar, tea, copra, and sisal by order of value for 1967. By order of tonnages exported during the same year, sugar came first, followed by cashew nuts, cotton, copra, sisal, and tea.[32] Cane sugar, sisal, and tea are all plantation crops produced for overseas markets. Cotton is essentially African-grown and destined to metropolitan Portugal's textile mills. Cashew nuts, formerly mainly an African collection item, are now being grown by Europeans on plantations. There exists both African and non-African ownership of coconut palm plantations, which supply copra and oil for internal needs and overseas export.

Cashew Nuts. The wild cashew tree is found on the sandy soils along the coastal and subcoastal belt of Mozambique, particularly in the north, where it continues into the south of mainland Tanzania. Until 1935, this natural wealth was little exploited, when sudden harvest shortages in western India, a long-established world supplier, led Indian traders to start cashew purchases in Mozambique. For almost two decades, local unshelled nuts were shipped to India, where hosts of women and children labored at home on the delicate operation of stripping off the thin shell containing an oily, caustic liquid and separating the two halves of the kernel without breakage. The nuts were then re-exported, principally to the United States.

A few years ago, suitable decorticating machinery was perfected for the first time in Mozambique, and several mechanized plants have been set up in the south, while others are under construction or in the experimental stages in the north. Higher profits have spurred African nut-collection and encouraged further European plantings. Planted cashew trees now rank second in the area in Mozambique, after the coconut palm and before sisal. The leading cashew region is still Moçambique District, where harvest was reported to be as high as 55,000–60,000 tons for 1967. Combined exports of shelled and unshelled nuts were 64,300 tons for that year, valued at about $18.1 million. Additional small exports of cashew-nut shell liquid (CNSL) for varied industrial uses brought the total export value of cashew-tree products to $18.8 million. The bulk of unshelled nuts goes to India, but, owing to the rapid development of mechanical shelling, Mozambique expects to be able to process the total crop at home by 1970, thus achieving a higher unit-value for its cashew-nut exports, and thus being able to supply the United States market directly. Domestic industry also plans to prepare cashew jams and juices from the pear-shaped stem on which the nut hangs.[33]

Cotton. Before the latest upsurge of cashew-nut exports, cotton was the largest export of Mozambique. Under the control of the Cotton Export Board (Junta de Exportação de Algodão) established in 1938, a system of concessionaries arose cooperating with local administrators, who prodded the Africans to work harder. Thus, cotton-growing became the dominant African cash crop of the north and an important source of income in other sections of Mozambique. While in Angola production remained almost stationary between 1949 and 1960, with a yearly average of 18,000–20,000 tons of unginned or seed-cotton, in Mozambique it nearly doubled during the same period. More than 140,000 tons were produced in 1960. After ginning, some 43,000 tons of fiber were obtained. Supported by this stream of cotton at prices lower than in the world market, the metropolitan Portuguese textile mills centered at Braga and Pôrto were thus able to build up a national industry employing 71,000 people and worth over $107 million per year.

Considerable protests were heard at times in Portugal and elsewhere as to the low level of fixed prices paid to the African grower, the contribution he was obliged to make to the Cotton Welfare Fund for each kilo sold, the system of concessionaries, and the coercion of Africans by the Mozambique administration to make them grow cotton. The latter outcry was particularly in evidence among some international organizations. Actually, what was called forced labor in cotton-growing consisted of each African being required to cultivate 1.25 acres of cotton, in addition to his normally grown food staples, if he could not prove that he was steadily employed elsewhere. Such cotton-growing for cash was especially enforced in northern parts of Mozambique, where the African had no tradition of cash-cropping and only limited employment opportunities. When the price of unginned cotton was raised in the early 1960's, and the concessionary regime and deductions for the Cotton Fund terminated, the farmer of northern Mozambique was so accustomed to growing cotton that he naturally persevered in the habit. The general economic awakening of the north was essentially due to two decades of cotton cultivation. Northern progress was evidenced by the emergence of numerous small trading settlements at the points of cotton collection in formerly empty country, the expansion of a regional road-network and public and private trucking services, and the construction of hospitals, infirmaries, and schools made possible because of the Cotton Welfare Fund. Moreover, many cotton-concessionaries reinvested their profits in other regional enterprises, such as tea plantations, cattle-raising, and industrial plants, thereby broadening the economic structure of the province. A considerable share of development capital has likewise come to the government from taxes on cotton.[34]

Total Mozambique seed-cotton harvest now varies from just under to well over 100,000 tons a year, varying according to weather conditions. In 1967, it was 130,000 tons. The area under cotton is estimated at about 750,000 acres, with some 500,000 African growers. Two-thirds of the harvest originate in the four northern districts of Cabo Delgado, Niassa, Moçambique, and Zambézia, where over one-half of the population of the province lives. Most cotton gins are there, and there is a cottonseed-oil extracting-plant in Monapo. For 1967, exports of fiber and linters were 39,433 tons, valued at $21.8 million. Total exports of cotton products inclusive of cottonseed, cottonseed-oil, and feedcake were 57,500 tons, worth $23.5 million.

Internal consumption of local fiber in Mozambique is somewhat higher than in Angola, about 2,500 tons. At present, the only important textile plant in which cotton is worked belongs to the Sociedade Algodoeira do Fomento Colonial (Soalpos), located at Vila Pery on the rail line between Beira and the Rhodesian border. Another textile mill is planned for the north. A few small establishments in Lourenço Marques produce knitwear and pharmaceutical cotton.

Sugar. As in Angola, sugar-cane cultivation and milling were until recently the monopoly of three large companies. Sena Sugar Estates Ltd., with head offices in London, owns large cane plantations on both banks of the main arm of the Zambezi delta, two crushing mills, and a sugar port at Chinde. Companhia Colonial do Buzi is installed on the lower Buzi River, west-southwest of Beira; besides its own cane fields, it buys cane for crushing from local small-farmers and also raises rice, cotton, and livestock. Sociedade Agrícola de Incomáti operates on the Incomáti at Xinavane, some 80 miles north of Lourenço Marques. The last two concerns are Portuguese.

At the time of the district census carried through 1961–62, the Buzi Company held about one-half of the total 96,700 acres under cane and had an output of 93,800 tons of the combined provincial production of 186,300 tons. Since then, the planted area has been expanding chiefly in the Incomáti valley, particularly as a fourth company, Marracuene Agrícola Açucareira (Maragra) began new plantations there in 1963, and started milling the cane in 1967. Sena Sugar Estates, with a total concession area of just over 50,000 acres and a processing capacity of 90,000 tons a year, has been held back by irrigation problems; recently, the company signed a $4.7-million contract with a British engineering firm to complete new irrigation installations.[35]

Total sugar production of Mozambique was nearly 200,000 tons, domestic consumption over 75,000 tons, in 1967. Exports for that year were 109,500 tons of raw sugar, over four times the amount exported by Angola, and 38,300 tons of molasses with a combined value of $11 million. Encouraged by the rise of fixed sugar prices and consumption in Portugal, a fifth large company, Açucareira de Moçambique, plans to begin operations with a total investment of $14.2 million and an intended yearly output of 60,000 tons. It would locate just inland from Beira and have a refinery of 10,000-ton capacity. A refinery of 20,000–30,000-ton capacity is also aimed at by Maragra.

Local authorities expect that, by 1970, the sugar production of Mozambique will reach 350,000 tons;[36] in the expectation of greatly increased traffic, a special sugar terminal, which will also handle the small sugar production of neighboring Swaziland, was recently completed at Lourenço Marques.

Tea. Throughout eastern Africa, tea is grown in many a highland with at least 60 inches of rainfall well-distributed during the year. Mozambique ranks third, after Kenya and Malawi, the two leading producers of tea in Africa.[37] Tea cultivation is concentrated in the western half of Zambézia District, extending from the forest-clad slopes of Mount Milange (Mlanje), which stands astride the common border with Malawi, to about 125 miles east and northeast. Within that zone are to be found some of the highest mountain massifs of the province, as well as the highest rainfall. Gurué, Milange, Tacuane (Lugela), and Socone are the focuses for tea plantations.

Approximately 37,800 acres are now under cultivation, producing from 9,000 to 10,500 tons of cured tea-leaf yearly; both Chinese and Indian types are grown, but they are generally referred to as the East African teas and are used in blending. About 40,000 Africans are employed on the tea estates. It is estimated that almost ten times as much land suitable for tea is available as is at present cultivated. However, installations call for substantial financing and, since the average Portuguese or African farmer lacks the necessary capital, any further tea expansion is likely to be tied in with the formation of cooperatives and establishment of centrally located factories to serve the leaf-processing needs of small tea-growers. One cooperative of that kind is already in operation. Until recently the large, self-contained tea plantation with abundant labor was the most usual.

Production in 1967 reached 15,000 tons, of which 10,000 tons came from the Gurué region. Exports for that year were 14,800 tons, worth $9 million, directed as usual to the United Kingdom, Portugal, and the United States.

Copra. The seaboard of Zambézia District boasts of being the largest coconut-palm plantation in the world. Coconut groves, many established on land reclaimed from coastal marshes and lagoons, stretch from Quelimane to António Enes and, more sparsely, along the seaboard of Moçambique District into that of Cabo Delgado. The leading corporate grower is the Companhia do Boror, with headquarters in Macuze, just northeast of Quelimane, the major copra-shipping port. Small coconut-palm plantations also exist in several coastal locations of the Manica e Sofala and Inhambane districts.

A total of some 200,000 acres is estimated to be planted with coconut palm through the province; Africans alone may own 5.4 million trees, two-thirds of which are fully bearing. Commercialized production of copra, the dried kernel of the coconut, is 50,000 to 60,000 tons per year, of which some 10,000 tons are marketed by African growers. Some copra provides coconut oil, popular in the eastern African cuisine and converted into soap. Feedcake and coir fiber for mattress-making are other by-products of the coconut palm. In 1967, some 42,900 tons of copra, worth $6.5 million, and 14,500 tons of oil and cake were exported, bringing the total to $8.9 million.

Sisal. Sisal cultivation in Mozambique began just after the beginning of the twentieth century. After World War I, German planters, formerly established in Tanganyika, preferred not to return to their confiscated plantations in British East Africa and settled in the northern coastal strip of Mozambique, which has very similar ecological conditions. One-fifth of the total sisal area in the province is still in foreign hands.

The local association of sisal producers, Associação dos Produtores de Sisal de Moçambique, has insisted on quality, despite frequently distressing world prices. Meanwhile, Angolan sisal exports soon doubled those of Mozambique. A substantial share of Mozambique's sisal is destined for United States markets.

In 1961–62, sisal concessions covered 132,000 acres in twenty-seven plantations.[38] Lean years since then have caused a small contraction. Except for an isolated plantation at Vila Pery in central Mozambique, sisal is mainly grown in the hinterland of the ports of Moçambique, Nacala, and Porto Amélia. In 1967, exports totaled 23,200 tons, valued at $3.4 million; in several earlier years they were in excess of 30,000 tons. It is not likely, however, that in the near future there will be a large increase in sisal exports, since a cordage factory was established in the province late in 1966, and its requirements of 7,000 tons a year will affect overseas shipments. Also, since several noted sisal plantations lie close to present insurgency-affected areas of the north, the planters have been handicapped in their operations.

Crops of Some Significance for Export and Internal Consumption

Prominent in this category are some grains like rice and maize and, to a lesser extent, wheat; oil seeds, among which peanuts are the foremost; and tropical fruits, mainly bananas and citrus. Manioc, beans, sorghums (*mapira*), and millets (*mexoeira*) are also important in subsistence farming; the export trade in manioc and beans, averaging only 3,000–4,000 tons yearly, is much smaller than similar exports from Angola.

Maize. Contrary to what occurs in Angola, where practically all maize is African-grown and represents a leading export crop, the maize production of Mozambique is, first, derived from both European and African farms, and, second, not as a rule sufficient to meet total domestic demand. Consequently, additional maize is likely to be imported from Transvaal, Rhodesia, or Angola. Nevertheless, maize probably occupies some 60,000 acres of non-African cropland and perhaps as much as one-fifth of African holdings. Estimated production is about 400,000 tons, of which 5 to 6 per cent enters internal trade under the supervision of the Instituto dos Cereais.

The main area of European maize-growing has long been the settlement belt along the Beira railroad between Vila Machado and the Rhodesian border; small European farmers moved into the *concelho* of Chimoio during the period of Companhia de Moçambique control. Other Portuguese small-farmers grow maize in Lourenço Marques District and on the floodplain of the Limpopo. African maize was formerly a crop of the interior uplands, but, during the last two decades, the draining of some subcoastal marshes (*machongos*) south of Inhambane, formation of African cooperatives, and adoption of more progressive methods of cultivation (like ox-drawn plows) have fostered marketable African maize-production in the south. On these heavy black soils, maize is often intercropped with rice.

Rice. Mozambican rice production is considerably larger than Angolan. The existence of many marshes and lagoons in the coastal lowland, together with the periodic occurrence of floods in the southern river valleys, naturally favors the

10—PA

crop. During World War II, because of the loss of Far Eastern sources of supply, a special division of the Department of Agriculture, Divisão do Fomento Orizícola, was entrusted with the encouragement of rice-planting. As was the case for cotton, a concessionary system was originally set up for rice. Recently, it was replaced by a network of authorized rice-hulling plants that buy directly from associations of growers or individual producers in a government-organized system of markets.

As the African farmer became rice-conscious, its cultivation concentrated within three zones, one in *machongos* of the south, a second on the central seaboard from the northernmost arm of the Zambezi delta down to the Pungué River flats behind Beira, and the third in some river valleys and basins of the north. In the last decade, some European farmers, notably at the *colonato* of Limpopo, have turned to mechanized rice-cultivation. Production of rice in husk was 93,000 tons for the agricultural year 1965–66, resulting in about 50,000 tons of clean rice. Present exports are around 4,000 tons, and it is hoped that much greater volumes can be shipped to the neighboring South African market in the near future.

Wheat. Wheat occupies only a limited acreage, all in the south. Production through the 1960's has varied from 7,500 to 13,000 tons a year, so most of the domestic demand continues to be met through imports. The quality of local grain is higher than in Angola. Both local and imported products are milled at the large flour plant in Matola; two other mills are under construction, at Lourenço Marques and at Beira. In the near future, wheat-growing might show some healthy increases, if the original goals of the *colonato* of Limpopo are realized: wheat was to be a main crop of the immigrant farmers there.

Oil Seeds. Peanuts are grown by Africans throughout the province, but the three southern districts and the northern Moçambique District, in particular, offer the necessary rainfall regime and the light soils favored by the plant. Total yearly production is around 125,000 tons of unshelled peanuts. About one-sixth of each harvest is marketed under the control of the same Instituto dos Cereais that handles grains. Nuts are locally milled for oil. The 1966 exports of peanut oil and seedcake were 17,900 tons valued at $4.1 million.

Sesame and sunflower seed are raised on a smaller scale and are processed at the same mills as peanuts and cotton seed. Africans living in the coastal belt of the Lourenço Marques, Gaza, and Inhambane districts collect and market seeds of the *Trichilia emetica* tree (*mafurra*). Oil from this tree is widely used in local soap-manufacturing; seedcake is exported. Total production of oil mills in the province ranged in the 1960's between 20,000 and 32,000 tons for edible oils, around 12,000 tons for inedible oils, and 44,500 tons of oil-seed cake for cattle feed.[39] Of this, 16,300 tons of oils and 37,500 tons of seedcake were exported in 1967, for a total value of $8.1 million. Another mill is under construction that would process as much as 75,000 tons yearly, to boost oil shipments to Portugal, notably for the sardine-canning industry. The government reportedly is placing emphasis upon further increases in oil-seed production for the next five years.

Fruit. Bananas and citrus have long been exported from Mozambique, the first chiefly being sent across the border to South Africa and Rhodesia, and sometimes as far as Zambia. Most banana production is derived from European and Asian-owned plantations along the Incomáti valley and from white farmers in the *concelho* of Chimoio—all located near rail transport.

Recently, banana production for export has risen to 25,000 tons. At times during the 1960's, plantations of the lower Incomáti have grievously suffered from recurrent floods; only now has the Portuguese administration embarked upon a program of long-needed protective works. Because of the flooding and a tropical cyclone in the fall of 1965, banana exports for 1967 were only 14,000 tons, worth $500,000. In contrast to Angola, large-scale expansion of banana cultivation in Mozambique is less assured. South Africa is actively encouraging banana-planting at home, and possible shipments to metropolitan Portugal are handicapped by long sea distances.

Citrus fruit production in the south has been modelled on production in Transvaal, for which Lourenço Marques is an important gateway. Cold-storage facilities at that port serve both the larger South African citrus traffic and domestic shipments. Emphasis in Mozambique has lately been on grapefruit, which seems to thrive particularly well in the ecological conditions of the south, but oranges, and to a lesser extent lemons and tangerines, are also of significance. Processing of juices is now being studied. For 1967, citrus-fruit exports were 10,800 tons, valued at $610,000.

Crops of Minor Significance

Among such crops, tobacco, *kenaf*, European potatoes, and vegetables are worthy of mention.

Tobacco cultivation, persistently pursued since the 1920's around Entre-Rios (Malema) in the westernmost sector of Moçambique District, has had many developmental problems, including not very suitable soils in the chief area and discrimination on the part of Portuguese buyers. Despite examples of successful tobacco-farming in Rhodesia and Malawi, Mozambique has not been able to move much beyond the manufacture of tobacco products for its own use. Total area planted in tobacco is now about 10,000 acres, and yearly production averages 5,000–5,500 tons. As in Angola, Virginia-type flue-cured tobacco is usually grown by Europeans while the darker air-cured leaf is grown by African growers. Exports have seldom risen above 1,000 tons per year.

The need for burlap bags for sugar and other crops led to experimentation after World War II by several concerns with some wild jute-type plants, and, more recently, *Hibiscus cannabinus*, known in the fiber trade as *kenaf*, has been planted inland from Beira. Production of around 6,000 tons is absorbed by a local weaving factory, which complements it with imported jute.

The growing of European-type of potatoes has been moderately successful in some uplands of the Tete and Niassa districts, but it is handicapped by the distance to main provincial markets. It is now promoted around Vila Pery and in the south, notably at the *colonato* of Limpopo. There is market-gardening of fresh vegetables near Lourenço Marques and other urban centers. Yet the volume of produce has remained lower than demand in the capital city. The Mozambique population has always tended to rely on better-organized South

African and Rhodesian producers for their everyday needs, rather than to strive for self-sufficiency.

Livestock-Raising[40]

Mozambique has fewer livestock resources than does Angola. Estimates in 1966 placed the total provincial herd at 1.1 million head of cattle (or roughly 1 head for 6 inhabitants), 431,000 goats, 106,000 sheep, 99,000 hogs, and some 16,000 donkeys, horses, and mules. About 70 per cent of cattle and 60 per cent of sheep are African-owned. Two-thirds of the province is still infested with the tsetse despite the valiant efforts of the Anti-Trypanosomiasis Team to eliminate the special type of bush favored by the fly.

The three districts south of the Save River contain seven-tenths of the cattle, close to one-half of the sheep, over one-third of the goats, and about one-third of the hogs of Mozambique. Gaza District, free of tsetse, is the leading cattle area, with some 451,000 head. African cattle raised in the upper Limpopo region reach fair size on shrubby vegetation and good mineral nutrients of local soils. But in this driest sector of the province, water for animals is notably scarce. Recently, drilling for underground water-reservoirs by the Geological Services has led to the construction of some artesian wells. The installation of the *colonato* of Limpopo has further contributed to the large number of cattle in Gaza District. Although rather heavily infested by the tsetse, Lourenço Marques District ranks second in number of cattle because of meticulous sanitary precautions taken by local European ranchers. It also contains the largest dairy herd, approximately 9,000 milking cows, to supply the city of Lourenço Marques with fresh milk. The ten-year-old Cooperativa de Criadores de Gado do Sul do Save was previously the only one to distribute dairy products. In the mid-1960's, a few Lourenço Marques firms also started to make butter and cheese. One of these firms, Protal, plans soon to add powdered and condensed milk to its line of products. The international Nestlé interests have also begun to construct a factory in Lourenço Marques.

The Tete and Manica e Sofala districts in the central zone have slightly less than one-fourth of all cattle and about two-fifths of all goats and hogs but only one-tenth of all the sheep. Cattle-herding has always been important in the fairly densely settled and well-watered Angoni highlands astride the border with Malawi; the tsetse fly, moreover, is absent there. The traditional reluctance to part with cattle and the distance to markets have thus far prevented the commercialization of Angoni beef. In 1966, however, a firm began considering the establishment in Tete of a slaughterhouse to produce frozen and canned meat.

Some cattle are raised in the vicinity of Quelimane on several large coconut plantations, principally for manure, and on tea plantations in the west to provide meat and milk for the staff. One-fifth of all Mozambique hogs are also in Zambézia District. Goats and fat-tailed sheep dominate in the three northern districts—their combined cattle herd is less than 25,000 head.

Slaughtering of livestock in Mozambique is still insufficient for local demand; in particular, Lourenço Marques and Beira often have great difficulty in securing the necessary supplies in dressed meat for their expanding population and active tourist trade. Several modern poultry farms on the city peripheries compensate in some measure for the lack, but there is no processed-meat industry in Mozambique comparable to that of Angola. As a result, imports of fresh and prepared meat have been quite high. To alleviate this, the Veterinary Service has been campaigning to expand the marketing of livestock among the Africans and to provide price adjustments for better-grade animals as an incentive to progressive farmers. The Service is now responsible for a special Livestock Development Fund (Fundo de Fomento Pecuário) and a program of cattle fairs throughout the province.

AGRICULTURE IN OTHER PORTUGUESE-AFRICAN PROVINCES

Portuguese Guinea[41]

Agriculture in this province is entirely in the hands of the Africans, with about 12 per cent of total area under cultivation. The Balanta and Fula, the foremost agriculturalists, continue to follow traditional African routines rather than adopt plow-and-oxen methods steadily promoted by local agriculture and veterinary services. Farming is synchronized with the rainy season; work begins in late March or early April, and harvest time is reached by the end of the year. Three-quarters of production is for subsistence.

Rice, grown both on the periodically flooded coastal lands and on dry land, is the principal crop, occupying over one-fourth of all cultivated area. With an estimated production of 170,000 tons, it is the staple food of the population, and it is traded widely, both internally and with adjoining tribes outside the control of the Portuguese administration; these latter sales do not figure in export statistics. Occasionally, some rice shipments are made to overseas markets.

The two leading export crops have long been peanuts (locally *mancarra*) and oil-palm products. Peanuts, largely grown in the northeast as an extension of intensive peanut-cultivation of Senegal, account for 60 per cent of provincial exports. The yearly volume of peanut production reaches 70,000–80,000 tons, of which 15,000–25,000 tons are exported together with some peanut oil and seedcake from a few local oil-extracting plants. Oil-palm kernels, gathered in the Bijagós island group and in the coastal zone between Cacheu and Bissau, account for about 30 per cent of exports. During 1967, combined exports of peanut and oil-palm products were depressed by the continuing guerrilla warfare in the peanut zone and were reduced to a value of only $2.7 million instead of the more usual $4.8 million. It is quite common for Africans of Portuguese Guinea to migrate for harvest season to aid peanut-farmers in neighboring countries.

Millets, sorghums, maize, beans, manioc, and sweet potatoes are secondary subsistence crops; sugar cane, sesame, and tropical fruits are also grown. For the last two decades, diversification of cash-cropping has been the preoccupation of government agronomists. Though ecological conditions in the north, for example, are favorable to cotton, a concessionary system envisaged through the 1950's, on the model of Mozambique, failed to materialize. Official attention has also been concentrated on further reclamation of coastal and riverine marshes (*bolanhas*), soil studies, improvement of palm fruit, and the possible collection

277

of wild cashew nuts. However, total allocations for spurring agriculture and other primary production in the provinces under the different *Planos de Fomento* did not surpass $4 million for the whole period from 1953 to 1967, since no agricultural settlement schemes were involved.

The livestock position in Portuguese Guinea is better than in either Angola or Mozambique. In the east, among the nomadic or semi-nomadic Fula, cattle are common. Local breeds have developed an unusual immunity to sleeping sickness, despite a heavy presence of the tsetse. There are approximately 250,000 head of cattle, roughly one for every two inhabitants; goats number 144,000, hogs 98,000, and sheep 54,000. There is no dairy industry, but limited slaughtering produces the necessary meat as well as annual exports of hides and skins worth about $68,000. Some 2,000 donkeys introduced from Senegal help in rural movements at the height of peanut harvests.

São Tomé and Príncipe

Agriculture on São Tomé and Príncipe islands contrasts sharply with that in Portuguese Guinea. Commercial farming is concentrated in São Tomé on some 110 plantations (*roças*) owned by Portuguese corporations or other absentee landlords and managed by Europeans or *mestiços*. On these is grown the chief export crop, the cacao bean, which currently represents some 70 per cent of total export value. A smaller number of plantations exist on Príncipe, where, because of low world-cacao prices, transport difficulties, and increasing costs of labor, many plantations are turning to copra. The creole population of the islands raises only produce for family consumption, the small surpluses being informally sold in the village markets.

Cacao-growing began in the islands in 1890, replacing the decayed sugar cultivation that had been based on slave labor. Introduction of cacao from Brazil proved so successful, on the fertile volcanic soils and in the equatorial insular environment, that São Tomé became the largest world-producer of cacao, with a 15 per cent share of the total in 1908. After a peak export year of 49,900 tons of beans in 1919, there has been a steady decline, however. Despite the high quality of its bean, São Tomé now ranks only sixth in African cacao-production and exports yearly only 8,000 to 10,000 tons. In contrast, Ghana, which originally received its cacao trees from São Tomé, produces around 250,000 tons.[42]

Various factors have been responsible for the continuing cacao crisis in the province: gradual exhaustion of soil fertility under intensive cultivation, erosion of cultivable land on the steep slopes, sudden diseases of the tree, periodic weakening of world prices, and the problem of manpower. The work on the plantations has constantly demanded many more laborers than the islands can muster.[43] A decade ago, 21,000 imported workers were needed for the year-round harvests of multiple-plantation crops. The cacao alone demanded much labor for two peak periods in cacao harvest, cacao-bean preparation through fermentation and drying, weekly cutting and stocking of wood fuel for the dryers, and reforestation to avoid timber exhaustion. In some more rugged areas lacking roads and mechanized transport, beans were transported by head-loads. Half of the laborers then were on contract from Angola, 30 per cent were from Cape Verde, and the rest were from Mozambique. Replacement of some of the manual operations by mechanized equipment and the closing down of some *roças* have currently reduced the labor requirements. The poverty-stricken Cape Verde Islands are now a main source of labor. Except for an extensive survey of agricultural potential of various island sections, initiated in 1956, most of the financing available to the primary production under successive development plans through 1953–67 has been earmarked for land purchase and distribution to Cape Verdian immigrants, to encourage their settling in São Tomé to substitute for the less willing arms of the creoles.

Other export crops are palm kernels, copra, and coffee. The oil- and coconut-palm areas occupy 10,000 acres each, the former often being located on the lower, interior forested slopes, the latter along the seashores. *Arabica* coffee, grown in some areas at elevations above 1,800 feet, and the lower altitude *liberica* coffee cover together about 6,000 acres. Production figures for 1967 stood at 10,400 tons of cacao, 5,400 tons of copra, 1,600 tons of kernels, 1,200 tons of palm oil, and 174 tons of coffee—all, except for the palm oil, destined for export.[44]

The raising of livestock in the islands is not significant, mostly because of the dominance of rainforest vegetation and plantation work. At present, the island records show only 3,300 head of cattle, 2,600 sheep, 1,000 goats, and 3,700 hogs. Poultry and other domestic fowl are fairly abundant.

Cape Verde Islands

Of all the Portuguese-African provinces, Cape Verde is the one where cultivation is fraught with the most hazards; yet this struggling agriculture is the indispensable basis of economy.[45] Subsistence crops like maize, beans, and manioc occupy in a disorderly manner most of the arable and level areas in higher islands. Ramshackle terraces attempt to control erosion in many places. Irrigation, usually indispensable to successful harvests, does not always contribute to economic development. For example, sugar cane, the peasant crop receiving the most irrigation, serves only for making local *grogue*, an alcoholic beverage. A deficient agrarian structure, paucity of technical assistance due to the meagerness of government funds, and lack of economical interisland transport all militate against the Cape Verdian farmer.

The most populous island, Santiago, is the most important agriculturally, with about 12,000 acres, or 5 per cent of the total area planted with maize, which is largely intercropped with beans. Some *arabica* coffee is grown in the more humid and sheltered valleys, at elevations of between 1,000 and 4,000 feet, and also citrus and other fruit trees are grown. Lately, commercial banana-growing under irrigation and peasant castor-bean cultivation have shown marked progress. Neighboring Fogo is noted for peanuts. Santo Antão and São Nicolau in the northern group have a range of crops similar to Santiago. Practically all other islands are [suitable only for pasturing livestock or for salt exploitation.

Agricultural products contributed only from 22 to 35 per cent of the total export value from the Cape Verde Islands through the 1960's. Bananas were the leading export crop in both weight and value. Other exports have been peanuts, coffee, European potatoes, castor beans, tomatoes, and the wild plant *Jatropha curcas* (locally *purgueira*), collected for oil-extraction and soap-making.

During the last two decades, the chief efforts of government agronomists have been directed toward an expansion of the irrigated areas, both to improve the food situation for the islanders and to widen the range of agricultural exports. Consequently, the largest share of development funds for agriculture, some $5.7 million, has been spent on hydrological studies. However, unless world progress in water desalinization adds a new source of water supply, further increases in irrigated land will continue to be limited by the low annual rainfall and the problems of storing water for the long periods of drought. Even the pastureland is now supporting its maximum capacity, with approximately 13,000 head of cattle, 24,000 goats, 12,000 hogs, some 13,000 donkeys, mules, and horses, and 2,500 sheep, in 1967. Donkeys, mules, and horses are a common form of transport in the countryside. Hogs, raised everywhere by peasants, are the principal source of meat.

AGRICULTURAL SETTLEMENT SCHEMES IN ANGOLA AND MOZAMBIQUE

Angola

Until about two decades ago, the maze of government regulations for the granting of concessions and the lack of sources of credit for land purchase and improvement hindered agricultural occupation of Angolan land by individual white settlers. The laws on land tenure, passed in May, 1919, guaranteed to the African the possession and use of a plot five times as large as the area he normally had under cultivation; he could not sell his land but could only pass it on to his heirs.[46] As agricultural settlement in Angola lagged, the capital-poor immigrant from Portugal rapidly succumbed to the urban lures of Luanda or Lobito, even if he had to live in the *muceques*. Only exceptionally brave souls were willing to risk a life of sweat, tears, sickness, and little profit for the glory of opening virgin land (*desbravamento do mato*).

An increasing poverty-doomed peasant class in Portugal, growing national emigration toward world areas other than Portuguese Africa, and the conviction that the best way to teach Africans better farming methods was through the example of a hard-working white farmer at last led the government to plan for subsidized settlement of peasants in Angola and Mozambique.

The first project in Angola, the *colonato* of Cela, was initiated in 1952 in the subplateau zone and the basin of a tributary to the Cueve River, some 200 miles southeast of Luanda and 90 miles east-southeast of Gabela. The area, at an approximate elevation of 4,000 feet, was then very sparsely occupied by a handful of white and African subsistence farmers, who were eventually resettled on the margins of the *colonato*. Due to the fact that only a moderate amount of rainfall (less than 45 inches) is received in the region, irrigation of at least a part of the future cropland was imperative; furthermore, marshy sections had to be drained. A thorough hydrological and potential land-use survey was conducted by Hydrotechnic Corporation of New York in collaboration with the Brigada de Estudos Agronómicos da Cela.

Prospective settlers were screened by a committee in Portugal, and the selected applicants were granted free passage to Angola for themselves and their families. In general, large families were chosen because of a prohibition against using African labor. Under the original plan, each family upon their arrival was to receive 50 acres of individually held land, of which 7.5 acres was already in irrigated and sometimes plowed fields, the rights to 100 acres of communal pastures, several head of livestock, farm implements and seed, a dwelling, sheds, and a cash allowance to sustain them until the first harvest. The costs of the installation were to be repaid over a 25-year period, through a specified share of future harvests, after an initial free occupancy of three years. For the first ten years, no interest on the loan was demanded, and thereafter a modest rate of 1.5 to 2 per cent was to be charged.

Five years later, close to 350 families lived within the *colonato* in thirteen hamlets, each with some welfare facilities and an administrative-technical-commercial township at Santa Comba Dão, named in honor of the birthplace of Oliveira Salazar. The total cultivated area was some 14,800 acres, with a crop value of $476,000. Maize, potatoes, rice, beans, some vegetables and fruit, and poultry were the main products. The more successful farmers fared rather well, were able to purchase tractors on a share-basis, and even sometimes brought a farm hand from Portugal at their own expense. Only a few had asked for repatriation, a possibility foreseen in the original contract. The revision of original plans was caused by several factors: constant demand for more irrigated cropland and motive power for crop-processing, necessary additional investment in water works, land limitations, and often-heard complaints in the provincial press that residents of Angola were not allowed the benefits of the project. Original plans had emphasized subsistence holdings and the transfer from Portugal of as many as 2,000 peasant families to Cela. An alternative type of occupancy was, therefore, devised. It offered larger farms of 75 acres and 250 acres and more numerous livestock to knowledgeable immigrant or local Portuguese farmers who could muster a guarantee capital ranging from $3,400 to $8,500. More valuable crops such as coffee, citrus fruits, hogs, and dairy produce were to be stressed. Prospective annual income from these new farms was estimated by the Junta de Povoamento Agrário de Cela to reach $6,800 and $17,000, respectively, while the original farms would gross only an average of $2,600. Since 1960, the *colonato* has functioned along these three patterns, and larger landholders have used laborers engaged in Portugal.[47]

The second project, the Middle Cunene scheme, was to comprise two *colonatos* in the south. The first was to be located along the Moçâmedes rail line about 100 miles east of Sá da Bandeira and was to draw on the water of the Matala dam reservoir and power from that hydroelectric plant; the second was to be farther downstream, not far from the South-West Africa border. The second *colonato* has not yet been developed. In the Matala area, settlement began after 1956, combining, unlike the situation in Cela, immigrant white peasants and local Africans. Each white settler was to receive 7.5 acres of irrigated land and about 65 acres of unimproved communal pastureland, with other endowments similar to those in Cela; subsequently, holdings were raised to 12.5 acres of irrigated land and 75 acres of pasture. Africans received slightly smaller holdings initially, until they could prove effective management. Limited assistance by local Africans to European farmers was not prohibited. In another difference between the *colonato* of Cunene and that of Cela, the Overseas Ministry in Lisbon exerted direct administration over the new project. By 1965, a total of 400 families had settled in four hamlets and a central township, Vila de Folgares. Maize, wheat, potatoes, and rice are now the *colonato*'s chief food crops; tobacco leaf cured locally and tomatoes processed into paste are the main sources of cash.

Surveys for a third extensive settlement project, inland from Luanda, were also begun late in the 1950's. This multiracial scheme was to embrace some 500,000 acres between the Cuanza and Bengo rivers. The study of necessary drainage, flood protection, and other hydraulic works was conducted by the Hydrotechnic Corporation. A main goal was to provide produce for Luanda, intensify cotton-growing in the region, and plant citrus fruit and oil palm for export. Sugar-cane cultivation was also contemplated, to supply the projected Companhia Açucareira de Cuanza. Technical differences of opinion between various organizations involved in surveying and planning, African uprisings in the north in the early 1960's, and the consequent government expenditure for defense have all slowed this project. A 2,500-acre pilot farm has functioned in the area for several years. Of late, arrivals of some Cape Verdian peasant families have been reported.

With the limelight focused on the more spectacular projects much discussed in Portugal and abroad, little publicity was given through the 1950's to smaller *colonatos* in Angola, designed specifically for Africans. As early as 1948, one was established near Caconda on the central plateau for 3,000 Africans. Others began later in the Loge valley, northwest of Carmona, and to the southeast of Damba. All now have several thousand acres under subsistence and cash crops cultivated in conjunction with livestock-raising; technical advice is received from resident agronomists, and some mechanical equipment is used. Farther-reaching goals were envisioned in a campaign initiated in 1954 for a change for Africans from shifting agriculture to permanent agricultural settlement within a network of rural centers through the Malange, Congo (now Uíge and Zaire), Cuanza Sul, Benguela, Huíla, and Moxico districts. According to this program, as many as half a million Africans were first to be introduced to soil conservation practices in their customary environment and subsequently regrouped in hamlets to make the provision of technical and welfare assistance more effective. There, elements of crop rotation, use of fertilizers, and other more advanced methods of agriculture were to be taught to them, the most progressive families eventually to become landowners of plots of up to 12.5 acres.[48]

In the present decade, the impetus toward intensified agricultural settlement has continued in Angola, despite the threat of African nationalism and despite some official opinions that industrialization and not agriculture should be put first. Some changes have taken place, however. All settlement programs were placed under the control of Junta Provincial de Povoamento early in the 1960's. Rather than invest enormous sums in one large site, the trend has been toward establishing smaller peasant settlements, frequently pluriracial and scattered throughout the province. Immigrant families may come from Cape Verde, the Azores, and Madeira, as well as from the Portuguese mainland. Special settlement privileges are also extended to soldiers having completed their term of service and wanting to remain in Angola to farm. Last, but not least, regrouping of the African population was speeded up in the northern districts as a consequence of guerrilla warfare, which called for a closer supervision of activities within that region and a better protection of loyal Africans, who have been at times dealt with more harshly by the insurgents than were the captured whites. In the last few years, over seventy new African villages, some with populations as high as 3,000 persons, were thus created among the Bakongo in the north, with educational and medical facilities. There is also a growing prosperity for African farmers in the north as a result of their planting coffee in the vicinity of their new villages.

Mozambique

Even more than in Angola, the Portuguese who went to Mozambique traditionally avoided life in the bush. In the mid-1950's, of a total European population of 60,000, over three-fourths lived in Lourenço Marques and Beira. The only two significant areas of rural European settlement were in the *concelho* of Chimoio along the line of the Beira Railway (survivors of an early colonization project by the Mozambique Company) and several somewhat more prosperous clusters in the south, mainly in the Incomáti valley.

Two agricultural settlement projects, differing in size and structure but with the common objective of grouping immigrant Portuguese peasants and local Africans, began in the 1950's. The larger and more publicized is the Limpopo Valley Scheme, with 30,000 acres under irrigated crops, where some 1,000 Portuguese and 500 African families are farming. Holdings vary according to family size, with 2.5 acres of irrigated cropland assigned per person, plus 20 acres of meadow and 60 acres of unimproved communal pastures per family unit. Other provisions are similar to those of *colonatos* in Angola, save for the repayment that requires that one-sixth of annual harvests be turned over to project-administrators for sale until the cost of settlement is repaid; no fixed period is laid down for final payments. Total indebtedness per family is about $6,800.[49] The *colonato* comprises thirteen hamlets with a chapel, infirmary, and school, and a central township at Guijá (or Vila Trigo de Morais, in honor of the Portuguese official who originated the scheme). Water for irrigation is supplied by a system of canals from the reservoir behind the Limpopo Dam, on which passes the rail line from Lourenço Marques into Rhodesia, completed in 1955. Principal crops cultivated are wheat, rice, maize, cotton, vegetables, and alfalfa for fodder—all marketed through farmers' cooperatives.

The second settlement project is located in the basin of the Revuè River (an important tributary of the Punguè), which was dammed in 1953. In two sites at the foot of the Rhodesian escarpment, Sussendenga and Zonuè, the beginnings of small *colonatos* with a few dozen Portuguese and African families have already been made. In the vicinity are to be established other homesteads on 625 acres each, instead of settlement in villages. Tobacco will be a leading crop, together with some fruit, *kenaf* fiber, dairy produce, and the usual subsistence staples.

Several African agricultural development schemes had already been started before the Limpopo and Revuè projects. The most successful one involved the partial drainage in 1951 of the Inhamissa marsh, in the floodplain of the lower Limpopo northward from João Belo, and the formation of African cooperatives to work reclaimed land. Two smaller local marshes were subsequently drained. Extensions to the Inhamissa area and better defense works against periodic floods have been continued since then, aiming at bringing into use some 100,000 acres on each side of the Limpopo. Rice is the principal crop there, but bananas, peanuts, pulses, and root crops are also grown, and livestock is raised. Though quite impressive, this scheme could greatly benefit from an increase in development funds.

As in Angola, the Junta Provincial de Povoamento has become the official agency in charge of immigration and settlement, and there is a tendency toward organizing smaller farm aggregates. Plans are to reinforce the settlement in the Chimoio, encourage tobacco cultivation in the north and ranching in the Angoni highlands, establish cooperatives of small tea-growers in the Guruè area, and, finally, give an impetus to the neglected European settlement around Vila Cabral in Niassa District. Nor has the spectacular been forgotten. The ambitious and multifaceted scheme to harness the Zambezi at Cabora Bassa and then to develop other resources of the Lower Zambezi Basin also foresees extensive resettlement of Africans and further immigration of Portuguese farmers.

An important question remains as to the success of these government-supported settlement projects, which envision thousands of families and tens of thousands of irrigated acres. Already, however, economic development has been much speeded, the Portuguese cultural influences deepened, and impoverished tenant farmers from many corners of Portugal and their offspring given a better chance in life. On the other hand, there has been a high expenditure per family and a greater use of funds for the benefit of Europeans than for Africans.

Possibly the greatest agricultural achievement during the last ten or fifteen years in Angola and Mozambique has been that, for the first time, financial support and access to technical knowledge have been put at the disposal of Europeans and Africans with strong backs and willing spirits. Previously, whatever their own effort, they had no adequate means of handling appropriately that precious commodity, the African land.

FORESTRY

Three Portuguese-African provinces export tropical timber, although the volume of these exports cannot compare, by any means, with that of leading African timber traders: Ghana, Nigeria, and Gabon. Until 1960, Angola led in timber shipments, reaching in that year a total value of $3.9 million. Subsequently, Mozambique moved to first place; in 1967, it exported 106,900 tons of timber products with a value of $5.6 million. Angola exported 94,000 tons and $4.3

million. Smaller Portuguese Guinea has considerably lower timber exports, amounting to about $50,000 in 1967.

In Angola, the most important region for logging is the Cabinda Enclave, containing the only provincial reserves of dense equatorial rainforest in the inland *concelho* of Maiombe and substantial forest patches through the sub-coastal belt. Felling is done by some fifty loggers, members of the Grémio de Madeiras do Distrito de Cabinda. The largest concessionary is the Companhia de Cabinda, founded in the 1920's, with approximately 318,000 acres; it operates two modern sawmills and has small plantations of cacao and coffee. Of the estimated total of 1.5 million acres of forest, about one-fourth is in government-protected reserves, the National Forests of Alto Maiombe and Cacongo.[50]

Characteristic handicaps of the logging industry in Cabinda have been a shortage of capital, heavy export taxation, lack of feeder roads, and inadequate port facilities. Logs are either floated down the Chiloango, the main watercourse, to the loading beaches of Lândana, or have to be trucked to Cabinda city wharves. Formerly, timber was exported through the deepwater terminal at Pointe-Noire in the Congo (Brazzaville). Cabinda also shares in the customary head-aches of all African tropical timber producers: the wide scattering of desirable tree species through the tangled mass of forest, long distances to the main timber markets in the Northern Hemisphere, and the poor acceptance in those markets of many tropical hardwood species.

Cabinda produces timber largely for export, though logs and lumber are also carried by coastal vessels to the rest of Angola. In 1967, timber exports totaled 91,475 tons; 21,600 tons were absorbed in the province. The diminutive size of the Enclave recommends restraint in the amount of timber felled annually; to avoid depletion of the natural wealth, visiting U.S. experts recommended a yearly maximum cut of 100,000–125,000 cubic meters. Over one-half of round-wood is directed to Portugal for sawing, cabinet-making, and plywood- and veneer-manufacturing. Railroad ties for South Africa are the largest item in sawn-timber traffic, which also comprises hardwood flooring and box boards.

Lighter tropical forest covers some parts of the northern interior of Angola, notably in the *concelho* of Dembos of the Cuanza Norte District, where the first coffee plantations began. Timber is logged there for domestic needs. The second most important timber-felling region of the province, however, is Moxico District, where the more open and drier *mata de panda* resembles the better known *miombo* forest of East Africa. The proximity of these woodlands to the Benguela Railway has permitted moderate exports through Lobito. Other timber from the area is used throughout the central zone as far west as the sawmill at Lobito, and the Benguela Railway also uses it for railroad ties, locomotive fuel, and charcoal-making.

For several decades, wood fuel was the main source of power for Angolan rail lines. As a consequence, the Benguela Railway Company undertook the planting of vast groves of fast-growing, imported eucalyptus along its route, to have an assured supply of fuel. Following that example, in 1955, the Companhia de Celulose do Ultramar Português (CCUP) was formed to expand in the upper Catumbela basin existing eucalyptus and cypress plantations for processing into wood pulp and subsequently manufacturing various grades of paper; the hydro-power plant at Alto Catumbela was built for the needs of that concern. At present, company softwood plantings reach 125,000 acres; total capital investment by the CCUP has been $11.9 million. In 1967, their pulpwood exports were 24,500 tons, and about 6,700 tons of packaging paper and cardboard were produced.

In Mozambique, the main logging areas are in Manica e Sofala District, within a woodland similar to Moxico District in Angola, and in gallery forests. Exploitation is facilitated by the Beira rail system, which gives rapid access to Rhodesian and Malawi markets. Inhamitanga and Inhaminga are the most important localities involved in timber traffic north of Beira; other timber comes from the western parts of the district. In all, some thirty concessions are in operation. Unlike the practice in Angola, practically all exports are in sawn timber, almost half of which are railroad ties shipped to South Africa through Beira. Construction timber, hardwood-flooring, and crates for Mozambique fruit exports are other significant products. Recently, a plywood-and-veneer plant started operating in Beira city.

Another region with a promising timber potential is Zambézia District, where closed moist forest is found in the western mountain massifs. However, difficulties of transportation to the seaboard have not encouraged local progress in the forest industry. Throughout the northern districts of Moçambique and Cabo Delgado, perhaps a dozen logging companies are functioning, but no more than 10 to 15 per cent of the annual cut comes from these areas. Other concessions are located south of the Save River, particularly in Gaza District. Mangrove bark is periodically collected by Africans in the coastal marshes and sold for the preparation of leather-tanning extracts.

While in Angola the afforestation effort has largely come through private enterprise, in Mozambique it is the Forestry Subdivision of the Department of Agriculture that has been mainly responsible for planting imported eucalyptus, pine, and cypress, as well as the spread of several local timbers.

In Portuguese Guinea, commercial logging started after World War II, with the Cape Verde Islands and metropolitan Portugal as the most important destinations for exports. The volume of exports, practically all in sawn timber, fluctuates annually, occasionally reaching 10,000 tons.

Loggers have principally worked subcoastal forest patches, being assisted in timber transport by the vast fluvial network of the province. An important area of dense forest on the southernmost seaboard, which surrounds the Cacine estuary near the Guinea border, had not been touched before 1962; at present, that area is occupied by guerrillas. The contribution of provincial forest resources to the general economy could probably be increased if proper safeguards against over-cutting were taken.

Though the mountainous islands of São Tomé and Príncipe still have a wealth of forest in many sections, fuel demands of local plantations place first call on timber that is presently available in accessible areas. A switch to imported petroleum products would, in most cases, not be economical, because of the cost and the difficulty of internal distribution. Conservation of much of the forest cover on the slopes is also essential as an anti-erosion measure.

FISHERIES

The Portuguese have traditionally been oriented toward fishing, and fish is a favorite item in the national diet. As early as the beginning of the nineteenth century, a sprinkling of pioneer fishing colonies could be found along the Angolan coast. Commercial development of the fish resources of Angola grew after World War II; these mostly used Portuguese manpower, because only a few African tribes along that coast had a liking for the sea. Now the Angolan fishing industry employs some 13,000 people, and it is the second largest processing industry in the province in declared capital investment. In Cape Verde and Mozambique, the fishing industry was somnolent until after 1960, though some fishing went on for the internal markets. Fisheries in Portuguese Guinea and São Tomé and Príncipe have not yet emerged from the stage of a subsistence activity, with modest sales of surpluses for local consumption.

Angola

The abundance of fish off the coast of Angola stems from two favorable factors: the existence of a fairly sizable area of continental shelf and the presence of a zone of upwelling coastal waters associated with both the South Atlantic trades and the convergence of two marine currents of differing temperature and salinity. The cool and more saline Benguela current, which originates in Antarctic waters, flows northward along the southwestern coast of Africa. During the southern hemisphere's winter, it reaches as far as the shores of Gabon; during the southern summer, it fans out at sea at about the latitude of Benguela. The warm (79°–86° F.) and less saline Guinea current flows south from the Gulf of Guinea as a surface water layer, and, during the southern summer, it reaches down to Moçâmedes. On the nutrients brought from the sea bottom by this marine circulation feed rich concentrations of plankton, smaller fish, and larger predatory fish, on which the fisheries of South Africa, South-West Africa, and Angola can draw.

Angolan sea-fisheries can be grouped in three regions.[51] The fairly homogeneous southern region centered on Moçâmedes and Porto Alexandre leads in the yearly volume of catch and the number of fish-processing plants. The central region, centered on Benguela, is second in catch but has the largest fishing fleet. The northern region has four separate centers: Luanda, Porto Amboím, Santo António do Zaire in the estuary of the Congo, and recently Cabinda. The main species of soft fish that are caught are horse mackerel (*carapau*), various kinds of *sardinha*, and jacks. Dog's teeth, Spanish and frigate mackerel, and little tuna are also common. Of particular significance to the small provincial canning industry are the tunas, principally the yellowfin (*albacora*) and the big-eyed tuna (*patudo*). Shrimp, spiny lobster, and mollusks are fairly abundant along the northern seaboard.

Large fluctuations in live catch have marked the last decade in Angola since the peak year 1956, with 420,500 tons and a value of $9.5 million. After 1957, the best year for exports of fish products, when a value of $16.7 million was reached, yearly catches dipped disastrously, creating a very difficult situation for an overbuilt and overborrowed processing industry, particularly as world prices for fishmeal, the leading product, started a downward trend. The government did not intervene until early in the 1960's, despite constant official talk, both of reorganizing the fisheries and of concentrating small, uneconomically operated plants into several large units. Thereafter, a technical agency, the Instituto das Indústrias de Pesca de Angola, patterned after the South African Commission, and a financial offshoot, Fundo de Apoio à Pesca, were established together with a Commissão Nacional de Coordenação e Apoio às Pescas. Local research laboratories, both on land and aboard two special ships, were added to the limited facilities of Lisbon-based Centro de Biologia Piscatória. Impetus for development came particularly from visits to Angolan waters of several Japanese factory-ships, which conducted excellent fishing seasons with the assistance of some local purse-seiners, while operating farther offshore than the customary fishing grounds. The success of the Japanese confirmed former predictions that deep-sea trawling might hold better prospects than coastal fisheries; it also flashed a ray of hope for many a demoralized fishing crew.

By the mid-1960's, the position of the industry showed considerable improvement, because of higher international fishmeal prices, bigger catches, government tax-exemptions on locally produced fuels for fishing vessels, and credits granted by the Banco de Angola to the Fundo de Apoio à Pesca. Conditions were also improved with the arrival on the scene of some metropolitan freezer-ships, able to operate for as long as 45 days at sea away from their land base at Moçâmedes; these vessels belong to a newly formed Sociedade de Armadores de Angola. Combined Portuguese–Japanese interests planned the financing of two factory-ships. A South African–Angolan investment company was also planned for exporting shellfish from Luanda by air. Renewal and modernization of the fishing fleet and industrial equipment continue. As a result, the rudimentary open-air curing of dried fish, the second-ranking fishery product of Angola, is being increasingly replaced by mechanical drying.

In 1967, the total catch of live fish was estimated at 289,600 tons, worth $7 million, over two-thirds of the fish being caught in the southern region. Probably 3,000 tons were consumed as fresh fish within the province. The output of over 345 provincial fish-processing plants was 40,400 tons of fishmeal, 4,800 tons of fish oil, 3,100 tons of canned fish, and 40,700 tons of dried fish, with a total estimated value of $16 million. Export value of fish products for the same year fell to $9.8 million from $14 million in 1966, owing to a glut in fishmeal on the world market. Practically all fishmeal and oil are exported to various European countries; one-third of the dried fish is retained in Angola, and the rest is sent to Mozambique and, notwithstanding political friction, to the Congo (Kinshasa). The United States buys one-half of all canned fish.

Mozambique

Though the Mozambican coast is longer than Angola's, the fishing potential remained largely unexplored through the postwar decades. Only shrimp and other shellfish from the bay of Lourenço Marques were caught to meet the demand of the hotel and restaurant industry of the capital city. Local fisheries were inadequate for market supply of fresh softfish, which was customarily imported from South Africa, while the beloved dry cod (*bacalháu*) and sardines were shipped in from Portugal and dried fish for the Africans came from Angola. At present, a main goal is to render the province independent from at least South Africa.

Two important new developments are the intensive fish surveys made all along the Indian Ocean shore by the Indústria de Peixe Nossa Senhora de Fátima (Inos) and the formation of the Sociedade de Armadores de Pesca em Moçambique (Sapem), using metropolitan Portuguese capital. Inos is principally backed by the Anglo-American Corporation of South Africa. Plants to prepare frozen-fish products are under construction in Quelimane, Porto Amélia, and Lourenço Marques, where a fishmeal factory is also being planned. Shrimp, crab, and other shellfish like spiny lobster should be in the forefront of future exports. Meanwhile, in 1967, total live catch was only 5,000 tons of softfish and 1,400 tons of crustaceans and mollusks; exports of about 1,300 tons of sea products, worth about $1 million, included shipments of coral and decorative seashells, a speciality of Moçambique Island.[52]

Freshwater-fishing in the two provinces by Africans living near the larger streams remains at a subsistence level—little of the freshwater catch is marketed outside the immediate areas. On the other hand, freshwater fish-farming in water reservoirs and artificially created ponds has had quite interesting results in Mozambique on several large tea and sisal plantations, located in the northern interior. Their success with *Tilapia* has encouraged the Mozambique Department of Agriculture to start a stocking-and-breeding campaign among African farmers in other interior regions. A similar move is discussed in Angola.

Cape Verde Islands

The islands are favorably located in regard to the cool Canary current, which supports, in the south, the developing fisheries of Senegal and Mauritania and, in the north, regular fishing by Spaniards. Only in recent years, however, did the traditional Cape Verdian subsistence fishing begin to assume commercial importance, with some modernization of equipment and cooling facilities. In 1967, the total catch by some 3,000 fishermen was 5,900 tons, valued at $509,500.[53] Fish exports currently represent 22 to 25 per cent of the yearly export trade of Cape Verde.

Noteworthy is the seeming wealth in tuna in deep-sea waters at some distance from the islands. In coastal fisheries, horse mackerel dominates, and there is an abundance of spiny lobster. Several processing plants financed with metropolitan capital are now operating on São Vicente, Brava, and some of the islets.

Further expansion of provincial fisheries, to augment the meager agricultural resources, has been the object of much study by the Portuguese Government. As much as $8.5 million was allocated specifically to fisheries development during the *Plano Intercalar* (1965–67). An agreement for the provision of technical assistance was also reported to have been signed between Lisbon and West Germany in 1966, relating specifically to a strong fishing-base in Cape Verde.

NOTES

1. Banco de Angola, "Estimativas Provisórias do Rendimento Provincial de Angola," *Boletim Trimestral*, No. 37 (January–March, 1967), p. 4. The secondary sector consisted of mining, manufacturing, construction, and energy production. The tertiary sector encompassed transports, trade, and finances (28 per cent), services (36 per cent), and administration and defense (9 per cent).

2. Eduardo Cruz de Carvalho, "Esboço da zonagem agrícola de Angola," *Fomento* (Lisbon), I, No. 3 (1963), 67–72, also containing a map at a scale of 1:4,000,000.

3. Banco de Angola, *Relatório e contas—exercício de 1967* (Lisbon, 1968), pp. 146–47. From this report are also derived the rest of 1967 data as to specific crops, livestock, fisheries, and timber given in this chapter.

4. *Ibid.*, p. 31.

5. *Coffea robusta* is the principal type of coffee grown in Africa. It is grown at lower altitudes and has properties different from the main Latin American species, *Coffea arabica*. On coffee in Angola, see Irene S. van Dongen, "Coffee Regions, Coffee Trade, and Coffee Ports in Angola," *Economic Geography*, XXXVII, No. 4 (October, 1961), 320–46. Useful details on northern coffee *fazendas* are also in Richard J. Houk, "Recent Developments in the Portuguese Congo," *Geographical Review*, XLVIII, No. 2 (April, 1958), 201–21.

6. *A economia do sisal* (Lisbon, 1965), pp. 32–34. See also O. J. A. de Menezes, *Cultura e beneficiamento do sisal em Angola* (Luanda, 1963).

7. Banco de Angola, *Relatório . . . 1967*, p. 40.

8. Angola's maize production is substantially covered in Marvin P. Miracle, *Maize in Tropical Africa* (Madison, 1966), pp. 185–93. Earlier fine sources of information on Angolan staples are J. de Barros Rodrigues Queiróz, "Generalidades sôbre a agricultura em Angola," *Mensário Administrativo* (Luanda), Nos. 65–66 (January–February, 1953), pp. 51–59; Nos. 69–70 (May–June, 1953), pp. 75–90; Nos. 73–74 (September–October, 1953), pp. 5–23; Nos. 83–84 (July–August, 1954), pp. 41–56; Nos. 91–92 (March–April, 1955), pp. 30–44, and Genaro F. Correia Mendes Vidigal, *O milho na economia da província de Angola* (Lisbon, 1953–54).

9. Banco de Angola, Economic Studies Department, *Economic and Financial Survey of Angola, 1960–65* (Lisbon, 1966), pp. 12–13.

10. *Jornal Português de Economia e Finanças*, December 15, 1966, p. 45.

11. Banco de Angola, *Relatório . . . 1967*, pp. 162–63.

12. Portugal, Província de Angola, Repartição de Estatística Geral, *Anuário estatístico* (1963), p. 93.

13. Banco de Angola, *Relatório . . . 1967*, pp. 47 and 162–63.

14. V. A. Canhoto Vidal, J. E. Mendes Ferrão, and J. J. Lopes Xabregas have extensively covered the oil palm in Angola in Vol. I of *Oleaginosas do ultramar português* (Lisbon, 1960).

15. William O. Jones in his *Manioc in Africa* (Stanford, 1959), pp. 126–33 and 155–58, and Bruce O. Johnston in *The Staple Food Economies of Western Tropical Africa* (Stanford, 1958), pp. 84–87, have attempted to give a picture of manioc in Angola, under the auspices of the Food Research Institute.

16. Useful information on some of these crops is in J. E. M. Ferrão, "Angola e o mercado metropolitano do tabaco," *Gazeta agrícola de Angola*, II, No. 2 (1965), 18–21; Banco de Angola, "A cultura do tabaco em Angola," *Boletim*

Trimestral, No. 38 (April–June, 1967), pp. 1–12; Júlio de Castro Lopo, "O amendoím na economia de Angola" and "Para a história do rícino de Angola," *Actividade económica de Angola*, No. 64 (September–December, 1962), pp. 5–13, and No. 66 (May–August, 1963), pp. 23–39.

17. Banco de Angola, *Relatório e contas—exercício de 1965*, pp. 48–49. Yet Kenya and Tanganyika somehow managed, after many initially unsuccessful experiments, to build a relatively prosperous wheat-production at the time of British administration, and Angola may study their methods.

18. Banco de Angola, *Relatório . . . 1967*, p. 62.

19. Based on figures from U.N., *Statistical Yearbook, 1965* (New York, 1966), pp. 125–32.

20. Alvin W. Urquhart, *Patterns of Settlement and Subsistence in Southwestern Angola* (Washington, D.C., 1963), p. 114. The memoir is a valuable source of information on the pastoral activities of some southern tribes.

21. Excellent recent Portuguese works on the livestock resources of Angola are by J. Lima Pereira, "Fomento da bovinicultura em Angola," *Fomento*, IV, No. 4 (Lisbon, 1966), 339–44, and V, No. 1 (1967), 29–42, as well as his earlier *Introdução ao estudo técnico-económico da criação de gado bovino em Angola* (Lisbon, 1962), p. 155. Eduardo Ferreira Soares de Albergaria, *Produtos animais de Angola* (Lisbon, 1963); J. B. Vieira da Silva, *Notas sôbre a criação de gado bovino em Angola* (Lisbon, 1960). Comprehensive individual studies on various Angolan livestock problems were also published in: Angola, *Pecuária* (*Anais dos Serviços de Veterinária*) (1958–59, 1960–61), while Armando Salbany was the first to define the pasture zones in "Reconhecimento geral preliminar dos tipos de pastos em Angola," *Agronomia Angolana*, No. 10 (1956), pp. 39–55.

22. Jacinto Ferreira, "Panorama pecuário das províncias de Angola e Moçambique," Banco Nacional Ultramarino, *Boletim Trimestral*, No. 55 (September, 1963), p. 12.

23. It would have 250,000 acres of land and 15,000 cattle. Other large ranches are of the CAOP on 75,000 acres, with 3,000 cattle raised mainly for meat supply to "Diamang," and of União Comercial de Automóveis on 750,000 acres with some 18,000 head.

24. In 1967, some 86,600 cattle, 181,800 hogs, and 62,700 goats were slaughtered for internal consumption. Total dairy production was 11.4 million liters of milk, 351 tons of butter, and 417 tons of cheese. Banco de Angola, *Relatório . . . 1967* (Lisbon, 1968), pp. 66–67.

25. Overseas Companies of Portugal, *Reports on Portuguese Africa*, No. 3, Economic Development (Lisbon, 1964), pp. 11–12, and Alberto Diogo, *Rumo à industrialização de Angola* (Luanda, 1963), pp. 110–11.

26. J. F. Rosário Nunes and G. C. Tordo, "Características especiais da abelha angolana," in *Prospecções e ensaios experimentais apícolas em Angola* (Lisbon, 1960), pp. 85–90.

27. Manuel Pimentel dos Santos, "Situação económica de Angola e Moçambique," *Fomento* (Lisbon), V, No. 2 (1967), 85; and José Júlio Cravo Silva, "Recursos económicos do ultramar português," *Boletim da Associação Industrial de Angola*, No. 66 (November, 1965–January, 1966), p. 10.

28. See Portugal, Província de Moçambique. Direcção Provincial dos Serviços de Estatística Geral, *Anuário estatístico, 1964* (Lourenço Marques, 1966), pp. 233–34 and 238, for most of the figures. See also Anibal Ferreira, "Panorama

económico agrário de Moçambique," *Fomento* (Lisbon), V, No. 3 (1967), 191.

29. Anibal Ferreira, *ibid.*, pp. 179 and 182.

30. The latest being Portugal, Província de Moçambique, Direcção Provincial dos Serviços de Estatística Geral, *Estatística agrícola, 1962* (Lourenço Marques, 1966).

31. Portugal, Ministério do Ultramar, Missão de Inquérito Agrícola de Moçambique, and Governo Geral de Moçambique, Direcção Geral de Economia, *Recenseamento agrícola de Moçambique* (Lourenço Marques, 1961–64), Vols. I–VIII.

32. Portugal, Província de Moçambique, Direcção Provincial dos Serviços de Estatística, *Boletim Mensal*, IX, No. 4 (April, 1968), 48–49. This release is also the source of trade data on the individual crops for 1966.

33. Banco Nacional Ultramarino *Boletim Trimestral*, Nos. 66–67 (2nd and 3rd quarters, 1966), pp. 32 and 38, and No. 69 (1st quarter, 1967), pp. 46–47.

34. A concise story of cotton-growing in Mozambique is in C. F. Spence, *Moçambique—East African Province of Portugal* (Cape Town, 1963), pp. 78–81. From this valuable source is also derived much information on other crops of Mozambique. A more exhaustive and precise study on cotton is by Nelson Saraiva Bravo, *A cultura algodoeira no norte de Moçambique* (Lisbon, 1963), esp. pp. 63–250.

35. Banco Nacional Ultramarino, *Boletim Trimestral*, Nos. 66–67 (2nd and 3rd quarters, 1966), p. 34.

36. U.S. Department of Agriculture, *Foreign Agriculture Circular*, Sugar FS2–67 (July, 1967), and Banco Nacional Ultramarino, *Boletim Trimestral*, No. 69 (1st quarter, 1967), p. 38.

37. U.S. Department of Agriculture, *Foreign Agriculture Circular*, Tropical Products, FTEA 2–66 (June, 1966).

38. *Estatística agrícola, 1962*, p. 70.

39. Santos, "Situação económica de Angola e Moçambique," *op. cit.*, p. 90.

40. Information on livestock raising in Mozambique is largely from Ferreira, "Panorama pecuário das províncias de Angola e Moçambique," *op. cit.*, pp. 21–33, various issues of Banco Nacional Ultramarino, *Boletim Trimestral*, and dispatches of the U.S. Agricultural Attaché in Salisbury, Rhodesia, to the Department of Agriculture, Washington, D.C., through 1966–67.

41. This section on agriculture in Portuguese Guinea is essentially based on the valuable work of A. Teixeira da Mota, *Guiné Portuguesa* (Lisbon, 1954), particularly II, 145–68 and 175–92, A. J. da Silva Teixeira, *Os solos da Guiné Portuguesa* (Lisbon, 1962), pp. 277–81 and 333–46, Carlos Bento Correia, *O amendoím na Guiné Portuguesa* (Lisbon, 1965), and information in Banco Nacional Ultramarino, *Boletim Trimestral*, No. 69 (1st quarter, 1967).

42. An outstanding source on São Tomé agriculture is Francisco Tenreiro, *A ilha de São Tomé* (Lisbon, 1961), particularly pp. 169–76 and 215–40. On Príncipe, see Raquel Soeiro de Brito, "A ilha do Príncipe," *Geographica* (Lisbon), No. 10 (April, 1967), pp. 2–18. The 1966 statistics are from Banco Nacional Ultramarino, *Boletim Trimestral*. See also Helder Lains e Silva, "Esboço da carta de aptidão agrícola de São Tomé e Príncipe," *Garcia de Orta* (Lisbon), VI (1957), 61–86.

43. The question of labor importations to São Tomé has several times in the century led to much discomfort to Portugal in international circles. In the years 1907–10, a boycott was declared on cacao from São Tomé by British

and American chocolate manufacturers because of working conditions in the islands as described in a field report; another effort to discredit the Portuguese through accusations of forced plantation labor was made in the early 1930's.

44. Banco Nacional Ultramarino, *Boletim Trimestral*, No. 73 (1968), p. 58.

45. Main sources on Cape Verde agriculture are Ilídio do Amaral, *Santiago de Cabo Verde—a terra e os homens* (Lisbon, 1964), particularly pp. 257–91, and António José da Silva Teixeira and Luís Augusto Granvaux Barbosa, *Agricultura do arquipélago de Cabo Verde—cartas agrícolas, problemas agrários* (Lisbon, 1958).

46. Vidigal, *op. cit.*, p. 16.

47. Data on the *colonatos* of Cela and Cunene were collected by the author when visiting them in the late 1950's. A detailed description of Cela is in George Kimble, *Tropical Africa*, Vol. I, *Land and Livelihood* (Garden City, 1962), pp. 180–85. In the mid-1960's, Cela had 226 families living in the older hamlets and 193 families being installed in 7 new hamlets, some of the residents being *mestiços*. Two African *colonatos* also functioned nearby. (See Angola, Junta Provincial de Povoamento, *Relatório das actividades 1964* (Luanda, 1965), pp. 44–50.)

48. An annotated bibliography on various schemes in Portuguese Africa is in U.S. Library of Congress, General Reference and Bibliography Division, *Agricultural Development Schemes in Sub-Saharan Africa—A Bibliography* (Washington, D.C., 1963), pp. 155–67.

49. António Trigo de Morais, "O colonato do Limpopo," *Estudos Políticos e Sociais* (Lisbon), No. 2 (1964), pp. 479–80. For further information on Mozambique agricultural schemes, see Spence, *op. cit.*, pp. 103–10, and R. J. Harrison Church, "The Limpopo Scheme," *Geographical Magazine* (London), July, 1964, pp. 212–27.

50. On forestry in the Cabinda Enclave, see Irene S. van Dongen, "La vie économique et les ports de l'enclave de Cabinda (Angola)," *Cahiers d'Outre-Mer* (Bordeaux), XV (1962), 5–24; an English version of the article was released by the Division of Economic Geography, Columbia University, as a technical report. See also Rui F. Romero Monteiro, "Panorama forestier de l'Angola" and "Le massif forestier du Mayumbe angolais," both in *Bois et Forêts des Tropiques*, No. 75 (1961), pp. 3–16, and No. 82 (1962), pp. 3–18, and his earlier "Aspectos da exploração florestal no distrito do Moxico," *Garcia de Orta* (Lisbon), V, No. 1 (1957), 129–46. Information on Mozambique and Guinea forests is from various releases of Banco Nacional Ultramarino.

51. Angolan fishing regions are described by Irene S. van Dongen in "Sea Fisheries and Fish Ports of Angola," *Boletim da Sociedade de Geografia de Lisboa*, January–July, 1962, 3–30. Data on subsequent catches are from Banco de Angola, *Boletim Trimestral*, No. 37 (January–March, 1967), 24. Provincial fisheries are also covered by Walter Marques in *Problemas do desenvolvimento económico de Angola* (Luanda, 1964), pp. 395–426.

52. Portugal, Província de Moçambique, Direcção Provincial dos Serviços de Estatística, *Boletim Mensal*, April, 1968, pp. 28 and 48.

53. Banco Nacional Ultramarino, *Boletim Trimestral*, Nos. 77–78 (1969), p. 51.

XIII

Minerals, Manufacturing, Power, and Communications

DAVID M. ABSHIRE

ANGOLA

Agriculture has long been the major source of Angolan wealth and has generally accounted for 63 to 69 per cent of the value of exports. Full mineral exploitation has lagged, owing partly to inadequate transportation facilities. Until the new policies of the 1960's, the Lisbon government deterred the establishment of Angolan industries, such as textiles, that would compete with those in the metropole. The result has been an economy precariously built on a postwar boom in the coffee trade.

The government attitude has changed, however, and developments are now at work to establish a more balanced economic foundation. These developments include production and transport of minerals, especially iron ore and petroleum, and emerging industrial activities. More impressive as a springboard for future agricultural and industrial expansion are new hydroelectric projects, which have now given Angola the muscle to move into a more advanced stage of development; the projects stand out, even in a continent that abounds in great rivers. This chapter will describe the background of these economic activities, identify some of their sources of invested capital, and outline new major projects.[1]

Mining

In the latter part of the nineteenth century, the search for minerals in Africa began in earnest, and, early in the twentieth century, several important finds were made. Today, mineral production in Angola includes iron ore, manganese, oil, diamonds, asphalt rock, and marine salt.

Diamonds. The most significant mineral has been diamonds, first found in November, 1912, by two prospectors in a creek of the Chiumbe River in Lunda District. This led to the founding of first the Companhia de Pesquisas Mineiras de Angola and then the Companhia de Diamantes de Angola (Diamang), in October, 1917. In the meantime, the first workings in the territory had begun in 1913. The concession granted by the government to Diamang covers much of the northeastern quarter of Angola. Headquarters of the diamond industry are at Dundo. The company has built a large hydroelectric plant of 12,000-kilowatt capacity

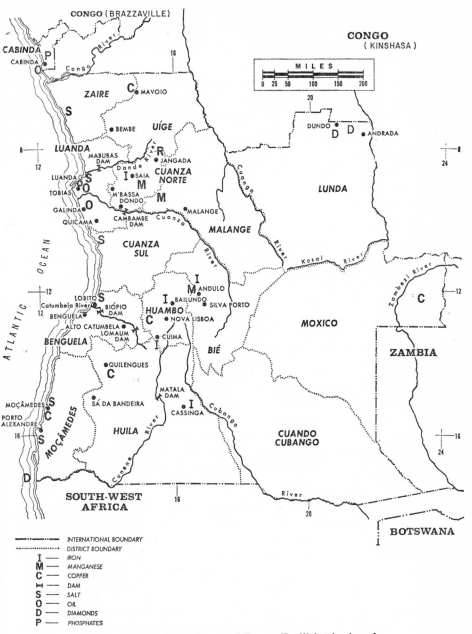

Major Mining Operations and Power Facilities in Angola
Adapted from U.S. Government, *Area Handbook for Angola*
(Washington, 1967) p. 301

295

on the Luachimo River and an extensive network of roads, and it operates an elaborate social welfare program for almost 30,000 workers, mostly Africans.

Diamonds have been found also in the offshore sediments deposited by the Cunene River. Such offshore deposits are exploited in South-West Africa, and several Portuguese business interests have been contemplating doing the same. In July, 1968, the Portuguese Government awarded an eighty-year concession to an American firm, Diversa, Inc., for prospecting for diamonds and oil between Lobito and Moçâmedes. A previous diamond concession, granted to João António Veiga, covers most of the Angolan coast from Ambriz to the South-West African border.

Angola's principal diamond fields, bordering Congo (Kinshasa), are a continuation of the noted diamond-yielding formations of the Kasai region of that country. The major mining sites are in the *concelho* of Chitato in Lunda District and in the basin of the Cuango River. The Liumba and Chiumbe rivers, the location of the diamond-placers, are important tributaries of the Cassai River. The gently undulating area is covered by a thick geological formation known as the Kalahari system, largely in sands. These alluvial diamond deposits are similar to those in South-West Africa (from which the term "Kalahari sands" is taken), but they are different from those of South Africa found in the so-called kimberlite pipes at Kimberley.[2]

Since 1920, Angola has produced diamonds in commercial quantity, and, until 1940, this production was one of the financial mainstays of Angola. During the past decade, over 1 million carats have been mined annually. This amounts to about 4 per cent of world production and ranges between 12 and 15 per cent of Angola's total value of exports. Diamang produced 1,288,500 carats in 1967, worth about $41.5 million, and 1,667,000 carats in 1968, worth about $58.8 million. About three-fourths of the production is gem stones and about one-fourth is of industrial quality.[3]

The present exploration contract of Diamang expires in 1971, ending its exclusive concession for prospecting in northeastern Angola by that time. However, the company should be able to establish definite mining claims on an area of some 50,000 square kilometers that has already been thoroughly prospected and mapped. The remainder of the former concession will then be released to independent prospectors.

Diamang, the oldest mining company in Portuguese Africa, provides an example of international ownership. Major shareholders include the Portuguese Government, British and Belgian firms (Société Générale and Forminiere), and an individual American, A. A. Ryan. The Angolan Government directly benefits from Diamang activities through a 50 per cent participation in company profits as well as dividends on its shares in the company. It also benefirs from increased foreign-exchange holdings, as Diamang has to contribute 25 per cent of its foreign-exchange earnings to the Angola Exchange Fund. Furthermore, on several occasions Diamang has advanced loans worth several million dollars to the Angola administration for development projects.[4]

Part of the diamonds produced in Angola are now sent to the Portuguese diamond-cutting company Sociedade Portuguêsa de Lapidação de Diamantes, a subsidiary of Diamang in Lisbon. Though other diamond shipments go directly to the United Kingdom for cutting, an increasing amount of diamond-cutting is now done in Portugal.[5] It must be kept in mind that almost the entire world output of diamonds is controlled by De Beers Consolidated Mines Ltd., a subsidiary of Anglo-American Corporation of South Africa. Except for the South American and Russian output, De Beers has contracts for the purchase of the world's output, including that of Diamang, and De Beers handles the marketing. Harry Oppenheimer, chairman of Anglo-American Corporation, is a board member of Diamang. The cartel allots quotas to producers, regulates prices, and controls the amount released for sale.

Petroleum. Although bituminous shales were mined in Angola prior to World War II, early drillings for oil by a Portuguese company and the American Sinclair Consolidated were unsuccessful.[6] The Companhia de Combustíveis do Lobito, financed by Belgian capital, was established in 1927 as a joint stock company to act as a distributor of oil products, household gas, and coal in Angola. By 1952, the company had been granted exclusive rights to explore for oil in the Congo and Cuanza river basins, the exploring activities being financed and carried out by Petrofina of Brussels, the largest industrial enterprise in Belgium. After three years of deep drilling in the Luanda area, petroleum was struck in 1955, in Benfica, near Luanda. The following year, the first tanker left Luanda with crude petroleum for processing in Portugal.

In 1957, with government approval, the Companhia de Combustíveis do Lobito formed another company, Companhia Concessionária de Petróleos de Angola (Petrangol), to which all rights were transferred. The Companhía de Combustíveis do Lobito holds about 12 per cent of the capital of the new company, the remaining major shareholders being the province of Angola (33.33 per cent) and Petrofina. With an initial capital of over $31 million, Petrangol constructed a $65-million refinery near Luanda, with a capacity of 650,000 tons per year. It is planned to raise the capacity to 1 million tons a year.

The production and refining of local crude and the distribution of imported petroleum products are now even more important than diamond-mining as an economic activity in Angola. Ranking second in importance after coffee, the gross product of petroleum, including retail sales and exports, has been rising steadily and has reached over $40 million annually.[7] A large increase in 1964 was a result of Petrangol's discovery of the major Tobias deposit, the largest existing onshore field, with reserves of 200–300 million barrels. The increase continued until 1967, when production was down somewhat, forcing Angola to import oil for the first time in many years.[8] Exports of crude oil outside the Portuguese areas were thus terminated temporarily.

At present, Petrangol has a production of 15,000 barrels daily, from seven deposits. As crude arrives from the producing fields by a pipeline 68 miles long, it is refined in Luanda and consumed locally as fuel oil, gas, gasoline, and kerosene. Formerly, some 9,000 tons of petroleum products were also exported annually to Congo (Kinshasa), and 200,000 tons of fuel oil and some Angolan crude, to be processed in the Sacor refinery near Lisbon, went to metropolitan Portugal. A second refinery, with a capacity of 500,000 tons a year, will be built by the Portuguese company Angol in Lobito by 1971. Within Angola, the distribution of petroleum is in the hands of five companies, two of them, Mobil Oil and Texaco, being U.S. companies, one Portuguese, Angol, and the others Shell and Combustíveis do Lobito. Aviation gas and lubricants for Angolan needs continue to be imported.[9]

Well to the north, extensive oil exploration has been conducted by another petroleum concern, the Cabinda Gulf Oil Company, a subsidiary of Gulf Oil Corporation in the United States. In the 1950's, Cabinda Gulf—noting that the French had discovered petroleum at Cape Lopes in Gabon and near Pointe Noire in the former French territory of Congo—undertook a seismographic survey of the whole Cabinda Enclave, but without great success. In July, 1966, it began offshore drilling and soon struck oil on the continental shelf about 15 miles from the town of Cabinda. In December, 1966, an agreement with the Portuguese Government renewed and extended the earlier exploration concession, covering most of the land area and continental shelf in the district of Cabinda. Further offshore and land discoveries have since been made in what appears to be a major oil field.

Cabinda Gulf invested over $125 million in the development of their discoveries in 1968 including a petroleum port, a storage park, and new telecommunications facilities. Cabinda oil first entered world markets late in 1968. The published production goal is 150,000 barrels a day, twice the amount of Portuguese oil needs, which would thus free the metropole from dependence upon the Middle East.[10] Although company releases have estimated the offshore reserves to be at least 300 million tons of crude, there are indications that much larger reserves actually exist. Actual production by 1970 may be double the published estimates. The Cabinda operation is already proving a major boost to the Angolan economy—from an area of Angola previously dependent economically on timber—in terms not only of petroleum exports but also of construction, communications facilities, and foreign employees. The Angolan provincial government will receive a surface rent and 12.5 per cent of the sales value of the extractions as royalties.

To the south, Portuguese interests have been hard at work conducting seismic soundings on the continental shelf to the north and south of the Cuanza River basin and in the sedimentary basin of the Congo River. A January, 1966, government contract stipulated that Petrangol join with Angol, previously only a distributor in which Sacor and Sonap held large interests. Required to increase its capital rapidly, Angol has formed partnerships with the French Compagnie Française des Pétroles (CFP), Texaco, and a consortiam of South African companies, to increase the area under exploration with emphasis on the Ambriz area and the eastern Cuanza basin. On shore, two more important deposits were discovered, one on the Catete road and the other in the Pinda region near Santo António do Zaire. These successes, added to those of Gulf Cabinda, have created great optimism over the importance of oil to the economic future of Angola.[11]

Iron. Another bright spot for Angola's future is in iron-ore production. The first production in Angola began in 1956 on the central plateau. In the mid-1960's,

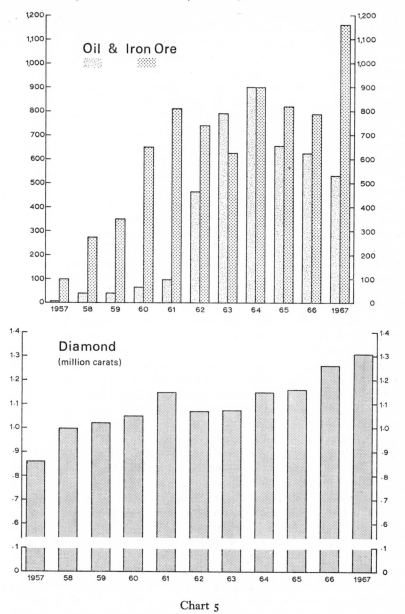

Chart 5

Production of Some Angolan Extracting Industries (in Millions of Tons), 1957–67

Source: Banco de Angola, *Relatório e contas—exercício de 1966* (Lisbon, 1967), p. 152, and *ibid.*, *1967* (Lisbon, 1968), p. 80.

production was 700,000–800,000 tons annually, from mines at Saia, near Malange, from Cuíma, Teixeira da Silva, and Andulo in the central zone, and from Cassinga in the south, which has been called a veritable mountain of ore. The most extensive reserves belong to the Companhía Mineira do Lobito (Lobito Mining Company) and its subsidiary, Sociedade Mineira de Lombige, which owns the Cassinga mines. Proven reserves at Cassinga exceed 1,000 million tons of high-grade hematite (43 to 63 per cent Fe) ore. Of the four types of iron ore in the world, hematite is by far the most important, because such deposits tend to be more extensive and easier to reduce. While the theoretical percentage of metallic iron in hematite ore is 70, it seldom occurs, and any percentage over 60 is classified as quite high grade ore. In Angola, unestimated but extensive deposits of medium-grade ore, banded hematite-quartzite, extend beyond the high-grade reserves.

Financing of about $100 million for the Cassinga development was completed in June, 1965, between the Portuguese Government, Lobito Mining Company, and the Krupp group of Essen, Germany, which coordinated the financing by German, Danish, Austrian, and U.S. banks. Operations of the Cuíma mines were terminated in 1967, owing to diminished reserves, but the closing was more than offset by the 560,000 tons produced at Cassinga.

Transportation of iron ore from Cassinga is provided by the Moçâmedes rail line, which had a link extended 55 miles to the mine in 1967. This spur to Cassinga was financed as the major portion of the Krupp loan to Lobito Mining. A bulk ore-handling port of 2.5-million-ton capacity has also been built north of Moçâmedes. These developments enabled iron-ore exports to Japan and, mainly, to West Germany, during the first half of 1968, to reach 1,105,000 tons, about the same as total exports for the whole of 1967. Annual exports of 7 million tons are envisioned.[12] With Cassinga and new deposits in the Cassala-Quitungo area of northern Angola, the value of iron ore will represent an increasing share of production of the territory. This promising situation is apparent to the Portuguese Government, which, in 1968, assumed the total interests of the financially overextended Sousa Machado family, founders of the Lobito Mining Company. Anxious to expand operations, the government intended to seek new capital, apparently from foreign sources.

Other Minerals. Several other minerals have been produced in Angola in smaller amounts at one time or another. There is now a renewed interest in copper-mining. The Mavoio copper deposits in northern Angola, belonging to Emprêsa de Cobre, were exhausted in 1962, but several concessions for prospecting and production are still operative. Emprêsa is now involved in a joint venture with the Japanese Nippon Mining Company, which is to invest $25 million in the exploitation of copper mines in northern Angola.[13] This will be an extension of the Mavoio vein, the Tetelo deposits, which contain low-grade but commercially exploitable ore. The Emprêsas Mineiras de Angola (Angolan Mining Company) holds a concession on some copper in the east-central panhandle. The Companhia Mineira do Lobito has a possibly rich copper deposit in Moçâmedes District, and it has begun a survey with the assistance of Krupp of Germany and Hojgaard Schultz of Denmark. By 1967, Anglo-American Corporation had begun to consider a major investment in Angolan copper, a development no doubt motivated by the rising costs of copper-mining in Zambia.

Gold has historically been washed in small quantities in some Angolan rivers, but gold production has lately become insignificant. In 1969, however, renewed production, in the Cassinga area, was planned, and rumors of veins near Malange were expanding.

Several types of manganese ores have been mined, since 1943, by Companhia do Manganês de Angola, largely along the Luanda rail line, and 33,000 tons were produced in 1967. There are some large manganese deposits in Cabinda Enclave now being studied for possible exploitation.

Production of mica, previously bought by the United States, came to a halt with the beginning of insurgency in the north. The most important mines are located in areas where regular access is still precarious. So far, foreign buyers have shown slight interest in the small production of scrap mica in the southern part of the territory. Some 50,000 tons of rock asphalt has been produced annually for the local market.[14]

Phosphate reserves in Cabinda Enclave and the coastal belt north of Ambrizete are officially estimated at 27 million tons. Four companies have applied for concessions to develop these deposits: Fosfangol, Cabinda Gulf, Coframet, and Companhia Mineira do Lobito. But the problems of shipping the phosphates overseas are great, due to the difficulty of constructing deep-water port installations on the northern coast. Angola's considerable limestone deposits are vital to cement production in Luanda and Lobito. Newly discovered sulfur deposits in southern Angola also seem promising. Small deposits of an excellent quality of marble in Moçâmedes District and other deposits, expedially around Gabela, are said to be commercially exploitable.

Marine salt extraction, which has averaged 66,000 tons per year, reached 77,000 tons in 1967, and it has long been an important activity in the province in many places along the coast, both for export to neighboring African countries and for processing in Angola's fishing industry. Areas around Ambrizete, Ambriz, Luanda, Lobito, Moçâmedes, and Porto Alexandre contribute to the bulk of the salt produced, of which 20,000–30,000 tons are exported.[15]

Power

The generation of electricity for industry and improved urban living and the provision of water supply for agricultural projects are common fruits of hydro-electric development in Africa. Africa has greater water-power potential than any other continent, and yet it has developed less than 1 per cent of the total hydroelectric power of the world. Until recently, it has been uneconomical to develop large hydroelectric projects there.

Although the Portuguese have displayed a traditional weakness in industrial organization as well as apathy toward foreign investment, strength in civil engineering is reflected in several projects that have been completed or planned in Angola and Mozambique. If the amount of power generated per head of total population is a measure of the actual or potential productivity of a country, Angola and Mozambique offer a favorable picture for less developed areas of the world. The power industry has been steadily developing in Angola, reaching, in 1967, a total production of 391 million kilowatt hours. Between 1958 and 1967, the average annual rate for electrical power expansion was 14.5 per cent. Electrification of thirteen towns was completed by 1966.

About half of all Angolan power is produced by the Sociedade Nacional de Estudo e Financiamento de Empreendimentos Ultramarinos (SONEFE). SONEFE is an autonomous state entity, not an ordinary private firm, which also has the franchise for Mozambique and other overseas provinces.

The five most important hydroelectric plants are at Cambambe, Mabubas, Lomaum, Biópio, and Matala.

1. Cambambe, the largest recently completed hydroelectric project in Africa after Kariba, is located on the Cuanza River near Dondo, about 120 miles southeast of Luanda. The specific location, near the ruins of the seventeenth-century *presídio*, is just downstream of the Cambambe rapids at the end of the navigable section of the lower Cuanza. This location should eventually provide for some irrigation developments in the lower basins of the Cuanza and Bengo rivers; it was chosen with the idea also of attracting aluminum smelting—an idea delayed by red tape until late in 1968.[16]

The first phase of the installation under control of SONEFE was started in 1959 and completed in December, 1962. The power plant has a capacity of 90,000 kilowatts, its major consumer being the city of Luanda and its industrial plants. A second stage is projected that will eventually increase the capacity to 260,000 kilowatts.[17]

2. Mabubas, 47 miles northeast of Luanda on the Dande River, was the first of Angola's important post–World War II hydroelectric plants. Completed in 1954 to provide power to Luanda, its potential of 17,800 kilowatts was soon outstripped by the city's demand. It is now used only as an emergency supplier for the Luanda area, being linked in a high-voltage grid with the Cambambe system. In 1967, it produced only 1.4 million kilowatt hours.

3. Lomaum, on the upper Catumbela River, is privately owned by Hidro-Eléctrica do Alto Catumbela. It has a 20,000-kilowatt plant built originally to furnish power to the paper-pulp mill near by. Since January, 1965, it has also supplied some power to Lobito, Benguela, and Nova Lisboa in a link system with a plant completed in 1957 at Biópio on the lower Catumbela River, inland from Lobito. This is one of the first examples of American financing: $5.4 million of the cost of this dam was paid through a loan from the Inter-American Capital Corporation of New York.

4. Biópio, located on the Catumbela River, inland from Lobito, was constructed in the mid-1950's for the needs of Lobito-Benguela area with a potential of 15,000 kilowatts.

5. The Matala project is located on the middle Cunene River. It dates from 1959, has a capacity of 27,000 kilowatts, and presently supplies power and irrigation for the Cunene agricultural settlement scheme and furnishes power for Sá da Bandeira, Moçâmedes, and Porto Alexandre. From an economic viewpoint, the dam is too small to be profitable—a typical example, common to less developed areas, of the results of inadequate economic feasibility studies. The

power station is excellent, though, and the uneconomical aspect of the project should soon be remedied through a joint Portuguese–South-West African project for a back-up dam that will provide the necessary further storage for Matala. Construction of this new $11.2-million dam at Gove will be financed by South African capital, half in the form of a twenty-year five per cent loan and half from invested capital. In return, Portugal has agreed to furnish South-West Africa with 90 million kilowatt hours per year, at a cost of 0.17 cents per kilowatt hour, and with a perennial supply of water.[18]

The use of Matala is only the beginning of a much larger scheme to harness the Cunene that emerged from agreements in 1965 between the Portuguese and the South-West African Government, represented by the Odendaal Commission and Dr. H. J. van Eck, Chairman of the Industrial Development Corporation. Plans center on a hydroelectric complex with a first dam to be built at Gove on the lower Cunene River and a major power station to be constructed at Ruacaná Falls. The regularization of the Cunene River and the construction of dams on the Angolan side will provide an installed capacity of 300,000 kilowatts and an output of 1,000 million kilowatt hours a year. The dams will have a total capacity of 7,000 million cubic meters, irrigating 375,000 acres by gravity and 875,000 acres through a rural distribution network.[19] Eventually the project would result in a common Angolan–South-West African power grid. One power line would run across the Angolan border into Ovamboland and thence to the Tsumeb mines, where power is urgently needed before the larger and nearer Ruacaná falls project can be constructed. A second power line will eventually link the generating plant at Ruacaná to the Matala-Tsumeb line. For some future date, another power line is planned between Ruacaná falls and Walvis Bay. The South-West Africans have expressed interest in further cooperation toward the construction of a series of power stations on the Cunene.

Made possible by the large market for cheap power in South-West Africa, these schemes should mean much to the economic development of southern Angola. Thousands of acres of land will be irrigated, making them suitable for the development of the cattle-raising industry. As for the South-West African area, it is believed that "the whole of South-West Africa will enter upon a new phase in its economic history once power from the Cunene scheme starts flowing."[20] The scheme has attracted considerable political attention, due to the controversy over South-West Africa and signs of increased economic cooperation between Lisbon and Pretoria.

Processing and Manufacturing

The bulk of industry in Angola is involved in processing local primary production. Until 1945, such processing largely consisted in simply preparing raw materials for export; since then, industrial production has progressed rapidly. Although the largest share of present manufacturing output is absorbed locally, over 12 per cent of Angola's exports are now in either manufactured or semiprocessed items. The upward trend in industrial export is expected to continue, as there has been a 13 per cent annual growth of industrial production since 1962. The value of total annual manufacturing production has reached $134 million.[21]

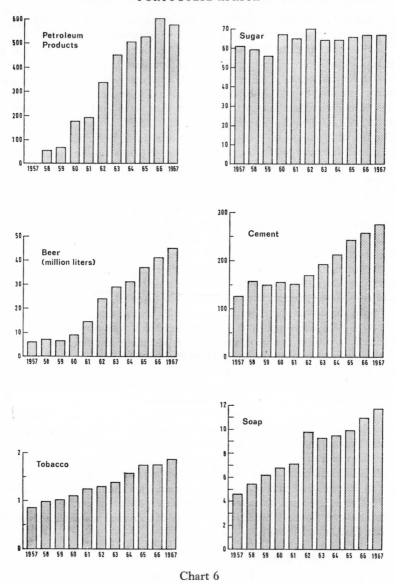

Chart 6

Production of Some Angolan Manufacturing Industries (in Millions of Tons), 1957–67

Source: Banco de Angola, *Relatório e contas—exercício de 1966* (Lisbon, 1967), pp. 82–102, and *ibid., 1967* (Lisbon, 1968), p. 81.

The capital investment in industrial plants amounted to $56 million in 1955 and $122.5 million in 1964. In 1967 alone, $21.8 million of new investments were made, with 62,570 persons employed.

Food-Processing. The most fully developed manufacturing sector is concerned with the preparation of food products for local consumption as well as export. The value of food-processing in 1967 reached almost $40 million, or 29 per cent of total production. Much of this sector has already been discussed in the agriculture chapter, as the processing of most food products must be viewed as connected with their very growth. This is true for such industries as coffee-hulling, sugar-refining, vegetable-oil extraction, meat and dairy production, wheat-processing, fish-product preparation, and rice-polishing. Major growth in recent years has been made in wheat- and rice-processing. Other important food-processing plants include those that produce noodles, chocolate and cocoa, yeasts, and bread.

Beverages and Tobacco. The second largest manufacturing sector is the production of beverages and tobacco, which account for $26.6 million, or 20 per cent of total production. Between 1962 and 1967, the value of beverages increased at an annual rate of 14.7 per cent, tobacco at 10.3 per cent. The oldest brewery, CUCA, is truly an economic power in the province, and its factories at Luanda and near Nova Lisboa are showpieces. In 1967, the value of beer production alone was $13.6 million. Other beverages produced include soft drinks, fermented fruit drinks, brandy, whisky, wine, and mineral waters.

Cigarette-making has flourished, especially with the increase of Portuguese troops in Angola. Of the four cigarette plants in Luanda, three are Portuguese-owned and the fourth is affiliated with the British-American Tobacco Company. The value of 1967 production was $9.2 million.

Textiles. Until 1966, there was only one major producer of cotton textiles, Sociedade Algodoeira de Fomento Colonial, Textang. Expansion of textile-manufacturing suffered for over two decades as a result of a 1944 law that prohibited new cotton mills in order to protect the textile industry of metropolitan Portugal. These earlier restrictions were lifted in 1966, and investment in the industry is expanding. The value of textile products, including spinning, weaving, and finishing of cotton and other fabrics, increased 16 per cent in 1967. This included a large increase in the production of sacking and other products derived from sisal. Another cotton textile mill is being completed at Dondo, near the Cambambe hydroelectric plant.

Other Major Industries. The range of manufacturing products in Angola is wide. To mention all of them is unnecessary in a summary view such as this; some deserve special attention, however. Important among them are cement, tires, paper, aluminum metal, and assembly of vehicles.

Two cement factories, one each in Luanda and Lobito, owned by the Champallimaud group of investors, produced 280,000 tons in 1967. This industry has benefitted from the urban construction boom of recent years. Tire production was long delayed in Angola, but after a five-year wait, Mabor, a Lisbon company (of which the General Tire Company of Akron, Ohio, has a 10 per cent interest), finally received needed protection for operating in Angola. The agreement grants a ten-year monopoly, assuring protection from both Portuguese and foreign competition. The annual production goal is 90,000 tires.

Paper-manufacturing has shown marked growth recently. The Companhia de Celulose do Ultramar Português, at Alto Catumbela, began production at the end of 1961. This is the largest company that produces paper in Angola; it holds an extensive plantation of eucalyptus trees for pulp and manufactures several kinds of paper and paper bags. Another small paper plant, producing cardboard and wrapping paper, is located at Luanda. Pulpwood exports in Angola reached 24,500 tons in 1967, with paper, paper bags, and cardboard coming to 6,700 tons.

Special mention should be made of the planned aluminum industry. Though Angola lacks bauxite, it has an excess of inexpensive electricity. In 1967, the Portuguese Government authorized Alumínio Português, a subsidiary of the French firm Pechiney, to obtain foreign financing to establish the industry. Bauxite will be imported from France, Greece, and Australia. Using the power and water supply of the Cambambe dam, the plant is to produce 25,000 tons of ingots annually, which will be shipped to Portugal for further processing and refining.[22] An electrometallurgical plant to manufacture "Sodeberg" electrodes is also to be established with foreign investment, guaranteed by the Angolan Government.[23] Sites for the new aluminum industry are at Dondo, Cambambe, and Dombe Grande. A steel industry is also planned near Cambambe.

A bus-assembly plant of Cicar, Companhia Industrial de Construções Mecânicas, has begun operations in Lobito,[24] and another assembly plant for automobiles, trucks, and agricultural machinery is being established in Luanda, where bicycles are presently manufactured.

Minor Industries. Among the many smaller industries, several stand out, such as paints and varnish; automobile batteries; brick and glassware; chemical products like industrial alcohol, pesticides, and explosives; plastics and rubber goods; metal drums and hoes; electric cables and conductors.

Construction

The rapid growth of population in the cities has led to a booming building industry, after a depression from 1960 to 1963 that followed a previous boom in the 1950's. In Luanda, the number of buildings completed and the area they occupy continue to set new records. Cabinda Enclave also is expected to show an increasing demand for housing. There, a new prefabricated village will be followed by permanent constructions, and many construction companies are anxious to participate.[25]

Certain urban areas of the province are actually being built up at a much faster rate than others, the highest paces being set in Luanda, Nova Lisboa, Lobito, Benguela, and Sá da Bandeira. In 1967, control of insurgency led to a resurgence of an earlier building boom at Carmona. With the expansion of industry in Luanda and the extension of a large industrial park outside the city, the appearance of Luanda is also being transformed. Radiating from the older commercial core, modern apartments and commercial office buildings are rising, the tallest being the twenty-four-story Banco Comercial de Angola, completed in 1966. This boom in construction has stimulated other industries, and small-scale manufacturing of bricks, tiles, and other construction materials is carried on in many places.

Much Luanda building activity is illegal. City-planning in Angola, especially in Luanda, is falling behind urban increases in population, with the result that substandard housing has developed in *muceques* and many people find it necessary to construct on unzoned land on the city's periphery, without the requisite authorization of the municipal government (see Chapter VII).

There have been two foreign investments of particular significance in heavy construction projects. One involves the General Trade Corporation, organized by French firms headquartered in Geneva. It is supported vigorously by French diplomacy and is especially active in the sale of French equipment. After competition with U.S. interests, General Trade received a $35-million contract from the Portuguese Government for sales and construction projects, including construction of the proposed Quiminha dam and construction and equipping of the ore-loading port at Luanda. The second foreign-financed construction effort of considerable size involves the Inter-American Capital Corporation, already mentioned. This United States company has provided loans for highways and the Catumbela paper plant, in addition to the Lomaum hydroelectric plant. The financing was linked to equipment sales through Evans and Edell, a wholly owned subsidiary.

There is a small steel-rolling mill near Luanda, and a number of engineering firms are engaged in repairs, partial construction or assembly of miscellaneous machinery, building of rolling stock for Angolan railroads, and ship construction. Sociedade Reunida de Fabricações Metálicas, or Sorefame, in Lobito has the most important workshop of the province and has had several contracts to furnish heavy dam equipment as far as Rhodesia and Sudan.

Telecommunications

Telecommunications in Angola are government-operated through an administrative bureau, the Department of Posts, Telegraphs, and Telephones. Commercial communications abroad by telephone and radio are in the hands of the Companhia Portuguêsa Rádio Marconi. Internal long-distance calls are handled through a radio network consisting primarily of a VHF network running along an axis from Carmona through Salazar (with branches to Luanda and Malange), Quibala, Nova Lisboa (with connections to Lobito and Benguela), Matala, and Sá da Bandeira. Automatic telephone systems were under construction, in 1966, in Benguela, Lobito, Catumbela, and Nova Lisboa. A telex ordered from a French company was to be installed in Angola to use the main VHF system.[26]

A central transmitter station at Mulenvos near Luanda is a part of the government's radio-broadcasting plan. There are broadcasting stations at Cabinda, Luanda, Novo Redondo, Lobito, and Moçâmedes, air navigation stations in twenty cities, and government stations for the various armed services and regular police. Private interests also maintain communications networks. The most modern of these is the one recently constructed for Cabinda Gulf by an American firm, Page Communications Engineers, to facilitate interchanges between Cabinda and Luanda. Diamang and the large coffee plantation of CADA additionally cover vast areas with transmitters, which are of tactical importance for the government in combatting possible infiltration. As yet, no television station has been begun.

MOZAMBIQUE

Over 90 per cent of Mozambique's population is engaged in agriculture. Though Mozambique is at present considerably behind Angola in industrialization, other sources of wealth are in the process of development in the province. The spectacular Cabora Bassa Power Scheme alone may produce an economic transformation in Mozambique.

Mineral Resources[27]

As noted in the historical chapters, the mineral wealth of Mozambique was reported to be fabulous, as ancient legends linked King Solomon's riches with Sofala and the land of Ophir. An early survey of the mineral resources of Mozambique was compiled by A. Freire de Andrade and published in Lisbon in 1900. The first field geological survey was carried out in 1911–14 for the Mozambique Company by the Imperial Institute in Great Britain. This was followed by other surveys, either directly by government departments or under contract to the Portuguese Government. The minerals that have been mined at one time or another and either used domestically or exported form a long list, including asbestos, bauxite, beryl, bismutite, coal, columbo-tantalite, diatomite, gold, graphite, ilmenite, kaolin, lepidolite, and mica. Other minerals in Mozambique include silver, chromium, copper, corundum, iron, tin, lead, semiprecious stones, and radioactive minerals. Thus far, the working of minerals has been of only limited significance, but very recent discoveries may change the picture.[28] New deposits of diamonds, asbestos, and manganese have been discovered in Mozambique at Catuane, on the border with South Africa. The companies holding the prospecting rights are Agro-Comercial Lda. and Gabinete Moçambicano de Organizações. The size of the deposits, however, is not yet known.[29] Finally, promising traces of uranium have recently been discovered, suggesting that Mozambique may become a major producer of that mineral.

The mineral of the greatest export value per ton has been columbo-tantalite, used in the manufacture of hard and tough steels; only small quantities of it are needed in the smelting. Although it will never be a large export in volume, the world supply is very short, and it therefore commands a very high price. It is exported to the United States and the United Kingdom.

A deposit of tantalite, regarded as the largest known in the world, was found at Murrua in northern Mozambique. It contains enough reserves to permit working for thirty years.[30] Ilmenite is found in heavy concentrations in the coastal sands north of the mouth of the Zambezi River, the heaviest deposits

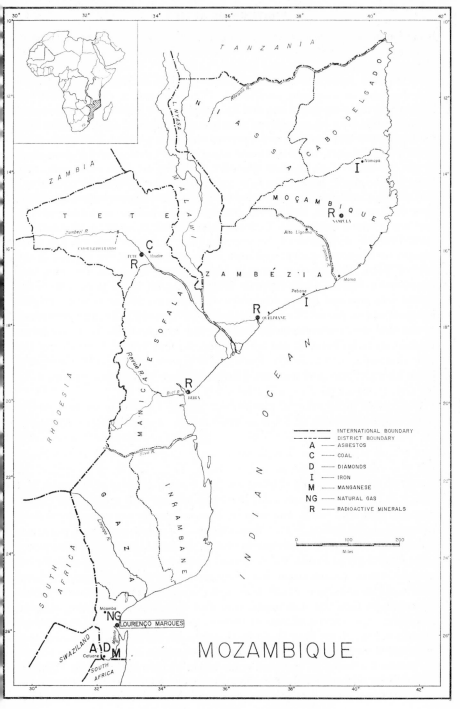

Major Mining Operations in Mozambique

being found on the beaches between Moma and Pebane, where it can be dug up almost pure in apparently unlimited quantities. It is exported to the United Kingdom on a small scale.

An iron-ore deposit comparable to that of Cassinga in Angola was discovered near Namapa, in Moçambique District. It is estimated to contain about 360 million tons of 60–64–grade iron ore. An estimated $50 million is to be invested in exploitation by a Japanese investment group, Sumitomo, under contract with the Portuguese Government, and a private rail line is planned, linking the mine to the port of Nacala, where a mineral wharf will be constructed for ships of up to 100,000 tons.[31] Iron ore has also been found in the Tete region and may become of economic importance with the Cabora Bassa hydroelectric scheme.

Until 1949, coal-mining was carried on in modest scale at Moatize, near Tete, by a Belgian company, the Société Minière et Géologique du Zambeze. The coal was shipped out on the Zambezi River, which is navigable downstream from Tete for six months of the year. In 1949, a railway line was laid from Moatize to Mutarara, providing direct transportation from the pithead to the port of Beira. This brought a much wider market within range, and a new company was formed, Carbonífera de Moçambique, for which 30 per cent of the capital was provided by the Mozambique Company, 60 per cent by Belgian interests, and 10 per cent by the Portuguese Government. The main consumers of the coal are Trans-Zambezia Railway and Caminhos de Ferro da Beira. Production varies between 200,000 and 300,000 tons yearly. The value of the 1967 production was $260,000. Some coal is exported occasionally, but quality is not high and transport costs are substantial. The Cabora Bassa project, making river transport possible, will relieve this situation.

Widespread distribution of potential oil-bearing formations favors a general belief that considerable oil exists in Mozambique. Anglo-American, Continental, Sunray, Clark, Skelly, and Texaco are among companies that have recently received oil exploration and exploitation concessions.[32] An offshore concession was granted to Hunt International of Dallas, Texas, late in 1967, around the mouth of the Zambezi. The Portuguese firm Sonarep plans to invest about $3.5 million during the next three years in oil-prospecting, with a target of 2 million tons by 1970; total North American investment over the same period has been estimated at $15 million.[33] The Mozambique Gulf Oil Company has pursued a drilling campaign for over a decade in southern Mozambique, and has discovered some natural gas at Panda, where limited reserves make expanded exploitation unlikely. Some consideration has been given, however, to a pipeline from southern Mozambique to South Africa and to a nitrous ammonia plant at Panda. Mozambique Gulf has also joined with Pan American Oil to start offshore petroleum exploration southeast of Beira in about 85 feet of water.[34] Although petroleum has not yet been found in Mozambique, the new mining concessions contributed almost $21 million in foreign exchange in 1967.[35]

Petroleum-refining of imported crude began in 1960 in Lourenço Marques. The refinery now can handle 800,000 tons of crude oil annually, with a value of more than $7 million. Presently, 40 per cent of the production is fuel oil, 35 per cent dieseline, and 25 per cent gasoline. The rapidly expanding market for petroleum products in South Africa, however, has led to a planned expansion of facilities by 250 per cent, to 2 million tons, by 1970.[36]

Power

In 1967, there were 688 power plants in the province, based largely on steam and totaling 258,263 kilowatts of installed capacity. Particularly noteworthy are the steam power plants at Lourenço Marques, with a total installed capacity of 42,000 kilowatts.

The harnessing of the Revuè River was initiated during the First National Development Plan (1953–58). This included flood-control, provision for irrigation, and building a hydroelectric power plant and the Chicamba Real dam. Another hydroelectric plant, completed in 1953, operates at Mavuzi, 31 miles south of Vila Pery. It supplies power to the Vila Pery textile mill, to the city of Beira, and to Umtali across the frontier in Rhodesia. Demand has grown so rapidly that in 1965, Sociedade Hidro-Elétrica do Revuè started an enlarged installation at Chicamba at a cost of $3.5 million, which should supply power to a prospective steel mill at Beira.

A hydroelectric scheme and irrigation project in the Maputo area, between Catuane and Bela Vista on the South African border, is also planned by the government. The project, which will cover an area of 99,000 acres on both sides of the Maputo River, will further irrigate part of the South African territory by canal from the dam.[37]

In 1956, the Limpopo dam was built to control the river and also carry the rail line to the Rhodesias. The dam provides irrigation for 75,000 acres and permits agricultural use of over half a million acres, including the lands of the Limpopo settlement scheme.

Far-reaching plans for the economic development of Mozambique, through the use of the great hydroelectric power potential of the Zambezi River, have now captured the interest of the Portuguese administration. It has been pointed out that the Zambezi's 85,000 cubic-feet-per-second water flow is only slightly less than the Nile's 93,000 cubic feet at Aswan.[38]

Announcement that a scheme to harness this potential was in preparation was made in August, 1966, by the governor-general of Mozambique. Funds were allocated for preliminary work on the hydroelectric power station and dam at Cabora Bassa, a gorge that constricts the Zambezi upstream of Tete. It was the Cabora Bassa rapids that stopped David Livingstone in his attempts to discover a navigable route into Central Africa over the Zambezi a century ago. The Zambezi River enters Mozambique territory at Zumbo, in Tete District, at a height of over 1,000 feet, and, in the course of its 200-mile stretch to the city of Tete, it drops 400 feet and thereafter flows 290 miles to the sea. The 60-mile-long, 300-yard-wide gorge of Cabora Bassa lies about halfway between Zumbo and Tete, with steep cliffs on either side. Various sites offer excellent locations for a dam. A British company is acting as consultant, and an international consortium has been formed for construction of the first stage, estimated at $315 million. The

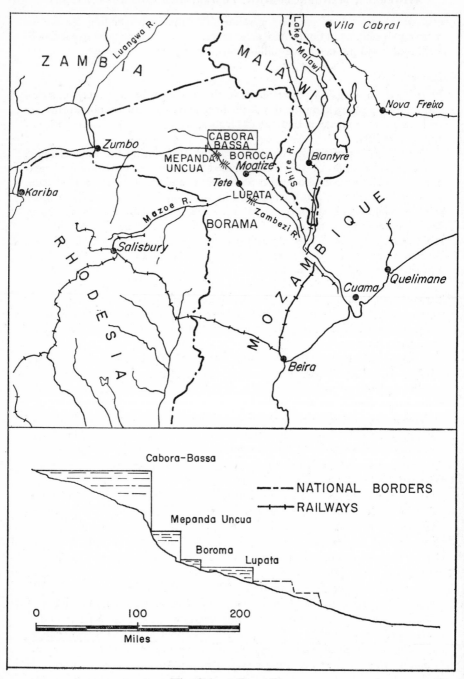

The Cabora Bassa Dam

consortium, Zamco, which holds a provisional contract, was organized by the Anglo-American Corporation of South Africa and is made up of French, German, South African, and Swedish concerns. The plans for the proposed scheme, drawn up by a Portuguese firm of consultants, Hidrotécnica Portuguêsa, call for a double-arch dam about 1,000 feet long and over 500 feet high, higher than the Kariba dam and expected to produce more power than the Aswan dam. A 150-mile-long lake will reach almost to Zumbo and will generate 17,000 million kilowatt hours a year, compared with the 8,000 million kilowatt hours for Kariba and 10,000 million for Aswan.[39]

Important though this hydroelectric scheme may be, it is only the first step in a far more extensively projected power development. Other dams below Cabora Bassa are envisaged at Mepanda-Uncua, at the Boroma and Lupata gorges, and at various smaller sites on tributaries of the Zambezi. It is expected that, altogether, hydroelectric power from the Zambezi valley will eventually total 50,000 million kilowatt hours a year and will offer the cheapest power in Africa.

The value of these projects goes much beyond the supplying of power. The over-all Zambezi Valley Development Scheme[40] looks toward the eventual development of an area covering 54,000 square miles, in which 1.5 million people, most of them Africans, now live in a subsistence economy. This will involve the agricultural use of 6.2 million acres, 3.7 million acres of which will be irrigated. Cattle, citrus, and food crops are to be raised in the highlands, sugar, cotton, and jute in the lowlands. About 600,000 acres of new forest will be planted, which, added to the existing 470,000 acres, will create the basis for a profitable timber industry. At the present time, the only important local industry is coal-mining at Moatize. The Zambezi scheme plans for the exploitation not only of these coal reserves but also of other important minerals. An iron and steel industry might be set up at Tete, 90 miles from the dam. A further development is to make the Zambezi navigable from Tete to the sea. Now the mouth of the river is blocked by a sand bar, the river channel is silted, and only a 10-mile section is truly navigable.[41] At the mouth of the Zambezi, a new seaport will be built at Cuama, capable of handling 40,000-ton freighters. Plainly, the Zambezi scheme stands out as a focal point for the development of the entire territory.

But the scheme has international implications in political, strategic, and economic terms. The important factor in the feasibility of the scheme was South Africa's present need for power and willingness to commit itself to the project. Over 800 miles of high-tension wires will tie Cabora Bassa into the South African grid at a point near Middleburg. Malawi, Zambia, and eastern Rhodesia are also potential customers. Zambia has abstained from exploratory participation, however, and has begun plans to develop a second hydroelectric project at the north bank of Kariba. Though Cabora Bassa and Kariba could supply total Zambian hydroelectric requirements, political factors have weighed heavily on President Kaunda's decision to develop Zambia's internal resources.

Processing and Manufacturing

Even more than in Angola, preparation of primary products dominates the Mozambican industrial scene. The proximity of the highly industrialized

Republic of South Africa and of Rhodesia has considerably retarded industrial development in Mozambique. This has been due to both the easy availability of superior merchandise at a relatively low cost and the opportunity for skilled technicians to find higher-paying employment elsewhere.

Nevertheless, recent years have seen a significant rise in industrial production. In 1967, the $20.7 million of new capital invested in industry more than doubled the $9.2 million invested in 1966.[42] Also in 1967, reduced imports of metal goods, machinery, and finished textiles showed the effects of attempts at import substitution.[43] In recent years, there has also been an indication that there will be increased decentralization of industry away from Lourenço Marques, its suburb Matola, and Beira. A closer examination by industry provides an insight into the scope of industrial production.

Food-Processing, Beverages, and Tobacco. Though much of the food-related industry, including the important sugar-refining activities, has been discussed in the agriculture chapter, some aspects deserve mention here. Of special interest to the economic future of Mozambique is the recent industrialization of abundant cashew fruit, including hopes to manufacture by-products such as juices, jams, and CNSL, the cashew-nut shell liquid used as a lubricant, an insecticide, and in the production of plastics. The largest enterprise so far has been Cajú Industrial, owned by the Banco Nacional Ultramarino. MOCITA (Industrial de Cajú Mocita Lda.), with a modern mechanized factory near João Belo, is owned by the Anglo-American and the Tiger Oats companies of South Africa and Outremare of Italy, which designed the equipment dealing with the nut itself. An English concern, Spence & Pierce Ltd., is located at Inhambane. Companhia Colonial D'Angoche at António Enes on the northern seaboard and SCAJU, a fully mechanized plant at Nacala (35,000-tons-a-year capacity), work the nut production of the north. SCAJU is owned by the powerful Portuguese industrial combine CUF. Factories are also planned at Porto Amélia and Nampula.[44] Production increased in 1967 over 1966 by 12 per cent.

A large grain mill of the Matola Industrial Company prepares flour, macaroni and spaghetti, and biscuits, much of it for export to Angola, São Tomé, the Cape Verde Islands, Madeira, and metropolitan Portugal, as well as to Zambia and Rhodesia.

The combined importance of the beverage and tobacco industries is much less in Mozambique than in Angola. The value of beverage production in 1966 was $9 million, while tobacco production was $7.1 million.[45] In 1967, formal plans were announced for the establishment of a $4.4-million wine industry, with bottling plants at Lourenço Marques, Beira, and Nacala.

Textiles. For years, all cotton fibre was exported, after ginning, to metropolitan Portugal. In the mid-1950's, the first thread and yard-goods factory began at Vila Pery. That textile mill has been enlarged, and another major textile concern has begun to install a spinning and weaving mill in Moçambique District. Textile production doubled in value between 1965 and 1967 alone.[46] Expansion of local manufacturing can be expected to reduce the level of cotton exports to Portugal.

Other Major Industries. The industrial development of Mozambique will rely heavily on the expansion of three major industries—cement, fertilizer, and steel. Cement production has risen from 25,000 long tons in 1947 to 240,000 in 1967, with plants in Matola, Nampula, and Nova Maceira, near Beira. Fibro-cement products are also made. Anticipating the Cabora Bassa hydroelectric project, Mozambique's only cement company, Companhia de Cimentos de Moçambique, owned by the Champallimaud group, plans to install a plant with a 60,000-ton capacity at Moatize. Other developments should soon bring total output to over 500,000 tons.

A fertilizer complex is being completed at Matola. Production goals are 120,000 tons, 30,000 of which will meet Mozambique's needs, the rest being for export. The project is also owned by a Portuguese subsidiary of the Champallimaud group, Sociedade Química Geral de Moçambique, with 10 per cent interest being South African and 15 per cent French.[47]

At Beira, a large steel plant is being installed by a Rhodesian firm and an industrial group of Mozambique (Textafrica, Cifel, and Sher). The first furnace has an initial daily work capacity of 30,000 tons, and a second furnace is to double that. Iron ore will be supplied mainly from the Tete region, electric power from the Chicamba dam on the Revuè River. The Champallimaud group also plans to construct an aluminum smelter near Tete, which will use raw materials from both Mozambique and Malawi and power from the Cabora Bassa dam. A subsidiary plant may be erected near Beira to manufacture potash.

Minor Industries. The expansion of other economic activity and industrial expansion has brought with it the growth of numerous smaller manufacturing plants. The production of glass bottles, ceramics, bricks, tiles, candles, and the like for local consumers has existed for many years. Recently, factories have begun making paper, electrical conductors, chemical laboratory apparatus, telephone equipment, and cardboard. Tires and tubes will be manufactured in Lourenço Marques by Firestone Portuguêsa, and Japanese capital is preparing to begin a match factory. There is a noticeably larger participation of foreign investors in Mozambican small industry than in Angolan, where capital and initiative are frequently Portuguese.

Telecommunications

Telecommunications in Mozambique are government-operated under the administration of the Direcção Provincial dos Serviços dos Correios, Telégrafos e Telefones. There is a Radio Club of Mozambique, which maintains a network of broadcasting stations in various parts of the province.

CAPITAL AND SKILLS

The two most important resources lacking in Angola and Mozambique are capital and skills, and the former without the latter is useless. S. Herbert Frankel, along with Colin Clark, has made the point that a supply of capital is only one of the factors that makes for economic development. By itself, capital

315

plays an inefficient role, for it is dependent upon the cooperative factors of labor, raw materials, organization, and so forth. Capital cannot be applied in a vacuum, and "much confusion has resulted from the fallacious belief that the supply of capital alone can solve the economic problems of development."[48] However, the inflow of foreign capital on proper terms and in proper form can mean not only new investment but also a way of attracting previously unavailable skills and much-needed technology. The prominent examples of such occurrences described here were the Krupp loan to Lobito Mining accompanied by German engineering know-how in building the necessary infrastructure for an economic operation, the international financing and know-how in the Zambezi power scheme, and the Gulf Cabinda operation. There were also smaller examples: first, the cellulose factory and the Lomaum hydroelectric project, financed by Inter-American Capital Corporation, also linked to equipment sales, and, second, the two separate joint ventures in new mechanized cashew-nut factories in Mozambique, both involving Italian firms with capital and advanced technological expertise.

Accelerated importation of foreign capital, especially foreign equity capital, along with skills and technical knowledge, seems to be forthcoming. This step should next be complemented by rapid training of skilled labor within the indigenous labor force. These two measures are the essential requirements of the Portuguese-African economy at a time when it has the absorptive capacity to receive these benefits.[49]

NOTES

1. Particularly valuable sources for this section include José Júlio Cravo Silva, "Recursos económicos do ultramar português," *Boletim da Associação Industrial de Angola*, No. 66 (November, 1965–January, 1966), p. 10; "Economic Summary—Angola," American Consulate General Dept. of State Airgram, No. A-100 (unclassified) (Luanda, January 20, 1966); *Standard Bank Review* (London), April, 1967, pp. 34–35; *Economic and Financial Survey of Angola, 1960–65*, 2nd ed., published by the Economic Studies Department of Banco de Angola (Lisbon); "Annual Economic Summary—Mozambique," American Consulate, Dept. of State Airgram, No. A-128 (unclassified) (Lourenço Marques, March 7, 1967); Walter Marques, *Problemas do desenvolvimento económico de Angola*, Vols. I and II (Luanda, 1964–65). See also various issues of *Boletim dos Serviços de Geologia e Minas* (Luanda), notably M. L. Teixeira Faísca, "Sôbre a exportação e produção de minérios em Angola" (July–December, 1960), pp. 59–72, *Ocorrências minerais* (1966), p. 59, and *Bank of London and South America Review*, II, 22 (October, 1968), 562–66.

2. Due to the thickness of the cover, 4 cubic meters of sandy overburden must be removed before diamonds can be taken from the gravel, which yields 40 carats per cubic meter. The diamond-bearing gravels are divided into upper and lower formations, the upper gravels containing a reconcentration of diamonds found in the lower formation. During the 1950's, some kimberlite (or lode) sources, such as in South Africa, were also found.

3. Although the large Chiumbe deposit was exhausted in 1961, resulting in a decrease in the rate of yield, a new deposit with estimated yields of up to 0.89

carats per cubic meter has been discovered, and the rate of increase has been constant, with bright prospects for the future. From 1962 to 1966, exports rose on the average of 11 per cent per year. Banco de Angola, *Relatório e contas —exercício de 1966* (Lisbon, 1967), p. 147. A considerable harassment of the industry is diamond-smuggling; in the first half of 1966, over 10 tons of coarse diamonds were found in the possession of smugglers. According to the 1966 company report, eighty-one arrests were made in 1966. *Notícias da Beira* (Beira), July 4, 1967.

4. United Nations, A/600/Rev. 1, pp. 234–36.
5. In 1957, Portugal took steps to enter the diamond cutting and processing industries, requiring diamond producers in the overseas territories (the only one being Diamang) to establish sorting and appraisal services in Lisbon and to support the establishment of a Portuguese diamond-cutting enterprise, the Sociedade Portuguêsa de Lapidação de Diamantes, which was organized in 1957 with headquarters in Lisbon. See Nicolas de Kun, *The Mineral Resources of Africa* (New York and Amsterdam, 1965), pp. 106–9; *International Financial Survey*, XIX, 32 (August 18, 1967), 255. Banco de Angola, *Annual Report and Economic and Financial Survey, 1967* (Lisbon, 1968), p. 31.
6. Richard J. Houk, "Prospects and Problems of Petroleum Production in Angola," *Tijdschrift voor economische en sociale geografie* (Rotterdam, August–September, 1958), pp. 185–91.
7. Since 1956, when crude production was 9,000 metric tons, production has risen to 104,428 tons, from 12 producing wells in 1961, and to over 1,000,000 tons in 1965.
8. *The Financial Times*, June 13, 1967.
9. De Kun, *op. cit.*, p. 108.
10. *Jornal Português de Economia e Finanças*, No. 170 (September 15, 1967), and No. 171 (October 15, 1967). Also see *The New York Times*, September 20, 1967.
11. Banco de Angola, *Annual Report and Economic and Financial Survey of Angola, 1966* (Lisbon, 1966), pp. 34–35.
12. See *Angola—Companhia Mineira do Lobito*, booklet issued by the Companhia Mineira do Lobito (Lisbon, 1965). Also see J. António Martins, *Minérios de ferro em Angola* (Luanda, 1962), *The Times*, (London) August 3, 1968, and *Bank of London and South America Review*, October, 1968, p. 564.
13. *Diário de Notícias* (Lisbon), June 17, 1967.
14. "Economic Summary—Angola," p. 31.
15. *Jornal Português de Economia e Finanças*, No. 170 (September 15, 1967).
16. The initial study to determine the feasibility of the project was conducted by Hydrotechnic Corporation of New York, followed by surveys and studies by the Brigada de Estudos do Cuanza, Bengo e Lucala of the Overseas Ministry. The final works were designed by another Portuguese firm, Hidroeléctrica do Zêzere, and the final construction was done jointly by Portuguese and South African firms Sociedade de Empreitadas Moniz da Maia e Vaz Guedes Lda. and S. A. Conrad Zschokke, with Sorefame (Sociedade Reunida de Fabricações Metálicas) in Lisbon supplying much of the hydroelectric equipment. Gonçalo Sarmento and P. C. Afonso, "The Middle Cuanza Development," reprinted from *Water Power*, July–August, 1962.
17. *Angola*, pamphlet issued by Overseas Companies of Portugal (no date or place of publication given).

317

18. *South African Digest,* November 22, 1968, p. 14.
19. The cost of the project on the Angolan side will amount to approximately $210 million. The annual revenue is estimated at $52.5 million. *Actualidade Económica* (Luanda), June 28, 1967.
20. *South-West Africa Survey, 1967,* published by the Department of Foreign Affairs of the Republic of South Africa (March, 1967), p. 79. See also "Economic Summary—Angola," pp. 63–64.
21. Banco de Angola, *Annual Report, 1967,* p. 42.
22. *Standard Bank Review,* April, 1967, p. 35.
23. *Jornal Português de Economia e Finanças,* No. 167 (June 15, 1967).
24. *Diário de Luanda,* May 19, 1967.
25. *Standard Bank Review,* September, 1967, p. 43.
26. *Diário de Luanda* (Angola), September 6, 1966. The governor-general of Angola is authorized to spend up to $1.6 million in telecommunication material in the period 1966–75. *Diário de Notícias* (Lisbon), September 14, 1967.
27. In addition to sources already mentioned, this section draws from C. F. Spence, *Moçambique: East African Province of Portugal* (Cape Town, 1963); *How to Invest in Moçambique,* published by the Directorate of Services of Economy and General Statistics (Lourenço Marques, 1961); João Carlos Alves, "Riqueza mineira de Moçambique: produção e exportação de minérios," *Boletim da Junta Nacional da Marinha Mercante,* September, 1962; and Banco Nacional Ultramarino, *Boletim Trimestral,* No. 73 (1968).
28. A supposedly rich vein of gold has been found in the region of Manica, next to the former Bragança mine. *Jornal Português de Economia e Finanças,* No. 196 (August 15, 1967). It is reported that important deposits of iron and copper ores and natural gas have been discovered in Mozambique. *Marchés Tropicaux et Méditerranéens,* April 1, 1967, and *Summary of World Broadcasts,* June 23, 1967.
29. *Diário* (Lourenço Marques), September 28, 1967.
30. *Africa Research Bulletin,* April 30, 1967, p. 722A.
31. *Diário de Notícias* (Lisbon), October 26, 1967; *Jornal Português de Economia e Finanças,* No. 171 (October 15, 1967); *African World,* October, 1967; *Standard Bank Review,* November, 1967, p. 38.
32. The latter three companies received prospecting rights for an initial period of three years during which minimum expenditures are to be $385,000 in the first year, $1.2 million in the second, and $2 million in the third year. The companies will pay a total of 3 million escudos in surface rent for the first three years and, upon first renewal of the concession, a surface rent of $7 per square kilometer. If oil is found, Mozambique will receive $100,000 as a bonus within three months of the opening of the first commercially exploitable well. Once production reaches 50,000 barrels a day for more than thirty consecutive days, Mozambique will be paid $1 million. As in the case of the other recent petroleum concessions, the state will receive 50 per cent of the profits and will have the right to 12.5 per cent of the value of the petroleum produced. *Diário de Notícias* (Lisbon), October 12 and 15, 1967; *Diário de Luanda,* October 14, 1967.
33. *Africa Research Bulletin,* October 31, 1967, p. 842A; *African World,* September, 1967; and *Barclays Overseas Review,* September, 1968, p. 26.
34. *Africa Research Bulletin,* April 30, 1969, p. 1318.
35. United Nations, Doc. A/AC. 109/L.538/Add. 2 (April 15, 1969), p. 18.
36. *Ibid.,* November 30, 1968, p. 1179.

37. *Ibid.*, October 31, 1967, p. 841A.
38. "Cahora [sic]-Bassa! Muscle for Mozambique," article in *News/Check* (September 9, 1966), p. 27.
39. *Ibid.*
40. See "A potencialidade de recursos do vale do Zambeze em Moçambique," in *Jornal do Comércio* (Lisbon), Suplemento ao No. 34406 (August 6, 1966), pp. 39–42; *Portugal Information Bulletin*, VI, Annex No. 4 (April 29, 1967) (Portuguese Embassy, London). According to the government, "it is the intention of the government to create body on a pattern similar to that of the TVA and other analogous bodies administratively and financially autonomous, with its own juridical character and governed by norms already tried and compatible with the efficiency and dynamism characteristic of the best private enterprises. . . ." *Posibilidades de fomento do vale do Zambeze*, 2nd ed. (Lisbon, 1963); "Missão de fomento e povoamento do Zambeze," *Bacia de Zambeze—Fomento e Ocupação* (Lisbon, 1963), covers the scheme in 16 volumes. A good, more condensed description, by A. F. A. Falcão, "A programação do desenvolvimento do vale do Zambeze em Moçambique," *Fomento* (Lisbon, 1963).
41. Under study is the building of a series of locks and the dredging of a 5-mile ship channel. The laying of a rail line from the sea at Chinde to the Tete area is also contemplated. See "Cahora-Bassa! Muscle for Mozambique."
42. *Barclays Overseas Review*, December, 1968, p. 26.
43. The Economist Intelligence Unit, *Portugal and Overseas Provinces*, No. 4 (1968), p. 14.
44. Foreign Agricultural Service, U.S. Dept. of Agriculture, Memo. No. MOZ-30 (from Salisbury), *Mozambique: Edible Tree Nuts: Cashew Nuts—Annual* (February 7, 1967).
45. *Standard Bank Review*, January, 1968, p. 34.
46. *Boletim Trimestral*, No. 73, p. 36.
47. *Africa Research Bulletin*, May 31, 1967, p. 741A; *Southern Africa*, June 19, 1967.
48. E. A. G. Robinson (ed.), *Economic Development for Africa South of the Sahara* (New York, 1964), p. 407.
49. A similar observation has been noted in *Angola: An Economic Survey*, published by the Standard Bank of South Africa Limited (Johannesburg, n.d.).

XIV

Transport Systems and
Their External Ramifications

FRANK BRANDENBURG

EARLIER chapters on the penetration and settlement of territories claimed by the Portuguese have revealed that lack of transport represented a major impediment to development. Until the arrival of the Europeans, the wheel had not come into use in Africa, south of the Sahara. After its introduction, the rugged terrain and other physical characteristics of the territories raised monumental barriers to its usefulness. Pack animals were often impeded by trypanosomiasis, carried by the tsetse fly, and other diseases, by the dense forests, and by the prodigal rains that can render roads impassable. Major obstacles exist even today, and the bush path often remains the ultimate reliance. As one authority has pointed out, there is hardly any commodity, whether cacao, coffee, or cotton on its way to export or salt and sewing machines on the way to the consumer, that does not begin or end its journey on a path. The means of transport along the path is most frequently the African woman, who may carry on top of her head burdens of up to a hundred pounds for hours on end.[1]

Alongside the preindustrial means of transport in Angola and Mozambique, there now exists an expanding system of roads, railroads, ports, airfields, and even a few pipelines. Almost everything required to build the present system had to be imported. Costs have, naturally, been high. Modern vehicles to utilize these facilities come from abroad. The presence of the two kinds of transport, traditional and modern, represents one of the two striking features of the transport network in Angola and Mozambique. The other is the interrelationship of local transport and African regional transport.

Basic sectors of the transport network of Portuguese Africa comprise indispensable links in the economic infrastructure of all southern Central Africa. Six countries—the Congo (Kinshasa), Malawi, Rhodesia, South Africa, Swaziland, and Zambia—depend upon the ports and railways of Portuguese Africa to a greater or lesser degree for essential imports and exports. The future of transportation systems in Angola and Mozambique thus depends on both territorial and extraterritorial development. Plans for the modernization and expansion of the railways and ports of Portuguese Africa have to take account of rate schedules based on price discrimination as to specific goods carried to and from countries of the interior. The improvement of airports, highways, bridges, and inland waterways are also at times affected by considerations of extraterritorial traffic.

The first half of the present chapter examines transport in the local settings of Angola and Mozambique. Critical and strategic dimensions of southern Central African transport are described in the second half of the chapter.

ANGOLA

Four aspects of the transport system of Angola are of overriding importance: ports, railroads, roads, and air facilities.

Ports

Lobito, Luanda, and Moçâmedes, in descending order of cargo handled, are the three major ports of Angola. Lobito is about equidistant from its two major competitors and has one of the finest natural anchorages in all Africa. Its harbor is protected by a sandspit that parallels the shore for 3 miles and is up to 400 yards wide. Mindful of the value of this natural shelter, unusual on the West African coast, the Portuguese call this sandspit "the gift of the sea." Behind this natural breakwater, the harbor is about 2 square miles in area and from 18 to 100 feet in depth. Lobito ranks as Angola's chief port, mainly because it is the terminus of the Benguela Railway, the only rail system crossing the entire width of Angola. The Benguela serves the productive highlands of central Angola and the wealthy mining region of the Katanga in Congo (Kinshasa) and, through linkages with other railways, further serves Zambia, Malawi, Rhodesia, and even Mozambique and South Africa. The Benguela offers not only the shortest route from mine to coast for Katanga minerals but also a route no longer than that to Beira in Mozambique for the Zambian mines. Moreover, since Lobito is on the Atlantic Ocean, it is as much as 2,500 miles closer by sea to European markets than the ports of Mozambique.

From its opening in the 1920's to the present day, the port at Lobito has been steadily improved to keep port facilities abreast of increasing amounts of tonnage and freight. At the southwestern end of the harbor is an L-shaped quay capable of berthing six large ocean vessels. The port's largest mineral loader has a 400-ton-per-hour capacity and is alongside a maize-storage elevator with a capacity of 20,000 tons.

Expansion of copper, zinc, and cobalt production in southern Katanga and manganese-mining and cotton-planting in southwest Katanga led to an increase of Congo transit through Lobito, until, by 1954, freight movements registered over 500,000 tons to and from Katanga. The increased tonnage includes coal, petroleum products, and various types of materials and machinery for hydro-electric and other construction projects in support of the Union Minière du Haut Katanga,[2] the Belgian mining company that produced all the copper in Katanga until it was nationalized by the Congolese Government in January, 1967. Between 1957 and 1966, mineral traffic was enlarged by Angolan iron-ore shipments from the Cuíma mines southwest of Nova Lisboa, which reached 500,000 tons in the peak year before operations ceased in August, 1967.

By the mid-1950's, Lobito's volume of trade first reached 1 million tons a year.[3] Tonnage has remained above that level since then, reaching 1.5 million tons in 1967, but is by no means all the volume that the port is capable of handling. Full use of present and potential port capacities depends largely on the transport and tariff policies of neighboring countries. Zambia's transit trade through Lobito has fluctuated widely in yearly volume from 60,000 to 250,000 tons.

Luanda, the second port and the capital city of Angola, also enjoys the advantages of a naturally sheltered and wide harbor and is connected to the interior by rail. Since 1960, the cargo handled by the port expanded to 1.2 million tons, in 1967. Berthing facilities can now accommodate five large ocean vessels, and further expansion is planned. Negotiations in 1966 involved contracts for the construction of an ore-loading port large enough to take ships of up to 100,000-ton capacity, to be financed by the General Trade Corporation Agreement, with French equipment. Unlike Lobito, Luanda is engaged exclusively in domestic trade, exporting the produce of the northern Angolan hinterland and supplying it, as well as the city itself, with necessities from abroad.[4] In fact, Luanda handles a larger volume of both domestic cargo and passengers than Lobito, with annual average embarkations and debarkations, since 1960, reaching about 30,000, or three times as many as Lobito.

Moçâmedes has been a weak third behind Lobito and Luanda, but it should overtake both no later than 1969 because of the Cassinga iron-ore mining venture. In 1967, the amount of cargo handled at Moçâmedes was 440,000 tons. The harbor at Moçâmedes lacks the natural endowments of its two competitors —it is smaller, shallower, and without a long sandbar for protection against the outer sea. However, a breakwater and modern port installations, including deep-water dockage, were built in the 1950's, equipping the port for capacities much greater than its present volume of traffic. Moreover, the Companhia Mineira do Lobito has built new installations at the northern end of the harbor to load its shipments of iron ore from Cassinga aboard ocean-going ore carriers. Storage areas at that site will hold 1 million tons, initially; a bucket-wheel-type reclaimer operating alongside the stockpiles is to deliver 3,000 tons of ore per hour to a conveyor belt leading to the loading docks for ore carriers of up to 100,000 tons. With the completion of new railway spurs and improvements along the main line of the Moçâmedes railroad, yearly shipments of ore through the port were expected to reach 5 million tons in 1969 and to increase eventually to 7 million tons annually.

Besides the three major ports, there are others that carry little or no international traffic but that do serve provincial coastal trade. They are Cabinda (which should shortly take on international importance due to oil exports), Ambrizete, Ambriz, Porto Amboím, Novo Redondo, Benguela, Cuio, Lucira, Porto Alexandre, and Baía dos Tigres. River navigation is today chiefly used for transporting sugar from mills near the Dande and Cuanza rivers to shipping points at their mouths or to Luanda. Some seasonal passenger traffic also moves along a section of the Cubango River.

Railroads

The railway system of Angola has served primarily as a means of moving the export and import trade of the province and of countries in the adjacent interior to domestic ports. Major parallel rail routes head eastward from Lobito, Luanda, and Moçâmedes; Angola has no north-south railroad. Railroad management favors the extension and interconnection of present lines.

The railway network is comprised of one international line, two major domestic lines, and two small local lines, as the accompanying list shows.

Benguela Railway (private)	
Main line, Lobito to Katanga frontier	836 *Miles*
Spur from Robert Williams to Cuíma	41
Other spurs, sidings, and yards	113
Moçâmedes railroad (state)	
Main line, Moçâmedes to Serpa Pinto	509
Spur from Sá da Bandeira to Chiange	77
Spur from Entroncamento to Cassinga	70
Other spurs, sidings, and yards	62
Luanda railroad (state)	
Main line, Luanda to Malange	264
Dondo Branch	34
Golungo Alto Branch	19
Bengo Branch (48 of original 58 miles closed down in 1960)	10
"Congo Railroad" Branch	7
Spurs, sidings, and yards	62
Amboím railroad (private)	
Porto Amboím line	76
Spurs, sidings, and yards	4
Cuio railroad (private)	
Cuio to Dombe Grande and Luacho	15

The Benguela Railway (Caminho de Ferro de Benguela), or CFB, is the monarch of Angola's railway system. The original concession to build the line was secured from Portugal by Sir Robert Williams, in 1902, on behalf of Tanganyika Concessions Limited, a promoter-developer of rich mineral deposits in the Katanga region of the Congo. For the line, Williams chose an old slave-trade route through Angola, terminating at the coastal settlement of Benguela. This route offered the shortest overland distance from the Katanga mines to the Atlantic seaboard; later, the better Lobito harbor was developed as the line's terminal. While Williams convinced his business associates of the advantages of building the Benguela Railway, opinion in Portugal apparently was divided, because of considerable fear that foreign investment in Angola "might prove a Trojan Horse for covetous imperialists."[5]

The Portuguese Government, unlike some of the more outspoken critics of the rail venture, recognized that non-Portuguese investors were indispensable for building the proposed line. Despite delays caused by difficulties encountered by the promoters in raising capital and overcoming technical problems—besides interruptions brought on by World War I—the line was finally completed as far as the frontier of the Congo in 1928, and the connecting line from there to the Katanga mines was finished in 1931.

The world recession of the 1930's intervened, and the price of copper dropped to $25 a ton. The company was forced to reorganize financially. The Benguela paid its first dividends in 1948 and has paid an annual dividend since.[6] Although the company annually reinvests part of its profits in the improvement of the line and rolling stock, expansion of its network has been handicapped by a clause of the original contract with the Portuguese Government, which foresees its being taken over ultimately by the latter in 2001.[7] Thus, in the 1930's, the Benguela Railway became one, but by no means the only, railroad link between the mineral wealth of Central Africa and the outside world. Other routes were the main rail lines of the Belgian Congo (now the Democratic Republic of the Congo), Northern Rhodesia (Zambia since 1964), Southern Rhodesia (now Rhodesia), Tanganyika (now joined with Zanzibar in Tanzania), and Mozambique. For political and economic reasons, the Belgians in the Congo gave preference to the long and slow *voie nationale*, which involves first a rail journey to Port Francqui on the Kasai River, then a river voyage to Kinshasa (Léopoldville), and another rail journey to the harbor of Matadi, within the estuary of the Congo River. Apart from the repeated transshipments, river navigation is sometimes impeded by low water levels during the dry season. Only after World War II did the Belgians fully accept the Benguela Railway and Lobito's magnificent harbor as the best way of breaking the bottleneck of the Congo's "national route," over which it was impossible to transport efficiently the mineral traffic piled up in Katanga.

Until 1960, facilitated by the dual role of Tanganyika Concessions as owner of the Benguela Railway and important stockholder in Union Minière du Haut Katanga,[8] the Benguela hauled about 20 per cent of Katanga's copper. This percentage climbed considerably in the period 1961–63, when disruptions of the Congolese transport system and the secession of Katanga cut the latter area off from the rest of the Congo; subsequently, it decreased to about 40 per cent. Prior to 1957, none of the copper from Zambia moved out through Angola. There followed a short period of copper shipments ending in mid-1960, when special discount rates introduced by a competitor ended the shipments, and a resumption of copper traffic in 1966, when Zambia's quarrel with Rhodesia over Rhodesian independence resulted for a time in the virtual cessation of all Zambian traffic over Rhodesian Railways to its normal outlets, Beira and Lourenço Marques.

During 1967, copper shipments on the Benguela Railway, from both Katanga and Zambia, showed a slight increase. However, railway sabotage, first in Katanga and then Angola, introduced new factors that decreased its reliability but not its importance. Not wishing to be at the mercy of the Portuguese in Angola, the Congolese Government was reported to be considering alternatives: either improving their internal route, the *voie nationale*, or building another railway from Luluabourg or Port Francqui to the mouth of the Congo River, to eliminate river transport entirely. Although the costs of a new railroad would be high, the British firm of LonRho seemed about to undertake the project late in 1968.[9] Zambia, which has also been wishing to reduce its dependency on Angola, Mozambique, and Rhodesia, has been trying to have a railroad financed to link Zambia to Dar es Salaam, Tanzania's port on the Indian Ocean. It signed recently an agreement with Communist China for an interest-free loan of $14 million to meet the expenses of the construction survey of the railroad.

The position of the Benguela Railway in the Angolan railroad system remains paramount. In 1967, it hauled some 829,000 passengers and 1.8 million tons of freight.[10] Many communities across the entire width of central Angola depend on the line for their daily livelihood, especially Nova Lisboa, where the major rail repair shops are located. Even if true, as Richard Hammond contends, that "any value it [the Benguela] might have had in opening up the hinterland of Angola itself was incidental,"[11] today the over-all economic development of Angola is linked with the state of the province's only international railway. A planned $240-million improvement of the line between Cubal and Lobito will double the capacity of the whole railway.

The Moçâmedes rail line lies in the south about halfway between the Benguela line and the border of South-West Africa, paralleling the two for about three-fifths of the width of Angola. Initiated in 1905 on an extremely modest scale by the Portuguese Government, the line was slowly pushed eastward with a view to encouraging agricultural colonization and general economic activity on the southern plateau, as well as that of possibly establishing a second international link with the rail system of Rhodesia. Funds made available under various development plans made possible the widening of the rail gauge and completion of the main line as far as Serpa Pinto, 466 miles inland from Moçâmedes, but still several hundred miles away from the Rhodesian border. While the stretch between Serpa Pinto and Rhodesia is unlikely to be completed in the near future, the Moçâmedes line now handles the iron ore along a new 30-mile spur from the newly developed mines at Cassinga, 400 miles to the port of Moçâmedes. More than 70 miles of the main line are in the process of being built to accommodate heavier train loads. When the project is completed, the railroad will be equipped with forty-five diesel locomotives and 600 cars. Unless the Benguela Railway can capture a greater share of the transit trade from Congo (Kinshasa) and Zambia or develop higher domestic traffic, the Moçâmedes rail system will soon surpass all other Angolan railways in freight movements. In 1966, the line carried only 135,700 passengers and 291,000 tons of freight. In 1967, freight tonnage more than tripled, to 938,000 tons.

The Luanda rail line in the north, the province's oldest railway, dating to the 1880's, was originally projected as a trans-Africa railroad. The main line now reaches 264 miles into the interior and serves the towns of Catete, Zenza, Salazar, Lucala, Cacuso, and Malange; spur lines further serve Dondo, Golungo Alto, and certain suburbs of Luanda. One 7-mile branch, the so-called Congo Railroad, was conceived before Congolese independence as the initial link to the far-distant Matadi-Léopoldville line in the Congo. Such eventual linking is now highly conjectural, though funds are being passively sought to extend the Congo Railroad to Carmona and to serve the coffee areas of Zaire and Uíge districts.

Long-standing plans for extending the main line of the Luanda beyond its present terminus at Malange were temporarily shelved early in the 1960's, pending the widening of the gauge from the long-used 1 meter to the standard African gauge of 3 feet 6 inches. This would ease the transport of manganese and iron ore from mines along that route.

In the expectation of increasing iron-ore traffic, particularly when the Luanda ore-loading port is constructed, a government contract was awarded in 1967 to an American firm for the purchase of ten diesel-electric locomotives. In 1967, some 569,000 passengers and 420,000 tons of freight were transported by the railroad.

The Amboím and Cuio railroads are short, privately owned lines. The first, initiated in 1925 by a company holding a concession to develop the port of Amboím and its hinterland, is the common carrier to and from the Gabela area. At the present time, that railroad survives only by virtue of the coffee shipments from the CADA plantation near Gabela. Its yearly freight traffic seldom surpasses 20,000 tons; the annual number of passengers is about 12,000.[12] The Cuio railroad, a narrower gauge line of the Companhia de Açúcar de Angola, serves that company's sugar and oil-palm plantations at Dombe Grande and Luacho.

Still unresolved are major questions concerning the advisability of constructing one or more lines on a north-south axis in Angola, extending the Moçâmedes line to Rhodesia or, alternatively, building a new line from the port of Baía dos Tigres to the frontier, which was considered late in the 1940's, along with extending the Congo Railroad, building new spurs for short distances from Luanda, and lengthening the Amboím to serve the *colonato* of Cela.

Roads

Road construction received high priority in the development plans of 1959–64 and 1965–67. As of 1967, the official highway network of Angola embraced about 15,100 miles of roads. The quality of the road network varies, however, from good stretches of paved highways to mere bush trails. In many areas, traffic on roads is difficult, if not impossible, during the rainy season. Local authorities in charge of such roads generally face financial and labor difficulties, which hinder improvements. Efforts of the Public Works Department have, on the other hand, resulted in an increase of paved roads from about 250 miles in 1960 to approximately 2,200 miles in 1967. In addition, there are some 1,240 miles of improved roads and 700 miles of leveled, all-weather dirt roads.

It is hoped that a network of paved, all-weather roads between all the major population centers will be completed by 1970. This is a rather ambitious undertaking for a territory that, by 1963, had merely 15,000 trucks and 36,000 automobiles. Yet, the dual needs of developing the interior and easing the defense burden has spurred endeavor.

Angola is working toward the ultimate completion of three main north-south highways and an equal number of east-west highways. The north-south highways include (1) a coastal connection from Santo António do Zaire on the Congo River to Luanda and Lobito, continuing to Vila Pereira d'Eça near the South-West African border; (2) a central route from Maquela do Zombo near the Congo border via Malange, Nova Lisboa, and Cassinga, to Pereira d'Eça; (3) an eastern route, from Dundo in the northeast to Luso, a major railhead on the Benguela Railway, and finally to Mavinga in southeastern Angola. The east-west highways include (1) the Luanda highway, paralleling the rail line to Malange and thence eastward to Henrique de Carvalho; (2) the Lobito highway, paralleling the Benguela Railway most of its distance to Teixeira de Sousa; (3) the Moçâmedes highway, paralleling the Moçâmedes rail line as far as Serpa Pinto and then southeastward to Neriquinha on the Cuando River, near the Rhodesian border. Already built is the stretch from Sá da Bandeira to the South-West African border, intended for the improvement of trade with South-West Africa and as an impetus for development of the southern part of the province.

Air Transport

Air services in Angola compare favorably with the most efficient and least expensive in Africa. Airfields capable of handling at least DC-3 type planes are located in thirty-three towns. Three airports, at Luanda, Luso, and Negage, can handle jet traffic. The facilities at Luso and Negage are for military aircraft. The President Craveiro Lopes Airport in Luanda serves the Portuguese Air Force, as well as international and domestic commercial air traffic, and has an excellent reputation among medium-size airports in Africa. Domestic aviation is in charge of the Divisão de Transportes Aéreos (DTA), an agency of the government of Angola, which also maintains airports and airfields. The DTA provides scheduled flights between all major population centers in Angola, flying DC-3's and Fokker Friendship aircraft. In 1967, DTA flew almost 2 million miles and over 10,000 hours, carrying 98,000 passengers and 2,100 tons of cargo and mail. International connections are maintained by the Portuguese national airline TAP (Transportes Aéreos Portugueses), flying between Lisbon, Luanda, Beira, and Salisbury, and by South African Airways between Johannesburg, Luanda, and Europe. A new service connecting South Africa with Brazil and the United States may stop in Luanda. Former flights between Luanda and Brazzaville, Luanda and Pointe Noire, and Luanda and Kinshasa have been interrupted for some time for political reasons, and special attention has been shown to the need for an expansion of airfields during the continuing military tensions in Angola.

MOZAMBIQUE

The economy of Mozambique is decidedly more dependent than that of Angola on income derived from transit trade with neighboring countries. Though the Benguela Railway forms an integral part of the transport network of southern Central Africa and is a vital artery for the interior of Angola, charges on goods carried between Lobito and the Congo border provide only a small fraction of Angola's income, and they essentially accrue to the privately owned CFB. In contrast, charges on goods carried between the ports of Mozambique and neighboring countries represent a major source of income for Mozambique. Such dependence has led some economists to characterize the monetized sector of Mozambique's economy as an economy of ports and railroads. The focus of this section of the chapter is on these ports and railroads and on developments in Mozambique's roads and air transport.

The Mozambique Government exercises an influence on the transport system much beyond the normal effects of controls and regulations, because it owns and operates provincial harbors, airlines, and much of the highway transport. It further owns and operates a significant part of the domestic railroad system for all railroads except the British capitalized Trans-Zambezia Railway, the Beira railroad owned by the Portuguese Finance Ministry in Lisbon, and the short rail line of the Sena Sugar Estates. Administration of the local government's transport complex is lodged in a single decentralized agency, the Mozambique Administration of Harbors, Railways, and Transport Services.

Ports

Nature bestowed several excellent harbors on the 1,746-mile coastline of Mozambique. The presence of these natural harbors was one of the reasons that prompted Vasco da Gama and his successors to plant the Portuguese flag along those shores of the Indian Ocean. Technological advances and new ocean routes have reduced the strategic importance of Mozambique's ports as stopovers between East and West. Yet World War II, the recent blocking of the Suez Canal, and the development of giant oil tankers have re-emphasized their strategic significance. However, the continuing importance of these ports lies mainly in their being convenient points of entry to the interior of Africa.[13]

Lourenço Marques and Beira are the two leading ports of the province. Together they account for about 90 per cent of the cargo handled by Mozambique's ports and, like Lobito in Angola, represent important outlets in the transport network of all southern Central Africa.

Lourenço Marques serves the domestic hinterland, Swaziland, the Transvaal, and some of Rhodesia and Zambia. It has an excellent harbor, with several channels sufficiently deep for large ocean-going vessels. Fifteen such vessels can be berthed at the same time along the port's 2 miles of waterfront. At the inner end of the harbor, some distance from the port's main facilities, are the quays of Matola, especially equipped for handling crude oil, mineral ores, and timber. The main port has electric coal-loaders, for handling Transvaal coal, and considerable refrigerated storage space for fresh fruit and fish. Lourenço Marques wharves are also used by vessels engaged in the active cabotage trade along the Mozambique coast. The port's trade, largely attributable to the transit movements, reached a yearly average of about 6 million tons late in the 1950's, twice surpassed 7 million tons a year in the first half of the 1960's, and in 1967 soared to 10.2 million tons.[14]

Beira is situated 15 miles from the open sea in the estuary of the Pungué River, five-sixths of the distance from Lourenço Marques northward to the mouth of the Zambezi River. It serves as the terminus for both the Beira Railway running westward to Rhodesia and the connection running northward toward Malawi and Lake Nyasa. Lacking the natural advantages of Lourenço Marques, Beira's harbor is shallow and requires continuous dredging to maintain the necessary depth of its single deep-water channel. It is difficult to enter and leave, especially at low tide, when the depth on the bar is only about 16 feet. It has been said that until 1942 Beira's competitive position was weakened by its operation by a British-Portuguese concessionary, the Mozambique Company. Administration of the port improved greatly after the Mozambique Government took over its management in 1948.

Present capacity of the port is eight large ocean-going vessels at once and 3.7 million tons of cargo a year, about half that of Lourenço Marques. Since late in the 1950's, the amount of cargo actually handled at Beira has averaged about 3 million tons a year, with some 3.5 million tons handled in 1967.

Secondary coastal ports include, from north to south, Mocímboa da Praia, Porto Amélia, Memba, Nacala, Moçambique, António Enes, Moma, Pebane, Macuze, Quelimane, Chinde, Mambone, and Inhambane. Quelimane and Nacala are the only secondary ports now handling more than 100,000 tons a year. Porto Amélia has a fine natural harbor and is expected to become the fourth port of the province.

Quelimane, situated on a channel of the Zambezi delta, the Bons Sinais River, is connected by rail to the Mocuba area, from which tea, sisal, and copra move to the port. Nacala, situated 30 miles north of the historical but now virtually abandoned port on Moçambique Island, is the principal port of northern Mozambique. Until 1908, Moçambique city was the capital of Mozambique, and it was long an important port of call on the Portuguese route to the Orient. A death blow was dealt to it in 1947 when a modern port was built at Nacala. Nacala, in the wide and deep Fernão Veloso Bay, has the finest harbor in eastern Africa and one of the best in the world. The bay is an enclosed water area 8 miles long and from 2 to 4 miles wide, nowhere less than 36 feet deep, with deep water close to the shore along the eastern side, where the port of Nacala stands. A relatively long rail route connects the new port and the northern interior.[15]

River traffic has almost totally lost out to rail, road, and air transport, although three of Mozambique's rivers—Incomáti, Limpopo, and Zambezi—are sectionally navigable for barges during part of the year. However, government plans for the development of the Zambezi river basin envision that the Zambezi will be converted into an important commercial inland waterway. Small river ports on the Zambezi include Marromeu and Luabo, from which sugar is shipped down to Chinde, and João Belo on the Limpopo, from which agricultural products are sometimes transported along the coast to Lourenço Marques.

Railroads

Like the rail system of Angola, the railroads in Mozambique were designed primarily for moving freight between the seaboard and the interior. Tentacles of the Mozambique network spread inland from six terminals on the Indian Ocean, never connecting one with the other. A link does exist, however, between the Lourenço Marques and the Beira systems in the interior through the Rhodesian Railways system.

Major rail routes run westward from Lourenço Marques, Beira, and Nacala, minor ones from Quelimane, Inhambane, and João Belo. The province's total length of track is about 2,250 miles shorter than Angola's, but the Mozambique system carries considerably more passengers and freight. In the mid-1960's, yearly movements averaged over 3 million passengers (3.2 million for 1967) and more than 10 million tons of freight (10.7 million for 1967).

The components of the railway system of Mozambique, as of mid-1966, were as follows:

Lourenço Marques network (state)
Lourenço Marques to Ressano Garcia main line	54 *Miles*
Goba (Swaziland) branch, to Goba	40
Xinavane branch to Xinavane and Magude	58
Lourenço Marques branches to Vila Luísa, Magude, and Malvérnia (on the Rhodesian border)	327
Spurs, sidings, and yards	—

Beira network (state and private)
Beira Railway or Beira-Umtali main line (Portuguese Finance Ministry)	195
Trans-Zambezia Railway, Dondo to Malawi border (private)	205
Tete line, Dona Ana to Tete (state)	158
Sena Sugar Estates line, Caia to Marromeu (private)	67

Mozambique network (state)
Nacala to Vila Cabral main line	589
Lumbo branch	27

Secondary lines (state)
Quelimane rail line, Quelimane to Mocuba	90
Gaza railroad, João Belo to Chicomo and Maúle	87
Inhambane railroad, Inhambane to Inharrime	61

The Lourenço Marques system, wholly owned by the Mozambique Government, serves primarily the transit traffic from the Transvaal, Swaziland, and Rhodesia and secondarily the growing domestic traffic from the Incomáti, Maputo, and Limpopo valleys. It grew from a line constructed late in the nineteenth century from Lourenço Marques to Ressano Garcia, to provide an outlet to the sea for the landlocked Transvaal. American, Portuguese, and Dutch concessionaries, between 1886 and 1894, were involved in that construction and extension to Pretoria, Komatipoort, and the Witbank coal fields. The Boers, who controlled the Transvaal Republic, relied then on the Portuguese line as a preferred alternative to British-controlled ports of the Cape. After the Boer War, the Lourenço Marques line retained a significant share of the Transvaal traffic because of the Convention Between the Governments of the Transvaal and the Portuguese Province of Mozambique Relating to Natives, Railways and Ports, and Commerce and Customs, signed in 1909. The agreement provided for 50 per cent of the Transvaal's seaborne traffic to flow through Lourenço Marques, in exchange for the right of the Transvaal to recruit African labor in Mozambique. With various amendments relating to the percentage of a guaranteed rail traffic and other matters, the agreement is still in force today. The original line continues to be the most significant of the entire Lourenço Marques system, carrying a large part of the Transvaal's exports of coal, chrome ore, and citrus.

Besides the main line to the Transvaal, branches were built to Magude and Xinavane in the Incomáti valley and to Vila Luísa north of Lourenço Marques. In 1912, a second rail line was begun from Lourenço Marques to Johannesburg through the Swaziland protectorate. Because of conflicting interests, this line was terminated at Goba in Mozambique. Traffic on this line has been increasing rapidly in recent years, mainly as a result of Swaziland exports of sugar, wood pulp, and iron ore and imports of petroleum. Modernization of the rolling stock and the port facilities at the Matola docks in Lourenço Marques, extension of the line to Manzini in Swaziland, and an efficient railroad management have combined to keep the southern part of the Lourenço Marques system abreast of the transit trade needs of the Transvaal and Swaziland. In 1966, the system moved some 2 million passengers and 8.9 million tons of freight.

One of the newest, and by far the longest, branch of the Lourenço Marques system connects Mozambique and Rhodesia at the border city of Malvérnia, moves thence to Bannockburn and the main trunk of the Rhodesia Railways, which serve the rich mineral regions of Zambia and the Congo. Opened in 1955, the Malvérnia line, or the Limpopo Railway, interconnects with the Xinavane and Vila Luísa branches at Magude, offering alternate routes. Completion of the line provided Mozambique with its second rail link to the Rhodesia Railways network, the first being the Beira Railway. Post–World War II congestion on the latter railroad and at Beira port was primarily responsible for the construction of the Malvérnia line. It is significant that the connection to Lourenço Marques quickly acquired an almost equal share of the highly coveted copper exports from Central Africa. By 1962, for example, 322,000 tons of such copper were transported over the Malvérnia route, compared with 336,000 tons over the Beira Railway.

The Beira-based network comprises the Beira Railway from Beira to Umtali in Rhodesia, the Trans-Zambezia Railways, and the Tete and Sena Sugar Estates line. Most of the business handled by the system concerns transit trade of Rhodesia, Zambia, the Congo, and Malawi. However, since completion of the spur lines to the coal fields at Tete and the Sena Sugar Estates, the Beira network has been steadily increasing the volume of domestic traffic and now accounts for almost one-fourth of the total rail freight of Mozambique. In 1966, it transported 775,400 passengers and 2.8 million tons of freight.

The Beira-Umtali section, the oldest and most significant in terms of tonnage, was built and financed by the British South Africa Company and its subsidiaries after an Anglo-Portuguese agreement of 1891 had provided for the construction of a rail line from Beira to assure the Rhodesias an outlet to the sea. Opened in 1899, it remained in non-Portuguese hands until its purchase in 1949 by the Portuguese Finance Ministry in Lisbon. Two years later, the Beira Convention between Great Britain and Portugal guaranteed to the port the traffic of the Federation of Rhodesia and Nyasaland (Zambia, Rhodesia, and Malawi) largely to insure its operation at full capacity and thereby justify the financing of port improvements needed by all users. It was further agreed that the short section of the Beira Railway between Umtali and the frontier of Mozambique would be sold to Rhodesian Railways.

Until the Malvérnia line of the Lourenço Marques network opened in 1955, the Beira Railway carried the great bulk of copper and other mineral exports from Zambia and agricultural commodities from both of the Rhodesias. Since 1955, except for small amounts shipped through South Africa and a few years when the Benguela handled up to 20 per cent of the copper tonnage and other mineral and agricultural exports from Zambia, the two Mozambique terminals of Beira and Lourenço Marques have largely divided the traffic from and to Zambia and Rhodesia. Also, until 1963, about 30 per cent of Katanga copper was shipped via the Beira-Umtali route. This percentage was stepped up between 1961 and 1963, when the Congolese "national route" suffered considerable destruction, but it has dropped to previous levels. All in all, the Beira Railway carries about 70 per cent of the total freight handled by the Beira network.

The Trans-Zambezia rail line, inaugurated in 1922, begins at the town of Dondo on the Beira-Umtali trunk, crosses the Zambezi River at Sena, and pushes northward to the Malawi border. The bridge over the Zambezi, which was completed in 1935, is almost 2 miles long and was once considered one of the longest in the world. Constructed, and still owned, by the British-capitalized Trans-Zambezia Railways Company, the private line is in fact owned by Portuguese and British interests, the latter holding the majority. It forms one of three integral parts of the 600-mile connection serving Malawi, which also includes Central African Railways, operating across the Mozambique-Malawi border, and Malawi Railways, operating inside Malawi. Freight volume on the Trans-Zambezia line rose from 176,000 tons in 1945 to over 1 million tons in recent years.

The state-owned Tete line, built between 1947 and 1950, begins at Dona Ana on the northern side of the Zambezi and travels 160 miles northwest to Tete and the coal fields at Moatize, which supply the entire Beira rail network with its coal needs. Another spur, the narrow gauge privately owned Sena Sugar Estates line, branches off the Trans-Zambezia at the town of Caia, near the south bank of the Zambezi River, and follows the river to Marromeu in the heart of the Sena Sugar Estates.

The northern Mozambique rail line is the newest and longest in the province. Its main eastern terminus is Nacala; for a long time, the inland terminal was Nova Freixo in the highlands above Lake Nyasa, but then the line was extended to Catur with plans to continue to Vila Cabral. Since the Nacala hinterland is attractive climatically and agriculturally and—although the tsetse fly still plagues much of the area—it is hoped that the line will open up this vast territory to settlement and commercial agriculture. In 1966, the line had a traffic of 476,000 passengers and 150,000 tons in freight. Original plans to terminate the northern Mozambique railroad on the shores of Lake Nyasa, perhaps at Porto Arroio, have been substituted by plans to connect with the railway of Malawi, giving that landlocked country a second rail outlet at Nacala. Malawi has shown great interest in access to a port less congested than Beira, across the common land border to Nova Freixo.[16] In mid-1968, Malawi received a South African loan for $15.4 million for the construction of a railroad to make that connection,[17] including a bridge across the Shire River at Liwonde.[18]

While the operation of the Beira and Lourenço Marques routes has been highly profitable, the northern Mozambique railroad has been a deficit operation for many years. The three minor lines of Mozambique also have suffered annual deficits. The longest of the three, between the port of Quelimane and the town of Mocuba on the Licungo River, mainly serves cotton, sisal, and tea producers. The Gaza railroad, from João Belo directly north to the rural towns of Chicomo and Maule, is a narrow-gauge line moving the timber and crops between the Changane River and the coast. It was constructed in the days before road transport, but presently most of the freight is transported from João Belo to Xinavane by road and thence by rail over the Lourenço Marques network. The Inhambane rail line between the port of Inhambane and the town of Inharrime, to the southwest, is also meeting severe competition from road transporters.

Roads

The construction, improvement, and maintenance of roads, a traditionally neglected aspect of Mozambique's transport network, has received fairly high priority in recent development plans, but actual expansion has been less than planned. As of 1967, the road network of Mozambique totaled some 16,100 miles, of which less than 800 miles were paved. Paved or gravel-surfaced roads included (1) a highway paralleling the Beira Railway from Beira to the Rhodesian border, (2) a connection from Vila Pery on the Beira line to Tete, (3) a coastal link between Porto Amélia and Mocímboa da Praia, and (4) the roads radiating from Lourenço Marques to Inhambane, Ressano Garcia, Namaacha, and Goba. Most other roads are little more than narrow lanes of packed dirt, often impassable in the rainy season. Many parts of the province are still virtually roadless. An immediate plan, however, is for extending the Inhambane highway as far as the Beira highway, to complete the province's first totally asphalted north-south road, linking Lourenço Marques to the Malawi border. Inauguration of such a trans-Mozambique highway may encourage greater use of local passenger cars, motorcycles, and commercial motor vehicles. The number of such vehicles has been increasing steadily—from 9,100 in 1948 and about 27,000 in 1956 to almost 60,000 in 1964. In 1964, the number of motor vehicles in Mozambique was as follows:[19]

Light vehicles	47,344
Heavy vehicles	8,455
Tractors	3,405
Motorcycles	3,519
Total	62,723
Of this total:	
Passenger vehicles	34,720
Transport vehicles	25,213
Total	59,933

It should also attract many more automobile tourists from neighboring countries, especially Rhodesia and South Africa.

Of particular interest in respect to road transport are the special road services maintained by the Mozambique harbors, railways, and transport departments. These services carry freight and passengers in rural areas and act as a feeder to the railways, particularly in areas of cotton-growing at the times of harvest.

Air Transport

The Mozambique Government not only regulates air transport but owns and operates the only internal airline. The Serviço de Aeronáutica Civil, a regulatory agency, has authority for performing the usual services carried out by civil aviation agencies. DETA (Direcção e Exploração dos Transportes Aéreos), a branch of the Mozambique Administration of Harbors, Railways, and Transport Services, offers domestic and international air flights. In 1967, DETA transported 68,000 passengers and close to 2,300 tons of freight and mail. Its fleet of ships consists of Fokker Friendships, Douglas DC-3's, and Lockheed Lodestars. Short-range jets are being purchased. Of the sixteen local airports served regularly by DETA, only three—Lourenço Marques, Beira, and Nampula—are used as international airports. DETA further provides scheduled flights to Johannesburg, Durban, Salisbury, Blantyre, and Manzini (in Swaziland). In addition, South African Airways flies regularly between Johannesburg and Lourenço Marques, as do Central African Airways between Salisbury and Lourenço Marques–Beira and TAP between Lisbon, Luanda, Salisbury, and Beira. Major improvements are being undertaken to extend the capacity of the Lourenço Marques airport.

Pipelines

The one existing pipeline in Portuguese Africa was completed in 1965 to pump crude oil from Beira to Umtali in Rhodesia for use at the Feruka oil refinery. The 180-mile-long pipeline cost almost $100 million. The British and U.N. embargo on oil shipments to Rhodesia led to the interruption of its use in 1966.

Some consideration has been given to a pipeline to provide natural gas to South Africa. Such a project awaits the discovery of fields that are more commercially exploitable than those already discovered.

AFRICAN REGIONAL TRANSPORT

Political changes in the countries neighboring on Mozambique carry serious implications for the future of transport in Portuguese Africa. From the Portuguese point of view, the reliance of neighbors in Africa on the transport facilities of Angola and Mozambique has been derived from the combined effects of location, existing transport facilities, and higher costs of alternative routes. However, recent events suggest that some pressures are developing that affect regional transport.

Tanzania and Zambia have already completed an oil pipeline and are continuing in their efforts to link Dar es Salaam and the rich copperbelt of Zambia by a railroad known popularly as the Tan-Zam. As mentioned earlier, Communist China provided an interest-free loan of $14 million to meet the expenses of a survey of the projected 440-mile railroad and sent engineers for this survey in May, 1968. The building of the railroad may be further financed by China.[20] Moreover, the British blockade of Rhodesia, following the unilateral declaration of independence made by Prime Minister Ian Smith in November, 1965, fanned anew the fires of discontent among those who condemn both the Portuguese presence in Africa and the utilization of their transport facilities. In these circumstances, the need for an analysis of the transport network of this part of Africa is obvious.

The Existing System

The early development of regional transport in southern Central Africa was largely a tale of rail transport and copper. Major railroads in the area were originally built primarily to haul minerals from the interior to coastal ports. Rail transport remains the cheapest means, and for practical purposes the only feasible means, of transporting most kinds of bulk freight over long distances. A notable exception is the pipeline from Beira to Rhodesia, which greatly reduced the dependence of Rhodesia on petroleum carried by rail, until its operations were suspended in 1966. A similar pipeline now exists between Zambia and Tanzania. Neither inland waterways, whose use still requires a series of costly and burdensome handlings, nor road and air transport, though gaining significantly in local transport systems, hold much promise of competing successfully with rail transport for long-distance mineral freight. So long as rail transport carries the great bulk of mineral freight from the interior, the railroads will also continue to haul a great deal of agricultural exports and general imports.

Copper is the most important single source of traffic and revenue for the rail system in this area of Africa. It is hauled on all major railways in southern Central Africa, including the CFB in Angola and the Beira and Lourenço Marques lines in Mozambique. Its significance is heightened by the fact that the copper mines of the Congo and Zambia are located almost exactly in the center of Central Africa. In recent years, exports from these mines have earned nine-tenths of Zambia's income in foreign currency and seven-tenths of the Congo's. Furthermore, the transport of copper has been the main subject of several agreements designed to guarantee traffic to specific rail routes. Given the importance of copper in the modern industrial world, there should be no doubt that its transport will continue to be the impetus for a great deal of controversy.

There are four existing routes by which the copper and other minerals of Zambia and Katanga reach ocean ports:[21]

1. The all-rail route from Katanga and Zambia to the ports of Beira and Lourenço Marques, via the Congolese Compagnie du Chemin de Fer du Bas-Congo au Katanga (BCK) and Rhodesia Railways connecting with Beira and Lourenço Marques railroads.

2. The all-rail route from Zambia and Katanga to the port of Lobito via the Rhodesia Railways and the BCK, connecting with the Benguela Railway.

3. The rail-river-rail route from Katanga to the port of Matadi in the Congo, via the BCK, the Kasai and Congo rivers, and the Chemin de Fer du Congo (Matadi-Léopoldville railroad).

4. Rail-lake-rail route from the Katanga and Zambia to the port of Dar es Salaam in Tanzania, via BCK, Compagnie des Chemins de Fer du Congo Supérieur aux Grands Lacs Africains (CFL), Lake Tanganyika, and East African Railways.

Copper from Zambia and Katanga could also be transported directly to the Republic of South Africa via the BCK and Rhodesia Railways, connecting with the rail system of Botswana and South Africa. This "old South African route" is now used for the transport of copper destined for domestic consumption in South Africa, but it is no longer used for the export of copper at the South African termini of Durban, Port Elizabeth, and Cape Town, as it was on a few former occasions.

In the postwar years, governments have exerted increasing influence on the transport of copper by taking over the ownership and management of railroads and by endorsing controls and agreements relating to the division of traffic among the various railways serving the region. In 1947 and 1948, Rhodesia Railways and Beira Railway changed from private to state ownership. Since the Malvérnia line of the Lourenço Marques system has been owned by the Mozambique Government from the outset of operations in 1955, only three of the major rail lines concerned with copper traffic are still privately owned. These are the Benguela Railway and the two lines in the Congo, but the latter are virtually controlled by the state, as is the rest of the transport system in the Congo.

The British, Belgian, Portuguese, and German administrations, along with such strong-minded individualists as Cecil Rhodes and Robert Williams, played major roles in determining present railway routes. "The division of traffic among the various railways," as Haefele and Steinberg observe in their study of transport in the area, "has been and is determined to a large extent by agreements among private companies and railways, by railway tariff policies, and by ocean shipping rates." Other factors, according to these authorities, include "political relations among the colonial powers or among the countries themselves, the chronological order in which the railways were opened, and the allocation of the original mining and railway concessions."[22]

Nearly all the colonial powers became involved in building railways. Only after the explorer Stanley had warned Leopold II, founder and ruler of the Congo Free State, that, without a railway connecting the lower to the upper Congo, his colony was not worth a two-shilling piece, did he decide to build a railway from Matadi to Stanley Pool (Léopoldville), grant a concession to an international consortium to carry out the work, and persuade the Belgian Parliament to lend him 10 million francs as part of the capital.[23] It was Leopold II who, in 1906, sponsored the Compagnie du Chemin de Fer du Bas-Congo au Katanga in order to bring the mineral wealth of Katanga to the port of Matadi, enlisting private capital and making it pay for the concession by the allocation of a large number of shares to the state.

Similarly, it was the British South Africa Company, founded by Cecil Rhodes, Prime Minister of the Cape Colony, in order to annex, administer, and develop as much country to the north as he could lay hands on, that built most of the railways that now connect Central Africa with the southern and southeastern seaboards of the continent. One historian has called these rail lines "the greatest single bequest of the Chartered Company to Central Africa."[24]

Rhodes himself had dreamed of an "all red" (that is, all British) Cape-to-Cairo railway, but he came up against opposition from both the Belgians in the Congo and the Germans in East Africa. If it was true, as used to be said, that the flag follows trade, in Africa the railways followed the mineral prospectors. The final alignment was determined by the discovery of deposits of lead and other ores at a site in Zambia that was given the name Broken Hill (after a similar mine in New South Wales) and of copper farther north on sites that are now part of the copper belt of Zambia. Starting from Mafeking in 1895, the railway reached Bulawayo in 1897, Broken Hill in 1906, and Elizabethville in 1910. Meanwhile, the Beira Railway had reached Umtali, near the Rhodesia frontier, and from there the connection with Salisbury and Bulawayo, and thus with Zambia and Katanga, was completed in 1902. Thanks to this system, it is possible today to make a train journey from the Atlantic to the Indian Ocean through Central Africa and to admire the wisdom of those who had the vision to conceive and the energy to build the railroads.

The last and least important route for exports from Katanga, to Dar es Salaam via Lake Tanganyika, has existed since the eve of World War I, but it was greatly improved, in 1956, with the completion of the rail link between Kamina and Kabalo in the Congo. This route requires two transshipments in crossing Lake Tanganyika and consumes a great deal more time than the Angola or Mozambique routes. The Congo portion of the route consists of the BCK railway as far as Kamina and the CFL line from there to Albertville, the lakeside terminus; the Tanzania portion comprises the East African Railways (Tanganyika Central Line) and port facilities at Kigoma and Dar es Salaam. The Tanzania portion was originally built by the German Government, but, after Tanganyika became a British mandate following World War I, Belgium was permitted to establish its own cargo-handling facilities at Kigoma on the Tanganyika side of the lake and at Dar es Salaam on the Indian Ocean. Only small amounts of Katanga copper have been shipped by this route,[25] but it has come in useful at times when other routes were closed, as, for example, in 1966 when the Congolese Government put a temporary ban on the Benguela Railway. At other times, as when the eastern provinces of the Congo were in a state of rebellion between 1964 and 1966, all traffic movements were suspended on the CFL network.

The influence of controls and agreements pertaining to the copper traffic is considerably more complicated than the layout of transport routes. One of the major factors affecting the direction of movements has been the policy of *tout par la voie nationale*, initiated in the Congo by Leopold II and promoted successively by Belgian colonial governments and the independent Congolese Government at Kinshasa. The "national route policy" in effect promotes the transport of Katanga copper by way of the cumbersome rail-river-rail route via the BCK railway, the Kasai and Congo rivers, and the Matadi-Kinshasa rail line. From Lubumbashi in Katanga to the terminus of this route at the port of Matadi, the distance is more than 400 miles farther than the 1,309 miles from Lubumbashi to Lobito via the Benguela Railway, and even 100 miles farther than Lubumbashi

337

to Beira via rail. Because of the longer distance and time required to reach port, and the lower security of shipments, success of the national route policy has depended on specially adjusted tariffs, much persuasion, and, more recently, compulsion, rather than on competitive advantages. Preference of the powerful mining companies for the shorter routes, especially the CFB, and the dependence of Katanga on coal from Rhodesia were among factors restraining total shipment of Katanga copper via the all-Congo route, but a strong reason was also inadequate capacity.

Before the Congo became independent in 1960, only about half the copper from Katanga was shipped by the all-Congo route. With the secession of Katanga, this route was totally interrupted and traffic on it was resumed only in 1968. Owing to the deterioration in the railway and river port installations and partial silting of the access channels, the Matadi route can now handle only about one-third of the Congo copper exports. The remainder has been going out through Lobito via the Benguela Railway (about two-fifths) and through Beira or Lourenço Marques via the Rhodesia Railways and the Mozambique railroads (about three-tenths). The Benguela Railway also hauls a sizable share of cobalt, manganese, zinc, and other minerals from Katanga, mostly from the northwestern region contiguous to the BCK rail branch that connects directly with the Benguela. Present plans to build a new railroad in the Congo to preclude use of the Congo River to reach Matadi would give added meaning to the Congolese sentiment for the *voie nationale*.

Another major factor that affects the division of traffic among the various rail lines is a series of agreements among the governments of the countries involved. The first agreement, signed in 1936 between the Rhodesia Railway and the Northern Rhodesia copper companies, provided that all copper produced would be transported over the Rhodesian network and that no hydroelectric power would be developed. In return, Rhodesia Railways agreed to observe fixed rates on copper and grant extremely low rates on transport of coal and coke from the Wankie colliery in Southern Rhodesia to copper smelters in Northern Rhodesia. This ensured the rail companies some balance in shipments over the section of the main trunk between Wankie and Ndola.

The Beira Convention of June 17, 1950, was signed by Portugal and Great Britain (the latter on behalf of Southern Rhodesia and the territories of Northern Rhodesia and Nyasaland), to remain in force for twenty years and as long thereafter as all parties to the agreement wished. The Portuguese promised to maintain the port of Beira and the Beira rail line in a state of efficiency adequate to the requirements of the traffic proceeding from the three British territories and to preserve Beira as a free port for goods proceeding to or from these territories. In return for its commitment to undertake the substantial investment required to improve and maintain port and rail facilities, Portugal was promised that all parties to the convention would make every effort to use the full working capacity of the port and railway in their existing state or at any stage of their progressive expansion. If anything prevented such an increase or appeared likely to do so, the parties agreed to consult together with a view to taking whatever reasonable steps were necessary in furtherance of the common objective.[26]

The Tripartite Agreement on November 7, 1956, between the CFB, the BCK, and the Rhodesia Railways was a consequence of the impatience of the copper companies with congestion and delays on the Beira route. It became effective January 1, 1957, for a period of four years. Rail rates on copper from Northern Rhodesia to Lobito were then equalized with those to Beira and Lourenço Marques. However, the amount of copper permitted to be shipped out via the BCK and Benguela to Lobito in the course of a year was limited to "10 per cent of the railing by the Northern Rhodesian Copper Mines to Beira and Lourenço Marques" at the time the agreement became effective, "plus 50 per cent of any additional tonnage which would be available for railing to Beira and Lourenço Marques in the future, subject to higher tonnage than 20 per cent of the total tonnage available for export overseas."[27]

However, soon after the renewal of the Tripartite Agreement in July, 1960, Rhodesia Railways introduced a special discount rate on the amount of copper authorized to be shipped out via the BCK and the Benguela. At the same time, Rhodesia Railways watered down the agreement still further by unilaterally announcing that no more than 36,000 tons of copper a year could move out on the BCK-Benguela route. The attractiveness of the discount rate, which BCK and Benguela declined to match, was such that the Northern Rhodesian copper companies failed to utilize even the 36,000-ton quota. As a result, from mid-1960 to 1963, virtually all Northern Rhodesian copper was shipped out via Rhodesian Railways and the Beira or Lourenço Marques lines.

Dissolution of the Federation of Rhodesia and Nyasaland led to another lengthy agreement on December 10, 1963, between the governments of Rhodesia and Zambia relating to Rhodesia Railways. The ownership and control of the line passed from the government of the Federation to the joint authority of the separate governments. Rhodesia and Zambia promised to accept the "obligations arising from agreements on railway traffic matters which the Government of the United Kingdom has made on their behalf or in respect of each Territory and recognize agreements to which the Railways are a party." There could be no doubt that such an obligation included the Beira Convention. The two governments also recognized their mutual interest in "the maintenance of the existing arrangements for the movement of their internal and external trade" over Rhodesia Railways "as a means of ensuring the viability of the Railways and the protection of their investment in the Railways."

In 1965, however, following the unilateral declaration of independence (UDI) by the Rhodesian Government of Ian Smith, movement of copper on the Rhodesian Railways abruptly ceased, owing to the refusal of Zambia to transfer currency for the payment of freight dues. After stocks had accumulated alarmingly, the traffic was partly resumed in the summer of 1966, and at the same time agreement was reached to ship 10,000 tons of copper monthly (about one-fifth of the total output) by the Katanga and Benguela railways. Finally, in 1967, as a result of the quarrel over UDI and the application of sanctions against Rhodesia, the two governments agreed to end their joint control and run the two portions of the rail line separately.

To summarize, the system existing prior to its dislocation by the Rhodesia-

339

Zambia dispute endorsed the almost total reliance on the Rhodesia and Mozambique railways for Zambia's copper exports and part of Katanga's copper export. Recent events, however, especially the Rhodesian crisis, have served to emphasize the importance of the Benguela Railway as the shortest and safest link between Central Africa and the ocean.

The Future of the Regional Transport System

It is not at all unlikely that the historical pattern of rail transport in southern Central Africa will undergo serious alterations in the immediate years ahead. No interested party can afford to neglect new elements introduced by events of recent years. Foremost has been the break-up of the Central African Federation, the independence of Zambia and Malawi, and the unilateral declaration of independence by Rhodesia, resulting in the separation of the economies of these former British territories. Rhodesian coal is still essential for smelting Zambian copper, but Zambia is rapidly developing its own coal resources. Zambia no longer has to look upon the main rail trunk through present Rhodesia as "a national route." Greater reliance on the Congo-Angola route has been forced on the Zambian copper companies, and they have found it more convenient. Alongside this reliance, Zambia has begun to look more seriously at the Tan-Zam project.

The Benguela Railway has the potential for handling greater traffic, and, by modest additions to its motive power and rolling stock, it could substantially expand its present capacity. Officials in Angola have confirmed to the author that the estimate that the Benguela's capacity could be expanded by 1 million tons a year outbound[28] represents a reasonable and feasible objective. Moreover, improvements in track alignment over the central Angolan escarpment in the Cubal area (Cubal Variant) will increase that capacity by an additional million tons a year. There is more doubt about whether the Benguela Railway can reduce or even remove the proviso, imposed by the former Union Minière du Haut-Katanga, nationalized by the Congolese Government at the beginning of 1967, which requires the CFB to carry a certain proportion of low-rated manganese ore to obtain the much higher rated copper traffic. Without the proviso, the capacity now taken up by manganese shipments (as high as 300,000 tons a year), could be reserved for copper movements.

Five major studies have examined the proposed Tanzania-Zambia rail link, as indicated on the accompanying map.[29] These studies indicate that, given existing agreements, such a route would not be economically justifiable. These studies have stressed the fact that (1) trade between Tanzania and Zambia, both presently and projected, is insufficient to justify the costs of building such a link; (2) if it were built, the potential diversion of freight could have severe financial repercussions on existing lines; (3) a large investment, beyond that required for the rail line proper, would be necessary to make the port of Dar es Salaam capable of handling additional traffic; and (4) improvements in the existing Great North Road from Dar es Salaam to Kapiri in Zambia, estimated by the World Bank to cost roughly $30 million in contrast to the $200–$300 million required to build the rail link, could easily take care of the trade between

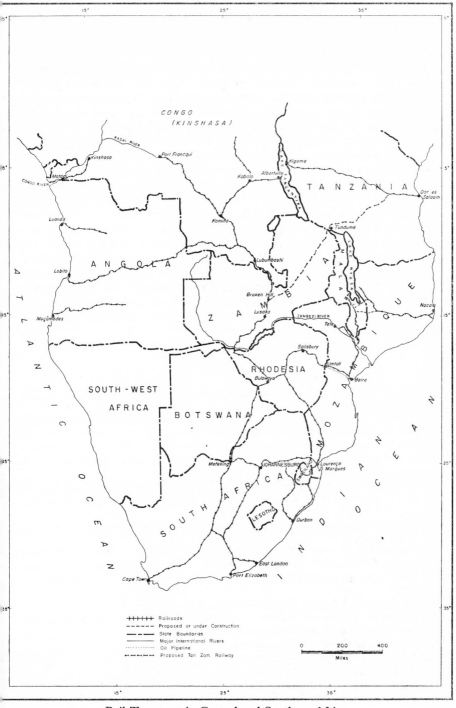

Rail Transport in Central and Southern Africa

the two countries. Because of these arguments, several Western countries refused to grant a loan to build the railroad.

On the other hand, a recent survey made by three consulting firms, headed by the British economist Maxwell Stamp and financed by Britain and Canada, estimated the probable cost of the railroad at $386 million (including the expansion of the Dar es Salaam terminal) and claimed that the link would be profitable because of the fast development of the Zambian economy since the World Bank survey.[30] Moreover, transport experts and economists in Zambia and Tanzania do not agree that the existing long-distance road connection between Kapiri and Dar es Salaam can handle per se the export and import needs of Zambia.

Other factors, however, may take precedence. Zambia sees the projected railroad mainly as a way of liberating itself from routes running through white-governed African countries. Tanzania agrees on this point and believes, furthermore, that it will help the long-postponed agricultural and mineral development of its soutwestern sector and result in additional income for the port of Dar es Salaam. The railroad would be the third largest foreign-aid project in Africa, after the Aswan dam in Egypt, financed by the Soviet Union, and the Volta dam in Ghana, financed by Western interests. The first stage for the building of the railroad began in mid-1968 when 200 Chinese engineers and technicians began a twelve-month survey of the area in Tanzania between Kidatu and Tunduma at the Zambian border.[31]

NOTES

1. George H. T. Kimble, *Tropical Africa: Land and Livelihood*, I (Garden City, 1962), 328–29.
2. Irene S. van Dongen, "Transportes Africanos Internacionais," *Jornal Português de Economia e Finanças*, VI, 63 (October 15, 1958), 13.
3. The best account, though much out of date, of Lobito port is W. A. Hance and I. S. van Dongen, "The Port of Lobito and the Benguela Railway," *The Geographical Review*, XLVI, 4 (October, 1956).
4. Luanda trade has been described in I. S. van Dongen, "The Port of Luanda in the Economy of Angola," *Boletim da Sociedade de Geografia de Lisboa*, January–March, 1960, pp. 3–43.
5. Richard J. Hammond, *Portugal's African Problem: Some Economic Facets* (New York, 1962), p. 16.
6. *Standard Bank Review* (London), September, 1966, p. 3. See also *Benguela Railway—Companhia do Caminho de Ferro de Benguela: Reports of 1960 and 1962*. Also *Tanganyika Concessions Limited: Report and Accounts* (July 31, 1966).
7. *Standard Bank Review*, September, 1966, p. 4.
8. Edwin T. Haefele and Eleanor B. Steinberg, *Government Controls on Transport: An African Case* (Washington, 1965), p. 18.
9. *West Africa* (London), November 9, 1968, p. 1331.
10. All data on port and railway movements are from Banco de Angola, *Relatório e contas—exercício de 1967* (Lisbon, 1968).
11. Hammond, *op. cit.*, p. 25.
12. Traffic over the Porto Amboím line and its terminal, as well as the development

of Moçâmedes terminal and its rail route, was studied by Irene S. van Dongen in her "Coffee Trade, Coffee Regions, and Coffee Ports in Angola," *Economic Geography*, October, 1961, pp. 339–44, and "Sea Fisheries and Fish Ports in Angola," *Boletim da Sociedade de Geografia de Lisboa*, January–June, 1962, pp. 13–17.

13. For an outdated but highly valuable discussion of the two ports, see William A. Hance and Irene S. van Dongen, "Lourenço Marques in Delagoa Bay," *Economic Geography*, XXXIII, 3 (July, 1957), 238–56, and "Beira, Mozambique Gateway to Central Africa," *Annals of the Association of American Geographers*, XLVII (1957), 307–35. Also see the more recent study by N. Manfred Shaffer, *The Competitive Position of the Port of Durban* (Evanston, 1965).

14. Portugal, Província de Moçambique, Direcção Provincial dos Serviços de Estatística, *Boletim Mensal*, March, 1967, p. 71. This source also provides other transport data for Mozambique. See also Banco Nacional Ultramarino, *Boletim Trimestral*, No. 73 (1968), pp. 38–41.

15. See Irene S. van Dongen, "Nacala, Newest Mozambique Gateway to Interior Africa," *Tijdschrift voor Economische and Sociale Geografie*, March, 1957, pp. 65–73.

16. Connected with this link-up by LonRho Company (a British enterprise that also controls the Beira pipeline) is the Malawi Government's offer for the controlling block of shares in Malawi Railways. Negotiations have been begun with contractors. The new railway will serve a proposed new port at Liwonde with railroad-water interchange. A survey has been undertaken to determine how the lake transport facilities could be better used. A projected Vipya pulp and paper scheme in Malawi would become a major benefactor of such transport to Nacala. "Malawi," *Standard Bank Review* (London), April, 1967, pp. 8–9.

17. *Washington Post*, May 9, 1968.

18. "Malawi", *Standard Bank Review* (London), April, 1968, p. 7.

19. Personal communication from the Economic Department of Portugal's Overseas Ministry.

20. *The Christian Science Monitor*, October 10, 1967; *Peking Review*, November 8, 1968, pp. 27–28.

21. Haefele and Steinberg, *op. cit.*, pp. 5–8.

22. *Ibid.*, pp. 10–11.

23. George Martelli, *Leopold to Lumumba* (London, 1962), p. 80.

24. A. J. Wills, *History of Central Africa* (London, 1964), p. 159.

25. See W. A. Hance and I. S. van Dongen, "Dar es Salaam, the Port and Its Tributary Area," *Annals of the Association of American Geographers*, XLVIII, 4 (December, 1958), 419–35.

26. U.K. Treaty Series, *Convention Between the Government of the United Kingdom and the Government of the Republic of Portugal, Relative to the Port of Beira and Connected Railways, Lisbon, 17 June 1950*, Cmd. Paper 8061 (London, 1950).

27. See *Tripartite Agreement Between the Companhia do Caminho de Ferro de Benguela, the Compagnie du Chemin de Fer du Bas-Congo au Katanga, and the Rhodesia Railways Relating to the Passage of Goods Traffic Between Lobito and the Rhodesia Railways* (Bulawayo: November, 1956).

28. Haefele and Steinberg, *op. cit.*, pp. 10–11.

29. These include *ibid.*, under a contract with the Agency for International Development of the U.S. Department of State; a joint study by the FAO and the Economic Commission for Africa, *Economic Survey Mission on the Economic Development of Zambia* (Ndola, 1964); an older survey prepared for the Colonial Office of the United Kingdom by Sir Alexander Gibb and Partners, a consulting firm, *Report on Central African Rail Link Development Survey* (London, 1952), 2 vols.; and reports of two survey missions from the World Bank.
30. *The Washington Post*, November 16, 1967.
31. *The Times* (London), June 21, 1968.

XV

Portugal and the African Territories: Economic Implications

ANDREW WILSON GREEN

THIS CHAPTER covers the economic situation and changes taking place in Portugal and Portuguese Africa as the result of Portuguese-African policies. Answers are sought to a number of questions. What is the cost to Portugal of its African involvement, and does Portugal have the economic capacity to carry this cost? Is Portugal's presence in Africa impeding the economic development of metropolitan Portugal? What would be the effect on Portugal of a change in its African policy? What would be the effect of a change in Portugal's African policy on Portuguese Africa?

Because answers to these questions cannot be given without an understanding of the basic structure of the present economy of metropolitan Portugal, one must begin with a survey of that economy and the effect on Portugal of its defense of the African provinces. Thereafter, an evaluation will be attempted of the costs and benefits of the most likely situations and policy choices confronting Portugal.

In an examination of the Portuguese economy, the persistence and stability of its main features are striking. Portugal is saddled with a backward and unproductive agriculture that occupies a disproportionate part of its active working force. In 1965, only 20.7 per cent of the Portuguese gross product at factor cost came from agriculture, fishing, and forestry; yet, in 1967, these activities still employed about 37 per cent of the Portuguese working force. As recently as 1952, agriculture, fishing, and forestry represented 30.7 per cent of gross national product at factor cost. The productivity of the land is low and not improving. It should be noted, however, that Portugal has substantially increased the area of land under cultivation in the last thirty years, perhaps unwisely, so that existing low productivity may be due to the entry into production of marginal land rather than failure to improve the productivity of the land formerly in use. As a consequence, the volume of agricultural production has increased substantially in absolute terms, but there has been no relative increase in recent years.[1]

There has lately been a significant expansion of industrial production in Portugal, at the rate of 8 to 9 per cent a year. Using 1960 as the index year of 100, industrial production has increased from 58 to 151 in the period 1953–65.

Foreign trade represents a significant part of the Portuguese economy, with imports varying from 20 to 25 per cent of gross national product and exports varying from 12 to 15 per cent. The importance of foreign trade has been increasing since World War II, as Portugal increased the importation of machines to modernize its economy and as its textiles and light industrial goods found wider markets abroad.

The export volume of Portugal has been dependent, to a large extent, on canned fish, wine, and cork. Dependence on these exports, however, has diminished from 38.6 to 25.6 per cent of exports in the period 1953–65. Textile exports, in contrast, have grown in importance from 12.6 per cent to 25.1 per cent of exports for the same period (see the accompanying table). Manufactured goods (excluding canned fish, wine, and cork but including textiles) now account for about 45 per cent of Portuguese exports.

Major Portuguese Commodity Exports (Percentage), 1953–65

	1953	1957	1961	1965
Cork products	19.2	16.5	14.7	9.8
Canned fish	9.5	11.8	12.7	8.5
Wine	9.5	8.9	8.2	7.3
Textiles	12.6	15.8	17.9	25.1
Total (in $ million)	$214	$282	$319	$563

Source: For 1953, 1957, and 1961; OECD, Études Economiques—Portugal (June, 1963), p. 19. For 1965; OECD, Études Economiques—Portugal (December, 1966), p. 56.

Portugal's trading partners change little from year to year but they are many; thus, Portugal is not dependent upon its trade with any one country. Since the end of World War II, the United States has lost its importance as a supplier while Western Germany has regained its importance as a supplier. The United Kingdom lost its importance as a customer in the 1950's, when exports to the United Kingdom fell from 20.3 per cent to 12.4 per cent, but, in 1966, the United Kingdom again took 19.2 per cent of Portuguese exports.[2]

In the mid-1960's, as compared to the late 1950's, imports from the United States rose rapidly, although the United States has not regained the importance as a supplier that it had in the immediate post–World War II period, as the United Kingdom and other EFTA countries have. Exports in recent years have shown a tendency to increase to EFTA countries, to the United Kingdom, and somewhat to the United States. The establishment of EFTA has had a marked effect on the pattern of Portuguese foreign trade. In the period 1959–64, the share of EEC countries in Portugal's foreign trade declined, while the share of EFTA countries in Portugal's foreign trade increased (see the accompanying table).

Portuguese-African provinces are important to Portuguese foreign trade, as they take about 24 per cent of all exports and supply about 13 per cent of imports. They have absorbed a much larger proportion of exports in the post–World War II period than they did in the pre–World War II period, although

Recent Trends in Portuguese Trade Origins and Destinations

		Per Cent Increase	Per Cent Share in Exports	
	1964*	over 1959	1959	1964
Exports to major markets				
EFTA	114.6	122.1	17.8	23.0
United Kingdom	63.2	91.5	11.4	12.7
EEC	106.8	62.1	22.7	21.5
United States	54.2	90.8	9.8	10.9
Portuguese overseas territories	127.7	56.9	28.0	25.7
Total	466.5	71.3	89.7	93.8

		Per Cent Increase	Per Cent Share in Imports	
	1964*	over 1959	1959	1964
Imports from major suppliers				
EFTA	167.3	69.0	20.8	22.3
United Kingdom	104.6	71.8	12.8	13.9
EEC	255.7	37.5	39.1	34.0
United States	81.1	180.6	6.1	10.8
Portuguese overseas territories	89.6	33.5	14.1	11.9
Total	698.3	57.9	92.9	90.9

* In millions of dollars.

Source: EFTA, EFTA Trade 1959–64 (Geneva, 1966), as adapted from tables C5 i and C5 v.

the proportion of Portuguese imports from its overseas territories has not increased. This increase in exports may reflect the demands of a greater number of Portuguese residents in the African provinces. On an individual basis in the last decade, there has been a tendency toward a relative reduction of exports to Angola and a substantial relative increase in imports from Angola, while Portugal's position in Mozambique's trade has remained constant. Traditionally, Portugal has enjoyed a favorable trade relationship with its overseas territories, particularly with Angola.[3]

The balance of trade between Portugal and its overseas provinces is not important in relation to metropolitan Portugal's over-all balance-of-payments position. In the period 1960–64, Portugal's over-all adverse trade balance with foreign countries was $1,000 million, and the positive trade balance with its overseas provinces was only $84 million. Despite a persistent adverse trade balance that runs from 7 to 9 per cent of GNP, and a tendency toward positive trade balances in the overseas provinces, Portugal's balance of payments is nearly always positive, except in years like 1961, when Portugal and the escudo zone were under pressure to meet the emergency arising from the outbreak of

Summary Balance of Payments of Escudo Zone (in Millions of Dollars), 1961–66

		1961	*1962*	*1963*	*1964*	*1965*	*1966*
Current transactions							
Metropolitan Portugal							
Trade		−269.4	−164.0	−185.4	−215.7	−298.4	−327.1
Invisibles		+9.9	+58.1	+76.5	+103.5	+172.1	+303.9
	Total	−259.5	−105.9	−108.9	−112.2	−126.3	−23.2
Metropolitan Portugal overseas provinces							
Trade		+84.7	+14.5	+24.2	+32.5	−27.3	−51.2
Invisibles		+29.4	+55.9	+62.7	+96.5	+118.9	+130.0
	Total	+114.1	+70.4	+86.9	+129.0	+91.6	+78.8
Balance on current account		−145.4	−35.5	−22.0	+16.8	−34.7	+55.6
Capital transactions*							
Short-term		+18.2	+28.2	+5.8	−5.9	+41.8	−18.2
Long-term		+38.7	+120.8	+89.3	+99.3	+65.3	+110.7
Balance on capital account		+56.9	+149.0	+95.1	+93.4	+107.1	+92.5
Overseas capital transactions		—	—	−0.2	−2.1	−5.7	−7.2
Errors and omissions		−7.8	−0.6	+1.9	+1.1	+2.6	−4.0
	Total	−96.3	+112.9	+74.8	+109.2	+69.3	+136.9

* Metropolitan Portugal only.

Source: For 1961–62, Xavier V. Pintado, *Structure and Growth of the Portuguese Economy* (July, 1964), table CIX; for 1963–66, Banco de Portugal, *Relatório Anual* (Lisbon, 1967).

rebellion in Angola (see the accompanying table). The adverse trade balance is normally met by private remittances of Portuguese nationals in foreign countries and from tourism.[4] With the anticipated growth of tourism in Portugal, no balance-of-payments deficit seems likely in the foreseeable future. However, the size of the adverse trade balance as a percentage of GNP appears to be increasing; it was 9.9 per cent of GNP in 1966.

Per capita GNP was about $457 in 1967.[5] Total GNP rose at an average annual rate of 6.3 per cent in the period 1959–65, as indicated by the national income figures at constant prices published by OECD, and the GNP per capita rose at an average annual rate of 5.8 per cent. In 1966, the increase of GNP appears to have been smaller and has been estimated unofficially at 4.7 per cent.[6]

In 1964, Pintado was of the opinion that "the Portuguese economy has not done very well." In his study for EFTA, however, he compared Portuguese economic growth with growth of other European Mediterranean regions— Spain, southern Italy, Greece, Turkey, and Yugoslavia—on the basis of 1961 figures. His comparisons show that Portugal has done better than southern Italy, Spain, and Turkey but not as well as Greece and Yugoslavia.[7]

A comparison of Portuguese economic growth with that of Western Europe is favorable to Portugal. In the period 1951–61, the annual rate of growth of income per capita was 4.0 per cent in Portugal, 2.9 per cent in all EFTA countries, and 3.6 per cent in all European OECD countries. While the annual rate of growth of Portuguese GNP was 5.7 per cent, that of EFTA countries was 3.4 per cent and of all European OECD countries, 4.4 per cent. Similar comparisons for other periods are likewise favorable to Portugal. OECD data show that, in the period 1958–65, Portugal had a higher increase of GNP per capita than all OECD countries except Japan and Greece.

The price level in Portugal has been quite steady, but there have been signs of modest inflation in recent years. For the period 1958–65, OECD figures show GNP at market prices as 12.8 per cent greater than GNP at constant prices, or an increase of 1.8 per cent annually, uncompounded. The level of prices increased by 2.6 per cent in 1966. OECD figures, ending in November, 1967, show for the Lisbon area, where prices are only slightly higher than in other parts of Portugal, an annual rate of change of the consumer price index as 3.4 per cent.[8]

Military expenditures on the basis of income figures published by the OECD were about 6.5 per cent of GNP in 1965 and 1966, or almost twice the level before the outbreak of the rebellion in Angola in 1961.[9] In 1966, military expenditures amounted to $263 million. This percentage varies between 3.8 and 5.8 per cent and is higher than in all other countries of Western Europe but considerably below that of the United States, with 7.6 per cent in 1965 and 11 per cent in 1966. The rate of fixed-asset formation appears to be higher than before the outbreak of the rebellion in Angola in 1961, for the period 1953–60, it averaged 14.9 per cent of GNP, and it is now occurring at the rate of about 17 per cent of GNP. A comparison of Portugal with OECD countries for 1965 shows that Portugal is investing the smallest proportion of GNP of any OECD country in fixed domestic assets. This indicates that Portugal has effected a rather remarkable performance in increasing its GNP as much as it has, with such a small level of investment. In other words, Portugal has enjoyed a high capital output ratio. It also indicates that Portugal has the capacity to generate a higher level of savings and investment and that it would enjoy a rapid rate of increase in GNP. A major Portuguese problem is stimulating domestic savings and investment and developing capital markets.

Government finances are conducted on a conservative basis, which means that the national debt is low in relation to current government revenue and that the amortization of existing debt is feasible. *Current* central government expenses for Portugal were 13.7 per cent of GNP for 1965, which is slightly less than the average of 14.8 per cent in other OECD European countries. For the period 1951–60, these expenses averaged 10.6 per cent and, for 1961–65, 14.1 per cent of GNP.

This increase in current governmental expenditures is roughly equivalent to the increase of military expenditures between the two periods, which has previously been noted to be equivalent to 3 per cent of GNP.

Total government expenditures, which includes capital expenditures, averaged 17.5 per cent of GNP for the period 1961–66. During the period 1961–65, military expenses averaged 40.9 per cent of central government expenditures.[10] In comparison with other countries, Portugal's defense expenditures are high as a percentage of total government expenditures (see the accompanying table).

Military Expenditures in Relation to Current Government Expenses, 1965

Country	(A) Current Government Expenditures	(B) Defense Expenditures	Per Cent (B/A)	Currency Units
OECD	212.8	77.5	32	U.S. dollars (billion)
OECD-Europe	73.1	20.2	27	U.S. dollars (billion)
EEC	42.7	11.3	26	U.S. dollars (billion)
Canada	7,176	1,693	24	Canadian dollars (million)
United States	125,226	52,262	42	U.S. dollars (million)
Belgium	107.4	24	22	Belgian francs (billion)
Denmark	10,614	1,970	19	kroners (million)
France	61.47	19.56	32	francs (billion)
Germany	69.60	18.01	26	marks (billion)
Greece	17,553	5,614	32	drachmas (million)
Italy	5,198	930	17	lire (billion)
Portugal	14,825	7,108	48	escudos (million)
Sweden	19,254	4,430	23	kroners (million)
United Kingdom	5,918	2,050	34	pounds (million)
Switzerland	7,035	1,465	21	Swiss francs (million)

Source: OECD, *National Account Statistics, 1956–65* (Paris, 1967).

The 1968 national budget called for defense expenditures of $273 million, or 35 per cent of the total budget. However, in the first eight months of 1968, emergencies raised military expenditures by one-fourth above the budget provisions and thus represented 48.7 per cent of total budgeted expenditures, a significant increase.[11]

Central government debt in relative terms has increased slightly since the outbreak of the rebellion in Angola. In 1962, central government debt was 27.4 per cent of GNP, and in 1966 this percentage was 29.2. Debt service and amortization were estimated to take 9.8 per cent of budgeted revenues in 1968. Comparing Portugal's public finances with other OECD countries, one finds that interest charges as a percentage of government revenues for 1965 are higher in seven countries and lower in eleven countries. If interest charges are compared with GNP, one finds that, in Portugal, they are higher than in seven OECD countries and lower than in eleven. Portuguese public debt should also be considered in relation to Portuguese gold and foreign-exchange reserves, which in 1966 amounted to $1.1 billion, in relation to a national debt of $1.2 billion.[12]

Money in circulation in Portugal has varied only slightly from 21 per cent of

GNP. The lowest percentage of money in circulation was 19.4 per cent of GNP, in 1951; the highest percentage was 23.2 per cent, in 1953.[13] Also evident is the determination of Banco de Portugal not to weaken the solidity of Portuguese currency by reducing the proportion of reserves held to support the increased money in circulation and the increased economic activity. Gold and foreign-exchange reserves have been maintained at a fixed ratio of 56 to 57 per cent of sight responsibilities. It is notable that, despite increased defense expenditures and the need for external public borrowing, Portugal managed to increase its gold and foreign-exchange reserves. Its policy in this regard is like that of a corporate treasurer who borrows money on long-term to place in the corporate cash account, so that short-term liquidity will not be jeopardized and so that the corporation will not lack cash when an immediate demand is made.

Some modest credit expansion has occurred since the outbreak of the rebellion in Angola in 1961, and bank deposits have expanded at a rate faster than money in circulation, so that gold and foreign-exchange reserves have been reduced in relation to the total credit volume in Portugal. This may account for the increased but moderate rate of price inflation since 1961, and it may also have assisted in the increasing pace of economic development in the first half of the 1960's.

It appears, thus, that Portuguese monetary authorities have attempted, as a general policy, not to stimulate economic activity by monetary manipulation but rather to adjust the monetary volume to the level of economic activity. In other words, while Portuguese monetary volume varies, it is kept in fixed relation to other economic variables, so as to operate with constant and predictable effect.

The correctness of the Salazar government in maintaining such large reserves of gold and foreign exchange has been a matter of discussion. Portuguese gold and foreign-exchange reserves continue to exceed one year's imports, and they are large in comparison with the reserves of similar countries. There seems to be little question that this policy has contributed to price stability in Portugal and has sheltered its currency from the effects of foreign-exchange speculation. With the exception of the need for defense imports in relation to the Angolan crisis of 1961, Portugal has not used its foreign reserves to offset the economic effects of fluctuations in foreign trade.

Nevertheless, it is questionable whether so large a part of Portugal's assets need be kept unproductive at the cost of assuring the stability that makes other assets productive. It is likewise questionable how far Portugal should borrow abroad when the proceeds, at least indirectly, end up in increasing the reserves of Banco de Portugal. On the other hand, if these reserves do not represent a diversion from investment, they at least contribute to the checking of any inflationary tendencies in the economy. Also, some of these reserves undoubtedly earn interest, so that the net loss to Portugal may be smaller than would seem at first glance.

Portugal's level of domestic savings has been low in relation to other countries. The 10.6 per cent in the period 1952–61 stands below Spain, where savings average 18.0 per cent of GNP, Greece with 11.4 per cent, Turkey with 12.9 per cent, and Yugoslavia with 25.5 per cent. At the same time, the rate of domestic investment was 16.3 per cent of GNP,[14] leaving an investment deficit of 5.7 per cent to be filled from external sources. Domestic savings are defined here as domestic investment plus the foreign-trade balance. Such a definition makes the domestic-savings deficit equivalent to the adverse trade balance. However, Portugal has added to its currency reserves and has maintained a positive balance of payments, overcoming its adverse trade balance by remittances and invisibles. If these two factors are taken into consideration, the Portuguese domestic-saving "deficit" may be nonexistent.

A study made by the International Development Association, which deplores the inadequacy of Portugal's domestic savings, nevertheless shows that, in the first half of the 1960's, the savings deficit (if account is taken of the remittance of emigrants and others) is only 3.2 per cent of GNP (omitting the abnormal year of 1961).[15] The study noted that no consideration has been made of "service transactions between the metropole and overseas provinces," because "statistical data on this surplus vis-à-vis the overseas territories are not available." Such data are now provided in the annual reports of Banco de Portugal, and they indicate that the overseas provinces contribute a considerable positive sum from invisibles to the metropolitan balance of payments, even after contributions of the metropolitan government to the overseas provinces are deducted. The contributions of invisibles by the overseas provinces for 1964, 1965, and 1966 were $63 millions, $21 million, and $38.5 million, respectively.[16] Since Portugal's nondebtor position depends on private remittances and invisible earnings from its overseas provinces, its ability to meet its domestic investment requirements without external borrowing might be dubious if it is separated from them in the future.

Whether Portuguese domestic savings are low because of inadequate demand for savings or inadequate supply of savings is uncertain. The interest rate paid by Portuguese banks is relatively low, at about 2 per cent. This low rate is not likely to attract new savings or foreign investments in today's money markets, although the interest will be received in currency subject to little price inflation, without risks. Portuguese households have the habit of thrift, as the large emigrant remittances show. It seems somewhat dubious that higher rates of interest would substantially increase household savings, while they would subject government finances to the stress of higher interest rates, which they are, nevertheless, quite capable of bearing at present. Since the capital output ratio of Portugal is high, this suggests that the absence of domestic savings may be due to the failure of individuals and enterprises to demand credit for productive undertakings and, possibly, to the failure of government and financial institutions to expand credit to take care of such needs. The circle seems vicious: there is no market because there is no credit, and there is no credit because there is no market. These reflections strengthen the view that the Portuguese must develop a securities market.

An alternative to the prudent expansion of credit for investment would be greater investment by the state in business enterprises. The Portuguese Government has shown no prejudice, in principle, against investment in public works and nationally owned industries. However, Portugal has, by and large, maintained a privately owned economy, and expansion of the government owned sector has certain disadvantages. Since the government is fighting a war, it may not wish to add to the burdens of public finance at this time. Extra taxation also dries up the normal sources of private investment. Investment through government debt is inflationary and may discourage private investment.

If Portugal fails to generate a higher level of private domestic investment, it may wish to have access to the foreign capital market. The recent external loans of the government and recent substantial private foreign investment in Portugal—such as the ship-building and repairing installations of Lisnave at Lisbon—indicate that Portugal has effective access to international capital markets.

From the foregoing data, it seems fair to conclude that Portugal's defense of its African provinces does not have, so far, a critical effect on the economic development of metropolitan Portugal and that the defense effort has been within its economic means. The increase of 3 to 3.5 per cent of GNP for defense expenditures over pre–1961 levels cannot be regarded as sufficiently large to exercise a powerful effect on Portugal's economic development.[17]

Of more pressing concern are reforms to provide more credit on a selective basis (including medium and long-term credit for industry), modernization of the many family-run companies, and improvement of agriculture, as already discussed. A fundamental issue is whether Portugal's educational effort is adequate to support development needs. Late in 1968, indications were that Dr. Alfredo Vaz Pinto, Caetano's minister of state, would give early attention to reforms in such areas.

EFFECTS OF A WITHDRAWAL FROM AFRICA ON PORTUGAL

This section will consider the benefits and costs to metropolitan Portugal of a conjectural withdrawal from its African provinces. As seen above, the cost to Portugal of both military defense and economic development of its African provinces does not, at present, exceed 4 per cent of its GNP, and the cost of the African defense alone is between 3 and 3.5 per cent of its GNP. Under the Third National Development Plan (1968–73), the metropolitan government further plans to contribute $235 million to overseas economic development, of which approximately two-thirds will be spent in the African provinces. This would represent about one-half of 1 per cent of estimated Portuguese GNP for that period. Presumably, if Portugal were to withdraw from its African provinces, these expenses for defense and for overseas development in Africa would be saved and would become available for other purposes.

Against this small saving must be balanced the loss of profits from trade with its African provinces, loss of investments in Africa, and loss of future profits from these investments. It seems only reasonable to suppose that, if the political connection with its African provinces were terminated, Portugal's trade with them would diminish. This trade is profitable to Portugal and to Portuguese business, however.

In the case of Mozambique, the loss should not be very significant. Trade with Mozambique, constituted 4.4 per cent of all Portuguese imports in 1964,

9.9 per cent of all exports. Angolan trade is more important. In 1964, Angolan trade constituted 7.9 per cent of Portuguese imports and 15.6 per cent of exports. Together, in 1964, Angola and Mozambique accounted for 12.3 per cent of Portuguese imports and 25.5 per cent of exports.[18] The loss of this amount of total trade would have a serious, but not critical, impact on the Portuguese economy. If imports and exports were to decline in the same ratio, the effect of the loss of this trade on the Portuguese balance of payments should be minimal. While Portugal's exports to overseas provinces constitute a larger proportion of its total exports than imports from these provinces constitute of its total imports, the exports to overseas possessions are only slightly larger in absolute amount than imports from the provinces.

The foreign exchange earned by the sale of Angolan coffee is not used by Portugal to pay for its trade deficit with other countries, but it pays for imports from Portugal and for Portuguese services to Angola. The net profit to Portugal from this trade is small or nonexistent. The favorable trade balance of Portugal with Angola is tending to disappear. Portugal's increasingly favorable trade balance with Mozambique is not sufficiently large, in absolute terms, to be significant. For all these reasons, Portugal's loss of trade with its African provinces should have little or no effect on Portugal's balance of payments or balance of trade.

With respect to Portugal's present investment income from its African provinces, the official balance of payments shows that there is no new net private investment by metropolitan Portugal in Portuguese Africa. Undoubtedly, private businesses do reinvest a substantial part of their earnings in Portuguese Africa. There are no figures available on the amount of such reinvestment, however. Private businesses receive a return on their present investment in Portuguese Africa, and they remit a substantial amount of that return to Portugal. For 1965, the net return on investments in Angola and Mozambique remitted to Portugal, as shown on the balance-of-payments statements, was $28 million, or about three-fourths of 1 per cent of 1965 Portuguese GNP. Such a loss of income would be substantial, but not critical, for the economy of metropolitan Portugal. The amount of private-investment income remitted to Portugal from its African provinces is just about equal to the contribution of metropolitan Portugal to the economic development of its African provinces.[19]

In addition to the possible loss of private-investment income, Portugal's withdrawal would cause the loss of its existing investments in the public sector. Schools, transport facilities, power stations, and other forms of publicly owned infrastructure would probably be taken over by the new governments without compensation. Investments in the private sector might be subject to nationalization without adequate compensation, or, even if such investments were not nationalized, in an unfavorable political climate, they would lose the greater part of their going and liquidation value. Figures on the total amount of private and public metropolitan investment in Portuguese Africa are not available, and it is thus impossible to estimate the possible loss of capital investments to metropolitan Portugal that would be due to withdrawal.

An evaluation of the losses that Portugal might suffer should also take into consideration the future income to be realized from oil production and the development of hydroelectric power. Cabinda has already entered into substantial petroleum production. Even though Portugal has not yet enjoyed substantial taxation revenues from this oil, the amount of potential revenues from it might solidify economic justification to its insistence on retaining the African provinces. The sale of hydroelectric power to South Africa from the Cunene and Zambezi projects should also provide substantial revenues, adding economic justification for staying in Africa.

An evaluation of the effects of withdrawal should also consider other consequences, including the closing of an outlet for emigration, psychological effects of withdrawal, and, finally, the human cost of staying, expressed in casualties among the armed forces. Removal of European population, which is now in the neighborhood of 400,000, would represent a further suffering for those involved, as well as impose a substantial economic burden on metropolitan Portugal, with a population 9.5 million, if they were to return home. This exodus would be twice the magnitude of decolonization of Algeria by the French in relation to the metropolitan population, and the economy of Portugal is far less able to bear such a decolonization than the economy of France was.

Against these considerations must be balanced the likelihood that future total emigration from Portugal to its African provinces might be lower than the current figure of 10,000–15,000 annually, because of labor shortage and wage rises in Portugal. Emigration to Africa is expensive, in terms of both support given by the government and private requirements. At least for the immediate future, there would be no great loss to the Portuguese people if the African outlets were closed while other outlets for Portuguese emigration remained open. In the long-term future, Portugal's capacity to send emigrants to Africa should increase, and the economic opportunity there may be greater than it is today.

Effects of a Withdrawal on Portuguese Africa

Many of the ways in which a Portuguese withdrawal would affect Portuguese Africa are implicit in what has already been said. Withdrawal would not mean for the overseas provinces a loss of any large amount of external investment for development, since metropolitan investment, both public and private, in its African provinces has not been large in absolute terms. (In relation to the size of metropolitan Portugal's economy, it has been substantial, since it constitutes about the same proportion of GNP as the foreign-aid program in the United States). It is uncertain, however, where substitute development funds would come from if Portuguese investment in Africa were to cease. Certainly, the United States, with its current balance-of-payments problem, is not likely to expand its foreign economic aid. The Soviet Union and the Chinese People's Republic, involved in Cuba, Vietnam, and elsewhere, may not wish to substitute.

The lack of firm future direction in the economic development of Portuguese Africa would doubtless have substantial adverse effect on economic development in the short run. Disregarding the size of their investment, the Portuguese in Africa have certainly started Angola and Mozambique on the road to modern development; much of that impetus would be lost. On the other hand, tight metropolitan direction of economic activities in Portuguese Africa has had adverse as well as beneficial aspects. Portuguese in Angola and Mozambique frequently complain that regulations issued by the metropole constitute obstacles to greater trade and other forms of economic growth.

A departure of substantial numbers of Portuguese would be detrimental to the economy of the provinces, at least in the short run. There seems little question that some Europeans are currently needed to operate the administrative and economic infrastructure and to conduct industrial activities. In a few years, these Europeans can undoubtedly be replaced by Africans. In addition to existing managerial skills in various enterprises, the Portuguese small-shopkeeper is considered a useful economic lubricant in the interior areas; the Portuguese personality is well adapted to the occupation of frontier trader. Yet Portuguese immigration has not been an unmixed blessing, as many of the metropolitan immigrants are not sufficiently skilled and end up in the slums of Luanda and other cities.

Withdrawal from Africa would reduce Portugal's importance as a market for the goods of Angola and Mozambique. Portugal presently takes about one-third of their exports, and the partial loss of this market would affect the prosperity of the two provinces. Portugal is also a very important supplier of Angola and Mozambique, in both cases accounting for about one-third of their imports. It would seem easier, however, to replace Portugal as a supplier than as a customer.

A decline in both export and import trade between Portugal and Angola and Mozambique should not create balance-of-payments problems for the two provinces, as the balance of trade of both of them with Portugal is negative. If, however, these provinces were to lose their export earnings to Portugal but continue their present level of imports, balance-of-payments problems would arise.

The effects of Portuguese withdrawal on the monetary structure of Angola and Mozambique seem about equally divided between adverse and beneficial. The solidity of the escudo as an international currency is undoubtedly of benefit to the African provinces. However, the system of interprovincial currency restrictions operates to the detriment of the provinces.[20] Likewise, currency restrictions between the metropole and the provinces result in the delay of payment for the import of goods until Banco de Portugal releases sufficient foreign exchange or exchangeable escudos to pay for them. The effects of such currency restrictions might be more in the nature of an inconvenience, however, since analysis of various balance-of-payments accounts indicates that no net balance of foreign exchange accrues to the benefit of metropolitan Portugal from Angola or Mozambique.

PORTUGAL'S DEFENSE OF ITS AFRICAN PROVINCES AND ITS RELATIONS WITH WESTERN EUROPE

Consideration will now be given to the problems of evolution of the Portuguese economy in relation to the need for closer economic ties with Western Europe.

Also, an evaluation will be attempted of the effect that Portugal's defense of its African provinces and its continuing political connection with them might have on the development of desirable economic ties with Western Europe.

There is reason to believe that Portuguese economy is at a critical phase in its evolution and that the continuation of the military effort in Africa may have adverse economic consequences that it has not had before now. Portugal is suffering a genuine labor shortage, with all the implied repercussions in the domestic economy. The shortage is caused by emigration, the development of industry, and the absence of young men: the continued presence of thousands of youths in Africa may exert a depressive effect on future economic development. Also, the defense effort in Africa now absorbs much energy and attention of Portugal's scarce administrative and managerial talent, needed to solve economic problems.

There have been sharp increases in the cost of labor in agriculture and construction,[21] the sectors most affected by emigration. These higher costs may induce a release of labor from agriculture. Portugal is thus witnessing a shift of labor from one sector of economic activity to another. The process may have its effect on Portugal's rate of growth, since the shift of labor from sector to sector is less likely to produce spectacular economic growth than the employment of hitherto unused labor. The latter process is the phase of economic evolution through which Portugal has just passed in the last decade.

The wage increase in agriculture is demanding improved techniques and the long-overdue mechanization of agriculture, which in turn calls for production or import of agricultural machinery, demanding increased investment in industry or foreign exchange to pay for imports. This should exert pressure on wages in industry at the same time that they are under pressure in agriculture. Eventually, as additional labor is released from agriculture, pressure on the supply of labor will diminish. In the meantime, deflationary monetary and fiscal policies may be indicated to assure that the limited available resources are used only for the most productive enterprises. Such monetary and fiscal restraint was applied by the Portuguese late in 1965,[22] which apparently resulted in reduced growth rates for 1966 and 1967.

The need for more efficient use of Portuguese labor means that Portugal will have to make a major effort to remedy the lack of skills on the part of its labor force and to create the managerial and technical skills necessary for an industrial economy. This demands an improvement in Portuguese education, both in quality and quantity.[23] There is general agreement that, in relation to the time spent in Portuguese educational institutions, the amount of subject matter mastered is low. In addition, Portugal must begin establishing a modern mass-educational system with a goal higher than merely general literacy. While educational problems are generally understood among the Portuguese, there may not be a sufficient sense of urgency about them.

Another solution to the anticipated shortage of labor in Portugal would be a cessation of emigration. This, in turn, demands an increase in domestic wages, and it implies a general increase in costs of production with the implication of decreased exports, increased imports, and so on. Keeping labor at home without

causing adverse economic disturbances means urgent creation of economic activities where labor is used more productively and a change in the structure of
the Portuguese economy and national mentality, together with an increased level
of investments.

Portugal may also find that continuing economic development will require a
higher level of savings and investment than in the past. It has achieved a
creditable economic performance in the last two decades, with a relatively low
level of savings and investment. An increased level will probably call for foreign
investment on a large scale, a need that has been much discussed but not, with a
few exceptions, actually resorted to significantly in the past, except for public
borrowing. The proceeds of this borrowing have been used, not for public
investment, but for increasing the currency reserves of gold and foreign exchange.

The probable necessity for increased investment means that a domestic
capital market should be further developed. The existing capital market is very
limited in Portugal. The average annual turnover of stocks and bonds in the
secondary market in both banks and stock exchanges in the five-year period
from 1962 through the first quarter of 1966 was only $43.5 million,[24] but there
has been a trend toward increased activity.

The primary market—that is, the issuance of new securities—shows similarly
increasing activity. New issues of stocks and bonds rose from $154 million in
1960 to $259 million in 1963, with the amount of $94.6 million in company
shares in 1963. About half of the new securities were government-debt,
however.

How to increase exports will be a persistent problem for the Portuguese
economy in the next decade. The increase in Portugal's balance-of-trade deficit
has already been noted. It will not be easy to increase exports as a share of
GNP. Consequently, Portugal may find that over-all economic growth requires a
strengthening of the domestic sector rather than striving for an expansion of
foreign trade. However, it would seem unwise for Portugal to regard the
improvement of its economy on the domestic level and production for export
as mutually exclusive alternatives. Both should occur.

The likelihood that neither internal development nor production for export
will in itself be sufficient to achieve a favorable solution to Portugal's problem
of over-all economic growth affects the perspective in which policy alternatives
are regarded. If the increase of exports cannot itself be a solution to Portuguese
economic problems, it would be imprudent to bend all policy choices toward the
accomplishment of this end. Applied to the matter of forming closer economic
ties with Western Europe, this means that it is imprudent to seek such ties
without regard to the cost of such a policy, since they are not in themselves an
assurance of prosperity and their absence is not a condemnation to economic
misery.

In this context, the desirability of forming closer economic ties with Western
Europe raises several questions. Is an increase in Portuguese exports truly
feasible, and what can Portugal do to that effect? Would an increase in Portuguese exports require closer political and economic ties with Western Europe
and, more particularly, entry into an expanded Common Market? Will Portu-

gal's entry into an expanded EEC require an abandonment of special political and economic relationship with its African provinces, much as England had to choose, in 1968, between maintaining its Commonwealth relationships and applying for admission into the Common Market? Definitive answers cannot be given to these questions, but relevant elements can be considered.

It is unlikely that Portugal will be able to gain much additional foreign exchange by increasing its exports of wine, cork, and fish. These commodities presently constitute a declining share of exports, and the demand for them is inelastic. On the other hand, Portugal may have missed the opportunity to exploit the seafaring skills of its fishermen in the development of long-range deep-sea fishing off the Spanish-owned Canary Islands. Some modest success might be realized by additional efforts in that direction.

The development of industrial exports is handicapped by the small scale of the Portuguese economy. Portugal will find it difficult to develop new industries for its restricted domestic market and, after these industries are developed, to seek export outlets for increase in profits. Much economic development will depend on an assurance of access, on competitive terms, to foreign markets *before* the development of such industries is begun. The 9.5 million people in metropolitan Portugal have but a very limited purchasing power. The 13.5 million people in Portuguese Africa have even less.

Increasing the scale of Portuguese economic activity means increasing its dependence upon the economies of the United States and Western Europe. Only at some time in the future will Portugal's African provinces add significantly to the expansion of the Portuguese market and contribute substantially to the enlargement of the Portuguese economy, though a possibility exists that substantial oil or mineral revenues could have an unforeseeable effect on the role of Portuguese Africa as a consumer.

There is no doubt, of course, that some industries are suitable for development on the limited scale of Portugal's domestic economy. Portugal can develop industries that have production high in value per unit, that do not demand expensive plants, large volume output, or much technological skill, and that can use Portugal's relatively low cost and unsophisticated labor. Textiles is one such industry, and Portugal has been active in developing export markets for its textile production.

It seems likely that, for a long time, Portugal will remain dependent on imports of some products of advanced technology, such as computers, aircraft, and automobiles. Yet, one is often surprised to find that an advanced technological product can, with ingenuity, be produced on a small scale. Thus, Portuguese entry into these areas is not precluded. Moreover, some parts of the total industrial process can be performed in Portugal, even though the entire production process might not be appropriate. Examples of such partial production processes are the auto-assembly plants and the diamond cutting facilities now located in Portugal.

Despite the small scale of the Portuguese economy, heavy industry is not, in principle, excluded. The excellent harbor of Lisbon and its location on major sea routes make ship-building and steel-making feasible, despite the insufficient size of the domestic market. This has been recognized by the installation of an infant steel industry at Lisbon and by the construction of the Lisnave shipyards there which can handle the largest tankers yet built and are fully competitive. Portugal's seaboard location is suitable for other types of heavy industry, such as oil and chemical plants, but these facilities require massive investment, which, in Portugal's case, means foreign investment.

The more that Portugal is able to integrate its economy with the mass markets of Western Europe, the more practical the production of mass-consumer goods and advanced technological goods in Portugal would be. This consideration would indicate the desirability of Portugal's entry into the Common Market, when and if England joins. Portugal would not wish to be economically isolated from the rest of Europe. It is unlikely, however, that Portugal will have the opportunity or the desire to join the Common Market before England does. As long as Western Europe is divided into two halves economically, Portugal must adhere to one half or the other, although which half does not make much difference. The gain in Portuguese exports to EFTA countries is balanced by the decline in exports to EEC countries. There would seem to be little advantage in switching from EFTA to the EEC if the opportunity arose.

If the Common Market were expanded, what would be Portugal's chance of being included? The obstacles seem twofold. There is first the political objection to Portugal's regime and to its African policy, which seem regressive and undemocratic to many Europeans. However, such considerations have not kept Portugal from EFTA, and it does not seem likely that this political objection would be sufficient to exclude Portugal from an expanded Common Market.

The second obstacle is the special economic relationship of Portugal with its African territories. France, in joining the Common Market, has maintained many of its special economic relationships with its former African territories, however. Imports from Angola and Mozambique to Portugal are not competitive with products of the EEC or EFTA countries. The EEC duty on them is likely to be low. It is even possible that Portugal's African provinces could be granted a special position, such as that enjoyed by the Dutch West Indies, if Lisbon were to offer those provinces greater autonomy.

CONCLUSION

Portugal is carrying the burden of defending its African provinces without critical strain on its government finances or its economic growth and with no change in its conservative fiscal and monetary policies. The Portuguese economy shows serious signs of developing a labor shortage, however. Consequently, the Portuguese defense effort should place a greater strain on the economy in the future than it has in the past. There is no reason to believe, however, that this strain will be intolerable at the present level of defense effort. This strain will be caused more by dynamic processes than by the relative economic cost of Portugal's African defense.

A fair conclusion is, thus, that Portugal is able to bear the military and economic burdens of its present level of defense effort in Africa indefinitely, and, if the need should arise, Portugal has the human and economic capacity substantially to increase its military effort. There is nothing in the present economic situation that indicates that a change of policy will be forced upon Portugal if it is reasonably determined to see its African policy through. Only if the level of military activity should increase would there be any necessity to revise this economic evaluation.

When full account is taken of all costs, Portuguese Africa is not now, and probably never was, economically profitable to Portugal, not even in the relatively prosperous post–World War II period. It is possible that prospective oil, power, and mineral revenues will make Portuguese Africa more profitable in the future. Whether future profits will justify the economic costs to Portugal of the defense of its African provinces remains unclear.

A Portuguese withdrawal from its African provinces would cause a substantial, but not serious, readjustment in the Portuguese economy. The Portuguese-African trade is not a sufficiently large part of total Portuguese trade that its cessation would lead to major economic adjustments. However, the reabsorption of large numbers of the 400,000 Europeans in Portuguese Africa would be a major economic burden for Portugal and could produce political crises.

Up to the present, Portugal's African policy has not prejudiced its economic relations with Western Europe, which are of increasing importance. Furthermore, Portugal's special economic and political relations with its African provinces are not altogether incompatible with future membership in an expanded EEC. Even if Portugal should be excluded from an expanded EEC, however, the eventuality would not be a crushing blow to future Portuguese economic development, though it would undoubtedly make its economic situation substantially more difficult. While closer economic ties with the United States might be a substitute for denied economic ties with Western Europe and the retention of its African provinces, it is probably in Portugal's economic best interest to choose expanded ties with Western Europe. However, such a choice is not currently presented, and it may be that an ultimate choice will never be forced upon Portugal.

NOTES

1. OECD, *National Account Statistics for 1956–65* (Paris, February, 1967), and *Études Economiques—Portugal—1966* (Paris, December, 1966), p. 36. X. V. Pintado, an economist, attributes the poor Portuguese agricultural performance to the small size of the average holding, the absence of tractors and other farm machinery, the underemployment of labor (inefficient or seasonal use of agricultural labor), the lack of pesticides, and the underforestation of marginal land. X. V. Pintado, *Structure and Growth of the Portuguese Economy* (Geneva, July, 1964). According to him, capital returns in Portuguese agriculture are average for the Portuguese economy's return on invested capital. The OECD report on Portugal for 1961 attributes the poor Portuguese agricultural performance particularly to lack of irrigation and, correlatively, to lack of investment (not only in irrigation but also in reforestation and animal husbandry), lack of reforestation, and the inefficient use of labor. OECD, *Situation et problems de l'economie dans les pays membres et associés de l'O.C.D.E.*

—*Portugal* (Paris: June, 1961), pp. 9–10. This publication is also the source of most statistical data cited further.

2. See OECD, *Overall Trade by Countries* (Paris: October, 1967), and EFTA, *EFTA Trade 1957–64* (Geneva, 1966), especially tables C5 i–C5 v.

3. See discussion of foreign trade of Angola and Mozambique in Chapter XI.

4. See Banco Totta Aliança, *Portugal—Some Facts About Its Economy* (Lisbon, 1968), p. 42.

5. This estimate was made by taking the 1966 gross national product of $4,027 million (Dillon Read & Co. in its prospectus for the 1967 Portuguese External Loan), increasing it by 4.5 per cent, the 1967 increase in gross national product (as estimated by the writer), and dividing by the estimated current resident population of 9.4 million.

6. *Bank of London and South America Review*, January, 1968, p. 81.

7. Pintado, *op. cit.*, pp. 22–30. The better performance of Yugoslavia (assuming that the statistics of a rigidly controlled socialist economy without a market structure can properly be compared with those of a market economy), is explained by the low point from which the Yugoslav economy started in the immediate post–World War II period, the enormous rate of capital investment of about 28 per cent of gross national product, and the rigid economic controls of the Yugoslav Government with its emphasis on industry. The superior performance of Greece appears due to a superior productivity of capital, a possible superior productivity of labor, a favorable capital output ratio in agriculture, and a transfer of labor from less to more productive sectors.

8. OECD, *Main Economic Indicators* (January, 1968).

9. Banque du Paris et des Pays Bas, Dillon Read & Co., Banca Commerciale Italiana, *Republic of Portugal $15,000,000 c/o External Loan Bonds Due 1977* prospectus (October 1, 1967).

10. The 1961–65 figures for military expenditures given by the OECD in its pamphlet *Études Économiques—Portugal—1966*, p. 20, are higher than those in its *National Account Statistics 1956–65* (Paris: February, 1967).

11. *Bank of London and South American Review*, January, 1968, p. 127, and Banque de Bruxelles, *Bulletin Commercial*, February 20, 1968.

12. Banco Totta Aliança, *op. cit.*, pp. 46 and 51.

13. Estimates made from graphs appearing in Portugal, *Estatísticas Financeiras* (Lisbon, 1967).

14. Pintado, *op. cit.*, tables IV and VI, pp. 22 and 25.

15. IDA, *Current Economic Position and Prospects of Portugal* (Geneva: November 1, 1965), table 25, p. 81.

16. Banco de Portugal, *Relatório Anual* (1966), p. 159, and (1965).

17. There is a tendency, however, in some circles to consider that the funds spent in Portugal's African defense exert an adverse effect on Portugal's economic development. For example, the *Bank of London and South America Review* (January, 1968) states (pp. 81–83) that the targets of the Third National Development Plan are unlikely to be achieved unless "further steps can be taken . . . to divert to development purposes some of the funds at present allocated to defense." Richard Hammond in his *Portugal's African Problems: Some Economic Facets* (New York, 1962), also argues (pp. 36–38) that the Portuguese defense effort is delaying a necessary change of Portuguese economic policies and class structure. Also, there is a tendency to be over-critical of Portuguese economic performance. In the judgment of this writer,

and according to the theories of Keynesian economics, the amount of funds expended for Portugal's African defense is not sufficient in magnitude to have exerted any significant effect on Portuguese economic development since 1961.

18. See Chapter XI.
19. The contribution of the metropolitan government to the economic development under the Third National Development Plan is two-thirds of $235 million over a 6-year period, or $28 million a year roughly, which compares with 1965 private investment income remitted to Portugal from Portuguese Africa of $28 million.
20. See Chapter XI.
21. Wages for rural men rose 59.5 per cent in Portugal between 1962 and 1967 while industrial wages in Lisbon in the same period only rose 32.4 per cent. Banco Totta Aliança, *op. cit.*, pp. 24–25. See also *Bank of London and South America*, January, 1968, p. 82.
22. *Ibid.*
23. See Chapter IX.
24. Banco Totta Aliança, *op. cit.*, p. 46.

PART IV

Political and International Issues

XVI

The Issues Internationalized

GEORGE MARTELLI

WHY HAS Portugal continued to reject decolonization, accepted in principle by all the other colonial powers, even while they insist on their intention to proceed about it in their own way and in their own time? Some of the reasons have been suggested earlier in this book:[1] the fact that Portugal's overseas empire was much older than any other; that, to this small, poor nation, overseas possessions were politically much more important than they were to rich and highly industrialized countries such as Great Britain, France, and Belgium; that, as a result of historical circumstances, Portugal's imperial role was more deeply planted in the national consciousness and it felt more deeply involved with the overseas peoples.

In addition, most Portuguese politicians have been convinced that the rapid decolonization of Africa, embarked on by other governments under pressure of internal and world opinion, often against their better judgment, was a mistake from the point of view both of the West's defending itself in the cold war and of the African peoples concerned. It must result, they thought, in the creation of a large number of independent states that would be independent only in name, since they were too weak to stand by themselves. Portuguese Foreign Minister Franco Nogueira believed that "many of the new nations will disappear, either to be integrated in larger units or to fall under the domination of new colonialisms."[2]

Other reasons were to be found in more recent history. Since the constitution of the New State was adopted in 1933, Portugal has lived outside the main currents of world opinion. Immersed in the task of internal reconstruction and ruled by an authoritarian government that discouraged foreign influences, it remained largely immune to the political movements flourishing outside. It was also near enough to the Spanish Civil War to fear Communism more than some other countries. Although its neutrality in World War II favored Allied interests, Portugal remained skeptical of the liberal ideas that were popular with the Allies, such as national self-determination and supranational government.

THE PRINCIPLE OF SELF-DETERMINATION

The first Allied leader to use the word self-determination was British Prime Minister David Lloyd George, who, during the period of peace-making at the end of World War I, told a meeting of the Trades Union Conference on January 5, 1918: "a territorial settlement must be securely based on the right of self-determination and the consent of the governed."[3] Self-determination was soon taken as the panacea for all political ills. U.S. President Woodrow Wilson himself was aware of the danger of balkanization and envisaged an international police force to keep the peace and protect the smaller nations. This was the genesis of the League of Nations.

Wilson had anticipated that, as a result of the war and the defeat of Germany and Turkey, many territories would be changing hands. As one of his Fourteen Points, he had laid down the rule that there should be "a free, open-handed, and absolutely impartial adjustment of all colonial claims, based upon a strict observance of the principle that in determining all such questions of sovereignty the interests of the populations concerned must have equal weight with the equitable claims of the government whose title is to be determined." It is worth noting that he said that the interest of the population should have only equal weight with the claims of the administering power.

It was in pursuance of this principle that, besides providing for collective security, the sponsors of the League sought to make special arrangements for the countries outside Europe that had been conquered by the Allies in the war, which included the German colonies in Africa and elsewhere and parts of the former Turkish empire. It was proposed that these should be administered internationally. The victors—France, the United Kingdom, and other members of the British Commonwealth—not wishing to be robbed of the fruits of their victory, naturally objected. As a compromise, a mandate system was devised and embodied in the covenant of the League. Under this system, the victors remained in possession of their conquests, but, inasmuch as they were inhabited by "peoples not yet able to stand by themselves," they undertook to apply the principle "that the well-being and development of such peoples form a sacred trust of civilization."[4]

Except in the case of "A" mandates, for the relatively advanced countries of Syria, Lebanon, and Palestine, nothing was said about self-government or independence. Subject to certain stipulations about trade and military bases, the mandatory was solely responsible for administering the territory, and no time limit was set. The only obligation undertaken was to regard the "well-being and development" of the population as "a sacred trust of civilization"—in other words, to make public acknowledgment of the acceptance of the educative mission that was now assumed on behalf of the international community. It was not envisaged that development could proceed at such a pace as to enable the burden to be laid down in the then foreseeable future. Although the League of Nations supervised the exercise of the mandates through the Permanent Mandates Commission, its powers to interfere were limited, and the scrutiny of the Commission, if at times embarrassing, was usually constructive.[5] The system, however, created a precedent for international intervention in colonial countries, by which the United Nations was to profit later.

During the years preceding World War II, the ruthless take-over by the Axis powers of weaker countries—Austria, Czechoslavakia, Albania, Ethiopia—

increased popular support for the principle of self-determination. When the war came, it was seen by most of the world as a war fought for freedom—that is to say, for the liberation of Europe from Nazi tyranny. Enshrined in the Atlantic Charter, the establishment of "the right of all peoples to choose the form of government under which they will live" was conceived as the major war aim of the Allies. Once in the air, the idea of freedom could not be confined to Europe. If the Czechs, Poles, Danes, and Norwegians were to be liberated from Germany, why not the Indians from Britain, the Indochinese from France, and the Indonesians from Holland? Among those who thought they should be was President Franklin D. Roosevelt. As recounted by Winston Churchill, the President used his influence to try to persuade the British Government to grant India self-government at the moment when the Japanese were preparing to invade India.[6]

At the Tehran conference, President Roosevelt had touched lightly on the colonial question, but he received no encouragement from Churchill, and Stalin showed little interest. At Yalta, during the discussion of the future United Nations, agreement was reached to establish a trusteeship system as successor to the League of Nations mandate system. It was to apply to the mandated territories, to territories detached from the enemy in the war, and to territories that might voluntarily be placed under trusteeship. There was no discussion of the existing colonies, nor was their future raised at Dumbarton Oaks, where the foundations were laid for the Charter of the United Nations.

It was thus left to the San Francisco conference to tackle the colonial problem. That conference set up a consultative group consisting of representatives of the five permanent members of the future Security Council,—the United States, the U.S.S.R., the United Kingdom, France, and China. The group hammered out the articles of agreements that were to be embodied in the controversial Chapter XI of the U.N. Charter, dealing with "non-self-governing" territories, and the less controversial Chapters XII and XIII, regarding the trusteeship system. Since Portugal was never concerned with the latter, we need not discuss it here, except to say that the right of supervision that it gave to the United Nations in respect of the trust territories was the thin end of the wedge for its subsequent involvement in non-self-governing territories.

THE QUESTION OF NON-SELF-GOVERNING TERRITORIES

The war having been fought for freedom, it was generally assumed that all people had the right to be "free," whatever that might mean in the varying contexts. In the cases of peoples with ancient civilizations, a high degree of culture, and a large educated class, such as the Indians, other Asiatics, and the Arabs, the right clearly could not be denied. For them, whatever the consequences, the principle of self-determination was felt to be paramount and to prevail over all other considerations.

For the peoples of tropical Africa, it was felt to be a different matter. The argument was that many Africans had made their first contact with European

369

civilization barely a century ago, some even more recently. With the exception of a small minority who lived in the towns or worked for the Europeans, the common social organization was that of the village, or at best the tribe, whose customs, superstitions, and way of life were frequently incompatible with accepted modern norms. The colonialists had drawn up frontiers which meant little to people whose horizons barely extended beyond their own villages. In most of the African colonies there was a small elite, which included some university graduates, most of whom had been sent to Europe to complete their education. But they were too few to form a ruling class or to provide even the nucleus of a civil service. It was considered that the colonial powers still had a duty to the African populations—to protect, to keep order, to administer the law, and to educate.

During the discussions of the Consultative Group, such views were defended, although not so explicitly, by the representatives of Britain and France against those of Russia, the United States, and China, who wanted it stated in the U.N. Charter that independence should be a goal of all non-self-governing territories. Britain and France argued that this was neither practicable nor realistic, and that the "hatching" of a number of small, independent political units unable to stand on their own feet would lead to confusion and be a threat to peace.

In the end a compromise was agreed upon. By substituting "self-government" for "independence" and by the use of other particular wording in Chapter XI, the U.N. Charter attempted both to satisfy the anticolonialists and to allay the qualms of the administering powers. The chapter is headed "Declaration Regarding Non-Self-Governing Territories," and it contains two articles, 73 and 74, of which only the former is relevant. Article 73 reads as follows:

Members of the United Nations which have or assume responsibilities for the administration of territories whose peoples have not yet attained a full measure of self-government recognize the principle that the interests of the inhabitants of these territories are paramount, and accept as a sacred trust the obligation to promote to the utmost, within the system of international peace and security established by the present Charter, the well-being of the inhabitants of these territories, and, to this end:

(a) to ensure, with due respect for the culture of the peoples concerned, their political, economic, social, and educational advancement, their just treatment, and their protection against abuses;

(b) to develop self-government, to take due account of the political aspirations of the peoples, and to assist them in the progressive development of their free political institutions, according to the particular circumstances of each territory and its peoples and their varying stages of advancement;

(c) to further international peace and security;

(d) to promote constructive measures of development, to encourage research, and to cooperate with one another and, when and where appropriate, with specialized international bodies with a view to the practical achievement of the social, economic, and scientific purposes set forth in this Article; and (*e*) to transmit regularly to the Secretary-General for information purposes, subject to such limitations as security and constitutional considerations may require, statistical and other information of a technical nature relating to economic, social, and educational conditions in the territories for which they are respectively responsible other than those territories to which Chapters XII and XIII apply.

Like all compromises, the text was full of ambiguities. The most significant of them was in the interpretation of "self-government": it did not necessarily mean democratic government, since many members of the United Nations were not democratic though undoubtedly self-governing. On the other hand, the U.S.S.R., a member state with an autocratic government, ruling vast and disparate populations spread over two continents, might be considered to be administering non-self-governing territories, even though it had no overseas possessions. Most people agree that the Soviets, who wanted "self-determination" inserted in the Charter, considered it a vehicle for the independence of dependent peoples other than their own.[7]

Although there is little doubt as to the meaning attached to it by the Soviets, the meaning that the Western powers attached to it is debatable. Carrington claims that, as General Jan Christiaan Smuts of South Africa drafted the Preamble to the Charter, he gave self-determination the connotation he had elaborated on in a paper he had circulated in Paris on December 16, 1918. To him it meant "a general theory of government by consent, with reservations in respect of minority groups for which it was inapplicable.[8] Leland M. Goodrich and Edvard Hambro do not think that "the words used . . . were intended to encourage demands for immediate independence or movements for secession."[9] On the other hand, other writers have stated that, although "direct debate on the controversial issue of the application of the principle of self-determination to colonial areas was avoided," nevertheless, "the problem was in the background."[10]

Whatever might have been the meaning of "self-determination" at San Francisco, most commentators take the view that the constant practice of the U.N. organs, the Declaration Regarding Non-Self-Governing Territories, and resolutions passed subsequently, all confirm that the principle of self-determination is now considered a basic and legal human right.[11] In a resolution passed in 1952, the General Assembly referred to "the right of all peoples and nations to self-determination in reaffirmation of the principle enunciated in the Charter of the United Nations."[12] In a later resolution, the General Assembly stressed that "self-determination is a prerequisite to the full enjoyment of all fundamental rights" and directed member states to "recognize and promote the realization of the right of self-determination of the peoples of Non-Self-Governing Territories." This would be done "according to the principles of the Charter of the United Nations in regard to each Territory and to the freely expressed wishes of the peoples concerned." The same resolution also directed the member states responsible for administration of non-self-governing territories to "take practical steps, pending the realization of the right of self-determination and in preparation thereof" and to "prepare them for complete self-government or independence."[13] This principle has been reiterated in several later resolutions. It has also been recognized by the Security Council.[14]

Who was to decide which territories were to be classified as non-self-governing? Although various definitions were proposed at the first session of the General Assembly, during the debates concerning the implementation of Article 73, the final decision was that any attempt at further definition was unwise. According to Goodrich, "it was tacitly admitted that the question of the meaning of the term would be considered in relation to the facts of each case."[15] Hans Kelsen, another authority, has written: "The Assembly may—in form of a recommendation—specify these territories. But a recommendation of the Assembly has no binding force; hence it depends finally on the Member States to decide which are the territories to which their obligations under Chapter XI refer."[16] This last was the view taken later by the Portuguese; it was the justification for their refusal to supply information on their overseas territories and the cause of their quarrel with the United Nations.

Then again, in regard to the principle recognized in Article 73 that the "interests of the inhabitants of these territories are paramount," who was to decide what these interests were? Since the Charter did not provide any alternative, it could only be left to the administering governments. Under paragraph b of the Article, member states undertook to "develop self-government, to take due account of the political aspirations of the peoples, and to assist them in the progressive development of their free political institutions," but with the qualification that this development should be "according to the particular circumstances of each territory and its peoples and their varying stages of advancement," which gave the administrations a loophole. At the same time, under paragraph c they undertook to "further international peace and security." But, supposing the two aims conflicted, and it appeared that the grant of self-government would be a threat to peace and security, which was to have priority?

The most important obligation under Article 73 and, in fact, the only one that was definite and binding,[17] was that of supplying information, under clause e. Even this was subject to severe restrictions. First, the information was to be of a technical nature relating to "economic, social, and educational conditions" and, furthermore, to be "subject to such limitations as security and constitutional considerations may require." It thus excluded information on political and constitutional matters, in contrast to what was to be supplied on the trust territories and, under Article 88, was to include information "on the political, economic, social, and educational advancement of the inhabitants." Second, the information was to be transmitted to the Secretary-General "for information purposes," thereby implying that it was not to be used for any other purpose, such as action by the United Nations.

However ambiguous its wording, a study of the text of Chapter XI, together with the discussions that preceded the drafting, make clear what the authors intended. First, since Chapter XI, unlike all the other chapters, was described in the title as a declaration, it was meant to be *declaratory*, as the Secretary-General stated—that is to say, a profession of ideals, a promise of good conduct.

It was not a contractual commitment nor a charter of independence; otherwise, the word "independence" would have appeared in the text, as it does in Article 76 with reference to the trust territories (although even here only as an alternative to "self-government," not as an obligatory objective).

On the other hand, it is evident that, once having undertaken to "develop self-government," the administering powers were left with entire discretion to decide what was meant by "self-government" and how best to develop it and at what pace, the pace being regulated "by the particular circumstance of each territory . . . and their varying stages of advancement."

There was, thus, no imperative for any member to do anything in any non-self-governing territory under its control that it did not consider appropriate to circumstances. This was the deliberate intention, since the colonial governments, which then included the United States as administrator of the Philippine Islands and other territories, would never have agreed to any reduction of their sovereign powers or admitted that the United Nations had any right to interfere in territories that came under their domestic jurisdiction.

That no such right was created by Chapter XI was successfully argued on repeated occasions during the early days of the United Nations. For example, at the sixty-fourth meeting of the General Assembly, the U.S. delegate, speaking of non-self-governing territories not under trusteeship, declared that "the United Nations has no authority to intervene in such territories. That authority remains with their own government."[18]

In 1947, during another debate in the Fourth Committee, the U.S. delegate referring to the San Francisco conference, stated, "It was realized then, and it remains true now, that in many non-self-governing territories sovereignty or jurisdiction rests in the administering states; and nothing was written into the Charter to change this fundamental fact. . . . Chapters XII and XIII materially alter the status of the non-self-governing territories coming within their scope. Chapter XI does not."[19] This, substantially, has been the argument sustained by the Portuguese Government in its long dispute with the United Nations, although the four other colonial powers, once rid of their colonies, no longer had any interest in defending their original points of view.

The original U.N. membership of fifty-one included a number (although nothing like as great as it was subsequently to become) of states, such as India, Syria, Egypt, Ethiopia, and Lebanon that had only recently achieved or recovered their independence and remained strongly anticolonialist. Together with the Soviet block they formed a vocal and active pressure group that became the spearhead of the General Assembly's attack on colonialism. This was launched against the administering powers in respect of both the trust and the non-self-governing territories. As regards the latter, the attack took the form of repeated attempts to alter the intention of Chapter XI of the Charter so as to turn it into an instrument of U.N. intervention in these territories.

As early as the first session of the General Assembly, in December, 1946, a resolution was passed that recommended that an *ad hoc* committee be set up to examine the information supplied under Article 73e. This was opposed by the delegates of France and the United States on the grounds that it constituted a modification of the Charter. They were overruled by the majority.[20] A year later, in a series of resolutions passed on November 3, 1947, the General Assembly invited the administering governments to render the information they were supplying "as complete and up to date as possible," encouraged them to include information "on the development of self-governing institutions" (although, as a political matter, this was excluded from the obligations undertaken in Article 73 e), and decided to set up a special permanent committee to examine the information and make recommendations.[21] Later, the General Assembly recommended the convening of conferences of "representatives of Non-Self-Governing peoples . . . in order that effect may be given to the letter and spirit of Chapter XI of the Charter and that the wishes and aspirations of the Non-Self-Governing peoples may be expressed."[22] The delegates of France and Britain pointed out that the proposal was an interference in matters that were "essentially within the domestic jurisdiction" of the administering powers and, in consequence, violated Article 2(7), but their protests had no effect.

And so it continued. Aiming at helping the non-self-governing territories, the General Assembly undermined the authority of the colonial administrations, forcing them to make concessions and quickening the pace of decolonization. During the first decade of existence of the United Nations, the Western powers, by standing together, usually with the support of the United States, were able to resist the international pressure. Resolutions of the General Assembly had the force of being only recommendations, and the administering powers were not obliged to comply. In theory, they could continue to go their own way. But the effect, in practice, as intended, was to create a climate of opinion hostile to the administering powers. Representing as it did the hopes for peace of a large section of humanity, the United Nations had something of the authority of religion, and its pronouncements were accepted as doctrine by many people in the world. They affected the Western countries as much as the rest, with the result that the anticolonialist current was strong also in America, Britain, France, and Belgium.

The other effect of U.N. anticolonialism was to encourage the revolutionary element in the non-self-governing territories.

As a result, the colonial governments were increasingly subjected to two kinds of pressure, one internal and the other external. In the territories that they controlled, growing agitation by nationalist parties, encouraged and sometimes financed from abroad, led to riots, the imprisonment of leaders, and more agitation. In the United Nations, pressure took the form of resolutions against the colonial powers. Countries with colonial possessions were faced with anticolonialist clamor from their progressive parties, while other parties began to resign themselves to "the wind of change," inasmuch as it seemed inevitable.

Exhausted by two world wars, Western Europe was little willing to carry the burden of imperial responsibility, which, in any case, was proving increasingly expensive. On the other hand, it was felt that, by surrendering gracefully to their demands, the colonial powers would gain the good will of the nationalists, thus enabling them to continue to exercise some influence, while putting themselves right with world opinion. Political and international pressures, as well as the burden of financial difficulties at home, caused these powers, led by Britain, to embark during the 1950's on the first steps of decolonization.[23]

PORTUGAL AND THE UNITED NATIONS

Portugal became a member of the United Nations in 1955. At that period, the colonial powers were still fighting against encroachment by the General Assembly on their sovereignty in the non-self-governing territories, and they had achieved some success with delaying tactics. But, in the previous year, the Bandung Conference of Asian, African, and European Communist countries had passed a resolution condemning colonialism "in all its manifestations" and declaring that "the subjection of peoples to alien domination and exploitation constitutes a denial of fundamental human rights, is contrary to the Charter of the United Nations, and is an impediment to the promotion of world peace and cooperation." This was to herald the mounting of a new offensive against the West, greatly encouraged by the retreat of Britain and France from Suez in 1956.

Following events in the United Nations, Portugal had seen how the Charter had been used to hasten the decolonization process. Determined not to submit to the same experience, it therefore disclaimed the possession of any non-self-governing territories. Angola, Mozambique, and Portuguese Guinea had officially been called colonies until 1951. Portugal revised its constitution in 1951 and reintroduced the term "provinces," which they had been called prior to 1910. It claimed that these overseas areas could not be considered as non-self-governing territories, since they were part of the national territory, a unitary state governed by one constitution. As the Portuguese foreign minister wrote, this constitution "did not recognize the existence within the nation of non-self-governing territories, and it would be unconstitutional for some parts of the nation to have one international status and others a different one. The interpretation and application of its constitution was a question of each Government alone, and the Portuguese government denied the United Nations the least competence in the matter."[24] In consequence, the Portuguese did not consider that Chapter XI of the Charter applied to them, and they had no intention of supplying information as required by Article 73e.

In the face of this act of defiance, the General Assembly appointed a committee of six,[25] the United States, the United Kingdom, the Netherlands, Mexico, India, and Morocco, to examine the "principles which should guide members in determining whether or not an obligation exists to transmit the information called for in Article 73e of the United Nations." After deliberating for nearly a year, the committee presented a report that set out twelve principles, summarized as follows:

1. Chapter XI applied to territories "of the colonial type" that had not attained "a full measure of self-government," and, under Article 73e, there was an obligation to transmit information on such territories.

2. Chapter XI embodied the concept of non-self-governing territories "in a dynamic state of evolution . . . toward self-government." Until this had been attained, the obligation to transmit information continued.

3. The obligation to transmit information was international and should be carried out with due regard to the fulfillment of international law.

4. There was prima facie an obligation to transmit information in respect of a territory that was geographically separate and distinct, ethnically or culturally from the country administering it.

5. If the effect of administrative, political, juridical, economic, or historical elements was to place the territory concerned in a subordinate position, they supported the presumption that there was an obligation to transmit information.

6. A non-self-governing territory could reach self-government by emergence as a sovereign independent state, free association with an independent state, or integration with an independent state.

7. Free association should be "the result of a free and voluntary choice by the peoples of the territory concerned expressed through informed and democratic processes." The associated territory should have the right to determine its internal constitution without outside interference.[26]

8. Integration with an independent state should be on the basis of complete equality.

9. Integration should come about after the integrating territory had attained an advanced stage of self-government with free political institutions, so that its "peoples would have the capacity to make a responsible choice"; it should be the result "of the freely expressed wishes of the territory's peoples acting with full knowledge of the change of their status."

10. The limitations required by security and constitutional considerations under Article 73e did not relieve a member state of the obligation to transmit economic, social, and educational information.

11. Responsibility for transmitting information under Article 73e continued until constitutional relations of the territory with the administering member precluded the latter from receiving statistical and other information relating to economic, social, and educational conditions in the territory.

12. Only in very exceptional circumstances could such information have a security aspect.

With these principles, formally adopted during its fifteenth session,[27] the Assembly immediately passed a resolution[28] stating that the territories under Portuguese administration "listed hereunder" were non-self-governing territories within the meaning of Chapter XI of the Charter, declaring that an obligation existed on the part of Portugal to transmit information on these territories under Chapter XI, and requesting that Portugal do so. The territories listed were the Cape Verde archipelago; Guinea, called Portuguese Guinea; São Tomé and Príncipe and their dependencies; São João Batista de Ajudá; Angola, including the enclave of Cabinda; Mozambique; Gôa and its dependencies, called the State of India; Macao and its dependencies; and Timor and its dependencies.

Portugal rejected both the report of the Committee of Six and the General Assembly resolution that arose from it and argued the reasons in a long statement during the debate of the Fourth (Trusteeship) Committee in the same session of the General Assembly.

The basic argument of Portugal was that its relations with its overseas territories were regulated by the national constitution and the United Nations had no authority to discuss national constitutions; to do so would be flagrant interference in the internal affairs of member states, which was expressly forbidden by Article 2(7) of the Charter.[29] Furthermore, it has always been left to the administering powers to decide to which of their territories the Declaration in Chapter XI applied and on which they were willing to transmit information. For the General Assembly to assume that function in regard to Portugal was a clear case of discrimination.

As regards the correct interpretation of Chapter XI, in the Portuguese view, this could be arrived at only by examining the Chapter within the context of the Charter. It would then be seen that the provisions for international supervision in Chapters IX and X (on international economic and social cooperation) and in Chapter XI were omitted. This made it clear that the latter had a different character. Dr. Nogueira has argued:

> In order to apply and administer the international system of economic and social cooperation, the Charter had created the Economic and Social Council. In order to apply and administer the international trusteeship system, it had established the Trusteeship Council. But no organ had been created for the system of non-self-governing territories, for the reason that as regards this system the Charter had not contemplated any positive action on the part of the United Nations. This is borne out by an analysis of the relevant sections of the Charter. In the articles regulating the working of both the first and second systems mentioned above, reference is made to the power of the Assembly to take decisions, to formulate recommendations, to discharge certain duties, to assume given responsibilities. A certain competence is thus attributed to the Assembly, and power is granted to it to exercise that competence. But nothing even remotely similar is allowed for in the case of the non-self-governing territories. The role of the United Nations concerning the latter was evidently intended to be passive, and it was the Member States alone who determined their respective policies.[30]

This was of course the argument advanced and sustained for many years by all the other administering powers, including the United States, Britain, and France. Portugal's distrust of the United Nations handling of international disputes increased when the seizure by India of Gôa, Damão, and Diu in 1961 was condoned by the U.N. majority.[31]

More serious to Portugal than the failure to condemn aggression, however, was the development in the United Nations of the idea that a "colonial situation" is, in itself, an aggression that automatically condemns the administering power and justifies any action taken against it. Repeated attempts have been made by the Communists and the Afro-Asians to have the Security Council declare the situation in the Portuguese provinces a "threat to peace."[32] Were this done, it would be possible to apply Chapter VII of the Charter, which provides for sanctions and, in the last resort, military action against the offender.[33] Those taking the lead against Portugal based their case on the doctrine that the Charter is an evolving and "dynamic instrument consisting of the original documents and interpretations resulting from the Security Council's and Assembly's actions and resolutions" and that "what may have been simply a solemn declaration is today a recognized, perhaps enforceable obligation."[34] This view is being increasingly advocated by several authorities on international law. For example, Wolfgang Friedmann thinks that "the General Assembly of the United Nations is exercising a far from unimportant role in the making and developing of international law."[35] Oscar Schachter attributes a very general character to the "principles and norms of the Charter" and says that they "require concretization."[36] The late Judge Hersch Lauterpacht, in the South-West Africa Voting Procedure Advisory Opinion, said that to decrease the value of the resolutions of the General Assembly, which he considered as "one of the principal instrumentalities of the formation of the community of nations represented by the United Nations," and to consider them as "nominal, insignificant, and having no claim to influence the conduct of the Members" would be "wholly inconsistent with sound principles of interpretation as well as with highest international interest."[37]

The Portuguese take the contrary view, that the Charter is a contract made among the members of the United Nations and that the essence of any contract in law is that it remains unaltered unless amended by mutual consent of the parties to it. Machinery for amending the Charter is provided in Chapter XVIII, Articles 108–9, but it has never been used. Its meaning cannot legally be changed simply by a vote of the majority.[38]

The Portuguese arguments were rejected by the U.N. majority. The General Assembly and its various committees have continued to accuse Portugal of violating the Charter. During the first 5 years of membership, Portugal could count on a certain support from NATO allies and this helped to inihibit the passing of any drastic resolutions aimed against Portugal.

THE DECLARATION ON COLONIALISM

In 1960, however, there was a dramatic change in the composition of the United Nations. Eighteen colonies became independent states and were admitted to the organization, bringing its total membership to 97, of which 30 had previously been non-self-governing territories. The result was to give a clear majority to the "independence now" bloc, consisting of Afro-Asian and Communist countries. The Communist powers took this opportunity to press the attack on the West, and, during the September meeting of the General Assembly, Khrushchev seized the initiative by demanding, as an urgent matter the inclusion in the agenda of "a declaration on the granting of independence to colonial countries and peoples." This was followed by a Soviet memorandum proposing, first that all colonial countries and trust and non-self-governing territories be granted "complete independence forthwith"; second, that all "strongholds of colonialism" in the form of possessions and leased areas in the territory of other states be eliminated; and, third, that all governments "abjure colonialism or any other special rights or advantages for some States to the detriment of other States."

The Afro-Asians then drafted a resolution on much the same lines and titled it Declaration on the Granting of Independence to Colonial Countries and Peoples. After a long preamble that concluded by proclaiming "the necessity of bringing to a speedy and unconditional end colonialism in all its forms and manifestations," the Declaration proceeded to lay down five main principles:

1. The subjection of peoples to alien subjugation, domination, and exploitation constitutes a denial of fundamental human rights, is contrary to the Charter of the United Nations, and is an impediment to the promotion of world peace and cooperation.

2. All peoples have the right to self-determination; by virtue of that right, they freely determine their political status and freely pursue their economic, social, and cultural development.

3. Inadequacy of political, economic, social, or educational preparedness should never serve as a pretext for delaying independence.

4. All armed action or repressive measures of any kind directed against dependent peoples shall cease in order to enable them to exercise peacefully and freely their right to complete independence, and the integrity of their national territory shall be respected.

5. Immediate steps shall be taken, in trust and non-self-governing territories that have not yet attained independence, to transfer all powers to the peoples of these territories, without any conditions or reservations, in accordance with their freely expressed will and desire, without any distinction as to race, creed, or color, in order to enable them to enjoy complete independence and freedom.[39]

After a long debate, the resolution was adopted by a vote of 90 to 0, with 9 abstentions—the United States, the United Kingdom, France, Belgium, Australia, South Africa, Portugal, Spain, and the Dominican Republic. The U.S. representative, James J. Wadsworth, Jr., gave as the reasons for abstention that the resolution remained silent on the contributions of the colonial powers, including the United States, to the advancement of the dependent peoples; that, by insisting on complete independence, it ignored the provisions made by the Charter for self-government within large political units; that the principles would result in political fragmentation and fly in the face of political and economic reality; that, contrary to the statement of the third principle, adequate preparation for self-government was a matter of elementary prudence; that the sweeping demand for the immediate transfer of power ignored the need for time in the progress toward independence; and that, since every territory was different, no one timetable could be imposed on all.[40]

None of this reasoning carried any weight with the Assembly, where it was continually argued that Portugal was not preparing its territories for self-determination. While the resolution had only the force of a recommendation, the declaration contained in it was henceforth regarded as a mandate for the United Nations to take every practical step for the liquidation of the remaining colonies at the earliest possible moment.

As a first step, a special committee of seventeen members was set up to examine the application of the declaration and to make recommendations. Later, the committee was enlarged to twenty-four, and it took over the functions of various other committees, including the Committee on Information from Non-Self-Governing Territories, established in 1949, and the Special Committee on Portuguese Territories, established in 1961. The latter had been set up, following the refusal of Portugal to cooperate with the General Assembly, in order to examine such information as was available on the territories and to formulate recommendations for the consideration of the Assembly.

At its first session in 1962, the Special Committee decided to instruct the secretary-general to collect and submit to it all the available information (including, that is, information on political matters) on the non-self-governing territories and also to receive written petitions and hear petitioners. In doing so, it expanded upon the Charter in three important respects. First, under Article 73e, information was to be supplied only by the administering powers, although there was no provision for a situation in which an administering power might refuse to supply the information; second, it did not include information on political and constitutional matters; and, third, although there was a provision in the Charter under the trusteeship system for receiving petitions, there was none in regard to non-self-governing territories. Only Portugal, however, raised, objections, since by this date the other colonial powers were no longer concerned with defending their interpretation of Chapter XI. The last of the British and French colonies in Africa, except for French Somaliland, had either been given their independence or were soon to receive it.

The Debate on Angola

On March 15, 1961, following some rioting in Luanda, the Security Council met at the request of its Afro-Asian members to consider the situation in Angola. A resolution introduced by Ceylon, Liberia, and the United Arab Republic called on Portugal as a matter of urgency to introduce reforms that would enable the Angolans to exercise the right to self-determination, and it also proposed the creation of a subcommittee to study conditions in the territory. Although supported by Russia and the United States, the resolution failed, because of abstentions, to obtain the necessary votes. The fact that it was given U.S. support was highly significant, however, indicating a change of policy consequent to the election of President Kennedy and the appointment of Adlai Stevenson as the U.S. delegate to the United Nations. Up to then, the United States had attempted a posture of restraint on colonial issues; for this reason the United States had abstained from voting on the declaration of colonialism. The Portuguese foreign ministry declared that it viewed "with gravest apprehension" the latest U.S. vote.

The outbreak of rebellion in Angola on March 15 placed Portugal in the forefront of U.N. concern, a position that, along with South Africa and, lately, Rhodesia, it has occupied ever since. In the course of the next 7 years, eight resolutions were voted by the General Assembly, five by the Security Council, all critical of Portugal's overseas policy and demanding radical change. Portugal has shown no sign of complying with any of these resolutions. A brief account of the debates will indicate the attitudes adopted at each stage by the major powers. While the Soviet bloc and the Afro-Asians consistently voted in favor of the resolutions, the United States and the United Kingdom—acting in concert on every occasion but two—sometimes approved, sometimes disapproved, and sometimes abstained from voting. Abstention is of course, a device adopted with the object of avoiding offense to either side that often results in the annoyance of both. It is frequently the least inconvenient course open to a world power like the United States, with so many ramifications to its foreign policy that some are bound to conflict.

Angola was first debated by the General Assembly on April 20, 1961, when a resolution[41] was passed—with U.S. approval and British and French abstention—calling on the Portuguese Government to "consider urgently the introduction of measures and reforms in Angola for the purpose of the implementation of General Assembly resolution 1514, XV." This was the Declaration on the Granting of Independence to Colonial Countries and Peoples already referred to. The General Assembly also decided to set up a subcommittee of five to investigate the situation in Angola.

On June 7, the Security Council met to consider an Afro-Asian resolution calling on Portugal to "desist . . . from repressive measures" in Angola and to give every facility to the U.N. subcommittee. Opposing the motion, the Portuguese contested the right of the United Nations to interfere and asserted that Portugal was the victim, not the perpetrator, of "unbelievable savagery" and "foreign-sponsored" violence. After 2 days of debate, the Security Council adopted the resolution,[42] softened by a Chilean amendment expressing hope of a peaceful solution, by 9 votes to 0, with Britain and France abstaining. Two of Portugal's NATO allies, the United States and Turkey, voted in favor.[43]

On December 19, the General Assembly, with U.S. and British approval, once again condemned Portugal for failing to comply with Chapter XI of the Charter and refusing to supply information as required by it.[44] But, on this occasion, the debate was overshadowed by India's invasion of Goa on the previous day and the fruitless efforts of the Western powers to obtain any support for a "cease-fire," or even an expression of disapproval, from the Security Council. As one of its most uncompromising critics has written, this was "perhaps the most flagrant example of what Portugal sees as the United Nations double standard of condemning Portugal while condoning the acts of its opponents."[45]

Early in 1962, the General Assembly reopened the question of Angola and considered, for the first time, a demand presented by Poland and Bulgaria for sanctions against Portugal. This was rejected in favor of an Afro-Asian resolution that reaffirmed the right of the Angolan people to self-determination and independence. The resolution called upon Portugal to desist from repressive measures and release all political prisoners; urged the government to undertake, without delay, extensive political, economic, and social reforms and, in particular, to set up freely elected and representative political institutions; and requested members of the United Nations to deny Portugal any support or assistance that might be used for suppression of the Angolan people.[46] While supporting the resolution—which was approved by all the NATO group except

France—the U.S. delegate, Adlai Stevenson, uttered a strong warning against the use of force to effect changes in Angola or any other colonial territories. According to the *New York Herald Tribune*, commenting on January 26, Stevenson's warning apparently took account of two sources of anxiety in the United States and among its Western allies: the fear that countries of black Africa might really try to form a military command to intervene on the side of the Angolan nationalists in the year-old revolt and the apprehension that the Soviets might send "volunteers" to Angola, carrying the seeds for general war in Africa.

When the matter of the Portuguese territories was next raised, at the end of the year, the Assembly went several steps further. A resolution[47] passed on December 14, 1962, while repeating and strengthening all the demands made in previous resolutions, urged all states to prevent the sale and supply of arms and military equipment to Portugal and requested the Security Council, in the event of noncompliance with the resolution, "to take all appropriate measures" to secure compliance. The resolution was adopted by 82 to 7—the seven against being the United States, the United Kingdom, France, Belgium, South Africa, Spain, and Portugal—with 13 abstentions.

This was the first time since the opening of the debate that the United States and Britain both defied the majority by recording a negative vote; they repeated the performance a few days later when a further resolution,[48] relating specifically to Angola, requested the Security Council to take all appropriate measures, *including sanctions*, to obtain Portugal's compliance. No doubt it was the demand for sanctions, hinted at in the first resolution and explicitly stated in the second, that caused them to object. At that moment, the U.N. force in the Congo was poised for the final battle with Tshombe's gendarmes, and, at the U.N. headquarters in Léopoldville, the idea was being canvassed of its being used next against the Portuguese in Angola. Such talk aroused alarm in the U.S. State Department and, especially, the British Foreign Office, which was already none too happy about Katanga.

In July of the following year, 1963, the Security Council, at the request of 32 African states, met again to discuss the Portuguese territories and to hear a delegation representing the OAU. The meeting was also attended by Portuguese Foreign Minister Nogueira, who rejected all accusations against Portugal, attributed the trouble in Angola to a "vast network of foreign interests," and invited the African governments to send delegates on a visit to the territories. This invitation, like a similar one subsequently made to the secretary-general, was refused. The meeting ended with the adoption of a resolution[49] by 8 votes to 0, with U.S. and U.K. abstentions, calling on Portugal to recognize the right of its African subjects to self-determination and independence, requesting all states to refrain from giving any assistance that would enable Portugal to continue repression, and to prevent the supply of arms and military equipment for this purpose. As part of a Security Council resolution, the last demand was mandatory, even on countries that abstained from voting for it. However, Portugal, having given assurance that arms would not be used in Africa, continued to receive its share of arms and equipment as a member of NATO.

In December, 1963, the General Assembly adopted a resolution[50] by 91 to

2—Portugal and Spain against—with 11 abstentions, including the United States and the United Kingdom, again requesting the Security Council to take action, this time to give effect to its own decisions of July. The Council met on December 11 and, in a new resolution[51] passed by 10 to 0, with France abstaining, called on members to comply with its July resolution. It requested the secretary-general to promote negotiations with Portugal and report back in six months. "African delegates," wrote *The New York Times*, "welcomed the fact that the United States and Britain, which abstained on the July 31 resolution, voted for it today."

A few weeks before the meeting of the Security Council, African delegates to the International Conference of Public Education at Geneva had walked out as a protest against the presence of the Portuguese. This was the beginning of a campaign designed to exclude Portugal from participating in any agencies of the United Nations and other international organizations. It was followed by Portugal's expulsion, in the same month, from the U.N. Economic Commission for Africa, a walkout of Afro-Asian and Soviet-bloc delegates from the U.N. Trade and Development Conference in Geneva in April, 1964, and the adoption of a resolution in May, 1965, by the executive committee of UNESCO, barring Portugal from taking part in the International Conference of Public Education and the International Conference on Illiteracy. Finally, the 19th World Health Assembly in May, 1966, suspended the right of Portugal to "participate in the Regional Committee for Africa and in the regional activities."[52]

In 1964, the General Assembly was paralyzed by a dispute over the question of payment for "peace-keeping operations," and most of its time was occupied in maneuvers to prevent Russia, as the chief defaulter, from being expelled from the organization. In consequence, the Portuguese territories, which normally would have figured on the agenda, were not discussed.

In the summer of 1965, the U.N. Committee on Colonialism (Committee of Twenty-Four) visited Africa, receiving delegations and petitions from thirteen nationalist parties from the Portuguese territories. Seven were Angolan, three were from Mozambique, one was from Portuguese Guinea, one was from the Cape Verde Islands, and one was from São Tomé e Príncipe. At its final session, the Committee, by 18 votes to 2 (U.S. and U.K.) with 3 abstentions (Australia, Denmark, and Italy), adopted a resolution[53] criticizing the NATO countries for their alleged support of Portugal and calling once again for sanctions. The U.S. representative, while observing that he could not accept the Portuguese view that "self-determination meant the agreement and consent of the population to a certain political structure, type of State, and administrative organization," said that the United States was against violent solutions and still believed in persuasion. The British representative, who had been heavily under fire over Rhodesia, took the same line.

This was the prelude to a new drive against Portugal during the 1965 session of the General Assembly. In November, however, the Security Council rejected an Afro-Asian demand for an economic boycott of Portugal, and the United States and the United Kingdom both abstained from voting on the resolution[54] finally adopted. This repeated the demands made in previous resolutions for the self-determination and independence of the Portuguese territories of Angola, Mozambique, and Portuguese Guinea, the immediate cessation of all acts of repression, withdrawal of all military and other forces employed for that purpose, and an unconditional political amnesty. It also added a new demand to open negotiations with nationalist representatives "with a view to the transfer of power to political institutions freely elected and representative of the peoples."

Having failed to obtain a vote for sanctions in the Security Council, the Afro-Asians made another bid in the Assembly, where they succeeded, on December 18, in putting through a resolution[55] calling for, among other measures, the rupture of diplomatic relations with and an international arms and trade boycott of Portugal. The vote this time was 66 to 26, with 15 abstentions. The small majority against Portugal indicated that, while almost all members of the United Nations were willing to condemn it publicly, only three-fifths were prepared to contemplate action against Portugal, despite the fact that most of them would not have been affected by it. Similar resolutions continued to be voted in 1966 and 1967 with no new development, except that, in 1966, the General Assembly recommended that the World Bank and other specialized agencies should not cooperate with Portugal, a recommendation that was respected in 1967.

In November, 1968, however, both the strength of the General Assembly resolution and the voting pattern changed. Previous references to Portuguese policy as a "crime against humanity" were dropped, as were requests that the World Bank suspend loans to Portugal. These changes represented the first time that African countries were willing to modify a previous harsh resolution on a colonial issue. In response, many countries that had voted against Portugal in 1967 chose to abstain, including the United States, Britain, Spain, the Netherlands, and Australia. The final result was 96 to 3, the three being South Africa, Portugal, and, significantly, Brazil. Some observers viewed this 1968 vote as a change of strategy by the African nations, which hoped to induce Western countries to more actively play an anticolonial role and to influence the new Caetano government at a time when liberalizing winds were whispering in Portugal.[56]

The 13 years of debate can be summed up by saying that, as the tenor of discussion on Portugal became more inflamed, the pressure of some to pass from words to deeds became more intense, so Washington and London and most other Western capitals became more cautious. Having succeeded for several years in keeping the demand for sanctions out of resolutions by diplomacy, they were prepared, when it was finally inserted against their advice, to risk the ire of the Afro-Asians by voting against it. If it were illustrated by a graph, Anglo-American support for the opponents of Portugal in the General Assembly would appear as a curved line rising from the abstentions of 1960, reaching its apogee in the affirmative votes of late 1961 and early 1962, and then descending to the "noes" of December, 1962, partly reviving with the abstentions of 1963, dropping once more to the "noes" of 1965 through 1967, and levelling with the abstentions of 1968. For the Security Council, a graph would have much the same shape.

The changes in tactics, if not in policy, thus depicted were the result not only of American and British reluctance to take drastic measures against a NATO ally, measures that, without any certainty of being effective, would further divide the Western alliance and risk more unrest in Africa. They also reflected a growing disillusionment with the consequences of too precipitate a decolonization. One independent African country after another had succumbed to civil war—the Congo, Sudan, Nigeria—or had been taken over by military dictatorship— Algeria, Ghana, Dahomey, Upper Volta, Sierra Leone, the Central African Republic—while most of the remainder became one-party states. All this caused second thoughts about the timing of self-determination.

NOTES

1. See Chapters II and III.
2. Franco Nogueira, *The United Nations and Portugal* (London, 1963), pp. 121–22
3. C. E. Carrington, "National Self-Determination," *Modern Age*, Summer, 1967, p. 251.
4. Article 22 of the League of Nations Covenant.
5. See T. B. Millar, *The Commonwealth and the United Nations* (Sydney, 1967), p. 121.
6. Winston Churchill, *The Second World War* (London, 1951), pp. 194 and 824. Another Prime Minister, Clement Atlee, recorded his impression that "Roosevelt, having been brought up to regard imperialism as a danger to world peace and to the freedom of small nations in the American tradition of the world, was never free from eyeing British policy with suspicion." *The Listener*, January 22, 1959, p. 155.
7. Carrington, *op. cit.*, p. 249.
8. *Ibid.*, p. 257.
9. Leland M. Goodrich and Edvard Hambro, *Charter of the United Nations: Commentary and Documents* (Boston, 1949), pp. 95–96.
10. Ruth B. Russell and Jeannette E. Muther, *A History of the United Nations Charter* (Washington, D.C., 1958), p. 811.
11. Obed Y. Asamoah, *The Legal Significance of the Declarations of the General Assembly of the United Nations*, preface by Wolfgang Friedmann (The Hague, 1966), p. 166; Rosalyn Higgins, *The Development of International Law Through the Organs of the United Nations* (London, 1963), p. 104.
12. U.N. General Assembly, Res. 545, VI (February 5, 1952).
13. Res. 637, VIII (December 16, 1952).
14. U.N. Security Council, *Resolution of June 9, 1961*, Security Council Official Record, 18th Year, Suppl. 4835 (April–June, July 31, 1963), and Suppl. 5380 and Corrigenda 1 (July–September) on Portuguese Territories.
15. Goodrich and Hambro, *op. cit.*, p. 408.
16. Hans Kelsen, *The Law of the United Nations* (London and New York, 1950), p. 556.
17. In his annual report for the period July, 1947, to January, 1948, Secretary-General Trygve Lie wrote: "The transmission to the Secretary-General of information on economic, social, and educational conditions in non-self-governing territories is an obligation specifically stipulated in the Charter

under Article 73e. The other provisions of Article 73 are of a declaratory character."

18. *Journal of the United Nations*, 63 (December 16, 1946), 683ff. The British delegate was equally emphatic when he said: "The Charter itself provides no organ for the supervision of the application of Chapter XI," while the French declared: "As regards Chapter XI particularly I would remind you that this Chapter is not in the same form as the other provisions of the Charter. It is entitled 'Declaration.' It contains a unilateral declaration by a certain number of states, and the Charter merely confines itself to recording it. This is absolutely clear: there can be no argument about it." *Ibid.*, p. 688. The Australian delegate made the same point when he told a subcommittee of the Fourth Committee, which deals with trusteeship: "The three chapters (XI, XII, and XIII) had a common root. But Chapter XI was a unilateral declaration on the part of administering states, while Chapter XII represented an international multilateral contractural undertaking." United Nations, Doc. A/C/4/68 (December 8, 1946), p. 10.

19. U.S. Mission to the United Nations, Press Release 251 (October, 1947).

20. *Journal of the United Nations*, 55, Suppl. 4-A/C (December 9, 1946), 77ff.

21. United Nations, Doc. A/519 (January 8, 1946), pp. 48ff.

22. A/64/Add. 1 (January 31, 1947), pp. 126ff.

23. David H. Wainhouse, *Remnants of Empire* (New York, 1964), pp. 6–7.

24. Franco Nogueira, *The United Nations and Portugal* (London, 1963), p. 78. As Nogueira points out in a footnote, India used the same argument over Kashmir.

25. U.N. General Assembly, Res. 1467, XIX (December 12, 1959).

26. The Assembly had already declared in a resolution passed in 1953, that, to be valid, any association between a non-self-governing territory and a metropole or any other country would have to fulfill certain conditions. It must result from the "freely expressed opinion of the population of the territory" arrived at "by democratic and informed means." "Geographical . . . ethnical, and cultural considerations" and especially "political advancement of the population sufficient to enable them to decide upon the future destiny of the Territory with due knowledge" were among other factors to be taken into account. General Assembly, Res. 742, VIII (November 27, 1953).

27. U.N. General Assembly, Res. 1541, XV (December 15, 1960).

28. Res. 1542, XV (December 15, 1960).

29. The Article reads, in part, as follows: "Nothing contained in the present Charter shall authorize the United Nations to intervene in matters which are essentially within the domestic jurisdiction of any state or shall require the Members to submit such matters to settlement under the present Charter."

30. Nogueira, *op. cit.*, p. 82.

31. The failure of the Security Council to order a cease-fire in Gôa caused Adlai Stevenson to declare: "We have witnessed tonight an effort to rewrite the Charter to sanction the use of force . . . when it suits one's own purpose. This approach can only lead to chaos and to the disintegration of the United Nations."

32. The idea that "domestic jurisdiction" has never been clearly defined and that action by international community can be taken in areas that not only are "a threat to peace" but are of "international concern" had been taking shape even while the Charter was being drafted and was developed during the debates of the "Spanish situation." The Security Council resolution on this clearly

established the point that "an investigation to ascertain facts cannot constitute intervention." Rosalyn Higgins, *The Development of International Law Through the Political Organs of the United Nations* (London, 1963). p. 78; see also Security Council Official Record, 1st Year, 1st Session, No. 2, 39th Meeting, p. 245. Although this resolution was later changed, "the idea had taken root that matters *prima facie* of domestic jurisdiction may be of international concern in certain circumstances." Higgins, *op. cit.*, p. 79. Later, the General Assembly also adopted a similar resolution (General Assembly Official Record, Res. 39, 1st Session, Part 2, Plen. 59th Meeting, p. 1222). The same author expressed the opinion that the Spanish case might provide "a sufficiently international case to remove it from the operation of article 2 (7), and permit action under Chapter VI," although Article 39 might not be applicable to it (Higgins, p. 80).

The underlying idea of a "potential threat" that was voiced in resolutions concerning South Africa was repeated in resolutions concerning the Angolan situation. The General Assembly stated its awareness that "failure to act speedily, effectively, and in time for ameliorating the disabilities of the African peoples of Angola is likely to endanger international peace and security." General Assembly, Res. 1603, XV (April 20, 1961). Meanwhile, the Security Council declared that it was "taking note of the grave concern and strong reactions to such occurrences throughout the continent of Africa and in other parts of the world. Convinced that the continuation of the situation in Angola is an actual and potential cause of international friction and is likely to endanger the maintenance of international peace and security." S/4835 (June 9, 1961). The limits of international concern were not precisely defined but the concept is becoming important at least "as a supplementary basis for United Nations jurisdiction," indicating that "states may be concerned about events happening within another state even if their interests are not directly involved or jeopardized." Higgins, *op. cit.*, p. 81.

33. A similar attempt was made in the case of Rhodesia at the end of 1965. However, it was the British Government that, in April, 1966, successfully invoked Chapter VII to justify its oil blockade of Beira, this being the first instance in the history of the United Nations when the Security Council authorized economic sanctions backed by force.

34. Patricia Wohlgemuth, *The Portuguese Territories and the United Nations* (New York, 1963), p. 28.

35. Wolfgang Friedmann, *The Changing Structure of International Law* (New York, 1964), p. 138.

36. Oscar Schachter in his first Hague Lectures of 1963, as quoted in *ibid.*, pp. 139–40.

37. International Court of Justice, Rep. 67 (1955), p. 122.

38. Most jurists respect this view, however, Friedmann considers international conventions as "framework documents" that are "developed and modified by practice," in a continuous "adjustment between common goals and conflicting national interests and policies of the participants." He thinks that, as it is almost impossible to achieve "formal amendments of an international constitutional document, such as the U.N. Charter," "consolidation of practices" and "*de facto* revisions" lead to this adjustment. Goodrich claims that "the practice not too commonly or widely challenged of interpreting the Charter as a constitution and not simply as a treaty" has been one of the prominent

features of the development of the United Nations. Leland M. Goodrich, "The Political Role of the Secretary-General," *International Organization*, Vol. XVI (1962), p. 726.

39. Full text of the resolution usually referred to as 1514, XV, will be found in General Assembly Official Records, A/PV/947 (December 14, 1960), p. 21.
40. For a fuller account of the debate see Wainhouse, *op. cit.*, pp. 11–12.
41. United Nations, Doc. A/Res. 1603, XV (April 20, 1961).
42. S/4835 (June 9, 1961).
43. Commenting on the debate, Arthur Krock wrote in *The New York Times* (June 13, 1961): "The perplexity of the U.S. Government created by the Afro-Asian activity in the U.N. against the Portuguese in Angola grows out of policies which require the Kennedy Administration to try simultaneously to ride two horses galloping in opposite directions. Our fundamental military alliance in NATO, and its strength, depend greatly on the unity which this government is ever urging. Our fundamental diplomatic policy is to demonstrate by votes in the U.N. and otherwise that the U.S. unreservedly supports movements for the independence of peoples everywhere."
44. United Nations, Doc. A/Res. 1699, XVI (December 19, 1961).
45. Wohlgemuth, *op. cit.*, p. 27.
46. United Nations, Doc. A/Res. 1742, XVI (January 30, 1962).
47. A/Res. 1807, XVII (December 4, 1962).
48. A/Res. 1819, XVII (December 18, 1962).
49. S/5380 (July 31, 1963).
50. A/Res. 1913, XVIII (December 3, 1963).
51. S/5480 (December 11, 1963).
52. World Health Organization, Press Release WP/31 (May 27, 1966), p. 4.
53. United Nations, Doc. A/AC. 109/124 and Corr. 1 (June 10, 1965).
54. S/218 (November 23, 1965).
55. A/Res. 2107, XX (December 18, 1965).
56. *Washington Post*, November 22, 1968.

XVII

The Nationalist Parties

MICHAEL A. SAMUELS

THROUGHOUT history, practically from the time of the original Portuguese conquest, there have been independence movements of greater and lesser importance in various parts of the Portuguese empire. These movements have generally failed, through the apathy or open opposition of much of the local and immigrant populations. The one important exception is Brazil, where independence occurred after the reluctant return of the king of Portugal to Lisbon after a stay in Brazil during the French occupation of Portugal; independence was practically bloodless and was perpetrated under the leadership of the crown prince.

The feeling, especially strong in Angola, that overseas Portugal was being neglected, if not smothered, in a sea of economic muddle and administrative red tape dates from the 1860's, when newspaper editorials began to criticize the Lisbon government for failing to develop Angola. In the period 1870–1922, early signs of Angolan nationalism appeared among the *mestiço* and *assimilado* communities, usually taking the form of newspaper comments or the organizing of political and cultural clubs. A resurgence of this feeling followed the *coup d'état* of 1926, when the new regime was preoccupied with putting the financial house of metropolitan Portugal in order. The European-dominated Pro-Angola Party, formed in the 1920's and dormant for some time, became active again in the 1950's. The openly pro-Delgado sentiment of 1958 in Angola (see Chapter VII) led to a series of arrests of European Portuguese in 1959. When the Movimento Popular de Libertação de Angola (MPLA) was founded in 1956, it originally included a number of white Angolans, but it has remained largely a *mestifço* party. As such, it might be seen as the contemporary incarnation of the earlier *mestiço, assimilado* protest. A similar European organization in Mozambique, Movimento Democrático de Moçambique, petitioned Premier Salazar in 1961 to loosen the economic system.

During the 1950's frustration was building up within Portuguese Africa as a result of a growing internal awareness of Portuguese repression, the spirit of coming African independence elsewhere on the continent, and the willingness of various international bodies to support dissent. This chapterconcerns the development of Portuguese-African nationalist organizations. Their development represents one branch of a continuation of earlier protest movements. The other branch reflects a curtailment of protest by some white, *mestiço*, and African leaders, who, after the outbreak of armed violence in Angola, have coalesced around the protection of the Portuguese army. Throughout the discussion of Portuguese-African nationalism, therefore, this second branch should be kept in mind. (It may display a sometimes multiracial similarity to the ideas among the white settlers of Southern Rhodesia that eventually led them unilaterally to declare their independence.)

A large number of nationalist organizations developed throughout Portuguese Africa in the 1960's. Some have been short lived. Some have consolidated through mergers. Others have changed little since their inception. Some propound theories of revolution and use tactics of guerrilla insurgency, while others have found ways of coexisting with the Portuguese. The recent growth of some of the major nationalist organizations will now be described.

ANGOLA

The oldest of the current revolutionary parties, União das Populações de Angola (UPA), began as União das Populações do Norte de Angola (UPNA), among a small group of Angolan Bakongo in 1957 in Léopoldville where several informal groups had existed among the Bakongo for some time.[1] A dispute over the succession to the Bakongo chieftancy in São Salvador the following year stirred new animosities. The dispute developed after tribal leaders had recommended an assimilated, educated successor for the Bakongo kingship, and the government had appointed another candidate. One result of the government selection was a strong split between Protestant and Catholic Bakongo, and UPNA took on a clearly Protestant image. During the early days, the party was clearly a tribal organization reflecting an all-Bakongo nationalism through the revival of the ancient Kongo Kingdom and a detaching of Bakongo regions from the rest of Angola. A June, 1957, petition from the party to the United Nations stated that it was "not introduced by the country called Angola, but by the Congo which is an ex-independent territory with no treaty with Portugal."[2]

It became difficult to commit public actions in Léopoldville. In 1958, the nephew of two UPNA founders, Holden Roberto, named after a British Baptist missionary, was sent to visit independent Africa. His first destination was Ghana, where, by December, he had met Kwame Nkrumah and George Padmore and had attended the First All-African Peoples Conference.[3] Roberto's experience soon convinced him that it was necessary to expand his party's focus. While in Accra, he changed the name of the party to União das Populações de Angola (UPA). Though by name it was a national Angolan movement, the party still inclined heavily toward its Bakongo and Protestant roots.

Under Roberto, UPA became heavily influenced by Patrice Lumumba, the first Prime Minister of the Congo, and soon was closely allied with him. Roberto also began a fortnightly newspaper, *La Voix de la Nation Angolaise*.[4] Published mostly in French, but also in Kikongo and Portuguese, the paper appealed to Congolese citizens and the large group of Angolan Bakongo working in the Congo, from whom the first Angolan freedom fighters were drawn.

The fall of Lumumba was a serious blow to Roberto. The new government in

Léopoldville was anti-Communist, had closed the Soviet-bloc embassies, and had expelled the representatives of Guinea and Ghana, thus denying Roberto the valuable assistance he had envisioned after his return from Accra. Because arms and money stopped arriving, UPA, when it launched its attack the following March, had to use *pangas*, the all-purpose African cutting tool, and homemade muskets.

The second important nationalist party, Movimento Popular de Libertação de Angola (MPLA), was founded in 1956 in Luanda at a secret meeting of "all Angolan anti-imperialist forces."[5] Major support within MPLA came from groups reflecting the growing Communist influence in Angola. The Angolan Communist Party was a branch of the larger Portuguese one and, given the lack of opportunity for participation in Angolan politics, had been able to build a following among discontented intellectuals and other urban disaffected, especially in Luanda, Malange, and Catete.

For several years, MPLA operated clandestinely in Angola, but in March, 1959, a number of the leaders were arrested and the party's very existence was threatened. As a result, a new office was opened first in Paris and later in Conakry, with the approval and assistance of Sékou Touré, and was taken charge of by two *mestiço* intellectuals, Mário de Andrade and Viriato da Cruz, who assumed the titles of president and secretary-general, respectively, of MPLA. Andrade, born in Cuanza Norte District in 1928, was first educated in Lisbon, where he became a member of the illegal Portuguese Communist Party, and later he studied in Paris. As a writer with an international reputation, he had been a delegate to the Afro-Asian Writers Conference convened at Tashkent, in the U.S.S.R., in 1958.

While in Conakry, MPLA sought to unite with similar organizations that advocated independence elsewhere in Portuguese Africa. At the Second All-African Peoples Conference in Tunis in January, 1960, a new united front was formed, the Frente Revolucionária Africana para a Independência Nacional das ColóniasPortuguesas (FRAIN), under the direction of Andrade. The headquarters of F RAIN were in Conakry, then functioning as a strong center of national liberation movements under the influence of the Russian ambassador, Daniel Semenovich Solod, who was known for his success, while serving in the Soviet embassy in Cairo, in spreading Russian influence in the Middle East.[6]

UPA refused to join FRAIN, in spite of pressure to join from various international supporters. According to one observer, "the major purpose of FRAIN appears to have been to undermine Roberto's position" by either subordinating him in the larger organization or embarrassing him by his refusal to cooperate.[7] Whether or not this tactic would have succeeded became academic after the outbreak of conflict in Angola. After the first outbreak of terrorism of March, 1961, Roberto assumed leadership of the continuing conflict. By so doing, he gained enough international prestige to cause the downfall of FRAIN. Another meeting, at Casablanca in April, 1961, led to the formation of the Conferência de Organizações Nacionalistas das Colónias Portuguesas (CONCP), which established a permanent secretariat in Rabat under the responsibility of Mozambican Marcelino dos Santos.

Meanwhile, Roberto was busy soliciting international support. His activities were successful, and, by October, 1961, the Algerian FLN, with the tacit support of President Habib Bourguiba of Tunisia, had both supplied and trained the growing UPA army. (There are indications that Roberto also received private American support.[8]) Congolese officials were also most helpful, although possibly a dispute between Roberto and President Joseph Kasavubu over Roberto's unwillingness to join fully in Kasavubu's pan-Bakongo dreams was averted only because of Kasavubu's own tenuous position.[9] The UPA took advantage of the increasing chaos in the Congo and added to its growing quantity of arms from the disintegrating Force Publique. Roberto's fortunes once more hit a zenith in August, 1961, when Cyrille Adoula, an old friend of Roberto, became Premier of the Congo.

By this time, American support for Roberto was also becoming apparent. During 1961, he made several trips to the United States, succeeding in gaining support, if nothing else, from several private sources. In December, he delivered a speech in Washington in which he called on the United States and other Western powers to abstain from giving any material assistance, including arms, to the Portuguese. In Léopoldville, he had entree to the American Embassy, which issued visas for his visits to America on the Tunisian passport he carried under the name José Gilmore.

As we have seen, this was the period when the members of the newly installed Kennedy Administration had decided to support African nationalism. They were looking for non-Communist leaders to whom they could give their blessings[10] and furnish aid, if not material then at least moral, with a clear conscience. Thus, other Angolan nationalist leaders also received visas to enter the United States. As James Duffy has written, "no less an authority on international Communism than the Central Intelligence Agency reportedly made an investigation of the UPA and satisfied itself that it was an authentic African nationalist party, free from any Communist association."[11]

Andrade was now in danger of being left out in the cold, so, in October, 1961, he moved the MPLA headquarters to Léopoldville. Here he was closer to the many Angolan refugees and *émigrés*, among whom a militant nationalistic spirit was more easily engendered. MPLA continued its attempt to create unity within the Angolan nationalist movement, but Roberto constantly rebuffed Andrade. Not only was Roberto wary of association with the Communist-supported leaders of MPLA, but, as one observer noted, Roberto "and his Negro aides distrust mulattoes and also fear that in merging with the Andrade group their position might be undermined by those who are better educated."[12]

Roberto was not, however, completely averse to coalitions. In March, 1962, UPA merged with the smaller Partido Democrático Angolano (PDA), which represented the Zombo tribe of the Bakongo,[13] to form the Frente Nacional de Libertação de Angola (FNLA). An early step of the FNLA was to create Angola's first government in exile, the Governo Revolucionário de Angola no Exílio (GRAE), with Roberto as Premier, PDA's Emmanuel Kunzika as vice-premier, Msgr. Manuel Mendes das Neves (the former vicar-general of Angola, who had been arrested in Luanda in April, 1961, on charges of complicity with nationalist activities), as second vice-premier, and an Ovimbundu, Jonas Savimbi, who had earlier been secretary general of UPA, as foreign minister.[14] There were signs that, at least among the leadership, GRAE was trying to disprove the criticism that it represented solely Protestant and Bakongo interests.

The split between the two movements had deepened a few weeks earlier, when the UPA chief of staff in Léopoldville, Marcos Kassanga, left the party, accusing his associates of waging a "fratricidal war" in which not only Portuguese but "8,000 Angolans were savagely massacred by tribal elements in the UPA."[15] To Kassanga, UPA remained a Bakongo organization.

In July, 1962, MPLA was further buoyed by the arrival in Léopoldville of Dr. Agostinho Neto, a physician and poet and one of the first contemporary Angolan nationalists. Neto had been arrested in Angola in 1960 but escaped, after periods in jail in both Cape Verde and Lisbon. Neto soon attempted to create a united front, but Roberto was unwilling to participate. The following December, MPLA elected Neto president, stated a foreign policy of "positive neutralism," and laid down minimum conditions for negotiations with Portugal.

One of Neto's first acts, within a month of his election, was to take a trip to the United States to seek financial assistance and attempt to dispel the belief that the MPLA was a pro-Communist movement. The fact that Radio Moscow, however, continued to support the MPLA and criticize the GRAE weighed heavily against the success of the trip.[16]

The affiliation of Neto with MPLA neither unified the movements nor forestalled the momentum of GRAE. As John Marcum has observed, "The Roberto policy of concentrating on three basic goals—building a military force, creating a mass political base, and securing the good will of the Government of the Congo—began to pay off at the African summit gathering in Addis Ababa in May, 1963."[17] This gathering resulted in the formation of the Coordinating Committee for the Liberation of Africa, which planned to go to Léopoldville to unite the movements.

June and July of 1963 saw a scurry of activity. GRAE sought to show that it was already a united front and not about to merge with anyone. Showing its early support, the Congo Government recognized GRAE late in June. A week later, the MPLA was rocked by a surprise event. After returning from a journalism conference sponsored by Communist China in Indonesia, Viriato da Cruz denounced Neto and formed his own splinter faction to rule the party. This immediately led to a violent clash with Neto and Andrade supporters. As a result, on July 12, the da Cruz followers quit MPLA and expressed a desire to participate in GRAE. It was clear, however, that they did so, not because of agreement with either Roberto or his movement, but because of the relative success of GRAE compared with MPLA.

Rebuffed by Roberto in his search for unity, Neto had not given up his idea of a confederation under his own leadership. His search found success in July, 1963, with the establishment of the Frente Democrática de Libertação de Angola (FDLA) through initiatives of Abbé Youlou in Brazzaville. This new group was doomed almost from the start by the ideological diversity of its various parties. Some of the groups that comprised FDLA were Mouvement de

Défense des Intérêts de l'Angola (MDIA), Ngwizani a Kongo (Ngwizako), the NtoBako, and União Nacional dos Trabalhadores Angolanos (UNTA). The MDIA had begun in 1961, when a group, under the leadership of Jean Pierre M'Bala, broke away from UPA. They favored pacifism and opposed Roberto's tactics of revolution and terrorism. The resultant policy of collaboration with the Portuguese was criticized in 1962 by the Special Committee on Territories Under Portuguese Administration, which visited MDIA's Léopoldville headquarters and claimed that it was being "used by the Portuguese Government solely for the purpose of being able to claim that it had the cooperation of some Angolan group."[18] Mid-1963 saw an internal struggle for power, and another former UPA adherent, Simon Diallo Mingiedi, who ousted M'Bala, led his followers into Neto's FDLA.

The Ngwizako was a nonviolent, royalist faction of the Bakongo begun in Léopoldville in 1960. Its supporters, many of whom were Catholics, had backed the 1955 Portuguese choice of king at São Salvador. Their major goal from the outset was similar to that of UPNA, the rights of the "twelve free and sovereign clans of the Congo" to "regain freedom and sovereignty as a Monarchy."[19]

The third collaborative party, NtoBako, began under the leadership of Angelino Alberto late in 1960. This party had the support of the Congolese party, Abako, and of Joseph Kasavubu and had dreams of a greater Kongo State.

These three parties were willing to collaborate with the Portuguese authorities. At one time or another, all received scholarships for youthful party affiliates to study in Lisbon.[20] Their joint collaboration alone does not seem surprising, but their entry into FDLA with the UNTA does. UNTA, largely a Communist-trained labor union associated with MPLA, was clearly more radical than the other three collaborators. The resultant FDLA coalition has been aptly described by John Marcum as a "heterogeneous group of half-parties"[21] reflecting the internecine splits so prevalent at the time.

When the representatives of the Coordinating Committee for the Liberation of Africa met in Léopoldville in mid-July, da Cruz further hurt the MPLA by revealing that its claims of having a meaningful fighting force in Angola were false. GRAE, on the other hand, was able to conduct a tour of its military training camp at Kinkuzu and invited the Committee to tour parts of Angola occupied by its forces. This show succeeded in convincing the Committee that GRAE was the only real fighting front in Angola. Their subsequent recommendations succeeded in gaining wide African recognition for GRAE. Another important consequence was the closing of the MPLA's offices in Léopoldville by the Congo Government.

A new MPLA headquarters in Brazzaville was aided by a *coup d'état* that brought the radical, Alphonse Massamba-Debat, to power. Here the MPLA proceeded to denounce the GRAE by radio and began the gradual development of a fighting force to regain esteem lost within independent Africa. Russian, Cuban, and Algerian support was forthcoming. It was a time for reorganization and military training to prepare for a new target: Cabinda.

The GRAE also began a period of consolidation as it waited for the material signs of recent support from the Organization for African Unity (OAU).

Though these signs were delayed, GRAE had succeeded in taking significant steps toward showing that its movement embraced more than just the Bakongo. Just as the horizon began to look bright for GRAE, adversity struck. The Portuguese army was becoming noticeably more efficient in dealing with GRAE insurgents, and PIDE intelligence operations were likewise becoming more efficient. Monetary support from the OAU liberation fund had been minimal. Internal organizational problems and increasing refugee demands began to present problems of morale.

Meanwhile, a number of GRAE's Ovimbundu cadres were becoming restless with Roberto's apparent refusal to extend activities far from Bakongo lands. Fraternal support for this position, and reaction to GRAE's admission, finally, of the MPLA-da Cruz group into the FNLA, led Roberto's highest-ranking Ovimbundu assistant, GRAE's Foreign Minister Jonas Savimbi, to resign at an OAU meeting in Cairo in July, 1964. He criticized Roberto's "flagrant tribalism" and his acceptance of support from "American imperialists." With Savimbi went most of the other Ovimbundu leaders in GRAE.

To compound Roberto's problems, a new government had come to power in the Congo, led by Moise Tshombe, who had been befriended by the Portuguese during his attempts at Katangan succession and also prior to his gaining power in the Congo. Tshombe was much less willing than his predecessors to move against his former Portuguese allies.

By the end of 1964, the fortunes of MPLA in Brazzaville had revived. Andrade had returned as an active party member. Russian support was now strongly in its favor, as shown by charges in December that Roberto had become a puppet of the United States and requests that MPLA be recognized as the true nationalist party.[22] That the tide had turned was clear when the OAU liberation committee recognized MPLA's growing effectiveness by giving it part of the funds previously set aside for GRAE.

For the first half of 1965, the two major parties exchanged charges on their own radio stations, with MPLA, through The Voice of Angola, operating out of Brazzaville and GRAE, through The Voice of Free Angola, operating out of Léopoldville. By May, GRAE had been expelled from the Afro-Asian Solidarity Conference in Ghana, which, in turn, recognized MPLA.

In June, 1965, Roberto's office in Léopoldville was attacked and sacked by supporters of Alexandre Taty, the dissident GRAE defense minister, and André Kassinda, formerly associated with a UPA trade union, who the previous April had begun the Conselho do Povo Angolano (CPA), an anti-Roberto, pro-Tshombe alliance. The Congolese army helped GRAE recapture its offices but not without the loss of valuable documents. This provided the opportunity for Tshombe to place new restrictions on GRAE operations, as both he and his friends, the Portuguese, desired. General harassment of GRAE's officials and the stopping of supplies to its major training camp were its major obstacles.

After the dismissal of Tshombe, in the fall of 1965, and the seizure of power by General Joseph Mobutu, who was a good friend of Roberto, the prospects for GRAE improved. Mobutu pledged himself to assist the movement, and the flow of arms and supplies was resumed. Relations between GRAE and MPLA remained unchanged, however.

Meanwhile, the MPLA was becoming more of a competitive force. Realizing that it had lost the first round of the international struggle for recognition and the national struggle of liberation to GRAE, it expanded its activities late in 1965 and in 1966. The expansion of MPLA insurgency into the Dembos area and into the far eastern portion of Angola from Zambia were important activities, especially since campaigns against Cabinda, after initial successes, had failed.

Since the MPLA had established itself as a fighting force, it resumed its international campaign aimed at unification of all Angolan nationalists under its leadership. Following a *rapprochement* between Léopoldville and Brazzaville, several African countries made determined efforts to effect a reconciliation. At the end of August, 1966, a meeting of the council of CONCP was held in Brazzaville, attended by Eduardo Mondlane (from Mozambique), Amilcar Cabral (from Portuguese Guinea), and Agostinho Neto and António Medeiros (from São Tomé and Príncipe). No representative of GRAE was present, but, on the day after the meeting, on August 29, Cairo radio announced that an agreement had been reached in Dar es Salaam for GRAE's amalgamation with MPLA in "one front." Neto claimed that the amalgamation bore witness "to the recognition of the MPLA as the leading organizing force in the armed liberation struggle against Portuguese colonialism in Angola," adding that it "favored the cause of opening a second front in the south of Angola, bearing in mind that the headquarters of the UPA are in Katanga [sic]."[23] These various announcements suggested less a genuine change of heart in the parties than a jockeying for position in areas where MPLA already had support.

In October, 1966, a more serious effort at reconciliation was made in Cairo, by a committee of the OAU under the chairmanship of Najib as-Sadr, head of the African department of the Egyptian foreign ministry. This meeting was one of several attempts by the OAU since 1964 to bring about consolidation. Delegations from MPLA and GRAE were present and submitted their views. On October 15, Cairo radio announced that an agreement had been signed for the cessation of all forms of hostile propaganda between the two organizations, supervision of their publications by a body affiliated with the OAU, immediate release of members of each organization detained by the other, and the formation of a joint committee under the auspices of the OAU to study and formulate "the final form of cooperation between the two organizations in military and political affairs." In fact, however, this agreement was more an OAU dream than an Angolan reality.

The chief significance of the agreement was that the status of Roberto's movement as the sole recognized representative of Angola's nationalism had begun to erode, and, in the eyes of other African countries, it rated no more than equal with its rival. The better educated leaders of MPLA had regained by diplomacy the ground they had lost initially by leaving the fighting to UPA.

With unification foiled again, the parties continued their separate tendencies. The most significant development came not from either of the two major movements, but from a new party. After leaving his position as GRAE's foreign minister, Jonas Savimbi had gone to Brazzaville, where he later tried to join the MPLA. By mid-1965, it was clear that the two groups had failed to harmonize their interests. After a year's study to complete a degree at the University of Lausanne, Savimbi moved to Lusaka. There he gathered his colleagues who had left GRAE with him in 1964, a number of students and former students from southern Angola, and groups of people from the Lovale and Chokwe tribes who had migrated from Angola. In March, 1966, meeting near Luso in Angola, Savimbi and his followers formed the União Nacional para a Independência Total de Angola (UNITA). Savimbi tried not to interfere with Zambia's concern that guerrilla activities not be based in Zambia, but begin operating from inside Angola.

Zambian restrictions were not fully accepted. On Christmas, 1966, first, and several times later the following March, UNITA attacks halted the Benguela Railway, thus hurting the economies of Zambia and the Congo. After Portugal threatened to close the railway completely, Savimbi was expelled from Zambia in mid-1967 and went to Cairo.

Though leaderless, UNITA still functioned. Its activities were directed along the eastern border and in the central Ovimbundu areas. Technical and material assistance, especially from China, was allowed to pass through Zambia. In mid-1968, Savimbi himself was reportedly back in Angola, and UNITA activities emphasized instilling a political consciousness among the rural population and conducting guerrilla activities along the eastern border, especially in the sparsely populated Cuando Cubango area. There was some indication that first UNITA and then MPLA cooperated with the South-West Africa People's Organization (SWAPO) to facilitate SWAPO's task of infiltrating the Caprivi Strip. UNITA continued to show that, in spite of its tardiness entering in the field, it remained a viable nationalist movement.

During the 1966 visit to Africa of the U.N. Special Committee on Colonialism, several other new groups presented petitions.[24] These included the Front Patriotique pour l'Independence du Kongo dit Portugais (FPIKP), an alliance of NtoBako, Ngwizako, and other Bakongo secessionists opposed to Roberto and favoring negotiations with Portugal for the restoration of the ancient Kongo Kingdom; Partido Nacional Africano (PNA), representing the Chokwe tribe and based in Tshikapa in the Kasai; and União Progressista Nacional de Angola (UPRONA).

Meanwhile, the two original movements continued their activities. In the wake of Savimbi's success in establishing UNITA within Angola and an apparently similar success in Portuguese Guinea, the MPLA decided to establish an internal base. The distance of Brazzaville from the fighting front, the obstacle of a hostile Congo (Kinshasa), and the importance of showing internal operations to gain international support, especially from the OAU, were important factors in MPLA's changed strategy. The changes brought new support. In its July, 1968, meeting, the OAU's African Liberation Committee withdrew its recognition of GRAE as a government in exile and put the more "representative" MPLA on an equal footing with the FNLA.[25] As a result, the MPLA could look forward to an important increase in international support.

With the nationalist conflict almost seven years old as of 1969, three major nationalist movements carried on the insurgency in Angola. While they had been developing, nationalist movements elsewhere in Portuguese Africa had by no means been quiescent.

PORTUGUESE GUINEA

The origins of the major nationalist party in Portuguese Guinea,[26] Partido Africano da Independência da Guiné e Cabo Verde (PAIGC) were similar to those of MPLA. In the mid-1950's, PAIGC organized clandestinely in Bissau, not purely as an intellectual movement; its founders sought to stir artisans and urban workers to make demands on the Portuguese authorities. Firm and violent police response to a strike at the Pigiguiti dock against the giant Companhia União Fabril (CUF) in Bissau caused changes in PAIGC strategy. Seeing this response as a sign of Portuguese ability and determination not to loosen control over urban life, the PAIGC leaders vowed to silence their urban organization and to begin a campaign to make the rural inhabitants more aware.

Credit for making success of this campaign belongs to the secretary-general of PAIGC, Amilcar Cabral, who founded the party along with Raphael Barbosa, the party president who was arrested in Bissau in 1962. After receiving a degree in agronomy in Lisbon, Cabral entered the government agricultural service in Guinea in 1950. His agricultural activities involved him more than most educated leaders with the lives of rural Africans. As a result, though himself a *mestiço* whose parents came from Cape Verde to settle in Bissau, Cabral was aware of the importance of the countryside to any basic program for Africa. Following this awareness, he was a firm advocate of the changed tactics after the events of 1950.

The policy of PAIGC is to unite Guinea and the Cape Verde Islands into an independent state. While Guinea alone has little economic or strategic significance, the Cape Verde Islands could be a valuable strategic asset. But the crowded nature of insular Cape Verde limits opposition there, so that many educated dissident Cape Verdians have been attracted to PAIGC, seeing Guinea as a necessary stepping stone to the independence of their own lands. Thus, although the party executives included people from all areas, a number of the leaders of the small PAIGC elite are *mestiços*, rather than black Africans.

Important to Cabral's strategy was the development of activity on three fronts: internal, neighboring, and international. Establishing the internal front meant giving the populace first an increased political awareness, then guerrilla and larger-scale warfare, and finally rural development schemes, as signs of PAIGC ability to bring positive benefits. Assistance from the neighboring countries of Senegal and Guinea was necessary for continuing insurgency. Training grounds, weapons depots, and food supplies were of course among the items most needed. Seeing this, special attempts were made to gain acceptance by Senegal, which had at first been more favorable to the less doctrinaire Frente para a Libertação e Independência da Guiné Portuguesa (FLING).

The international scene was no less important. Major funds, arms supplies,

398

and constant anti-Portuguese pressure could be solicited only in international circles. As the Organization for African Unity (OAU) developed, it would become a useful source of moral and material assistance. Arms and training were needed and were found with little difficulty from the Soviet Union and various of its Eastern European allies.

In its attempts to appeal to the rural population, PAIGC was aided by the highly undeveloped nature of the countryside. Roads were few and administration was inadequately developed. Patiently awaiting the proper internal preconditions before launching into open conflict, PAIGC slowly built a party machinery within Guinea. Neither of the major Angolan parties had done this.

The PAIGC machinery has proved quite intricate. At one time, Ronald Chilcote described the party as being organized by territorial regions, zones, sections, and groups. The group or cell is based on places of work or residence. Five groups constitute a section, and sections are subdivided into 13 regions, while regions comprise at least two zones. The party structure is similar to that of Communist parties everywhere.[27] Recently, the party has adapted its organization to local conditions within the framework of its Marxist orientation.

The party changed its tactics first to sabotage in 1962 and then to open guerrilla warfare. Early guerrilla successes heartened the PAIGC command and, by 1964, at a meeting of party leaders, an over-all military command was established. Although major party efforts had become and have continued to be military, social and administrative activities also played a significant role. Military successes that have brought between one-third and two-thirds of the territory of the province under the control of PAIGC have been followed by the establishment of schools, an economic infrastructure, and medical facilities.[28]

As PAIGC began to develop a meaningful party organization with real responsibilities and an over-all theory, Cabral revived his associations with dissidents from other areas of Portuguese Africa, some of whom he had known as a student in Lisbon and when he worked in Angola. This was first facilitated by the presence of MPLA offices after 1959 in Conakry. PAIGC then joined MPLA in the establishment of FRAIN in Tunis in 1960 and, after that organization failed, continued in CONCP a year later. CONCP sought to be identified with the more successful insurgents. It also represented the organizations that received the most radical support internationally.

The major rival nationalist movement, the Frente para a Libertação e Independência da Guiné Portuguesa (FLING), developed in 1953 as a weak amalgam of several groups begun independently of one another. The oldest of these was Movimento de Libertação da Guiné (MLG), which considers itself descendent from the first modern African voluntary association in the area, the Liga Guineense, founded in 1911. The MLG, which has maintained a strong dislike for Cape Verdians and, by extension, for PAIGC, is concerned only with Guinea. As nationalist activity spread after about 1961, MLG found support and shelter under the regime of Léopold Senghor of Senegal. Under the leadership of François Mendy and with support especially from Manjaco refugees, MLG had subdivisions in both Bissau and Conakry, but its major activities were in Senegal. The MLG continued a somewhat independent posture within FLING until late in 1964, when some members of the party affiliated themselves with PAIGC.

Other parties that were part of FLING included União das Populações da Guiné (UPG) led by Henri Labery, formerly associated with Cabral; União Popular para a Libertação da Guiné (UPLG); the Malinke-oriented Rassemblement Démocratique Africain de la Guiné (RDAG); and União dos Naturais da Guiné Portuguesa (UNGP). The UNGP, independent from FLING until late in 1963, favored independence from Portugal without violent revolution. UNGP President Benjamin Pinto Bull, a secondary school teacher in Dakar, talked with Portuguese officials in Lisbon in July, 1963, the same month in which his brother Jaime was appointed to the second highest administrative position in Portuguese Guinea. Disappointed with his discussions, Pinto Bull returned to Dakar, emphasized the need for a more realistic policy, and eventually led his followers fully into the FLING camp.

Internecine squabbling between FLING and PAIGC as apparent as that in Angola continued in the international arena until 1967. Nevertheless, to most observers, though portending a sometimes ethnically motivated rivalry in the future, this squabbling did not hide the fact that PAIGC was much more active in the insurgency than FLING. It has been the constant interest of the OAU to bring these two parties together. From its first meeting in 1963, unity became a major OAU goal. After the second OAU meeting in July, 1964, in Cairo, it began to become clear that that organization was planning to give assistance to the parties most active in the insurgency. FLING chose to interpret this as a challenge to its own development rather than as an impetus for working with PAIGC, and Senegal reportedly forestalled sole recognition to PAIGC. In October, 1964, Senghor tried unsuccessfully to bring the two parties together. After these attempts failed, Senghor began to cooperate more fully with PAIGC. One Portuguese observer has expressed the belief that "this attitude reflected his desire to keep PAIGC from falling totally under the protection of independent Guinea. If PAIGC were to govern Guiné-Bissau one day, it would not be convenient for Senegal to be looked at with resentment for not having helped in the independence struggle."[29]

The PAIGC-FLING rift symbolized the radical-moderate division of independent African states apparent early in the 1960's. This rift still found expression after the March, 1965, meeting of OAU foreign ministers in Nairobi. The Guinean representative announced that PAIGC had been recognized as the only liberation movement. In Senegal, this report was denied. Nevertheless, Senegal had now committed itself to letting the PAIGC use its territory for training facilities and attacks into northern Portuguese Guinea.

During the years 1965–68, use of radio broadcasts for propaganda, internal campaigns of political awareness, and an expanded international campaign for assistance and recognition continued. Cabral himself became known as Africa's most successful revolutionary, through not only his apparent military successes, but also his lectures on revolution at the Cercle Frantz Fanon in Milan and at the Tricontinental Conference at Havana. Trips to Sweden, the Soviet Union, and China brought arms and scholarships.

Contrary to other similar revolutionary movements, the major PAIGC, emphasis was on its political organization rather than its military one. The latter has been divided into three types of force: guerrilla units, a militia, and the army. Examples of some young military leaders are two among seven who were trained in Nanking, China, Oswaldo Vieira (Ambrósio Djassi) and "Nino," a former Bissau electrician.[30] The emphasis on military tactics and concern over a strong exile base has kept Cabral from forming a government in exile, as GRAE has in Angola. Recent PAIGC development is discussed in Chapter XVIII. Meanwhile, in 1966, the leadership of FLING passed to Benjamin Pinto Bull. Occasional reports tell of FLING military activities, but it seems as if they continue not to be active but to await a Portuguese withdrawal from which they could benefit. In 1967, a third party surfaced, the Bloc Démocratique de Guinée-Bissao (BDG), which claimed to represent civil servants and others and offered to join other parties in forming a government in exile.[31]

MOZAMBIQUE

Urban movements of *mestiços*, assimilated Africans, and Europeans have existed in Mozambique continuously since the 1920's.[32] These movements—included among which were Associação Africana, Associação dos Naturais de Moçambique, and Instituto Negrófilo—though often merely social or debating clubs, provided the best opportunities for politically interested Mozambicans to exchange views about their province. As the independence decade of the 1960's began, however, none of these groups had developed into a political organization similar to what had transpired in Angola and Portuguese Guinea. Neither had there been much organizing of Mozambicans living in neighboring countries.

The earliest of the Mozambican nationalist parties was União Democrática Nacional de Moçambique (UDENAMO) formed among Mozambicans working in Southern Rhodesia and Nyasaland under the leadership of Adelino Gwambe in 1960. A second party, composed chiefly of Mozambicans working in Kenya, Tanganyika, and Uganda, began in Dar es Salaam in February, 1961. As its name Mozambique African Nationalist Union (MANU) showed, it derived much support from similar African nationalist unions in Kenya (KANU) and Tanganyika (TANU), with which some MANU leaders had been involved during their formative periods. This was especially true of the MANU president, Matthew Mmole, while its secretary-general, M. M. Mallinga, had worked as a union organizer in East Africa with Tom Mboya. A third group, União Africana de Moçambique Independente (UNAMI), began in Nyasaland among people originally from Mozambique's Tete District. By mid-1961, all three of these groups were located in Dar es Salaam.

Despite certain tensions among the parties, by April, 1961, MANU and UDENAMO had agreed to send Gwambe as their joint representative to the Rabat conference, where CONCP was formed. Strong pressures from African leaders convinced the leaders of the three parties, to unite into the Frente de Libertação de Moçambique (FRELIMO), early in 1962. The first officers of FRELIMO included Eduardo Mondlane (president), Uria Simango

401

(vice-president), David Mabunda (secretary-general), Matthew Mmole (treasurer), Paulo Gumane (deputy secretary-general), and Leo Milas (publicity secretary).

Born in Gaza District of southern Mozambique and the son of a chief, Mondlane went first to a local government school and then to a mission school. In 1944, he won a scholarship to a high school in Transvaal, and in 1948 he entered the University of the Witwatersrand to continue his studies in social sciences. After the South African Government refused to renew his permit, he returned to Mozambique but was arrested there on suspicion of subversion. He was discharged with a recommendation that he should be sent to a Portuguese university to continue his studies. Receiving a scholarship from the Phelps-Stokes Fund of New York, he entered the University of Lisbon in 1950, being the first African from Mozambique to do so. There he met Neto, Andrade, and other future leaders of Portuguese Africa. However, owing to continued harassment by PIDE, he had his scholarship transferred to Oberlin College in Ohio, where he was graduated in 1953.

After further studies at Northwestern University, where he obtained his M.A. and Ph.D degrees in sociology, and after a further year's research at Harvard, Mondlane joined the trusteeship department of the United Nations, where he remained for five years. As an international civil servant, he was able to visit Mozambique, and, when he resigned from the United Nations in 1961 to teach at Syracuse University, he openly joined the nationalist movement. He arrived at Dar es Salaam in June, 1962.

At its first congress, held in September, 1962, FRELIMO adopted a program for developing unity among the Mozambicans, promoting literacy and the training of cadres, encouraging the formation of trade unions and students' and women's organizations, cooperating with national organizations in other Portuguese territories, procuring all "means of self-defense," preparing the people "for any eventuality," and appealing for financial support and diplomatic, moral, and material aid for the "cause of freedom in Mozambique."[33]

During the organizing process, personal rivalries developed that led to the firing of Mabunda and Gumane by Leo Milas. The first two proceeded to Cairo where, in May, 1963, they reconstituted UDENAMO, which had merged into FRELIMO. Another party, UDENAMO—monomotapa, had previously been formed in Uganda by Gwambe, who never agreed to join FRELIMO. Moreover, Mmole was also expelled, and he reconstituted MANU. A series of other expulsions and the growth of more political parties led to the establishment of another unified organization, this time among the opponents of FRELIMO, the Comité Revolucionário de Moçambique (COREMO) in Lusaka in June, 1965. COREMO's first president, Adelino Gwambe, lasted less than a year before being succeeded by Paulo Gumane, who had worked among Mozambicans in South Africa.

Discussion of expulsion and reorganization may give the impression that FRELIMO was floundering during this period. On the contrary, its growth as a party rivaled that of any group elsewhere in Portuguese Africa. A major reason for its growth was the growing numbers of disaffected Makondes crossing the Rovuma River from Mozambique. These Makonde provided the great mass of

FRELIMO adherents. The leadership, however, remained tribally representative of Mozambique.

FRELIMO has aspired to be a truly national party, embracing the whole population of Mozambique and cutting across tribal divisions. In this respect, it had a closer affinity, at least in theory, with Andrade's MPLA than with Roberto's UPA; in practice, however, it came to resemble the latter. While Mondlane himself came from the south of the province, his guerrillas were recruited almost exclusively from two tribes inhabiting the north, the Makonde and the Nyanja, both of whom, like the Bakongo, overlap international borders. This made it easy to organize training camps in Tanzania, but the result of relying so largely on two tribes was to alienate others. This was especially the case of the Makua, one of the largest ethnic groups in Mozambique, traditionally hostile to the Makonde.

FRELIMO also was gaining international assistance. From the United States came private funds for the Mozambique Institute, a secondary school run by Mondlane's American wife in Dar es Salaam. This institute aimed to prepare Mozambicans to attend universities wherever FRELIMO could arrange scholarships. Other assistance, designed specifically for military training, came from Algeria, the Soviet Union, and several other nations. Mondlane also claimed that most of the help for his political and military programs came from independent African states. This aid was frequently channeled through the OAU's African Liberation Committee, whose headquarters are also in Dar es Salaam. The recognition by the OAU, in 1963, of FRELIMO as the sole recipient of aid for Mozambique proved of great assistance; over two-thirds of total aid since then has come from African sources.[34]

While gradually building its insurgency capabilities, FRELIMO party organization showed signs of weakness. Several incidents of 1968 emphasized the potential weakness of the bonds holding together the various factions of FRELIMO. Chief among these were incidents leading to the closing of Mozambique Institute for several months. Perpetrator of these incidents was Mateus Gwenjere, a young African priest who had worked in Mozambique until mid-1967. Gwenjere, young, militant, impatient, and antiwhite, felt that Mondlane was moving too slowly and seemed too eager for eventual compromise.[35] His militancy had been infectuous among the Institute's students. His views are known to be shared by many of the Mozambicans who went abroad to study in the early 1960's and who must decide whether and how to enter the independence struggle.

In May, 1968, rivals of Mondlane invaded FRELIMO's main office in Dar es Salaam and attacked three staff members, killing one. In spite of that incident, however, FRELIMO managed to hold its second congress in Mozambique in July. At this congress, all the leaders were re-elected, in spite of signs of dissent among Makonde representatives from Cabo Delgado District. Aware of the need to give more representation to some of the young people who had gained positions of responsibility over the previous few years, FRELIMO increased the number of representatives on its central committee from 24 to 44.[36]

The changes in the FRELIMO organization barely had time to operate before another incident seriously disturbed party peace. Early in February, 1969, while working at a desk in Dar es Salaam, Mondlane himself was assassinated. The effects of this blow to the structure of nationalist parties in Mozambique remains to be seen.

NOTES

1. There exist many sources for a study of contemporary Angolan nationalism. See especially George Houser, "Nationalist Organizations in Angola," in John A. Davis and James K. Baker, (eds.), *Southern Africa in Transition* (New York and London, 1966), pp. 157–79; João Baptista Nunes Pereira Neto, "Movimentos subversivos de Angola—tentativa de esboço sócio-político," *Angola* (Lisbon, 1964), pp. 343–85; John Marcum, "The Angola Rebellion: Status Report," *Africa Report*, February, 1964, pp. 3–7, and "Three Revolutions," *Africa Report*, November, 1967, pp. 9–22. Another major source is the large number of U.N. documents, especially proceedings of the Special Committee on Territories under Portuguese Administration and the Sub-committee on the Situation in Angola, both established in 1961, and the Special Committee on the Situation with Regard to the Implementation of the Declaration on the Granting of Independence to Colonial Countries and Peoples (Committee of Twenty-Four), which took over the functions of the former Special Committee in 1962.
2. Houser, *op. cit.*, p. 167.
3. *Ibid.*, p. 168.
4. Mário Pasquale in *Le Peuple de Lausanno* (Lausanne), January 17, 1963.
5. Houser, *op. cit.*, p. 163.
6. Pieter Lessing, *Africa's Red Harvest* (London, 1962), p. 18.
7. Andrew Westwood, "The Politics of Revolt in Angola," *Africa Report*, November, 1962, p. 9.
8. *Ibid.*, p. 10.
9. Some of the groups intimated as providing direct support to Roberto were the American Committee on Africa, the Ford Foundation, and the AFL-CIO, one of whose leaders, Irving Brown, met Roberto in Léopoldville in 1961.
10. Hella Pick, in the *Manchester Guardian* (March 22, 1962), reported a rumor that Roberto had been given "fairly solid White House blessing."
11. James Duffy, *Portugal in Africa* (London, 1962), p. 218.
12. Lloyd Garrison in *The New York Times*, May 14, 1962.
13. For more on the PDA, see Houser, *op. cit.*, pp. 162–63.
14. *The Christian Science Monitor*, April 5, 1962.
15. The *Observer* (London), March 18, 1962.
16. *The Baltimore Sun*, December 21, 1962.
17. Marcum, "The Angola Rebellion: Status Report," p. 4.
18. United Nations, *Report of the Special Committee* (August 15, 1962), p. 160.
19. United Nations, Doc. A/AC109/Pet. 58.
20. See Antoine Matumona, "Angolan Disunity," *Angola: A Symposium* (London, 1962), pp. 123–25.
21. John Marcum, "The Angola Rebellion: Status Report," p. 6.
22. *Pravda*, December 16, 1964.
23. Report of a Tass correspondent from Brazzaville, Russia for Abroad broadcast, August 30, 1966.

24. Draft report of the Special Committee on Territories Under Portuguese Administration, United Nations, Doc. A/AC 109/L345.

25. *Africa Research Bulletin*, V, No. 7 (August 15, 1968), 1115.

26. Major sources for a study of nationalist parties in Portuguese Guinea include Gérard Chaliand, *Lutte Armée en Afrique* (Paris, 1967); Ronald Chilcote, "The Political Thought of Amilcar Cabral," *The Journal of Modern African Studies*, VI, 3 (1968), 373–88; and João Baptista Nunes Pereira Neto, "Movimentos subversivos da Guiné, Cabo Verde, e São Tomé e Príncipe," *Cabo Verde, Guiné, São Tomé e Príncipe* (Lisbon, 1966).

27. Chilcote, *op. cit.*, p. 385.

28. I. William Zartman, "Guinea: The Quiet War Goes On," *Africa Report*, November, 1967, pp. 68–69.

29. Hélio Felgas, *Os movimentos terroristas de Angola, Guiné, Moçambique* (Lisbon, 1966), p. 60.

30. Zartman, *op. cit.*, p. 67.

31. Marcum, "Three Revolutions," p. 18.

32. Much of the discussion of nationalist parties in Mozambique has been drawn from *ibid.*; Eduardo Mondlane, "The Struggle for Independence in Mozambique," in Davis and Baker, *op. cit.*, pp. 197–210; Ronald A. Chilcote, *Portuguese Africa* (Englewood Cliffs, 1967), pp. 119–22; and João da Costa Freitas, "Movimentos subversivos contra Moçambique," in *Moçambique* (Lisbon, 1965), pp. 319–37.

33. Basil Davidson, "Africa After Salazar," *West Africa* (London), October 5, 1968, p. 1169.

34. Helen Kitchen, "Conversation with Eduardo Mondlane," *Africa Report*, November, 1967, p. 50.

35. Stanley Meisler, "Mozambique Rebels Disagree," *Washington Post*, June 30, 1968.

36. Davidson, *op. cit.*, p. 1169.

XVIII

Conflict in Portuguese Africa

GEORGE MARTELLI

THE MAJOR consequence of the development of nationalist organizations directed against continued Portuguese possession of its overseas provinces was the initiation of armed conflict. For the most part, the members of these organizations, many of whom were accustomed to living away from their tribal homes in Portuguese Africa, in such neighboring capitals as Kinshasa, Conakry, and Dar es Salaam, or recent arrivals denied the opportunity for internal political activities, began their operations outside the areas they sought to liberate. As of 1960, neither the sense of frustration nor the state of organization of the nationalists gave the Portuguese serious cause for concern. Within eight years, however, first early terrorism and, later, increasing effectiveness through well-trained and equipped guerrilla insurgents provided a continual challenge to the Portuguese stay in Africa.

Since the style and dimensions of the conflict have varied within each territory, they will be treated separately, after which there follows a discussion of some of the changes generated within the Portuguese military itself.

ANGOLA

In August, 1960, a number of white, *mestiço*, and African Angolans were condemned by a court in Luanda for the crime of subversion against the Portuguese state, and they were sentenced to prison terms of varying severity. On the following January 23, Henrique Galvão, a former Portuguese colonial official, with a party of Portuguese and Spanish desperados, seized the Portuguese luxury liner "Santa Maria" while the ship was cruising in the Caribbean. According to his own account, Galvão's plan was to sail to the Spanish island of Fernando Póo, collect reinforcements there and in Spanish Guinea, and then proceed to Angola. Had he done so, he and his followers, all of whom were in opposition to the Salazar regime, would have been immediately arrested, so it seems likely that publicity was the major goal of their actions. In the end, they changed plans and sailed to the Brazilian port of Recife, where the ship was surrendered to the authorities.[1]

The foreign journalists who had gathered in Luanda to cover the story were treated, instead, to an attack, not by Galvão, who never materialized on the scene, but by partisans of the MPLA on the central prison of Luanda, in an unsuccessful attempt to free the political prisoners. The initial attack, on February 4, was against an old fortress, São João, which at the time was being used not for political prisoners but as a common jail. The rebels, armed with machetes and rifles, hoped to release those whom they erroneously considered political prisoners to join the fighting. The prison guards drove the attackers back to the steep slopes that rise to the opulent Miramar residential district. Another attack was made on the police headquarters. Eight members of the security force and thirty-six Africans were killed, and a total of sixty-three Africans and Europeans were wounded.[2] During the funeral procession next day, European demands for reprisals led to serious rioting, in which more people were killed and wounded and many were arrested.

It appears that the MPLA actions were not intended to be coordinated with the actions taken by Galvão, who, by that time, had tamely interned himself in Brazil. When general unrest broke out in the north, under the leadership of the UPA, the MPLA did not again initiate attacks in Luanda. They had apparently been discouraged by the lack of popular backing of their first attempt and by the violence of the Portuguese response.

The next major event occurred in northern Angola. Attempts had been made during the previous few years to organize the local people into resistance groups. Customarily, this was accomplished by UPA representatives infiltrating from the Congo and summoning meetings of the villagers in the bush, an easy matter, since the Bakongo territory bridges the frontier. On March 15, as a culmination of previous preparation but somewhat precipitously, perhaps, large bands of terrorists, a number of them trained in the Congo, armed with machetes, cutlasses, and homemade muskets launched concerted attacks on European settlements over an area extending about 250 miles along the Congo border and as far south as the area of Carmona, 100 miles northeast of Luanda. On the first day, between 200 and 300 Europeans and many Africans were killed and mutilated on farms and plantations at or near Maquela do Zombo, São Salvador, Quitexe, and Masimba.[3] The Portuguese had no troops in the area and few metropolitan troops anywhere in Angola. There were only two regiments of infantry in the whole province, composed mostly of Angolans, and these were concentrated at Luanda in case of a further attack on the capital. The two regiments, totaling about 3,000, each had two training battalions of recruits and one fighting battalion. One regiment was normally in Nova Lisboa on the Benguela Railway; the other was stationed outside Luanda. There was also an armored cavalry group, part in Silva Porto and part in Luanda.

For a week or so, the massacre continued, in the course of which several hundred Europeans and more than 6,000 Africans loyal to Portugal were killed.[4] The only defense was by African police, assisted by groups of settlers, mostly armed with sporting guns, who fought the terrorists and carried out reprisals on villages suspected of harboring them. Only with the arrival of the first troop reinforcements from Portugal was an organized attempt made to restore the former situation. For many months, life remained precarious. Every road was liable to ambush. The bush provided impenetrable cover. The insurgents, if pressed, had only to retire across the frontier. But, by the end of the year, they

,ad been driven into the more inaccessible areas, and outside these the Portuguese authorities were again in control. By then, it was unofficially estimated that 2,000 Europeans and 50,000 Africans had been killed.[5]

Initially, there were two zones of attack, one along the frontier with the Congo and the other about 100 miles to the south, in the northern portions of the districts of Luanda and Cuanza Norte, where the available cover for guerrilla activities is excellent. Both are coffee-growing areas in which contract laborers were numerous and where the confiscation of African land for the construction of plantations had caused much dissatisfaction. The maximum extension of zones under rebel control was reached by June, 1961, when they included parts of the districts of Congo, Luanda, Cuanza Norte, and Malange. By October, all towns and administrative posts had been reoccupied by the Portuguese forces, and, thereafter, guerrilla operations were reduced and limited mostly to the bush.

Preparation for the original attack had taken place in the Congo during the first few months of 1961. Though some terrorists were local residents whose long-festering emotions burst under the prodding of the UPA, many others had been trained and supplied by individual members of the Congolese army. Most of the arms were machetes, which also came from the Congo; some other weapons had been stolen from, bought from, or given by the U.N. forces.

According to the Portuguese, an important role in the affair was played by foreign Protestant missionaries,[6] some of whom were later arrested and expelled. They were suspected of encouraging the attack, having advance knowledge of it, and failing to inform the authorities. Protestant missionaries claimed that their refusal of the offer of arms for their own protection had been wrongly interpreted as proof of their connivance with the nationalists. The missionaries were apparently the only white people in the district spared by the terrorists, and some of the catechists and preachers trained by the missionaries were seen at the head of the bands. Some Roman Catholic priests, all African, were also implicated.

Meanwhile the vicar-general of Angola, Msgr. Manuel Mendes das Neves, had been detained on April 1, on suspicion of complicity with terrorist activities, and was subsequently dismissed from his ecclesiastical post. On April 15, the archbishop of Luanda, Msgr. Alves de Pinho, and four other bishops issued a pastoral letter. While condemning the attacks as "criminal acts . . . characterized by complete disregard for human life," the letter also declared that

> legitimate and just aspirations deserve to be taken into consideration [and] disillusioned people fighting against privation are a prey to despair and are apt to be carried away by dangerous ideologies and promises which cannot be fulfilled. Poverty is a bad counsellor and a threat to tranquility and peace. . . . The Church is entirely within the limits of its mission in advising citizens to unite for . . . the creation of a more perfect social order based upon justice and peace.[7]

Since the outbreak of the rebellion, much of the debate over the attitude and actions of the Portuguese Government regarding its African populations has been beclouded by charges and countercharges of atrocities committed by both sides during the conflict. During the period of the initial attacks, both Europeans and Africans were perpetrators of atrocities.

A notable feature of the attacks was the resurgence of primitive animism among the terrorists, exemplified by their belief in magic and the practice of savage atrocities. Many of them apparently went into action drugged with hemp and believing that the enemy's bullets would be turned to water by their *dawa*.[8] The terrorists were drawn almost entirely from the Bakongo, and the revolt did not extend to areas of other tribes. As a result, the initial trouble was confined within the Bakongo and Dembos areas in the north, about 7 per cent of the total territory of Angola. The terrorists initially numbered not more than 4,000 or 5,000 of a total population of nearly 5 million. The Portuguese custom of arresting members of any organized opposition group is an inadequate explanation for the lack of any spontaneous and sympathetic uprising anywhere else in Angola.

The committing of atrocities was later admitted by Holden Roberto in an interview with the Belgian journalist Pierre de Vos, published by *Le Monde* (Paris) in July, 1961, and was justified by him on the grounds that terror was necessary in order to scare the Portuguese into "seeing reason." Accusations of atrocities were also levelled against the Portuguese. They were first made by Baptist missionaries and then taken up by members of the British Labour Party, although a number of observers on the spot, including British journalists, denied them. An official British fact-finding mission, however, consisting of the British consul general at Luanda and the military and air attachés at the British embassy in Lisbon reported that some Portuguese did commit atrocities, but these were mostly the acts of settlers who responded to terrorism with their own brand of reprisals. For the most part, these took place before the arrival of Portuguese troops.[9] After their arrival, the government placed greater restraint on settlers than ever before. The report of the British fact-finding commission showed that there had been "cases of arbitrary and repressive conduct by some members of the police" but that members of the mission had been impressed very favorably "by the sense of duty among senior officials and military commanders" whom they met.[10] Likewise, the atrocities committed by the insurgents proved to be mostly a phenomenon of the original outbreak.

The unsettled conditions in northern Angola led to great human instability. Tens of thousands of people fled from their homes for fear of the violent Portuguese reprisals or to escape the terrorism. Many of them took refuge in the Congo, while others moved south toward Luanda. According to a report of the Red Cross in Léopoldville, most of them, far from showing signs of oppression, were healthy and well cared for.[11] Though most of the refugees stayed in the Congo, some of them later returned and were resettled by the authorities with the help of the army, which began an ambitious program of social rehabilitation, welfare, and education. The main object of this was to win the "hearts and minds of the people," by giving them a sense of security and providing for their needs. New villages were built under the protection of the army and schools, dispensaries, and social centers set up under its aegis. This program has had considerable success, and, by attracting the population to come and live in safe zones, it deprived the insurgents of a source from which to extort food. Those who remained in the Congo were cared for by refugee organizations. The number in the Congo is hard to determine, but estimates range between 200,000 and 600,000.[12]

The Portuguese had been unconcerned about local grievances and were unprepared for any trouble in Angola, even after the Congo erupted. Except at the military bases already mentioned, there were no troops stationed in any part of the province. Government was represented by civilian officials, African police-men, usually unarmed, and a limited secret police (PIDE) establishment. But, in the weeks of the March events, the Portuguese decided to defend Angola at all costs; Lisbon acted with great energy. Troops were dispatched at once and steadily reinforced until they reached a total of 50,000, some of whom were later transferred to Portuguese Guinea or Mozambique.

The army first sought to reoccupy all posts and settlements up to the nor-thern frontier, reopen communications, and provide protection for the white farmers. Then they settled down to sustain a protracted antiguerrilla war.

The failure of the guerrillas to achieve more than a nuisance value after their early success could be attributed to various factors, including inadequate training and leadership, quarrels between the various nationalist groups, insufficiency of foreign aid, failure of nationalist campaigns of political education, and lack of popular support. In guerrilla warfare, the insurgent forces must have two things operating in their favor: the willing help of the population and freedom of movement at certain times. In the affected zone of northern Angola, which included the mountainous Dembos area northeast of Luanda, an area of about 80 square miles in which the terrain is difficult, the Portuguese policy of group-ing the previously scattered population into villages gradually succeeded in separating the local inhabitants from the insurgents, thus removing the possibi-lities of labor and logistic assistance. Consequently, the guerrillas found it diffi-cult to rely upon local sources of food and shelter. It was also difficult for the rebels to "melt into" the local villages. In addition, the Portuguese kept the rebels in a state of constant movement, pushing them back and forth across the rugged countryside, hitting at them whenever possible, and causing them to be deprived of an important advantage: superior knowledge of the terrain. Once this advantage was lost, the rebels were put on an equal footing with the regular military forces, composed for the most part of metropolitan Portuguese.

Because of the terrain, ground actions were often unproductive. It was not unusual for a Portuguese patrol to have to march for two or three days to find and engage the rebels, shoot it out for a day or two, and then trek back to camp. Thus, a minor operation could take a week or more and had to be supplemented by extensive reconnaissance activities as well as occasional bombing.[13]

The fortunes of the insurgency sunk to their lowest ebb in 1965, when the Tshombe government in the Congo, friendly with the Portuguese, clamped down on its support, and GRAE dissidents turned openly against Roberto and sacked his offices in Kinshasa. The rivalry between MPLA and GRAE was in full blossom, as evidenced by a January, 1965, broadcast by the MPLA's Voice of Angola, from Brazzaville, declaring that Roberto refused

> to bring about unity among the Angolan peoples, and even opened the doors to the murder of Angolans who did not belong to his party. . . . Such so-called leaders as Holden Roberto, who are working in the interests of the imperialists, will lead our country into bloodshed and fratricide. They are not worthy of the support of the Angolan people and they must be unmasked.[14]

The quarrels of the nationalist parties, combined with the beginning of repacification of the country by the Portuguese military forces, caused the nationalist campaigns to come to a virtual standstill. In a Belgrade interview of September, 1965, Agostinho Neto saw fit to reiterate his party's position when he stressed that "two preconditions are indispensable for the success of the liberation struggle of the people of Angola—unity between MPLA and FLNA (UPA) movements and assistance from independent Africa."[15]

The Attack on Cabinda

The first attacks in the north of Angola were almost exclusively the work of Holden Roberto's party, UPA, although the MPLA was involved in the continuing unrest in the Dembos area around Nambuangongo. After the outbreak of internecine disputes and the expulsion of the MPLA from Léopoldville, the latter moved its headquarters to Brazzaville, and, in 1964, started using this as a base for directing operations against Cabinda, the interior of which contains one of the densest forests in Africa. Forced to operate from strategic villages because of the difficulty of the terrain, the Portuguese military forces slowly succeeded in checking guerrilla activities. The rebel forces, entering Cabinda from the Congo (Brazzaville) border only at night, avoided engagements with the Portuguese forces whenever possible. Extensive use was made of booby traps and antipersonnel mines by both sides.

The main victims of the guerrilla attacks in the Enclave were not the Portuguese forces but the African populations. Because of their manpower shortage, the MPLA infiltrators abducted entire families, using the women and children as hostages to assure continued service of able-bodied males. The kidnapped were then taken to the base at Ilipanga, just over the border in the Congo (Brazzaville), where the men and boys were trained in guerrilla techniques and the women and children were put to work at domestic chores.[16]

As in the other Portuguese territories, the insurgents in Cabinda repeatedly claimed control of large parts of the territory. Realizing the psychological value of such claims, the MPLA leaders issued frequent communiqués announcing military successes. These were usually exaggerated, however, and often inconsistent. For example, speaking at an "Afro-Asian Economic Seminar" in Algiers in February, 1965, MPLA representative Luis d'Almeida stated that "part of Cabinda, or one-quarter of the territory, has already been freed."[17] The following September, Agostinho Neto claimed the rebels controlled about half the territory. Since seven months separated the statements, it might be assumed that the rebel movements had made progress in the interval. However, when one of the authors of the present volume visited Cabinda in February, 1965, and again in September, 1965, he learned that little had changed in the interval between his visits. The rebels did not, in fact, control either one-quarter or one-half of Cabinda. Furthermore, the very nature of guerrilla warfare in rural areas with inadequate governmental administrative control makes it difficult to determine actual success. Control of land areas, the old yardstick for determining military victory, has proven to be inadequate in the age of guerrilla warfare. Guerrilla forces can claim control over the area of land in which they can operate relatively freely and keep the defending forces off balance. The defending forces can claim the areas surrounding their military forts and the areas that supply the towns they occupy. In fact, neither side is correct, as lands claimed by each are in constant threat by the other. The most accurate estimates, however, usually come from the defending forces, which can defend the towns relatively easily and, by use of superior weapons, can limit massed attacks by the insurgents and destroy rural areas cooperating with them.

The motive for the Cabinda attack was more political than military. Roberto's government in exile had won initial recognition and aid from other African countries because it was doing the fighting. It was therefore essential for the MPLA to establish a similar claim. After its ejection from the Congo and retreat to Brazzaville, Cabinda was the only Portuguese territory in which it was able to operate.

The 60,000 inhabitants of the enclave, however, gave the intruders little encouragement. Many of those Cabindans who were politically conscious had their own nationalist party, the Front pour la Liberation de L'Enclave de Cabinda (FLEC), which had been founded in Brazzaville (hence the French nomenclature), during the regime of the conservative Fulbert Youlou, and was tolerated by his radical successor, President Alphonse Massamba-Debat. They wanted not only independence but also separation from the rest of Angola, which made any cooperation with MPLA impossible.

The discovery, in 1965, by the Cabinda Gulf Oil Company of considerable petroleum reserves off the coast of Cabinda strengthened the determination of the Portuguese to hold on. It also gave a boost to the economy and created new jobs that attracted back some of the Cabindans who had taken refuge beyond the frontier. In face of the apathy, if not hostility, of the bulk of the population, the MPLA Cabinda campaign lost its impetus and, by 1967, had practically collapsed. Sporadic incidents in 1968, especially in the area around Buca Zau, showed that some insurgency continued.

Although basically unsuccessful, the campaign served its purpose of furthering the claim of MPLA to be recognized as a fighting force and thus to qualify for financial aid from the OAU through its Liberation Committee. From 1964 onward, it has received more money from the committee than its rival, GRAE. In 1967, Roberto complained that, since 1964, he had been given a mere $73,000 by the committee.[18]

The Eastern Front

Between 1962 and 1965, world attention was focused on events in the neighboring Congo. Roberto's movement depended largely on the Congolese Govern-

ment in Kinshasa, where he had his headquarters, and on the provincial authorities in the lower Congo, where his military bases, training camps, and refugee
centers were situated. Without their good will, its functions were limited.
Although the Adoula government was sympathetic and cooperated with
Roberto, it had its hands full, coping with the secession of Katanga, and, after
this had been ended, with the Mulelist rebellion that broke out in Kwilu, in
1964, and subsequently spread to the eastern provinces. Operating from bases in
neighboring countries and primed with Maoist doctrine, the Congolese rebel
leaders sought to exploit the miserable conditions of the rural population. These
rebels had little use for Roberto, who was described by one of them, Gaston
Soumaliot, as "the number two enemy of the Congo after Tshombe."[19]

After Tshombe's return from exile to head a new central government, and his
successful repression of the rebellion with the help of white mercenaries, he
adopted a policy of cooperation with the Portuguese in Angola and, at first
discreetly and then more openly, discouraged the liberation movements. This,
combined with its internal squabbles, came near to finishing GRAE, but it was
saved by the dismissal of Tshombe, followed by Mobutu's *coup d'état* in the fall
of 1965. Mobutu reversed the Tshombe policy, declared himself on the side of
revolution, and promised full support for GRAE. In October, 1966, he formally
broke off relations with Portugal after a Kinshasa mob had sacked its embassy.

A further consequence of Mobutu's more cooperative policy was the reactiva-
tion of an earlier insurrection in the Cassange cotton-growing region in the
district of Malange, about 300 miles east of Luanda. In this area GRAE forces,
operating from bases in the Kwango region of the Congo, made several raids
across the frontier toward the end of 1966 and reportedly occupied some villages
briefly. The area is sparsely populated, and the attack had little impact except to
cause a dispersion of Portuguese forces, a major GRAE objective.

At about the same time, GRAE set up an office in Katanga with a view to
launching another offensive along the eastern border. New activity in eastern
Angola by the MPLA and the newly organized UNITA spurred this action.
Aware of the Bakongo stigma attached to its heritage, the party chose southern
leaders here. Still, GRAE made little headway with the local population.

Further south, near the border of Zambia, Jonas Savimbi's UNITA began its
activities. UNITA chose to work within Angola in the vicinity of the Benguela
Railway line. Use of Zambian territory was minimal, as was the total UNITA
operation at the time. Since Savimbi favored a careful program to gain local
support, he attempted a long-range campaign to politicize the masses. Activities
by the UNITA guerrillas, however, did not show such vision. Early in 1967,
they twice interrupted the Benguela Railway, thus holding up vital copper
exports for several weeks. These tactics so angered the owners of the Railway
and the Portuguese, Congolese, and Zambian governments that, by mid-1967,
Savimbi himself became *persona non grata* in Lusaka and was forced to move his
headquarters to Egypt. Nevertheless, the clandestine politicizing of the populace, especially among the Chokwe and the Ovimbundu, continued.

Soon after the founding of UNITA, in March, 1966, the MPLA showed a
resurgence, opening its own second front in much the same area, also with

headquarters in Lusaka. During 1967, operating from bases just over the frontier, MPLA guerrillas ranged widely over the thinly populated scrub country in the districts of Moxico and Cuando Cubango in eastern Angola.

By the end of 1967, the MPLA announced, in Brazzaville, that "a year after the opening of our eastern front our valiant guerrillas in the east are already on the threshold of the district of Bié" and that the population was "enthusiastically following the directives of the MPLA, providing guerrilla detachments, setting up popular militia units, and creating the necessary conditions for supplying the guerrillas." At the same time, they accused the Portuguese of "bombing centers of population supporting our organization," burning crops, and forcing the people to live near their garrisons.[20]

Opposing the more than 3,000 MPLA guerrillas in the east[21] were over 5,000 Portuguese troops, with headquarters at Luso on the Benguela Railway. Throughout 1968, guerrilla activity in the region increased; there were ten clashes in January alone, some occurring as far inland as Serpa Pinto and Silva Porto, 300 miles from the Zambian frontier. The MPLA fighters were better armed than those of UNITA. Weapons captured from them included Kalashnikov and Simonov automatic weapons of recent date made in Russia and China.[22] The major bases in Zambia were at Balovale and Sikongo. Other bases existed at two border points, Shangombo and Chavuma.[23]

By 1967, the eastern front had eclipsed the northern. As a result, the prestige of the MPLA increased at the expense of GRAE. Likewise, other African countries have recently supported the former much more than the latter. The triumph of the MPLA over its rival could also be regarded as victory for the Communist powers that had consistently backed it with arms, money, and propaganda.[24]

Another result was the transfer of the center of Angolan revolutionary activity from Brazzaville and Kinshasa to Lusaka, whose Liberation Center already played host to Rhodesian, Mozambican, and South African movements. This reflected the decision of Zambia's President Kenneth Kaunda to become more involved in southern African problems.

Depending as it does, even more than the Congo, on the Benguela Railway for the export of copper, Zambia is at the mercy of the Portuguese should they ever decide to take reprisals for support of MPLA by denying Zambia the use of Angolan ports and railways. Recent actions toward the building of both the Tan-Zam and a new Congo railway have resulted from this political situation. Apart from the fact, however, that the ports and railways are important earners of foreign currency for Portugal, to use them as a political weapon would be counter to the principle invoked by Portugal's foreign minister, in connection with the blockade of Rhodesia, that landlocked countries have a right of access to the sea, and such use would have far-reaching international repercussions.[25] Nevertheless, the weapon is there to be used in the last resort.

Short of actually closing the frontiers to the copper, by temporarily interrupting or delaying shipments, Portugal is in a position to restrain both Zambia and the Congo from becoming too aggressive in supporting the rebels. Kaunda's support of Angolan nationalists has provided more than economic concern for Zambia. Three events of 1968 indicated the possible growth of military and political threats. Though denied by the Portuguese, Zambia claimed a bombing raid by Portuguese planes on the western border on March 22. A further clash in November was admitted by both sides.[26] In December, villages in Barotse Province of Zambia were attacked by a group claiming to be partisans of the Zambian opposition party, the African Nationalist Congress, which had trained on Angolan soil.[27] These were early signs that insurgency might be a two-edged sword.

More than seven years after the first outbreak of insurgency in northern Angola, the military situation was broadly as follows: a northern zone of sporadic disturbances extending along the frontier with the Congo, with incidents occurring as far south as Ambriz, being operated by GRAE from bases in the lower Congo; a pocket of resistance in the Dembos mountains under the MPLA; a northeastern zone, more or less dormant, operated independently of GRAE, from bases in the Kwango region of the Congo; and an eastern zone, increasingly active, operated militarily by the MPLA, mainly in the Lunda, Moxico, and Cuando Cubango districts from bases in Zambia, and by UNITA in the extreme southeastern corner, and politically, through propaganda, by UNITA among the Chokwe and the Ovimbundu.

Meanwhile, from their respective broadcasting stations in Kinshasa and Brazzaville, the spokesmen for GRAE and MPLA kept up an unrelenting campaign of mutual recrimination. Early in 1968, for example, in the Voice of Free Angola program, the GRAE propagandists denounced an alleged plot by MPLA to persuade the OAU to withdraw its recognition of the government in exile. In September, 1968, the OAU met in Algeria and confirmed an earlier report of its African Liberation Committee, stating that MPLA was clearly making the most progress in the continued insurgency. As a result, official recognition was removed from the GRAE as a government, and its political arm, the FNLA, was placed on an equal footing with the MPLA.

Following the attack on Angola, nationalist parties of Portuguese Guinea and Mozambique began to accelerate their activities. By 1962 in the former, and 1964, in the latter, insurgency had begun. The pattern of each evolved differently from the insurgency in Angola.

PORTUGUESE GUINEA

After its failure as an urban organization in the 1950's, PAIGC began political and military training in the Republic of Guinea and a covert expansion of its political force through the development of small cells in rural areas of Portuguese Guinea.[28] In July, 1961, while PAIGC was organizing, the MLG, which later became a subdivision of FLING, launched the first attack, on towns bordering Senegal on the north. This incursion eventually led to Senegal's breaking diplomatic relations with Portugal over an alleged violation of Senegalese air space by the Portuguese air force. This MLG attack was an isolated action, however.

Since then PAIGC has been responsible for almost all of the conflict. By mid–1962, it felt enough confidence in its internal preparations to begin its guerrilla operations. Operating originally from bases in independent Guinea, it began incidents of sabotage to communications facilities and attacks in a number of areas where Portuguese control seemed least strong. By 1963, widened attacks on Portuguese army facilities and occasionally on towns became common. In those first years of insurgency, PAIGC efforts were directed from independent Guinea and were concentrated in the south.

The methods used to spark revolt were twofold. Small groups of men crossed the frontier from the south and summoned meetings in the bush, where they persuaded Guineans to join them in the fight against the Portuguese, sometimes on pain of having their villages burned. They recruited many of their supporters from the younger men of one tribe, the Balanta. Meanwhile, internal organizing was taking place on the village level. When the first attack was made, the Portuguese, with only two companies of infantry in the province, found themselves heavily outnumbered. There were barely enough troops to defend the main centers. For many months, the rebels were masters of a large tract of territory extending east and south of Bissau, the capital, to the frontier. To escape the danger of growing hosilities, about 50,000 Africans left their homes and took refuge either in the Republic of Guinea or in Senegal, but mostly in the latter.

The largest tribe, the Muslim Fula, and some smaller groups remained loyal to Portugal. Fula chieftains asked for arms to defend themselves against the guerrillas and were given 10,000 rifles by the Portuguese. Besides the addition of assistance, this gesture of arming the civilian population was an attempt to refute guerrilla claims to have all the population with them. African volunteers were recruited to defend their own villages, and a local militia was formed to act as auxiliaries. With the arrival of Portuguese reinforcements in 1963 and the later appointment of a new governor and commander-in-chief, General Arnaldo Schultz, who had been highly successful in Angola, the tide turned for a time against the guerrillas. Most administrative posts were reoccupied and garrisoned, and the large numbers of Africans who had fled from the attack, either into the bush or over the frontier, were encouraged to return to their villages, many of which, having been destroyed by the guerrillas, had to be rebuilt with the help of the Portuguese army.[29] By 1965, the situation had been stabilized: the insurgents held a strong military initiative and continued to operate much at will; all centers of population were in the hands of the Portuguese, who could also penetrate all parts of the territory with the exception of the island of Como, the rebel stronghold in the swampland south of the capital, where the PAIGC withstood a major Portuguese assault.

In the central district, east of Bissau, small bands of guerrillas, operating from hideouts in the bush, adopted tactics of mining roads and mounting ambushes. They also fired at Portuguese patrol boats from the banks of the rivers. Attempts to pursue them were made only when firm information could be acted on, which seldom resulted in contact with the rebels but occasionally led to the discovery of caches of arms. Portuguese defense had been restricted by the lack of roads in Guinea, although increasing numbers have been built in recent years. One of the first tasks of the army, after the arrival of reinforcements, was to build airstrips in all outlying districts.

By establishing garrisons at key points along the southeastern frontier, the Portuguese aimed at sealing off the routes by which the rebels infiltrated from independent Guinea. This was not possible, of course, since there is always another path, especially where the frontier runs through forest. However, the main direction of infiltration eventually shifted from the southeast to the east, first, and then to the north, showing the partial success of the Portuguese defenses, the generalization of the conflict, and the ease with which the insurgents could maneuver.

The other reason for posting troops near the frontier was to give protection to the population and encourage people to resettle, by providing medical services, schools, essential goods when these were lacking, and help with crops and in building new homes. As in Angola, the main object of this pacification campaign was to win the allegiance of the people by offering them a better way of life than that held out by the nationalists.

Under Governor Schultz, who became known for his advocacy of the creation of fortified villages, a typical procedure was for the Portuguese to enter an abandoned village and secure themselves from attack by erecting around it a double fence of barbed wire, equipped with an alarm system, and then constructing an inner defense line of earth and timber bulwarks, pillboxes, and underground shelters for protection against mortar fire. In theory, as the village would be secured, some of the inhabitants would start to drift back and receive food, clothes, medical attention, and tools. As life became organized, the number steadily would increase until the population was almost back to normal.

Occasional guerrilla attacks against the garrison were usually beaten off. The Portuguese commander was frequently a young lieutenant doing his compulsory service. He would build a new village outside the defensive perimeter as a symbol of renewed confidence in law and order. This would be more solidly constructed, of mud bricks baked in the sun, often including a mosque, a school, and a hospital.

Such a village would have a corps of African volunteers under command of the village headman. Some would take rifles when working in the fields, as much as a status symbol as for fear of attack. Not all such villages had Portuguese garrisons, but there was always a garrison within radio communication that could send reinforcements in the event of an alarm. Villages occasionally actually beat off an attack without asking for help.

Besides providing security, the presence of the army brought benefits to the countryside, such as better communications, housing, and services. For example, a district officer who previously had pleaded in vain for a new water supply for some village would find his request immediately answered by the local commander, as well as troops supplied to do the work. As in Angola, there has been more material progress since the emergency than had been seen for many years before it.

In the first few years of the conflict, attacks on fortified villages were rare. The guerrillas shot from the nearest cover, usually several hundred yards away, and, in the ensuing exchange of shots, the most likely casualties were livestock straying into the line of fire.

This system of defense, effective when it was attempted, was the Portuguese answer to the continuing claims made by Amilcar Cabral that his movement controlled between one-third and one-half of the territory. Most of this territory was either forest or marsh, with very little population, and the PAIGC guerrillas could move about freely in it without the risk of encountering any Portuguese.

The success of the Portuguese pacification campaign and the inconstancy of PAIGC's successes led the PAIGC to announce, in 1965, their own program of education and other social services for the area they controlled. The later execution of this program demonstrated the organizational capacity and following of the rebels.

During 1966, PAIGC advances continued, and the forces on both sides were increased. From an estimated several hundred in 1962, the number of guerrillas rose to 3,000 by 1964, at least twice that by 1966. They also contained a higher proportion of men trained abroad and were better led and better armed, with bazookas, mortars, and automatic weapons. In the same period reinforcements brought the Portuguese force to between 20,000 and 30,000 regular troops and six companies of local militia, apart from the civilian volunteers organized as "self-defense" groups in the villages.

The PAIGC forces received initial training at a base camp at Kindia, near Conakry, in the Republic of Guinea, which was staffed for a time by Russian instructors who were afterward replaced by Algerians. Here the guerrillas received their arms and supplies. The arms, including mortars, bazookas, and machine guns, were mostly from Eastern Europe with some new weapons from China. In 1965, the Algerians reportedly concluded an agreement with the U.S.S.R. by means of which any Algerian equipment sent southward for use in liberation movements would be replaced in kind by the Soviet Union. The three routes used to supply the rebels in Portuguese Guinea have been: (1) by sea, from Algeria via Conakry; (2) overland, from Algeria via Mali and thence to Conakry or Dakar; (3) by sea, from Cuba via Conakry.

By 1967, a modus vivendi had been established between PAIGC and Senegalese leaders. Most of the PAIGC incursions from Senegal were made across the northern frontier and came from a base camp at Kolda in Senegal, which appeared to have replaced the camp at Kindia in the Republic of Guinea as the principal training and supply center of PAIGC, although Cabral's own headquarters remained at Conakry.

Why the attack on the north had been expanded was not clear, but there could have been several reasons: failure to win over the southern tribes, better conditions in the north for living off the land, better conditions in Senegal for the majority of the refugees, or a more welcoming attitude on the part of the government of Senegal than previously. Another possibility was a change in the sources of PAIGC's foreign aid. The camp at Kolda allegedly included Cubans on the staff.

By the end of 1967, Cabral claimed to control half the territory, and several Western observers whom he had invited to visit the liberated zones accepted the claim. One of these, Basil Davidson, who spent two weeks with the guerrillas, described his experience when accompanying them on three sorties, one from a landing on the coast and the other two across the northeast frontier.[30] After travelling about 80 miles inside the territory, mostly on foot, he reported that "the Portuguese no longer have any hold on four-fifths of their land frontiers or about half their coast line, now firmly in guerrilla hands." He also confirmed PAIGC claims to "practically undisputed possession of rather more than half the villages and rural areas," to be "operating successfully with mobile or guerrilla units in most of the rest of the country" and to be "beginning to close in on all but the biggest two or three towns."

Davidson witnessed "several air bombardments of villages and rice fields by small jet bombers" and was present when a napalm canister hit a nationalist ack-ack emplacement, incinerating one gunner and badly burning the other. He afterward visited the wounded man in a guerrilla hospital "not far from Cacine," in the extreme south of the territory. This was one of the two hospitals which PAIGC claims to operate in liberated zones. He was told by Cabral that PAIGC had 470 men and women in training in Europe as doctors, nurses, mechanics, electricians, agronomists, and the like, and that military supplies and civilian training facilities were provided chiefly by the Soviet Union, Czechoslovakia, Yugoslavia, and the German Democratic Republic.

Other press reports appearing about the same time gave a similar impression of nationalist successes. Thus, in a dispatch from Conakry, Russell Warren Howe wrote:

> Portugal concedes that more than half of this maze of swamp and jungle is out of its control. Mr. Cabral concedes that he occupies none of the urban centers. All but three of these, however, have been hit by nationalist mortar and bazooka shells. . . . Recent visitors escorted by Mr. Cabral's forces around parts of Portuguese Guinea found African morale high.[31]

The propaganda success scored by the nationalists prompted the Portuguese to reply in kind. A visit to Portuguese Guinea in February, 1968, by Portuguese President Américo Tomas was meant as "evidence that Lisbon is determined to retain the nearly worthless tropical territory, despite the high cost of the five-year guerrilla war there" and despite the army assessment of the area as "militarily undefendable."[32] To remove doubts of Lisbon's decision, on his arrival at Bissau, the President declared:

> Guinea does not stand in so-called Southern Africa but that does not matter, for we attach to it the same importance as to other sacred portions of national territory. Within the healthy principles that are the guidelines of our collective life, our decision to defend it against foreign attacks could not be any other. It is a part of the same body, which to function perfectly must be kept intact.[33]

In spite of this symbol of continuing commitment, however, the Portuguese may still have been considering finding some way to extricate themselves from the area through the middle of 1968.

Throughout the summer, reports of PAIGC victories continued. Governor

Schultz's replacement was even forced to withdraw from several key centers in the northeast and south. At the time of the change of government in Portugal, there was some speculation that the opportunity would be taken to reduce their commitment in Guinea or to withdraw altogether. However, the announcement of the new Prime Minister, Marcello Caetano, promising that another 7,000 troops were to be sent to Guinea showed that there was no change of policy.[34]

Portuguese forces still retained counterstrike capabilities, largely because of a squadron of twelve Fiat jets, which gave them the power to reach any part of Guinea in a few minutes. This to some extent offset the fact that the insurgents now had high-powered automatic rifles, heavy mortars, and modern antiaircraft guns and that their attacks on military camps and convoys were increasingly effective and daring. Undoubtedly the nationalists had help from many civilians, as a result both of spontaneous loyalty, signs of success, and threats.

By the same token, a major reason given by the Portuguese for holding on in Guinea was their moral obligation to protect the loyal section of the population. Even if it were true that the nationalists controlled half the territory, as they claimed, this was not the same as controlling half the inhabitants, a great number of whom, possibly the majority, were living in towns or fortified villages under Portuguese protection. Many of them feared that in the event of a national victory, they would be exposed to reprisals. Other important factors in the Portuguese determination include their own tradition in Africa, the economic interests of CUF, and a fear of consequences for Angola and Mozambique.

If the Portuguese were still in Guinea, it was not due entirely to superior force but also to the willingness of at least a part of the population to cooperate with the government, once they were sure that it had no intention of withdrawing, was resolved to remain indefinitely, and had the will and means to secure their protection. As a Portuguese officer observed to one of the authors of this chapter: "The Americans can never win in Vietnam, because everybody knows that sooner or later they will be leaving. Here we shall win because everybody knows we are staying."

MOZAMBIQUE

In Mozambique, the Portuguese took precautions to avoid the surprises of Angola and Guinea.[35] They cleared a zone adjoining the northern frontier and obliged its population to move elsewhere. They also constructed airstrips and roads for the military. When the conflict began, they had a considerable force in the area. In making these preparations, steps were taken to clear rural areas and establish most of the population in fortified villages, where the inhabitants could work safely on the land by day and be protected from attack at night. As a result of the Portuguese actions, several thousand Makonde migrated to Tanzania.

The Makonde, who inhabit both sides of the Rovuma River, the border between Mozambique and Tanzania, resisted Portuguese attempts to assimilate them. The new migrants and others who had been living there for some years formed the first recruitment pool for anti-Portuguese activities. After the onset of insurgency, the numbers of migrants to Tanzania expanded.

The insurgency in Mozambique started in August, 1964, with a raid across its northern frontier by a small force headed by a former MANU leader who had quarreled with FRELIMO. After killing a Dutch priest and some Africans who were out hunting with him, the raiders withdrew toward Tanzania, but they were intercepted by Portuguese troops and a number, including the leader, were killed.

This premature action may have forced the hand of FRELIMO and obliged it to launch its own attack a month later. Several small bands of guerrillas had crossed the Rovuma River from Tanzania, and one of these struck first, against a Portuguese military outpost at Mueda on the Makonde plateau.

The first FRELIMO insurgents were led by men who had received their training in Algeria. By late in 1964, the force amounted to 250. They operated in small groups in the Makonde plateau, raiding villages and killing the headmen if they were cooperating with the Portuguese. They would then retire to some sanctuary on the edge of the plateau, where it was difficult for troops to pursue them, before launching another attack. Later they took to mining roads, ambushing convoys (in which mortars were sometimes used), sniping at Portuguese patrols, and occasionally making a night attack on some Portuguese garrison. Casualties were slight and little harm was done, except to some sisal plantations in the vicinity of Mocímboa da Praia, which the authorities closed down rather than taking the trouble of defending them.

The policy of establishing fortified villages was partially successful, but, between the defended positions, movement was unsafe and could be made only in convoy. This situation continued on the Makonde plateau with little change. The guerrillas also tried to infiltrate to the coast and thence southward, but they did not get further than the vicinity of Quissanga, 100 miles south of Cabo Delgado, where they were in the territory of the predominantly hostile Makua.

During the first half of 1965, the insurgency spread to the district of Niassa, further west, where Nyanja tribesmen, also based in Tanzania, engaged in the same kind of guerrilla warfare. This soon extended along the shore of Lake Nyasa, and for a short time threatened the Portuguese as far south as Nova Freixo, an important railhead.

Like the Makonde, the Nyanja have strong ties outside Mozambique. The majority of them live in Malawi and, of those who speak a European language, even in Mozambique, probably more speak English than Portuguese. This can be explained partly by the influence of Anglican missions, which, since the end of the nineteenth century, have been established on the island of Licoma[36] (which, although close to the eastern, and therefore Portuguese, side of the lake, belongs to Malawi) and at Massumba, in Niassa District of Mozambique. As a result, most Nyanja Christians are Protestants. Another reason for the prevalence of English was the fact that the Niassa Company, given a charter in 1891 to develop the district, was controlled by British finance capital.

After being cleared from the Nova Freixo region, guerrilla activity was concentrated in a fairly narrow zone running south from the Tanzanian border along the eastern shore of Lake Malawi to Vila Cabral and Catur, where the railway terminates. A start had been made to extend the line to Vila Cabral, but this was abandoned because of the continuing FRELIMO threat. The Portuguese have a naval base at Metangula, from which they patrol the lake and where there is a fortified village with several thousand inhabitants.

In Niassa District, as in Cabo Delgado District, the system of concentrating the population in fortified villages proved very effective. In Niassa, moreover, the defense of many of the villages was left to local militia, usually, but not always, under command of a European NCO. As in Guinea, the villages were surrounded by barbed wire, usually with watchtowers, sometimes with an inner perimeter of bunkers and slit trenches. The villagers were free to go in or out but were expected to return at night, which they normally did. Nearly all contained schools provided by the government with African teachers, as well as dispensaries.

Another area of insurgency was in the vicinity of Milange, close by the frontier with Malawi in Zambezia District. In the summer of 1965, two FRELIMO units, who had presumably come from Malawi, operated for a short time as far inland as Tacuane, the center of a tea-growing country, where they killed several headmen and some Portuguese before being rounded up or shot.

Later there was some infiltration from Zambia, organized by COREMO from headquarters in Lusaka, but this was ineffective and was not taken very seriously by the Portuguese. Since at that time there were no known training camps for Mozambican guerrillas in Zambia, it was thought that the infiltrators' mission was political rather than military, in accordance with the COREMO plan for preparing the population for "a massive uprising at a propitious time of COREMO's own choosing."[37] Under this plan, small guerrilla units were to remain permanently in Mozambique, but, after making a few attacks in Tete District, the raiders usually retired across the frontier.

By late in 1967, FRELIMO was faced with the fact that its activities were being contained in two relatively small areas, the northeastern corner of Cabo Delgado District, mainly the Makonde plateau, and the northwestern corner of Niassa District. Furthermore, within these areas at least 250,000 people, perhaps half the population, were living in fortified villages under Portuguese protection,[38] and the number of such villages was constantly increasing. This situation led FRELIMO to search for another front. With the Cabora Bassa dam looming as a major project to cement the Portuguese position, FRELIMO sought to impede or harass those who were involved in the area. As a result, infiltration into Tete District began in mid-1968. As 1969 began, Eduardo Mondlane reported that his intention was "to paralyze the work on the dam, or to make it more costly than the contractors had calculated."[39] The Portuguese, for their part, reportedly with some South African assistance, began to fortify their defenses in that area.

The failure of FRELIMO to make gains further south was due partly to the effectiveness of Portuguese counteraction, both military and administrative, but even more to tribal opposition. Although the FRELIMO hierarchy reflected no tribal emphasis, nevertheless, with their bases in Tanzania, they were obliged to recruit fighters from those who were already living there or just across the frontier, nearly all of whom were either Makonde or Nyanja. To the south of these two tribes lived other, more numerous and important tribes. When the guerrillas tried to penetrate beyond their own tribal territory, they found their progress blocked by either apathy or hostility from the African population. We have already noted the enmity between the Makonde and the Makua, the latter being one of the two largest ethnic groups in Mozambique. The Portuguese have recruited the Makua into defensive forces and have not hesitated to make use of tribal enmities. To a lesser extent, friction existed between the Christian Nyanja and the Muslim Yao.

Although there were, no doubt, nationalist supporters in other parts of the country, they remained inactive. There were practically no acts of sabotage outside the areas of guerrilla warfare. Such organization as FRELIMO had in the big towns, Beira and Lourenço Marques, seems to have been broken up in the early days of PIDE (the Portuguese security police), which has continued to keep a surveillance on suspected FRELIMO sympathizers.

As in Angola, nationalist claims of success have been consistently exaggerated and have helped to confuse the picture. Portuguese estimates have also under-estimated their own casualties, since they only report those who die in battle, omitting casualties in accidents, which may include mine explosions and the deaths of injured soldiers. Nevertheless, Portuguese authorities must inform the next of kin of the dead and, if there were a wild discrepancy between the published and the true figures, the fact would become apparent. Therefore, it seems likely that Portuguese figures are fairly accurate. Many examples of the divergent information can be found. In one of these, during November, 1967, FRELIMO claimed that its forces had killed over fifty Portuguese, while the Portuguese admitted to only three.[40] Estimates of casualties for the first four years of the insurgency are likewise difficult to determine. By September, 1968, FRELIMO claimed to have killed 1,500 Portuguese troops.[41] That estimate varied greatly from the figure of 5,000 claimed by FRELIMO's vice-president, Uria Simango, in a statement at Dar es Salaam early in 1968.[42] Portuguese estimates are considerably below both numbers.

Foreign Aid

Eduardo Mondlane boasted in 1965 that he received "money from the West and arms from the East," as much of both as he needed. Some of his funds were also provided by the African Liberation Committee (first referred to as the Committee of Nine and later of Eleven) which was set up in 1963 by the Organization of African Unity, with an office in Dar es Salaam. In March, 1967, however, he told an interviewer in Tunis that aid received from the OAU was being reduced month by month but that FRELIMO received substantial aid from the U.S.S.R., China, Yugoslavia, Czechoslovakia, and Bulgaria.[43] The reliance on Communist sources reflected an unwillingness of Western countries to provide assistance. The aid received from Western countries was "mostly from churches and humanitarian pro-African committees, and is designated for our educational, refugee, and other humanitarian programs."[44]

The sites for the training and refugee camps were provided by the Tanzanian Government, and nearly all the arms and military equipment came from Communist countries, as shown from captured material. The principal training camp was installed at Kongwa, 100 miles west of Dar es Salaam. Financed by the OAU and one of the sites of a British groundnut (peanut) scheme that failed shortly after World War II, Kongwa was already partially equipped. Old buildings were rehabilitated and new ones constructed with a view to accommodating up to 12,000 people, mainly refugees and rebels from Rhodesia, South Africa, and the Portuguese territories. A smaller camp, to which recruits were sent for "boot training," was located at the small port of Bagamoyo, a short distance north of Dar es Salaam. Some of the leaders were given a course in guerrilla warfare at the Tlemcen base in Algeria. The operations were launched from bases in the south, in a chain from the Indian Ocean to the shore of Lake Nyasa: Lindi, Mtwara, Newala (where FRELIMO forces first gathered in the fall of 1964 in preparation for their entrance into Mozambique), Masasi, Tunduru, Songea, and Mbamba Bay. A road connected these bases, and the entire area was insulated from daily Tanzanian life by the Selous Game Preserve. While primarily designed to support operations in Mozambique, the bases were also used by rebels seeking to re-enter Zambia and Malawi.

The instructors were reported to include East Europeans, Algerians, Cubans, and Chinese. Captured weapons were the usual heterogeneous collection: the rifles of East European, West European, and American origin and the more sophisticated arms, such as mortars and bazookas, from China or Russia. Toward the end of 1967, new weapons made their appearance, notably the Kalashnikov AK47 automatic rifle and a new rocket launcher, both of Chinese manufacture.[45]

The Border Situation

Most manpower available for the continuing insurgency derives from among the Mozambicans who have migrated to Malawi, Kenya, Zambia, and Tanzania in the past two or three decades.[46] The liberation groups claimed that 7,000 refugees had entered Tanzania before September, 1964, when the first raids were launched across the frontier, but this was probably an overestimate. By 1968, the figure had risen to over 10,000 and, including families, possibly much higher. It would be a mistake to assume, however, that all refugees were involved in political activities. Many of them were simply escaping, after being caught in crossfire. Some became involved in refugee projects such as communal agricultural schemes in southern Tanzania making them less willing to join the ranks of the fighters. For this reason, such schemes did not find favor with the nationalists.[47]

After the first few years, the Committee of Nine concluded that the nationalist political leaders and refugee groups did not make able and dedicated fighters. A possible alternative that was considered was the raising of an international brigade of mercenaries, officered by professionals and recruited from all races. However, such a force presented both practical difficulties of recruitment and organization and a potential challenge to the authority of the host government. That idea soon lost favor.

The Rovuma River line and the region immediately to the south comprise a natural defensive area for Mozambique. The banks of the Rovuma River and its valley are, for the most part, rugged and wild. Most of the migratory groups from Mozambique to Tanzania have not crossed the river directly but have moved upstream in small boats along the banks, a distance of more than 30 miles, passing the 5-mile-wide zone cleared by the Portuguese. The Portuguese tactical advantage along the entire river line has been vastly enhanced by air reconnaissance, using helicopters and light aircraft. During 1963, new airstrips were built at Umtamba, Midumba, Ngamba, Mueda, and Palma in order to support reconnaissance efforts and to provide bases for fighters and transport aircraft. In addition, Mueda and Palma were joined by a new road. The Portuguese have also constructed a naval base at Porto Amélia, to assist in surveillance operations. Their main military headquarters is at Nampula, connected by rail to the new port at Nacala, one of the largest natural harbors in East Africa.

The central flank—bordering Malawi and Zambia—may be an area of greater vulnerability than the Tanzanian border. Lake Nyasa has already served as a waterway to support infiltration. However, there was always an extremely strong political tie between Banda's government and the Portuguese. Economically, Malawi has strategic interests which are closely tied to the southern part of Africa. (Malawi and Portugal alone opposed the U.N. resolution on South-West Africa in October, 1966.) Malawi is dependent upon Beira for transit, and its two most important cities, Zomba, the capital, and Blantyre-Limbe are flanked to the east, south, and west by Mozambique. When the projected railway between Nova Freixo and Malawi is completed, Nacala will become the chief outlet for Malawi. Because of the vulnerability of the Lake Nyasa area, it was believed that the Portuguese had plans to counter a number of contingencies, such as an increase in infiltration from Tanzania along the lake routes, or a changed political situation in Malawi itself. Reportedly, the plans included the movement of forces across Lake Nyasa and into Malawi and were capable of being implemented, since the southern portion of Malawi near the end of Lake Nyasa is no more than 60 miles wide, of which the lake constitutes 35 miles. The Portuguese have completed a lake base for marine commandos at Port Arroio, from which, according to one observer, "it would take no more than three or four hours to seal off the southern end of Lake Nyasa."[48]

The vulnerability of the Zambian-Mozambique border is different from the Malawi–Lake Nyasa area, inasmuch as it is further removed from major areas of Portuguese settlement. Portuguese relations have never been as close with the Zambian Government, as with Malawi, yet Portuguese political and trade relations with Zambia continued even after the Rhodesian unilateral declaration of independence (UDI). Zambia retains a dependency upon Beira, and, to a lesser extent, Lourenço Marques, for transit purposes. In the UDI crises, Kaunda played a delicate political game of *realpolitik* by making calculated public demands and assuming a posture aggressive enough to maintain internal political support. Similarly, he gave no more than token support to the liberation movements in the early years. However, geography and a deeply felt sense of commitment to what Kaunda has seen as an African necessity have tended more and more to make Lusaka a capital of revolution for the whole of southern Africa. By 1967, he had agreed to allow Angolan insurgents to expand their operations from Zambia. Subsequently, a training camp was also sanctioned first for Rhodesian and South Africa freedom fighters and later for Mozambicans. Zambian bases were used in mid-1968 by a group of guerrillas who attempted unsuccessfully to pass through Mozambique to South Africa. Portuguese defensive activities in the area began to worry the Zambian Government.

To sum up, so long as the conflict remains confined to the north, where the terrain and the wildness of the country favor the guerrillas, the military challenge to the Portuguese is limited, and there is no great danger to the rest of Mozambique. Furthermore, if the guerrillas succeed in advancing southward, the flat, open terrain would favor the Portuguese, and the nationalists might also be faced with the threat of action by Rhodesia and South Africa to remove the potential danger to their territories.[49] Nevertheless, between 40,000 and 60,000 Portuguese troops are necessary to carry on the present Portuguese policy. How much the defense effort can continue to expand is questionable.

THE PORTUGUESE MILITARY

With the development of conflict in each of its territories on the African continent, the Portuguese have themselves witnessed a decade of change that affected their own military establishment.[50] In 1961, only a few thousand troops guarded an empire. By late in 1968, an estimated 120,000 to 150,000 troops fought a continuing struggle with an enemy whose numbers were increasing, whose tactics were maturing, and whose materiel was improving.

The immediate response to the 1961 uprising was to send troops to Angola. Later responses included the recruitment of more troops, the extension of military service obligations, modernization of equipment, and the expanded use of military officers in administrative positions formerly filled by civilians. What had been seen as military necessities have led to a greater reliance on the military and to a greater military presence, both in Portuguese Africa and within the government in Lisbon.

A major change in the decade was the growth of the Portuguese military establishment. The total strength of the armed forces in 1964 was about 80,000, about three-fourths of whom were in the army, with the rest divided almost evenly between the navy and the air force. By mid-1968, that figure had surpassed 180,000, the numbers were still increasing, and the emphasis (over 80 per cent) was clearly on the army.[51] Although some of the troops were committed to the Portuguese participation in NATO, for the most part their purpose was to fight in Portuguese Africa. Though exact information was lacking, the general newspaper consensus suggested 40,000 to 60,000 in Angola, 40,000 to 60,000 in Mozambique, and 25,000 to 30,000 in Guinea. The requirements of a particular conflict often required more of one branch than another. Thus, there was a greater naval effort in Guinea than in the other territories.

The deepening of the Portuguese military commitment brought changes in national service requirements. Previously all youths had been required to serve for two years upon reaching age twenty-one. Those who wished at that age to continue their schooling could do so, since they would later be available as officers. The new manpower needs, however, forced a change of policy. In 1967, military service was opened to women, the age of entrance was lowered to eighteen, the foreign travel of sixteen-year-olds was carefully limited, and the total service obligation was lengthened to four years, through a mandatory two-year tour of duty in Africa. Although these new laws also apply to Africans, it is difficult to determine how diligently they are applied.

Instructions in counterinsurgency tactics were being used in the training of the Portuguese army by 1962, following precedents developed by the British in Malaya. Later, elite commando units began to be trained in Angola as well as in metropolitan Portugal. These units were trained to embody the total mission of the Portuguese military.

Broadly speaking, that mission was threefold: to defend territorial borders, to ensure internal security, and to develop a program of psychosocial activity. As has been suggested before, a major tactic used by the Portuguese joined all parts of that mission. The principle of fortified villages, often associated with Governor Arnaldo Schultz of Guinea, has also been used in northern and eastern Angola and in northern Mozambique. Its success seems to have varied from area to area. It has been most successful in northern Angola, where repatriated Bakongo are now participants in a thriving, coffee-based rural economy, and least successful in Portuguese Guinea, where many of the hamlets have been overrun by PAIGC forces.

The Portuguese have traditionally relied on African allies to fill military needs. Immediate manpower needs after 1961 and a lack of confidence in the general trust previously given native Africans led to an over-reliance on Portuguese troops. By 1968, however, there were signs that the Portuguese were again resorting to African troops. An observer estimated that 19,000 troops in Angola were "locally recruited" and racially mixed.[52] It remained clear that the Portuguese were neither unwilling nor unable to find Africans to fight for Portugal.

Other than in the official military units, Africans were also part of local militia that frequently handled the major defense burdens of the fortified villages and other rural towns. The Portuguese have armed these militia and occasionally use militiamen in wider combat. Civil defense units (Voluntários e Defesa Civil), which sometimes act as vigilantes, Public Security Police, and the secret police (PIDE) are also part of the defense effort.

An important advantage that the Portuguese maintain over the nationalist insurgents is the capacity to manufacture much of their own military equipment, including vital river-patrol craft. Nevertheless, though self-sufficient in most army material, Portugal has to rely on foreign sources for its major naval and air equipment.[53] Although Portugal is a member of NATO, it is restricted from using NATO equipment in African wars. A major asset to the Portuguese, however, has been the ability to acquire jet planes from West Germany and helicopters from France.

The combination of increased material needs and larger troop demands has been costly to Portugal. Defense expenditures have risen substantially until they amount to slightly less than half of current government expenditures. Although it was shown in Chapter XV that the Portuguese economy can tolerate these expenses, the burden has not passed unfelt.

It is difficult to obtain an accurate figure for Portugal's annual military expenditure, because of the separation between what are considered "extraordinary" defense expenditures and other allocations for military purposes that appear elsewhere. Moreover, in order to present a balanced budget, estimated revenues and expenditures are usually considerably lower than actually anticipated, and the real situation can be known only after the accounts have been approved, usually two years later.[54]

Portugal's Budget Allocations for Extraordinary Overseas Forces
(in Millions of Dollars), 1961–68

Years	Initial	Supplementary	Total
1961	32.3	51	83.3
1962	51	61.1	112.1
1963	59.5	56.6	116.1
1964	59.5	62.9	122.4
1965	68	74.5*	142.5*
1966	85	63.6	148.6
1967	119	59.6	178.6
1968	136	—	—

* As revised in the 1967 budget.

Source: Portugal, Diário do Governo (Lisbon, 1961–67).

The Portuguese, of course, maintain other defense requirements, but since 1962, the Extraordinary Overseas Forces have absorbed an average of two-thirds of total defense allocations.

Portugal's Military Budget (in Millions of Dollars), 1962–67

Year	Extraordinary Overseas Forces	Total Defense Allocations	Total Ordinary Budget
1962	112.1	193.7†	280.1
1963	116.1	198.7†	307.2
1964	122.4	222.6†	326.3
1965	142.5	246.8†	364.1
1966	148.6	213.5	374.1
1967	178.6	267	428.6
1968	136*	280.9	575.1

* Initial allocation.
† Actual expenditure.

Sources: Figures for EOF and total ordinary budget allocations from Portugal, Orçamento geral do estado (Decree 48,164), in Diário do governo (Lisbon), I, 298 (December 26, 1967). Total defense allocations for 1962–65 from Portugal, Projet de loi d'autorisation des recettes et des dipenses pour 1966 (Lisbon), p. 227, Table 14, and ibid., 1967 (Lisbon), p. 243, Table 10. For 1966–67, Portugal, Rapport sur le budget general de l'etat pour 1967 (Lisbon), p. 75. For 1968, Diário do governo (Lisbon), Table XXXIII.

CONCLUSION

By late in 1968, the nationalist challenge to Portuguese rule in Africa was more than seven years old and no end to it was in sight. While the disturbance was confined to limited areas of the three territories affected, and life elsewhere went on much as usual, the containment of the liberation movement continued to require an army of at least 120,000 men and to absorb 40 per cent of the national budget. Every Portuguese called up for national service had to face a two-year tour of duty in Africa; and the fact that this, and the drain on the nation's resources for defense expenditures, might continue indefinitely weighed increasingly on the national consciousness and pocketbook. Was there any way of breaking the deadlock, by one side or the other forcing a decision?

One possibility was a great increase in Portugal's use of military force, bombing, artillery, and armor. Apart from the expense involved, the use of bombers, for example, has proven relatively unsuccessful in other areas against insurgents operating as guerrillas. For every guerrilla killed or captured there is always a replacement, and short of occupying or destroying the country that provides him with a base, there is no means of preventing foreign supplies from reaching him. Massive retaliation would also not be in accord with Portuguese policy. Portugal's strongest point has always been the loyalty, or at least neutrality, of the majority of the population, and to increase repression, for example by large-scale napalm bombing, would have thrown this away.

Another possibility was an increase in rebel effectiveness through the introduction into the insurgent forces of more efficient equipment and weapons, of which there was already evidence by 1967, and the provision of badly needed training in the field by the attachment of foreign instructors, as was done in the Congo. However, experience suggested that neither better weapons nor better training would make a major difference, until the bulk of the population had first been won over.

Another possibility was that of firmer action by the United Nations, accompanied by the cessation of arms supplies to Portugal by NATO allies; but neither of these seemed very likely, at least while the war in Vietnam continued, and experience with Rhodesia did not hold out any hope that sanctions against Portugal would be effective. Finally, therefore, it boiled down to who would tire first, the Portuguese or their opponents. Were there any weakening on the part of Portugal, it would presumably have appeared after the retirement of Dr. Salazar. But this did not occur; on the contrary, one of the first acts of his successor was to confirm that the struggle would continue. As for the liberation movements, although some might tire, there would always be others willing to take up arms against the Portuguese and colonialism. After all, it did not cost the organizers much, since all the guerrillas asked for was their keep, a rifle, and occasional opportunities for battle spoils, while for the political leaders, their exile was made tolerably comfortable by the funds they received for the movement. On the other hand, the cost to the Communist countries, who were the main suppliers of arms and supplies, was a small price to pay for posing as the champions of the "oppressed" colonial peoples, thus enhancing their standing in the United Nations and their influence in the world, especially with the developing nations. Given the resolve of both sides, all signs pointed to a long continuation of the conflict in Portuguese Africa.

NOTES

1. Galvão acted as a subordinate to General Humberto Delgado, who ran for the Portuguese presidency in 1958 and later became leader of the exile opposition, with headquarters in Brazil. This operation was conceived as having two phases: first, the seizure of the "Santa Maria" and attraction of world-wide support as conducted by rebels against the Salazar and Franco regimes; second, a surprise attack upon the Spanish-held island of Fernando Po, followed later by an operation to take control of Luanda, supposedly with the help of local rebel forces. Galvão's anticipation of the help of Angolan rebels, and, in fact, his attempt to gain the support of the Africans in the crew of the "Santa Maria," should not be interpreted as his support for the immediate liberation of the Portuguese territories. He asserted, in 1961, that the "immediate and absolute independence of Angola . . . in the situation found at present in the Portuguese colonies, after 30 years of Salazar's colonialism, can only lead Angola to the chaotic situation which exists in the Congo." He felt that the nationalist groups later formed did not represent "more than a minute minority of Angolans with a capacity for self-determination" and that, anyway, self-determination for Africa should occur only after "the return of the Portuguese nation to a regime of representative democracy." As for the revolution, which he personally hoped to foment in Portuguese Africa, he primarily looked to, in his words, "the white inhabitants of Angola and Mozambique shown by popular vote to be clearly anti-Salazar." The "Santa Maria" thus excited international attention, at a time when a change of government had taken place in Washington and was about to take place in Brazil. The ship surrendered at Recife on February 2, but not before there had been considerable speculation as to whether the seizure portended a wider rebel effort against the Portuguese Government. These events had led to an alert in Angola. (See Henrique Galvão, *Santa Maria: My Crusade for Portugal* (Cleveland, 1961), pp. 223–24 and 233.) Galvão had been high inspector of colonial administration from 1946 to 1949 and served in the National Assembly for Angola, where, in 1948, he delivered a critical report on native problems in Portuguese colonies. In 1952, he directed the presidential campaign of Admiral Quintão Meireles. The following year, he was tried and sent to prison, but he escaped in 1959. For a book that challenges Galvão's *Santa Maria: My Crusade for Portugal* and deflates most of his claims, see Beth Day, *Passage Perilous: The Stormy Saga of the Santa Maria* (New York, 1962).

2. *Keesing's Contemporary Archives*, XIII, 18070.

3. *Ibid.*

4. Ronald Waring, "The Case for Portugal," in *Angola: A Symposium, Views of a Revolt* (London, 1962), p. 31, adds that this "was the biggest slaughter of Europeans which has taken place in Africa in this century and it passed almost unnoticed in the world press."

5. Douglas Wheeler, "Reflections on Angola," *Africa Report*, November, 1967, p. 58.

6. A statement of the point of view of at least one of these Baptist missionaries

may be found in Clifford Parsons, "The Making of a Revolt," *Angola: A Symposium: Views of a Revolt*, p. 59.

7. *Keesing's Contemporary Archives*, XIII, 18071.

8. A Kikongo word for the magic that certain tribes believed would turn their enemy's bullets into water.

9. Hugh Kay, "A Catholic View," *Angola: A Symposium: Views of a Revolt*, p. 89.

10. Parsons (*op. cit.*, p. 67) says: "During the first assaults many European settlers suffered appalling deaths with their families, a terrible and repugnant feature of the uprising that has been well-publicized by the Portuguese authorities." Parsons also declares that "the evidence of atrocities by Portuguese civilians and troops is far too formidable to be denied, and indeed even Portuguese sources have concentrated on making excuses rather than persisting in early denials. . . . Allowance must be made for those Portuguese who had lost those who were dear to them. . . . But it can never justify the measures taken against Africans all over the country who, because they were intelligent and educated, were considered potential leaders."

11. Kay, *op. cit.*, p. 96.

12. Pieter Lessing, *Only Hyenas Laugh* (London, 1964), p. 125. John A. Marcum, "Three Revolutions," *Africa Report*, November, 1967, p. 16, lists a figure of 400,000 in 1967.

13. One is tempted to draw parallels with the war in Vietnam, but, apart from the fact that both wars are waged by guerrillas supplied from abroad, there is little similarity between them. The Portuguese have historical and linguistic advantages not enjoyed by American troops in Southeast Asia: the Portuguese have been in Angola for nearly 500 years, and much of the population speaks Portuguese. Parsons (*op. cit.*, p. 78) makes this point: "The Portuguese presence has been a unifying factor. The use of Portuguese as a first language in school has created a medium of communication that was denied to the Congolese where primary education until quite recently was wholly in the vernaculars." Then again, the Portuguese are defending what they consider their own possessions, not merely assisting a foreign government to resist aggression.

14. The Voice of Angola, Congo (Brazzaville) broadcast in Portuguese to Angola, January 17, 1965.

15. Belgrade Tanug Service in English, September 20, 1965. Neto also mentioned that a meeting between the two warring factions was scheduled to take place at Cairo. The results of the meeting (if, indeed, it took place) are not known.

16. The Junta de Investigação do Ultramar, through its Centro de Estudos Políticos e Sociais, has published a series of papers by various authors, analyzing the tactics used in the revolts in Portuguese Africa and the methods suitable for combating them. One of the contributors, Joaquim Franco Pinheiro, has shown that terrorism is a very important tactic methodically used by the subversives in order to gain dominance over a native population through fear. "Natureza e Fundamentos da guerra subversiva, " *Subversão e contra-subversão* (Lisbon, 1963), p. 36.

17. *L'Alger Républicain*, March 10, 1965, quoted in "Smashing Their Chains," *Information Bulletin of the Communist and Workers' Parties* (Prague), No. 12, p. 49.

18. Marcum, *op. cit.*, p. 10.

19. *Ibid.*, p. 16.
20. The Voice of Fighting Angola, broadcast, monitored by BBC, November 19, 1967.
21. According to Agostinho Neto, *Summary of World Broadcasts*, No. 2805, Part 4 (June 26, 1968).
22. *The Times* (London), March 11, 1968.
23. *The Star* (Johannesburg), August 5, 1968.
24. Marcum (*op. cit.*) states that both the Soviet Union and China provided training, arms, and funds and the Cubans provided technical assistance, including instruction in the techniques and strategy of Castro-style revolution.
25. Letter from Franco Nogueira to the secretary-general of the United Nations, February 3, 1967.
26. *The Financial Times* (London), December 12, 1968.
27. *Africa Research Bulletin*, V, No. 11 (December 15, 1968), 1244.
28. Much of the following discussion of conflict in Portuguese Guinea derives from the sources listed in note 26 of Chapter XVII.
29. The Portuguese army, according to the semiofficial newspaper *Diário da Manhã*, has trained and armed Africans in almost 400 hamlets and has put Africans in command of them. *The New York Times*, January 15, 1968.
30. Basil Davidson, quoted in *The Times* (London), November 10, 1967.
31. *The Christian Science Monitor*, January 12, 1968.
32. *The New York Times*, January 15, 1968.
33. *The News* (Lisbon), February 10, 1968.
34. *Manchester Guardian*, November 28, 1968.
35. Much of the following discussion of conflict in Mozambique derives from the sources listed in note 32 of Chapter XVII.
36. Licoma has also been used as a staging area from Tanzania into Malawi by the exiled parties in opposition to Dr. Hastings Banda, led by Henry Chipembere, an ex-minister. The support given to this opposition by other African nationalists was one of Banda's reasons for cooperating with the Portuguese, the other being Malawi's economic dependence on Mozambique.
37. Marcum, *op. cit.*, p. 20.
38. *The Times* (London), March 11, 1968.
39. *The New York Times*, January 23, 1969.
40. In the Battle of Britain, the Royal Air Force claimed three or four times as many "kills" as were discovered actually to have occurred when the official German records were examined at the end of the war. If ten guerrillas fire at a Portuguese soldier and he is killed, more than one of them may claim to have shot one man and the total killed will be inflated.
41. *Le Monde* (Paris), September 27, 1968.
42. Dar es Salaam Radio, broadcast in English, monitored by BBC, March 5, 1968.
43. *Tunis-Afrique Presse*, in French, monitored by BBC, March 7, 1967.
44. See Helen Kitchen, *op. cit.*, p. 31.
45. *The Times* (London), March 11, 1968.
46. Colonel Arnold H. Humphries, *The East African Liberation Movement: Adelphi Papers No. 16* (London, 1965), p. 5.
47. *Ibid.*
48. Pieter Lessing in *The Christian Science Monitor*, March 19, 1963.
49. James M. Dodson, "Dynamics of Insurgency in Mozambique," *Africa Report*, November, 1967, p. 53.

5ɔ. Much of the material in this section derives from an excellent report found in United Nations, Doc. A/7200, Part II (November 7, 1968), pp. 57–73, and from Edgar O'Ballance, "The War Potential of Portugal," *Military Review*, XLIV, No. 8 (August, 1964), 84–90. For special emphasis on Angola, see Allison B. Herrick, *et al.*, *Area Handbook for Angola* (Washington, D.C., 1967), pp. 377–88.

51. *The Military Balance, 1968–69* (London: The Institute for Strategic Studies, 1968), p. 27.

52. *U.S. News and World Report*, June 10, 1968.

53. Statement by former Portuguese Secretary of State for Air, Brigadier General Kaulza de Arriaga, quoted in United Nations, Doc. A/AC109/L388, para. 24.

54. United Nations, Doc. A/7200, pp. 58–59.

XIX

Strategic Implications

DAVID M. ABSHIRE

SEVERAL EVENTS of the late 1960's sharpened the strategic importance of southern Africa. They include the vacuum left in the Indian Ocean by the scheduled British withdrawal from East of Suez, the growing Soviet presence in the Middle East and the waters surrounding it, and the increased use of the route around the Cape of Good Hope as a result of the 1967 Suez Canal closing and the construction of larger tankers. Even were it not for these developments Portuguese Africa has particular strategic significance, due to its geographic position in relation to the remainder of Southern Africa and to the South Atlantic.

Before specifically discussing Portuguese Africa, it is well to note that the Western powers have a national security interest in Africa as a whole. In two world wars Africa's large quantities of strategic raw materials were important to the West's security and later to the development of economic power, trade, and influence of the non-Communist great powers. In a military sense, these raw materials are not now of the importance that they were in those wars. With stockpiling, synthetics, and alternate sources in the Western hemisphere, they would no longer play a vital role in a general war, even a protracted, nonnuclear one. But if by the term "strategic" we mean to include the range of economic forces that mesh with the political, technological, and military to develop or undermine great-power influence, African resources are certainly strategic.

In the years just before the 1967 Arab-Israeli crisis that resulted in the closing of the Suez Canal, there had been a general downgrading of Africa in U.S. policy-making, a downgrading likewise reflected in Congressional appropriations. Annual U.S. AID appropriations to Africa averaged about $200 million between 1961 and 1966, declined to $184 million in fiscal year 1967, and to $157 million for fiscal year 1968, after which the figure was expected to be "substantially further reduced as a result of drastic over-all cuts in aid appropriations."[1] U.S. policy was certainly influenced by the view that Europe had primary responsibility for the security of Africa, as the United States had for the security of the Western hemisphere. Nevertheless, this basic attitude was at times disturbed by policy problems resulting from U.N. actions, fear of Soviet or Communist Chinese intervention, and the renewed importance of the Cape route after the Suez Canal was closed. Between June 5, 1967, and August 1, 1968, more than 20,000 ships, flying the flags of some 50 states, were forced to sail round the African continent.[2] The closing of the Suez Canal also gave short-term emphasis to the

434

development of sources of oil west of Suez. Thus, Nigerian and Angolan oil fields provide one form of "oil insurance" for Europe.[3]

PORTUGUESE STRATEGIC POSSESSIONS

The Portuguese hold important positions along major maritime and air routes of the world: the Azores, Madeira, the Cape Verde Islands, Portuguese Guinea, São Tomé and Príncipe, Angola, and Mozambique. Because of their pivotal positions, the Portuguese possessions could become economically and strategically important in certain conflict situations. Military patrol aircraft operating from these areas could effectively survey the eastern South Atlantic, the western Indian Ocean, and the seas south of the Cape. Portugal itself has neither the naval nor the air power to turn this fact to world significance. An arrangement, however, with any one of the world's great powers to be based in these areas could be of real consequences in terms of controlling maritime routes around Africa or influencing submarine activities in the Atlantic and Indian oceans.

As the American naval strategist and historian Alfred Thayer Mahan frequently pointed out, Britain's strategic power was based upon its control of the narrow seas. Subsequently, during the two world wars, U.S.–U.K. strategy depended upon control of the Suez Canal. Now no longer assured of its use, both powers have become increasingly dependent upon the alternate maritime routes around Africa. From Portuguese possessions in the Atlantic, a strong naval and air power could potentially control a substantial portion of the Atlantic and at the same time the gateway to the Mediterranean. Metropolitan Portugal, Madeira, and the Azores in effect constitute a strategic triangle in the North Atlantic.

The Portuguese African territories become all the more significant in view of Portugal's membership in the North Atlantic Treaty Organization. In addition, the headquarters of Iberian-Atlantic, NATO Command formed in December, 1966, after the French pullout in 1965, is stationed in Sintra, Portugal. One of the main functions of the NATO Command is the protection of shipping routes from northern Europe to Africa and North America.[4]

A consideration bearing heavily on U.S. relations with Portugal, as mentioned earlier, is the significance to U.S. security of the Azores, which the United States has been using for naval and air force bases since 1951, and which has sometimes been called the single most important airbase the United States has anywhere.[5] Besides providing a strategic air transport base, the islands serve the U.S. Navy as a vital communications center and constitute the hub of its antisubmarine operations in the eastern Atlantic.

The Azores assist the U.S. Navy in protecting American shores from the menace of the Soviet Union's growing nuclear submarine fleet. The time and distance factors inherent in the Atlantic undersea battleground are important. The best U.S. Navy patrol aircraft, the turboprop P3, now operating from the Azores, can carry equipment with which to protect convoys and ferret out hostile underwater craft in the mid-Atlantic, flying less than three hours en route and remaining on airborne station therefore several hours. However, should these antisubmarine planes be denied the use of the Azores bases, they would have to fly four or five hours to and from the mid-Atlantic and thus severely restrict their on-station time.[6] Nevertheless, in recent years, normal use of the Azores has shown a significant decline: Although in 1962 it was estimated that approximately 80 per cent of U.S. military air traffic depended upon the Azores,[7] by 1968 that dependence had dropped to less than 20 per cent.

The need for retaining American rights to the air bases, however, is heightened by a growing emphasis upon U.S. capability to execute the strategic deployment of ground forces in conventional warfare. In 1963, exercise Big Lift was successfully conducted, in which the entire personnel of a U.S. armored division was moved from Texas to Germany by air, the hardware being shipped by sea using the facilities at the Azores. Big Lift proved that planes cannot do such jobs without shipping and the use of such bases as the Azores.[8]

With increased tensions in the Middle East, the Azores have assumed a reinforced importance due to two major factors. First, there is a growing reluctance of West European nations to grant overflight and transit rights for a U.S. airlift into the Middle East. Second, the new transport, the C-5, has the necessary range to reach terminal air bases in the Middle East from the Azores without interim refueling stops and without overflying any West European or North African states.

GENERAL CONSIDERATIONS

Portuguese Guinea has a naval base of some significance at Bissau. The Cape Verde complex, while physically separated from the African continent, is a centerpost of the South Atlantic "strait" between Latin America and Africa. Because of the volume of shipping and other maritime communications between Latin America, Africa, and Europe, the Cape Verde complex, with its air base at Sal, the only facility of its kind in the area, functions as a significant link in both sea and air communications. The Portuguese have constructed an operational naval base in the Cape Verde Islands. Cape Verde could also provide an en route air base for the airlift of the forces of any great power into Africa.

The island of São Tomé has also proven useful for purposes of an airlift to the African mainland. The human tragedy that developed during the Nigerian civil war led the Portuguese Government in 1968 to sanction the use of São Tomé as a base for international church organizations sending food and medicine to Biafra.

Because of a unique relation with the Congo, Angola serves as the door to one of the most minerally rich parts of Africa. Mozambique has become a door of equal or greater importance by draining the Copperbelt and other productive areas of Zambia, Rhodesia, and Transvaal. Both Angola and Mozambique secure the strategic flanks of South Africa, the wealthiest and most powerful area in Africa, and the most sensitive in terms of U.S. and U.K. policies.

From its base at Santo António do Zaire on the south bank of the mouth of the Congo River, the Portuguese navy today is in a position to observe shipping along the entire navigable portion of the river, where the Congolese are accelerating their economic activities. The Congo River is an international waterway open to shipping of all nations, and the Portuguese have made no attempt to interfere with any commerce. With a small naval force, the Portuguese could initially seal off the river and could continue to disrupt the flow of Congo River traffic. In the event of further disorder in the Congo, Angola could serve as a base of operations to restore order. Its size and proximity offer obvious advantages over the British-owned Ascension Island.

A high percentage of the world shipping turning the Cape and continuing on to the eastern coast of Africa and into the Indian Ocean passes through the Mozambique Channel. Mozambique has several excellent harbors. For example, the bay where the new port of Nacala is located is so large that it could accommodate the entire U.S. Seventh Fleet. If Portuguese rule continues in Mozambique, or if an independent Mozambique is pro-Western, this would be important at a time when the British have decided to withdraw from east of Suez and phase out all their aircraft carriers by the end of 1971. Significantly, Russian naval vessels for the first time in about sixty years have visited the Persian Gulf and Moscow is negotiating with India for Indian Ocean bases. Furthermore, the Rhodesian Unilateral Declaration of Independence of November, 1965, and the subsequent sanctions imposed upon Rhodesia highlighted the strategic position of Mozambique's railways and ports.[9]

Separated from the north by more than a thousand miles, Lourenço Marques, the capital of Mozambique, has difficulty in communicating with the administration in outlying areas. The need for improved accessibility to the northern sector of the province prompted the Portuguese to build their principal jet airstrip at Beira. The major runway, completed in the fall of 1965, can handle the largest aircraft now flying. Jet flights from Lisbon land first at Luanda and then at Beira. From there, traffic to Lourenço Marques is by propeller aircraft, while Nampula in the north has a new jet airport that can accommodate Boeing 707's.

Should unrest come to eastern Africa, or should the United States become militarily engaged with a major Communist power, the extensive air and port facilities offered by Mozambique could well become an important support factor to a possible U.S. involvement in the Indian Ocean area. Although there is strong political opposition in the United States to cooperative arrangements with the Portuguese in Africa, the opposition is less than that against cooperative military arrangements with South Africa, due to its policy of apartheid. The potentialities of Mozambique's harbors notwithstanding, South African harbors are the only ones in Africa south of the Sahara that have docking, bunkering, and repair facilities for major naval vessels. They have great potential value in antisubmarine warfare. The only naval base and graving yard in that part of the globe is the Simonstown base, 30 miles from Cape Town. South Africa would also be important for overflying rights.[10] In case either the Suez Canal or the Panama Canal is closed, the Cape is the only route open to all ships in all seasons. The ports of Mozambique should be viewed with these facts in mind.[11]

THE MILITARY BALANCE

The military balance is crucial to any strategic considerations about Portuguese Africa—especially since the line of the Zambezi in Central Africa and the northern borders of Angola and Mozambique have been characterized as the "battle line" between black and white Africa. It is appropriate, then, to ponder the "order of battle," as it is called in the intelligence community. If this is done, it becomes all the more obvious why the African states have turned to the United Nations, as discussed earlier, in an attempt to gain support of the Great Powers in redressing the balance, currently so unfavorable to them.

Greatly significant is the often-overlooked fact that Portugal has the strongest land forces existing in sub-Saharan Africa, which for the most part has only weak military forces. Metropolitan Portugal's army strength in 1968 totaled about 200,000, its navy consisted of 15,000, and its air force 13,500 men.[12] The Portuguese have, furthermore, shown themselves fully committed to using their military strength to defend their African interests. About 75 per cent of the army was committed in Africa during 1968. These forces were supplemented by police and security forces, which in Angola numbered well over 5,000 and in Mozambique over 8,000; in Portuguese Guinea, there were perhaps 14,000 additional African militiamen under arms. In contrast, the nationalists, even at the height of the Angolan insurgency, have never exceeded 7,500; in Mozambique they probably number about 5,000, and in Portuguese Guinea about 5,000.

The two largest military establishments among independent black African states belong to Ethiopia and Nigeria. Ethiopia has a regular army of approximately 40,000 men organized into three divisions of nine battalions each, an Imperial Bodyguard of divisional size, a tank battalion, a medium artillery battallion, and an airborne battalion. The air force has approximately 1,800 men in four fighter-attack squadrons and one transport squadron.[13]

The Nigerian armed forces have a strength of approximately 100,000 men organized into three divisions and several smaller separate units. The divisions have light field and anti-aircraft artillery and mortar support. There are also a limited number of light armored vehicles. The air force consists of a small number of MiG-15 and MiG-17 fighters and Ilyushin bombers, as well as transport aircraft.[14] Much of the present strength of the Nigerian armed forces has developed as a result of its current civil war. Neither its maintenance nor its use in the future can be accurately predicted.

Among nearby independent African states, there are no military forces comparable in size to those of Portugal. In 1965, Congo (Brazzaville) had armed forces estimated at no more than 700; in the same year, Congo (Kinshasa) had 35,400 regular forces, mostly of very poor military quality, and 15,000 police and security forces, none of them very reliable. The stabilization of recent years has led to some improvement in these Congolese forces, however.

Tanzania entered statehood with a small army of fewer than 1,350, with 5,000 police and security forces. Since the first African officers were not commissioned until 1961, and, until 1963, all officers over captain's rank were British, African military leadership in the Tanzanian army remains at a low level. When, in 1964, an army battalion mutinied against British officers, some 500 British Royal Marines brought in by helicopter from ships based at Aden[15] were able to restore order in a few hours. Since the mutiny a new army of 1,700 has been formed. No navy is maintained. The air force of 400 has exclusively transport aircraft.

Zambia, the country that feels most threatened by the white minority regimes of southern Africa, has been expanding its defense establishment. By late in 1968, however, it had an army of only 4,000, including 200 in the air force. A further 6,000 police were considered internal security forces. Concern for defense in 1968 led Zambia's President Kaunda to put first priority on the obtaining of ground-to-air defensive missiles and helicopters from Britain, Italy, or whatever other source would provide them. Furthermore, there were two RAF fighter-bomber squadrons based on Zambian territory in case of need in the Rhodesian crisis; they were perhaps more for show than for use.

Malawi's regular armed forces numbered only 1,000 in 1968, but internal security forces were 5,900. In 1965, Rhodesia had a regular army of 3,400, part-time forces in the region of 7,000, and internal security forces of 7,400, backed by strong reserves, all with a high level of efficiency. The Royal Rhodesian Air Force (RRAF), with many seasoned officers from World War II, is a strong force with about 80 planes; in 1965, they included 15 Canberra bombers, 12 Vampire fighter bombers, 12 supersonic Hawker Hunter fighters, and a reconnaissance squadron of Provosts. This air force, the largest in Africa, with the exception of Egypt's and South Africa's, and undoubtedly the most efficient for its size, would, in any coordinated campaign with Portugal, greatly enhance the capability of Portuguese ground forces. The growth of insurgency in Rhodesia in 1967 and 1968 led to an expansion of military preparedness and actual cooperation with South African defense forces.

South Africa has small regular forces, but with the Citizen Army and the Kommandos, it has the strongest potential military power south of the Sahara. There are only, 5,700 men in the regular army, but 22,000 men are in training in the Citizen Army. Including regulars, men in training, and men who have completed training, South Africa planned to have a total army strength of 60,000 men in 1969. With 3,000 men and 1,000 more in training, its expanding navy is already the largest in sub-Saharan Africa. It has two destroyers, six frigates, a survey ship, and several minesweepers and inshore vessels. Three Daphne class submarines are being built in France. The air force consists of 4,700 men, with 3,000 in training, eight squadrons of Citizen Air Force, and over 250 aircraft. There are 58,000 Kommandos, a militia consisting of infantry units, armored cars, and air squadrons having 250 nonmilitary privately owned aircraft.[16]

From the foregoing summary of military strength in Africa south of the Sahara, it is clear that, for the foreseeable future, Portugal, Rhodesia, and South Africa, acting together, would enjoy a strong military advantage over any force that opposing formations would be able to muster.

POLICY DILEMMAS

The withdrawal of colonial powers from Africa beginning in the 1950's brought immediate political changes on the world's horizons. Because of the dramatic expansion of U.N. membership, it soon became apparent that, should the newly independent African nations align themselves with the East rather than the West,

439

a rapid erosion of Western influence would occur. The choice for the principal Western powers then became clear: support the demands of the bloc of new African states or face increasing isolation in the United Nations.

Many of the rulers of the new countries of Africa, in spite of pressing domestic problems, have been interested in the "liberation" of the southern part of the continent. Their motivations are many, but in the forefront are emotions that "go deep to the level of loyalties, or racial pride, or very different perceptions of history and justice."[17] A December, 1960, resolution of the U.N. General Assembly insisted that "inadequacy of political, economic, social, or educational preparedness should never serve as a pretext for delaying independence." This resolution, vigorously promoted by new African states (and, for quite different reasons, by the Communist representatives in the U.N.), was followed by even more aggressive pronouncements from certain African leaders.

While Kwame Nkrumah and some others demanded immediate independence for all Portuguese Africa, more moderate leaders registered doubts (frequently off the record) about "independence now" for Portuguese Africa. At the meeting of the OAU held in Cairo in 1964, Dr. Banda of Malawi firmly and clearly stated his unwillingness to be involved in preventive action against Portugal and South Africa. Waldemar Nielsen noted in 1965 that "it would appear that the OAU, given its many problems, has moved Angola and Mozambique significantly downward in its list of priorities."[18]

Furthermore, as suggested in another chapter, there is evidence that Ben Bella's overextended support of liberation movements was one reason for his overthrow in June, 1965; the same may be true of Nkrumah's overthrow. On the other hand, although Banda has not changed his stand and has even established diplomatic relations with South Africa, both Nyerere of Tanzania and Kaunda of Zambia have grown increasingly hostile to the Portuguese presence in Africa. When they visited Kinshasa, the capital of the Congo, on Mobutu's invitation in June, 1966, they decided "to consolidate the front against South Africa."[19] The OAU also decided at its meeting in Kinshasa in September, 1967, to encourage African "freedom fighters" against white-ruled parts of southern Africa. The over-all strategy for them would be determined by a military committee of the OAU, with two-thirds of OAU's annual budget set aside to aid the struggle.[20]

However, it was reported that, in a closed door session of the OAU council of ministers in Addis Ababa in February, 1968, some of the delegates were not enthusiastic about increasing the credits of their Liberation Committee. One chief of delegation reportedly said that these funds "were going up in smoke," and another protested by claiming that the money was being spent in luxury hotels frequented by the leaders of the liberation movements.[21] The subsequent OAU meeting in Algiers, later in the year, reflected this critical feeling.

The United Kingdom and the United States, while disclaiming imperial interest in Africa, have sought to base their appeal to the new countries on the principles of disinterested economic aid and assistance in finding "the African way to development," a path neither wholly capitalist nor wholly socialist. The French have clearly been interested in furthering the cultural, political, and economic influence of France in their former colonies, and give development assistance through FIDES (Fonds d'Investissement pour le Développement Économique et Social). The Communist nations have sought to employ their standard appeal to the new nations by impugning the motives of the West and claiming that Western interests, far from being disinterested, are but a mask for the gradual repartitioning of the continent into neocolonialist spheres of interest. This was continuously harped on through Moscow radio broadcasts during U.S. Vice-President Hubert Humphrey's trip to Africa in January, 1968. For example, a broadcast on January 10, 1968, said: "It is plain from what the U.S. Vice-President said in the Africa House that the main aim of his trip is an attempt to find the ways and means to step up American neocolonial domination in Africa."[22]

Soviet and Communist Chinese Interests

The fundamental strategic interest of the Communist powers in Africa is a function of their quest for the expansion of their political, economic, and military influence. The character of Soviet interest, of course, differs in some respects from that of Communist China. The dissolution of NATO and the complete fractioning of West European political and economic unity has long been a basic Soviet objective. For the Soviet Union, Africa forms the southern flank of Europe. To the Chinese, Africa is a major area of the world in which to pit the colored against the white races and to pit the southern underdeveloped world against the northern industrial world. The evidence of the high priority they have given to Africa in their world strategy is found in their moves toward building the Tan-Zam Railway. Their actions may have spurred interests in Southern Africa to assist Congo (Kinshasa) in expanding its own rail network. Such a network would further lessen the economic viability of the Tan-Zam route.

Until 1965, when Peking suffered important setbacks in its attempts to gain influence in Africa, the mainland Chinese had concentrated on Africa's eastern shores. At first this was thought to be a function of the "international division of revolutionary labor," but, as the Sino-Soviet split widened, it became clear that it was because Peking saw the greatest potential gains in these African countries historically oriented toward Asia. For their part, the Russians also have shown great interest in eastern Africa by giving extensive arms aid and sending technicians to Somalia in the Horn of Africa and training its civil servants in the U.S.S.R. Most recently, aid has included MIG-15 and MIG-17 fighters.[23]

Especially in view of the setbacks in Africa suffered by the Chinese after 1965, it may seem unlikely that Communist powers will make important advances in Africa on the basis of rapid governmental upheavals. Nigeria provides one case illustrating increased Russian influence in the wake of a major disturbance. Western long-range planning must take into account the possibility that African governments may eventually become more influenced by Soviet and Chinese aid, or, in their unstable conditions, more vulnerable to radical charismatic leadership. Still-persisting racial discrimination in the West disenchants young Africans, the leaders of tomorrow, gives opportunities to the Communists, and weakens the pro-Western stand of moderate African leaders.[24]

Some of the African countries may simply become so anti-European or anti-NATO that major Western powers would be denied any use of their maritime or air facilities. In North Africa, the United States has been forced by Morocco to dismantle its extensive strategic air bases. As a result of the Middle East war of 1967, Libya had also asked the United States to remove its Wheelus Air Force Base but, in February, 1968, changed its decision. The other American installation that is left in Africa is the Kagnew Communications Center in Eritrea, Ethiopia, which has become a target of local political attack and controversy.

THE QUESTION OF SANCTIONS

With the Rhodesian Unilateral Declaration of Independence of 1965, the policy dilemmas involved in taking sides in sanctions against all or part of southern Africa became particularly acute for U.S. and U.K. decision-makers. The relatively small success of sanctions against Rhodesia led to strong demands by African leaders and others for "complete mandatory sanctions backed by threat of force" to prevent Portugal and South Africa from helping Rhodesia.[25] A spokesman for the Africans, President Kaunda of Zambia, asked for a "total blockade against Rhodesia" that would involve Portugal and South Africa "backed by the compulsory powers of the United Nations" in order to "bring South Africa and Portugal into line and 'crush' the Smith regime."[26] According to some who favor a total blockade, sanctions against Rhodesia cannot be successful while Rhodesia can get support from Portugal and South Africa. They think that "it is possible to enforce a tight blockade by controlling or immobilizing the communication lines between Rhodesia, South Africa, and Mozambique."[27]

There have also been demands for sanctions against South Africa because of (1) South Africa's refusal to surrender the government of South-West Africa established under the League of Nations mandate and (2) South Africa's policy of apartheid. Since these issues could lead to sanctions against South Africa, they have serious strategic and security implications for the Portuguese as well. Sanctions against South Africa could hardly be successful unless extended to Portuguese Africa, for the same reasons that made the sanctions against Rhodesia only partly successful.

In the South-West African crisis, the U.N. General Assembly adopted a resolution on October 27, 1966, recommending a take-over by the United Nations of the administration of South-West Africa and establishment of a committee to study means of including the use of force or economic sanctions against South Africa.[28] Adoption of sanctions has also been urged as a means of intervening in the South African racial situation.[29]

The range of actions advocated against South Africa, and perhaps against Rhodesia and Portuguese Africa, encompasses limited economic sanctions against one or several countries, total economic sanctions, and intervention by military force. For the time being, these proposals are more hypothetical than real in that, among other reasons, the major powers that would have to execute them are either opposed to them or unwilling to implement them. Waldemar Nielsen has noted that "for the United States to take a clear and steady stand against mandatory sanctions against South Africa will inevitably subject it to criticism and perhaps to some propaganda defeats. But any course other than rejection of such measures would be a violation of its own responsibilities as a world leader and contrary to the interest of its own citizens and of all mankind."[30]

The opposite case, nevertheless, is still argued in black Africa and among some influential writers on the United Nations, and therefore should be analyzed in practical terms. Any U.N. action on sanctions must be approved by the Security Council and is, therefore, in theory subject to veto by any one of the permanent members. The practice of expressing disapproval by abstaining rather than registering a negative vote, however, has made it easier to get a resolution passed by the Council. On the other hand, a Uniting for Peace Resolution of November 3, 1950, made it possible, in theory, for members to take action without the consent of the Security Council.

The application of sanctions in the form of an economic blockade against the countries involved would not necessarily be an act of war. A pacific blockade, by definition, obviously is not. The "Cuban Selective Interdiction and Quarantine" in 1962 was not an act of war, but, had it not been respected, it could have led to hostilities. Neither a unilateral nor a collective embargo or boycott is an act of war, because any nation has the sovereign right to control its international trade. Collective sanctions under Articles 39–41 of the U.N. Charter can be regarded as the use of force short of war but, unless accepted by the opposing side, may lead to hostilities. In southern Africa, to judge by the results of the sanctions against Rhodesia, economic sanctions, unilateral or collective, would probably require a tight sea and land blockade to be effective. This could well bring armed conflict.[31]

It has been argued that such a result could jeopardize the existence of the United Nations, financially and constitutionally. Furthermore, because of South Africa's self-sufficiency in almost all necessities except oil, which it has been heavily stockpiling, even a total blockade might not have decisive effect upon the South African economy for several years.[32] On the other hand, in view of the economic interdependence of the countries of southern Africa, a blockade of South Africa, if effective, would affect not only South Africa but also Angola, Mozambique, Rhodesia, Malawi, Zambia, Botswana, Lesotho, and Swaziland, causing hardship and deprivation in varying degrees. Zambia has already suffered from the sanctions against Rhodesia as "fuel shortcomings and transport limitations" have reduced its copper production.[33] Botswana, Malawi, and Congo (Kinshasa) have also suffered to such an extent that they felt forced to notify the United Nations that even their political structures might suffer as a result.[34]

What has been observed about South Africa applies throughout southern Africa: "When the blockade starts to hurt, the Africans will bear the first brunt. As it hurts more, the character of the regime, its economy breathing heavy, will grow sterner."[35] Far from averting violence by this economic strategy, "the world will have promoted violence: the violence of hunger, the violence of fear and hate."[36] Furthermore, the three former British protectorates—Botswana,

Swaziland, and Lesotho—whose economies are entirely dependent on South Africa, would have to be supplied by extensive airlift operations.

Collective embargoes have rarely been applied and, when applied, have rarely been effective.[37] An attempt to blockade South Africa, for example, could hardly be effective without the full cooperation of Portugal, unless, of course, the blockade was also extended to Mozambique and perhaps Angola. In that event, the decision would have to be taken whether or not to infringe upon Portuguese territorial waters, where Portuguese shipping moves along the African coastline, with far-reaching financial as well as military implications.[38]

It is inconceivable that Portugal would voluntarily join in any U.N. action against South Africa. Much of the economy of Mozambique is intimately tied to South Africa, and any interruption in normal economic relations between the two countries could cause a serious economic crisis in Lisbon. Moreover, South Africa is the most important military ally of Portugal in defense of African interests. It follows that Portugal would automatically reject involvement in any sanctions against South Africa and that those who proposed and implemented them, anticipating the Portuguese attitude, would have to urge that the sanctions be extended to Angola and Mozambique.

The economic vulnerabilities of Portuguese Africa under selective or total sanctions should therefore also be considered. Coffee would be the most obvious "limited sanction area" for Angola; and, in this connection, it has been reported that some consideration has been given in Luanda to the possibility, however remote, of Angolan coffee being refused on the world market.[39] In an earlier chapter it was noted that Angola vies for third place as a world coffee-producer, with annual sales of more than $120 million. Such sales could be drastically reduced, if not completely stopped.

Similar sanctions were attempted in the case of Rhodesian tobacco, but it continued to be sold at secret auctions, and a portion eventually found its way to British markets. Moreover, the experience of Rhodesia suggests that although sanctions and other such measures may hurt the economy of a country and impose much hardship on its population, they tend not to weaken but rather to strengthen the will to resist. Just as South Africa could rely on Portugal for assistance in evading the worst effects of sanctions, so could Portugal rely on South Africa, if the positions were reversed.

These observations on strategic considerations and contingencies lead to three conclusions. First, the United States and, to a lesser extent, the United Kingdom have had to recognize that Portugal controls certain strategic assets that are a constraining factor on diplomatic policy toward Portuguese Africa. Foreign Minister Franco Nogueira late in 1968 hinted that Portugal, in the future, might try to elicit Western support, both politically and economically, for its African policies, in return for the base agreements.[40]

Second, as of 1969, the balance of African military power lay decisively with the complex of white-controlled areas of southern Africa, and, third, the economic weapons of sanctions contained complicating factors that increasingly ruled them out by the two major powers.

NOTES

1. Joseph Palmer II, Assistant Secretary of State for African Affairs in a speech before the Chicago Council on Foreign Relations, December 5, 1968.
2. *Moscow News*, August 17–24, 1968.
3. J. E. Hartshorn, "Oil and the Middle East War," *The World Today*, April, 1968, p. 135.
4. *The New York Times*, June 25, 1967.
5. *Congressional Record*, 87th Cong., 2nd Sess., Vol. 108, Part I, p. 1126.
6. "Big Lift in Retrospect," *The New York Times*, November 20, 1963, p. 42.
7. *Congressional Record*, 88th Cong., 2nd Sess., p. 13994.
8. *Ibid.*, p. 1127 (remarks made at Washington press conference, January 24, 1962).
9. *Manchester Guardian*, September 11, 1964.
10. *United States–South African Relations*, Hearings Before the Subcommittee on Africa of the Committee on Foreign Affairs, House of Representatives, 89th Cong., 2nd Sess., Part I (March 1, 2, 3, 8, 10, 15, and 17, 1966), pp. 105–10; Part II (March 23, 24, and 30, 1966), p. 318.
11. Rudolf Gruber, "The Strategic Importance of the Cape," *Perspective*, August, 1967, pp. 4–5.
12. *The Military Balance, 1967–68* (London: The Institute for Strategic Studies, 1967), p. 26.
13. Unless otherwise noted, information on the size of African military establishments has come from S. H. Steinberg (ed.), *The Statesman's Year-Book, 1968-69* (London and New York, 1968).
14. The *Observer* (London), November 10, 1968, *The New York Times*, February 5, 1969, and April 3, 1969, and *The Washington Post*, April 24, 1969.
15. Helen Kitchen (ed.), *A Handbook of African Affairs* (New York, 1964), pp. 225–26. Corrections from Robert C. Sellers, *1966 Reference Handbook of the Armed Forces of the World* (Washington, D.C., 1966).
16. *The Times* (London), December 19, 1967.
17. Lincoln Bloomfield, *The United Nations and U.S. Foreign Policy* (Boston, 1967), p. 203.
18. Waldemar Nielsen, *African Battleline* (New York, 1965), p. 26.
19. Immanuel Wallerstein, "Penetrating the Continent," *The New Leader*, September 25, 1967, p. 7.
20. *The Christian Science Monitor*, September 20, 1967.
21. *Le Monde* (Paris), February 23, 1968.
22. Foreign Broadcast Information Service, *Daily Report*, January 11, 1968.
23. *The Military Balance, 1967–68*, p. 53.
24. *The New York Times*, June 27, 1967.
25. *The New York Times*, January 2, 1967.
26. The *Observer* (London), November 5, 1967.
27. Colin Legum, "Naught for Our Comfort on the Rhodesian Front," in *ibid.*, November 12, 1967.
28. For detailed information concerning the South-West African problem, see *United States–South African Relations*, Part III, pp. 394–97, and also "Issues before the 22nd General Assembly," *International Conciliation*, 564 (September, 1967), 59–65.

29. For detailed information on this subject, see two studies that openly and unequivocally urge the adoption of sanctions as a means of intervening in the South African situation; Colin and Margaret Legum, *South Africa: Crisis for the West* (London and New York, 1964), and Ronald Segal (ed.), *Sanctions Against South Africa* (London, 1964). A third study, Amelia C. Leiss (ed.), *Apartheid and the United Nations* (New York, 1965), prepared under the auspices of the Carnegie Endowment for International Peace in March, 1965, does not make policy recommendations, as do the first two, but discusses some of the practical implications entailed in the application of coercive measures. Another study, sponsored by the South African Foundation, *South Africa and United States Policy*, examines the question of sanctions from a South African perspective. A subcommittee of the United States House of Representatives has investigated the problem (*United States–South African Relations*). Also see "Issues Before the 20th General Assembly," *International Conciliation*, 554 (September 1965), pp. 94–101; United Nations, Doc. A/5957 (S/6605, August 16, 1965), Annex I; "Issues Before the 21st General Assembly," *International Conciliation*, 559 (September, 1966), pp. 113–19; "Issues Before the 22nd General Assembly," *International Conciliation*, 564 (September, 1967), pp. 103–7.

30. Nielsen, *op. cit.*, p. 86. As for the question of apartheid, in 1964 Ambassador Adlai Stevenson told the Security Council that the United States could not support "the concept of an ultimatum to the South African government which could be interpreted as threatening the application of coercive measures in the situation now prevailing, since in our view the Charter clearly does not empower the Security Council to apply coercive measures in such a situation." Thus the United States Government, although on record as being against the policy of apartheid, has rejected the contention that such a policy constitutes a "threat to the peace." Consequently, it is reasonable to conclude that the United States may not support any collective measures taken as a consequence of the internal political and racial policies of the South African Government.

31. *United States–South African Relations*, Part II, p. 318.

32. Even then, in the opinion of the British delegate to the United Nations, "a total economic boycott, if it could be adequately enforced, would have appreciable consequences for the South-African economy, but would fail to cripple it." S/6210, Annex VIII, p. 164.

33. *The Times* (London), February 28, 1968.

34. *The New York Times*, September 6, 1968.

35. Peter Ritner, "The Problem of Sanctions," *Commonweal*, May 28, 1965.

36. *Ibid.*

37. An embargo was invoked, belatedly, half-heartedly, and ineffectively, by the League of Nations against Italy for the invasion of Ethiopia. In the Korean War, the United Nations called on member states to put an embargo on strategic materials and many responded but with their own interpretation of what was strategic. British shipping to North Korea and China continued and was the subject of Congressional attacks in the United States. The industrial nations of Western Europe have refused to observe strategic control of trade with the Communist nations of Eastern Europe, China, North Vietnam, North Korea, and Cuba. A good example of the nonfeasibility of a collective embargo is the arms embargo imposed upon South Africa with several U.N. recommendations, one being the Security Council recommendation of June 18, 1964.

Although the United States and Great Britain, in spite of financial difficulties, have been enforcing it, other nations, notably France, have been supplying arms to South Africa since 1964.

38. Leiss, *op. cit.*, p. 109.
39. Andrew Borowiec, "Portugal Spurs Angola's Development," *Washington Evening Star*, October 20, 1966.
40. *The New York Times*, December 29, 1968.

XX

Emerging Policies and Alternatives

DAVID M. ABSHIRE

THREE WEEKS after 79-year-old Dr. Salazar was incapacitated by a stroke, President Américo Tomas of Portugal, on September 26, 1968, announced the appointment of Dr. Marcello Caetano as Prime Minister. Salazar's longstanding refusal to groom a successor allowed President Tomas freedom to act in accord with the constitutional provisions for naming a successor, and the three-week illness afforded time to confer with and align military and political leaders as well as gain the official approval of the council of state.

Some foreign observers had expected that the succession events, whenever they occurred, would involve factionalism, instability, and perhaps even a revolt that would shake Portugal from its unbending African policy. On the contrary, however, the elderly President Tomas acted with decisiveness, quickly brushed aside some right-wing military opposition, and presided over an orderly transition —a transition that was greeted calmly and almost with docility among the population in Portugal as well as in Portuguese Africa. Significantly, the position of chief of staff of the armed forces had been filled, in Salazar's last cabinet reshuffle, by General Venáncio Deslandes, who had been comparatively progressive as governor of Angola in 1962 and had later been ambassador to Spain. Deslandes was retained in the new government.

Professor Caetano, like Professor Salazar, is a product of the university world, but he had also formerly been a newspaper reporter. He had served as overseas minister. In 1959, he had been relieved of his position as minister of state because of his persistence in pushing for a law to reform press censorship. In 1962, he resigned as rector of the University of Lisbon in protest over police intervention in student riots. Unlike his predecessor, he had traveled widely, and his directorship in several companies had given him contact with the business community and, no doubt, its support in the power transfer.

In the opening weeks of the new government, Caetano indicated that he would liberalize censorship and the corporate state, to a degree at least. Some concrete actions followed. A liberal lawyer, Mário Soares, a critic of the regime, was returned from exile in São Tomé. For the first time university students were to be allowed to elect their own representative committees. Likewise, members of the government-sponsored trade-union syndicates were to elect their own officials, rather than have them appointed by the government.

But Caetano's pronouncements on African policy made it clear that the new

448

government would continue the commitment to Portuguese rule in Africa, and certainly his acceptance of this policy was the precondition of his acceptance as prime minister. In speaking to the Portuguese National Assembly on November 27, 1968, Caetano asserted that Salazar's African policy was the only one possible to the Portuguese nation:

> Could the Portuguese watch impassively the savage destruction of civilized life? . . . Could the Portuguese let racial hostility grow and a chasm develop between two ethnic groups whose ability to live and collaborate together intimately are indispensable to the progress of southern Africa? . . . The territories are going to mature to full economic and cultural development so as to permit the progressive participation of natives in the responsibilities of administration and government.

This reference to natives, however, broke a recent tradition of not referring to Africans separately from other citizens. Caetano denied any alliance, written or otherwise, with South Africa or Rhodesia, because of the "distinct racial policies, and it is known how much we are determined to proceed on and perfect our policy of non-discrimination and of frank conviviality."[1]

Despite the stress on unbending continuity in African policy, the end of the Salazar era in Portugal provides a base from which to view the prospects for change in Portuguese Africa. It is important first to assess what the events from 1961 to 1968 had meant in terms of Portuguese rule.

From Salazar to Caetano

The Salazar government, climaxing the Portuguese experience of almost 500 years in Africa, had defied the "winds of change" in its determination to stay, to fight as necessary, to govern, and to consider the overseas provinces as part of Portugal itself. In some ways, this attitude was an enigma. The wealthy industrialized European powers that could perhaps have afforded the cost of staying had all left. At least until the mid–1960's, Portuguese Africa had not been economical for the metropole. Any concept of an imperialistic Portuguese Government's successfully exploiting its African possessions in the past century for economic advancement is a myth, even though many individual Portuguese benefitted. Traditionally, Portugal has invested more in Africa than it has received, bankrupting itself in the process. Recently, Portugal has borne defense costs, part of which otherwise could have gone into its own development, and certainly its commitment of administrative and managerial talent to Africa robs the metropole. Yet Portugal's African commitment is not measured by the Portuguese in cost-benefit terms.

The Portuguese case contrasts with that of the Belgians in the Congo. According to Oliver and Atmore, "The independence of the Congo was in fact far from being a triumph of African nationalism. It was, rather, a result of Belgian irresolution, and of the inability of a small country like Belgium to stand up to international pressures."[2] The Belgian case, of course, involved a liberal democracy with free debate on African policy, something Portugal lacks.

Similar international pressure against Portugal had indeed been enormous. Yet, gripped by the strong hand of Salazar for 40 years, most of the Portuguese ruling classes, much of the business class, and a large segment of the common people became resolute in their self-styled mission in Africa, despite both the international pressures and local insurgency. As recently as 1962, there had been discussions within the government about the ways in which Angola could be brought to independence, or at least to full political maturity within the Portuguese state. As Pedro Theotónio Pereira, the Portuguese ambassador to the United States, publicly stated at that time,

> We hope to develop these provinces, to raise the standard of living, and to use their rich resources in the interest of all. We are, however, determined that self-determination must be a process of political evolution from within and must rest in the hands of the people concerned and not with outside terrorists and agitators.[3]

Many Portuguese have always envisioned that their African possessions might break away eventually, as Brazil did in 1822. But they envisioned independence as a goal to be reached only after the mature development of their multiracial societies as Portuguese communities, and certainly not under threat of force from any quarter—internal or external. They constantly revived the analogy of Brazil, while ignoring the difference in their demographic situations. Plainly, Brazil's peoples are mostly of European or African-slave ancestry, while Portuguese Africa's peoples are mostly of indigenous African ancestry.

Westerners from the liberal democracies viewed the course of independence quite differently from the Portuguese. In 1961 and 1962, some British and American diplomats expected that independence would take place as in the Congo or as in Kenya and that, in some way, this independence would be guided by a one-man one-vote pattern. In their minds, there was little doubt that the new government would be black, as in the Congo and Kenya. There was a strong hope that the new government would have the vision to ensure a congenial place for the Portuguese who make up most of the skilled part of the population of Portuguese Africa. Portugal was expected to play a caretaker role, and, for this, the Kennedy Administration made a promise of aid. It certainly must have been envisioned that Great Britain and the United States would give the needed underwriting for the United Nations to play an additional peace-keeping role during a period of transition.

After 1962, the emphasis of liberal Western diplomats shifted away from a push toward immediate independence. President Kennedy himself made a shift in attitude about a year before his death. The new approach, obviously influenced by events in the Congo, called for a Portuguese declaration of intent for offering independence within a stated period of time. A five- or ten-year period was often mentioned, but the stress was upon having a fixed timetable at the end of which there would presumably be a plebiscite.

The Portuguese argued that it would be political suicide for them to talk in terms of a fixed timetable for departure. They reasoned that a rich Britain or France could talk of such timetables in their decolonization, but not a poor

Portugal, and not even a Belgium that moved a timetable from ten to five years, and then, once it became a lame-duck power, to six months. The reasoning was that, once a government has announced that it may depart, all those who look to it for protection may "trim their sails," and soon it will have no supporters at all. The withdrawing power can become locked in a pattern of uncontrollable events as new political forces vie for power.

Added to this Portuguese view was a political problem in Portugal itself. If ever Salazar or his successors believed that Portugal should or must give up political control of Portuguese Africa, it would have been difficult to announce openly that such control would terminate at a given date in the future, so enormous would be the political impact in Portugal. A Portuguese soldier will not fight and die, a Portuguese tax-payer will not tolerate more taxes, and a Portuguese peasant will not see hospitals better in Africa than in his village, if it is announced that in a few years hence the object of such sacrifices will no longer be Portuguese. Even an authoritarian government depends upon a measure of public participation and support. Ironically, the greater the conflict in Portuguese Africa, the more difficult it became for the Portuguese freely and rationally to discuss options for Angola and Mozambique, although Portuguese Guinea may be an exception to this observation.[4]

A result of the fighting that began in 1961 and of the diplomatic attack from the international community was the development of a heightened nationalism and a sense of involvement that Salazar would not have imposed earlier. Yet, what had happened was not out of character with Portugal's response to the challenge to its overseas ambitions, represented by the British ultimatum of 1890, an ultimatum that created not only anger and resentment but an awareness of its possessions that was previously lacking. We have seen, in an earlier chapter, that the turn-of-the-century threat to the colonies and what the Portuguese considered the duplicity of their traditional ally, Great Britain, sparked the very energies and determination that made possible the overseas development of the decades before World War I. The 1961 challenge of what the Portuguese took as an external invasion, along with decolonization demands from the international community, involved, for the first time, not only the governing class or the economic elite but much of the Portuguese nation, in defense of a new nationalism that turned out to be more militant and active than black nationalism in Angola. Between 1961 and 1968, thousands of Portuguese from the streets of Oporto, Coimbra, and Lisbon and from the fields of the Ribatejo and the Algarve for the first time gained a firsthand experience in the African possessions for which they previously had cared little.

Whatever the extent of the increased national ideology for continued commitment to rule in Africa, there were, of course, countervailing psychological factors as well. There were people who felt that their sons were fighting to save a fever-ridden, worthless territory—Portuguese Guinea. Some student groups and intellectuals also showed antiwar sentiment. Mário Soares publicly called for a change in overseas policy, although even his proposed decolonization was to take place well in the future. On New Year's day, 1969, 150 Catholics in a Lisbon church staged a five-hour peace vigil to call for peace in Portuguese

Africa.[5] There was certainly a chance, still small as of early in 1969, that such discontent could spread to become disruptive of the national commitment.

The continuing overseas war had other very practical, unplanned, and unanticipated consequences in Portugal. First, increased military manpower requirements were the initial reason (followed, of course, by migration to Europe) for Portugal's moving from an underemployed to an overemployed economy. Thus, the forcing up of unduly low urban wages benefitted morale and induced pressures for agricultural reform and factory modernization. Until about 1965, when a labor shortage began to appear, due particularly to the large migration to West Europe, the war in Africa brought, on balance, more benefits than liabilities for the economy of Portugal.

Second, and far more important, the African war expanded the Portuguese army four times in size since the war's outbreak. Inevitably, the army became committed to staying in Angola and Mozambique (Portuguese Guinea being another matter) for some very personal reasons: Soldiers serving in Africa received much higher pay than those who served in the metropole, and many built up savings, while others became involved in business activities there. The military expansion also brought perquisites and advantages to the officers in higher ranks.

This same army, along with the police, ultimately controls the balance of power in Portugal. Not surprisingly, the acceptance by the military of President Tomas' appointment of Marcello Caetano in September, 1968, came after Caetano showed a willingness to continue the defense of Angola and Mozambique. Thus, it is not an exaggeration to say that at the time of Salazar's passing from power, the institutionalized commitment of Portugal to rule in Africa was greater than at any time in its recent history.

Another striking change in national attitude and determination took place among the Portuguese white population in Angola and Mozambique. Before 1961, they were becoming increasingly restless and resentful toward Lisbon. Some manifested a growing desire to declare their own independence. The overseas territories seemed to claim only a low, second priority in Lisbon, and the vast development schemes of Norton de Matos and others seemed a vanished dream. Salazar himself had never visited the overseas territories. Dissatisfaction, particularly in the Benguela area, was sharpening. PIDE, the secret police, first appeared in Africa to watch disloyal whites more than Africans.

After 1961, with the continuing warfare and unsettled conditions elsewhere in Africa, the attitude among the white population changed. A vast majority concluded that a continuation of Portuguese rule was necessary. Such a conclusion was further facilitated by the fact that overseas development, their major concern, had been shifted by Salazar himself to primary rather than secondary priority. The change of attitude also resulted from the large numbers of Portuguese troops whose very presence legislated against any precipitous activities by Europeans. The passing of Salazar led to some questioning of the possible orientation of the European Portuguese in Africa, but such questioning was directed only to the contingency of Lisbon's faltering in its determination to stay in Angola and Mozambique.

452

Although the war hardened the Portuguese will to stay in Africa, it did accelerate changes in other ways. Of course, many of the political reforms that came after the debates of 1962 had previously been in the making. A major innovator was the scholarly, reform-minded Adriano Moreira, who had become overseas minister a year before the beginning of the insurgency. The government began to strengthen its economic ties in Europe, with new views of trade and investment. (The Carmona-Salazar government had come to power in 1928, in part on a policy of not accepting outside financing to bail Portugal out of its bankruptcy.)

In 1959, the government took a momentous step: It joined EFTA. Two years later came a change in Portugal's economic policies toward its African territories. Dr. Teixeira Pinto, noted for his writings about the need for outside investment and loans, was made economic minister. Younger economists, such as Vasco Cunha d'Eça and Xavier Pintado, deeply influenced by the need to abandon medieval economics and to modernize, worked their influence in and out of government. The de Mello family of CUF (Companhia União Fabril), the corporate giant that dominates Portugal, and the leaders of the large Portuguese companies overseas, such as Queiroz Pereira and Jorge Jardim, moved toward more dynamic development policies, under the influence of increasing business contacts with developed countries. New sets of policies and, even more important, new attitudes were forthcoming in development planning. The long-held Salazarian policy of excluding foreign capital and relying on scarce Portuguese capital began to diminish. At long last, the modernization of Portugal became possible, owing to this turnabout in economic policy, both in the metropolitan area and overseas. The Caetano government indicated an even greater receptivity to foreign investment. Significantly, Caetano gave the key post of minister of state to one of the most modern-minded of Portuguese businessmen, Dr. Alfredo Vaz Pinto, formerly chairman of the Portuguese airline TAP. Especially with the new attitudes and the discovery of new iron-ore and oil resources, the near future offered the hope for an Angola and a Mozambique that could carry their own defense burdens and offer a profit. In the more distant future, the overseas economy could become more important than that of the metropole.

THE AFRICANS

But what of the attitudes of the Africans? They, not the whites, make up 97 per cent of Portuguese Africa. They were there before the Portuguese arrived nearly five centuries ago and their well-being and rights should be the ultimate concern. Otherwise there can be no semblance of increasingly representative government in Portuguese Africa, where the vast majority is black.

Much of that vast majority of the population was not involved in the revolutionary movements and remained rather apolitical. Like the lower-class Portuguese in the metropole, they were not politically attuned or sharply affected economically. It is, of course, impossible to gauge accurately non-white opinion in Portuguese Africa. But, on the other hand, one can note that increasing numbers of the African population began to participate in social, cultural, and

453

economic changes. An acceleration of modernization was an obvious new force, particularly in terms of urbanization, the broadening of a limited consumer market, improved agricultural techniques, and widespread educational opportunities for the young.

In any developing society, tensions increase: the field-worker decides he prefers the factory before job openings occur; people from the country move to the cities and end up in slums, away from traditional tribal structure and with a lost sense of identity. Many of those in the bush resent new methods of agriculture and the invasion of technicians into their traditional surroundings. And in Portuguese Africa, particularly, many resent Europeans who hold petty jobs that they themselves desire. The hand of a paternalistic society hung heavy over all, but control of the media and elimination of politics did much to hold rising expectations more in line with opportunities.

The lack of party politics delayed the development of local political leaders and resulted in a certain political docility among the African population. At the same time, conflicts among different tribes were held in abeyance, in contrast to the continuing conflicts between the various nationalist movements in Portuguese Africa and within independent states such as Nigeria, the Sudan, and the Congo. Especially in Angola, there was a steady movement toward over-all unity, interdependence, and cohesiveness. In short, many Africans also benefitted by the events of the 1960's, through an increasingly rapid economic development combined with continued stability free from tribal conflict. There were nowhere the blood baths or ethnic conflicts of Nigeria or the Sudan nor the conflicts known earlier in the Congo.

In exchange for this externally imposed peace and order, those who were more politically attuned continued to be denied the exhilaration of the politics of independence. Thus, African initiative was stifled, and the Africans did not develop their own full measure of self-reliance. As W. P. Kirkman, writing about Rhodesia, has noted, "the desire to run one's own affairs is a natural human instinct, not just an African quirk, and it is not determined or diminished by economic consideration."[6] James Duffy, in 1962, argued that "there can be no easy answer to the problems of Portuguese Africa. Independence may not itself be the answer, but there will be no satisfactory answer without it."[7] It is indeed true that, over the world, black men are seeking black solutions to their problems, and there has risen a resentment of the white man's attempted answers, even of his economic benefits, if such can in any way be identified with colonialism or neocolonialism. In Africa, such an attitude relates to black identity and a lingering bitter resentment of the bygone slave trade, past practices of forced labor, and the period of foreign domination.

Robert Gardiner, distinguished Ghanaian head of the U.N. Economic Commission, emphasized to this author that Africa is for the Africans, and the Portuguese will not be Africans. So long as there is an idea of a "civilizing mission," some pattern is being imposed from the outside, and this is implicit paternalism. At the same time, he notes that there are differing viewpoints among African leaders. President Banda of Malawi, adjacent to Mozambique and within the South African economic orbit, believes in economic cooperation, rather than isolation, throughout southern Africa, and believes that the economic development in Portuguese Africa now benefits Malawi. He explains his position to other black African diplomats by asserting that the railroads of Mozambique will eventually be African, so that all economic development and interdependence is to be encouraged. Some Africans of former British Africa are resentful of the many ways—cultural, economic, and even military—that states of former French Africa have maintained their ties with the former metropole. To them, an independent Angola and Mozambique could, if independence evolved under the aegis of Portugal, offer a similarly distasteful situation.

It is quite appropriate, therefore, that Victor Ferkiss has observed that the future of Portuguese Africa poses the question of African identity more clearly than has any former colonial territory. This would be true, he says, even if Angola and Mozambique were to become independent while yet forming part of a Lusitanian cultural community, an action that would conflict with the spirit of pan-Africanism: "The very ties of culture which might bind an interracial Angola and Mozambique together and to extra-African countries would be a rejection of most of what is symbolized by *négritude* and the African personality." Ferkiss notes that "independent states of black Lusitanians, states based not on traditional African cultural bonds but on a universalistic mystique, run counter to African cultural nationalism."[8] African nationalists could not easily accept this situation, which clashes with their goals, and an independent Angola and Mozambique could be torn apart "not only by racial, social, and tribal divisions but by a conflict between those seeking to reinstate purely African identifications and those opting for a nation primarily nonwhite in race but consciously Western in culture."[9]

FUTURE ALTERNATIVES

This leads to the consideration of alternative political prospects for these entities. There are, at least theoretically, several possibilities: independence under African rule; continuation of the present system, with political control resting in European Portugal; an autonomous but multiracial rule; and a loose commonwealth arrangement, either in the form of an independent Euro-African Lusitanian republic or in federation with Portugal.

No one can accurately predict the character of African rule, but it affords some insight to examine the attitudes and forecasts of some of the nationalist leaders. The leader of the most active nationalist movement in Guinea, which has the least concentration of whites of any of the provinces, is a *mestiço*. Amilcar Cabral, probably the most able of the revolutionary leaders, speaks as a Cape Verdian in terms not necessarily acceptable to other Guineans. Cabral's attitudes contain a stronger ideological content than those of most other revolutionary leaders in Portuguese Africa, and he has significant affiliations with the international Communist movement, as evidenced by his appearances at the Cercle Frantz Fanon of Milan and the Tri-continental Conference of Havana. He has also been influenced by the writings of Régis Debray, although Debray's thesis runs counter to Cabral's.[10]

455

In contrast to Cabral, Benjamin Pinto Bull, headquartered in Dakar, is much more oriented toward the political attitudes of French-speaking Africa, and he apparently would envision a socialistic, non-Marxist state along the lines of Senegal. John Marcum writes:

> Pinto Bull and his associates are gambling that if Lisbon is forced by rising taxes, casualties, and common sense to come to terms with African nationalism, it will hand over power to men with whom it could most easily create a Portuguese version of the Francophone Organization Commune Africaine et Malgache.[11]

It is unlikely, however, that Lisbon would negotiate the turnover of power to any opposition group, as to do so would be an act of betrayal to the Africans who had fought with the Portuguese. In fact, the most consistent Portuguese allies in Guinea are the Fula, who would be unable to defend themselves without outside assistance.

In the case of Benjamin Pinto Bull, it is possible to conceive of negotiations for a coalition arrangement. It is interesting to note that his brother, Jaime Pinto Bull, has served as secretary-general of Guinea as well as in the Lisbon legislature, even though he later resigned as secretary-general over "broken promises."

One might question the possibility for survival of an independent Guinea-Bissau under any terms. Though Gambia does provide a precedent of a tiny, still-existing West African state, at the present time a merging of the two Guineas, or a conflict between Senegal and Guinea over Guinea-Bissau, seems more likely. The fact that Cabral is a *mestiço* but not a native Guinean could make him a target for internal dissension. A further unsettling factor is the historic tribal conflict. The problem of tribal peace has been exacerbated by recent fighting. The Fula fear that a Portuguese withdrawal would expose them to the kind of gross reprisals that befell the Ibo in Nigeria, the Tutsi in Ruanda, and the Fouta Djalon in Guinea (Conakry). Clearly, any picture suggests an instability that might not be any less a decade or two hence than it is now.

It is for Mozambique that the most clearly stated future direction has been outlined by a nationalist leader. Before his death, Eduardo Mondlane planned that an "independent Mozambique will be a democratic, modern, unitary, single-party state. Our model is the neighboring Tanzania"[12] He went on to say that "we do not intend to be either a capitalist or communist, but rather a socialist state." This means that a new government led by the FRELIMO of Mondlane would correct the policy of "selling many of the concessions to private foreign companies. . . . The natural resources of the country—the land, the minerals, and everything that God has given this country—should belong to its people, not to foreigners." Mondlane's contention was that another reason for an independent Mozambique to embrace state socialism was that private ownership means private capital: the native people of his Mozambique "have no capital, none whatsoever," they would have no chance to inherit any from the Portuguese, and thus "what is available is the state. The state will have control of all natural resources, and the people will invest their energies in the activities of the state." Any private interest would have to deal with the socialist state.[13]

There are, however, difficult obstacles to FRELIMO's achieving success. When the insurgency began in 1964, Mondlane sought a Mozambique-wide effort, but this did not succeed. Although FRELIMO elites represent a geographical and tribal diversity, fighting elements became restricted principally to Makonde and Nyanja. Thus, Mondlane became entangled in a tribal situation that tended to make enemies of other tribes, and the pro-FRELIMO support from the Makonde and the Nyanja was far from ideal in that both were border tribes rather than from the Mozambique heartland. There are no indications that FRELIMO yet represents a true Mozambican nationalism that would be attractive to a majority of the population.

FRELIMO's best hope had been that Lisbon would weary of the economic or political cost of its efforts. By 1969, however, there had developed a new contingency that South Africa and Rhodesia might fill any void left by the departure of Portugal. The strategic realities indicate that any abdication of Lisbon rule would result in South African power filling the vacuum, perhaps along with Rhodesia. If Lisbon were to do what now appears inconceivable— negotiate a transfer of power to FRELIMO at the time of Portugal's departure— the white Mozambicans might initiate a unilateral declaration of independence (UDI) and invite South Africa and Rhodesia to come to their defense. The Cabora Bassa hydroelectric power scheme suggests that these two countries would be willing to assume the burden of defense, at least south of the Zambezi line. Barring the total collapse of South African and Rhodesian power, it is thus improbable that most of Mozambique in the foreseeable future could come under the control of a government hostile to these powers. On the other hand, as both Edwin S. Munger and Larry W. Bowman have correctly observed, South Africa can well abide a protective cushion of black-ruled states economically dependent on it, like Malawi, Lesotho, and Botswana and can even have greater advantages than from white-ruled states that attract conflict.[14]

The Angolan situation perhaps offers problems still different from those of Mozambique or Portuguese Guinea. Holden Roberto speaks from a Bakongo tribal base, and the organizational structure of his GRAE shows this. Thus, there has been a tendency to project an overlay of Bakongo desires on all Angola. He demands immediate independence and opposes any "veiled or disguised integration with the Portuguese."[15]

The general character of the model Angolan state of the major nationalist movements would appear to be first anti-Portuguese and then socialistic. As in the case of Mozambique, the principles, means, and capital for economic development would be different from present policies, or even from future policies under an independent but pro-Portuguese Angola. This latter possibility has gained increased encouragement among Western officials.[16] Of course, one must allow for the fact that the most militant of leaders could change after independence, as did Dr. Hastings Kamuzu Banda of Malawi.

Angola is already much more of a nation than Mozambique, but the fabrics of nationhood are more Luso-African than black African. Yet it could be that

457

beneath these fabrics Angola may be more seriously split ethnically. Of special significance, however, is Angola's *mestiço* population, which in its character and attitudes, carries an influence out of all proportion to its numbers. Moreover, a unifying Angolan black nationalism has not developed. The insurgency has been heavily affected by the continuation of tribal loyalties. As discussed earlier, a precipitate withdrawal of the Portuguese presence would be likely to result in tribal antagonisms and, possibly, civil war. The Ovimbundu might stand as the centralist group, opposed to the regionalists who have some of their roots outside Angola. Neighboring states would exert influence over border groups such as Zambia, the Chokwe, Congo, and Bakongo, and South Africa and the southern part of Angola. For the latter, there is indeed a historical precedent, since, in 1878, the white settlers of Moçâmedes requested annexation by the English Government. A similar situation may arise now that the South African Government's commitment to the Cunene development project has increased its economic strategic interest in southern Angola.

Over the longer term, one can postulate for Angola, even more than for Mozambique, a possible process of gradualism leading to multiracial independence. Especially in the Benguela area and in some of the northern coffee areas, there is a nascent black middle class. In Angola, although not in Mozambique, Africans have begun to enter the professions. These and other groups may tend to be cognizant of the stake they have in a continuation of the present type of economic development and the need for technical assistance from Brazil and Portugal. If the nationalist leaders do not achieve more success, they might modify their policies in a pragmatic deal with some of the whites, *mestiços*, and blacks in the establishment. Any such scenario would, of course, be ruled out by a rapid increase of insurgency that exacerbated tribalism and that further increased the control of the Portuguese army over the Angolan governmental and political structure.

Local Control or Gradual Semiautonomy

The preceding discussion about gradualism raises the possibility of a more abrupt development of a white UDI. There was some speculation about this contingency after Rhodesia's UDI. Could a government in the post-Salazar era alter Portuguese resolve to the point where local groups might suddenly declare independence for Angola and Mozambique? After all, many whites now feel more Angolan and Mozambican than European Portuguese; their interests and homes are no longer in the metropole. Localism and particularism in the military and administration had been limited, however, by the policy of the Salazar regime of not allowing officials to remain in one position or province for long. Thus, if a person gained local popularity, he was transferred, as was the popular governor, Venáncio Deslandes, in 1962.

Will the presence of the army, ostensibly fighting African nationalist insurgency, prevent unilateral actions by local white residents? Some observers have argued that such an army, in the wake of any instability in Portugal, might incite, rather than prevent, such actions. A more plausible possibility, however, would be a realization in Lisbon that increased economic interest in Europe would mean decreased importance for Africa. This might result in Lisbon's deciding that it would be to its advantage to move toward some sort of confederation—with or without complete independence as the goal. Such a confederation will be impossible until there is widespread use of the Portuguese language, however. As education spreads both language and literacy, the option of a Portuguese community becomes more feasible.

This type of confederation would differ from Rhodesia, by being bilateral rather than unilateral. Another important difference from Rhodesia would be the complexion of the government itself. It is unlikely that such a government would be a typical white minority one, because the Portuguese racial legacy is so different from that of other colonial powers. Nor would it follow the tradition of Kenya or Congo (Kinshasa). Rather, the group which would evolve, though possibly subordinated to certain economic interests, would more likely be multiracial, with *mestiços* playing an important role and Africans increasingly having some share in power.

A last possibility is the continuation in some form of the "one nation" concept. If this were to be successful administratively and economically, it still would demand an increase in the present centrifugal direction of evolving, little by little, toward semiautonomy, with greater decentralized, decision-making, and local initiative. Of course, one might assume that the Portuguese over the next few decades could maintain their African presence, if necessary by force, in the face of rapidly rising nationalism. In this situation, aid could come from Rhodesia and South Africa. But Portugal's strength in Africa—its staying power—is in part built around the conviction that the majority of the population is either with Portugal or neutral and not in active opposition. In all probability, Portugal could not sustain a repeat of Algeria and struggle against an actively discontented majority. Many Portuguese now admit their surprise, in 1961, when insurgency did not become an Angola-wide revolt. Had such been the case, Portugal would have been forced out.

By 1969, it was very evident that the Portuguese officials recognized, more than ever, that there was no purely military answer to defeating the guerrillas and that ultimate success could lie only in offering more benefits than the nationalists and in winning the minds of the Africans, who are bound to become less docile as the years go by.

RISING EXPECTATIONS

What of the 1970's, with the rising expectations of the African population? Certainly the benefits offered to the Africans will increase, but so also will the demands of the Africans increase. Will these people really choose to be black Portuguese and loyal citizens? Can the Portuguese assimilate this population enough to retain its support? Dom Sebastião Soares de Resende, late the bishop of Beira, predicted that, early in the 1970's the full impact of the educational revolution would begin to be felt among the Africans. That will be the time of testing. Only then will questions and problems of assimilation have meaning.

The magnitude of the Portuguese problem with assimilation should be viewed in comparison to the French experience, because imperial France had a similar policy aim. Michael Crowder has written that

> the French found themselves quite unable to pursue a full-scale policy of assimilation in their African territories. Indeed the difficulties and above all the costs of applying such a policy, which if pursued to its logical conclusion would have involved the political, cultural, and economic assimilation of twenty million Africans to the same standards enjoyed by the metropolitan French, led to its abandonment everywhere except in the *quatre communes* in Senegal.[17]

The Portuguese have progressed further constitutionally with their assimilation policy than did the French, whose postwar policy extended only to the four communes in Senegal. They also have progressed further than the French in convincing themselves of its workability as well as their "mission" in Africa. Moreover, Angola and Mozambique are moving into a time of dynamic economic development.

As for the future, Portugal's staying power may well depend on a new efficiency that can only be the product of greater decentralization and more local initiative involving whites and blacks in the political and administrative structures of Angola and Mozambique. Paradoxically, General Deslandes, chief of staff in Lisbon during the Salazar–Caetano transition, was the great advocate of precisely this kind of decentralization when he was governor-general of Angola in 1962.

Might the post-Salazar governments take decisive steps to Africanize part of the government in Lisbon? Might a future regime even consider moving the capital, or at least the legislative branch, to Luanda? Or, perhaps give political reality to an already aptly named "Nova" Lisboa? As for the possibilities of a new Portuguese government's pursuing such steps, one must not underrate the future influence not only of senior officials like Caetano and Deslandes who know Angola and Mozambique firsthand, but of the younger ones who have served in specialized positions in Africa and returned to the Overseas Ministry in Lisbon, and whose future influence could be decisive.

As for the governmental bureaucracy, many of the Africans currently filling positions are *mestiços* These could become mistrusted by black Africans. Can the filling of positions by black Africans be accelerated as educational advance makes them available? In any event, a vast Africanization of the government may well be necessary if the Portuguese are to have long-range staying power in Africa during the turbulent times ahead when confronted with a new generation of Africans.

The problem is not solely that of governmental policy. A further factor will be the attitudes of the private sector of Portuguese businessmen. Will the large private companies encourage the educating and training of Africans as well as absorbing them and giving them important responsibilities in supervisory and management positions? Diamang, for example, has 30,000 black employees.

Meanwhile, an increase in the number of European settlers who are in direct economic competition with the Africans may create increasing racial tension.[18]

Will dangers of a racial backlash be recognized and avoided in Portuguese Africa? If not, the present direction of development toward a nonracist society could be reversed. Lisbon serves now as a restraining influence on the Europeans who fear African competition and desire to change Portuguese official policy.

Much will depend upon how the Portuguese handle internal situations as the conflict continues. The most counterproductive action the Portuguese Government could take, if insurgency were to become more widespread, would be to overuse the secret police and to institute repressive measures of the type that governments generally tend toward, especially as a means of gaining vital intelligence information. During the peak of any emergency, such as that in Angola in March, 1961, ruthless measures may be practiced for internal security, without proper police restraint. Terror begets terror, reprisal leads to counter-reprisal, until the innocent are victimized and brutality increases on both sides—as part of the classical course of revolution and guerrilla warfare.[19] The Portuguese officials have recognized the adverse and dire consequences of their more repressive actions in the early years of the war, and even PIDE is now being used, in part, to convince Africans in northern Mozambique, for example, that even supporters of FRELIMO are well treated when they fall into Portuguese hands.[20]

Another Portuguese strength under the Salazar regime, in contrast to some earlier Portuguese regimes, was the existence of a strong, noncorrupt governmental structure along with the relative ability, in Angola and Mozambique, to provide the population security and protection in turn for its loyalty, or at least its nonopposition. There has been an effective authority structure; it can even be argued that the undemocratic and hierarchical nature of the government has served as an advantage in the insurgency situation. The strong hand of Lisbon also has served as a restraint on repressive measures of the type in evidence at the outbreak of the fighting in Angola.

When Marcello Caetano came to power in September, 1968, there were indications that the new government would take definite steps in the direction of true reform. What the new direction of 1968 will mean for Portuguese Africa remains to be seen. Despite the fact that Portugal is bearing the burden of the war without undue strain, it does cost an amount that could otherwise be available for economic development. The war has several other effects, one already noted: it hinders the dialogue that could soften the more rigid Portuguese attitudes and lead to an evolution toward self-determination as well as more immediate decentralization, along the lines once formulated by Caetano and Deslandes during the Salazar regime. Then, too, the war perpetuates an abnormally large centralized military establishment, and it distracts Portugal from turning her attention to self-modernization, in which integration into the European economy might take precedence over holding on to the African possessions.

Constructive Change

Time will be needed to bring the entities of Portuguese Africa to the political goals that free men wish for them. If one goal is constructive political change, the question arises of how best to achieve it. In the preceding chapter, attention

461

was given to certain proposals to try to produce political change in southern Africa by military force or by sanctions. George Ball rejects both as impractical and counterproductive and, therefore, subscribes to the same policy he proposes vis-à-vis the Soviet Union: to try to open doors rather than close them, to create contact rather than isolation, to broaden rather than rigidify the attitude of the ruling group, and to give more liberal elements within it a chance to build influence. Ball has emphasized the need to distinguish among the various entities in southern Africa, by stressing that "that area is not a monolith."[21]

Many experienced diplomats like Ball question whether the present liberation movement leaders, when so divided among themselves, could and would offer to Portuguese Africa truly free representative government. Tribal warfare and economic recession resulting from the withdrawal of Portuguese authority and capital, it is argued, might well result in attempts at restoration of authority based upon far more authoritarian, repressive, and discriminatory measures than presently exist in Portuguese Africa. It is commonly argued by many practical diplomats that, for the next decade, the Portuguese, if willing, are better able to provide the environment and requisites for development objectives than could the nationalist leaders, split by their own quarrels. Ball's solution would include cooperation with Portugal in developing both the metropolitan areas and the African provinces, so that an eventual self-determination would allow for both pride and honor.[22]

The ultimate question is obvious: What is best for the majority of the population in Portuguese Africa? One might answer that the goals set by Article 73 of the U.N. Charter can appropriately be applied to Portuguese Africa. Its territories have not obtained separate self-government, and the interests of the inhabitants must be the major guide in any evolution toward self-government that takes account of the political aspirations of the people and assists them in the development of free political institutions, according to the particular circumstances and stages of advancement. Article 73c notes the importance of the consideration of international peace and security. Because Portugal has made such strides in the last decade in terms of advancing the economic, social, and educational condition of the Africans, it is especially regrettable that they have not taken the initiative in complying with item c in transmitting to the secretary-general such requested information. It is also regrettable that the evolution of Portuguese thought in the flexible direction of a broader concept of self-determination was halted and perhaps reversed by the war. It may well be that the Caetano government will move in more flexibly despite the war, and it would appear that a deescalation of conflict would rapidly accelerate both reform and progress.

Whether one is satisfied with the official statement of the Portuguese goal in Africa—and almost no U.N. members are—there is little doubt that Portuguese rule will continue in the foreseable future. But this does not mean a static situation, for the Portuguese have initiated a vast educational revolution for Africans. Thus, valuable time is being bought, and this will allow for development. At a later date, there should be a better chance for the proper application of the principle of self-determination, applied at the right time and in the right circumstance. Effective representation—true self-government—necessitates choice, under circumstances in which it can be intelligent and meaningful.

If present trends continue, the hope for increased representative government and even, eventually African majority rule will probably be found in the leverage that Africans, within ten years, will themselves be exercising by means of the present establishment rather than through the divided and disorganized nationalist groups with tribal biases. These will be years filled with many changes, in the metropole and overseas. Portuguese Africa exists under an authoritarian European regime, but it reaps the advantages of the greater Portuguese acceptance of racial coexistence and the Portuguese ability, coming from an underdeveloped home country, of using resources rather wisely.

It is a fortunate but peculiar fact of the political process in Portuguese Africa that the role of opposition has been filled, in part, by the internationalization of the issue in the United Nations. Here there has been not only debate and criticism but also a close scrutiny of health, education, and social conditions—a scrutiny not ordinarily given to independent one-party governments or authoritarian Communist powers which lack also opposition and criticism within the polical system. While the Portuguese Government, in reacting to criticism, has in no way agreed to move toward genuine self-determination, it has indeed changed on many issues, both social and economic. As for the racial aspects, the U.N. spotlight here, too, has probably had a beneficial aspect in leading the Portuguese to take pride in accelerating integration and assimilation efforts.

The civil war in Nigeria brought home to the Organization of African Unity, as well as to the world in general, the basic issue as to whether a redrawing of colonial boundaries could be permitted as a result of the many trends toward separatism in independent African states. The specter of a series of secessionist movements was seen by most African leaders as disastrous, an invitation to foreign intrigue, and an encouragement of tribal differences. Angola and Mozambique, once independent, could not escape such problems.

In the Nigerian conflict, two of the few uniting elements were the common use of the English language among the literate population and the existence of an economic infrastructure. For Angola and Mozambique, paradoxically, the spread of the Portuguese language and economic development may establish internal cohesion for these areas to exist as independent entities—neither under Lisbon nor as a battleground for the interests of neighboring states or even of some of the great powers as in the Congo and Nigerian conflict situations.

Nevertheless, for most African leaders, each continued year of Portuguese rule marks another year of white foreign domination in Africa; each such year, under the present development policies, also marks another step in the amalgamation of unified wholes. Paradoxically, true and effective Mozambican or Angolan nationalism, whether as seen from Lisbon in terms of the Lusitanian community or from Addis Ababa in terms of black African independence, has a better chance of developing in such circumstances than in a cauldron of tribal conflict and international rivalries.

It is not accidental that the European power first to arrive in black Africa is the last to depart. There is something to Gilberto Freyre's Luso-tropicology that points to the Portuguese tendency for adaptation and assimilation in tropical countries, and coexistence with other races. This has provided a staying-power stronger than wealth and power might have provided. In the coming crucial decade of educational development, if there can truly be a coequal assimilation of African and Portuguese values, in a way that appreciates both rich heritages, Angola and Mozambique might take their places in tropical Africa as free and stable societies that would give reality to the Manuelian dream of five centuries ago. They may help show the modern world that the world's oldest continent, unlike some others, is congenial to and mature enough for multiracial societies, mixing men of diverse colors and ethnic backgrounds into one.

NOTES

1. Speech delivered by Dr. Marcello Caetano before the National Assembly on November 27, 1968. *Notícias de Portugal*, Vol. XXII, No. 1126 (Lisbon, November 30, 1968).
2. Roland Oliver and Anthony Atmore, *Africa Since 1800* (London, 1967), p. 251.
3. Speech before the Commonwealth Club of San Francisco, March, 1962.
4. Most Portuguese thinkers, whatever their ultimate visions of their overseas empire, have been united in opposition to such timetables as a manner of foreign interference. Armando Cortesão of the University of Coimbra, involved with Portuguese colonial policy since 1914, summed up one Portuguese position, "The day will come when Angola and Mozambique will become completely self-governing or independent, as happened in Brazil," he wrote in 1962 at the height of the diplomatic crisis with the United States and the United Kingdom over Portuguese policy toward Africa. But he stressed that, in timing and execution, "no one should tell us what to do." To Cortesão's way of thinking, those who would so tell Portugal include both the Americans and the Soviets, whose respective "neo-colonialism in Africa is a staggering phenomenon." He specifically pointed the finger at the United States in infiltrating Africa through "the great American trusts" as well as through heavily subsidized "subversive action by American Protestant missions in our overseas territories." Armando Cortesão, *African Realities and Delusions* (Lisbon, 1962), pp. 22–26.
5. *The New York Times*, January 2, 1969.
6. W. P. Kirkman, *Unscrambling an Empire* (London, 1966), p. 107.
7. James Duffy, *Portugal in Africa* (Cambridge, Mass., 1962), p. 229.
8. Victor C. Ferkiss, *Africa's Search for Identity* (New York, 1966), p. 201.
9. *Ibid.*
10. John A. Marcum, "Three Revolutions," *Africa Report*, XII, No. 8 (November, 1967), 17.
11. *Ibid.*, p. 18.
12. Helen Kitchen, "Conversation with Eduardo Mondlane," *Africa Report*, XII, No. 8 (November, 1967), 51.
13. *Ibid.*
14. Edwin S. Munger, *Foreign Affairs*, January, 1969, p. 385; Larry W. Bowman, *International Studies Quarterly*, September, 1968, p. 252.

15. United Nations General Assembly, 22nd Session, Agenda Item 66(a), A/6700/ Add. 3 (October 11, 1967), p. 187.

16. Arthur J. Goldberg, "The United States, the United Nations, and Southern Africa," *Department of State Bulletin*, February 20, 1967.

17. Michael Crowder, *Senegal, A Study of French Assimilation Policy* (London, 1967), p. 4.

18. In the southern part of the United States after the Civil War, the Jim Crow laws on segregation and discrimination came with, and not before, the agrarian reform movements of the 1890's and only after the planter class had lost political power to the pressure groups of the small white farmers, the "Red Necks," who viewed the Negro as an economic threat.

19. Hugh Kay, an observer basically sympathetic to the Portuguese and the difficult problems of their government, has a well-expressed recommendation worth quoting and worth consideration by that government: "There are far too many people in political detention and there is no doubt that the Security Police (the PIDE) are too much a law unto themselves. Stories of torture and murder in the PIDE prisons are hard to prove or disprove. Frankly, I believe such things happen, as is almost inevitable in any secret police organization. It is plainly imperative that the PIDE should be fundamentally reformed and integrated with the regular police (like Scotland Yard's Special Branch), or into the army." Kay, "A Catholic View," *Angola, A Symposium: Views of a Revolt* (London, 1962), p. 103.

20. Anthony Astrachan, "Portugal Aims at Hearts and Minds in Struggle to Hold Mozambique," *Washington Post*, December 25, 1968.

21. George W. Ball, *The Discipline of Power* (Boston, 1968), p. 245.

22. *Ibid.*, p. 250.

NOTES ON THE CONTRIBUTORS

DAVID M. ABSHIRE received his doctorate from Georgetown University and is presently Executive Director of its Center for Strategic and International Studies. He is editor of *National Security*, contributing author for *Détente: Cold War Strategies in Transition*, and author of *The South Rejects a Prophet*.

NORMAN A. BAILEY received his doctorate from Columbia University and is now Professor of Political Science at The City University of New York (Queens). He is editor of *Latin America: Politics, Economics and Hemisphere Security* and author of *Latin America in World Politics*.

FRANK BRANDENBURG completed his doctoral studies at the University of Pennsylvania and has been a staff member of both The National Planning Association and The Committee for Economic Development. He is author of *Private Enterprise in Latin America* and *The Making of Modern Mexico*.

ANDREW WILSON GREEN, who received his doctorate at the University of Pennsylvania, also holds graduate degrees in law and business administration. As a practicing lawyer for twelve years, he published several articles on legal problems. His book on the role of the Court of Justice of the European Communities in the process of European integration will be published in 1970.

GEORGE MARTELLI, formerly diplomatic correspondent of the London *Daily Telegraph*, has published numerous books on historical and current topics, including *Léopold to Lumumba*, *Italy Against the World*, and *The Man Who Saved London*. His most recent article on Portuguese Africa appeared in *The Reporter*, December 29, 1966.

MICHAEL A. SAMUELS, a senior staff member at the Center for Strategic and International Studies, received his doctorate from Columbia University. His doctoral dissertation, "*Instrução* or *Educação?* A History of Education in Angola, 1878–1914," will soon be published by Teachers College Press. He is the author of "Methodist Education in Angola," published in *Stúdia*, in Lisbon, and "The New Look in Angolan Education," published in *Africa Report*.

IRENE S. VAN DONGEN studied agricultural production of Angola as a Fulbright research fellow in Portugal and worked extensively in Portuguese Africa on a Columbia University–Office of Naval Research, Geography Branch, contract. Now teaching at California State College, Pennsylvania, she is the author and co-author of a number of publications in the field of African geography.

INDEX

Abako political party, Congo (Kinshasa), 120, 394
Abreu e Brito, Domingos de, 99
Afonso, Diogo, 107
Afonso Henriques, King of Portugal, 34
Afonso I, King of Kongo (Nzinga Mvemba), 38, 94, 95, 178
Afonso II, King of Portugal, 34
Afonso III, King of Portugal, 34
Africa, 33, 49; demographic character of, 205–6; fauna of, 29; first discoveries in, 35; flora of, 29; interior expeditions in, 45; peoples of, 107–27; Portuguese administration of, 41, 49; racial categories in, 30; regional transport in, 334–42; slave traders in, 51; Soviet interests in, 441–2; Spanish domination and stagnation in, 41
African Liberation Committee, 423
African National Congress, 415
Agricultural education, 188
Agricultural settlement schemes, 280–4
Agriculture: in Angola, 254–67; in Cape Verde Islands, 279–80; in Mozambique, 16, 268–77; in Portuguese Africa, 222, 253–84; in Portuguese Guinea, 277–8; in São Tomé e Príncipe, 278–9
Água Rosada e Sardonia, Dom Aleixo, 64
Air transport system, 9, 17, 327, 334
Ajaua people, 14, 123
Alberto, Angelino, 210, 394
Albuquerque, Afonso de, 40, 97
Albuquerque, Mousinho de, 75, 76, 81, 102
Algeria, aid to nationalists, in Portuguese Africa from, 392, 394, 418, 424
Aljubarrota, 34
Almeida, Francisco de, Viceroy of India, 40, 46, 95, 97
Almeida, Francisco de, Governor of Angola, 42
Almeida, Jerônimo de, 42
Almeida, João de, 78
Almeida, Luís de, 411
Alvares Cabral, Pedro, 41, 45
Alvaro, King of Kongo, 39
Alves, Carlos, 210
Alves, Custódia, 210
Ambo language group, 114, 122
Amboím railroad, 326
Ambriz, Angola, 68
Ambundu people, 114, 117
Andrada, Paiva de, 72
Andrade, Mario de, 391, 392, 395, 402, 403
Andrade Corvo, João de, 68–9
Anglo-Portuguese treaty, 34, 50
Angola, 1–10, 30, 31, 33, 39, 40, 42, 51, 52, 53, 78–81, 83, 96, 99, 101, 103, 112–4, 136, 138, 140–1, 149, 153, 160–2, 178–86, 195–8, 203, 208, 210, 219, 221, 226, 227, 237–8, 258–9, 260, 262–7, 270–2, 280–8, 294–303, 305, 307–8, 314, 380–5, 389–98, 423, 424; abolition of slave trade in, 62; administrative districts of, 4; administrative process in, 146–50, African population of, 206; agricultural census in, 255; armed forces' influence in, 154; associations of class in, 155; attitudes and society in, 208–11; banking in, 154, 231; Bantus in, 30; Brazilian economic control of, 50; British-Portuguese conflict in, 68–70; budget of, 234; capital and skills in, 315; central watershed of, 3, coastal plain of, 2; commercial regulation in, 158–61; conflict in, 406–15; construction in, 306–7; corporate structure in, 152; Corps of Local Militia, 139; currency unit of, 230; diamond discovery in, 83; diamond industry in, 9; directed economic system in, 221; dry season of, 3; early racial policies in, 95; economic partnership with Portugal, 9; economy of, 219–51; effect on Portugal of withdrawal from, 354; electoral process in, 157–8; exchange system in, 233; expansion into, 70; exports of, 9, 255–64; external financial and economic relations of, 238–9; external trade of, 239–46; final conquest of, 76–7; future of, 457–8; Goans in, 211; governor-general of, 135–6; gross domestic product in, 227; immigration into, 1, 225; import trade of, 9; interior plateau of, 2; internal financial situation in, 230; land area of, 1; legal structure in, 140; mineral development in, 222; mining in, 9; mixed ownership in, 221; money supply in, 232; peoples in, 112–23; planalto of, 2; police and security forces in, 139, 438; Political, Penal, and Civil Statute, 140; population of, 5; ports of, 321–2; processing and manufacturing in, 303–6; Psycho-Social Service in, 194; public utilities in, 224; racial policy in, 97; racial types in population of, 208; rainfall in, 4; regional and local government in, 137; revenue and expenditures, 235; sea terminals in, 9; strategic importance of, 435, 436; temperature of, 3; tribes in, 114; vegetation of, 4; vulnerability of, to sanctions against South Africa, 443; wage-earners in, 170; wage levels in, 170–1; white population of, 205
Angola Metropole Bank, 83

467